Guide
to Research on
North American
Indians

ARCTIC
OCEAN

ESKIMO

KUTCHIN   ARCTIC   ESKIMO

ALEUT

ESKIMO

TLINGIT   ESKIMO

NORTH –   SLAVE   HUDSON BAY

HAIDA TSIMSHIAN BEAVER   ESKIMO
WEST   BELLA COOLA   CHIPEWYAN
         BELLA BELLA   SUBARCTIC
KWAKIUTL   SIKSIKA   NASKAPI
NOOTKA   (BLACKFOOT)   CREE   CREE   MONTAGNAIS   BEOTHUK
COAST SALISH   KAIGANI PLAINS
        KUTENAI   (BLOOD)   CREE
   PUYALLUP COLVILLE   PIEGAN   MICMAC
   NISQUALLY SPOKAN COEUR   MALECITE
CHINOOK   D'ALENE   OJIBWA (CHIPPEWA)   PASSAMAQUODDY
TILLAMOOK YAKIMA PLATEAU   ABENAKI
        WALLA WALLA FLATHEAD   HIDATSA   OJIBWA   HURON PENOBSCOT
           NEZ PERCE   CROW   MANDAN   WYANDOT   OTTAWA   PENNACOOK
   KLAMATH CAYUSE   GROS VENTRE (ATSINA)   MAHICAN
YUROK MODOC   BANNOCK   ARIKARA   WINNEBAGO   MOHAWK ESOPUS
 HUPA NORTHERN SHOSHONI TETON   SANTEE MENOMINEE NEUTRAL ONEIDA NIPMUC WAMPANOAG
      PAIUTE (SNAKE) DAKOTA YANKTON DAKOTA SAC   POTAWATOMI ONONDAGA WECQUAESGEEK NARRAGANSET
CALI-   GOSIUTE   NORTHERN PONCA DAKOTA FOX   CAYUGA HACKENSACK PEQUOT
FORNIA WASHO GREAT BASIN CHEYENNE PLAINS OMAHA KICKAPOO EASTERN SENECA RARITAN MOHEGAN
                      PAWNEE IOWA   WOODLAND SUSQUEHANNOCK WAPPINGER
         SOUTHERN   UTE   OTO   KASKASKIA MIAMI   (CONESTOGA) DELAWARE
         PAIUTE   ARAPAHO KANSA   PEORIA WEA PAMUNKEY NANTICOKE
CHUMASH   SOUTHERN MISSOURI ILLINOIS   CHICKAHOMINY POWHATAN
                  CHEYENNE   PIANKASHAW   MATTAPONY
      HAVASUPAI NAVAHO JICARILLA KIOWA OSAGE SHAWNEE OCCANEECHI PAMLICO
   MOHAVE WALAPAI HOPI APACHE KIOWA   TUTELO NOTTOWAY
CAHUILLA YAVAPAI ZUÑI PUEBLO APACHE QUAPAW   CHEROKEE TUSCARORA
   YUMA SOUTHWEST   YUCHI CATAWBA
COCOPA PIMA WESTERN COMANCHE WICHITA CHICKASAW SOUTHEAST ATLANTIC
   PAPAGO APACHE   CADDO   OCEAN
          MESCALERO   TUNICA CHOCTAW CREEK YAMASEE
PACIFIC   APACHE   SERI   LIPAN   NATCHEZ ALABAMA
                      APACHE   MOBILE
OCEAN   TARAHUMARA   SEMINOLE

                  YAQUI NORTHERN KARANKAWA   CALUSA
TRADITIONAL   MEXICO   TAINO
CULTURE AREAS   GULF OF MEXICO
AND TRIBAL LOCATIONS   TAINO
NORTH AMERICA   CIBONEY
                  TARASCAN   YUCATAN   CIBONEY
              TLAXCALAN   MAYA
               AZTEC
              MESOAMERICA

From *The Indian in America*, p. 45, by Wilcombe E. Washburn. Copyright © 1975 by Wilcombe E. Washburn. Reprinted by permission of Harper & Row, Publishers, Inc.

Guide
to Research on
North American
Indians

ARLENE B. HIRSCHFELDER
MARY GLOYNE BYLER
MICHAEL A. DORRIS

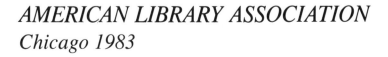

AMERICAN LIBRARY ASSOCIATION
Chicago 1983

Designed by Vladimir Reichl

Composed by Automated Office Systems Inc.
  in Century on a Text Ed/VIP phototypesetting
  system. Display type, Caslon, composed by
  Continental Composition, Inc.

Text printed on 50-pound Antique Glatfelter,
  a pH-neutral stock, and cover printed on
  B-grade Holliston cloth by Malloy Lithographing, Inc.

Bound by John H. Dekker & Sons

Library of Congress Cataloging in Publication Data

Hirschfelder, Arlene B.
    Guide to research on North American Indians.

    Includes indexes.
    1. Indians of North America — Bibliography.
I. Dorris, Michael.   II. Byler, Mary Gloyne.
III. Title.
Z1209.2.N67H57   1983   016.970004′97   82-22787
[E77]
ISBN 0-8389-0353-3

For my husband, Bill, and
my mother, Lula Owl Gloyne. MGB

To my wife, Louise Erdrich. MD

To my extraordinary parents who have always
inspired me with their love for learning. ABH

CONTENTS

PART IV RELIGION, ARTS, AND LITERATURE

PREFACE

This bibliography is intended to serve as a basic guide to the literature for general readers, students, and scholars interested in the study of American Indians—Native Americans. A vast body of literature about Native Americans has accumulated over the years. The sheer mass of this material often proves a serious obstacle to scholarly and casual inquiry alike. Imre Sutton, in his introduction to *Indian Land Tenure: Bibliographical Essays and a Guide to the Literature,* observes, "the mass of material on the Indian awaits the willing compiler, bibliographer, or classifier who would sort, classify, and evaluate what is in print on any number of subjects useful to students of Indian affairs."[1]

Efforts at organizing this material range from a five-volume, 40,000-entry bibliography covering ethnographic works published through 1972 to a reference encyclopedia listing 2,500 titles with brief annotations and a series of highly selective bibliographies consisting of critical essays evaluating from 175 to 275 works on specific topics. All of these important research tools are among the works described in this bibliography.

From the mass of material, approximately 1,100 books, articles, government documents, and other written materials in twenty-seven fields of study have been selected and annotated for this guide. Lengthy annotations identify the tribal territories, time frame, and point of view of each work. No attempt has been made to be exhaustive in the coverage of any topic. The goal is to present a selection of scholarly materials in the varied disciplines that will be useful both as a source of immediate information and as a reference tool that will lead investigators further into the intricacies of individual fields.

All of the selections are in English. They range geographically across the United States, including Alaska, and chronologically from ancient eras to contemporary life and thought. Canadian writings treating those tribes located along, and spilling over, the United States–Canadian border have been included, as well as important works about Canadian natives. Important works about Central and South America and Mexico have also been included. For the most part, however, this guide is limited to Native Americans of the United States—a restriction dictated by the large number of materials available.

1. p. 61 (New York: Clearwater, 1975).

Selected works are organized into twenty-seven chapters under four broad subject headings. Each chapter treats a specific topic. The standard pattern in each chapter is: an essay; a list of works treating the topic in a general way; works treating the topic in several geographic areas (the Northeast, Southeast, Plains, Southwest, Basin-Plateau, California, Northwest Coast, and Alaska) and bibliographies related to the topic covered. The essays trace the main lines of scholarly inquiry of the works listed and are keyed to the books cited. Although this arrangement has been followed in most of the chapters, complete uniformity has not been possible.

Works about archival materials are included, although the materials themselves are not listed. Books and articles dealing almost exclusively with the ways of life—ethnographies—of particular Native American groups (e.g., Hopi, Kiowa, Seneca, etc.) have been excluded. For such material, readers are referred to George Peter Murdock and Timothy J. O'Leary's *Ethnographic Bibliography of North America* (p. 5).

In choosing works for inclusion, availability was kept in mind so that works reasonably accessible in a good library or through a library were sometimes favored over those more difficult to obtain. For the most part, nonprint and unpublished materials as well as unpublished academic dissertations have been excluded. For such material the reader is referred to reference works such as Frederick J. Dockstader's *The American Indian in Graduate Studies: A Bibliography of Theses and Dissertations* (p. 2). The terminal date of publication for the majority of the books and articles cited is 1979. There are occasional exceptions; some of the books listed were published as late as 1982.

Some books and articles included in this guide contain dated opinions and terminology. However, the information they contain was considered important enough to justify a cautious reading. Every effort has been made to eliminate works in which racism and ethnocentric bias overwhelm the information the author purports to present. Nevertheless, the reader is urged to be alert to the more subtle forms of racism and ethnocentric bias that pervade the literature about Native Americans.

Native American has been used interchangeably with *American Indian* or *Indians,* and *nation, group,* or *people* with *tribe.* Over the centuries, spellings of the names of American Indian nations have varied considerably. In most instances, the authors have tried to use spellings preferred by Indian groups. For example, Navajos have declared a preference for *j* over *h,* and the Blackfeet have expressed similar declarations of preference for *Blackfeet* over *Blackfoot. Abenaki, Athapaskan, Cahuilla, Goshute, Mesquakie, Munsee, Muskogean,* and *Sac* have been used instead of other spellings. In most cases, spellings adhere to modern usage.

The authors regret that it was necessary to omit a number of valuable works owing to constraints imposed by space. No doubt other bibliographers would have omitted some of the titles included here and added others, and specialists in particular fields will regret omissions as much as we do. The authors take joint responsibility for the whole work.

The authors thank the following people for their good advice and assistance as they prepared this volume: John J. Bodine, William Byler, Fred Eggan, Michael D. Green, Bertram Hirsch, William Leap, Cesare Marino, Peter Nabokov, Roger C. Owen, Jacqueline Peterson, Chester Sprague,

Jack Stokely, Helen Hornbeck Tanner, Steven Unger, and James Van-Stone. We also want to thank the librarians of the American University Library, the Anthropology Library of the Smithsonian Institution, the Library of Congress, and the Martin Luther King Public Library, all of Washington, D.C.; the New York Public Library; the Newberry Library of Chicago; and the White Plains Public Library in New York.

PART I   *Introductory Material*

---

1   GENERAL SOURCES

In this section, the readers can locate bibliographies that treat individual tribes (the Apaches, Cherokees, Creeks, Delawares, Navajos, Ojibways, Sioux, etc.), culture areas (the Northeast, Northwest, Plains, and Subarctic as well as California, Delaware, and Maryland), and specific topics including folklore, language, literature, social science research and writings, Native American authors, health and disease, historical demography, astronomy, law and constitutions, economic development, missions, U.S. policy, Indian-white relations, evaluations of media materials, ethnography, education, and contemporary affairs. There is a bibliography that contains listings of the library collections of the Peabody Museum of Archaeology and Ethnology (p. 5).

There are two major series of bibliographies. The Newberry Library Center for the History of the American Indian has prepared thirty critical bibliographies intended as guides to reliable sources and studies in particular fields of the general literature. Some of the volumes are devoted to culture areas; others treat selected individual tribes; and a third group speaks to significant contemporary and historical issues. The standard format for the bibliographies is intended to be useful to both beginning students and advanced scholars. Each bibliography has two main parts: an essay, organized by subheadings, and an alphabetical list of all works cited. All citations in the essay are directly keyed to the more complete publication data in the list and each item in the list carries a reference to the page number where it is mentioned in the essay. There are usually between 175 and 275 items in each bibliography. The series has other features. There are two sets of recommended titles: a list of works recommended for the beginner and a group of volumes that constitute a basic library collection in the field. Asterisks denote works suitable for secondary school students. There is variety in the kinds of sources because these critical bibliographies support the study of ethnohistory.

The second series, entitled the Native American Bibliography Series, is published by Scarecrow Press, Inc. The goal of this series of bibliographies is to publish comprehensive bibliographies of service to scholarship with all important items annotated to make them useful to students and to others beginning research in the field. During the 1980s a score or more of these bibliographies, each containing several thousand entries, will be published. Except for those tribes that have received little notice in books and journals, each tribe will be treated in a separate volume. *Bibliography of the Sioux,* the first of the comprehensive bibliographies in the series, contains the first complete listing of the major materials on the Sioux Indians. Entries within each of the thirty-three topics in the volume are arranged alphabetically. Nearly half of the 3,300 entries are annotated.

ABLER, THOMAS S., and SALLY M. WEAVER. *A Canadian Indian Bibliography 1960–1970.* Toronto: University of Toronto Press, 1974. 232pp. Illustrated.

Scholarly material published between 1960 and 1970 on Canadian Indians and Métis is included in this bibliography. Works on physical anthropology, biomedicine, and archaeological and linguistic studies have been excluded. Source materials include books, monographs, journals, theses, unpublished papers, and reports. Newspaper and popular magazine articles are omitted. Works by Indian authors are indicated. Eskimo materials are included only when they include comparison with Indian cultures. A special case law digest section includes cases from 1867 to 1972. Sections include articles by tribe, bibliography, general and comparative studies, bills and acts, Indian administration and government policy, history, demography, material culture, education, economics, social organization, politics and law, medicine, religion, oral literature, music and dance, and urban issues. About 3,040 works are cited and most are annotated. Two maps show linguistic regions and Canadian Indian tribes and culture areas.

AMERICAN INDIAN HISTORICAL SOCIETY. *Index to Literature on the American Indian: 1970–1973.* San Francisco: Indian Historian Press.

This volume and succeeding ones are annual subject indexes, selecting a "fair sampling(s)" of the enormous amount of periodical and book literature published on Native Americans, both popular and scholarly. The first volume lists 63 subject areas chosen and 257 periodicals that were searched for articles. Each volume indexes under subject several hundred publications devoted to American Indians, emphasizing those written, edited, and published by Native American organizations or tribes, religious schools, and groups. The addresses, publication schedules, and prices are given.

ASSOCIATES OF THE JOHN CARTER BROWN LIBRARY. *The Mirror of the Indian.* Philadelphia: Pickering Press, 1958. 57pp. Illustrated.

One-half of this work is devoted to abstracts of sixteenth- to eighteenth-century sources by Spanish, French, and English authors on Indian subjects. Divisions are geographic and include Mexico, the Southwest, the Southeast, Virginia and Maryland, Pennsylvania, New York, New England, the Old Northwest (of the British colonial frontier), and Canada. Works cited include linguistic sources, personal observations, massacre accounts, early ethnographies, etc. There are five illustrations from sixteenth- and seventeenth-century manuscripts depicting Native Americans.

BUTLER, RUTH LAPHAM. *The Newberry Library: A Checklist of Manuscripts in the Edward E. Ayer Collection.* Chicago: Newberry Library, 1937. 293pp.

This annotated checklist of the roughly 2,000 manuscripts in the Ayer Collection of the Newberry Library is divided into seven sections including one on general aboriginal North American topics, one on Native American languages, and one on Hawaiian languages. Nearly 1,500 of the entries deal with Native American materials. The 250 entries dealing with Indian languages are subdivided by particular languages.

DOCKSTADER, FREDERICK J., comp. *The American Indian in Graduate Studies: A Bibliography of Theses and Dissertations.* Contributions from the Museum of the American Indian, Heye Foundation, vol. 15. New York: Museum of the American Indian, 1957. 399pp.

An uncritical bibliography, this book lists 3,684 theses and dissertations, presented for graduate degree requirements at 203 colleges and universities in the United States, Canada, and Mexico between 1890 and 1955, which deal in any way (in at least one chapter) with North, Central, and South American natives. The selection includes all academic fields. Some of the studies are briefly annotated and there is a topical index. The Museum published a supplementary bibliography in 1974 which covers theses and dissertations written between 1955 and 1970.

FOGELSON, RAYMOND D. *The Cherokees: A Critical Bibliography.* Bloomington: Indiana University Press, 1978. 98pp.

This work is part of the bibliographical series of the Newberry Library Center for the History of the American Indian. A list of 6 works is provided for beginning reading and 15 titles are recommended for inclusion in a basic library collection. Works suitable for secondary school students are indicated throughout. The author excludes materials published in the Cherokee language. A bibliographic essay contains sections on basic reference works; general sources; prehistory and archaeology; the colonial period; the revolutionary period; nineteenth-century renaissance; removal; Cherokees in the West; the Eastern Cherokees; language; ecology, natural history, material culture, and social organization; world view, religion, and medicine; and personality and biography. There are 347 sources cited.

GIBSON, A. M. "Sources for Research on the American Indian." *Ethnohistory* 7, no. 2 (Spring 1960): 121–36.

The author gives a general summary of selected

research centers with substantial material on American Indians. In addition, he discusses collections of the U.S. government archives, describes holdings of over thirty other centers, and cites published documents and other aids.

GREEN, MICHAEL. *The Creeks: A Critical Bibliography*. Bloomington: Indiana University Press, 1979. 114pp.
This work is part of the bibliographical series of the Newberry Library Center for the History of the American Indian. Five works are recommended for beginning reading and 18 works are suggested for inclusion in a basic library collection. Works suitable for secondary school students are indicated throughout. The author begins with a description of the dynamics of the Creek Nation as a confederacy of tribes. A bibliographic essay includes sections on southeastern archaeology, Creek ethnography, and historiography (with subcategories, general studies, sixteenth and seventeenth centuries, eighteenth-century contact, 1783–1813, the Creek War, removal, resettlement in Indian Territory, Civil War, late nineteenth-century allotment, and twentieth century). There are 216 sources cited.

GRUMET, ROBERT STEVEN. *Native Americans of the Northwest Coast: A Critical Bibliography*. Bloomington: Indiana University Press, 1979. 108pp. Illustrated.
This work is part of the bibliographical series of the Newberry Library Center for the History of the American Indian. Six works are recommended for beginning reading and 24 works are suggested for inclusion in a basic library collection. The author's bibliographic essay begins with a description of the Northwest Coast and its peoples. Sections include general works, archaeology, regional history, art, the potlatch, the north culture provinces (Tlingit, Haida, Tsimshian, and Northern Kwakiutl), the Wakashan culture province (Southern Kwakiutl, Bellacoola, and Nootka), and the Coast Salish–Chemakum culture province (Coast Salish of British Columbia and Coast Salish and Chemakum of western Washington State). There are 222 works cited. A map shows the location of tribes and culture provinces.

HEIZER, ROBERT F. *The Indians of California: A Critical Bibliography*. Bloomington: Indiana University Press, 1976. 68pp.
This work is part of the bibliographical series of the Newberry Library Center for the History of the American Indian. A list of 5 works is provided for beginning reading and 16 works are recommended for inclusion in a basic library collection. Works suitable for secondary school readers are indicated throughout. The introductory section of a bibliographic essay presents works on historic demography and early ethnographic studies. Additional sections include the study of Indian civilization, native world view (which includes archaeological works), general and specific demography, Indian-white relations to 1870, the reservation period and urbanization, and Indians and the law. There are 193 works cited.

———, and ALBERT B. ELSASSER. *A Bibliography of California Indians: Archaeology, Ethnography, Indian History*. New York: Garland Publishing Co., 1977. 267pp. Illustrated.
Over 3,300 sources are listed here in two general sections: prehistory (archaeology) and history from the European discovery of California in 1542. Some ethnographic works appear in the second section, but, by the authors' admission, the collection is not comprehensive. Subsections in the prehistory section include archaeology by geographic region and by material culture aspect (shell and bone, pottery, basketry and textiles, charmstones, petroglyphs and pictographs, bone analysis, etc.). The history section is divided by topics that include six subject ethnographies, Spanish/Mexican contact, Anglo conquest, the aftermath of conquest, Indian nationalism, works written by Indians, and source materials. Two maps are of (1) archaeological areas and (2) California tribes and territories. The work includes an author and tribal index. Brief annotation is included for those works whose titles do not provide adequate information about the subject matter.

HELM, JUNE. *The Indians of the Subarctic: A Critical Bibliography*. Bloomington: Indiana University Press, 1976. 91pp.
This work is part of the bibliographical series of the Newberry Library Center for the History of the American Indian. Five works are recommended for beginning reading and 15 works are suggested for inclusion in a basic library collection. Works suitable for secondary school students are indicated throughout. A bibliographic essay includes sections on misconceptions of the Subarctic, basic reference works, ethnographies, prehistory, history and historical materials, Indian accounts and personal histories, contemporary conditions, native newsletters and newspapers, traditional Indian culture and society, language, and bibliographies and series. There are 272 sources cited.

HIPPLER, ARTHUR E. *Eskimo Acculturation: A Selected, Annotated Bibliography of Alaskan and Other Eskimo Acculturation Studies*. Fairbanks: Institute of Social, Economic, and Government Research, University of Alaska, 1970. 209pp.
The 199 sources of this annotated bibliography of cultural change among Alaskan Eskimos were selected on the basis of their contribution toward understanding the processes and details of cultural change. The annotations include in some cases value judgments about the work's shortcomings. Section 1 contains an alphabetical list by author with the date, title, reference to abstract number, and the page where cited. Section 2 contains complete bibliographical information including abstracts listed alphabetically by author for Alaska Eskimos; Northwest Eskimo groups; works dealing with specific Northwest Eskimo groups including Kauwerak, Kingikmiut, Kowagmiut, Malemiut, Noatagamiut, Nunamiut, Selawigmiut, and Taremiut; Southwest Alaskan Eskimos; Asiatic Eskimos and other Siberian aborigines; and Canadian Eskimos and Indians. There are works dealing with aspects of all or most of the four major divisions

(Greenland, Canada, Alaska, and Asia), works dealing generally with Alaska's native population, and miscellaneous works on Greenland Eskimos, Aleuts, and Alaskan Indians. The third section lists the sources under four headings: precontact and earliest white contact through 1866; middle contact, 1867–1914; late contact, 1915–40; and contemporary, 1941 to the present.

HODGE, WILLIAM. *A Bibliography of Contemporary North American Indians*. New York: Interland Publishing, 1976. 296pp.

This bibliography concentrates on contemporary (post-1875) Native Americans and their communities, both reservation and urban. The author includes a study guide to Indian life before 1875 and to contemporary American Indians. The bibliography of 2,594 works is partially annotated. Sections include bibliography, anthropologists and Indians, history, professional Indians of various kinds, material culture (food getting, food habits, arts and crafts, artists), social organization, population dynamics, reservation/rural communities, linguistics and language, culture dynamics, migration patterns, urban living, economics, the anthropology of development, personality and culture (including folklore), formal education, politics, social control, music and dance, religion, health-disease-poverty, Canadian government documents, U.S. publications, current periodicals, arts and crafts (supplies), museums, and maps. A subject index is provided.

HOEBEL, E. ADAMSON. *The Plains Indians: A Critical Bibliography*. Bloomington: Indiana University Press, 1977. 75pp.

This work is part of the bibliographical series of the Newberry Library Center for the History of the American Indian. It presents the difference between the Plains culture area approach traditionally popular with scholars and the reality of cultural diversity in the Great Plains. A list of 5 works is provided for beginning reading and 15 works are recommended for inclusion in a basic library collection. Works suitable for secondary school readers are indicated throughout. A bibliographic essay contains sections on the Plains as a natural and cultural area, archaeology, initial contact with Europeans, the introduction of the horse, and works specific to each of the nineteen principal Plains tribes. There are 205 works cited.

HOOVER, HERBERT T. *The Sioux: A Critical Bibliography*. Bloomington: Indiana University Press, 1979. 78pp.

This work is part of the bibliographical series of the Newberry Library Center for the History of the American Indian. Five works are recommended for beginning reading and 15 works are suggested for inclusion in a basic library collection. Works suitable for secondary school readers are indicated throughout. A bibliographic essay includes sections on general histories (the tribes and special monographs), autobiographies and biographies (Sitting Bull, Crazy Horse, Red Cloud, and others), battles and wars, observations and influences of non-Indian groups (explorers and traders, Catholic missionaries, Congregational and Presbyterian missionaries, Episcopal missionaries, and captives), special Sioux groups (including the Assiniboines), and culture (general studies, language, religion, legends, and other cultural materials). There are 213 sources cited.

IVERSON, PETER. *The Navajos: A Critical Bibliography*. Bloomington: Indiana University Press, 1976. 64pp.

This work is part of the bibliographical series of the Newberry Library Center for the History of the American Indian. A list of 5 works is provided for beginning reading and 18 works are recommended for inclusion in a basic library collection. Works suitable for secondary school readers are indicated throughout. Emphasis is placed on the Navajo people's "success in maintaining its traditional culture while adapting to the massive pressures of Euro-American society." The bibliographic essay includes sections on basic texts and studies, bibliographies, Navajo accounts and documents, newspapers and newsletters, origins and early history, the Long Walk Era, stock reduction and contemporary history, social organization and language, government and law, education, economy, and health and religion. There are 189 sources cited.

JONES, WILLIAM K. "General Guide to Documents on the Five Civilized Tribes in the University of Oklahoma Library Division of Manuscripts." *Ethnohistory* 14, no. 1–2 (Winter–Spring 1967): 47–76.

The author lists and briefly describes the collections concerning the Five Civilized Tribes (Cherokees, Chickasaws, Choctaws, Creeks, and Seminoles) held by the Division of Manuscripts of the University of Oklahoma Library. There are papers of former principal chiefs, tribal governors, and other leaders; collections of materials on Indian schools; official papers of tribes; personal papers of prominent tribesmen; and files of non-Indian collectors. The guide is divided into three sections: maps, microfilms, and collections of manuscripts. Each collection is briefly described and inclusive dates of the collections are given.

KLEIN, BARRY T., ed. *Reference Encyclopedia of the American Indian*. 2nd ed. 2 vols. Rye, N.Y.: Todd Publications, 1973.

A subject and title bibliography is included in this work along with information on relevant government agencies, magazines and periodicals, museums, libraries, reservations, urban centers, etc. The title bibliography lists about 2,500 books in print relating to the native peoples of North America (north of the Rio Grande). Entries are annotated and works suitable for young people are indicated with an asterisk. The subject bibliography is a listing of the titles from the first bibliography, filed under appropriate categories. The work includes a list of publishers and their addresses. Volume 2 is a "Who's Who" listing of Native Americans.

MARKEN, JACK W. *The Indians and Eskimos of North America: A Bibliography of Books in Print through 1972*. Vermillion: University of South Dakota Press, 1973. 200pp.

The author lists books on American Indians and Eskimos in print as of 1972, along with information on price, number of pages, availability in paperback, and, for children's books, appropriate grade levels. Where the author is known to be a Native American, this is noted. Little additional annotation appears. Approximately 4,000 books are listed in six sections (bibliography, handbooks, autobiographies, myths and legends, reprints in *American Journal of Archaeology* and *Ethnology*, and a miscellaneous category). Works of fiction by non-Indian authors are not included except for children's books and a representative group of twentieth-century novels by white authors. A subject index is provided for categories with three or more references.

MELODY, MICHAEL E. *The Apaches: A Critical Bibliography*. Bloomington: Indiana University Press, 1977. 86pp.

This work is part of the bibliographical series of the Newberry Library Center for the History of the American Indian. A list of 6 works is provided for beginning reading and 20 titles are recommended for inclusion in a basic library collection. Works suitable for secondary school students are indicated throughout. The author introduces the popular misconceptions of the "Apache peoples as savages" and replaces them with the reality of Apache peoples as "victims of deception, dishonest Indian agents, governmental [U.S.] inertia, treachery, murder, and massacre." The Apache "fought nobly for their land, families, and way of life." Sections in the author's bibliographic essay include a general description of Apache life and linguistics, bibliography, basic ethnographic works, area-specific ethnographic works (Western and Eastern Apache), basic historical materials (subdivided into general works, the Spanish/Mexican period, and the American period), the Bascom Affair, military affairs, the reservation period, mythology, religion, ritual, art and basketry, costume, government, language and linguistics, and photographs. There are 223 works cited.

MURDOCK, GEORGE PETER, and TIMOTHY J. O'LEARY. *Ethnographic Bibliography of North America*. 2nd ed. 5 vols. New Haven, Conn.: Human Relations Area Files Press, 1975. Illustrated.

Often referred to as "the Bible" of Native American bibliographies, this work provides a basic coverage of the published literature on the native peoples of North America through (and including) 1972. Nearly 40,000 entries appear without annotation. Volume 1 is a general bibliography with one "general North America" section and fifteen sections which are geographic-region-specific. The general section includes five subject bibliographies subsections. Volumes 2–5 are detailed bibliographies on cultures in four geographic regions (Arctic and Subarctic, Far West and Pacific Coast, eastern United States, and Plains and Southwest). Each contains an ethnic bibliography (i.e., section on other bibliographies). All volumes contain a guide for using the work. General ethnic maps of North America appear in all the volumes and detailed ethnic maps of particular geographic regions appear at the beginning of corresponding chapters.

PEABODY MUSEUM OF ARCHAEOLOGY AND ETHNOLOGY, Harvard University. *Author and Subject Catalogues of the Library*. 53 vols. Boston: G. K. Hall, 1963.

Bibliographic information for over 230,000 sources available in the Peabody Museum collection is indexed in this work by author and by subject. The collection includes materials on Europe, Africa, Asia, and Oceania, but the emphasis is on North and Central America. The original work concentrates on volumes and pamphlets. Numerous supplementary volumes make the catalogs current to 1979. There is a greater emphasis on periodical literature in these supplements. The card catalog format has minimal annotation.

PORTER, FRANK W., III. *Indians in Maryland and Delaware: A Critical Bibliography*. Bloomington: Indiana University Press, 1979. 107pp. Illustrated.

This work is part of the bibliographical series of the Newberry Library Center for the History of the American Indian. Five works are recommended for beginning reading and 16 works are suggested for inclusion in a basic library collection. A bibliographical essay includes sections on primary sources, bibliographies, county and state histories, archaeology, culture areas, tribes (Nanticokes, Piscataways, Susquehannocks, and others), subsistence strategies, material culture, language, population and demography, early voyages, explorations and descriptions, missions, land tenure and reservations, migration, strategies for survival, Indian survivals in the East, and triracial isolates. There are 230 sources cited. One map shows selected sites and tribes in the region.

PRUCHA, FRANCIS PAUL. *A Bibliographical Guide to the History of Indian-White Relations in the United States*. Chicago: University of Chicago Press, 1977. 454pp.

Published by the university press for the Center for the History of the American Indian of the Newberry Library, this guide cites sources dealing with Indian-white relations from early contact to the present. The author writes from a historical rather than an anthropological perspective, and, thus, classification of sources is more by general topic rather than by tribe. Organizational categories include materials in the National Archives, guide to federal documents, guide to manuscripts, guides to miscellaneous sources (newspapers, maps, oral histories, travel accounts, Indian periodicals, etc.), federal Indian policy, the Bureau of Indian Affairs, treaties, land tenure, warfare, trade and traders, missions and missionaries, legal status, education, health, social and economic development, works by tribe, and special topics (Indian captivities, writings, delegations, place-names, and images of Native Americans in Euro-American art). In general there is no annotation, although remarks on sources appear at the beginning of some of the sections. The work contains an index.

RONDA, JAMES P., and JAMES AXTELL. *Indian Missions: A Critical Bibliography*. Bloomington: Indiana University Press, 1978. 85pp.

This work is part of the bibliographical series of the Newberry Library Center for the History of the American Indian. Five works are recommended for beginning reading and 15 works are suggested for inclusion in a basic library collection. Works suitable for secondary school students are indicated throughout. The work begins with a discussion of ethnocentrism and early missionaries' accounts of their experiences with Native Americans, followed by a discussion of more contemporary works which attempt to portray Native American response to the mission invasion. A bibliographic essay includes sections on denominational variety (Anglican and Episcopal, Baptist, Catholic, Methodist, Moravian, Mormon, Presbyterian and American Board missions, and Quaker), mission goals, methods of conversion (mission towns, institutional education, and Indian churches), and Indian responses (conversion, theological criticism, syncretism, revitalization, and armed resistance). There are 211 works cited.

SNOW, DEAN R. *Native American Prehistory: A Critical Bibliography*. Bloomington: Indiana University Press, 1979. 75pp.

This work is part of the bibliographical series of the Newberry Library Center for the History of the American Indian. Five works are recommended for beginning reading and 15 works are suggested for inclusion in a basic library collection. Works suitable for secondary school readers are indicated throughout. The author begins by noting the difference between the present-day fields of archaeology and prehistory; his sources focus on prehistory and tend to be "competently written, up-to-date, and nontechnical syntheses." Most of the titles are books and sources represent all of North America including Meso-America. A bibliographic essay includes sections on general works in archaeology, general works on North American prehistory, Meso-American background, the earliest Americans, and regional works (Eastern Woodlands, the Great Plains, the Desert West, the Far West, and the Arctic and Subarctic). There are 204 works cited.

SPOFFORD, AINSWORTH. "Rare Books Relating to the American Indians." *American Anthropologist* 3, no. 2 (1901):270–85.

A bibliographic essay of rare sources dealing with Native Americans is contained in this work. The author provides brief descriptions of works in Latin, Spanish, English, and French. Early bibliographies, explorers' accounts, histories, missionary narratives, linguistic works, and captivity narratives are included. In some cases the locations and the latest costs paid as of 1901 are given. Nearly forty books are cited.

TANNER, HELEN HORNBECK. *The Ojibwas: A Critical Bibliography*. Bloomington: Indiana University Press, 1976. 78pp.

This work is part of the bibliographical series of the Newberry Library Center for the History of the American Indian. A list of 5 works is provided for beginning reading and 16 works are recommended for inclusion in a basic library collection. Works suitable for secondary school students are indicated throughout. The author explores the controversial criteria that distinguish a tribe from a band or a clan. A bibliographic essay includes sections on the origins of the terms "Ojibwa" and "Chippewa" to describe kindred groups who have occupied the expanse of land from the eastern end of Lake Ontario westward to Lake Winnipeg, Manitoba, and the Turtle Mountains, North Dakota, along with accounts of travelers, explorers, and missionaries, regional studies, anthropological contributions, languages and traditions, portrayal of Ojibway life, and sources for advanced research. There are 275 sources cited.

THORNTON, RUSSELL, and MARY K. GRASMICK. *Bibliography of Social Science Research and Writings on American Indians*. Center for Urban and Regional Affairs, Publication No. 79-1. Minneapolis: University of Minnesota, 1979. 160pp.

Sources appearing in some 150 scholarly journals of history, sociology, geography, political science, economics, and American and ethnic studies through 1976 are cited in this bibliography. Anthropological journals are not included in the review because of the large number of articles and the availability of other relevant indexes. There is no annotation. Sources are listed according to the social science discipline of the journal in which they appear. Over 100 of the 160 pages of this work list history articles.

TOOKER, ELISABETH. *The Indians of the Northeast: A Critical Bibliography*. Bloomington: Indiana University Press, 1978. 77pp.

This work is part of the bibliographical series of the Newberry Library Center for the History of the American Indian. A list of 5 works is provided for beginning reading and 15 titles are recommended for inclusion in a basic library collection. Works suitable for secondary school students are indicated throughout. The Northeast is defined as the area extending from Newfoundland to North Carolina and from the Atlantic Ocean to the Upper Great Lakes. The author's bibliographic essay includes sections on introductory ethnographic, language, and archaeological works; history; coastal Algonquian cultures; Northern Iroquoians; and Upper Great Lakes Societies. There are 270 works cited.

UNRAU, WILLIAM E. *The Emigrant Indians of Kansas: A Critical Bibliography*. Bloomington: Indiana University Press, 1979. 80pp. Illustrated.

This work is part of the bibliographical series of the Newberry Library Center for the History of the American Indian. Five works are recommended for beginning reading and 12 works are suggested for inclusion in a basic library collection. Works suitable for secondary school students are indicated throughout. The author provides titles dealing with the forced removal of more than 10,000 Native Americans of more than twelve tribes from the Old

Northwest to the future Kansas in the decade and a half after 1830. A bibliographic essay includes sections on historical setting and cultural identification; federal Indian policy; removal; conflict between federal land and Indian policies; tribal leadership and factional response; missionaries; the impacts of malnutrition, disease, and alcohol; and expulsion from Kansas. There are 187 sources cited and two maps that show emigrant Indian reserves in January and July, 1854.

WESLAGER, C. A. *The Delawares: A Critical Bibliography.* Bloomington: Indiana University Press, 1978. 84pp.

This work is part of the bibliographical series of the Newberry Library Center for the History of the American Indian. A list of 6 works is provided for beginning reading and 22 works are recommended for inclusion in a basic library collection. Works suitable for secondary school students are indicated throughout. A bibliographic essay includes sections on introductory works, Lenape origins, seventeenth-century accounts, early relations with Europeans and other tribes, Lenape migrations, subdivisions and clans, traditional religion and missionaries, language, and specialized studies. There are 224 sources cited.

WHITESIDE, DON (Sin a Paw). *Aboriginal People: A Selected Bibliography Concerning Canada's First People.* Ottawa: National Indian Brotherhood, 1973. 345pp.

This is a bibliography of major published works; unpublished speeches, reports, and proceedings of conferences; and newspaper articles dealing with Canadian natives. Emphasis is given to works written by Canadian aboriginal people (Indian authorship is indicated in an author index). Sections include general concerns; history by tribe; population distribution; values, traditions, tales, crafts, and biographies; religious beliefs, experiences, and ceremonies; aboriginal rights and treaties; Indian acts; Indian administration; prejudice and discrimination; aboriginal conferences; resistance; community development and internal organization; economic development; other social and cultural changes; urbanization; formal education; health, housing, welfare, and poverty; crime and nontreaty legal matters; and aboriginal people in other than North American countries. The work is indexed by author and by subject.

2 GENERAL STUDIES

This section contains books that offer introductions to different aspects of Native American studies. There are collections of papers that have sociological, anthropological, or historical focuses. There are books that introduce Native American studies in topically organized formats. There are works on contemporary Indian affairs, culture contact and culture change, the impact of Native Americans on American culture, and one that contains a directory of federal and state Indian reservations. There are two works profusely illustrated with photographs, one that concentrates on Native Americans as they were and one that shows them as they are today. There are handbooks on Native American groups in the United States, Canada, Middle and South America; regional handbooks that deal with the Native American peoples of California and the Northeast, Southeast, and Southwest areas of the United States. These handbooks offer brief descriptions of every linguistic stock, confederacy, tribe, subtribe or tribal division, and settlement known to history or to tradition. There are general studies of the Native American groups of the North American Great Plains, the Great Basin-Plateau, the Northwest Coast, and Alaska. While this section is concerned with North American studies generally and with Native American groups in the United States particularly, works on Canada and Middle and South America are offered here for those who are interested.

American Indian Dictionary Series. Newport, Calif.: American Indian Publishers, 1981.

A multivolume reference series, these books present information on Native Americans of the Western world. *The Dictionary of Indian Tribes of the Americas,* four volumes, includes tribes of the entire hemisphere from the Aleuts of the Arctic region to the Onas near the Antarctic. The tribal entries are arranged alphabetically with each article a complete treatise on a tribe. There are hundreds of maps that show the locations of the groups. *The Dictionary of Daily Life of Indians of the Americas A to Z,* two volumes, includes information on the daily life of Indians of the Western Hemisphere. Articles deal with such topics as agriculture, athletics, ball games, birth customs, boats, body decoration, cards and card games, Carlisle In- dian School, dolls, food and drink, hats and headdresses, marriage customs, spices, etc. Besides *Tribes* and *Daily Life,* dictionaries are being planned for Biography, Religion, and other subjects. The articles have been written by Indian and non-Indian historians and anthropologists.

BAHR, HOWARD M.; BRUCE A. CHADWICK; and ROBERT C. DAY. *Native Americans Today: Sociological Perspectives.* New York: Harper & Row, 1972. 547pp.

Forty-two empirical studies of Indian people, pieces that demonstrate principles or variables relevant to the sociology of minority-majority relations, are included in this anthology. The organizing topics are: The Setting; Patterns of Prejudice and Discrimination; Indian Education; Acculturation and Identity; Crime and Deviant Behavior; The Urban Indian; and Red Power, Action Programs, and the Future. Individual pieces are footnoted and some contain bibliographies.

BEUF, ANN H. *Red Children in White America.* Philadelphia: University of Pennsylvania Press, 1977. 155pp. Bibliography.

This study examines the relative importance of prejudicial discrimination and institutional and cultural racism in determining children's racial feelings. The racial attitudes in a group of Native American preschool children and a control group of non-Native American children were investigated to discover whether or not the attitudes differ and, if so, to identify the social sources of such differences. The author establishes that cultural and institutional racism does exist with regard to Native Americans, has a profound influence on the lives of the children from even rather isolated communities, and plays a vital role in establishing negative self-images. The author concludes that social-structural changes are necessary.

COLLIER, JOHN. *Indians of the Americas: The Long Hope.* New York: New American Library, 1947. 191pp.

Discussing the ways of American Indians from the Paleolithic Age to the mid-1940s, the author reviews the policies of Spain and the United States toward American Indians, and describes four centuries of Western European impact on the cultures of the Native American peoples of the Americas—both south and north of the Rio Grande—from Incas and Aztecs to modern Sioux, Iroquois, Cherokees, Pueblos, and Navajos. He discusses federal Indian policy which until 1933 determined the spoilation of the Indians and tells of the newer, more creative policy put into effect during the late 1930s. Throughout the book the author conveys the indestructible spiritual lifeways and world view of Indian societies.

CROSBY, ALFRED W., JR. *The Columbian Exchange: Biological and Cultural Consequences of 1492.* Contributions in American Studies, no. 2. Westport, Conn.: Greenwood Press, 1972. 268pp. Illustrated. Bibliography.

This biohistory examines the impact of Columbus's voyages on the global ecosystem. The transatlantic migrations of peoples, plants, animals, and germs are surveyed. The author discusses the role of smallpox in the exploitation of Native Americans, the biohistory of syphilis, European animals in America, the influence of American foods on European demography, and consequences of the continuing Columbian exchange. Guesswork, eyewitness accounts, apocrypha, suggestive statistics, and scientific evidence are synthesized in this consideration of the interaction between the ecosystems. Three maps of distributions of blood groups and old prints illustrate the book.

DELORIA, VINE, JR. *Custer Died for Your Sins: An Indian Manifesto.* New York: Avon Books, 1970. 272pp.

The author, a Yankton Sioux, delivers a bitter attack on the stereotypes and myths that have been built up by white society about Native Americans. He discusses laws and treaties, termination policy, anthropologists, missionaries, government agencies, humor, the "red and the black," leadership, modern society, and offers a redefinition of Indian affairs.

DOZIER, EDWARD P. "The Concepts of 'Primitive' and 'Native' in Anthropology." In *The Concept of the Primitive,* edited by Ashley Montagu, pp. 229–56. New York: Free Press, 1968.

The views of anthropologists toward the societies they traditionally have studied are considered in terms of the main currents of anthropological theory. The author holds that such views and development of theory bear important relations to one another. The article examines the negatively charged terminology by which anthropologists characterize people they study (illiterate, primitive, savage, crude, uncivilized, etc.) and urges anthropologists to seek and use a less tainted, more appropriate, classification system.

DRIVER, HAROLD E. *Indians of North America.* 2nd ed., rev. Chicago: University of Chicago Press, 1969. 632pp. Illustrated. Bibliography.

The major portion of this book utilizes a topical approach to describe Indian cultures from the Arctic to Panama before contact with Europeans. Thirteen culture areas serve as a framework for organizing information into chapters treating origin and prehistory, language, subsistence patterns, horticulture, narcotics and stimulants, housing and architecture, clothing, crafts, art, music and dance, exchange and trade, marriage and family, kin groups and kinship terminology, property and inheritance, government and social controls, violence, feuds, raids and war, rank and social classes, sodalities and ceremonies, life cycle, education, religion, magic, medicine, and personality and culture. There are four chapters on ethnohistory and culture change after 1492, with emphasis on the twentieth century in the United States, Alaska, Canada, and Greenland. The concluding chapter is on achievements and contributions. There are forty-five maps that show the distribution of particular culture traits, photographs, and other illustrations.

———, and WILLIAM C. MASSEY. *Comparative Studies of North American Indians.* Transactions of the American Philosophical Society (n.s.), vol. 47, part 2, pp. 165–456. Philadelphia: American Philosophical Society, 1957. Illustrated. Bibliography.

The authors offer a series of broad generalizations about North American Indian cultures (including Meso-American and circum-Caribbean) together with the data upon which they are based. Most of the data are given in a series of 163 schematic maps on which territories of individual tribes are differentiated by means of boundary lines. There are descriptive and relational generalizations. The descriptive generalizations are concerned primarily with the geographical descriptions of single traits or small clusters of variants on a single topic. The relational generalizations are concerned with correlations between the traits of one topic with those of another topic. The four divisions are Subsistence, Material Culture, Economics, and Social Organization. There is one oversized map of Indian tribes of North America.

FARBER, JOSEPH C., and MICHAEL DORRIS. *Native Americans: 500 Years After.* New York: Thomas Y. Crowell, 1975. 333pp. Illustrated. Bibliography.
The book contains hundreds of photographs taken by Joseph C. Farber as he traveled throughout North America photographing Native Americans as they live today. The photographs are clustered in geographical areas which include Alaska, the Far West, the Southwest, the Plains, the Great Lakes, the Northeast, and the Southeast. The concise text by Michael Dorris discusses the history of Native Americans on the North American continent. Each section is introduced with a note about the current status and historical context of the tribes in that area. There is a list of the locations photographed and a selected list of readings.

HALLOWELL, A. IRVING. "The Impact of the American Indian on American Culture." *American Anthropologist* 59, no. 2 (April 1957):201–17.
The author considers studies about the influence of Indians on American culture written by Alexander F. Chamberlain, Clark Wissler, Frederick Jackson Turner, Bernard De Voto, and others. He suggests that the significance of the impact not be confined exclusively to exchanges of objects in trade or more complex cultural borrowings in the narrowest sense. In addition, he tells how Indians exerted an influence on the American mind especially in the fields of literature, music, and art.

HODGE, FREDERICK WEBB. *Handbook of Indians of Canada.* Published as an Appendix to the Tenth Report of the Geographic Board of Canada. Ottawa: 1913. 632pp. Illustrated. Bibliography. Reprint ed.: Mamaroneck, N.Y.: Kraus Reprint Co., 1969.
This *Handbook* treats only tribes residing wholly or in part in Canada. The aim is to give a brief description of every linguistic stock, confederacy, tribe, subtribe, tribal division, and settlement known to history or to tradition as well as the origin and derivation of every name treated, whenever it is known, and to record under each every form of the name and every other appellation that could be learned. These synonyms are assembled in alphabetic order as cross-references in an appendix. There is a map showing the territory occupied by the natives of Canada, Alaska, and Greenland and maps showing the areas in which Indian title has been quieted by treaties with the natives.

———, ed. *Handbook of American Indians North of Mexico.* 2 vols. Bureau of American Ethnology Bulletin 30, parts 1 and 2. Washington, D.C.: Government Printing Office, 1907–10; part 1, 972pp.; part 2, 1,221pp. Illustrated. Bibliography. Reprint ed.: New York: Pageant Books, 1959.
Containing work begun in 1873 and completed in 1910, the *Handbook* treats all the tribes north of Mexico including Eskimos and those tribes south of the boundary more or less affiliated with those of the United States. The aim is to give a brief description of every linguistic stock, confederacy, tribe, subtribe or tribal division, and settlement known to history or to tradition as well as the origin and derivation of every name treated, whenever it is known, and to record under each every form of the name and every other appellation that could be learned. These synonyms, in alphabetic order, are assembled as cross-references in part 2. Under the tribal descriptions a brief account of the ethnic relations of the tribe, its history, its location at various periods, statistics of population, etc., are included. Accompanying each synonym, the earliest known date always being given, a reference to the authority is noted, and these references form a bibliography of the tribe for those who desire to pursue the subject further. There are illustrations throughout the two volumes and the second volume contains the bibliography.
The Smithsonian Institution is working on a new twenty-volume series, entitled *Handbook of North American Indians,* that will give an encyclopedic summary of what is known about the prehistory, history, and cultures of the aboriginal peoples of North America who lived north of the urban civilizations of central Mexico. For individual titles, see below under Northeast, Trigger; Southwest, Ortiz; and California, Heizer.

JENNESS, DIAMOND. *The Indians of Canada.* National Museum of Canada Bulletin 65, Anthropological Series no. 15. Ottawa: National Museum of Canada, 1960. 452pp. Illustrated. Bibliography.
Information about the Indians of Canada is presented here in two parts. The first part is topically arranged under Languages, Economic Conditions, Food Resources, Hunting and Fishing, Dress and Adornment, Dwellings, Travel and Transportation, Trade and Commerce, Social and Political Organization of Primitive Migratory Tribes, Iroquoians and Pacific Coast Tribes, Social Life, Religion, Folklore and Traditions, Oratory and Drama, Music and Art, Archaeological Remains, and Interaction of Indians and Whites. The second part discusses tribes of culture areas including Eastern Woodlands, Plains, Pacific Coast, Cordilleras, Mackenzie and Yukon River Basins, and Eskimos. There is a map of linguistic and tribal divisions and many photographs.

JENNINGS, JESSE D., and ROBERT F. SPENCER, *et al.* *The Native Americans: Ethnology and Backgrounds of North American Indians.* 2nd ed., rev. New York: Harper & Row, 1977. 584pp. Illustrated. Bibliography.
This book is intended as a textbook at the college or university level or as an introductory text for the general reader. Regional scholars focus on traditional culture patterns in describing representative tribes from each of the major culture areas of North America. The first chapter synthesizes information on prehistory; concluding chapters discuss urban adaptation and problems related to the changing conditions of Native Americans in contemporary

America. Areas and representative groups discussed are: Arctic and Subarctic—Eskimos and Athapaskans; Northwest Coast—Tlingits, Haidas, Tsimshians, Kwakiutls, and Nootkas; Western North America—(Plateau) Sanpoil-Nespelims and Klamaths, (California) Hupas, Pomos, Luiseños and Mohaves, (Basin) Shoshones; Southwest—Zuñis, Navajos; Great Plains—Mandans, Teton Dakotas and Kiowas; Northeast—Iroquois, Penobscots, and Ojibways; and Southeast—Natchez and Creeks. A list of suggested readings follows each chapter and a "Guide to American Indian Tribes" is provided.

JONES, CHARLES, ed. *Look to the Mountain Top*. San Jose, Calif.: H. M. Gausha, 1972. 121pp. Illustrated. Bibliography.

Articles by contemporary authors discuss various aspects of Native American life. Part 1 contains papers on Native Americans as ecologists, Native American arts, the literature of the first Americans, Native American women—a legacy of freedom, American Indians as warriors, religions, healing arts, farming and wild foods, economic conditions, the basis of Indian law, and the politics of the American Indian. Part 2 presents maps of Native American lands 1492–1972, a historical chronology, and articles on writing systems, examples of oratory, a discussion of stereotypes, the growth of arts and crafts and where to buy them, some recipes, and a book list.

KROEBER, A. L. *Cultural and Natural Areas of Native North America*. University of California Publications in American Archaelogy and Ethnology, vol. 38. Berkeley: University of California Press, 1939; reprint ed.: Mamaroneck, N.Y.: Kraus Reprint Co., 1965. 232pp. Maps.

Identifying seven major culture areas, or geographical units, for North America, this volume also lists eighty-four subdivisions or subareas. A brief discussion of the history of the concept of culture areas, climaxes, and boundaries is followed by an area-by-area description of the cultures and their areas with specific attention to geographical and ecological factors. The author also examines cultural development in relation to environmental and historical forces.

LEACOCK, ELEANOR BURKE, and NANCY OESTREICH LURIE, eds. *North American Indians in Historical Perspective*. New York: Random House, 1971. 498pp. Illustrated. Bibliography.

The focus of this book is on recent Indian history and its exemplification of constantly emerging ways of dealing with and adapting to new circumstances. The essays include "Americans Called Indians," a brief review of Indian adaptations to varying types of environment, "The Coastal Algonkians: People of the First Frontiers," "Creek into Seminole," "The Iroquois in History," "The Chippewa of the Upper Great Lakes: A Study in Socio-political Change," "The Plains Indians: Their Continuity in History and Their Indian Identity," "The American Southwest," "The Ute and Paiute Indians of the Great Basin Southern Rim," "California," "The Tlingit Indians," "The Hunting Tribes of Subarctic

Canada," "The Changing Eskimo World," and "The Contemporary American Indian Scene." There is a map and photographs of natives.

LEVINE, STUART, and NANCY OESTREICH LURIE, eds. *The American Indian Today*. Baltimore: Penguin Books, 1968. 352pp. Illustrated. Bibliography.

This book contains a collection of papers which provide some basic information about the history of Native Americans, their relationships with the U.S. government and its colonial predecessors, and introduces specific problems which face these people, giving examples of the situation in specific places around the nation. Cases in point are: the "isolated" Eastern Cherokees, Oklahoma Indians today, factional conflict among the Prairie Potawatomi, the current status of the Huma Indians, and limitations in acculturation among the Nez Percé. Additional papers discuss the problems presented by an educational program that is largely irrelevant to the people it is supposed to educate, explore the mutual learning experiences of tribes and attorneys they hire, and investigate the contemporary trends and attitudes in Indian affairs. A map shows the distribution of American Indians in 1950.

LINTON, RALPH, ed. *Acculturation in Seven American Indian Tribes*. New York: Appleton-Century, 1940. 526pp.

A series of acculturation studies of seven American Indian tribes, all prepared by scholars in accordance with a single plan or outline, are contained in this volume. The groups considered are the Puyallup of Washington, the White Knife Shoshone of Nevada, the Southern Ute of Colorado, the Northern Arapaho of Wyoming, the Fox of Iowa, the Alkatcho Carrier of British Columbia, and the San Ildefonso of New Mexico. The work concludes with a theoretical discussion of acculturation and the processes of culture change and culture transfer.

LITTON, GASTON. "The Resources of the National Archives for the Study of the American Indian." *Ethnohistory* 2, no. 3 (Summer 1955):191–208.

The author discusses the basic forms of archival materials which began to accumulate in 1789. The first category of correspondence forms the heart of the archival resources on Indians. These diverse files of correspondence contain the fullest and the frankest exchange on all matters of the Indians' relationship to the federal government, the states, the Indian tribes and individuals, and the general public. The second category consists of a series of reports covering a wide gamut of governmental business with the Indians. There are maps, photographs, motion pictures, and census rolls. There is little archival material from 1789 to 1800 due to a fire. The author explains the various federal agencies which have deposited their materials in the archives including the War Department, Army, Superintendent of Indian Trade, Indian Territory Division, Appointment Division, U.S. Court of Claims, Indian Claims Commission, General Land Office, Public Health Service, Pension Office, Geological Survey, etc. The archives are being microfilmed.

LYON, JUANA P., ed. *The Indian Elder: A Forgotten American*. Final Report on the First National Indian Conference on the Aging. Washington, D.C.: National Tribal Chairmen's Association, 1978. 595pp.

This report contains the recommendations and resolutions of some 1,500 Indian and Alaskan natives, representing 171 tribes, who met to speak of their needs and offer suggestions for action to improve the quality of their lives. The proceedings of the conference include statements by individuals and remarks by a panel of tribal elders. An appendix contains responses to a questionnaire submitted to groups in an effort to gather reliable data pertaining to American Indian elderly, presents statements on tribal sovereignty and government, excerpts from selected Congressional reports and testimony, and reprints area reports on programs and needs of older Native Americans from across the nation.

MALLERY, GARRICK. *Picture-Writing of the American Indians*. Bureau of American Ethnology 10th Annual Report, 1888–1889. Washington, D.C.: Government Printing Office, 1893; reprint ed.: 2 vols. New York: Dover Publications, 1972. 822pp. Illustrated. Bibliography.

This report on picture writing of American Indians places emphasis on the meaning of pictures and the differences between the styles of picture writing of the various tribes. Included are nearly 1,300 pictures and 54 plates illustrating the material which the author discusses. The subjects of pictography are classified and studied under the following headings: knotted cords, notched or marked sticks and wampum; mnemonic pictures for remembering songs, traditions, treaties, and accounts; the calendars (winter counts) of Lone-Dog and Battiste Good; maps, notices of visits, condition and warning; tribal designations, clan designations, tattoo marks (especially the Haida); designations of authority, property, and personal names; religious symbols of the supernatural and of mythic animals; symbols used on charms and amulets, in religious ceremonies, and in the burial of the dead; pictographs of cult associations, of daily events, and of games; historic records such as the Indian account of the Battle of the Little Bighorn; records of migrations, hunts, and notable events; biographical records; significance of colors; picture writing as it became conventionalized, and more. There are also sections on the interpretation of pictographs, on the detection of frauds, and comparative material from other cultures. There is a special section on petroglyphs (rock writing). Descriptions, with illustrations, are presented of petroglyphs in North America, including those in several provinces of Canada, in many of the states and territories of the United States, in Mexico, and in the West Indies. A large number from Central and South America also appear, followed by examples from Australia, Oceania, Europe, Africa, and Asia, included chiefly for comparison with the picture writings in America.

MCNICKLE, D'ARCY. *They Came Here First: The Epic of the American Indian*. Rev. ed. New York: Harper & Row, 1975. 310pp.

Some 25,000 years of American life are interpreted and explained from a Native American point of view. The author describes the process by which Native Americans have survived and adapted and yet retain separate and identifiable traditions faithful to their own past. Part 1 discusses Native American prehistory, physical characteristics, linguistics, the development of cultures and agriculture, law systems, language, and religion. Part 2 describes the second discovery of America and discusses first contacts between Europeans and Native Americans, and explores the policies of Spain, France, and England toward Native Americans. Part 3 chronicles the years from 1775 to the 1970s, focusing on Native American reactions to the theft of their lands and the assaults on their ways of life.

MEDICINE, BEA. *The Native American Woman: A Perspective*. Austin, Tex.: National Educational Laboratory Publishers, 1978. 107pp. Illustrated. Bibliography.

The material contained in this book is addressed to the need for organized data in analyzing women's roles in Native American culture. The author discusses Native Americans and anthropology, with the focus on a bias favoring males; the Native American woman in ethnographic perspective, with suggested approaches of study; the Native American woman in historical perspective, with examples of degrading and derogatory views that persist in historical accounts; the Plains Native American woman which discusses, expands, and corrects the literature. Concluding chapters examine the situation of the Native American woman in transition and identify issues and challenges facing the contemporary Native American woman. The author, born and raised on the Standing Rock Reservation in South Dakota, combines scholarship and traditional knowledge in this consideration of the problems encountered in the study of women's roles in Native American societies.

NATIONAL GEOGRAPHIC SOCIETY. *The World of the American Indian*. Washington, D.C.: National Geographic Society, 1974. 399pp. Illustrated.

This volume contains 440 illustrations, 362 in full color, and texts by ten scholar-authors that show Indians as they were—their beliefs, customs, crafts, appearance—and that provide an understanding of what they are today. The texts describe the arrival of people on this continent and trace their spread across the land, developing cultures as varied as the regions they settled. There are chapters on archaeology, native languages, the clash between Indians and whites, and the current struggle of Indians to determine their own future. The chapters that concern the diverse cultures of Indians are entitled: "Nomads of the North," "Woodsmen and Villagers of the East," "Farmers and Raiders of the Southwest," "Fishermen and Foragers of the West," and "Horsemen of the Plains." There is a supplement that lists all the tribal groups of the United States and Canada that are shown on the book's back pocket map.

NEWCOMB, WILLIAM W., JR. *North American Indians: An Anthropological Perspective.* Pacific Palisades, Calif.: Goodyear Publishing, 1974. 278pp. Bibliography.

This book provides readers with an introduction to Indians of North America. An introductory chapter touches on the concept of culture, origins and cultural development, biological nature, aboriginal population, and languages of North American Indians. In subsequent chapters the environmental setting, prehistory, and history of each culture area are sketched in before the salient features of the cultures are summarized. Chapters are entitled "Southeastern Farmers," "Northeastern Hunter-Farmers," "Plains Bison Hunters," "Subarctic Hunters and Fishermen," "Desert Gatherers," "Southwestern Farmers," "Plateau Fishermen-Gatherers," "California Gatherers," and "Northwest Coast Fishermen." The author concludes with a comparative summary of culture areas.

NICHOLS, ROGER L., and GEORGE R. ADAMS, eds. *The American Indian: Past and Present.* Waltham, Mass.: Xerox College Publishing, 1971. 295pp. Bibliography.

Twenty-four articles are arranged chronologically in this book to demonstrate the changing position of Native Americans within the country throughout its history. Brief headnotes provide background information and place each essay in its historical context. Many of the essays are footnoted.

OSWALT, WENDELL. *This Land Was Theirs: A Study of the North American Indian.* 2nd ed. New York: John Wiley & Sons, 1973. 617pp. Bibliography.

Chapters in this book are devoted to geographically representative tribes, each chapter covering the same range of topics but with some variation in topical order. There is a diversified representation in terms of culture, society, and language. The final chapter summarizes the position of Indians in modern American and Canadian life. Tribes included are the Chipewyan, hunters and fishers of the Subarctic; the Caribou Eskimo, hunters of the tundra; the Kuskowagamiut, riverine Eskimos; the Cahuilla, gatherers of the desert; the Fox, fighters and farmers of the woodland fringe; Pawnee, horsemen and farmers of the prairies; Yurok, salmon fishermen of California; Tlingit, salmon fishermen of the Northwest; Hopi, farmers of the desert; Iroquois, warriors and farmers of the eastern woodlands; Eastern Cherokee, farmers of the Southeast; and Natchez, sophisticated farmers of the deep South. There are maps and photographs of natives.

OWEN, ROGER C.; JAMES J. F. DEETZ; and ANTHONY D. FISHER. *The North American Indians: A Sourcebook.* New York: Macmillan, 1967. 752pp.

This collection of articles is intended as a general introduction to the study of the aboriginal populations of North America, the articles grouped according to culture area. The editors have included descriptive articles, those representative of the major theoretical points of view (historical, psychological, configurational, structural, functional, evolutionary), and articles that cover the major topical areas,

as well as provide examples of writings from various time periods. The first section presents articles on demography, culture areas, physical characteristics, languages, religion, and music. Area papers deal with Eskimos, northern hunters in Canada, peoples of the Basin-Plateau, the Northwest Coast, California, Southwest Native American groups, the Plains, and the Eastern agriculturists. The last section contains essays on Native Americans in the modern world. Sources of the articles are fully identified. A list of 251 educational films is organized into regional categories consistent with the organization of the book.

PRICE, JOHN A. *Native Studies: American and Canadian Indians.* Montreal: McGraw-Hill Ryerson, 1978. 309pp. Bibliography.

Twenty-one chapters in this book are organized in a sequence for use as an introduction to Native American groups in the United States and Canada. The first chapter discusses the rise of native studies as a new, interdisciplinary, academic subject. The body of the text has three clusters of chapters: genesis and traditional heritage, Native American urbanization and institutionalization, and modern problems and their solutions. The last chapter examines the need to bring science and humanism together in future native studies.

SMITHSONIAN INSTITUTION. Bureau of American Ethnology Bulletins and Annual Reports. Washington, D.C.: Government Printing Office, 1887–1971.

This series consists of forty-eight Annual Reports and 200 Bulletins. The first forty-seven Annual Reports contain, in addition to an administrative report, ethnological papers and monographs covering all phases of aboriginal life plus numerous archaeological surveys. The forty-eighth Annual Report includes an index to the preceding reports. The Bulletins contain articles, memoirs, and monographs on language, arts and industries, institutions and organizations, myths and beliefs, ethnobotany, ethnogeography, bibliographies of Indian languages, physical anthropology, and archaeology. Bulletin 200 has a list of publications of the Bureau of American Ethnology with an index to authors and titles. The bulletins and annual reports have been microfilmed by the Microfilming Corporation of America.

SPICER, EDWARD H., ed. *Perspectives in American Indian Culture Change.* Chicago: University of Chicago Press, 1961. 549pp. Illustrated.

This book contains six comparative studies of American Indian cultures which have in common a systematic framework of investigation considering the whole series of changes in Indian ways of life from the earliest contacts with Europeans to the present. The aim of the studies is to discover whether there are any fundamental similarities in responses of different Indian groups to similar conditions of contact. The conditions of change are described in each case and compared and related to the whole picture of cultural change. The studies show differences in the dominant processes of change and kinds of adaption within the cultures studied. The six groups studied are the Yaquis, Rio Grande Pueblos, Mandans, Navajos, Wasco-Wishrams, and the Kwakiutls. The studies point to the existence of similar social and cultural processes at work under the surface of reservation life. The last chapter analyzes the relationship between the type of contact and the type of change and generalizes about the relationships. There are twelve maps and ten tables which summarize the contact history of the six groups and other aspects of culture change. References follow each essay.

STEWARD, JULIAN H., ed. *Handbook of South American Indians.* 7 vols. Bureau of American Ethnology Bulletin 143. Washington, D.C.: Government Printing Office, 1946–59. Illustrated. Bibliographies.

This comprehensive study centers attention on the culture of each South American group studied as it was at the time of its first contact with Europeans. Archaeological information is included when available, as is postcontact information. Volumes 1–6 treat the marginal groups, the Andean cultures; the tropical forest groups; the circum-Caribbean area; comparative ethnology; physical anthropology; and linguistics and cultural geography. Volume 7 is an index to the previous six volumes.

SWANTON, JOHN R. *The Indian Tribes of North America.* Bureau of American Ethnology Bulletin 145. Washington, D.C.: Government Printing Office, 1952. 726pp. Illustrated. Bibliography.

The author lists the tribes, their subdivisions, and villages in each of the forty-nine states (excluding Hawaii), Canada, the West Indies (Haiti, Cuba, Puerto Rico, and Jamaica), Mexico, and Central America. Also included is the origin of the tribal name, a brief list of the more important synonyms, the linguistic connections of the tribe, its location, a brief sketch of its history, its estimated and actual population at different periods, and the "connection in which it has become noted," particularly the extent to which its name has been perpetuated geographically or otherwise. There are four maps illustrating the locations of the Indian tribes of North America.

U.S. DEPARTMENT OF COMMERCE. *Federal and State Indian Reservations and Trust Areas.* Washington, D.C.: Government Printing Office, 1974. 604pp. Illustrated.

This work is a directory of federal and state Indian reservations, Alaskan native villages, and Indian trust lands in Oklahoma. Lands and reservations are cataloged by thirty-one states: Alaska, Arizona, California, Colorado, Connecticut, Florida, Idaho, Iowa, Kansas, Louisiana, Maine, Massachusetts, Michigan, Minnesota, Mississippi, Montana, Nebraska, Nevada, New Mexico, New York, North Carolina, North Dakota, Oklahoma, Oregon, South Dakota, Texas, Utah, Virginia, Washington, Wisconsin, and Wyoming. Typical information given for Alaskan native villages, federal or state reservations, rancherias, or communities includes land area, acres allotted, land status, location of tribal

headquarters, as well as brief remarks on culture, history, government, economy, climate, transportation, community facilities, recreation, labor force, and education. There are photographs of historical and contemporary Indian life and artifacts.

WALKER, DEWARD E., JR., ed. *The Emergent Native Americans: A Reader in Culture Contact.* Boston: Little, Brown, 1972. 818pp. Bibliography.

This reader chronicles the changes in Native American cultures north of Mexico that have been brought about by exposure to Euro-American influences. The articles emphasize the processes that have eroded, transformed, and, in recent times, are revitalizing Native American cultures. The first section contains articles about acculturation theories, methods, and general trends. Articles in subsequent sections treat policies of native administration that have largely determined the outcome of acculturation among Native Americans; population decline and recovery, revealing the impact alien diseases have had on Native Americans; technoeconomic change, second only to population decimation in overall acculturational impact; new religions, primary forms of acculturation among Native Americans; changing social relations, a fundamental part of acculturation in North America; changing values and beliefs; conflict and social problems; persistence and resurgence which illustrate the spirit of revitalization among Native Americans; and Native Americans living in urban areas and Pan-Indianism.

WAUCHOPE, ROBERT. *Handbook of Middle American Indians.* 16 vols. Austin: University of Texas Press, 1964–76. Illustrated. Bibliography.

The first eleven volumes in this study treat the natural environment and early cultures of Middle America, discuss the archaeology of southern Mexico, northern and southern Middle America, social organization, ethnology, and physical anthropology. Volumes 12–15 are a comprehensive guide to ethnohistorical sources. Volume 16 is a unified list of sources cited and artifacts illustrated in the previous volumes.

YINGER, J. MILTON, and GEORGE EATON SIMPSON, eds. "American Indians Today." *The Annals of the American Academy of Political and Social Science* 436:1–151. Philadelphia: American Academy of Political and Social Science, 1978.

Twelve articles in this issue examine various aspects of Native American life and of the relationship of American Indians to the government and the larger society. For the most part, the articles update a previous issue of *The Annals* (George E. Simpson, and J. Milton Yinger, "American Indians and American Life." *The Annals of the American Academy of Political and Social Science,* vol. 311, 1957). Articles discuss the economic basis of Indian life; education since 1960; religion; health care; the Bureau of Indian Affairs since 1945; identity, militance, and cultural congruence; legislation and litigation; the Indian Claims Commission; current social and demographic trends; the impact of urbanization on Native Americans; and integration.

NORTHEAST

RITZENTHALER, ROBERT E., and PAT RITZENTHALER. *The Woodland Indians of the Western Great Lakes.* Garden City, N.Y.: Natural History Press, 1970. 178pp. Illustrated. Bibliography.

This book deals mainly with the culture of the Central Algonquians of the western Great Lakes area from the time when Europeans first arrived in the area until there was considerable change due to contact. Chapters discuss the food quest, the life cycle, social organization, material culture, religious and ceremonial life, shamanism and curative techniques, games, music, and folklore. Groups who lived in the area include the Chippewas (Ojibways), Ottawas, Potawatomis, Menominees, Crees, Sacs, Foxes (Mesquakies), Kickapoos, Miamis, Peorias, Illinois, Shawnees, Prairie Potawatomis, and Winnebagos.

TRIGGER, BRUCE G., ed. *Handbook of North American Indians: Northeast.* Vol. 15 *Handbook of North American Indians,* William C. Sturtevant, gen. ed. Washington, D.C.: Smithsonian Institution, 1978. 924pp. Illustrated. Bibliography.

A summary of what is presently known of the aboriginal culture forms and practices of the Native American groups who now live in the northeastern United States and southeastern Canada, or who lived there during the most significant or best documented period of their history, is provided in this volume. A history of the research reviews the literature and suggests sources. Sections on individual tribes contain information on marriage customs, kinship patterns, burial customs, and other social institutions. Areas treated are the Coastal Region (Atlantic Coast down to, and including, the northern half of the coast of North Carolina), the St. Lawrence Lowlands region, and the Great Lakes-Riverine region. Sections at the end of most chapters provide general guidance to important sources of information on the topics covered.

SOUTHEAST

HUDSON, CHARLES M. *The Southeastern Indians.* Knoxville: University of Tennessee Press, 1976. 573pp. Illustrated. Bibliography.

This volume traces the main outlines of the prehistory, social institutions, and history of the Native American groups of the southeast United States. The author describes the regions and discusses linguistics, physical characteristics, religion, social organization, subsistence, ceremony, art, music, and recreation. A final section brings the groups into modern times.

SWANTON, JOHN R. *The Indians of the Southeastern United States.* Bureau of American Ethnology Bulletin 137. Washington, D.C.: Government Printing Office, 1946. 943pp. Illustrated. Bibliography.

This is a topically arranged book which considers Indians who lived in Georgia, Florida, Alabama, Mississippi, Louisiana, northeast Texas, southern Arkansas, south and west South Carolina, part of North Carolina, and nearly all of Tennessee and marginal districts. The author begins with a discussion of the geography of the Southeast, a classification of southeastern tribes, their population, the relation of the aboriginal population to the natural areas, prehistoric movements, the history of these Indians from the period of the first white contact until the expedition of Hernando de Soto, and the post-de Soto period. There are sketches of around 175 southeastern tribes and their populations. Chapters focus upon interpretations of tribal names, physical and mental characteristics, the influence of language, raw materials used by southeastern Indians, the annual economic cycle, food, horticulture, hunting, fishing, domestication of animals, preparation of vegetable foods, treatment of meats, preservation of food, tobacco, housing, clothing, ornamentation, the use of stone, pottery, miscellaneous household items, implements used in hunting and fishing, war, transportation, materials and baskets, dyeing, mnemonic devices, artistic development, musical instruments, and societal and ceremonial life. There are 13 maps and 107 plates that illustrate the text.

GREAT PLAINS

HOEBEL, E. ADAMSON. *The Cheyennes: Indians of the Great Plains.* Case Studies in Anthropology. New York: Holt, Rinehart & Winston, 1978. 135pp. Illustrated. Bibliography.

A descriptive interpretation of the traditional culture of the Cheyennes is the subject of this book. Part 1 discusses prehistory and early history. Part 2 describes social structure, family, kindred and band, societies, law and justice, religion, subsistence, trade, warfare, world view, and personality. Part 3 covers the years between 1850 and 1978, discussing war with the United States, reservation days for the Southern Cheyennes, religious survival, modern political and social action, and socioeconomic needs and potential.

LOWIE, ROBERT H. *Indians of the Plains.* Garden City, N.Y.: Natural History Press, 1963. 258pp. Illustrated. Bibliography.

The theme of this book is the culture of the Native American groups that inhabited the North American Plains from the Mississippi River to the Rocky Mountains. Lifeways are described from the time Europeans first arrived in the area until there was considerable change due to contact. Chapters discuss material culture, social organization, recreation, art, religion and ceremonialism, prehistory, history, and acculturation. Groups included are the Algonquian Blackfeet, Cheyennes, Arapahos, Gros Ventres, Plains Cree and Plains Ojibway (Chippewa); the Athapaskan Sarsis and Kiowa Apaches; the Kiowan Kiowas; the Siouan Mandans, Hidatsas, Crows, Dakotas, Assiniboines, Iowas, Otos, Missouris, Omahas, Poncas, Osages, and Kansas; and the Uto-Aztecan Wind River Shoshones, Comanches, and Utes.

NURGE, ETHEL, ed. *The Modern Sioux: Social Systems and Reservation Culture.* Lincoln: University of Nebraska Press, 1970. 352pp. Bibliography.

Papers in this collection discuss the status of contemporary Dakota Sioux on the Pine Ridge and Rosebud Reservations in South Dakota. The nature of the culture that has emerged as a result of the meeting and commingling of the Dakotas and European immigrants is considered in the light of a century of interaction, in war and peace. Articles discuss culture change and the dynamics of societal interrelations; community development and programs; social systems and reservation culture; economy; traditional and contemporary diet; culture change; political and religious systems; individuals in the social system; and contemporary music and dance.

ROE, FRANK G. *The Indian and the Horse.* Norman: University of Oklahoma Press, 1955. Bibliography.

This book contains a comprehensive overview of the coming and influence of the horse among the Native American groups of the Great Plains. The author presents data on the role of the horse as a controlling factor in some aspects of the Great Plains societies and documents various aspects regarding horses—ownership, treatment, etc. The author argues that the arrival of the horse did not change, but intensified, cultural traits already in existence, enabling the people to do more easily what they always had done, and that those who were mobile remained so, those who were traders remained traders, and those who were sedentary remained sedentary.

SATTERLEE, JAMES L., and VERNON D. MALAN. *History and Acculturation of the Dakota Indians.* Agricultural Experiment Station, Department of Rural Sociology, Pamphlet 126. Brookings: South Dakota State University, 1973. 76pp. Bibliography.

An anthropological overview of the Dakota peoples is presented in this book. A brief discussion of the origin and prehistory of Native Americans is followed by a historical sketch of the Dakota Sioux and a description of the structure of eastern and western Dakota culture (kinship, economy, religion, government). Acculturation as a social process, its implications for the Dakotas, and problems due to acculturative dysfunctions and pressures are also considered. The work terminates with a summary and conclusions.

SOUTHWEST

DOWNS, JAMES R. *The Navajo.* New York: Holt, Rinehart & Winston, 1972. 136pp. Illustrated. Bibliography.

Various aspects of Navajo life in a pastoral community are described within the framework of the ongoing, unending work required to keep sheep and cattle herds and maintain a social and cultural system based on these activities. The author discusses Navajo society, social units (family, home-stead, and outfit), the clan, kinship and kinfolk, residence, mobility and land tenure, the animals, crops, religion, wealth and traders, headmen and chairmen, and change and continuity.

DOZIER, EDWARD P. *The Pueblo Indians of North America.* Case Studies in Cultural Anthropology. New York: Holt, Rinehart & Winston, 1970. 224pp. Illustrated. Bibliography.

A study depicting the culture of a group of related peoples of the southwestern United States, this work describes their adaptation through time to their changing physical, socioeconomic, and political environments. The author presents prehistoric and historic background information, discusses population and settlement patterns, kinship, lineage and clan, ceremonial organization of the Eastern and Western Pueblos, and gives an overview of general Pueblo characteristics.

————. "The Pueblo Indians of the Southwest: A Survey of the Anthropological Literature and a Review of Theory, Method, and Results." *Current Anthropology* 5, no. 2 (1964):79–97. Bibliography.

A representative selection of the anthropological literature on the Pueblo Indians is surveyed chronologically under topical headings. Current methods, theory, the results of investigations, and the main contributions of Pueblo studies to the development of anthropology are discussed. Topics are archaeology, linguistics, ethnology and social anthropology, culture and personality, culture change, and the present.

ORTIZ, ALFONSO, ed. *Handbook of North American Indians: Southwest.* Vol. 9 *Handbook of North American Indians.* William C. Sturtevant, gen. ed. Washington, D.C.: Smithsonian Institution, 1979. 700pp. Illustrated. Bibliography.

This volume summarizes scholarly knowledge of the history and cultures of the Native American groups of the southwestern United States from earliest prehistoric times to the present. Articles present information on individual tribes, covering prehistory and social organization including marriage customs, kinship patterns, burial customs, religion, and social institutions.

————, ed. *New Perspectives on the Pueblos.* A School of American Research Book. Albuquerque: University of New Mexico Press, 1972. 340pp.

Scholars discuss the Pueblos of the North American Southwest from various points of view. An ecological perspective on the Eastern Pueblos is followed by discussions of Pueblo prehistory, Rio Grande ethnohistory, Pueblo social organization, linguistics, ritual drama and the Pueblo world view, the ritual clown, Pueblo religion, literature, ethnomusicology, acculturation process, and population dynamics. References follow the discussions.

GREAT BASIN–PLATEAU

D'AZEVEDO, WARREN L.; WILBUR A. DAVIS; DON D. FOWLER; and WAYNE SUTTLES. *The Current Status of Anthropological Research in the Great Basin, 1964.* Social Sciences and Humanities Publications, no. 1. Reno: Desert Research Institute, 1966. 379pp. Illustrated. Bibliography.

Papers in this collection provide a basic assemblage and assessment of the information available on Great Basin peoples—the Northern Paiutes, the Southern Paiutes, Utes, Northern Shoshones, and Washos. Part 1 contains articles on ethnohistory, environmental manipulation, social organization, linguistics, prehistory, theoretical problems, and tribal distributions and boundaries. Part 2 presents comments on the papers. There are maps.

RAY, VERN F. *Cultural Relations in the Plateau of Northwestern America.* Publications of the Frederick Webb Hodge Anniversary Publication Fund, vol. 3. Los Angeles: Southwest Museum, 1939; reprint ed., 1964. 154pp. Illustrated. Bibliography.

The Plateau is the area between the Rocky Mountains (on the east) and the Cascade Mountains (on the west), extending to the big bend in the Fraser River on the north and southward into the Colorado Plateau. The author examines the conditions under which the cultural diversity of the Native American groups of the Plateau area was developed and describes the conceptual structures of various significant complexes in Plateau culture. Social life—social culture and stratification, religious life, customs, etc.—is emphasized over material culture. Groups discussed include the Carriers, Chilcotins, Shuswaps, Lillooets, Lower Thompsons, Lake Kutenais, Kalispels, Flatheads, Coeur d'Alenes, Sanpoils, Wenatchis, Kittitas, Klikitats, Yakimas, Teninos, Umatillas, and Cayuses. There are maps.

CALIFORNIA

BEAN, LOWELL J., and THOMAS C. BLACKBURN, eds. *Native Californians: A Theoretical Retrospective.* Ramona, Calif.: Ballena Press, 1976. 452pp. Bibliography.

Sixteen articles in this volume discuss California ethnography. Geographically, all of California is represented, the collection presenting an overall picture of aboriginal California society. The majority of the authors hold that the complexity of California Native American society has been greatly under emphasized in the past.

HEIZER, ROBERT F., ed. *Handbook of North American Indians: California.* Vol. 8 *Handbook of North American Indians,* William C. Sturtevant, gen. ed. Washington, D.C.: Smithsonian Institution, 1978. 800pp. Illustrated. Bibliography.

This volume provides a summary of what is presently known of the aboriginal culture forms and practices of the Native Americans of California. Tribal sketches are supplemented by essays on such subjects as trade, music, religion, and myths. See particularly "Social Organization," by Lowell John Bean, in which the author refutes an earlier view that California Indian societies were simple by describing a world of hunters and gatherers whose singularly complex social systems were similar to those of horticulturists and some agriculturists with presumably greater technological advantages. Bean discusses basic social units, levels of organization, social mechanisms, and social institutions.

————, and M. A. WHIPPLE, eds. *The California Indians: A Source Book.* 2nd ed., rev. Berkeley: University of California Press, 1971. 619pp. Illustrated. Bibliography.

Articles in this collection provide an introduction to various aspects of the cultures of Native American groups in California. Selections are organized under topical headings which include general surveys (cultures, linguistics, physical characteristics), archaeology, historical accounts, material culture and economy, and social culture (kinship, law, childhood, warfare, religion, urban living). A final essay presents information on population, economic conditions, education, and health. A classified bibliography lists published works arranged by culture areas and subjects.

KROEBER, A. L. *Handbook of Indians of California.* Bureau of American Ethnology Bulletin 78. Washington, D.C.: Government Printing Office, 1925. 995pp. Illustrated. Bibliography.

The author reviews some or all of such topics as population, material culture, land and civilization, law and customs, houses, religion, arts, geography, and politics of Indians in California. The tribes discussed are the Yurok, Karok, Chimariko and Wiyot, Tolowa, Hupa, Chilula, Whilkut, Athapaskan southern groups, Yuki, Huchnom and Coast Yuki, Wappo, Pomo, Coast and Lake Miwok, Shasta groups, Achomawi and Atsugewi, Modoc, Yani and Yahi, Penutian family, Wintun, Maidu, Miwok, Costanoans, Yokuts, Esselen and Salinans, Chumash, Washo, Shoshonean stock, Paiute, Mono and Koso, Chemehuevi, Kawaiisu and Tubatulabal, Seranno divisions, Gabrielaño, Juaneño, Luiseño, Cupeño, Cahuilla, Diegueño and Kamiah, Mohave, and Yuman tribes. There are maps, drawings, and photographs of artifacts. Native American groups from California have pointed out that this volume contains information that is incorrect.

NORTHWEST COAST

DRUCKER, PHILIP. *Cultures of the North Pacific Coast.* San Francisco: Chandler Publishing, 1965. 243pp. Illustrated. Bibliography.

This study recreates the unique patterns of culture of Native American groups along the western coastline of northern North America from Yakutat Bay, Alaska, on the north to Cape Mendicino, California on the south, as they existed before the arrival of Europeans. Habitat, economy and technology, social and political organization, and religion and ritual are described. The author contends that these cultures were very different from cultures north and south of the area, although in the same environment, because human use of environmental resources depends upon historical and other factors and not on simple automatic responses to geographical surroundings.

GUNTHER, ERNA. *Indian Life on the Northwest Coast of North America as Seen by the Early Explorers and Fur Traders during the Last Decades of the Eighteenth Century.* Chicago: University of Chicago Press, 1972. 277pp. Illustrated. Bibliography.

The author, in an ethnohistorical approach, reconstructs the cultures of the Northwest Coast Indians utilizing information in eighteenth-century diaries and journals. During extensive travels she sought out contemporaneous sketches from archives and examined eighteenth-century objects found in European collections and museums in order to establish the continuity and depth of Northwest Coast life and the areal extent of certain similarities.

MCFEAT, TOM, ed. *Indians of the North Pacific Coast.* Seattle: University of Washington Press, 1966. 268pp.

This book brings together key writings, many otherwise available only in out-of-print volumes or hard-to-find journals, by seventeen authorities in the field. Part 1 is an introduction to the area; part 2 deals with social organization; and part 3 examines the potlatch and part 4 presents viewpoints on rank and class. Ceremonialism, deviance, and normality are discussed in parts 5 and 6. An appendix provides culture element distributions. Groups treated include the Tlingits, Haidas, Tsimshians, Bellacoolas, Kwakiutls, Nootkas, and Salish.

ALASKA

BIRKET-SMITH, KAJ. *The Eskimos.* London: Methuen & Co., 1959; reprint ed.: New York: Crown, 1971. 275pp. Illustrated. Bibliography.

Originally published in Danish in 1927, and in English in 1936, this edition is updated to 1971. The author examines all of the important elements of Eskimo life, including all Eskimo groups. Methods of survival, social and family organization, religion and politics are discussed, the origin and development of Eskimo culture is outlined, and early contact with Europeans explored. A concluding essay by Diamond Jenness in the 1971 edition proposes assimilation as a solution to current social and economic problems. Although the book reflects an anthropological style and approach that is dated, it still contains useful information on Eskimo culture. There are photographs.

GRABURN, NELSON H. H., and B. STEPHEN STRONG. *Circumpolar Peoples: An Anthropological Perspective.* Pacific Palisades, Calif.: Goodyear Publishing, 1973. 236pp. Bibliography.

This book provides a broad guide to the anthropology of the wide circumpolar regions by focusing on particular problems and presenting brief but holistic sketches of the lifeways and history of a number of peoples of the North. An introductory chapter discusses geography, ecology and demography, physical anthropology, and common cultural characteristics. Subsequent chapters present general ethnographic sketches, discuss kinship, culture history, and offer culture descriptions and analyses. Groups studied include the Samek (Lapps), Northern Yakuts, Chuckchi, Athapaskan Indians, Kutchin, Northern Naskapi, Aleuts, and Eskimos. A closing section discusses modern conditions of the native peoples of Siberia, Alaska, and Canada. The bibliography lists additional bibliographies, journals, and ethnographic films.

LANTIS, MARGARET, ed. *Ethnohistory in Southwestern Alaska and the Southern Yukon: Method and Content.* Lexington: University Press of Kentucky, 1970. 311pp. Illustrated. Bibliography.

In this book, five anthropologists employ a combination of archaeological, ethnographic, and archival research methods in a cultural analysis of the Aleuts, the first people to be discovered in Alaska; the Indians and Eskimos of southwestern Alaska, especially those of the interior; and the Indians who live on the boundary of the Yukon Territory and British Columbia. The first part of the study approaches the subject from four different viewpoints: archaeology, archival history, social history, and folk history. Each of the authors seeks to reconstruct the first contact between the native peoples and Western civilization, discussing both their methods and their results. The second part indicates the effect of conquest on the nonmaterial culture of the Aleuts. The editor assembles archival materials, some of them translated from the Russian, from the age of north Pacific discovery, 1750–1810. She also considers historical sources and their use for the study of the Aleut social system up to the present. The bibliography includes Russian as well as English sources for the study of Aleut culture and history. There are five maps and photographs of Eskimo lifestyle.

SPENCER, ROBERT F. *The North Alaskan Eskimo: A Study in Ecology and Society.* Bureau of American Ethnology Bulletin 171. Washington, D.C.: Government Printing Office, 1959; reprint ed.: New York: Dover Publications, 1976. 490pp. Illustrated. Bibliography.

This study of the Eskimos of the Point Barrow region describes both their traditional folkways and the changes brought about by the introduction of a moneyed economy. The author traces the relations within the family and community, the life cycle, concepts of ownership and status, customary law, language, folklore, supernatural beliefs, shamanism, the Messenger Feast, and many other aspects of Eskimo society and tradition. He presents their legends, creation myths, and children's stories as well as detailed descriptions of the hunts of the inland and coastal Eskimos and of the mythologies surrounding the hunts. Among the questions the author examines are the extent to which the whalers' overall social patterns differ from those of the caribou hunters', and the effects of the opening of a naval petroleum reserve at Point Barrow on traditional social ways. There are four maps and photographs of Eskimos and their village life.

PART II

History and Historical Sources

3 GEOGRAPHY AND CARTOGRAPHY

This section includes selected works that illustrate different aspects of the discipline of geography and their application to the study of Indians. Social scientists have investigated the physical geography of various tribes, have explored the ethnogeographical experience of Indian groups, and have mapped locations and movements of tribes in historic and contemporary times.

A number of works describe the physical geography of tribes: the topography, soils, climates, fauna, and flora (Shimken [p. 21], Kniffen [p. 21], Waterman [p. 22], Ruttenber [p. 20]; see also the works in section 13, Subsistence Patterns). Studies concentrate too on the geographical concepts of various Indian peoples (Waterman, Ruttenber, Harrington [p. 21], Shimkin; see also the works in section 13, Subsistence Patterns). The writers note in lists and tables and on maps the aboriginal geographic terms that name places in the environment, physical features, houses, and other aspects of particular regions unique to different tribes.

Two atlases trace the historical experience of tribes by depicting the changing patterns of Indian village locations and movements of tribes to new areas (Tucker [p. 20], *Atlas of Great Lakes Indian History* [p. 20]). The *Atlas of Great Lakes Indian History* also covers such topics as natural vegetation, subsistence patterns, distribution of late prehistoric cultures, transportation routes, epidemics, land cession treaties, reservations, trade and missionary activities, Indian warfare, and changes in European sovereignty. DeVorsey (p. 21) explains how old maps can be used to reconstruct Indian cultural and physical landscapes. Maps are also used in Neils's study (p. 20) dealing with patterns of Indian urban migrations to illustrate contemporary distributions of Indians in counties, states, or reservations, and their migrations to cities. And Kelsay's volume (below) contains a list of descriptions of cartographic records that pertain to Indian affairs.

KELSAY, LAURA E., comp. *Cartographic Records of the Bureau of Indian Affairs*. Special List no. 13. Washington, D.C.: National Archives and Records Service, General Service Administration, 1954, 1977.
This list consists of revised descriptions of cartographic records in Record Group 75 dating from the early 1800s to the mid-1960s in various divisions of the Bureau of Indian Affairs and several field offices. The introduction tells where other cartographic records pertaining to Indian affairs can be found in the records of the National Archives. There

19

are brief summary descriptions of the types of maps that can be found in the Central map files and the divisions of Land Irrigation, Forestry and Grazing, Education, Extension and Industry, Statistics, Civilian Conservation Corps-Indian Division, Roads, Soil and Moisture Conservation Operations, Industrial Development, and Plant Development, as well as in the records of several field offices. There are detailed descriptions of maps found in each of the divisions given under numbered entries by state or the United States as a whole. There is an appendix of township plats, maps, and diagrams of lands in Indian reservations and adjacent areas, 1850–1935.

NEILS, ELAINE M. "Patterns of Indian Urban Migration and Characteristics of Urban Indians." In *Reservation to City: Indian Migration and Federal Relocation.* University of Chicago Geographical Research Paper, no. 131, pp. 14–45. Chicago: University of Chicago Department of Geography, 1971. Illustrated. Bibliography.

The author depicts the general Indian paths of migrations from 1890 to 1960 with special emphasis on the post-1930 period. She discusses population growth rates and locational changes; geographical distribution of Indian population over time; and migration patterns in-state, out-of-state, to cities, to rural areas, to urban destinations or to areas near reservations, and to destinations distant from home. She describes demographic, social, and economic characteristics of Indian urban populations. There are eleven figures and six tables that illustrate the concepts. The figures include maps which show density of Indian population by states, tribes resettled in Oklahoma, distribution of tribes across the country, the 1960 distribution of Indian lands and population by county, federal Indian reservations, Indian in-migrants to states from outside State Economic Areas, percentages migrating to California, and the Indian population of cities, 1930–60. The work is based on published government and secondary works and papers.

NORTHEAST

RUTTENBER, E. M. *Footprints of the Red Men: Indian Geographical Names in the Valley of the Hudson's River, the Valley of the Mohawks, and on the Delaware: Their Location and the Probable Meaning of Some of Them.* New York State Historical Association Proceedings of the Seventh Annual Meeting, vol. 6. Cooperstown: New York State Historical Assn., 1906. 241pp. Illustrated.

This work contains a compilation of hundreds of Algonquian and Iroquoian geographical names from the Mohawk, Hudson, and Delaware River valleys, the places and physical features to which these names belonged, and the meanings of these aboriginal names. The study begins with an explanation regarding linguistic methods used by the various European scribes to record the geographical names, the methods used to interpret them, the structure of polysynthetic Algonquian dialects and how they differ from Iroquoian construction, and the problems in pronouncing sounds as originally

spoken in these two language families. The author also includes a number of names that no longer exist but that illustrate both the dialect spoken in the valley and the local geography of the Indians. The book is arranged by geographical regions and includes an alphabetical index of names, two maps, and photographs of places to which certain names belonged.

TANNER, HELEN HORNBECK, ed. *Atlas of Great Lakes Indian History.* Norman: University of Oklahoma Press, forthcoming. ca. 200pp. Illustrated. Bibliography.

This *Atlas* contains thirty-eight maps which trace the changing patterns of Indian village locations and movements of tribes of the Great Lakes region during the period from 1615 to 1871, when treaty-making between the Indian tribes and the federal government came to an end and white dominance of the Great Lakes was secured. In addition, there are 125 pages of explanatory text and accompanying illustrations. Since the *Atlas* treats the Great Lakes region as a cultural whole, covering both the Canadian and the American sides, the mapped area extends from Montreal in the east to Winnipeg in the west delineating the northern boundary and the Ohio River marking the southern boundary. In addition to village locations, the *Atlas* covers such topics as natural vegetation, subsistence patterns, distribution of late prehistoric cultures, transportation routes, epidemics, land cession treaties, reservations, trade and missionary activity, Pontiac's War, the War of 1812, Black Hawk's War, the frontier in transition, and changes in European sovereignty. One map presents the entire region from the perspective of contemporary European and Indian observers north of the Straits of Mackinac. The *Atlas* depicts the historical experience of the Iroquois League, Huron, and other western Iroquois (whose eighteenth-century survivors were called Wyandots), the Ojibways, Ottawas, Potawatomis, Delawares, Shawnees, Kickapoos, the Miamis and their allies, the Kaskaskias and other Illinois tribes, the Menominees, Sacs and Foxes, Winnebagos, and Eastern Dakotas. There are short-form bibliographies accompanying each map.

TUCKER, SARA JONES. *Indian Villages of the Illinois Country.* Illinois State Museum Scientific Paper, vol. 2. Part 1: Atlas. Springfield: State of Illinois, 1942. Unpaged. Illustrated.

This volume presents a selection of fifty-four maps chronologically arranged from 1670 to 1835 that show which Indian tribes occupied Illinois and the areas in which they lived. These maps show the sites of villages, the tribes' movements to new areas, and the contacts between various tribes. Many of the original maps were field sketches designed by the explorers to acquaint their superiors with the territory covered, while others were the work of professional map makers who tried to bring together all known facts of the region. Preceding the plates is a section called "Notes on the Maps" which provides the names of the authors of the maps, when the maps were made, the personal knowledge the authors had of the country shown on their maps, and the parts the authors played in the events of the period.

SOUTHEAST

DeVorsey, Louis, Jr. "Early Maps as a Source in the Reconstruction of Southern Indian Landscapes." In *Red, White, Black: Symposium on Indians in the Old South,* edited by Charles Hudson, pp. 12–30. Southern Anthropological Society Proceedings, no. 5. Athens: University of Georgia Press, 1971. Illustrated. Bibliography.

The author demonstrates the use and value of historical cartography in two of his attempts to reconstruct aspects of mid-eighteenth century southern Indian cultural and physical landscapes. He describes the use of many manuscripts and small- and medium-scale printed maps to reconstruct the Southern Indian Boundary line which separated the British colonies from Indian tribal lands in the prerevolutionary Southeast and the use of many large-scale surveyor maps of granted properties to reconstruct the aboriginal forest cover of eastern America in the late eighteenth century. Illustrations include a map of the Southern Indian Boundary line on the eve of the American Revolution, reproductions of three early maps which were used in reconstructing the boundary, a copy of a 1784 survey plat, and two survey maps. The bibliography lists the early maps.

Myer, William E. *Indian Trails of the Southeast.* Bureau of American Ethnology 42nd Annual Report, 1924–1925, pp. 727–900. Washington, D.C.: Government Printing Office, 1928. Illustrated. Bibliography.

The author studies the aboriginal trail system in all of the southern states south of the Ohio and Potomac Rivers and east of the Mississippi River. There is a list of 125 trails, many of which are described in detail in the text, including The Great Indian Warpath Trail, six branches of the southern West Virginia trail, the Southern Appalachian Trail, and trails in Kentucky, Tennessee, and Mississippi. There is an archaeological map of the state of Tennessee, the trail system of the southeastern United States in the early colonial period, and two other maps. The work is based on field work as well as published primary and secondary works.

GREAT PLAINS

Rydjord, John. *Indian Place-Names: Their Origins, Evolution, and Meanings.* Norman: University of Oklahoma Press, 1981. 380pp. Illustrated. Bibliography.

The author discusses the origin, evolution, and meanings of Indian place-names in Kansas from the Siouan, Algonquian, Shoshonean, Caddoan, Iroquoian, and other tongues. He explains how the great variety of Indian place-names in Kansas resulted from attempts to create a permanent Indian frontier in the West where Indians from the East were urged to settle. Consequently, Kansas has Indian place-names not only from its early native inhabitants (Siouan, Caddoan, and Shoshonean tribes), but also from the Algonquians, Iroquoians, and other eastern groups. Because there is much disagreement among experts regarding the origin, evolution, and meaning of Indian names, the author includes a variety of interpretations, even contradictory ones. There are illustrations of Indians and seven maps. The bibliography lists manuscripts, government publications, newspapers, diaries, memoirs, journal articles, general works, guides, and other materials.

SOUTHWEST

Harrington, John Peabody. *The Ethnogeography of the Tewa Indians.* Bureau of American Ethnography 29th Annual Report, 1907–1908, pp. 37–636. Washington, D.C.: Government Printing Office, 1916. Illustrated. Bibliography.

Presenting geographical knowledge of the Tewa Indians of the upper Rio Grande valley, New Mexico, around 1910, the author begins with cosmographical and meteorological information followed by an alphabetically arranged list of terms denoting geographical Tewa concepts. He provides a treatment of place-names by dividing the region in which Tewa place-names are more or less numerous into twenty-nine areas, each of which is shown on a map and explained in the text. Names of places in Spanish, English, and various non-Tewa Indian languages are included. A list of tribal names and one of names of minerals known to the Tewa conclude the work. There are thirty maps of Tewa regions and over twenty-five photographs of Tewa geographical scenes. The book is based on fieldwork and unpublished and published primary and secondary works.

GREAT BASIN–PLATEAU

Shimkin, D. B. *Wind River Shoshone Ethnogeography.* California University Anthropological Records, vol. 5, no. 4, pp. 245–325. Berkeley: University of California Press, 1947. Illustrated. Bibliography.

The author sketches the habitat of the Wind River Shoshone of Wyoming between 1825 and 1875, regionalizing the habitat according to variations of several geographical factors: topography, physiography and soils, climate, and biota. He studies Shoshone adaptation to the environment and the nature of economic conditioning within this culture. There are nine maps, ten photographs that show ecological zones, a table of sixty-six place-names in English and Shoshone, and a table of plants and animals used by the Indians. The bibliography lists published primary and secondary works.

CALIFORNIA

Kniffen, Fred B. *Pomo Geography.* University of California Publications in American Archaeology and Ethnology, vol. 36, no. 6, pp. 353–400.

Berkeley: University of California Press, 1939. Illustrated.

The author describes the variation in natural resources and conditions peculiar to the section of middle-western California occupied by the Pomo linguistic group. There are descriptive treatments of three striking natural Pomo areas, Clear Lake, Russian River, and Coast Pomo including information on groups occupying each area, the yearly cycle of economic activities, location of villages, densities of population, and concomitant nonmaterial traits such as political boundaries, trade relations, and land ownership. There are maps of each of the three Pomo areas and photographs of landscapes of each of the three environments. See also: Omar C. Stewart, *Notes on Pomo Ethnogeography.* University of California Publications in American Archaeology and Ethnology, vol. 40, no. 2, pp. 29–62. Berkeley: University of California Press, 1943. Illustrated. Bibliography.

WATERMAN, T. T. *Yurok Geography.* University of California Publications in American Archaeology

and Ethnology, vol. 16, no. 5, pp. 177–314. Berkeley: University of California Press, 1920. Illustrated. Bibliography.

The author discusses the geography of Yurok Indians along the Klamath River and the adjacent region in northwest California. He discusses the Yurok way of life; geographical concepts; direction terms; place-names; distribution of towns; town and settlement; house and personal names; forms of real property; and descent and inheritance. He concludes by dividing Yurok territory into eleven arbitrary rectangles for the purpose of showing the distribution of place-names and provides notes for thirty-four maps of township plats which show the positions of Indian houses and place-names. There is an alphabetical list of place-names found in these maps, two other maps that show Yurok territory location, and one of northwest California showing the distribution of Yurok place-names outside Yurok territory. There are over thirty-five photographs of Yurok environments. The work is based on fieldwork and published secondary works.

4   ARCHAEOLOGY AND PREHISTORY

Prehistory is by definition a period of time before recorded history. Therefore, the only way we have of knowing anything about prehistoric Native Americans is through the traces which they have left behind of their activities. Archaeology is the science of recovering and studying these traces. On the basis of the archaeologists' work we can begin to build a picture of the history and culture of prehistoric Americans. Brennan (p. 24), Martin (p. 26), Snow (p. 26), and Wormington (p. 27) give basic introductions and surveys of North American archaeology. For an introduction to prehistoric Native American history, see Jennings's *Ancient Native Americans* (p. 26) and *Prehistory of North America* (p. 25) as well as Willey's *An Introduction to American Archaeology* (p. 27). Jennings and Norbeck (p. 26) and Taylor and Meighan (p. 26) treat prehistory for graduate and advanced study.

Archaeology itself is a changing field. Fagan (p. 24) treats some of the major developments in American archaeology since the Spanish conquistadores, including Thomas Jefferson's attempts at excavation. Huddleston (p. 25) examines the literature and opinions of sixteenth- and seventeenth-century European archaeologists. Wilmsen (p. 27) distinguishes six periods of time in the history of American archaeology in which different conceptions of American Indians were dominant. Willey and Sabloff (p. 27) distinguish five periods of time in the development of archaeology as practiced in the Americas.

The practice of archaeology also develops in particular ways in particular geographic regions. Each regional section includes at least one history of that area's archaeology. Brose (p. 28) outlines the history of archaeology in the northeastern United States. Stoltman (p. 29) treats the southeast United States; Frison (p. 30) and Jelks (p. 30) review Great Plains archaeology. Kidder (p. 31) and Rohn (p. 32) discuss Southwestern archaeology. Warren (p. 33) and Sprague (p. 33) trace the history of archaeology in California and the Northwest. Dekin (p. 34) gives an introduction to Arctic archaeology.

How to reconstruct the culture and history of a people from skimpy evidence is always a problem for archaeologists. Generally they speculate about the history and culture of a people from material traces of human activity. This use of human remains and artifacts is the primary method for gaining knowledge of earlier peoples. However, it is also possible to use data about the environment and geography of an area to help reconstruct a picture of an ancient people. Fitzhugh (p. 28) and Wood (p. 31) use the findings of geologists and palynologists as well as information on environmental changes. Griffin (p. 28), Quimby (p. 28), Muller (p. 29), Frison in *Prehistoric Hunters of the High Plains* (p. 30) and Wedel in "The Prehistoric Plains" (p. 31) use knowledge of the environment and its changes to infer more about the peoples they are studying. Prehistorians also try to link historic tribes with prehistoric cultures in order to try to get a clearer idea of what the prehistoric society may have been like. Perhaps the best example of this technique is in the study of Alaskan prehistory. In Alaska tribes are still living much as they did before exposure to Western culture. Dumond in *The Eskimos and Aleuts* (p. 34) uses linguistic and physical similarities and differences between present-day Eskimos and Aleuts to help understand their prehistory.

One of the most fascinating questions in North American archaeology is how and when human beings first came to live in North America. Archaeologists are constantly finding new evidence and always reinterpreting old and new evidence. Consequently, there are many theories about who the first people were and how they got here. Wauchope (p. 26) discusses various myths regarding the origins of Native Americans. Huddleston (p. 25) reviews the history from the sixteenth and the seventeenth centuries of the debate over the origins of Native Americans. Hopkins (p. 25) provides several articles about the Bering Land Bridge; Jennings in "Origins" (p. 25) and Shutler (p. 26) present material and arguments concerning the origins of Native Americans.

The constant debate over the question of the origins of human beings on the continent gives a glimpse of how the fields of archaeology and prehistory operate. Although the archaeologist can produce scientific data, that data must be interpreted by the prehistorian, who will interpret and reinterpret the evidence. Consequently, at any one time various prehistorians may be arguing several different theories of American Indian prehistory. We will never know without a doubt exactly the history and cultures of those ancient peoples.

BRENNAN, LOUIS A. *Beginner's Guide to Archaeology: The Modern Digger's Step-by-Step Introduction to the Expert Ways of Unearthing the Past.* New York: Dell, 1974. 378pp. Illustrated.

The author considers the basic techniques and precautions in explaining how the archaeologist works: the finding and recognition of sites, excavation procedures, deciphering finds, and recognizing and exposing artifacts are discussed. The history of human beings in the Western Hemisphere is outlined over some 40,000 years. The main trends in current archaeology are identified, including key concepts for placing sites chronologically and geographically within a cultural tradition, and a section discusses the search and use of relevant literature. The role of the nonprofessional, or citizen archaeologist (not to be confused with vandals or

"pot hunters"), is described. There are state by state guides to sites, resources, and regulations with recommended books for each.

FAGAN, BRIAN. *Elusive Treasure: The Story of Early Archaeologists in the Americas.* New York: Scribner's, 1977. 358pp. Illustrated.

This book identifies some of the major controversies that arose during the growth of American archaeology from the time of the Spanish conquistadores to about 1900. Drawing upon written accounts of early travelers and archaeologists, the author describes De Soto's plundering of archaeological sites in the present-day United States, details Fray Marco's 1637 expedition, discusses "lost" civilizations, the Moundbuilders' story, and Jefferson's amateurish excavations on the Ravenna River.

FITTING, JAMES E., ed. *The Development of North American Archaeology: Essays in the Development of Regional Traditions.* Garden City, N.Y.: Doubleday Anchor Books, 1973. 309pp. Illustrated. Bibliography.

This volume is meant to serve as a supplemental reader in North American archaeology courses and as a source book for regional archaeological bibliography and interpretation for amateur and professional archaeologists alike. Regional scholars summarize the history of ideas for every region in North America: the Arctic, Canada, northeastern United States, southeastern United States, the Plains, the Southwest and Intermontane West, California, and the Pacific Northwest. Significant trends, important expeditions, and major works are identified. There are maps of the various regions and each author provides a bibliography of pertinent regional material.

FORBIS, RICHARD G. "The Paleoamericans." In *North America,* edited by Shirley Gorenstein, pp. 17–35. New York: St. Martin's, 1975. Bibliography.

The author discusses and analyzes the roots of North American prehistoric cultures from approximately 9500 B.C. to 6000 B.C. using the Llano cultural complex as a reference point to discuss earlier and later cultural patterns.

GORENSTEIN, SHIRLEY, ed. *North America.* New York: St. Martin's, 1975. 209pp. Illustrated. Bibliography.

Regional scholars present summaries of what is known concerning prehistoric cultural developments in five significant areas of North America. A chapter on Paleo-Americans is followed by chapters on the Arctic and Subarctic, eastern North America, the American Southwest, the Far West, and one speculates on the possibilities of continuous prehistoric contact with the Old World. Authors also present interpretations of the processes by which cultures change and evaluate alternative explanations.

HENRY, JEANNETTE, ed. *The American Indian Reader: Anthropology.* San Francisco: Indian Historian Press, 1972. 174pp.

Native American anthropologists consider the subject "The Anthropologist: The Man and the Discipline" in four articles in this volume. Alfonso Ortiz presents an anthropologist's perspective on anthropology; Beatrice Medicine discusses the anthropologist as the Indian's image maker; and in "Indians Who Never Were," D'Arcy McNickle describes some of the problems contemporary Indians face because of archaeological and ethnological attitudes and opinions. Three articles examine archaeological ethics and racist attitudes. Other articles in the collection treat various archaeological subjects.

HOPKINS, DAVID M., ed. *The Bering Land Bridge.* Stanford, Calif.: Stanford University Press, 1967. 594pp.

This volume presents articles relating to theories about and the history of the Bering Land Bridge.

Twenty-seven scientists from six countries, representing a dozen disciplines, contributed to the collection. Papers examine many lines of evidence, summarize and analyze data from two continents and an island in the North Atlantic, formulate a chronology of the seaways and land bridges in Beringia, and reconstruct the character of the seascapes that prevailed there in the past.

HUDDLESTON, LEE ELDRIDGE. *Origins of the American Indians: European Concepts, 1492–1729.* Austin: University of Texas Press, 1967. 179pp. Bibliography.

This essay concerns the debate over the origins of Native Americans in the two centuries before it became distinguished from the question of the origins of their cultures and before it began to take on the characteristics of a scientific dispute. The author examined primary sources and investigated the literature of the sixteenth and seventeenth centuries to discover what the opinions of Europeans of the period were, how the opinions were derived, and how they'changed.

JENNINGS, JESSE D. "Origins." In *Ancient Native Americans,* pp. 1–41. San Francisco: W. H. Freeman, 1978. Bibliography.

This article is meant to serve as an introduction to the reams of data available on the increasingly deep (chronologically) story of the Paleo-Americans. The author reviews the evidence for the earliest humans to arrive in North America, discusses evidence dated at 27,000 B.P. (+/−), examines significant climatic changes between 20,000 and 10,000 years ago, and describes the adaptations early inhabitants made to the expansion of life zones and resources and to continuous population increase. There are references and recommended sources.

———. *Prehistory of North America.* New York: McGraw-Hill, 1968. 391pp. Illustrated. Bibliography.

Intended for use as a text for college students and as a guide to further study through bibliographic citation of important published sources, this work is organized into culture "stages" and describes the archaeological evidence which suggests the presence of human beings in North America in prehistoric times. Based on the evidence, the author discusses the development of North American culture over a period of some 12,000 years, identifying similarities and relationships as they occurred through time and space. An introductory chapter defines the terms used in the text and explains the techniques used in dating and classifying materials recovered. A chapter discussing theories regarding the peopling of North America includes a brief discussion of the physical anthropology of early Americans. Earliest cultures are reconstructed in light of the archaeological evidence and subsequent chapters trace their growth and development in various geographical areas of the United States, including the Arctic region. Ethnography and language in relation to archaeology are discussed and a final chapter summarizes the text.

———, ed. *Ancient Native Americans*. San Francisco: W. H. Freeman, 1978. 698pp. Illustrated. Bibliography.

This text is designed to be used at the graduate or undergraduate level. Eight chapters reconstruct the prehistory of the major culture areas of North America. Subsequent chapters treat Central and South America, and pre-Columbian transoceanic contacts. Each chapter is written by a specialist in the area covered, references receive full citation at the end of each chapter, and recommended sources of information are listed.

———, and EDWARD NORBECK, eds. *Prehistoric Man in the New World*. Chicago: University of Chicago Press, 1964. 633pp. Illustrated. Bibliography.

Designed mainly for specialists and university students, this book contains eighteen papers that review and appraise facts and theories concerning the prehistoric cultures of North and South America. An essay on early human occupation systematizes available data and establishes a hemispheric classification under categories representing developmental stages. Areal specialists review the literature and present interpretations of the succession and nature of the prehistoric cultures of the Arctic and Subarctic, the western coast of North America, the Desert West, the Greater Southwest, the Great Plains, the Northeast Woodlands, and the southeastern United States. Speculative articles considering transpacific contact, cultural diffusion, and cultural similarities are followed by a linguistic overview. Specialized bibliographies accompany each essay.

MARTIN, PAUL S.; GEORGE I. QUIMBY; and DONALD COLLIER. *Indians before Columbus: Twenty Thousand Years of North American History Revealed by Archaeology*. Chicago: University of Chicago Press, 1947. 582pp. Illustrated. Bibliography.

Intended for the lay public and for students taking introductory courses in anthropology, this volume discusses the nature and purposes of archaeology and traces the basic trends of cultural development of the earliest human inhabitants of the United States, including Alaska. Although written before radiocarbon dating, this book is a convenient source of reference for brief accounts of prehistoric cultures and for what was known at the time of its publication. The authors summarize the archaeological evidence and outline cultures chronologically for the Southwest, eastern North America, the Pacific Slope and the Far North. A chapter on prehistoric arts and industries discusses objects of stone, copper, bone, and shell; the textile arts; and trade and commerce. There are 122 illustrations.

RILEY, CARROLL L.; CHARLES L. KELLEY; CAMPBELL W. PENNINGTON; and ROBERT L. RANDS, eds. *Man across the Sea: Problems of Pre-Columbian Contacts*. Austin: University of Texas Press, 1971. 551pp. Bibliography.

Articles in this collection explore various aspects of the questions and controversies concerning the possibilities of pre-Columbian contacts between the peoples of the American continent and other conti-

nents. Section 1 examines some of the theories and methodologies involved in the diffusion controversy. Section 2 includes papers on pre-Columbian contact or alleged contact across both the Atlantic and Pacific oceans. Section 3 considers the problems of plant dispersal around the world and, especially, the possibilities of pre-Columbian spread of plant domesticates. Introductory and concluding sections interpret the data and suggest needed research.

SHUTLER, RICHARD JR., ed. "Papers from a Symposium on Early Man in North America." *Arctic Anthropology* 8, no. 2 (1971). 142pp. Illustrated.

Papers in this collection consider the question of the earliest human occupation of North America in light of data resulting from research conducted between 1960 and 1970 at a large number of archaeological sites dating prior to 6000–5000 B.C. Scholars review the research and present regional surveys, discuss new discoveries, and present new insights. Articles discuss time, environment and human beings, reconstruct lifeways, and formulate a technological perspective. A general overview concludes that no firm date for first human arrival can be given as yet.

SNOW, DEAN. *The Archaeology of North America*. New York: Viking, 1976. 272pp. Illustrated. Bibliography.

This volume, in non-technical language, summarizes the major points in covering Native American cultures from the Atlantic to the Pacific, from Alaska to northern Mexico, from the Ice Age to the seventeenth century. There are chapters on the Eastern Woodlands, the Great Plains, the Desert West, the Far West, the Arctic, and Subarctic. Each chapter is preceded by a map indicating the geographic area to be discussed. Chronologies trace cultural development in each area. Outstanding developments for each area are listed.

TAYLOR, R. E., and CLEMENT W. MEIGHAN, eds. *Chronologies in New World Archaeology*. San Francisco: Academic Press, 1978. 587pp. Bibliography.

Designed for "higher-level" studies, this volume contains papers by regional scholars in which they review archaeological literature, summarize the data, and arrange it chronologically. Information is compiled for western Arctic and Subarctic, eastern United States, Diablo Range (western Gulf of Mexico), North American Plains, Great Basin, American Southwest, California, Meso-America, Caribbean, and northern Chile. A summary section reviews the text and covers geographic areas not included. References are listed at the end of each article.

WAUCHOPE, ROBERT. *Lost Tribes and Sunken Continents: Myth and Method in the Study of American Indians*. Chicago: University of Chicago Press, 1962. 155pp. Illustrated. Bibliography.

The author examines various theories regarding the origin of Native Americans and discusses the people who proposed them. Subjects covered include the Egyptian theory, Atlantis, Mu, the Lost Tribes of Israel, the legends of the Mormon Church, and racist beliefs. He also considers the anthropological evidence for belief in an Asiatic origin of American Indians and touches on widely held fantasies.

WILLEY, GORDON R. *An Introduction to American Archaeology: Volume I, North and Middle America.* Englewood Cliffs, N.J.: Prentice-Hall, 1966. 530pp. Illustrated. Bibliography.

This book is intended as an introductory culture history of pre-Columbian America. Geographically, it covers North America, Mexico, and the northern half of Central America. Chronologically, it begins with the first appearance of human beings in these areas and traces the growth, development, modification, or dissolution of major cultural forms and patterns through time and in interrelationship with each other up to the point at which they are replaced or transformed by European ones. The author interprets the archaeological evidence in natural environmental contexts and in the light of contemporary ethnographic and ethnohistorical information.

————, and JEREMY A. SABLOFF. *A History of American Archaeology.* San Francisco: W. H. Freeman, 1973. 252pp. Illustrated. Bibliography.

The authors provide a history of the development of the discipline of archaeology as it has been, and is being, practiced in the Americas. Their emphasis is on the doing of archaeology and with the way problems of culture history have been conceived by archaeologists and how those conceptions have changed through time. They divide the development of American archaeology into five periods: the speculative, 1492–1840; the classificatory-descriptive, 1840–1914; the classificatory-historical, concerned with chronology, 1914–40; the classificatory-historical, concerned with context and function, 1940–60; and the explanatory, concerned with explaining culture and society, 1960– .

WILMSEN, EDWIN N. "An Outline of Early Man Studies in the United States." *American Antiquity* 31 (1965–66):172–92. Bibliography.

This article traces the fluctuating modes of thought concerning the origins of American Indians from the time of the Spanish Conquest to the 1960s. Early studies are related to the broader aspects of archaeology in Europe as well as in North America. Six periods are discussed, in each of which different conceptions of American Indians were dominant: 1520–1780; 1780–1859; 1859–90; 1890–1925; 1925–50; and 1950–65. The author considers the meaning of the term "early man" in each period and describes the developments in other fields of inquiry that influenced the conceptions that evolved in each of these periods. A concise summary of the development of Paleo-Indian studies provides the background for later developments in the field.

WORMINGTON, H. M. *Ancient Man in North America.* The Denver Museum of Natural History Popular Series, no. 4. Denver: Denver Museum of Natural History, 1957. 322pp. Illustrated. Bibliography.

This volume presents a survey of North American archaeology and explains developments that have occurred since the third edition of the book appeared in 1949. The author presents summary descriptions of over 200 archaeological sites at which tools and implements made by human beings were discovered in association with the remains of extinct animals. There are brief discussions of the Pleistocene (Glacial) and Holocene (Recent) epochs, archaeological methodology, theories regarding human skeletal remains of presumed antiquity and routes by which people first may have entered America. The major part of the book is about archaeological sites, the "stone industries" and Paleo-Indians (people who occupied North America prior to 6,000 years ago). In addition to sites in the United States, including Alaska, the author describes major sites in Mexico, Central America, and Canada. A section of this book presents a list of key projectile point and knife types, with illustrations and definitions.

EAST

FORBIS, RICHARD G. "Eastern North America." In *North America,* edited by Shirley Gorenstein, pp. 74–102. New York: St. Martin's, 1975. Bibliography.

The author traces prehistoric cultural development in eastern North America from the Arctic to the Gulf and from the Rockies to the Atlantic from about 8000 B.C. to A.D. 1000. Three cultures, the Archaic, the Woodland, and the Mississippi, and their phases and complexes are described; two stages, the Archaic (Mesolithic) and the Formative are delineated. The author focuses on the content of lifeways and on major changes in the organization of society.

GRIFFIN, JAMES B. "Eastern North American Archaeology: A Summary." *Science* 156, no. 3772 (1967):175–91. Illustrated.

The major themes of the prehistoric occupation of eastern North America over some 15,000 years are traced in this synthesis of archaeological information regarding the area east of the Rocky Mountains from the Gulf of Mexico to the forest zone of Canada. The author reconstructs prehistoric lifestyles and describes the development of different cultural traditions through time.

————, ed. *Archeology of the Eastern United States.* Chicago: University of Chicago Press, 1952. 392pp. Bibliography.

This collection of twenty-nine essays constitutes a summary of the archaeology of the United States east of the Rocky Mountains. The majority of the articles are regional in scope and present an interpretation of the succession of prehistoric human cultures in the various geographical regions. Several of the papers deal with the problem of relating historic tribes to prehistoric cultures and sites in the area. Areas treated include: the northeastern United States; the Middle Atlantic states; Ontario; the Ohio region; the Upper Great Lakes; the Northern, Central and Lower Mississippi Valley; the

Northern Plains; the Illinois Valley; the Lower Ohio Valley; the Tennessee area, North and South Carolina, Alabama, and Florida. Papers also deal with physical anthropology, the ethnological cultures and their archaeological backgrounds, Hopewellian dress in Illinois, dendrochronology, and radiocarbon dates.

MASON, RONALD J. "The Paleo-Indian Tradition in Eastern North America." *Current Anthropology* 3, no. 3 (1962):227–46.
This article correlates and evaluates the evidence for the existence of the Paleo-Indian in eastern North America. After an examination of archaeological evidence, the author analyzes the role of the hunting of Late Pleistocene big game and concludes that the Llano hunters were the first humans to inhabit the East.

NORTHEAST

BROSE, DAVID S. "The Northeastern United States." In *The Development of North American Archaeology,* edited by James E. Fitting, pp. 84–116. Garden City, N.Y.: Doubleday Anchor Books, 1973. Bibliography.
This chapter contains a concise history of the development of archaeology in the northeastern United States. The author discusses major trends and ideas beginning with the theme of the Moundbuilders.

FITTING, JAMES E. *The Archaeology of Michigan: A Guide to the Prehistory of the Great Lakes Region.* Garden City, N.Y.: Natural History Press, 1970. 274pp. Illustrated. Bibliography.
This volume chronicles the changing adaptive patterns of the aboriginal peoples of the state of Michigan over some 12,000 years, exploring the interrelations of prehistoric cultures and environmental variations. The author discusses the earliest inhabitants, traces the disappearance of their environment due to climatic changes, outlines the return of people to the area when the ecosystem could support them, and describes subsequent populations and settlement patterns through the Archaic, Woodland, late prehistoric, and early historic periods.

FITZHUGH, WILLIAM W., ed. "Papers from a Symposium on Moorhead and Maritime Archaic Problems in Northeastern America." *Arctic Anthropology* 7, no. 2 (1975). 147pp. Illustrated.
Nine papers in this collection deal with the prehistory of New England, Atlantic Canada, Labrador, and Greenland. In an interdisciplinary approach, archaeologists, geologists, palynologists, and a dating specialist provide information on sea/land changes together with deglaciation and vegetation history. Archaeologists give regional views of recent finds, discuss cultural origins, regional patterns and relationships, models of mortuary behavior, trade, population continuity and classification, and present new interpretations.

FUNK, ROBERT E., and CHARLES F. HAYES, III, eds. *Current Perspectives in Northeastern Archaeology: Essays in Honor of William A. Ritchie.* Researches and Transactions of New York State Archaeological Association, vol. 18, no. 1. Rochester and Albany: New York State Archaeological Assn., 1977. 173pp. Illustrated.
Thirteen essays in this volume examine archaeological and historical-prehistorical research, archaeology, history and ethnohistory, and suggest new approaches to consider. Papers discuss Paleo-Indian sites, early and middle Archaic occupations of upstate New York, the Laurentian tradition, prehistoric occupation of the Upper Ohio Valley, Oneida archaeology and early history, and examine the impact of European contact on Iroquoian and Algonquian art styles, and describe the social structure of Frontenac Island.

GRIFFIN, JAMES B. "The Midlands and Northeastern United States." In *Ancient Native Americans,* edited by Jesse D. Jennings, pp. 221–79. San Francisco: W. H. Freeman, 1978. Bibliography.
Geographically this article deals with New England and the Middle Atlantic states, the Great Lakes area (Michigan, Illinois), eastern Ohio, northern West Virginia, Pennsylvania, northern New Jersey, New York, and the Upper St. Lawrence. The author discusses the complex interrelationships of the aboriginal populations of the region and their ecological adjustments to the resources of the area from 17,000–10,000 B.C. to A.D. 1200.

QUIMBY, GEORGE IRVING. *Indian Life in the Upper Great Lakes: 11,000 B.C. to A.D. 1800.* Chicago: University of Chicago Press, 1960. 182pp. Illustrated. Bibliography.
This book is directed to the general reader or beginning student. The author presents a regional overview of the chronological developments in the Upper Great Lakes area, including the drainage basins of Lakes Superior, Huron, and Michigan. The first part of the book describes prehistoric settlements in the area in light of archaeological evidence. The second half discusses the historic cultures of the Miami, Sac, Fox (Mesquakie), Winnebago, Menominee, Chippewa, Huron, Ottawa, and Potawatomi peoples. The author explores the importance of ecological adaptation to the area and presents an appraisal of the work of other scholars.

RITCHIE, WILLIAM A. *The Archaeology of New York State.* Garden City, N.Y.: Natural History Press, 1965. 355pp. Illustrated. Bibliography.
In this study, the author reconsiders published archaeological data and opinions and utilizes previously unpublished information from newly discovered archaeological sites in reconstructing human prehistory in New York from ca. 7000 B.C. to A.D. 1600. Four cultural stages are discussed and the human activities implied by the artifacts, food debris, settlement patterns, site distributions, and other evidence are examined for each cultural unit. The information is integrated from a historical developmental viewpoint.

STRUEVER, STUART, and JOHN CARLSON. "Koster Site, the New Archaeology in Action." *Archaeology* 30, no. 2 (1977):93–101.

This article describes archaeological excavations at the Koster Site, above St. Louis, Missouri, in the Lower Illinois Valley, which have been underway since 1969. In a multidisciplinary approach (botany, zoology, nutrition, human biology, statistical analysis and employing new interpretive techniques, the authors reconstruct prehistoric life at Koster from about 7000 B.C. to A.D. 1200. On the basis of the evidence, the authors conclude that human beings made a much better adjustment to the new postglacial landscape of plants and animals than had been previously supposed. The authors suggest further reading. A more detailed account of the work at this site is contained in *Koster,* below.

————, and FELICIA ANONELLI HOLTON. *Koster: Americans in Search of Their Prehistoric Past.* Garden City, N.Y.: Doubleday Anchor Books, 1980. Illustrated. Bibliography.

The authors give a progress report of the ten-year-long dig in which a team of scientists reconstructed prehistoric people's relationship to the environment, using computers to sort out its conclusions.

TRIGGER, BRUCE G., ed. *Handbook of North American Indians: Northeast,* pp. 14–69, 322–33, 560–68, 580–82. Vol. 15 *Handbook of North American Indians,* William C. Sturtevant, gen. ed. Washington, D.C.: Smithsonian Institution, 1978.

This encyclopedic summary of what is known of the prehistory, history, and cultures of the aboriginal peoples of the northeastern United States contains a section on the general prehistory of the area up until A.D. 1000. A brief essay highlighting the theoretical and methodological aspects of American archaeology is followed by three chronologically successive papers. Subsequent chapters contain articles pertinent to the late prehistory (approximately A.D. 1000 to A.D. 1400–1700) of the East Coast from North Carolina to New Foundland, the St. Lawrence Lowlands Region, the Illinois area, and the Upper Great Lakes area.

SOUTHEAST

HUDSON, CHARLES M. "Prehistory and Early History." In *The Southeastern Indians,* pp. 34–119. Knoxville: University of Tennessee Press, 1976.

This section reviews the archaeology and outlines the human prehistory of the area that now includes Georgia, Florida, South Carolina, western North Carolina, Alabama, Mississippi, Louisiana, southeastern Arkansas, Tennessee and the portions of Missouri, Illinois, and Kentucky that border the Tennessee River. The author discusses some persistent myths concerning the peoples of the Southeast and describes four traditions, or cultural patterns, as they followed each other through time, reconstructing the probable lifestyle of the people of each phase.

MULLER, JON D. "The Southeast." In *Ancient Native Americans,* edited by Jesse D. Jennings, pp. 281–325. San Francisco: W. H. Freeman, 1978.

This article traces cultural development in the southeastern United States from ca. 10,000 B.C. to A.D. 540. The author reconstructs a regional sequence of events and examines social and ecological processes that caused changes through time.

PHILLIPS, PHILIP; JAMES A. FORD; and JAMES B. GRIFFIN. *Archaeological Survey in the Lower Mississippi Alluvial Valley, 1940–47.* Papers of the Peabody Museum of American Archaeology and Ethnology, vol. 25, 1951; reprint ed.: Mamaroneck, N.Y.: Kraus Reprint Co., 1968. 472pp. Illustrated. Bibliography.

This book contains a detailed report of extensive field research conducted from 1940 to 1947 at eighteen sites in the lower Mississippi River valley. The authors describe the geographic setting of the area and discuss the scope and methodology of their fieldwork. Pottery collections are classified and analyzed as to distribution and seriation, and related to the stratigraphy of the sites. Archaeological sequences for the sites are correlated with the drainage history of the Mississippi River and occupation site plans are analyzed. A final section reviews work done, summarizes the archaeology of the area, and presents a general picture of eastern archaeology based on the authors' findings. Figures 76–113 identify ceramics recovered.

STOLTMAN, JAMES B. "The Southeastern United States." In *The Development of North American Archaeology,* edited by James E. Fitting, pp. 117–50. Garden City, N.Y.: Doubleday Anchor Books, 1973. Bibliography.

The author presents a concise history of the development of archaeology in the Southeast, focusing on the growth of techniques by which archaeological data were gathered.

WEBB, WILLIAM S., and DAVID L. DEJARNETTE. *An Archeological Survey of Pickwick Basin in the Adjacent Portions of the States of Alabama, Mississippi and Tennessee.* Bureau of American Ethnology Bulletin 129. Washington, D.C.: Government Printing Office, 1942. 536pp. Illustrated. Bibliography.

This volume reports excavations undertaken at nineteen archaeological sites along the Tennessee River in Tennessee, Alabama, and Mississippi. The authors describe the physiography of each site, discuss the material recovered, and offer conclusions regarding the way of life of the people. The sites include five earth burial mounds; two villages; nine shell mounds, or middens, used as habitation and burial sites; two domiciliary earth mounds; and one village used by manufacturers of shell-tempered pottery. The authors, on a comparative basis, place the sites in the Southern Aspect of the Hopewellian Phase. Some 316 plates placed at the end of the text show sites, burials, house remains, and artifacts.

GREAT PLAINS

FRISON, GEORGE C. "The Plains." In *The Development of North American Archaeology,* edited by James E. Fitting, pp. 151–84. Garden City, N.Y.: Doubleday Anchor Books, 1973. Bibliography.

This chapter contains a concise history of the development of archaeology in the North American Plains from Canada to central Texas and from the flanks of the Rocky Mountains to the western border of the states west of the Mississippi River.

————. *Prehistoric Hunters of the High Plains.* New York: Academic Press, 1978. 457pp. Illustrated. Bibliography.

This book reconstructs the prehistoric cultures of part of what is commonly called the Northwestern Plains, an area that includes Wyoming, southern Montana, western South Dakota and Nebraska, and the extreme southwestern corner of North Dakota, plus an area along the northern border of Colorado. The author examines the cultures against the archaeological evidence of some 11,000 years. He discusses the Northwestern Plains as an ecological area for prehistoric hunting and gathering, reviews the archaeological record of the area, investigates means of game procurement employed by prehistoric hunters, and considers adaptive hunting strategies designed to cope with changing times.

GUNNERSON, JAMES H. *An Introduction to Plains Apache Archaeology: The Dismal River Aspect.* Bureau of American Ethnology Bulletin 173, pp. 131–260. Washington, D.C.: Government Printing Office, 1960.

Archaeological materials recovered from more than eighty sites scattered over four states in the Central Plains are considered in this report. The sites, dated from around the opening of the eighteenth century, yielded information indicating an Athapaskan influence reaching from central Nebraska to New Mexico. The report contains detailed lists of all finds, offers explanations of subsurface details, reviews previous work, presents information concerning many aspects of the material culture of the Plains Apache (Athapaskans), and documents the late phases of the Athapaskan occupation of the Plains and Southwest. The author presents general summaries and offers conclusions regarding the basic pattern of the area and its relationship to other patterns.

JELKS, EDWARD B.; E. MOTT DAVIS; and HENRY F. STURGIS. *A Review of Texas Archaeology.* Texas Archaeology Society Bulletin, vol. 29, part 1. Austin: Texas Archaeology Society, 1958. 254pp. Illustrated. Bibliography.

The papers in this collection review the archaeology of northeast, central, and southwest (Trans-Pecos) Texas and the central and southern sections of the Texas coast. In addition to a listing of references cited, there is a section entitled "Texas Archaeology: A Guide to the Literature" which lists 1,287 books and articles.

PRICE, JAMES E., and JAMES B. GRIFFIN. *The Snodgrass Site of the Powers Phase of Southeast Missouri.* Anthropological Papers Museum of Anthropology, University of Michigan, no. 66. Ann Arbor: University of Michigan Press, 1979. 178pp. Illustrated. Bibliography.

This report is a detailed account of archaeological excavations conducted at a site in southeast Missouri that is one of eight villages associated with the Powers Phase, a Middle Mississippian manifestation dating ca. A.D. 1275–1350. The villages form a radial pattern to the east and to the south of Powers Fort, a large civil-ceremonial center in Butler County, Missouri. The Powers Phase project represents the first major research project to excavate an entire Mississippian settlement and examine the distribution of its contents in an attempt to differentiate social segments through the presence or absence of attributes. In addition, the report seeks to provide evidence to determine the level of social complexity and patterned lifeways that existed among a prehistoric village population.

WEDEL, WALDO R. *An Introduction to Kansas Archaeology.* Bureau of American Ethnology Bulletin 174. Washington, D.C.: Government Printing Office, 1960. 723pp. Illustrated.

The author reports on research conducted in 1937, 1939, and 1940; reviews archaeological, ethnohistoric, and geographical data bearing on the aboriginal inhabitants of Kansas; and discusses the scattered evidence of preceramic occupation in most parts of Kansas. Based on the evidence, he suggests a Plains Woodland occupation in about A.D. 1 to 800; following Woodland, but apparently not derived from it, the Central Plains tradition (or phase) dating from approximately the eleventh to the fifteenth century; the Great Bend aspect of the protohistoric Wichita and Quivira from A.D. 1540 to 1640; and the Dismal River aspect, representing the Plains Apache of about 1700. The skeletal material from Kansas is discussed by T. D. Stewart in an appendix.

————. *Prehistoric Man on the Great Plains.* Norman: University of Oklahoma Press, 1961. 355pp. Illustrated. Bibliography.

This study reviews the human prehistory of the North American Plains, an area of some 800,000 square miles of semiarid grassland that now encompasses the states of Kansas, Nebraska, South Dakota; parts of Texas, Colorado, Missouri, Wyoming, Iowa, Montana, North Dakota; and the Canadian provinces of Manitoba, Saskatchewan, and Alberta. The author traces the presence of humans in the various subareas (Central, Southern, Middle, and Northeastern Plains) through examination of the artifact assemblages and faunal remains from principal archaeological sites. He challenges the belief that migratory nomadism was the only culture which ever flourished on the Great Plains, arguing that the native peoples of the Plains at different times and in different degrees exercised certain options offered by the environment and were by choice hunters, foragers, semisendentary farmers, or combinations of the three. Further, he argues that the horse was just another cultural adaptation made by some of the people.

———. "The Prehistoric Plains." In *Ancient Native Americans,* edited by Jesse D. Jennings, pp. 183–219. San Francisco: W. H. Freeman, 1978.

This article updates a summary review of Plains archaeology and culture history prepared in 1964 ("The Great Plains," in Jesse D. Jennings, *Prehistoric Man in the New World,* pp. 193–220. Chicago: University of Chicago Press, 1964). The author focuses on the environmental stresses of the Plains, linking cultural changes with climatic fluctuations that have been characteristic of the area for millennia. The time span treated is 10,000 B.C. to A.D. 1850.

WOOD, RAYMOND W., and R. BRUCE MCMILLAY, eds. *Prehistoric Man and His Environments: A Case Study in the Ozark Highlands.* New York: Academic Press, 1976. 271pp. Illustrated. Bibliography.

The authors report on more than a decade of interdisciplinary field research that has centered on the postglacial deposits in Rodgers Shelter, a deep rock shelter in west central Missouri, and on five nearby spring bogs. Papers detail the investigations and subsequent analyses of the sites, and summarize overall conclusions. This study proposes a preliminary model for the paleoecology of the western Ozark Highlands for the last 35,000 years and offers an interpretation of how human beings adapted to and exploited the Ozarks for the 10,500 years they are known to have lived in the area, the homeland of the probable ancestors of the historic Osage people who were moved to Kansas and Oklahoma in 1823.

SOUTHWEST

BREW, JOHN OTIS. *Archaeology of Alkali Ridge, Southeastern Utah, with a Review of the Prehistory of the Mesa Verde Division of the San Juan and Some Observations on Archaeological Systematics.* Papers of the Peabody Museum of American Archaeology and Ethnology, vol. 21. Cambridge, Mass.: Harvard University, 1946; reprint ed.: Mamaroneck, N.Y.: Kraus Reprint Co., 1968. 345pp. Illustrated. Bibliography.

This report is based on excavations carried out in southeastern Utah from 1931 to 1933. Thirteen sites were excavated; 234 rooms, including 195 storage and living rooms were cleared along with twenty-nine subterranean and semisubterranean pit houses and kivas. In addition to the buildings, ten refuse mounds were examined. The text reviews the archaeology of the area and of the Southwest in general as it bears on the area. Archaeological principle and theory are considered. The author describes the sites, artifacts, and house remains; traces the development of the Pueblo kiva and house architecture; discusses burial customs, stone, bone, and antler objects; and analyzes ceramic and pottery decorations.Illustrations are grouped at the back of the book.

GUMERMAN, GEORGE J., and ROBERT C. EULER. *Papers on the Archaeology of Black Mesa, Ari-* zona. Carbondale: Southern Illinois University, 1976. 186pp. Bibliography.

This is a collection of papers reporting the results of archaeological surveys and excavations carried out in advance of construction of a 274-mile slurry pipeline and strip-mining in the Black Mesa area on the Navajo and Hopi reservations in the northeast corner of Arizona, the first archaeological work to be done in the area since 1936–37. The first part of the book contains reports of the excavations and analyses of the materials recovered, such as maize cobs and animal bones. The second section consists of theoretically based papers on social organization, population growth, and cultural-environmental correlations. For an account that is mainly descriptive see: George J. Gumerman, *Black Mesa: Survey and Excavation in Northeastern Arizona, 1968.* Prescott, Ariz.: Prescott College Press, 1970.

HAURY, EMIL W. *The Stratigraphy and Archaeology of Ventana Cave, Arizona.* Albuquerque: University of New Mexico Press, 1950. 599pp. Illustrated. Bibliography.

The author provides a detailed report of excavations undertaken at a site on the Papago Reservation in southwestern Arizona with the consent and assistance of the tribe. The report summarizes the archaeology of the region and describes the cave being excavated, the geological layers, fossil vertebrates, modern flora and fauna of the cave remains, artifacts, burials, and the pictographs and skeletal remains discovered. The author dates the materials, correlates the findings, proposes cultural sequences, and concludes that the modern Papagos are descendants of the Desert Hohokam, who, in turn, drew from the racial and cultural reservoir of the Cochise culture.

HESTER, JAMES J. *Blackwater Locality No. 1: A Stratified Early Man Site in Eastern New Mexico.* Rancho de Taos, N.M.: Fort Burgwin Research Center, Inc., Southern Methodist University, 1972. 238pp. Illustrated. Bibliography.

Some twenty field parties, beginning in 1932, accumulated archaeological evidence from the site of a prehistoric pond in Blackwater Draw, an extinct river bed at the head of the Brazos River in east central New Mexico. The pond, termed Blackwater Draw Locality No. 1, functioned as one of the more permanent water holes in the Llano Estacado area of eastern New Mexico-northwestern Texas from approximately 15,000 to 6000 B.P. The evidence, as presented in this detailed examination, indicates that the pond was visited periodically by Paleo-Indian hunters in search of game. The text reviews past research and reports new field work, describes artifacts recovered, and offers a summary and conclusions.

KIDDER, ALFRED VINCENT. *An Introduction to the Study of Southwestern Archaeology with a Preliminary Account of the Excavations at Pecos.* New Haven, Conn.: Yale University Press, 1962. 377pp. Illustrated. Bibliography.

Originally published in 1924, this work contains a summary of the knowledge then available about

Southwestern archaeology. The present volume updates the text in a section that briefly sketches developments that took place between 1924 and 1961. The first part of the book describes excavations at Pecos ruins in New Mexico in 1915–16 and 1920–22. The author then summarizes Southwestern archaeology, dividing the area into regions and discussing the archaeological remains in each region chronologically, working from the historic pueblos back in time to the prehistoric pueblo remains.

LIPE, WILLIAM D. "The Southwest." In *Ancient Native Americans,* edited by Jesse D. Jennings, pp. 327–401. San Francisco: W. H. Freeman, 1978.

This paper summarizes what is known about prehistoric cultures of the southwestern United States from roughly 9000 B.C. to A.D. 1700. The author discusses cultural development in the various regions of the area and defines regional traditions, describing changes and interrelationships through time. Opposing interpretations are cited.

LONGACRE, WILLIAM A., ed. *Restructuring Prehistoric Pueblo Societies.* Albuquerque: University of New Mexico Press, 1970. 247pp. Illustrated. Bibliography.

Papers by participants in an advanced seminar on prehistoric Pueblo social organization focus on the methodology and theory for achieving strong inferences about the nature of social organization in extinct Puebloan societies. The articles discuss economic, political, and kinship systems; change and migration; ecological determinants of community location and patterns of resource exploitation; and ecological change and its effects on Pueblo migration and community integration. Recovery of pertinent data for the testing of hypotheses about many aspects of extinct cultural systems is stressed, reflecting a trend away from a basically inductive approach toward a more explicitly deductive one.

MCGREGOR, JOHN C. *Southwestern Archaeology.* 2nd ed. Urbana: University of Illinois Press, 1965. 511pp. Illustrated. Bibliography.

This book is intended as an introduction to the study of Southwestern archaeology. Northern Arizona is dealt with in greatest detail with outlying areas treated as somewhat peripheral. The first part of the book discusses archaeological theory and principles in general, and gives a brief history of Southwestern archaeology. The second part is a historical reconstruction of the cultures of the area beginning with the earliest evidences of human occupation some 13,000 years ago. The author compares early cultures at given times and discusses evolutionary processes affecting them.

ROHN, ARTHUR H. "The Southwest and Intermontane West." In *The Development of North American Archaeology,* edited by James E. Fitting, pp. 185–211. Garden City, N.Y.: Doubleday Anchor Books, 1973. Bibliography.

The author discusses the development of archaeological studies in the southwestern United States, including the Colorado Plateau, focusing on events and developments that have exerted a lasting influence on the knowledge of culture history in the areas or on the practice of archaeology in general.

WASHBURN, DOROTHY K. "The American Southwest." In *North America,* edited by Shirley Gorenstein, pp. 103–32. New York: St. Martin's, 1975. Bibliography.

This article reviews the preceramic period (approximately 6000 to 300 B.C.) in the southwestern United States, and the three major ceramic traditions which followed it: the Anasazi of the high plateau area of northern Arizona and northwestern New Mexico; the Mogollon of the mountainous zone of east central Arizona and west central New Mexico; and the Hohokam of the southern Arizona desert. Some other cultures of the Southwest are discussed briefly.

WORMINGTON, H. M. *Prehistoric Indians of the Southwest.* Denver: Denver Museum of Natural History, 1947. 191pp. Illustrated. Bibliography.

The author reconstructs the history of the earliest peoples to inhabit an area that includes New Mexico, Arizona, southern Utah, and the southwestern corner of Colorado. An introductory chapter explains archaeological tools and techniques, while subsequent chapters discuss successive cultures of the Southwest with descriptions of artifacts, physical remains, and architecture. A summary of what then was known about the prehistory of the area is followed by an appendix listing outstanding exhibit sites, modern Pueblos, and local museums.

FAR WEST:
GREAT BASIN–PLATEAU
AND CALIFORNIA

AIKENS, MELVIN. "The Far West." In *Ancient Native Americans,* edited by Jesse D. Jennings, pp. 131–81. San Francisco: W. H. Freeman, 1978.

The author discusses the great variety, and some similarities, among the aboriginal populations of California, the Great Basin (Nevada, Utah, southeastern Oregon, and eastern California) and the Plateau (Idaho, northeastern Oregon, and eastern Washington) and describes prehistoric lifeways of the three distinctive geographic provinces.

CRESSMAN, L. S. *Prehistory of the Far West.* Provo: University of Utah Press, 1977. 248pp. Illustrated. Bibliography.

This book contains a synthesis of the prehistory of the area of western North America lying between the Rocky Mountains and the Sierra/Cascade mountain chain, and the adjacent Pacific coast. This volume assembles the data on the cultural development in the region. The author reviews the geography of the major physiographic areas of the region, discusses the earliest evidence for the first human arrivals, examines the evidence for physical types of past and present occupants, and draws upon linguistic and cultural evidence to discuss changing patterns of adaptation to various environmental challenges. He also surveys archaeological work in the area and presents observations and conclusions.

HARRINGTON, MARY R., and RUTH D. SIMPSON. "Tule Springs, Nevada, with Other Evidences of Pleistocene Man in North America." *Southwest Museum Papers,* no. 18. Los Angeles: Southwest Museum, 1961. 146pp. Illustrated. Bibliography.

Chapter 1 reviews some thirty key archaeological sites that have yielded evidence of human occupation in association with the remains of animals that became extinct around 6000 B.C. Archaeological evidence from Tule Springs in Clark County, Nevada, is reviewed and analyzed, the data summarized and considered in light of archaeological evidence from other sites in the area. The authors show that human beings were in the Tule Springs area 28,000 years before the present time; that they were there contemporaneously with Pleistocene mammals including camels, bison, horses, mammoths, and ground sloths; that juniper and oak were burned in cooking fires; and tentatively describe the people who camped at the site as food gatherers with a predeliction for hunting.

HEIZER, ROBERT F., ed. *Handbook of North American Indians: California,* pp. 25–79. Vol. 8 *Handbook of North American Indians,* William C. Sturtevant, gen. ed. Washington, D.C.: Smithsonian Institution, 1978.

Articles in this section provide a summary of the available knowledge about the prehistoric peoples of California. Subjects include: post-Pleistocene archaeology, 9000–2000 B.C.; the development of regional prehistoric cultures; protohistoric and historic archaeology; Indian/Euro-American interaction, and archaeological information from non-Indian sites. Each author has attempted to utilize and cite all the important sources available.

———, and M. A. WHIPPLE, eds. "Archaeology." In *The California Indians: A Source Book,* pp. 131–243. Berkeley: University of California Press, 1971. Bibliography.

Eight articles in this section discuss prehistoric cultures of the west coast of North America, San Francisco Bay shellmounds, culture sequences in central California, a suggested chronology for southern California coastal archaeology, the antiquity of San Francisco Bay shellmounds, the prehistory of the Santa Barbara area, speculations on the prehistory of northwestern California, and rock art in California.

IRWIN, HENRY T. "The Far West." In *North America,* edited by Shirley Gorenstein, pp. 133–64. New York: St. Martin's, 1975. Bibliography.

This chapter summarizes salient points concerning the prehistory of the area that lies between the Rocky Mountains and the Pacific Ocean, a very large, physically diverse area. The author points out basic structural elements in the archaeological past in four separate, but not culturally independent, regions: the Great Basin (southeastern Oregon, southern Idaho, Utah, Nevada, southeastern

California); the Plateau (northeastern Oregon, eastern Washington, Idaho, western Montana); the Northwest Coast; and California. In a modified historical approach, the author uses linguistic and ethnographic data as guidelines for speculations concerning earlier peoples.

SHINER, JOEL L. *The McNary Reservoir: A Study in Plateau Archaeology.* River Basin Survey Papers, no. 23. Bureau of American Ethnology Bulletin 179. Washington, D.C.: Government Printing Office, 1961. 266pp. Illustrated. Bibliography.

This report discusses excavations conducted at the site of the McNary Reservoir on the Columbia River on the Washington-Oregon border. Nine sites are described. The author considers the architecture, material culture, and economy in a discussion of cultural change in the region. A comparative survey of Plateau sites is followed by a description of Plateau culture in the early historical period.

WARREN, CLAUDE N. "California." In *The Development of North American Archaeology,* edited by James E. Fitting, pp. 213–49. Garden City, New York: Doubleday Anchor Books, 1973. Bibliography.

The author presents a history of the development of archaeology in California and discusses new directions.

NORTHWEST COAST

DRUCKER, PHILIP. *Indians of the Northwest Coast.* Garden City, N.Y.: Natural History Press, 1963. 224pp. Illustrated. Bibliography.

This volume recreates the culture of the Native American groups who inhabited the coast of North America from southeast Alaska to northern California. The author first describes the land, people, and prehistory of the area and then considers each aspect of the culture. A final chapter reviews traits and complexes, defines subareas, draws inferences regarding relationships between the subareas, and between them and the neighboring culture areas.

SPRAGUE, RODERICK. "The Pacific Northwest." In *The Development of North American Archaeology,* edited by James E. Fitting, pp. 251–85. Garden City, N.Y.: Doubleday Anchor Books, 1973. Bibliography.

The author traces the development of archaeology in the Pacific Northwest, identifying major discoveries and trends.

ALASKA

BANDI, HANS GEORG. *Eskimo Prehistory.* Translated by Ann E. Keep. College: University of Alaska Press, 1969. 226pp. Illustrated. Bibliography.

This book gives an outline of Eskimo prehistory in various parts of the Arctic, tracing the main lines of development. The first section examines early studies of Arctic prehistory, beginning with attempts by nineteenth- and early twentieth-century

European archaeologists to view Eskimo culture as a survival of the European Paleolithic. Short chapters discuss language and physical characteristics. The second section surveys important Arctic archaeological sites, reports archaeologists' interpretations of their own material, and examines controversies. A third section considers theories on the origin of the peoples of America. The author reviews theories of American archaeologists and presents his own. He attributes the uniformity in Eskimo culture to an expansion some 1,000 years ago of the Thule culture from Alaska as far as Greenland and its subsequent retreat to Alaska a few centuries ago.

CAMPBELL, JOHN M., and LINDA SEINFELD CORDELL. "The Arctic and Subarctic." In *North America,* edited by Shirley Gorenstein, pp. 36–73. New York: St. Martin's, 1975. Bibliography.

The authors reconstruct the culture history of the Eskimos (Inuits) and Athapaskans in the Arctic and Subarctic; drawing on archaeological evidence from sites in Alaska and Canada.

DEKIN, ALBERT A., JR. *Arctic Archaeology: A Bibliography and History.* New York: Garland Publishing, 1978. 279pp.

This volume is designed to lead to the resources for the study of Arctic archaeology and to an understanding of how these studies contributed to the current understanding of archaeology in the Arctic. The author presents a historical narrative of the development of Arctic archaeology, chronicling the research and publications involved.

DUMOND, DON E. "Alaska and the Northwest Coast." In *Ancient Native Americans,* edited by Jesse D. Jennings, pp. 43–93. San Francisco: W. H. Freeman, 1978.

This article discusses the prehistoric cultures of interior and coastal Alaska from before 4000 B.C. to A.D. 1000 and of the Pacific Northwest Coast before and after 5000 B.C.

———. *The Eskimos and Aleuts.* London: Thames & Hudson, 1977. 180pp. Illustrated. Bibliography.

This study outlines the prehistory of Eskimos (Inuits) and Aleuts in Alaska and examines their earliest cultural remains in the Aleutian Islands, the Alaska Peninsula, and the Arctic Zone from Point Barrow to eastern Greenland. The author considers the physical characteristics and linguistic similarities of Eskimos and Aleuts, describes the regional development of cultures—beginning with archaeological remains from Old Crow Flats in the Yukon Territory which have been dated between 27,000 and 24,000 B.C.—and relates varied technical traditions to one another in a reconstruction of historical developments.

BIBLIOGRAPHIES

JOHNSON, LEROY, JR., and DAVID L. COLE. *A Bibliographic Guide to the Archaeology of Oregon and Adjacent Regions.* Special Publication of the Museum of Natural History. Eugene: University of Oregon, 1969.

This bibliography includes archaeological literature dealing with Oregon, southeastern Idaho, northeastern California, and southwestern Washington. There are 447 works listed. Each reference is coded and keyed to the categories of geographic area and region, artifact typological and distributional studies, ceramics and stone sculpturing, pictographs and petroglyphs, technical subjects, historic archaeology, book reviews, and bibliographies.

MOELLER, ROGER W., ed. *Archaeological Bibliography for Eastern North America.* Washington, Conn.: Eastern States Archaeological Federation and American Indian Archaeological Institute, 1977. 198pp.

This unannotated bibliography lists material dealing with the states east of the Mississippi River, including the eastern provinces of Canada. Selected articles from other areas and disciplines considered useful in interpretation and techniques are included. Some 8,000 entries published between 1959 and 1976 are organized alphabetically by author under eight subject headings: culture history, artifacts and features, ecology, techniques, reviews, theory, mathematics, and physical anthropology. Also, some 1,500 titles cover all aspects of archaeology and related fields in eastern Canada.

SNOW, DEAN R. *Native American Prehistory: A Critical Bibliography.* Bloomington: Indiana University Press, 1979. 75pp.
See annotation on page 26.

5   DESCRIPTIVE NARRATIVES

Personal observations in written form, an enormous accumulation of materials, constitute one of the indispensable sources of information on American Indian life and history. These documents provide detail, human interest, and occasionally, intelligent and penetrating observations not found in other historical sources. Most of these personal records have been written by whites who observed Indians and recounted information about them in their diaries, memoirs, correspondence, government reports, travel journals, speeches, and other documents. Personal accounts have been written by, among others, European, Russian, and American fur traders, travelers, and explorers, by people held captive by Indians, by missionaries, U.S. government officials and bureaucrats, naturalists, officials of the Spanish government in the Southwest and elsewhere, English and French officials in the United States and Canada, and by U.S. Army officers and enlisted men.

This section contains a small, representative sample of narratives ranging from captivity, travel, and war narratives to letters, journals, and memoirs of fur traders, missionaries, and government officials. They were written from the sixteenth through the twentieth centuries.

These personal records vary, however, in their reliability as historical and anthropological sources. The narrators were not all trained historians or anthropologists who knew how to write dispassionate, balanced, and accurate accounts. It is essential when reading firsthand reports to know the purpose of the writer. Documents intended as confidential records of events—to aid one's own memory—are usually more reliable firsthand sources than records intended for the public. The latter materials may suppress incriminating, embarrassing, or very private information and provide apologia instead.

Firsthand accounts which describe the history of Indian-white relations or convey ethnographic information are usually told from the white point of view. They are invariably permeated with the inherent biases of Western culture. Many of the observers, caught up in the events and opinions of their time, regarded Indians as "savages," "primitives," obstacles to the progress of white civilization, or passive victims of white assimilation. Many of the accounts are filled, therefore, with archaic jargon that reflects the particular prejudices or biases of a period. Nevertheless, despite the jargon and the underlying beliefs, the observations contain invaluable information about Indians, their way of life, and their relations with other tribes and whites. It is imperative that readers study the documents carefully in order to sift out the outdated opinions and demeaning terminology.

SCHOOLCRAFT, HENRY R. *Historical and Statistical Information Respecting the History, Condition, and Prospects of the Indian Tribes of the United States: Collected and Prepared Under the Direction of the Bureau of Indian Affairs.* 6 vols. Philadelphia: Lippincott, Grambo & Co., 1851–1857. Illustrated; reprint ed.: New York: AMS Press, 6 vols. and index.

This work is one of the first comprehensive studies of American Indians to appear in the United States. The intent was to provide a compendium of statistics and information on the Indian peoples of the country. The six volumes contain 336 full-page plates, many in color, representing thousands of the scenes and objects named.

Volume 1. 568pp. Schoolcraft discusses the origins and traditions of several tribes and the Ante-Columbian epoch, examines ancient artifacts, physical geography, tribal organization and government, mythology and oral traditions, and pictography. He reprints census returns and other statistical documents of the Iroquoian- and Algonquian-speaking tribes, Dakota groups, Chickasaws and Cherokees, and Indian populations of newly acquired states and territories.

Volume 2. 608pp. Schoolcraft discusses antiquities, physical geography, tribal organization, history and government, numeration and pictography of several tribes, the Cherokee syllabry, legends, physical types, grammar and vocabularies, and craft skills. He reprints statistics and populations for 1820 and 1850. The 1763 French *Journal of the Siege of Detroit* is reproduced.

Volume 3. 635pp. Schoolcraft discusses clothing, antiquities, physical geography, tribal organization, history and government, traditions, songs, physical types, principles of Indian languages, vocabularies, grammar, technological skills, witchcraft, magic and demonology, Winnebago medicine, and aboriginal nomenclature. He reprints the statistics and populations of various tribes from 1806 to 1851.

Volume 4. 668pp. Schoolcraft discusses antiquities, physical geography, tribal organization, history and government, pictography, oral traditions, public speaking, physical types, Indian vocabularies, arts and crafts, demonology, witchcraft and magic, medical knowledge of Indians, and Indian nomenclature. He reprints statistics and populations of various tribes, writes six biographies, and includes two papers on religion and one on migrations of Indians.

Volume 5. 712pp. Schoolcraft discusses antiquities, geography, tribal organization, history and government, physical types, the Chippewa language, Indian art, religion and mythology, demonology, magic and witchcraft, Indian nomenclature, vocabularies, medical knowledge, and Indians as

physicians. He reprints Major C. Swan's 1791 journal of the Creek Nation, gives a sketch of federal Indian policy, reprints statistics and population figures, writes six biographies, and includes thirty-four papers on various topics in the appendix.

Volume 6. 756pp. Schoolcraft traces the history in chronological order of Indian-European contacts in Florida, Louisiana, New Mexico, Virginia, New England, and Maryland. He discusses Indian wars in New England, tribes in Pennsylvania and the Carolinas, relations between Indians and European powers in North America from 1700 to 1750, the conquest of Canada, and the history of Indian tribes during the American Revolution. He describes events from the 1783 peace treaty to the surrender of the lake posts by the British in 1796, embittered relations with Indians west of the Mississippi to 1825, federal Indian removal policy and its effects on tribes east and west of the Mississippi River, and the conditions of tribes until the 1850s. He concludes with a discussion of the decline of Indian tribes and some additional comments on Indian cultures.

Volume 7. Nichols, Frances S. *Index to Schoolcraft's* Indian Tribes of the United States. Bureau of American Ethnology Bulletin 152. Washington, D.C.: Government Printing Office, 1954. 257pp. The index is arranged by subject and tribe. A brief biography of Schoolcraft is included.

————. *Narrative Journal of Travels, through the Northwestern Regions of the United States extending from Detroit through the Great Chain of American Lakes to the Sources of the Mississippi River performed as a Member of the Expedition under Governor Cass in the Year 1820.* Albany: E. & E. Hosford, 1821. 419pp. Illustrated.

————. *Notes on the Iroquois: or, Contributions to the Statistics, Aboriginal History, Antiquities, and General Ethnology of Western New York.* New York: Bartlett & Wilford, 1846. 285pp.; reprint ed.: Millwood, N.Y.: Kraus Reprint Co., 1975.

————. *Personal Memoirs of a Residence of Thirty Years with the Indian Tribes on the American Frontiers: With Brief Notices of Passing Events, Facts, and Opinions,* A.D. *1812–*A.D. *1842.* Philadelphia: Lippincott, Grambo & Co., 1851. 703pp.; reprint ed.: New York: AMS Press, 1978.

————. *Travels in the Central Portions of the Mississippi Valley Comprising Observations on its Mineral Geography, Internal Resources, and Aboriginal Population.* New York: Collins & Hannay, 1825. 459pp.; reprint ed.: Millwood, N.Y.: Kraus Reprint Co., 1975.

WASHBURN, WILCOMB E., selector and arranger. *Narratives of North American Indian Captivities.* New York: Garland Publishing, 1975. 111 vols.

This is a series of facsimile reprints devoted to North American captivity narratives dating from the late seventeenth century to the end of the nineteenth century. There are 311 titles in the 111 volumes, including all of the more familiar narratives as well as many from little-known sources, such as journals, newspapers, and broadsides. In some cases, multiple editions of the same captivity narrative are published where the changes have been of unusual magnitude. These narratives contain some of the most detailed information on the activities and policies of the North American Indians, furnish eyewitness accounts of the inner workings of Indian tribal societies, and help reconstruct the history and development of Indian customs, religions, languages, and attitudes toward the outside world. The introductory volume by Washburn, entitled *The North American Indian Captivity,* contains a general introduction to the history and development of the captivity genre, one of the most popular literary forms. The series begins with the first printed account of a New England Indian captivity by Mrs. Mary Rowlandson in 1682.

NORTHEAST

BIGGAR, HENRY P., ed. *The Works of Samuel de Champlain.* 6 vols. Toronto: Champlain Society, 1922–36. Illustrated.

These six volumes contain the narratives from Champlain's discoveries in New France and his observations and history of Indians from 1599 to 1632.

Volume 1. 1599–1607. 469pp. This volume includes the period 1604–07 when Champlain explored and mapped the Acadian and New England coast as far south as Nantucket Sound. The volume includes Champlain's descriptions of countries, coasts, rivers, ports, and harbors and observations on the beliefs, superstitions, manner of life, and mode of warfare of the Indian inhabitants. Champlain's drawings and maps are included.

Volume 2. 1608–13. 351pp. Champlain describes the founding of Quebec in 1608, his fight with the Iroquois on Lake Champlain in 1609, his visits to the St. Lawrence in the summers of 1610 and 1611, and his 1613 journey up the Ottawa River as far as Allumette Island. The volume also contains maps and drawings by Champlain and six contemporary documents relating to his career between 1610 and 1618. These include his marriage contract, hiring a servant, a petition to the king, and extracts from letters of the Chamber of Commerce.

Volume 3. 1615–18. 418pp. Champlain describes his visits to the Hurons near Lake Simcoe in 1615, the Huron expedition across Lake Ontario against the Iroquois in 1615, his winter in Huron country, his return to France in 1616, and an account of his visit to the St. Lawrence in 1618. This volume also contains the first two books of Part 1 of *The Voyages,* the edition of his discoveries which

Champlain brought out in 1632 in Paris. There are maps and drawings by Champlain in this volume.

Volume 4. 1608–20. 373pp. This volume contains the remainder of Part 1 of *The Voyages,* Books 3 and 4, and an appendix that contains an addition to Champlain's marriage contract.

Volume 5. 1620–29. 330pp. This volume contains Part 2, Books 1 and 2 of *The Voyages.*

Volume 6. 1629–32. 330pp. This volume contains Part 2, Book 3 of *The Voyages.* The second part of the 1632 edition contains an account of events in New France from 1620 to 1632, including the capture of Quebec by the English in 1629 and its restoration to France in 1632 by the treaty of St. Germain-en-Laye. The volume contains a summary of Champlain's discoveries made in New France, identification tables of Champlain's maps, his treatise on seamanship, and an index to the six volumes.

BURRAGE, HENRY S. *Early English and French Voyages Chiefly from Hakluyt, 1534–1608. Original Narratives of Early American History,* vol. 7. New York: Scribner's, 1906, 1930. 451pp. Illustrated.

This volume contains a selection of materials from early English and French voyages that tell of Indians in the Northeast and Southeast during the sixteenth and early seventeenth centuries. There are three narratives from Cartier's voyages, narratives of the voyages of M. Hore, M. John Hawkins, Jesus of Lubec, Francis Drake, Sir Humfrey Gilbert Knight, Captain Arthur Barlowe, Master Ralph Lane, John White, John Brereton, Martin Pring, and Captain George Waymouth. Most of the documents come from Hakluyt's *Principall Navigations, Voiages, and Discoveries of the English Nation* first published in 1589. There are three maps and a facsimile page from the third volume of Hakluyt's "Voyages."

HECKEWELDER, JOHN. *History, Manners, and Customs of the Indian Nations Who Once Inhabited Pennsylvania and the Neighboring States.* Edited by Reverend William C. Reichel. Pennsylvania Historical Society Memoirs, vol. 12. Philadelphia: 1876; reprint ed.: New York: Arno Press, 1971. 465pp.

The first part of Heckewelder's book, published in 1819, deals with historical traditions of the Indians, their account of the first arrival of the Dutch at New York Island, of European conduct towards them, and of the fate of the Lenapes and kindred tribes, and the Iroquois. He then gives an account of Indian government, education, languages, signs, oratory, metaphorical expressions, names, intertribal communication, political maneuvers, marriage, aged, wars, treaties, observations of whites, food and cookery, dress and ornaments, dance, scalping, health and disease, remedies, physicians and surgeons, superstitions, initiation of boys, Indian mythology, suicide, intemperance, friendship, funerals, preachers, and computation of time. Also included are brief biographies of Tamanend and Teedyuscung and comparisons of Indians and whites. The last part has correspondence pertaining to Indian languages and lists of words, phrases, and short dialogs.

KENTON, EDNA, ed. *The Indians of North America. Selected and Edited from Jesuit Relations and Allied Documents, 1610–1791.* 2 vols. New York: Albert & Charles Boni, 1925; reprint ed.: New York: Vanguard, 1954.

This two-volume edition clarifies and condenses the period in American history with which the *Jesuit Relations* are concerned. The excerpts selected from the seventy-three volume *Relations* tell the story of Jesuit missionaries in North America from the establishment of the first Acadian mission in 1611 to the final surrender of the Jesuit estates to Canada in 1789. Excerpts included are Marquette's manuscript, Coquart's *Memoir upon the Posts of the King's Domain,* an economic document, *Journal des Jesuites,* a running story of daily life at Quebec kept by the superiors there from 1645 to 1668, and the account book of the Jesuit Mission farm near Detroit with entries from 1753 to 1756. Reuben Gold Thwaites's historical introduction to the seventy-three volume edition is also included.

KINIETZ, W. VERNON. *The Indians of the Western Great Lakes, 1615–1760.* Ann Arbor: University of Michigan Press, 1940. 427pp. Illustrated. Bibliography.

In this volume, the author presents "synthetic ethnographies" of the Ottawa, Miami, Huron, Potawatomi, and Chippewa who were residents of Michigan from 1615 to 1760. Using direct quotations from the letters and journals of European traders, missionaries, and officials he tells the story of the five tribes in the years before contact with white people which changed their centuries-old way of life. Topics considered for each tribe are location of the tribe, characteristics, dress and ornament, economic life, social life, legends, music, and religion. The appendix consists of the 1709 *Memoir Concerning the Different Indian Nations of North America* by Antoine Denis Raudot. There is a map and there are several tables. The bibliography is composed only of those works which are cited in the text. There are critical notes after the entries indicating the investigator's opinion of the value of the work.

LINCOLN, CHARLES H. *Narratives of the Indian Wars, 1675–1699.* Original Narratives of Early American History, vol. 12. New York: Scribner's, 1913. 316pp. Illustrated.

This volume contains narratives of King Philip's War by John Easton, "N.S." presumed to be Nathaniel Saltonstall, Richard Hutchinson, a captivity narrative by Mrs. Mary Rowlandson, and Cotton Mather's history of the war with Indians from 1688 to 1698. There are two maps and a photograph of the original title page of Mather's "Decennium Luctuosum."

MCKENNEY, THOMAS L. *Memoirs, Official and Personal: With Sketches of Travels among the Northern and Southern Indians; Embracing a War Excursion, and Descriptions of Scenes along the Western Borders,* vol. 1. New York: Pawe & Burgess, 1846. 340pp. *On the Origin, History, Char-*

acter, and the Wrongs and Rights of the Indians; With a Plan for the Preservation and Happiness of the Remnants of That Persecuted Race, vol. 2. New York: Pawe & Burgess, 1846. 136pp. Illustrated. Reprint ed.; Lincoln: University of Nebraska Press, 1973.

In the first volume, McKenney discusses the duties and problems of holding public office; describes the organization of the Bureau of Indian Affairs; his trip to the Great Lakes to negotiate with the Indians; a war expedition against the Winnebagos; passage down the "Ouisconsin" and Mississippi Rivers to Chickasaw, Creek, and Choctaw countries; and his trip back to Washington. Concluding chapters deal with government plans for improving the condition of the Indians, obstacles to their improvement, and the use of government power in dealing with Indians. The appendix contains McKenney's remarks on the proposed abolition of the Indian factory system, a document examining charges against McKenney, and letters. The second volume contains McKenney's plan for preserving "remnants of the Indian race, and their advancement into the higher privileges of their nature . . ." as well as his views on the origin of Indian tribes, their customs, works of art, and mistakes of our forefathers. There are etchings of the Indian way of life.

MORSE, REVEREND JEDIDIAH. *A Report to the Secretary of War of the United States, on Indian Affairs, Comprising a Narrative of a Tour Performed in the Summer of 1820, under a Commission from the President of the United States, for the Purpose of Ascertaining, for the Use of the Government, the Actual State of the Indian Tribes in Our Country.* Washington, D.C.: Davis & Force, 1822. 400pp. Illustrated.

The author gives an account of Indian tribes after his trip to the Great Lakes to illustrate "their actual condition," including information on soil, climate, modes of life, customs, laws, political institutions, principal leaders, number of schools, teachers, plan of education, and disposition to "civilization." The first part contains a general summary of various Indian nations in New England, New York, Ohio, Michigan, the Northwest Territory, Indiana, Illinois, Kentucky, Pennsylvania, Virginia, South Carolina, Georgia, Florida, Alabama, Mississippi, and Tennessee. The author makes suggestions for conducting Indian trade and "civilizing" Indians. The appendix contains speeches by Morse and Indians, a map of the United States, and a statistical table of all Indian tribes within U.S. limits containing their names, numbers, and place of residence, keyed to the map and to pages of the text. There are tables of annuities paid by the United States to Indian tribes under treaties, estimates of land purchased from Indians, and the number of schools established for educating Indians. There is a drawing of a Pawnee.

THWAITES, REUBEN GOLD, ed. *The Jesuit Relations and Allied Documents, 1610–1791.* 73 vols. Cleveland: Burrows Brothers, 1896–1901.

Each year, Jesuit missionaries in New France

sent back to their superiors in France or Quebec a report, or relation, of their activities. These reports comprise the *Jesuit Relations* written from 1632 to 1673 which were published annually in Paris and to which Thwaites added personal letters, memoirs, journals, state and church records, and other ecclesiastical or secular archives that threw additional light on the more formal *Relations*. The reports are a combination of travel literature, exploration, adventure, and ethnography revealing the folklore, religion, mythology, manners, morals, speech, and daily life of Montagnais, Hurons, Iroquois, Abenakis, Algonquians, Ottawas, Illinois, and Crees. The *Relations* and allied documents are presented in chronological order with notes to help the reader; English translations beside the original French, Latin, or Italian texts; sources of each document; and additional bibliographical data as to other editions. All maps, old portraits, engravings, and facsimile texts that appeared in previous editions are reproduced. The last two volumes contain analytical indexes.

SOUTHEAST

BARTRAM, WILLIAM. *The Travels of William Bartram: Naturalist's Edition.* Edited by Francis Harper. New Haven, Conn.: Yale University Press, 1958. Illustrated. Bibliography.

This is an annotated and indexed edition of Bartram's *Travels through North and South Carolina, Georgia, East and West Florida, the Cherokee Country, the Extensive Territories of the Muscogulges, or Creek Confederacy, and the Country of the Chactaws; Containing an Account of the Soil and Natural Products of Those Regions, Together with Observations on the Manners of the Indians* (Philadelphia: James & Johnson, 1791. 522pp.), a work on natural history and the cultures of the southeastern Indians. This version contains, in addition to the original work, a preface, an introduction by Harper containing an account of Bartram's life and his *Travels*, a commentary which elucidates his route and which explains geographical, historical, and various other matters, and an annotated index providing identifications of Bartram's plants and animals, biographical notes on persons, definitions of unusual or unfamiliar terms, information on Indian tribes, and the location of geographical features. There is a bibliography of publications, manuscripts, maps and atlases, a section on variant orthography, punctuation, and composition, and a general index to the preface, introduction, and commentary. There are reproductions of Bartram's drawings, the map of his route, sites, and other maps of the Southeast.

HODGE, FREDERICK W., and THEODORE LEWIS. *The Spanish Explorers in the Southern United States, 1528–1543.* Original Narratives of Early American History, vol. 16. New York: Scribner's, 1907. 411pp. Illustrated.

This volume contains three narratives that provide information about Indians in the southern United States in the sixteenth century. The first narrative of Alvar Nuñez Cabeca de Vaca, edited and briefly discussed by Hodge, concerns his explorations from Florida to Texas, 1528–36. The second narrative of Hernando de Soto by the Gentleman of Elvas, briefly discussed by Lewis, concerns his explorations through Florida, Georgia, North and South Carolina, Tennessee, Alabama, Mississippi, Arkansas, Texas, and Indian Territory. De Soto relates the earliest history and cultures of the Indians residing in these states. The third narrative of Coronado by Pedro de Castaneda, edited and discussed by Hodge, concerns Coronado's explorations from Mexico City to Colorado, Texas, Kansas, and Nebraska. This narrative contains information on Pueblos and Indians of the Great Plains. There are two maps and a facsimile page of Cabeca de Vaca's "Relacion."

LAWSON, JOHN. *Lawson's History of North Carolina Containing the Exact Description and Natural History of That Country, Together with the Present State Thereof and a Journal of a Thousand Miles Traveled through Several Nations of Indians Giving a Particular Account of Their Customs, Manners, Etc., Etc.* London: 1714; reprint ed.: Richmond, Va.: Garrett & Massie, 1937, 1952. 259pp.

This volume contains a biographical sketch of Lawson, his journal, begun in December, 1700, which includes a description of North Carolina and an account of the Indians of North Carolina discussing housing, food, clothing, traders, warfare, vices, skills, hunting, ceremonies, beliefs, practices of priests, health disorders, intertribal conflicts, and language. He provides a small dictionary of "Tuskeruros" words.

U.S. CONGRESS. SENATE. *Correspondence on the Subject of the Emigration of Indians, between the 30th November, 1831, and 27th December, 1833. Furnished in Answer to a Resolution of the Senate, of 27th December, 1833, by the Commissary General of Subsistence.* 5 vols. S. Doc. 512, 23rd Cong., 1st sess., 1834–1835; reprint ed.: New York: AMS Press, 1973. New foreword by Brantley Blue. New introduction by John M. Carroll.

On December 27, 1833, the U.S. Senate adopted a resolution directing that it be furnished by the Commissary General of Subsistence copies of all correspondence from November 30, 1831, dealing with the subject of the "immigration" or removal of the Indian tribes from southeastern United States to what is now Oklahoma. The report was later issued as Senate Document 512 and was published in Washington, D.C. The Commissary provided the Senate with letters and instructions of the Commissary's office to agents and others on the subject of Indian "emigration" from the winter of 1830–31 to December, 1833, letters from agents addressed to the Commissary on the subject of "emigration," other letters referred to him from the War Department and the Office of Indian Affairs, and abstracts of disbursements of agents employed in Indian emigration and of expenditures not chargeable to that service. There are over 4,200 pages of correspondence.

GREAT PLAINS

BARNABY, THOMAS ALFRED. *The Plains Indians and New Mexico, 1751–1778. A Collection of Documents Illustrative of the History of New Mexico.* Coronado Cuarto Centennial Publications, 1540–1940, vol. 11. Albuquerque: University of New Mexico Press, 1940. 232pp.

This volume contains a collection of documents pertaining to the relationship of Plains Indians, primarily Apaches and Comanches, with the Spanish in New Mexico during the eighteenth century. There is a historical introduction about the relationship between the Spanish in New Mexico and the Plains Indians who were antagonistic to the Pueblo peoples allied with the Spanish. The introduction and documents trace the contacts of Plains Apaches and Comanches with the New Mexico province and interrelations between the Apaches and Comanches.

BLAIR, EMMA H., ed. *The Indian Tribes of the Upper Mississippi Valley and Region of the Great Lakes as Described by Nicholas Perrot, French Commandant in the Northwest; Bacqueville de la Potherie, French Royal Commissioner to Canada; Morrell Marston, American army officer; and Thomas Forsyth, United States agent at Fort Armstrong.* 2 vols. Cleveland: Arthur H. Clark, 1911–12. Illustrated. Bibliography. Reprint ed.; Mamaroneck, N.Y.: Kraus Reprint Co., 1969.

These volumes contain descriptive accounts by two French and two American observers covering the years from 1680 to 1827. The first volume contains Perrot's account written during 1680 and 1718 and published in 1864 and Bacqueville de la Potherie's account published in 1716 which convey information about the customs, character, and beliefs of the North American Indians and their relations with white people who appropriated their lands. The second volume contains works by two American officials who made reports after Indians passed under control of the United States. Major Marston's 1820 account and government agent Forsyth's 1827 account both concern the customs of Sac and Fox tribes. The appendixes contain a biographical sketch of Perrot, notes on Indian social organization, mental traits, religious beliefs, and migrations based on ethnological writings and letters describing the character and condition of Sioux, Potawatomi, and Winnebago tribes written for this book by missionaries and others. There is a map and several illustrations showing Indians and scenes. There is an annotated bibliography of manuscript and book sources.

CATLIN, GEORGE. *Letters and Notes on the Manners, Customs and Condition of the North American Indians.* 2 vols. London: By the author, 1841; reprint ed.: New York: Dover, 1973. Illustrated.

These two volumes contain fifty-eight letters, 312 sketches, and several maps that Catlin made during eight years of travel (1832–39) among Plains tribes of North America. Catlin's remarks are confined chiefly to the Plains people he visited that were "beyond the frontier . . . without the taints of civilized encroachments." He focuses on the appearance of the Indians, particularly in his collection of sketches which contains many portraits of women and men. He also drew buffalo and buffalo hunts, dwellings, villages, landscapes, ceremonies, war objects, pipes, and facsimiles of paintings on robes. There is an appendix of several different Indian vocabularies and an account of the destruction of the Mandans.

DENIG, EDWIN T. *Five Indian Tribes of the Upper Missouri: Sioux, Arikaras, Assiniboines, Crees, Crows.* Edited and Introduction by John C. Ewers. Norman: University of Oklahoma Press, 1961. 217pp. Illustrated. Bibliography.

Denig, a fur trader, describes the life and customs of five Indian tribes of the Upper Missouri before 1860, the Sioux, Arikaras, Assiniboines, Crees, and Crows. He spent twenty-three years of his life trading with Indians. The introduction by Ewers gives a biography of Denig who was born in 1812, his relationship with other traders, and a history of the manuscript. There is a map of Indian tribes of the Upper Missouri in 1855 and paintings of Indians.

HOWARD, OLIVER O. *My Life and Experience among Our Hostile Indians: A Record of Personal Observations, Adventures, and Campaigns among the Indians of the Great West.* Hartford: A. D. Worthington, 1907. 570pp. Illustrated.

This memoir by an important figure in the frontier army who had a career as an Indian fighter and Indian diplomat contains observations about the tribes with which he came in contact. Howard's memoir reveals sympathy for his Indian adversaries, the feeling that the conflicts were due to white provocation and that Indians were tragic victims of the "dominant" race. He tells of his military career fighting Indians in Florida, Minnesota, the Plains, Arizona, Oregon, Washington, Idaho, and Alaska. The last four chapters concern intermarriage of white men and Indian women and characteristics of American Indians including sign language, oratory, horsemanship, and humor. The book is loaded with dated language and opinions; it represents, however, views of the time. There are thirty-six photographs of Indian clothing, war and everyday objects, children, battlefield scenes, lifestyles, and a portrait of Howard.

LARPENTEUR, CHARLES. *Forty Years a Fur Trader on the Upper Missouri, the Personal Narrative of Charles Larpenteur, 1833–1872.* Chicago: R. R. Donnelley, 1933. 388pp. Illustrated.

Larpenteur's narrative is a source of information on the fur trade of the Upper Missouri in the nineteenth century. A frank picture of the treatment of the Indians by the fur traders operating under American influences, it contrasts with that of such traders as Henry, Long, MacKenzie, and Hubbard, all of whom used Mackinaw as an operational base. The introduction contains a historical setting of the journal. There is a map of Larpenteur country.

LEWIS, MERIWETHER, and WILLIAM CLARK. *Original Journals of the Lewis and Clark Expedition,*

1804–1806. 8 vols. New York: Dodd, Mead, 1904–5; reprint ed.: Edited by Reuben Gold Thwaites. New York: Antiquarian Press, 1959.

Volume 1. This volume contains discussions on previous explorers, brief biographies of Lewis and Clark, the story of Lewis and Clark's Journals, and bibliographical works arranged in five groups: Jefferson's Message, 1806–08; Counterfeit Publications, 1809–51; Gass, 1807–1904; Genuine History, 1814–1904; and Miscellaneous, 1804–1904. The volume also contains the journals and orderly books of Lewis and Clark from River Dubois to Two-Thousand-Mile-Creek, January 30, 1804, to May 5, 1805.

Volume 2. This volume contains the journals from Two-Thousand-Mile-Creek to the Shoshone Camp on Lembi River, May 6, 1805, to August 20, 1805.

Volume 3. This volume continues from the Shoshone Camp on Lembi River to Fort Clatsop, August 21, 1805, to January 20, 1806.

Volume 4. This volume covers Fort Clatsop to Musquetoe Creek, January 21 to May 7, 1806.

Volume 5. This volume covers from Musquetoe Creek to St. Louis, May 8 to September 26, 1806.

Volume 6. This volume contains scientific data accompanying the journals including data on geography, ethnology, zoology, botany, mineralogy, meteorology, and astronomy.

Volume 7. This volume contains the journals of Sergeant Charles Floyd, May 14 to August 18, 1804, and Joseph Whitehouse, May 14 to November 6, 1805, and an appendix of 137 documents.

Volume 8. This volume contains an atlas.

Throughout the volume there are maps, facsimiles of journal pages, manuscript sketches, and portraits of Lewis and Clark. See also: Donald Jackson, ed., *Letters of the Lewis and Clark Expedition with Related Documents, 1783–1854.* Urbana: University of Illinois Press, 1962.

PIKE, ZEBULON MONTGOMERY. *The Expeditions of Zebulon Montgomery Pike, to the Headwaters of the Mississippi River, through Louisiana Territory and in New Spain, during the Years, 1805–6–7.* 3 vols. A New Edition, Now First Reprinted in Full From the Original of 1810, With Copious Critical Commentary, Memoir of Pike, New Map and Other Illustrations, and Complete Index by Elliot Coues. New York: Francis P. Harper, 1895.

Volume 1. This volume contains the original 1810 preface, a new preface written by Coues in 1895, and Coues's memoir of Pike. It also includes the narrative of Pike's expedition from St. Louis to St. Paul, August 9 to September 21, 1805; St. Paul to Leech Lake, September 22, 1805, to January 31, 1806; and Leech Lake to St. Louis, February 1 to April 30, 1806. There is a chart of the meteorological observations made by Pike in 1805 and 1806 on the Mississippi, a chapter of Pike's correspondence, Pike's remarks on the fur trade, his review of the geography of the Mississippi River and the ethnography of the Indian tribes he met on the River and its confluent streams, and a vocabulary of Mississipian place-names in English, French, and Indian. There is a portrait and a facsimile of Pike's letter.

Volume 2. This volume contains Pike's Arkansas journey from July 15, 1806, to February 26, 1807, and his Mexican tour from February 27 to July 1, 1807. The volume also contains Pike's dissertation on Louisiana; his observations on soil, rivers, animal and vegetable production and other notes; Lieutenant Wilkinson's report on the Arkansaw *(sic)*; correspondence between Pike and Wilkinson; Pike's observations on New Spain; and the congressional report and other documents bearing on the compensation of Pike and his companions.

Volume 3. This volume contains an alphabetical index of names. There are six maps reproduced from the 1810 edition and a "Historico-Geographical Chart of Upper Mississippi River" by Coues. See also: Donald Jackson, ed., *The Journals of Zebulon Montgomery Pike, With Letters and Related Documents.* Norman: University of Oklahoma Press, 1966. 2 vols.

THWAITES, REUBEN GOLD, ed. *Early Western Travels, 1748–1846. A Series of Annotated Reprints of Some of the Best and Rarest Contemporary Volumes of Travel, Descriptive of the Aborigines and Social and Economic Conditions in the Middle and Far West, during the Period of Early American Settlements.* 32 vols. Cleveland: Arthur H. Clark, 1904–7; reprint ed.: New York: AMS Press, 1966.

Volume 1. Journals of Conrad Weiser, 1748, Ohio region; George Croghan, 1750–1765, Ohio, Lake Erie region; Christian Frederick Post, 1758, Ohio region; and Captain Thomas Morris, 1764, Detroit area.

Volume 2. John Long's Journal, 1768–1782, St. Lawrence River, Lakes Ontario and Superior region.

Volume 3. Andre Michaux's Travels into Kentucky, 1793–1796, Francois Andre Michaux's Travels West of the Allegheny Mountains, 1802, Ohio, Kentucky, and Tennessee areas; Thaddeus Mason Harris' Journal of a Tour Northwest of the Allegheny Mountains, 1803, Ohio area.

Volume 4. Fortescue Cuming's Tour to the Western Country, 1807–1809, Ohio, Kentucky, Mississippi Territory, West Florida.

Volume 5. John Bradbury's Travels in the Interior of America, 1809–1811, Trans-Mississippi region.

Volume 6. Henry Marie Brackenridge's Journal up the Missouri, 1811; Gabriel Franchere's Voyage to the Northwest Coast, 1811–1814, Columbia River region.

Volume 7. Alexander Ross' Adventures of the First Settlers on the Oregon or Columbia River, 1810–1813.

Volume 8. Tilly Buttrick's Voyages, 1812–1819, Ohio, Kentucky, and Louisiana areas; Estwick Evan's Pedestrious Tour, 1818, western New York, Ohio, Michigan Territory, Indiana, Illinois, and Louisiana Territories.

Volume 9. James Flint's Letters from America, 1818–1820, New York, Pennsylvania, Ohio, Kentucky, Indiana.

Volume 10. Thomas Hulme's Journal, 1818–1819, Pennsylvania, Ohio, Illinois; Richard Flower's Letters from Lexington and the Illinois, 1819, Kentucky; Flower's Letters from the Illinois, 1820–1821; John Wood's Two Year's Residence, 1820–1821, Illinois.

Volume 11. William Faux's Memorable Days in America, 1819–1820, Part 1: South Carolina, Pennsylvania, New York, West Virginia, Indiana, Kentucky, Illinois, Washington, D.C., Maryland, Virginia.

Volume 12. William Faux's Memorable Days in America, Part 2; Adlard Welby's Visit to North America, 1819–1820, Illinois, Ohio, Kentucky, Pennsylvania, Indiana, New York.

Volume 13. Thomas Nuttall's Travels into the Arkansas Territory, 1819.

Volumes 14–17. Edwin James' Accounts of Major S. H. Long's Expedition, 1819–1820, area from Pittsburgh to the Rocky Mountains.

Volume 18. James O. Pattie's Personal Narratives, 1824–1830, area from St. Louis to California; Doctor Willard's Inland Trade with New Mexico, 1825, and Downfall of the Fredonian Republic, Texas area, and Malte-Brun's Account of Mexico.

Volume 19. George W. Ogden's Letters from the West, 1821–1823, Ohio Valley and Kentucky; William Bullock's Journey from New Orleans to New York, 1827; Dr. Josiah Gregg's Commerce of the Prairies, 1831–1839, Part 1: Santa Fe Trail, New Mexico area.

Volume 20. Gregg's Commerce of the Prairies, Part 2.

Volume 21. John B. Wyeth's Oregon, or a Short History of a Long Journey, 1832; John K. Townscend's Narrative of a Journey Across the Rocky Mountains, 1834, Missouri to Oregon.

Volumes 22–24. Maximilian, Prince of Wied. Travels in the Interior of North America, 1832–1834, Trans-Mississippi area.

Volume 25. Comprising the Series of Original Paintings of Charles Bodmer to Illustrate Maximilian, Prince of Wied Travels in the Interior of North America, 1832–1834. Eighty-one black-and-white plates and map.

Volume 26. Edmund Flagg's The Far West, 1836–1837, Part 1: Illinois, Missouri, Ohio.

Volume 27. Flagg's The Far West, Part 2; Father Pierre Jean De Smet's Letters and Sketches, 1841–1842, Rocky Mountains.

Volume 28. Thomas Jefferson Farnham's Travels in the Great Western Prairies, etc., 1839, Part 1: Oregon.

Volume 29. Farnham's Travels in the Great Western Prairies, etc., 1839, Part 2; De Smet's Oregon Missions and Travels Over the Rocky Mountains, 1845–1846.

Volume 30. Joel Palmer's Journal of Travels Over the Rocky Mountains, 1845–1846.

Volumes 31–32. Analytical Index to the Series.

WALKER, JAMES R. *Lakota Society*. Edited by Raymond J. DeMallie and Elaine A. Jahner. Lincoln: University of Nebraska Press, 1982. 206pp. Illustrated. Bibliography.

This book contains the primary accounts of the informants of the agency physician of Pine Ridge Reservation, Dr. James R. Walker, and Walker's syntheses of the organization of traditional Lakota society. Part 1, "The Structure of Society" records the organization of bands and camps and the relationships among them. There is detailed information on family, marriage, and the kinship system. Part 2, "Hunting, War, Ceremony, and Art" offers material on day-to-day life in a Lakota camp, and part 3, "Time and History" gives Walker's reconstruction of Lakota methods of measuring and counting time. Three winter counts are included. There are ninety-six illustrations and a bibliography. Also see: James R. Walker, *Lakota Belief and Ritual*. Edited by Raymond J. DeMallie and Elaine A. Jahner. Lincoln: University of Nebraska Press, 1980. 329pp. Illustrated.

SOUTHWEST

BOLTON, HERBERT EUGENE, ed. *Spanish Exploration in the South-West, 1542–1706*. Original Narratives of Early American History, vol. 2. New York: Scribner's, 1916, 1930. Illustrated.

This volume contains a selection of documents that illustrates the history of the Southwest and provides information about Indians. There are brief historical introductions to each document. The first section includes materials relating to the exploration and plans for settling California. Materials included are the "Relation of the Voyage of Juan Rodriguez Cabrillo," the "Diary of Sebastian Vizcaino," and "Brief Report of the Discovery of the South Sea" (Father Ascension). The second section concerns the exploration, founding, and settling of the Province of New Mexico and its adjacent regions. Materials included are from the Rodriquez, the Espejo, and the Onate Expeditions. The third section concerns the exploration and settlement of Texas. Materials included are from the Bosque-Larios Expedition, the Mendoza-Lopez Expedition to the Jumanos, and the De Leon-Massanet Expeditions. The fourth section on Arizona contains materials on the Jesuits in Primeria Alta. There are three maps.

HACKETT, CHARLES WILSON. *Revolt of the Pueblo Indians of New Mexico and Otermin's Attempted Reconquest, 1680–1682*. Coronado Cuarto Centennial Publications, 1540–1940, vols. 8 and 9. Albuquerque: University of New Mexico Press, 1942. 267pp., 430pp.

These volumes contain a collection of Spanish documents drawn up during the progress of the Pueblo Indians' 1680 revolt against the Spanish in New Mexico, the defense of the Spanish, the retreat, the reorganization, and the Spanish reconquest. The collection includes acts of the cabildo of Santa Fe, sworn declarations by witnesses to events, orders of the governor, letters written by him and other persons prominent in the period, proceedings of juntas or councils, acts of the government at Mexico City, etc.

HAMMOND, GEORGE P., and AGAPITO REY. *Don Juan de Onate, Colonizer of New Mexico, 1595–1628*. Coronado Cuarto Centennial Publications, 1540–

1940, vols. 5 and 6. Albuquerque: University of New Mexico Press, 1953. 1,187pp.

Onate established the first European settlement in New Mexico. There are extensive documents on the founding of New Mexico and the treatment of Indians in New Mexico during the late sixteenth and early seventeenth centuries.

————. *Narratives of the Coronado Expedition, 1540–1542.* Coronado Cuarto Centennial Publications, 1540–1940, vol. 2. Albuquerque: University of New Mexico Press, 1940. 413pp.

This volume contains a collection of Spanish letters, reports, muster rolls, instructions, and historical narratives, and Coronado's testimony on the management of his expedition, the charges leveled against him, and his absolutory sentence. These documents contain information on southwestern Indians in the sixteenth century. There are introductions to each document.

————. *The Rediscovery of New Mexico, 1580–1594.* Coronado Cuarto Centennial Publications, 1540–1940, vol. 3. Albuquerque: University of New Mexico Press, 1966. 341pp.

This volume contains narratives from the explorations of Chamuscado, Espejo, Castano de Sosa, Morlete, and Leyva de Bonilla and Humana. These documents contain information on southwestern Indians in the sixteenth century. There are introductions to each narrative.

GREAT BASIN–PLATEAU

POINT, NICOLAS, S. J. *Wilderness Kingdom: Indian Life in the Rocky Mountains, 1840–1847. The Journals and Paintings of Nicolas Point, S. J.* New York: Holt, Rinehart & Winston, 1967. Illustrated. Bibliography.

The volume contains the illustrated diary of a missionary, Father Nicolas Point, S. J. who, between 1840 and 1847, lived among the Flatheads, the Coeur d'Alenes, and the Blackfeet of Montana and Idaho. The journal notes and 285 paintings, including maps, by Father Point which have been reproduced in this volume offer firsthand information about the customs, habits, family life, religion, hunting and war ceremonials, dances, and clothing of the Indians. The introduction contains a biography of Father Point. The appendix contains a story of the progress toward publication of Father Point's manuscript by Joseph P. Donnelly, S. J., who translated and introduced the journals and paintings. The unannotated bibliography contains published primary and secondary works.

CALIFORNIA

HEIZER, ROBERT F., ed. *The Indians of Los Angeles County: Hugo Reid's Letters of 1852.* Southwest Museum Papers, no. 21. Los Angeles: Southwest Museum, 1968. 142pp. Illustrated. Bibliography.

This volume contains the unabridged printing and analysis of twenty-two letters by Reid which deal chiefly with the Gabrieleño and the Fernandeño Indians of present-day Los Angeles county. The letters contain ethnographic notes about life before the first arrival of the Spanish as well as the history of the missions of San Fernando and San Gabriel. The letters discuss the Indians' lodges, government, laws and punishment, religion, food and clothing, marriage, birth, burials, medicine, diseases, customs, utensils, sports and games, legends, conversion to Christianity, and effects of the Spanish on traditional Indian life. In the introduction, Heizer discusses Reid's life and the history of the reprinting of the letters. He also adds explanatory notes to aid the reader in understanding the letters. There is an unannotated bibliography of published primary and secondary works.

NORTHWEST COAST

HOWAY, F. W. "Voyages of the *Columbia* to the Northwest Coast, 1787–1790 and 1790–1793." *Massachusetts Historical Society Collections,* vol. 79, pp. 1–518. Boston: 1941.

Four journals, two by Robert Haswell, one by John Hoskin, and one by John Boit, give firsthand ethnographic information about Haidas, Kwakiutls, Nootkas, and other Indians of California, Oregon, and Washington. The explorers describe food, dress, ornaments, housing, villages, physical appearances, domestic life, music, medicine, religion, amusements, canoes, language, vocabulary, government, the role of women, weapons, manners, and trade. They tell of attempted attacks on the *Columbia*. The journals are footnoted with explanatory notes. See also: Erna Gunther, *Indian Life on the Northwest Coast of North America* (pp. 18, 168).

ALASKA

RASMUSSEN, KNUD JOHAN VICTOR. "The Alaskan Eskimos as Described in the Posthumous Notes of Dr. Knud Rasmussen." Edited by H. Ostermann. In *Report of the Fifth Thule Expedition, 1921–1924. The Danish Expedition to Arctic North America in Charge of Knud Rasmussen* 10, no. 3, pp. 1–292. Copenhagen: Gyldendalske Boghandel, Nordosk Forlag, 1952. Illustrated. Reprint ed.: New York: AMS Press, 1976.

This report contains the notes by Rasmussen about Alaskan Eskimos and the journey itself, particularly focusing on how he was transported about the Arctic. The editor gives Rasmussen's ethnographical notes on hunting bear and wolf, customs when hunting, whaling ceremonies and customs, phases of life, religion, and miscellaneous items. Rasmussen also retells myths and tales and explains some ceremonies. The appendix contains Alaskan Eskimo ethnological documents and reports prepared in English and given to Rasmussen. There are photographs of Rasmussen's journey and his varying modes of transport, Eskimos, settlements, and drawings of masks.

BIBLIOGRAPHY

Cox, EDWARD GODFREY. "North America." In *A Reference Guide to the Literature of Travel Including Voyages, Geographical Descriptions, Adventures, Ship Wrecks, and Expeditions,* vol. 2: *The New World.* University of Washington Publications in Language and Literature, vol. 10, pp. 34–197. Seattle: University of Washington Press, 1938.

The author gives a chronological listing of travel literature from 1563 until 1937. He gives the title, language the literature was written in, when and where the document was published and reprinted, and the translator's name. Some of the items are annotated.

FREIDEL, FRANK, ed. "Books of Travel and Description." In *Harvard Guide to American Literature.* 2 vols, pp. 149–161. Revised ed. Cambridge, Mass.: Harvard University Press, 1974.

Books of travel often contain numerous references to American Indians. This unannotated listing includes a list of "Lists and Discussion," works which describe some of the travelers, discuss the observations in the accounts, or list by type or section the more important works and a list of "Collections of Narrative and Travel." There is a lengthy alphabetical list which is a selection from "the best and most representative travels in the United States, divided into four periods: from the beginning to 1789, from 1789 to 1865, from 1865 to 1900, and from 1900 to 1950.

MATTHEWS, WILLIAM, comp. *American Diaries: An Annotated Bibliography of American Diaries Written Prior to the Year, 1861.* University of California Publications in English, vol. 16. Berkeley: University of California Press, 1945. 383pp.

This bibliography contains diaries and journals from the English-speaking world of America and Canada written from 1629 to 1860 that have been published completely or in substantial part. The compiler provides a few biographical details about the diarists and gives dates of when and where (periodicals, books, etc.) the diaries were published. He briefly notes the contents to give a rough characterization of the document and to indicate the chief subjects, places, and persons dealt with and he occasionally provides a word of evaluation. Many of the earlier diaries, particularly those written during the seventeenth century, have entries about Indians.

6 AUTOBIOGRAPHIES AND BIOGRAPHIES

Biographies and autobiographies often provide valuable insight into the lives and cultures of Native Americans. They also record a variety of responses to the intrusion of an alien culture. Autobiographies, in particular, offer an opportunity to explore beliefs, values, and customs different from those brought here by people from other lands. Traditional lifeways have long been a subject of fascination. Left Handed (p. 49), Standing Bear (p. 49), and Sweezy (p. 49) describe manners, customs, and family life before and after contact with Europeans. Two Leggings (p. 49) and Plenty-Coups (p. 48) describe the process of gaining status in a warrior society. Bennett (p. 49) and Mitchell (p. 49) tell of more recent times.

Much of the interaction between Native Americans and Europeans involved violence. These encounters produced tragedies on both sides. European tales of such encounters are well known. Not so well known are the stories of Native Americans: Kaywaykla (p. 49) recalls being driven from his home, hunted down and taken to Florida by force, and imprisoned there. Tubbee (p. 47) describes being taken from his family as a child, enslaved by a white man, and only much later rediscovering and embracing his own heritage. Cuero (p. 51) tells of a people displaced and impoverished by Europeans hungry for land.

The struggle over land led to conflicts from which leaders emerged: Geronimo (p. 49), Chief Joseph (p. 50), and Black Hawk (p. 48) have recorded their stories. Sitting Bull, in three pictographic records (p. 48), depicts episodes from his life during the period before the Battle of the Little Bighorn in 1876.

But the conflict in the long run, perhaps even more persistent, is the one arising from the confrontation of widely differing cultures. Williams (p. 47), Lame Deer (p. 48), Rogers (p. 48), Whitewolf (p. 49), Nowell (p. 50), Attungoruk (p. 51), and Senungetuk (p. 51) bear witness to the endurance and strength of the human spirit in describing the tension, confusion, anguish, and joys in lives complicated by pressures from an alien culture. Crashing Thunder (p. 48) narrates a life marked by frustration and loss of identity. His sister, Mountain Wolf Woman (p. 48) recounts the peaceful unfolding of a harmonious, although far from simple, life. Ricard (p. 47) discusses his lifelong struggle on behalf of his people.

45

Responses to the confrontation between cultures are as varied as the individuals involved. Apes (p. 47) became a Christian and, eventually, a preacher; Goodbird (p. 48) also became an enthusiastic Christian. Eastman (p. 48) attended college, became a doctor, practiced medicine, and later worked on behalf of Native Americans. Two Hopi women, Qoyawayma (p. 50) and Sekaquaptewa (p. 50), chose to bridge two cultures, combining traditional and nontraditional ways of life.

The question of which Native Americans represent genuine leadership in the eyes of their own people is not addressed here. The collective biographies in this section present individuals commonly identified as leaders by non-Indian writers; sometimes they are so viewed by Native Americans.

Two collective biographies are in the chapter on art: *Art and Indian Individualists,* by Guy and Doris Monthan (p. 264) and *American Indian Painters,* by Jeanne Snodgrass (p. 265).

COLLECTIVE BIOGRAPHIES

DOCKSTADER, FREDERICK J. *Great North American Indians: Profiles in Life and Leadership.* New York: Van Nostrand Reinhold, 1977. 386pp. Illustrated. Bibliography.

Biographies of 300 Native Americans, now dead, whose lives span the years from the sixteenth century to 1977 are collected here. Each biography includes birth and death dates, true names, where appropriate, and English translations and family background. Each person is described against the historical context of his or her time and place. Emphasis is on the significance of each individual to Native American people. While persons of general familiarity are included, the total collection stresses lesser-known and more recent individuals.

EASTMAN, CHARLES A. (Ohiyesa). *Indian Heroes and Great Chieftans.* Boston: Little Brown, 1918. 240pp. Illustrated.

The author relates incidents from the lives of fifteen men representing a new kind of leadership that evolved in response to changed conditions brought about by contact with the invading Europeans. Much of the information is either directly from the leaders profiled or from people who knew them personally. Included are: Red Cloud, Spotted Tail, Little Crow, Tamahay, Gall, Crazy Horse, Sitting Bull, Rain-in-the-Face, Two Strike, American Horse, Dull Knife, Roman Nose, Chief Joseph, Little Wolf, and Hole-in-the-Sky. The word "savage"—in common use at the time—is used by the author, usually ironically; however, it has since been recognized as a term generally employed in the interest of racism, rather than as an accurate description.

EDMUNDS, RUSSELL DAVID. *American Indian Leaders.* Lincoln: University of Nebraska Press, 1980. 257pp. Illustrated.

This volume contains essays about Old Briton, Joseph Brant, Alexander McGillivray, Red Bird, John Ross, Satanta, Washakie, Sitting Bull, Quanah Parker, Dennis Bushyhead, Carlos Montezuma, and Peter MacDonald. A section of photographs depicts the leaders. Each chapter has notes and a map.

GRIDLEY, MARION E. *American Indian Women.* New York: Hawthorn, 1974. 178pp. Illustrated. Bibliography.

The author presents brief biographies of eighteen Native American women whose lives span the years from colonial time to the 1970s. Included are: Wetamoo, Pocahontas, Mary M. M. Bosomworth, Nancy Ward, Sacajawea, Sarah Winnemucca, Winema, E. Pauline Johnson, Susan La Flesche Picotte, Gertrude S. Bonnin, Roberta C. Lawson, Pablita Velarde, Maria Montoya Martinez, Annie Dodge Wauneka, Esther Burnett Horne, Maria and Marjorie Tallchief, Wilma L. Victor, and Elaine Abraham Ramos.

———. *Contemporary American Indian Leaders.* New York: Dodd, Mead, 1972. 201pp. Illustrated.

The author has chosen twenty-six Native American men and women who represent a variety of viewpoints, a cross section of vocations, and a wide political range. Biographies are arranged alphabetically by name.

JOSEPHY, ALVIN M., JR. *The Patriot Chiefs: A Chronicle of American Indian Leadership.* New York: Viking, 1961. 364pp. Illustrated. Bibliography.

The author presents the biographies of nine Native American military men, philosophers, and statesmen, selected to provide variety in backgrounds and cultures, geographic areas and historic periods, and particular large scale problems that led to crises and conflicts. Biographies are arranged chronologically. Included are: the real Hiawatha, King Philip, Popé, Pontiac, Tecumseh, Osceola, Black Hawk, Crazy Horse, and Chief Joseph. A map at the beginning of each chapter shows locations of tribes, important battles, and present-day state boundaries.

LIBERTY, MARGOT, ed. *American Indian Intellectuals.* 1976 Proceedings of the American Ethnological Society. New York: West Publishing, 1976. 248pp. Illustrated.

Biographical sketches profile sixteen Native Americans of the nineteenth and early twentieth centuries linked by a theme of awareness of unique lifeways in danger of vanishing and a dedication to the task of preserving something for the future. An introductory essay places the individuals portrayed in the context of their times, deals with some key aspects of American anthropology—a milieu to which most of the men and women portrayed had important ties—and addresses the issue of exploitation of Native Americans by anthropologists. There are personal vignettes of Ely S. Parker, Sarah Winnemucca, Francis La Flesche, Charles Alexander Eastman, James R. Murie, George Bushotter, Emmet Star, Richard Sanderville, Arthur C. Parker, Alexander General (Deskahe), Jesse Cornplanter, Long Lance, John Joseph Mathews, Flora Zuni, and Bill Shakespeare.

Significant American Indians. Chicago: Children's Press, 1975. 77pp. Illustrated.

Brief biographies of 177 Native Americans are arranged alphabetically within broad chronological periods of North American history. The periods covered are: 1580–1820, 1821–65, 1866–99, 1900–1935, and 1936– .

U.S. BUREAU OF INDIAN AFFAIRS. *Famous Indians: A Collection of Short Biographies.* Washington, D.C.: Government Printing Office, 1976. 50pp. Illustrated. Bibliography.

The lives of twenty-two Native American personalities are sketched. Included are: Powhatan and Pocahontas, Massasoit and King Philip, Popé, Joseph Brant, Pontiac, Sacajawea, Tecumseh, Sequoya, John Ross, Black Hawk, Cochise, Seattle, Red Cloud, Crazy Horse, Sitting Bull, Wovoka, Chief Joseph, Quanah Parker, and Geronimo.

WALDMAN, HARRY, et al. *Dictionary of Indians of North America.* 3 vols. St. Clair Shores, Mich.: Scholarly Press, 1978. Illustrated.

These volumes contain biographical information on some 1,700 Native Americans, covering males and females from the twelfth century through the present. Entries are arranged alphabetically by name.

AUTOBIOGRAPHIES

NORTHEAST-SOUTHEAST

APES, WILLIAM. *A Son of the Forest: The Experience of William Apes, a Native of the Forest.* New York: Published by the author, 1831. 214pp.

Apes, a Pequot, born in 1798 in Massachusetts, describes his childhood and the different people who raised, owned, or hired him. He discusses his life in the army and the strong influence of Christianity, which led him to become a preacher. An appendix of "general observations" presents Apes's views on the true character of Native Americans.

RICARD, CLINTON. *Fighting Tuscarora: The Autobiography of Chief Clinton Ricard.* Edited by Barbara Graymont. Syracuse: Syracuse University Press, 1974. 224pp. Illustrated.

Ricard, born in 1882, completed this story of his life shortly before his death in 1971. In it he recalls a childhood of poverty, his stint in the army during the Spanish-American War, his brutal treatment in a Canadian jail, and he discusses his legal battles with New York State, the U.S. Government, and Canada. This is the life struggle of a man who fought for the welfare of his people.

TUBBEE, OKAH. *Sketch of the Life of Okah Tubbee, Alias William Chubbee.* Springfield, Mass.: H. S. Taylor, 1848. 84pp.

Taken from his Choctaw family as a young boy, enslaved by a white man, Okah Tubbee describes his childhood experiences in Natchez, Mississippi, and his later life in the South in the first half of the nineteenth century. His first encounter with Native Americans in Mississippi and the rediscovery of his heritage are recalled. A brief autobiography of Tubbee's wife is included.

WILLIAMS, TED C. *The Reservation.* Syracuse: Syracuse University Press, 1976. 254pp. Illustrated.

A series of reminiscences by a Tuscarora man who grew up in Lewistown, New York, entwines the many levels of life on a reservation, including the pragmatic and the political. In a narrative style that sometimes is earthy and ribald, the author touches on many aspects of Tuscarora culture, conveying the ingenuity of the Tuscaroran people in surviving under severe handicaps.

GREAT PLAINS

ANONYMOUS. *The Autobiography of a Fox Woman.* Edited by Truman Michelson. Bureau of American Ethnology Annual Report 40, pp. 291–349. Washington, D.C.: Government Printing Office, 1925.

This autobiography provides a narrative account by a Fox woman of her life during the late nineteenth and early twentieth centuries. Customs and beliefs of the Fox at the time are described.

BLACK EAGLE. "Xube, a Ponca Autobiography." Edited by William Whitman. *The Journal of*

American Folklore 52 (1939):180–93. Millwood, N.Y.: Kraus Reprint, 1979.

Black Eagle, a Ponca born in Oklahoma in 1889, who possessed a limited amount of *xube* (supernatural power), covers his early experiences with the supernormal and the supernatural in this narrative.

BLACK ELK. *Black Elk Speaks: Being the Life Story of a Holy Man of the Oglala Sioux.* As told to John G. Neihardt. Lincoln: University of Nebraska Press, 1961. 281pp. Illustrated.

This autobiography of one of the great spiritual leaders of the Oglala Sioux was first published in 1932. Black Elk, who was born in 1863, narrates a moving account of his life from early childhood to the massacre at Wounded Knee in 1890.

BLACK HAWK. *Black Hawk: An Autobiography.* Edited by Donald Jackson. Gloucester, Mass.: Peter Smith, 1955. 206pp. Illustrated.

This autobiography is based on an 1833 narrative given by Black Hawk, a Sac, through an interpreter. Black Hawk, born in 1767, discusses his struggles with other Native American groups, his differences with the United States, and his final flight from the Army.

CRASHING THUNDER. *Crashing Thunder: The Autobiography of a Winnebago.* Edited by Paul Radin. University of California Publications in American Archaeology and Ethnology, vol. 16, no. 7, pp. 381–473. Berkeley: University of California Press, 1920; reprint ed.: New York: Dover, 1963. 91pp.

In this life story, translated by an interpreter for the editor, the narrator recounts a life of crises, frustrations, and violence, underscored by a loss of cultural values. The inner struggle of a man clutching at inadequate substitutes, until his final conversion to the peyote religion, is revealed. Information on Winnebago culture is also incorporated into this frank account of the author's life.

EASTMAN, CHARLES ALEXANDER (Ohiyesa). *From the Deep Woods to Civilization: Chapters in the Autobiography of an Indian.* Boston: Little Brown, 1916. 206pp. Illustrated.

This autobiography of a Sioux covers the author's life from his fifteenth year to the second decade of the twentieth century. He discusses his college life, medical training and practice of medicine, and work among Native Americans.

———. *Indian Boyhood.* New York: Dover, 1971. 247pp. Illustrated.

First published in 1902, this autobiography covers the first fifteen years of the author's life. Customs, religions, legends, games, and the history of the Santee Sioux before the reservation period are included. The first paragraph of the dedication presents sentiments that are out of keeping with the rest of the book.

GOODBIRD, EDWARD. *Goodbird, the Indian: His Story.* Edited by Gilbert L. Wilson. New York: Fleming H. Revell, 1914. 80pp.

Goodbird, a Hidatsa, born about 1869 and raised as a Christian, extolls the role of Christianity in Native American life. Information about his birth, childhood, life in a mission school, and religious beliefs were related to Wilson in 1913.

LAME DEER, CHIEF JOHN and RICHARD ERDOES. *Lame Deer: Seeker of Visions.* New York: Simon & Schuster, 1972. 288pp. Illustrated.

Born in 1903 in South Dakota, Lame Deer, Sioux shaman and raconteur, gives a lively and imaginative account of his life. Conditions on the Rosebud Sioux Reservation, South Dakota, are described and aspects of modern Sioux religion discussed.

MOUNTAIN WOLF WOMAN. *Mountain Wolf Woman, Sister of Crashing Thunder: The Autobiography of a Winnebago Woman.* Edited by Nancy Oestreich Lurie. Ann Arbor: University of Michigan Press, 1961. 142pp.

At age seventy-five, Mountain Wolf Woman tells of her earliest memories, records everyday events of her life, and details the peaceful unfolding of a harmonious, but far from simple life marked by the incorporation of new experiences and new ways of earning a living. Information on Winnebago culture in Wisconsin and Nebraska is included.

PLENTY-COUPS. *Plenty-Coups, Chief of the Crows.* Edited by Frank Bird Linderman. Lincoln: University of Nebraska Press, 1962. 324pp.

At eighty, Chief Plenty-Coups discusses his boyhood, describes how he attained the status of chief, and details his participation in the tribal life of his people. This book was originally published in 1930 under the title *American, the Life Story of a Great Indian, Plenty-Coups, Chief of the Crows.*

PRETTY SHIELD. *Red Mother.* Edited by Frank Bird Linderman. New York: John Day, 1932. 256pp.

Using sign language and with the help of an interpreter, Pretty Shield, a Crow born in Montana in the 1850s, relates incidents from her childhood and early maturity. Some Crow myths, tales, and history are included.

ROGERS, JOHN (Chief Snow Cloud). *Red World and White: Memories of a Chippewa Boyhood.* Norman: University of Oklahoma Press, 1974. 153pp.

This book, originally published in 1952, reveals something of the life and customs of both the Chippewas and whites. These recollections of Way-Quah-Gishig (John Rogers), from the age of six in 1896 until 1914–15, show the thinking and learning processes of a youth forced to cope with two cultures as well as rapid social and cultural change.

SITTING BULL. *Three Pictographic Autobiographies of Sitting Bull.* Edited by M. W. Stirling. Smithsonian Miscellaneous Collections, vol. 97, no. 5. Washington, D.C.: Smithsonian Institution, 1938. 57pp.

Three pictorial records by Sitting Bull, a Sioux, illustrate feats which won him special standing among his people. The three records are known as the Kimball, Smith and Pettinger Pictographic Records and contain respectively fifty-four, twenty-two, and thirteen drawings. Interpretations accompany the drawings, which cover the period before the Battle of the Little Bighorn (1876).

STANDING BEAR, LUTHER. *Land of the Spotted Eagle.* Boston: Houghton Mifflin, 1933. 259pp.
Chief Standing Bear, a Sioux, discusses his early life and describes the manners, customs, morals, and characteristics of his people.

———. *My Indian Boyhood.* Boston: Houghton Mifflin, 1933. 259pp.
Standing Bear, a Sioux, who was a member of the first class at Carlisle Indian School (1879), describes his home, school, and reservation life; his marriage; and efforts on behalf of his tribe.

SWEEZY, CARL. *The Arapaho Way: A Memoir of an Indian Boyhood.* As told to Althea Bass. New York: Clarkson N. Potter, 1966. 88pp. Illustrated.
Sweezy, born in 1881, recalls the old ways of Arapaho culture. Illustrations by the author depict dances, hunts, games, dress, and ceremonies.

TWO LEGGINGS. *Two Leggings: The Making of a Crow Warrior.* Edited by Peter Nabokov. New York: Thomas Y. Crowell, 1967. 226pp.
This first-person account of the everyday life of a nineteenth-century Crow Indian reveals the strivings, successes, and failures of a status seeker. The account provides information on the religious and social values of a Plains Native American group.

WHITEWOLF, JIM. *Jim Whitewolf: The Life of a Kiowa Apache Indian.* Edited by Charles S. Brant. New York: Dover, 1969. 144pp.
Born in Oklahoma during the second half of the nineteenth century, Whitewolf dictated his life story in 1949–50. A tribal society under white influence is described.

WOODEN LEG. *Wooden Leg: A Warrior Who Fought Custer.* As told to Thomas B. Marquis. Lincoln: University of Nebraska Press, 1962. 389pp.
This narrative of a Cheyenne warrior who fought against Custer at the Battle of the Little Bighorn (1876) includes observations on Cheyenne daily life and tribal customs from the mid-1850s to the 1920s.

SOUTHWEST

ANONYMOUS. *Autobiography of an Acoma Indian.* Edited by Leslie A. White. Bureau of American Ethnology Bulletin 136, Anthropological Papers no. 32, pp. 326–37. Washington, D.C.: Government Printing Office, 1943.
This is an autobiographical sketch given in 1941 by a seventy-three-year-old Acoma man. Acoma history and daily life are revealed and a pueblo culture subjected to the inroads of an alien culture is described.

BENNETT, KAY. *Kaibah: Recollections of a Navajo Girlhood.* Los Angeles: Western Lore Press, 1964. 253pp. Illustrated.
This autobiographical story of a Navajo girl and her family in New Mexico covers the years from 1928 to 1935. Each chapter presents a vignette of Navajo life as recalled from her childhood by the author.

CHONA, MARIA. *Autobiography of a Papago Woman.* Edited by Ruth Underhill. Memoirs of the American Anthropological Association vol. 46. Menasha, Wisc.: American Anthropological Assn., 1936. 64pp.
At ninety, Chona recalls her past, presenting a picture of the role and status of a Papago woman during the last quarter of the nineteenth and the early part of the twentieth centuries.

GERONIMO. *Geronimo's Story of His Life.* As told to and edited by Steven M. Garrett. Newly edited by Frederick W. Turner III. New York: Dutton, 1970. 190pp.
In 1905–6, while still a prisoner at Fort Sill, Oklahoma Territory, Geronimo, an Apache, dictated the story of his life to an interpreter. Ranging freely over the events of his life, Geronimo gives both a cultural and historical account of the Apaches.

KAYWAYKLA, JAMES. *In the Days of Victorio: Recollections of a Warm Springs Apache.* As told to Eve Ball. Tucson: University of Arizona Press, 1970. 222pp. Illustrated.
The author, born about 1873, recalling his youth in the Southwest, tells how Apache families were driven from their homes, hunted down, and, in 1886, forced aboard a train and taken to Florida prisons. Information on Apache daily life is included.

KUNI, PAUL; BLIND TOM; et al. *Walapai Ethnology.* Edited by A. L. Kroeber. Memoirs of the American Anthropological Association no. 42, pp. 205–29. Menasha, Wisc.: American Anthropological Assn., 1935.
Four brief biographies reveal various facets of the culture of the Walapai in the Southwest during the last quarter of the nineteenth century and the first quarter of the twentieth. Information on the acculturation process as the Walapai see it is included.

LEFT HANDED. *Son of Old Man Hat: A Navajo Autobiography.* As told to Walter Dyk. Lincoln: University of Nebraska Press, 1967. 378pp.
Left Handed narrates, through an interpreter, the story of his life from his birth in 1838 to his marriage some twenty years later. Navajo sex mores are discussed in a frank manner, and family relationships, customs, and philosophy of life are dealt with. This is a reprint of a 1938 edition.

MITCHELL, EMERSON BLACKHORSE and T. D. ALLEN. *Miracle Hill: The Story of a Navajo Boy.* Norman: University of Oklahoma Press, 1967. 230pp.
Mitchell records his life from birth in a hogan to his coming of age. His relationship with his tribal family and environment and his contact with the outside world are described.

MITCHELL, FRANK. *The Autobiography of Frank Mitchell, 1881–1967, Navajo Blessingway Singer.*

Edited by Charlotte Frisbie and David P. McAllester. Tucson: University of Arizona Press, 1978. 446pp. Bibliography.

Frank Mitchell, born in 1881, tells of his early life, details his adult years, and describes his ceremonial life. An epilogue by the editors includes details about the events surrounding Mitchell's death and records his final words to his family. This book, eighteen years in production, includes genealogical data, census data, and a chronology of Mitchell's life.

MR. MOUSTACHE. "A Navajo Personal Document with a Brief Paretian Analysis." Edited by Clyde Kluckhohn. *Southwestern Journal of Anthropology*, vol. 1, pp. 260–83. Albuquerque: University of New Mexico Press, 1945.

A brief life story of a Navajo man born in 1868, told through an interpreter. Ways in which social conditioning is accomplished are revealed and data on the values of Navajo society are presented.

OLD MEXICAN. *Old Mexican: A Navajo Autobiography*. As told to Walter Dyk. Viking Fund Publications in Anthropology, no. 8. New York: Johnson Reprint, 1947. 218pp.

Old Mexican narrates his life story from 1871, when he was five, to 1919. He emphasizes adult life in Navajo society.

PRINCE, ANNA; JOSEPH HOFFMAN; PALMER VALOR; et al. *Western Apache Raiding and Warfare*. Edited by Keith H. Basso from notes of Grenville Goodwin. Tucson: University of Arizona Press, 1971. 330pp. Illustrated.

Chronologically arranged, autobiographical narratives by six Western Apaches cover events that occurred during the 1850s and 1860s, providing information on Apache daily life, raiding, and warfare. The second part of the book contains very brief statements about specific aspects of Apache raiding and warfare.

QOYAWAYMA, POLINGAYSI (Elizabeth Q. White). *No Turning Back: A True Account of a Hopi Indian Girl's Struggle to Bridge the Gap between the World of Her People and the World of the White Man*. As told to Vada F. Carlson. Albuquerque: University of New Mexico Press, 1964. 180pp.

The life story of a Hopi woman, born about 1892, who decides at an early age to live in a nontraditional manner. Information on Hopi legends, ceremonies, religion, and philosophy is included.

SEKAQUAPTEWA, HELEN. *Me and Mine: The Life Story of Helen Sekaquaptewa*. As told to Louise Udall. Tucson: University of Arizona Press, 1969. 262pp.

A Hopi woman describes a rewarding life marked by her ability to choose and combine traditional and nontraditional ways of life.

TALAYESVA, DON C. *Sun Chief: The Autobiography of a Hopi Indian*. Edited by Leo W. Simmons. New Haven, Conn.: Yale University Press, 1942. 460pp.

Born in 1890, Don Talayesva describes his first

ten years in the Hopi village of Oraibi, Arizona, and details his life in boarding schools in Arizona and California during the next ten years. Sexual matters receive frank treatment.

GREAT BASIN–PLATEAU

CHIEF JOSEPH. "Chief Joseph's Story." *North American Review* 269 (1879):415–33; reprint ed.: Billings: Montana Indian Publications, 1972. 31pp. Illustrated.

Chief Joseph delivered this oration in Washington, D.C. in 1879. In it he recounts events from his life, tracing the history of Nez Percé contact with non-Indians beginning in 1779 and continuing through the 1877 war between the Nez Percé and the United States, to the time of his surrender, betrayal, and exile to Oklahoma Territory.

HOPKINS, SARAH WINNEMUCCA. *Life among the Paiutes: Their Life and Claims*. Edited by Mrs. Horace Mann. New York: G. P. Putnam's Sons; Boston: Cupples, Upham, 1883; reprint ed.: Bishop, Calif.: Chalfant Press, 1969. 268pp.

Sarah Hopkins, born about 1844 near Humbolt Lake, Nevada, describes her Paiute life and activities until 1882. Paiute history, customs, and experiences as the number of white settlers increased are discussed. Injustices suffered by the Paiutes, as well as by other nearby Native American groups, are highlighted.

LOWRY, ANNIE. *Karnee: A Paiute Narrative*. Edited by Lalla Scott. Reno: University of Nevada Press, 1966. 149pp.; reprint ed.: Greenwich, Conn: Fawcett, 1973. 160pp.

This narrative life story of a Paiute woman, born about 1860 in Nevada, includes a biography of her mother, Sau-tau-nee. Paiute history, legends, beliefs, and pre and postcontact customs are described.

NEWLAND, SAM, and JACK STEWART. "Two Paiute Autobiographies." As told to Julian Haynes Steward. *University of California Publications in American Archaeology and Ethnology* 33, no. 5, (1934):423–38; reprint ed.: Mamaroneck, N.Y.: Kraus Reprint Co., 1965.

Stewart and Newland, both nearly one hundred years old, narrate brief accounts of their lives. The two men, who reached maturity before 1841 when non-Indians arrived, reveal widely divergent personalities and also give insights into the dynamic aspects of Paiute culture.

NORTHWEST COAST

NOWELL, CHARLES JAMES. *Smoke from Their Fires: The Life of a Kwakiutl Chief*. Edited by Chellan Stearns Ford. Hamden, Conn.: Archon, 1968. 248pp.

Nowell, born in 1870, tells the story of his life, commenting on Kwakiutl society before and after contact with Europeans. This is a reprint of a 1940 edition.

SEWID, JAMES. *Guests Never Leave Hungry: The Autobiography of James Sewid, a Kwakiutl Indian.* Edited by James P. Spradley. New Haven, Conn.: Yale University Press, 1969. 310pp.

Sewid, a chief by heredity, tells the story of his life and discusses the organizational and civic concerns of a growing Kwakiutl community in the Northwest.

CALIFORNIA

ALLEN, ELSIE. *Pomo Basketmaking: A Supreme Art for the Weaver.* Healdsburg, Calif.: Naturegraph, 1972. 67pp. Illustrated.

An autobiography of the late Elsie Allen accompanies detailed descriptions, drawings, and photographs of how to make baskets. Mrs. Allen, born in California in 1899, represents the fourth generation of Pomo basket weavers.

CUERO, DELFINA. *The Autobiography of Delfina Cuero, a Diegueño Indian.* As told to Florence C. Shipek. Interpreted by Rosalie Pinto Robertson. Banning, Calif.: Malki Museum Press, 1970. 67pp.

Mrs. Cuero, born around 1900, in the course of narrating her life story reconstructs the culture of her youth, details the search of a displaced people for a place to live, describes the struggle to feed and clothe her children, and demonstrates the close relationship between environment and religious expression.

YOUNG, LUCY. "Out of the Past: A True Indian Story." As told to Edith V. A. Murray. *California Historical Society Quarterly* 20, no. 4 (1941):349–64.

At the age of ninety, in 1939, Lucy Young, a Wailaki, dictated this memoir in which she recalls her childhood and the occurrences of everyday life in California. The major part of the narrative takes place in 1862.

ALASKA

ATTUNGORUK. "The Autobiography of an Alaskan Eskimo." Edited by James W. Van Stone. *Arctic* 10, no. 4 (1957):195–210.

An Eskimo man, born in Point Hope, Alaska, in 1928, recounts events in his life from childhood through his first jobs, trips to Fairbanks and Anchorage, and his return to Point Hope. The problems presented by conflicting moral codes are illustrated.

HUNTINGTON, JAMES. *On the Edge of Nowhere.* As told to Lawrence Elliott. New York: Crown, 1966. 183pp.

The author, an Athapaskan born in Hughes, Alaska, in 1916, describes his parents and discusses raising his sisters and brothers, daily life on the tundra, dogsled races, and his adulthood.

SENUNGETUK, JOSEPH. *Give or Take a Century: The Story of an Eskimo Family.* San Francisco: Indian Historian Press, 1970. Illustrated.

The author describes the joys and tribulations of his family as they move from their Alaskan village and a century filled with the customs, traditions, and lifeways of an ancient time into a new century in which they are confronted and confused by the mores, social life, and technology of a different culture.

BIBLIOGRAPHIES

"BIOGRAPHY AND AUTOBIOGRAPHY." In *A Comprehensive Bibliography of the Studies of American Minorities* 2:809–19. New York: New York University Press, 1976.

This bibliography lists collective biographies, individual biographies, and autobiographies, including some non-Indians whose life stories focus on Native Americans. This list is arranged alphabetically by author with one or two sentence annotations.

HIRSCHFELDER, ARLENE B. *American Indian and Eskimo Authors: A Comprehensive Bibliography.* New York: Association on American Indian Affairs, 1973. 99pp.

This bibliography identifies material narrated or written by Native Americans and Eskimos. Authors are initially identified by tribe. This list is followed by an alphabetical listing of the authors and their works. Brief annotations accompany each entry.

LITTLEFIELD, DANIEL F., JR., and JAMES W. PARINS. *A Biobibliography of Native American Writers, 1772–1924.* Native American Bibliography Series, no. 2. Metuchen, N.J.: Scarecrow, 1981. 343pp.

The bibliography, covering the period from colonial times until the American Indians were granted citizenship, contains over 4,000 entries done solely by Indian authors writing in a foreign language, English. Material by Indian people written down by non-Indians has been omitted. The book lists political essays and addresses, satirical pieces written in various dialects, myths and legends, original poetry and fiction, published letters, historical works, personal reminiscences, and other genres. There is an introduction discussing Indian writings, an alphabetical listing of Native American writers with tribal designations followed by a listing of Native American writers known only by their pen names. There is a section containing biographical statements about the authors and indexes of writers by tribal affiliations and by subject.

PROVINCIAL LIBRARY. *Indians of the Americas: Biography.* Saskatchewan: Provincial Library Bibliographic Services Div., 1973. 13pp.

The library lists biographies and autobiographies of famous Native American people that are arranged alphabetically by author. A title index is provided and books suitable for young readers are indicated.

SYLVESTRE, GUY. *Indian-Inuit Authors: An Anno-*

tated Bibliography. Ottawa: Information Canada, 1974. 108pp.

Sections of this bibliography list works by Canadian Indian and Métis authors and Canadian Inuit (Eskimo) authors. Each entry includes a brief description. Author and illustrator's indexes are included.

U.S. DEPARTMENT OF THE INTERIOR. *American Indians and Persons Involved in Indian Affairs.* 8 vols. Boston: G. K. Hall, 1966.

This index to Native American biographical and historical materials was developed over some thirty years in the library of the Bureau of Indian Affairs and in 1949 was consolidated with other materials to form the library of the Department of the Interior. Arranged alphabetically by subject and name, it offers extensive listings of Indian agents, other Bureau of Indian Affairs personnel, Native American chiefs, and historically prominent Indians. The listings include material found in books, journals, documents in other libraries, and in personal collections.

7   LAND TENURE AND RESOURCES

The history of contact between American Indian nations and the United States might well be viewed as a contest for possession of the land. In 1492 native peoples thoroughly inhabited, if not densely populated, North America and utilized their territories in a wide variety of ways. Most tribes were dependent on agriculture for subsistence. To a greater or lesser degree all of them hunted and/or fished and many gathered roots, berries, and other wild foods as a regular part of their diet. (See Subsistence Patterns.) Because of this strong and vital relationship with the land and its resources, Indian peoples felt a powerful bond with the particular area of the earth they traditionally inhabited. It figured prominently in their belief systems and was inextricably entwined with their self-conception and world view. Basehart (p. 58) discusses the Mescalero Apache relationship to the land; Clemmer (p. 59) tells of Native Nevadan subsistence patterns and beliefs; Snyderman (p. 58) discusses the basic Indian philosophy toward the land; and Bishop (p. 60) and Martin (p. 60) explore land and resource utilization of some Subarctic native groups.

Natives had several different land tenure systems. Cooper (p. 58) describes three systems that operated among Indians living largely east of the Mississippi River and south of the St. Lawrence and Great Lakes, on the Plains, and in several other places. Davidson (p. 60) tells of family hunting territories west of the Rocky Mountains and MacLeod (p. 58) describes family hunting territories of the Delawares in the Northeast.

From a European standpoint, however, Indians lacked written validation to certify their ownership. Under the rules of European law, land belonged absolutely to a people because of certified title, not simply because of traditional usage. The Europeans therefore refused to recognize the clear ownership of land by the Indians, though they could not escape conceding their occupancy and possession. Consequently European nations developed a legal concept which came to be known as aboriginal claim: Indian tribes which had lived in a territory "from time immemorial" had a *claim* to it. Through treaty negotiations with the "discovering" European power (or later the United States) this claim was extinguished for much of the aboriginal territory, in exchange for a formal recognition of on-going Indian title to the remaining portion. This system, by no means equitable or fair in that it reflected the self-interest and legal understandings of only one of the treaty participants, had the effect of greatly reducing the size of the area controlled by indigenous North American peoples. It also left those peoples with small cores of territory, theoretically uncontested in their ownership. Royce (p. 57) has prepared a detailed schedule of land cessions from 1787 to 1894.

Treaty-making came to an end in 1871; the only Indian reservations created thereafter were those decreed by executive order. An article entitled "Tribal Property Interests in Executive-Order Reservations (p. 57) discusses the legal status of executive order reservations. In the 1830s, the Supreme Court defined reservations as "domestic, dependent nations" recognizing their internal sovereignty, and subsequent Supreme Court decisions have continued to affirm the special status of tribal lands. They exist in a category, different, separate, and superior—in sovereignty—to that of states. Barsch and Henderson (p. 55) and Kickingbird et al. (p. 56) discuss tribal sovereignty. Such judicial principles have not, however, succeeded in preventing further alienation of Indian lands, for the most part by illegal or unconstitutional means. The contest for the land, despite every promise and guarantee to the contrary, goes on.

The issues of Indian land tenure are broad and varied. Hall (p. 55) discusses the disputed definitions concerning the meaning and intent of the trust relationship which exists between a tribe and the federal government. White (p. 58) considers questions involving taxation, Jones (p. 56) and Chambers and Price (p. 55) describe land leasing, and Nelson (p. 57) deals with water rights. Some contemporary disputes over land ownership stretch well back into the eighteenth and nineteenth centuries. Goodman and Thompson (p. 59) describe the century-old struggle between Hopis and Navajos over disputed land. Some disputes have been imperfectly resolved by the federally initiated Indian Claims Commission. Lurie (p. 57) reviews the origins, functions, and performance of the ICC. Some disputes, involving tens of millions of acres, have yet to be adjudicated at all. Kickingbird and Ducheneaux (p. 56) document Indian land claims to approximately 100 million acres.

In some instances, tribal lands which have been taken through unethical or illegal means have been returned to Indian ownership. Whatley (p. 59) reviews the Taos Blue Lake controversy and Shames (p. 58) tells of the Menominee struggle to reverse termination.

The courts have struggled with decisions, often unpopular with non-Indians, upholding treaty accords giving preference to Indians in the exercise of fishing and hunting rights in their current and former lands. Hobbs (p. 56) considers the legal history of Indian hunting and fishing rights, and the American Friends Service Committee (p. 60) discusses how fishing rights of three Washington State fishing tribes have been ignored by authorities of state fisheries.

In still other cases, most notably in Alaska, Congress has been forced to renegotiate the settlement of native claims in territories previously undefined in terms of title. The Alaska Native Foundation/Robert R. Nathan Associates, Inc. (p. 61), the Alaska Federal-State Land Use Planning Commission (p. 61), Arnold (p. 61), and the Federal Field Committee for Development Planning in Alaska (p. 61) discuss Alaska native land claims and resource development.

And with increasing frequency, similar competitions over the use and occupancy of land have taken place in Canada, though the history and legal precedents there are different and less advantageous to native litigants. Watkins (p. 60) and Richardson (p. 60) tell of the struggles of two Canadian tribes to preserve their lands.

Issues of Indian land tenure may well become more pressing and hotly debated in the immediate future. Recent investigations have indicated that much of the United States' remaining energy resources lies beneath existing reservations. Questions of the management and development of these minerals involve astronomical amounts of money and test again the principles of tribal sovereignty and self-determination. The American Association for the Advancement of Science et al. (below), Kelly (p. 59), and the U.S. Commission on Civil Rights (p. 58) consider energy resource development on native lands. The wealth of Indian lands, once thought to be worthless, represents at long last an opportunity for tribes to reach economic self-sufficiency and to foster the continuity of their ancient and varied cultures. As ever, they must protect their remaining territories from the greed of entrepreneurs and land-grabbers.

Sutton (p. 61) has written a guide to the literature of Indian land tenure which also contains eight essays that critically discuss the relevant literature.

AMERICAN ASSOCIATION FOR THE ADVANCEMENT OF SCIENCE, MONTANA INTERTRIBAL POLICY BOARD, and MONTANA STATE UNIVERSITY, comps. *Conference on Energy Resource Development and Indian Lands.* Billings: The compilers, 1978. 68pp. Illustrated. Bibliography.

The work includes contributions by Charles Lipton, Wallace and Page Stegner, John Fialka, and numerous others. Topics considered by these writers include manpower training, sovereignty, EPA regulations, conservation/reclamation, intertribal cooperation, state/Indian planning, developing technology, leasing alternatives, water rights, socioeconomic issues, federal energy policy, and federal trust responsibility. Some of the articles are reprinted from other periodical publications. Also included is an unannotated bibliography of materials on American Indian Energy/Natural Resources—policy, assessment, planning, and development.

BARSCH, RUSSEL LAWRENCE, and JAMES YOUNGBLOOD HENDERSON. *The Road: Indian Tribes and Political Liberty.* Berkeley: University of California Press, 1980. 301pp.

This book concerns the rights of Indian tribes on tribal reservations. The rights of individual Native Americans are not considered except in those cases where the nature of such rights relates to the political status of tribes as well. The historical development of the doctrine of tribal sovereignty and the repercussions on the control of land and resources are discussed. Other sections deal with tribal sovereignty and federal courts and the development of a theory of "Tribe" in the American nation. The work is well footnoted but there is no bibliography.

CHAMBERS, REID PEYTON, and MONROE E. PRICE. "Regulating Sovereignty: Secretarial Discretion and the Leasing of Indian Lands." *Stanford Law Review* 26 (1974):1061–96.

The authors consider the potential implications and the reality of the leasing of Indian trust lands. They discuss how the use of Indian land by non-Indian lessees is now very substantial. Indian trust land totals slightly over fifty million acres, of which about seven million acres are leased to non-Indian farmers or ranchers and another eight million acres are covered by mineral leases. Explaining how leasing by a tribe or an individual owner is subject to approval by the Secretary of the Interior, who derives the power from trust responsibility, the authors consider the unclear standards which limit the secretary's discretion in exercising this power. The work reviews particular cases, the history of Indian leasing policy (beginning in 1763 with a Royal Proclamation establishing a boundary line between British colonies and "Indian country" along the Appalachian Mountains), and possible leasing policy goals. The authors suggest ways in which the secretary's approval power could be limited in order to more properly benefit the tribes.

HALL, GILBERT L. *The Federal-Indian Trust Relationship.* Washington, D.C.: Institute for the Development of Indian Law, 1979. 128pp. Illustrated. Bibliography.

Hall reviews the U.S. American Indian trust relationship. "Over the years this concept has been invoked inappropriately to justify U.S. action in dissolving tribal governments, taking Indian lands, mismanaging Indian natural resources, and otherwise violating Indian property and political rights."

He explains how the federal trusteeship has also played an important role in assisting Indians to protect those same property and political rights. Sections review the nature of the trust responsibility, the trust responsibility and the U.S. government, and the trust relationship from an Indian perspective. Appendixes deal with treaties which establish a trust relationship, select relevant federal court cases, recommendations of the American Indian Policy Review Commission, and resolutions of the National Congress of American Indians. Trust lands are inventoried by reservation, and information as to tribal ownership, percent allotted, total acreage, population, per capita earnings, and type of government is given.

HOBBS, CHARLES A. "Indian Hunting and Fishing Rights." *George Washington Law Review* 32 (1963):504–32.
Hobbs examines the legal history of U.S. Indian hunting and fishing rights from 1890 to 1963. He provides a synopsis of Federal Indian policy, general English Common Law principles relating to hunting and fishing rights, and a synthesis of a 1963 understanding of Indian hunting and fishing rights. Other sections deal with regulation of and jurisdiction over Indian hunting and fishing both on- and off-reservation. The usual sources of Indian rights are cited, including: (1) an automatic indicent to ownership of a reservation, (2) explicit treaty guarantees, and (3) aboriginal user right. Hobbs explains that Indian rights are tribal rather than individual, and that they are compensable. He also discusses how off-reservation Indian hunting or fishing may be subject to nearly the same conservation regulations as non-Indians or to no state regulation whatsoever, and argues that no dominant legal trend with regard to conservation regulation had emerged as of 1963. The work is extensively documented.

———. "Indian Hunting and Fishing Rights II." *George Washington Law Review* 37 (1969):1251–73.
Here Hobbs reviews important legal history regarding Indian hunting and fishing rights, focusing on developments between 1964 and the date of publication. He explains that during this period there were fifty to one hundred prosecutions of Indians throughout the United States for violation of state hunting or fishing regulations and that sixteen court opinions were handed down, including two by the Supreme Court. The two Supreme Court cases, *Puyallup Tribe* v. *Department of Game* and *Menominee Tribe* v. *U.S.*, are discussed in detail. Other sections include the Tulee Case, the Columbia River situation, and Klamath hunting rights. There is a general discussion about the regulation of hunting and fishing rights on- and/or off-reservation, including who may exercise these rights and under what circumstances. The work is extensively documented.

JONES, GARY T. "Enforcement Strategies for Indian Landlords." *American Indian Law Review* 2, no. 1 (1974):41–60.
This work deals specifically with sources of relief for tribes or Indian allotees in the event of a breach of contract by a lessee of Indian land and in general with the issue of leasing tribal trust lands. The author discusses how "Long-term development leases are initiating dramatic changes in reservation land use . . ." and he describes specific relevant leasing cases. Three general enforcement strategies are analyzed: (1) Department of Interior regulations, (2) state courts, and (3) tribal courts. The potential benefits for tribes and Indian allotees of an effectively administered lease are summarized. The work is extensively documented.

KICKINGBIRD, KIRKE, and KAREN DUCHENEAUX. *One Hundred Million Acres*. New York: Macmillan, 1973. 240pp.
This work documents Indian land claims to approximately 100 million acres which include presently held tribal and Indian allotted lands; submarginal, restoration, and surplus federal lands; and lands belonging to terminated and nonfederal tribes. The foreword by Vine Deloria, Jr., contrasts the mythological Indian-that-never-was with the reality of America's contemporary native peoples. An introductory section reviews contact and briefly summarizes the history of federal Indian policy as it relates to Indian land and contemporary issues and concerns. Other sections include the nature and status of Indian lands, removal, allotment, Oklahoma statehood, Alaska native lands, Indian reservation lands occupied by the Bureau of Indian Affairs, submarginal lands title transfer, Flathead lands, Warm Springs Reservation, the Crow-Northern Cheyenne land dispute, Menominee lands, Klamath/Modoc/Yahuskin Snake lands, Nisqually lands, Indian communities without federal recognition (Tonto Apache, Burns Pointe, Little Shell Chippewa, Tunicas, Hoemas, Coushattas, Appalachialalas, Lumbees, Cheraur, Haleiwa, Waccamaw, Machapunga, Pamunkey, and Mattaponi), urban lands, and recommendations for a new federal policy for Indians and Indian lands. The work includes an index.

———; LYNN KICKINGBIRD; CHARLES J. CHIBITTY; and CURTIS BERKEY. *Indian Sovereignty*. Washington, D.C.: Institute for the Development of Indian Law, 1977. 68pp. Illustrated.
The authors explain: "This book is intended to provide a context for the word sovereignty—particularly as it relates to American Indian Nations. . . . it is not designed to advocate American Indian beliefs of what the law should be. This volume is designed to display the law as it currently exists." Sections deal with the nature of sovereignty; sovereign powers; Indian sovereignty and the Congress, executive branch, and U.S. courts; and contemporary Indian nations. Taxation, control over land and natural resources, law and order and Indian nations, the Indian Self-Determination Act, and 1978, 1979 Supreme Court decisions are considered. The work is extensively documented.

KINNEY, J. P. *A Continent Lost—A Civilization Won: Indian Land Tenure in America*. Baltimore:

Johns Hopkins University Press, 1937. 366pp. Illustrated. Bibliography.

This is a period piece written by someone who feels that Native Americans in the United States have "little racial prejudice to overcome." He argues that the American Indians may have lost 97 percent of their lands but they have "won a civilization," i.e., a chance to lead a European lifestyle. Sections include Indian land tenure during the colonial period, removal, allotment, and the development of reservation resources, particularly timber. There are illustrations of Indian lands and homes and tables that depict the historic area of Indian lands from 1871 to 1933. One map depicts the traditional location of North American tribes.

LURIE, NANCY OESTREICH. "The Indian Claims Commission." *Annals of the American Academy of Political and Social Science* 436 (March 1978):97–110.

The author reviews the Indian Claims Commission Act of 1946 (P.L. 79–726), which was intended to facilitate the addressing of grievances of Indian tribes against the United States. Sections deal with the origins and functions of the commission, its performance during its second decade, the issues of fair market value of lands and the offset provision, and Indian grievances. The author notes that "despite exceptionally broad grounds for suit stated in the 1946 Act, the Commission has favored narrow construals and parsimonious settlements." Thirty footnotes refer readers to related literature.

NELSON, MICHAEL C. *The Winters Doctrine: Seventy Years of Application of "Reserved" Water Rights to Indian Reservations.* Arid Lands Resource Information Paper no. 9. Tucson: University of Arizona Office of Arid Land Studies, 1977. 147pp. Illustrated. Bibliography.

This work deals in detail with the nature and legal basis of Indian water rights. Sections consider historical growth in population and water consumption in the United States, the development of the Winters Doctrine (the legal basis for Indian water rights), powers of the tribes, aboriginal water rights, water law in the western United States, relevant case law development, the nature of Indian water rights attached to various classes of lands, waters affected by Indian water law, sale and lease of reserved water rights, and jurisdiction in water rights litigation. Court cases are listed and described chronologically and by court level. Two maps depict Indian lands in the West and the lands of the Five Tribes of the Lower Colorado River. The work is available from the National Technical Information Service (U.S. Department of Commerce) as PB 272 299.

ROYCE, CHARLES C., comp. *Indian Land Cessions in the United States.* Introduction by Cyrus Thomas. Bureau of American Ethnology Annual Report 18, 1896–97, part 2, pp. 527–997. Washington, D.C.: Government Printing Office, 1899. Illustrated.

The introduction by Cyrus Thomas includes a discussion on the principles maintained by the United States and by other governments in regard to the rights of the Indians to soil. Thomas examines the policies of Spain, France, and England in acquiring land from Indians. He treats the policy and methods adopted by different colonies in their dealings with Indians in regard to their lands. He considers the U.S. policy of obtaining or extinguishing Indian title to land from the Articles of Confederation until 1887, the year the Dawes Act was passed. There is a list of treaties and acts of Congress authorizing allotments of land in severalty from 1830 to 1895, as well as a detailed schedule of land cessions indicating the number and location of each cession or reservation from the organization of the federal government to and including 1894, descriptions of the tracts ceded or reserved, the date of the treaty, law, or executive order governing same, the name of the tribe or tribes affected, and historical data and references bearing on the tribes. There is a designation of each cession on the sixty-seven maps that follow the schedule and a list of land cessions by tribes.

"Toward a New System for the Resolution of Indian Resource Claims." *New York University Law Review* 47 (1972):1107–49.

The work notes that the success of tribal self-determination depends greatly upon protecting tribal land bases, water, and other natural and human resources. "However, the mechanisms and procedures under which the Federal government has operated in seeking to protect . . . assets . . . have proven inadequate." The work reviews the nature of Indian grievances (breach of federal fiduciary duty, abuse of guardianship, and state and local government violations of Indian rights), recurrent problems, mechanisms of governmental relief, and mechanisms of judicial relief. A final section deals with proposals for changes which include changes in existing remedial mechanisms to provide long-term relief *and* to lessen the hardship caused by the delay and expense involved under current procedures and the creation of an independent Indian agency to insure government protection of tribal rights, unhampered by conflicts of interest. The work is extensively documented.

"Tribal Property Interests in Executive-Order Reservations: A Compensable Indian Right." *Yale Law Review* 69 (1960):627–42.

The work deals with the nature of Indian reservation lands created by executive order. In 1871 Congress prohibited further use of the treaty power in Indian affairs and thereafter 23 million acres of land became classified as Indian lands by presidential order. A Supreme Court case (*Sioux Tribe* v. *U.S. 316 U.S. 317* [1942]) and federal district court case (*Confederated Bands of Ute Indians* v. *U.S. 330 U.S. 169* [1947]) established that executive-order lands confer only a right of use or occupancy subject to the pleasure of Congress which may terminate such rights without legal liability for compensation. The article discusses how congressional statues in 1927 and 1936 effectively conferred title to executive-order lands of tribes as well as tribal rights to energy and mineral resources. The work considers Alaska native lands prior to the Alaska

Native Claims Settlement Act. The article is extensively documented.

U.S. COMMISSION ON CIVIL RIGHTS. *Energy Resource Development: Implications for Women and Minorities in the Intermountain West.* Washington, D.C.: Government Printing Office, 1978. 221pp. Illustrated.

Twenty-three articles, six of which concern Native Americans, are included in this work. Some of the more general articles deal with Indians and energy tangentially. The articles dealing with Indians consider coal development on the Northern Cheyenne reservation, Northern Cheyenne coal sales 1966–73, water rights and the energy crisis, energy development and conservation policies affecting reservations, the impact of energy development on Indian people, and the Council of Energy Resource Tribes and resource development on tribal lands. Some of the articles contain bibliographies.

WHITE, JAY VINCENT. *Taxing Those They Found Here: An Examination of the Tax Exempt Status of the American Indian.* Albuquerque: Institute for the Development of Indian Law, University of New Mexico, 1972. 191pp.

White discusses how taxation of Native Americans is a complicated subject, involving tribal governments, treaty rights, congressional powers over individuals and tribes, and state agencies and governments. His work provides a historical overview of the theories of taxation which affect Indian income derived from trust lands. Sections include treaties, statutes, and attributes of sovereignty; tax-exempt Indians and the courts; and two sections dealing with relevant tax law in Washington State. Most of the major relevant legal cases are reviewed and an appendix contains opinions of the court for *Chouteau* v. *Burnet, Squire* v. *Capoeman, Ghahate* v. *Bureau of Revenue, Commissioner of Taxation* v. *Brun, McClanahan* v. *State Tax Commission, Tonasket* v. *State,* and *Stevens* v. *Commissioner.* Public Law 280 is also reproduced in the appendix.

NORTHEAST

COOPER, JOHN M. "Land Tenure among the Indians of Eastern and Northern North America." *Pennsylvania Archaeologist* 8, no. 3 (July 1938):55–59. Illustrated.

Summarizing land tenure systems of Indians living largely east of the Mississippi River and south of the St. Lawrence and Great Lakes, on the Plains, in the northern coniferous belt, and on barren lands, Cooper gives a tentative theory of the factors that seem to underlie the several different land tenure systems. Three diagrams show land tenure among gardening people, tenure of the family hunting ground system, and the trap-line system. The author discusses how ownership in severalty, rather than communal ownership, was the prevalent form of tenure for gardening plots and how both ownership in severalty and communal ownership prevailed among the hunting peoples. He discusses

three different forms of ownership in severalty: the family hunting ground system, the trap-line system, and the allotment system. The material is based on fieldwork and secondary sources.

MACLEOD, WILLIAM C. "The Family Hunting Territory and Lenape Political Organization." *American Anthropologist,* n.s. 24, no. 4 (October–December 1922):449–63.

The author discusses the existence of the hereditary family hunting territory as the basis of the social organization of the Lenápe tribes of the Delaware River valley. He contrasts the autonomous nature of the family group and its complete sovereignty over its hereditary territory among the Delawares with the complete absence of this autonomy and the institution which underlies it among the Iroquois. He describes the features of the Delaware hunting territory and relates the data to political organization based on a band of families.

SHAMES, DEBORAH, ed. *Freedom with Reservation.* Madison, Wis.: National Committee to Save the Menominee People and Forests, 1972. 116pp. Illustrated. Bibliography.

This work deals with the struggle of the Menominee people to reverse termination of federal recognition. (Their struggle was won a few years after the publication of this book.) Research and non-Menominee individuals, federal and state government documents, newspaper articles, and other published materials are the basis for this book. Sections include a brief history of the Menominee nation from initial treaties with Europeans to termination; the mechanics and general effects of termination; economic development; the impact of termination on health, education, and welfare; and a history of the organization, Determination of Rights and Unity for Menominee Shareholders (DRUMS). A map depicts the erosion of the Menominee land base between 1827 and 1972. The work includes a pictorial section of the Menominee people and land.

SNYDERMAN, GEORGE S. "Concepts of Land Ownership among the Iroquois and Their Neighbors." In *Symposium on Local Diversity in Iroquois Culture,* edited by William N. Fenton, pp. 15–34. Bureau of American Ethnology Bulletin 149, no. 2. Washington, D.C.: Government Printing Office, 1951. Bibliography.

Snyderman examines the basic Indian philosophy toward the land, the relationship of various segments of the society to land ownership, and changes in the philosophy wrought by white conquest. He also refers to statements by Indians that express their thoughts on these matters.

SOUTHWEST

BASEHART, HARRY W. "The Resource Holding Corporation Among the Mescalero Apache." *Southwestern Journal of Anthropology* 23 (1967):277–91. Illustrated. Bibliography.

The author argues that the mid-nineteenth-century pre-reservation Mescalero Apache operated as a unitary resource holding corporation. Aboriginal territory and resources (game, mescal, datil, piñon nuts, etc.) are described along with traditional mobility. Basehart discusses how a unitary resource holding corporation implies freedom of access for all Mescalero to any resources in Mescalero territory. He explains how "no Mescalero had exclusive right to any resource by virtue of discovery or prior exploitation." A map depicts traditional Mescalero Apache territory and migration patterns.

GOODMAN, JAMES M., and GARY L. THOMPSON. "The Hopi-Navaho Land Dispute." *American Indian Law Review* 3, no. 2 (1975):397–417. Illustrated.

This work reviews "a century-old struggle between two groups of Native Americans over the ownership of 2.5 million acres of semiarid land . . . ." The authors explain that "It is a legal conflict deeply rooted in pre-European settlement patterns, contemporary resource management questions, and policies of the federal government toward Native American peoples." They also discuss how "The disputed land is referred to as the Joint Use Area and may contain exploitable coal deposits of from 2.5 to 25 billion tons." The work contains a map of the Joint Use Area and surrounding region as well as extensive documentation.

KELLY, LAWRENCE C. "The Navaho Indians: Land and Oil." *New Mexico Historical Review* 38, no. 1 (1963):1–28.

Kelly documents Navajo population and reservation land base growth since 1868 and the consequences of the discovery of oil on the reservation in 1922. He describes an attempt made by non-Indians to acquire title to oil lands, but explains how the tribe confirmed its ownership of title in 1927 and its legal sovereignty over portions of Navajo national lands created by executive order. He also documents the failure of an attempt to allot Navajo lands.

ORTIZ, ROXANNE DUNBAR. *Roots of Resistance: Land Tenure in New Mexico, 1680–1980*. Berkeley and Los Angeles: University of California Press, 1980. 202pp. Illustrated. Bibliography.

This study is a socioeconomic interpretation of the history of northern New Mexico focusing on land tenure patterns and changes. The study dispels stereotypes of Mexican and Pueblo Indian people in New Mexico, provides a case study in capitalist development in a colonized area, and sheds light on land questions in northern New Mexico today. The author tells how a subsistent land tenure system in northern New Mexico was destroyed under capitalist control through the introduction of mercantile capitalism, followed by monopoly capital supported by the U.S. government. The study begins with the development of the indigenous Pueblo Indian land use system prior to colonization, then treats the first colonial period of land tenure in northern New Mexico characterized by conquest and imposition of Spanish colonial institutions, 1598–1693. The third

chapter covers the Spanish colonial period from 1692 to 1821; the fourth deals with the historical period during which New Mexico was part of Mexico, 1821–48; the fifth with the period when, under U.S. territorial rule, land was capitalized; and the sixth with an analysis of the effects of capitalist development on indigenous Pueblo Indians and on Mexican agricultural communities of northern New Mexico. There is a bibliographical essay discussing archival materials, published primary and secondary works, bibliographies, and guides to materials, followed by an extensive listing.

WHATLEY, JOHN T. "The Saga of Taos Blue Lake." *The Indian Historian* 2, no. 3 (1969):22–28. Illustrated. Bibliography.

The work reviews the history of the Taos Blue Lake controversy, which dates from 1906 when 130,000 acres of land used by the Taos pueblo were taken and incorporated into the National Forest System. The lands were a traditional source of plant and animal resources and the site of many sacred shrines important in Taos religion. The sixty-year struggle of the tribe to recover some 48,000 acres of land is documented. Since publication, title to the relevant lands was restored to the tribe. There is a photograph of the pueblo.

GREAT BASIN–PLATEAU

CLEMMER, RICHARD O. "Northern and Eastern Nevada 1858–1971: Land Use Patterns and Aboriginal Rights." *The Indian Historian* 7, no. 1 (1974):24–41, 47–49. Bibliography.

Clemmer reviews and compares traditional European and Native Nevadan land resource-use ethics. The impact of the 1880 Homestead Act on Paiute, Shoshone, and Goshute subsistence patterns is described and treaties between the three Nations and the United States are examined. The illegal alienation of lands and mineral resources from the Western Shoshone bands are chronicled. The author considers the current conflict between native Nevadans and the state over the use of piñon nuts and wild game (on lands never ceded by the relevant tribes), and the possible legal implications of the fact that Indian title to all of Nevada remains intact.

RATCLIFF, JAMES L. "What Happened to the Kalapuya? A Study of the Depletion of Their Economic Base." *The Indian Historian* 6, no. 3 (1973):27–33. Bibliography.

This work documents the destruction of the Kalapuya Nation, a group of eight to sixteen communities in the Willamette Basin in Oregon. In 1770, the Kalapuya numbered at least 3,000; by 1842, thirty years after the first Europeans occupied their territory, the tribe had virtually ceased to exist. Their demise has been attributed to European disease (particularly smallpox and typhus) and the depletion of their traditional resource base. The author examines the traditional Kalapuya economy of hunting, fishing, root digging, berry gathering, and intertribal trade, and how European settlement destroyed their resource base leading to widespread hunger and starvation.

WHALEN, SUE. "The Nez Percés' Relationship to Their Lands." *The Indian Historian* 4, no. 3 (1971):30–33. Bibliography.

The author reviews traditional Nez Percé belief about land, land tenure, and resources. The Nez Percé relationship to land is briefly compared with the typical European relationship to land. The emphasis is on the pre- and early contact period of Nez Percé society but contemporary testimony is included as well.

NORTHWEST

AMERICAN FRIENDS SERVICE COMMITTEE. *Uncommon Controversy: Fishing Rights of the Muckleshoot, Puyallup, and Nisqually Indians.* Seattle: University of Washington Press, 1970. 232pp. Illustrated. Bibliography.

This work concerns the unique fishing rights of three Washington State fishing tribes—Muckleshoot, Puyallup, and Nisqually—and how these rights have been ignored and misunderstood by state fisheries authorities, non-Indian commercial fishermen, and sports fishers. General Federal Indian policy and treaties between the relevant tribes and the United States are reviewed, including Medicine Creek and Point Elliot. Other sections deal with reservation history, the law of Indian fishing rights in Washington State, the present controversy, and the fish and their environment. The Committee discusses how the treaties generally state, with regard to fishing rights, that "the right of taking fish at all usual and accustomed grounds and stations is further secured to said Indians in common with all citizens of the Territory. . . ." Also, the Committee examines the Boldt decision which interprets treaty rights as 50 percent of the total catch, not to include fish taken from reservation waters which are not under jurisdiction of the state. Two maps depict present Washington Indian reservations and the history of Indian land cessions. Seven figures portray fish yield statistics.

DAVIDSON, DANIEL S. *Family Hunting Territories in Northwestern North America.* Indian Notes and Monographs, no. 46. New York: Museum of the American Indian, Heye Foundation, 1928. 34pp. Illustrated.

Davidson discusses family holdings in land throughout a great part of northwestern America west of the Rocky Mountains, looking at Northwest Coast tribes in general and at the Tlingit land system in particular. He concludes by comparing land systems in the Northeast and Northwest focusing on such concepts as boundaries, patrilocal residence, and clan territories, arguing that although one system was devoted to hunting (Northeast) and one to fishing (Northwest), the points of similarity appear to outweigh the differences.

SUBARCTIC

BISHOP, CHARLES A. "The Emergence of Hunting Territories Among the Northern Ojibwa." *Ethnology* 9 (1970):1–15. Bibliography.

The author considers land tenure and game resource utilization among Northern Algonquians in general (Crees, Ojibways, Naskapis, Montagnais) and the Ojibways in particular. Arguing that fixed and demarcated hunting territories for use by particular extended families were not a part of Ojibway culture of the Osnaburgh-Lac Seul (Ontario) region until at least the 1820s or early 1830s, he explains how this land tenure and game rights system grew out of greater competition for resources following European invasion and expansion.

MARTIN, CALVIN. *Keepers of the Game: Indian-Animal Relationships and the Fur Trade.* Berkeley: University of California Press, 1978. 226pp. Illustrated.

Martin explores the traditional conservation-oriented management of wildlife resources by the tribes of present-day eastern Canada (Micmacs, Crees, Montagnais, Naskapis, Ojibways, etc.) and changes in management practices brought about by European contact and the disastrous influx of European diseases. He reveals the currently popular Euro-American stereotype of "Ecological-Indian" as another ethnocentric perception and maintains that the advent of European diseases and decimation of Native American populations were largely responsible for the breakdown in the traditional relationship of mutual courtesy between wildlife and the Eastern Algonquian tribes. Sections include an ecological interpretation of European contact with the Micmacs, the Ojibway Cosmos and the early fur trade, and an analysis of the paradox of overhunting. The work includes a map of the eastern subarctic and a map of tribal areas. Related works are described in a notes section.

RICHARDSON, BOYCE. *Strangers Devour the Land.* New York: Knopf, 1976. 330pp. Illustrated.

This work chronicles negotiations between the East James Bay Cree people and the governments of Canada and Quebec, and the James Bay Development Corporation leading to the famous James Bay Settlement. The author explains that the James Bay Project, when completed, will inundate a major portion of Cree and Inuit hunting lands, burial grounds, and some community sites. In the course of the work, the author provides insight into Cree culture and feelings of individuals about their relationship with the land and the animals they hunt. Much Cree testimony (in translation) is included. The author notes that although the land settlement included almost $150 million, there are ambivalent feelings in Cree communities as to "whether the settlement is a victory or a disaster." Two maps depict eastern Canada and the James Bay Municipality. Numerous photographs depict Cree individuals and Cree land. In a notes section, major published works are described.

WATKINS, MEL, ed. *Dene Nation: The Colony Within.*

Toronto: University of Toronto Press, 1977. 189pp. Illustrated.

Watkins has compiled twenty papers concerned with the efforts of the Déné Nation (Athapaskan-speaking peoples of the Northwest Territories of Canada) to block construction of a pipeline through their claimed lands in the Mackenzie River valley. Most of the papers are based upon presentations to the Berger Inquiry (inquiry into the pipeline by Justice Thomas R. Berger of the Supreme Court of British Columbia), and several are authored by native people. Subjects include Déné testimony, resources (the mapping project, a trapper's life, Déné diet, the Déné economy, distribution of economic benefits of the pipeline, and development), and rights (colonialism, politics and the Déné, education, aboriginal rights, and the Déné Nation and the confederation). The work includes a proposal to the government and people of Canada. Three maps depict the boundaries of Déné land, the Fort McPherson area, and the Great Bear Lake region. Several of the papers include a reference list.

ALASKA

ALASKA FEDERAL-STATE LAND USE PLANNING COMMISSION. *Alaska Native Claims Settlement Act 1971–1979: Policy Recommendations.* Commission Study 44. Anchorage: The Joint Federal-State Land Use Planning Commission for Alaska, 1979. 261pp. Illustrated.

The work presents policy recommendations of the Alaska Federal-State Land Use Planning Commission. Sections include a general summary and findings chapter; effects of the Act on land and land use; economic consequences of implementation of the Act; generic problems of implementation; impact of the Act on federal, state, and local governments; and social implications. Each section is written by a different author or set of authors. There are numerous maps and figures. Some sections contain reference lists but most are not extensively documented.

ALASKA NATIVE FOUNDATION/ROBERT R. NATHAN ASSOCIATES, INC. *Implementing the Alaska Native Claims Settlement Act.* Washington, D.C.: Robert R. Nathan Associates, 1972. 336pp. Illustrated.

The work reviews the background and "naked" provisions of the Alaska Native Claims Settlement Act. Other sections include enrollment, native land selection, managing financial resources, long-term planning, and assessing development of regional corporations. Thirteen tables summarize regional population; twenty-three maps depict the territory of native associations and councils. A copy of the Act is appended.

ARNOLD, ROBERT D., comp. *Alaska Native Land Claims.* Anchorage: Alaska Native Foundation, 1976. 348pp. Illustrated. Bibliography.

This book deals with Alaska natives, their lands, and their destiny. Half of the book is devoted to history before the passage of the Alaska Native Claims Settlement Act; the remaining half deals with the Act's provisions as implemented in 1975. Sections include early Alaskan history, U.S. Indian policy and Indian lands in the lower forty-eight states, Alaska natives and their land, the land claims struggle, an introduction to the Alaska Native Claims Settlement Act, Settlement Act Organization (Native Corporations), the money settlement, the land settlement, and a view of the future. There are numerous maps and photographs. A copy of the Act and a list of references are included.

FEDERAL FIELD COMMITTEE FOR DEVELOPMENT PLANNING IN ALASKA. *Alaska Natives and the Land.* Washington, D.C.: Government Printing Office, 1968. 565pp. Illustrated. Bibliography.

According to one of its compilers, the work is a record of all relevant, available data and information on the native peoples, the land, and resources of Alaska, traditional resource use; present resource use and ownership; and future needs of native peoples, the state of Alaska, and the federal government. Sections include an overview of contemporary Alaska natives, village Alaska, land and ethnic relationships, natural resources, land claims, economic development, and decision-making frameworks. Nearly 300 figures and numerous maps are included.

BIBLIOGRAPHIES

SUTTON, IMRE. *Indian Land Tenure: Bibliographical Essays and a Guide to the Literature.* New York: Clearwater Publishing, 1975. 290pp. Illustrated.

This work consists of eight general essays with critical discussions of the relevant literature. Subjects include the structure and content of the general literature, aboriginal occupancy and territoriality, land cessions and the establishment of reservations, land administration and land utilization, aboriginal title and land claims, title clarification and change, tenure and jurisdiction, and land tenure and culture change. There is also a section of bibliographic and cartographic sources, a fifty-three page general bibliography, and subject, tribal, and geographical indexes. Six maps depict tribal territory and reservations, Indian redistributions relative to land cessions and reservation, Indian reservations as of 1974, samples of reservation tenure, legal jurisdiction over Indians, and water, dams, and Indian lands.

8 POLITICAL ORGANIZATION

Political organization is concerned with the way in which people who live in a particular territory are integrated internally with respect to each other and to outsiders. For the purposes of his study (p. 65), Driver determines that societies which "have no territorial organization larger than the residential kin group will be classed as lacking true political organization while those with territorial ties based on nonkinship factors will be classed as possessing it."[1] Driver surveys the existence of societies defined as having no true political organization which include the Arctic Eskimos, and native peoples of the Great Basin, Baja California, and northeastern Mexico. He also discusses borderline systems of territorial organization ranging from family groups to true tribes of several thousand people which include peoples of the Subarctic, the Northwest Coast, the Plateau, California, and the Southwest. Finally, he cites the Plains, Prairies, and the Northeast and Southeast where some Indians had tribal organization in the historic period.

Lowie (p. 65) discusses the lack of totalitarian concentration of power of most Indian societies in North America in aboriginal and historic times, ascribing it to the dominant Indian separatism and libertarianism which precluded the creation of the semblance of a modern state. He argues that Indian societies with populations around 10,000 rarely if ever referred to permanently integrated political units. He discusses the counteracting trends that made manifestations of coercive authority fall short of permanent results. Discussing sundry attempts made at centralizing power, he argues that in cases where attempts were successful supernaturalism and religious beliefs were used to obtain political influence and bring about more complex political developments.

Deep political divisions, or factions, prevailed in Indian societies at the time of contact with Europeans despite the fact that consensus was a professed political ideal for most Indian groups. Metcalf (p. 66) discusses political divisions within Indian communities which predated white contact and endured into the contact era, influencing postcontact Indian politics and the course of Indian-white relations. For example, he discusses contests for political supremacy within Indian societies and describes how

1. Harold E. Driver, *Indians of North America* (Chicago: University of Chicago Press, 1969), p. 287.

some Indians exploited the white presence to further their goal to rule. Fenton (p. 65) examines traditional roots of political behavior in four Indian societies and argues that the persistence of old forms of political behavior which included factions persisted in new situations. Clifton (p. 68) studies a prolonged factional conflict in one Prairie Potawatomi community which resulted from stresses of acculturation situations and Brugge (p. 69) discusses Pueblo factionalism.

Several works describe aspects of political organization and leadership in the prereservation and reservation periods. The political organization of the Iroquois League was first described by Lewis Henry Morgan in his classic account *League of the Ho-de-no-sau-nee or Iroquois* (p. 67). Grinde (p. 67) argues that the Iroquois political and philosophical tradition influenced the formation of the United States. He discusses the ancient Constitution of the Five Nations and shows how its structure and philosophy are reflected in the 1754 Albany Plan of Union.

Wallace (p. 67) defines and discusses general concepts of political organization of Indian groups in the Northeast based on tribe and tribal territory, ethnic confederacies, alliances, amalgamations, adoptions, and satellite relationships which tended to unify an area socially and culturally. J. Smith (p. 67) examines Ojibway political organization and leadership and considers the effects migrations and social and economic changes had on the leadership in the nineteenth century. Gearing (p. 68) explains how the Cherokees shared a culture but not an overall political organization by being divided into independent, politically sovereign villages that formed a jural community of peaceful coexistence among Cherokee people. He looks at the eighteenth-century village decision-making process. Green (p. 68) describes the development of the Creek National Council as a tribal governing body.

Miller (p. 67) compares the concept of authority of Europeans and Central Algonquians represented by the Foxes of the Great Lakes area during the late seventeenth and eighteenth centuries. He describes how the Foxes conceived of authority and organized collective action in a different way from European society, which had as its fundamental building block the vertical authority relationship. The Fox concept of power included the belief that it was dangerous and immoral for one individual to exercise substantial control over others, so the society coordinated collective action in a different way. M. G. Smith (p. 69) discusses the councils, the most important political institution among the Plains tribes in the nineteenth century, and gives brief facts about the governments of over twenty groups. Williams (p. 70) describes Navajo political organization before the development of twentieth-century political institutions. Collins (p. 70) explains that the Upper and Lower Skagits of Washington had no formal political organization but rather had informal leaders of several types who specialized in directing undertakings concerned with subsistence, warfare, or religion. She traces shifts in the social and political organization of the Skagits after white contact in the nineteenth century and argues that whites imposed a formal structure on what had been informal. Weyer (p. 70) discusses chieftanship among Alaskan Eskimos.

Several works treat the contemporary period. Fowler (p. 68) explores how the Northern Arapahoes of the Wind River Reservation have succeeded in legitimizing new authority relations through the creation and use of effective political symbols. Shepardson (p. 69) and Williams (p. 70) analyze modern political developments in the Navajo tribe of Arizona, New Mexico, and Utah. Williams describes the development and function of three contemporary Navajo political structures, the tribal council, district grazing committees, and chapters—local political organizations introduced and promoted among the Navajos as part of the directed culture change program of the government—and their incorporation into the Navajo way of life. Shepardson deals with the interaction of four authorities, traditional Navajo, modern Navajo, the federal government, and the local states and discusses the institutionalization of the Navajo Tribal Council into Navajo life. Fisher (p. 69) explains the two sets of officials in Pueblo government, one of preconquest origins and the other postconquest. He discusses the Spanish set of offices found among all the Pueblos, except Hopi, which represents the Pueblos in their transactions with outsiders, and the priestly offices, the real Pueblo authority which originated in pre-Spanish times. Fisher also reviews the close connection between Pueblo religious organization and political structures.

During the twentieth century, there has been an increase in collective Indian political activity. Historically, the tendency among Indian societies was to remain autonomous tribes. The Iroquois League, the Five Civilized Tribes of Oklahoma, and the Creek Confederacy of the Southeast were the exceptions. Josephy explains:

> The Pan-Indianism of today . . . has resulted from numerous forces, including relocation, education, government programs, social gatherings, and political strivings, that bring Indians of different tribes and backgrounds into contact with each other, and from the modern means of transportation which have encouraged and eased mobility. . . . These associations have led gradually to an increasing feeling of unity among many Indians and an emphasis on recognition that they are Indians as well as members of particular tribes. Pan-Indianism has been felt strongly in parts of Oklahoma, where many tribes dwell, but it has grown also among Indians elsewhere. It is reflected . . . by joint political action of many tribes in behalf of one or a few of them . . .[2]

Thomas (p. 66) examines the growth of Pan-Indianism, a common interest among tribal groups in opposing white people and the creation of political alliances. He argues that the commonality was brought to a head by the reservation system, in the way whites related to different tribes as "Indians," and by the pressure for assimilation which pushed Indians closer together. He describes how traits of the Plains area have come to symbolize a new identity of "Indian" for many tribal groups and how the new identity sets up a new structure of interaction among individuals of differing tribal groups. He also explains the nationalistic direction of Indian leadership.

Tribes as legal entities, in nearly all instances, are a post-white contact development. During the nineteenth century, many tribes began to write constitutions and laws. The Museum of Anthropology at Colorado State

---

2. Alvin M. Josephy, *The Indian Heritage of America* (New York: Bantam Books, 1969), p. 29.

College (see Fay, below) and Scholarly Resources (p. 69) have both published collections of charters, constitutions, and by-laws of selected Indian tribes. These documents reflect present-day Indian tribal organization and government procedures. Hargrett's bibliography (p. 70) lists 225 constitutions, laws, ordinances, and other documents produced by tribal governments during the nineteenth century until 1934.

BERKHOFER, ROBERT F., JR. "The Political Context of a New Indian History." *Pacific Historical Review* 40, no. 3 (August 1971):357–82.

Berkofer argues that political perspectives offer one way of reconstructing and organizing Indian history to suggest its complexity and diversity. He also explains that due to the rise of political anthropology, anthropologists see the nature and degree of cultural persistence and change entwined with politics and power. Discussing three studies of eighteenth-century Cherokee politics and diplomacy to illustrate current approaches to Indian scholarship, he considers the implications of these approaches for the writing of a new Indian history. The prevalence of factionalism and its effects in Indian life provide an awareness of the possible political context of historical and anthropological sources and he cites the relationship between factionalism and persistence and change in Indian political systems. He argues that focusing on the politics and changing governmental systems offers one way of organizing a general history of American Indians while preserving the diversity and complexity of the individual histories and suggests tracing the complex history of persistence and change from jural communities within tribes to tribal-wide political arenas, from confederacies and regional cooperation to contemporary national organizations. Finally, the author feels that the political context affords a glimpse of Indian history from an Indian point of view because it concentrates on Indians as individuals coping with the world through their leaders and reveals a fuller range of Indian opinion and action.

DRIVER, HAROLD E. "Government and Social Controls." In *Indians of North America*. 2nd ed., rev., pp. 287–308. Chicago: University of Chicago Press, 1969. Bibliography.

The author surveys the existence of societies having no territorial organization larger than the residential kin group, which he defines as having no true political organization, and societies with territorial ties based on nonkinship factors, defined as possessing it, from European contact through the historic period. He discusses the failure of Arctic Eskimos, Great Basin, Baja California, and northeast Mexican peoples to develop political organization and describes Subarctic, Northwest Coast, Plateau, California, and Southwestern peoples that exhibit borderline and mixed systems of territorial organization ranging from family groups to tribes of several thousand people. A survey of the Plains, Prairies, Northeast, and Southeast where some Indians had tribal organization in the historic period is followed with an examination of the state organization of Aztecs in Meso-America and theories

about the reasons for the differences in political organization.The chapter is based on published secondary works.

FAY, GEORGE EMERY, comp. and ed. *Charters, Constitutions, and By-Laws of the Indian Tribes of North America*. Occasional Publications in Anthropology, Ethnology Series. Greeley: Museum of Anthropology, Colorado State College, 1967.

To facilitate the study and understanding of present-day Indian tribal organizations and government procedures, the Museum of Anthropology of Colorado State College has assembled a large number of Indian tribal charters, constitutions, and by-laws to be reproduced as a series of publications. The materials have been published in related groupings, e.g., by culture (the Sioux tribes of South Dakota) or by geographical areas (the tribes of the eastern United States). The Museum has also reproduced a series of treaties, land cessions, and other U.S. congressional documents relative to American Indian tribes, such as military engagements between the U.S. troops and Plains Indians, and minutes of Indian tribal council meetings.

FENTON, WILLIAM N. "Factionalism in American Indian Society." In *Actes Du IVᵉ Congres International Des Sciences Anthropologiques et Ethnologiques* 2, pp. 330–40. Vienna: Verlag Adolf Holzhausens NFG, 1955. Bibliography.

Fenton studies factionalism in four American Indian societies who were formerly of distinct cultures—the Klamath of Oregon, the Blackfeet of Montana, the Iroquois of New York, and the Taos Pueblo of New Mexico—who still inhabit reservations located in their original geographical provinces. He argues the thesis that "self-government inevitably flows from accustomed ways of political behavior and shines through to modify whatever form of government is imposed on Native peoples." Beginning by discussing distinctions between factions and true political parties, he then examines traditional roots of political behavior in the four groups which are reflected in the persistence of old forms of political behavior in new situations.

LOWIE, ROBERT H. "Some Aspects of Political Organization Among the American Aborigines." In *Comparative Political Systems: Studies in the Politics of Pre-Industrial Societies*, edited by Ronald Cohen and John Middleton, pp. 63–87. Garden City, N.Y.: Natural History Press, 1967. Bibliography.

This article focuses on the lack of totalitarian concentration of power in most North and South American native societies in aboriginal and historic times, the author ascribing it to the dominant native separatism and libertarianism which precluded the creation of the semblance of a modern state. He begins by giving examples of the tendency to separate to illustrate that it was general among Indian peoples, except for the Incas and explains that the Creek and the Iroquois attempts at consolidation were "unimpressive" in a world perspective. Arguing that Indian societies with populations around 10,000 rarely, if ever, referred to permanently integrated political units, he then discusses the manifestation of coercive authority in aboriginal America, but notes that counteracting trends made them fall short of permanent results. The functions of titular and strong chiefs, two types of civil leaders, and factors that may have strengthened the titular chiefs in the American milieu are examined, and he considers other agencies besides the chiefs that assumed state coercive functions such as the military clubs. Finally, Lowie generalizes that there were sundry attempts toward centralizing power, and in cases where it was achieved he argues that supernaturalism and religious beliefs were used to attain political influence and more complex political developments, particularly by the Incas. Throughout the article there are comparisons made to other societies in the world.

METCALF, P. RICHARD. "Who Should Rule at Home? Native American Politics and Indian-White Relations." *Journal of American History*, 6, no. 3 (December 1974):651–65.
Metcalf examines the existence of deep political divisions in Indian societies at the time of white contact, despite consensus being a political ideal for most Indian societies. He explains the existence of political divisions within Indian communities predating white contact that endured into the contact era and which influenced postcontact Indian politics and the course of Indian-white relations. Examples are given of political leaders who wished to supplant the ruling leaders and exploited the white presence to further that goal, the Pequot Uncas-Sassacus rivalry in the 1630s and the Sac Blackhawk-Keokuk contest for supremacy within the tribe during the 1820s. The author also explains how Choctaw chief Pushmataha dealt with challenges to his political power and with the white presence in terms of internal politics and continuing indigenous disputes. The article is based on published primary and secondary sources.

OFFICER, JAMES E. "Politics of the American Indian." *The American Way* 5, no. 3 (March 1972): 24–29.
In this article, the author discusses the ways in which Indians participate in politics in contemporary America. He examines the nature of the reservation system and its relationship to the rest of society, explaining that most Indian reservations are not subject to the political jurisdiction of states in which they are located and that reservation Indians have usually ignored what goes on within state and local political systems. In addition, he shows that reservation Indians generally have concentrated their attention on their own tribal governments and on influencing the federal government,

that they have developed skills in tribal politics and in dealing with congressional people and federal bureaucrats. Citing examples of Indian political activity across America, Officer discusses the activities of the National Congress of American Indians, an organization he calls the most important collective voice of reservation Indians in contemporary times. A discussion of the need for Indians to involve themselves in local politics concludes the article.

THOMAS, ROBERT K. "Pan-Indianism." In *The American Indian Today,* edited by Stuart Levine and Nancy O. Lurie, pp. 128–40. Baltimore: Penguin Books, 1968.
Thomas surveys the historical development and present breadth and direction of Pan-Indianism. He begins with a discussion of the growth of a common interest among tribal groups in opposing white people and the creation of political alliances. Arguing that the historic roots of modern Pan-Indianism were found in a developing commonalty that Indians began to conceive of particularly in the Plains area, he explains how the conmonalty was brought to a head by the reservation system, in the way whites related to different tribes as "Indians," and by the pressure for assimilation which pushed Indians closer together. The author also describes how traits and institutions of the Plains area have come to symbolize a new identity of "Indian" for many tribal groups in the United States and how the new identity sets up a new structure of interaction among individuals of different tribal groups. Finally, he discusses how American Indian leadership is becoming nationalistically Indian and how Pan-Indianism is developing institutions which deal with people outside the community. The article is based largely on field work.

WITT, SHIRLEY HILL. "Nationalistic Trends Among American Indians." In *The American Indian Today,* edited by Stuart Levine and Nancy O. Lurie, pp. 93–127. Baltimore: Penguin Books, 1968.
This is a review of the historical antecedents which may have led to the development of American Indian nationalism, defined as a devotion to group interests, unity, and independence and an exploration of twentieth-century factors in Indian nationalism. The author surveys examples of historic Indian nationalism such as the Iroquois League and the Five Civilized Tribes of Oklahoma which were exceptions to the tendency to separate into autonomous tribes, reviews twentieth-century affairs, and the establishment of several intertribal organizations and Indian political activity. She concludes with an analysis of factors in the increasing contemporary, collective Indian political activity and cites the goals of Indian nationalism. The paper is based largely on published secondary works.

NORTHEAST

FENTON, WILLIAM N. "Collecting Materials for a Political History of the Six Nations." *Proceedings of the American Philosophical Society* 93, no. 3 (June 1949):233–38.

The author evaluates the source materials for the study of the political history of the Six Nations who form the League of the Iroquois Confederacy. Dividing the materials into two kinds, native traditions and rituals associated with the founding of the League and accounts by European and American observers of their official relations with the Iroquois, he discusses sources including published monographs by various ethnologists, particularly Lewis H. Morgan's *League of the Ho-de-no-sau-nee or Iroquois* (below) published in 1851, the classic attempt to describe the political structure of the Iroquois, and manuscript materials on the League. He also examines sources on the social and political organization of the tribes, election of chiefs, laws, and the ritual lore and practices which attend the perpetuation of the principal Iroquois institution, the Condolence Council. Fenton suggests French, English, and Dutch manuscripts, as well as material from the 1754 Albany Congress, that reflect the impact of the League and its institutions on Europeans. In addition, he gives examples to illustrate the kind of materials available to study.

GRINDE, DONALD A., JR. "The Background: The Iroquois United Nations" and "The Iroquois and the Legacy of the Revolution." In *The Iroquois and the Founding of the American Nation*, pp. 1–17, pp. 125–38. San Francisco: Indian Historian Press, 1977. Bibliography.

In these two chapters, the author discusses the social, economic, and political organization of the Iroquois Confederacy with its government of balance and compromise, concepts of federalism, and its legacy of democratic unity and balance. He argues that the formation of the United States during the eighteenth century was influenced by Iroquois political and philosophical traditions. The first appendix contains a copy of the Constitution of the Five Nations, the ancient constitution of the Iroquois which tells of the principles of Iroquois government. The second appendix contains a copy of the Albany Plan of Union developed at the 1754 Albany Congress which Benjamin Franklin admits was similar to and inspired by the League of the Iroquois. Grinde maintains that the Albany Plan and the laws of the Iroquois Confederacy are strikingly similar in their structure and philosophy.

MILLER, WALTER B. "Two Concepts of Authority." *American Anthropologist* 57, no. 2., part 1 (April 1955):271–89. Bibliography.

This article compares the concept of authority of Europeans and Central Algonquians represented by the Fox tribe of the Great Lakes area during the late seventeenth and eirhteenth centuries. The author begins by examining three relationships in European society that curtailed the exercise of authority: the sixth-century English lord, the sixteenth-century Jesuit Superior, and the seventeenth-century French king. He examines present-day European societies that share certain characteristics of these earlier prototypes, especially the vertical authority relationship, the fundamental building block of European society. Describing how the Foxes conceived of authority and organized collective action in a different way, Miller looks at the Fox system of religion, the Fox pantheon, and the concept of power which implied it was dangerous and immoral for one individual to exercise substantial control over others. He describes three formal positions of authority, the village chief, the war leader, and the ceremony leader, and tells of the village council which functioned to implement collective action. He concludes with a discussion of how Fox society lacked vertical authority and coordination of collective action, and how it utilized the device of role-relationships combining the right to direct, permanent incumbency, differential prestige, functions, and access to procedural rules. The article is based on published primary and secondary works.

MORGAN, LEWIS HENRY. *League of the Ho-de-no-sau-nee or Iroquois*. Rochester: Sage & Brother, 1851; reprint ed., Secaucus, N.J.: Citadel Press, 1962. 477pp. Illustrated.

This is a classic account, and the first scientific study of an American Indian tribe, that attempts to describe Iroquois political structure. In the new introduction, William N. Fenton explains that Morgan's account was "long on social organization and the mechanics of a kinship state," and short on history. Also, Fenton says that "though not entirely free of the ideas of savagism and primitivism, from which his predecessors never escaped, Morgan sought to describe the Iroquois in their own terms and fairly succeeded." All of the original illustrations appear in the reprint edition.

SMITH, JAMES G. E. *Leadership among the Southwestern Ojibway*. Publications in Ethnology, no. 7. Ottawa: National Museum of Man, 1973. 36pp. Illustrated. Bibliography.

In this account, Smith deals with the Ojibways (Chippewas) who moved into Minnesota, Wisconsin, and Michigan in the late seventeenth century, and looks at how the interaction of historical incidents and social processes affected leadership in the late prereservation period of the nineteenth century, when major land cessions were made, and during the reservation period. He also examines the social consequences of the Ojibway's southern migration that included increasing population density, technological innovation, warfare with the Sioux, land cessions, and their eventual settlement on reservations with limited economic resources as well as limited political autonomy. He cites the political organization and leadership problems imposed by the social and cultural context against the background of the late prereservation and contemporary reservation periods and suggests that in both periods the major characteristics were the segmented social structure of the Ojibways, restrictions of a limited economic base, decision-making processes based on egalitarianism and consensual democracy, distrust in interpersonal relations, the fear of those possessing power, and the lack of cooperation over a long period of time. There is a map.

WALLACE, ANTHONY F. C. "Political Organization and Land Tenure Among the Northeastern Indians, 1600–1830." *Southwestern Journal of Anthropology* 13, no. 4 (Winter 1957):301–21. Bibliography.

Wallace describes aspects of the political organization and land tenure of Indian tribes of the northeastern United States during the prereservation period, 1600–1830. He briefly defines and discusses the general concepts of political organization in the Northeast based on tribe and tribal territory, ethnic confederacies, alliances, amalgamations, adoptions, and satellite relationships which tended to unify an area socially and culturally. In addition, he mentions tribal splitting, intertribal trade relationships, and war and then discusses general principles of tribal land tenure in the Northeast involving concepts of boundary, permissive hunting and trespass, conquest, succession after abandonment, and after the arrival of whites, of sale. There is an unannotated bibliography of published primary and secondary accounts.

SOUTHEAST

GEARING, FREDERICK O. *Priests and Warriors: Social Structures for Cherokee Politics in the 18th Century.* Memoirs of the American Anthropological Association, vol. 64, no. 5, part 2. Menasha, Wisc.: American Anthropological Assn., 1962. 124pp. Reprint ed.: Millwood, N.Y.: Kraus Reprint, 1974. Illustrated. Bibliography.

This is a study of eighteenth-century Cherokee political life in terms of village decision-making and decision-making by the emerged Cherokee state in the 1760s. The author focuses on the personnel and procedures which helped villagers decide how to resolve conflicting interests and implement public policy decisions. He begins with an analysis of the four to five social "structural poses" (the way a human society sees itself to be organized at a moment) of Cherokee villages of South Carolina, Georgia, and Tennessee as the male inhabitants organized successively for the various tasks of hunting, punishing in-group murder, conducting war, holding general councils, and negotiating peace. He explains that until 1730 Cherokees shared a culture but not an overall political organization by being divided into politically independent sovereign villages that formed a jural community of peaceful coexistence among the Cherokee people. The author then describes the Cherokee ethos which disallowed disharmony, tells of the council and war organizations which were the village political structures, explains how the Cherokee ethos shaped relations among warriors, and describes the political behavior of younger and older men. He cites the efforts made by the peace chiefs of various villages between 1730 and 1760 to extend the village power structure to the entire jural community, describes the failure of the priest-state to create a structure analogous to the village council, and explains how the exigencies of war and diplomacy brought war chiefs to power after 1750 in an attempt to create another tribal-wide governmental organization. Finally, he discusses how the efforts of the war chiefs were stymied by tribal schisms of 1776 caused by the American Revolution. There are seven figures illustrating "structural poses" and lineages and one map.

GREEN, MICHAEL D. *The Politics of Indian Removal: Creek Government and Society in Crisis.* Lincoln: University of Nebraska Press, 1982. 268pp. Illustrated. Bibliography.

This study, the first detailed analysis of Creek political and social history during the two decades from the Creek War to the removal of the Creeks, also gives a full account of the development of the National Council as a tribal governing body. The author shows how the efforts of the Creek Nation to avoid removal strengthened the authority of the National Council, which previously had limited influence, making it a more powerful governing body. He also emphasizes internal political and social factors and stresses the influence of culture and culture change. There are three maps.

GREAT PLAINS

CLIFTON, JAMES A. "Factional Conflict and the Indian Community: The Prairie Potawatomi Case." In *The American Indian Today,* edited by Stuart Levine and Nancy O. Lurie, pp. 184–211. Baltimore: Penguin Books, 1968.

Clifton studies the history, course, character, and outcome of the prolonged factional conflict in one Prairie Potawatomi community, representative of other reservation Indian communities, defining factionalism as overt, unregulated disputes resulting from stresses of acculturation situations. He examines the historical roots of conflict between the acculturated Mission band and the conservative Prairie band of Potawatomis engendered by white demands. He studies the factional conflict in the 1930s during which time the conservative faction organized and emerged as a reform movement, a series of overt conflicts became prominent in reservation life, conservatives prosecuted a claims case which served as a rallying point and intensified the factional conflict, efforts at control failed, and the dispute ramified into various aspects of community life. He examines the Prairie band's rejection of the Indian Reorganization Act constitution, their battles with the Bureau of Indian Affairs, and their blunders which opened the way to a resurgence of assimilated elements. The author looks at the permissive membership provisions of the 1961 Prairie band Constitution by which the conservatives lost control of the reservation. He shows how several modes of conflict resolutions were attempted and failed. He concludes by discussing the point that Potawatomi factionalism has not spread much beyond the political sphere and shows that ambiguity concerning definition of membership in the Potawatomi tribe has contributed to intragroup conflicts. The article is based partly on fieldwork.

FOWLER, LORETTA. *Arapahoe Politics 1851–1978: Symbols in Crisis of Authority.* Lincoln: University of Nebraska Press, 1982. 374pp. Illustrated. Bibliography.

The author explores how, in response to the new

social realities of domination by white Americans, the Northern Arapahoes of the Wind River Reservation have succeeded in legitimizing new authority relations through the creation and use of effective political symbols. She discusses their reworking of an ethos associated with a traditional age-grade social structure, the willingness of the elderly ceremonial priests to endorse necessary innovations, and the younger men who served as intermediaries with outsiders to accept the elders' guidance. She tells how old symbols embodying ideas about age, authority, and the supernatural took on new meanings when they were manipulated to enable the middle persons to interact with white people. The photographs, maps, and bibliography reflect the extensive field work and archival materials on which the work is based.

SCHOLARLY RESOURCES. *The Constitutions and Laws of the American Indian Tribes.* Series 1: 20 vols. Series 2: 33 vols. Wilmington, Del.: Scholarly Resources, 1973–75.

These two series contain fifty-three volumes that present the complete collection of the written constitutions and laws of the Chickasaws, Osages, Cherokees, Choctaws, Muskogees, Creeks, Sacs and Foxes, and Indian Territories from the mid-nineteenth century until 1906 when tribal governments in Indian Territory were arbitrarily abolished. Some of the texts are written in native languages. Other volumes in this series concern meetings of the General Council of the Indian Territory with delegates representing over twenty-five tribes.

SMITH, MAURICE GREER. *The Political Organization of the Plains Indians.* University Studies of the University of Nebraska, 24, nos. 1, 2 (January–April 1924):84pp. Lincoln: University of Nebraska Press. Bibliography.

Smith summarizes material available for the study of the political organization of Plains Indians, generally in the nineteenth century, with special reference to the councils. He begins with a discussion of cultural characteristics of the Plains Indians and then presents brief facts about the government of the Blackfeet, Sarsis, Plains-Ojibway, Plains Cree, Assiniboines, Gros Ventres, Cheyennes, Kiowas, Comanches, Flatheads, Kutenais, Nez Percés, Shoshones, Bannocks, Utes, Western Teton Dakotas, Eastern Santee Dakotas, Mandans, Hidatsas, Crows, Arikaras, Pawnees, Wichitas, Caddos, Iowas, Omahas, Osages, Poncas, and Kansas. In addition, he deals with the council, the most important political institution among the Plains tribes, and its chief characteristics. The bibliography lists published primary and secondary works.

SOUTHWEST

BRUGGE, DAVID M. "Pueblo Factionalism and External Relations." *Ethnohistory* 16, no. 2 (Spring 1969):191–98. Bibliography.

The author discusses how Pueblo Indians have been allied with Apaches and Navajos against non-

Indians and how they fight among themselves. Citing several documented instances of such alliances from 1583 to the 1860s, he argues that diverse economic, religious, and kin interests have motivated political alignments both within the tribes as well as externally. The bibliography lists published primary and secondary works.

FISHER, REGINALD G. "An Outline of Pueblo Government." In *So Live the Works of Men,* edited by Donald D. Brandt and Fred E. Harvey, pp. 147–57. Albuquerque: University of New Mexico Press, 1939. Bibliography.

Fisher deals with Pueblo politico-religious structures in contemporary times by explaining the two sets of officials in Pueblo government, one preconquest and the other postconquest in origin. He describes the postconquest or Spanish set of offices found among all the Pueblos except Hopi and its important functions of concealing the existence of priestly officials from Spanish and English-speaking intruders and representing the Pueblos in their transactions with foreigners. He discusses the priestly offices, the real Pueblo authority which originated in pre-Spanish times and reviews Pueblo religious organization because of its close relationship to political structures. He considers the ultimate authority of Pueblo government resting in a council whose function is best described as judicial, discusses the head priest official, the executive phase of Pueblo government, and the role of moieties, kiva groups, societies, orders, fraternities, or clans in Pueblo political life, as well as noting that various offices of Pueblo politico-religious structure derive from supernatural sources.

SHEPARDSON, MARY. *Navajo Ways in Government: A Study in Political Process.* Memoirs of the American Anthropological Association 96, vol. 65, no. 3, part 2. Menasha, Wisc.: American Anthropological Assn., 1963. 132pp. Illustrated. Bibliography.

Shepardson describes and analyzes modern political developments in the Navajo tribe of Arizona, New Mexico, and Utah up to 1960 and argues that the Navajo Tribal Council is fully institutionalized in Navajo life and in the life of the surrounding states. The first part of the work is devoted to the background of Navajo life, including a sketch of Navajo history, the physical and demographic setting, economic development, and the traditional groupings in the social structure. The second part deals with the interaction of four authorities, traditional Navajo, modern Navajo, the federal government, and the local states. The author describes the four types of authority, their field of jurisdiction, values and goals, concrete units of government, and component political roles. She discusses the historical development of self-government among Navajos, the institutionalization of the Navajo Tribal Council, local participation in the modern political system, and the Navajo tribal elections of 1955 and 1959. She analyzes the component roles, how they are defined and by whom, methods of recruitment and compensation, limits of authority and accountability, and the types of situations in which the political role players must act. She also examines conflicts within a role, conflicts between roles, and conflicts among the role definers who compose the system. In the conclusion, the author offers a general theoretical analysis of the factors that tend to promote or inhibit the institutionalization of a modern political system in a stateless, tradition-oriented society. There is a map and a bibliography of published secondary works.

WILLIAMS, AUBREY W., JR. *Navajo Political Process.* Washington, D.C.: Smithsonian Institution, 1970. 75pp. Illustrated. Bibliography.

The author examines the development and function of three contemporary political structures, introduced and promoted among the Navajos as part of the directed culture change program of the government, and their incorporation into the Navajo way of life. He points out significant factors in Navajo history, culture, geography, and demography to establish a sociocultural baseline and explains traditional Navajo political organization prior to the development of twentieth-century political institutions. He describes the period around 1900 in which a rift developed between informal local leaders and formal Navajo leaders appointed by the government. He describes the administrative units into which contemporary Navajos were organized by the government, focuses on the beginnings of tribal self-government with the Navajo Tribal Council first elected in 1923, district grazing committees, and chapters, local political organizations, ninety-six of which existed at the time the book was written. The author examines Navajo political behavior, the cultural meanings Navajos ascribe to Anglo-American political principles and actions, shows how Navajos incorporated Anglo-American principles of political organization without the corresponding cultural content, and concludes that the major function of the Navajo chapters within the political system is to provide a structure that allows transfer of Anglo-American principles of government to Navajo culture with a minimum amount of opposition and conflict. There are six maps and photographs that illustrate chapter activities.

NORTHWEST COAST

COLLINS, JUNE MCCORMICK. "Growth of Class Distinctions and Political Authority among the Skagit Indians during the Contact Period." *American Anthropologist* 52, no. 3 (July–September 1950):331–42. Bibliography.

Collins traces the shifts in social and political organization of the Upper and Lower Skagit Indians of Washington after white contact in the nineteenth century and argues that whites gave a formal structure to what had been informal. She begins with a reconstruction of Skagit social and economic organization in prewhite times, explaining that there was no formal political organization but rather informal leaders of several types who specialized in directing undertakings concerned with subsistence, warfare, or religion. Describing the shifts in the Skagit system of social ranking and innovations in political

organization after white contact in the nineteenth century, she shows that class distinctions which already existed in Skagit society became greatly emphasized after white contact. She also describes how leadership emerged in response to having to deal with whites, to direct warfare and defense, and to take charge of new religious sects.

ALASKA

WEYER, E. M. "The Structure of Social Organization among the Eskimo." In *Comparative Political Systems: Studies in the Politics of Preindustrial Societies,* edited by Ronald Cohen and John Middleton, pp. 1–13. Garden City, N.Y.: Natural History Press, 1967. Bibliography.

The author surveys early twentieth-century social and political organization among Eskimos, particularly those of Alaska. He first discusses the social organization of Eskimos into villages and households and documents how the size of the social unit varies in response to seasonal phases which necessitate different modes of life. He examines how the office of chieftainship has developed to a higher degree among Alaskan Eskimos than in any other Eskimo group and provides over twenty documented observations of the nature of Eskimo leadership.

BIBLIOGRAPHY

HARGRETT, LESTER. *A Bibliography of the Constitutions and Laws of the American Indians.* Cambridge, Mass.: Harvard University Press, 1947. 124pp. Illustrated.

This bibliography contains an annotated list of 225 documents produced by tribal governments during the nineteenth century until 1934. There are printed constitutions, statutes, cession acts, and resolutions passed by Indian tribes of the United States as well as constitutional convention ordinances, resolutions, council rules, and a few volumes of Indian Territory local ordinances. John R. Swanton discusses, in his introduction, the documents listed in the bibliography which reflect efforts by the tribes to adjust to new conditions brought about by European intrusions, demands for land cessions, and the urging of missionaries and government agents to develop tribal-wide governments. He discusses the problems of adaption of the southeastern Cherokees, Creeks, Choctaws, Chickasaws, and Seminoles and chronicles their loss of autonomy in a list of events. All the documents are arranged chronologically by the date of their printing under tribes listed alphabetically. There are brief histories preceding each of the following: Cherokee, Chickasaw, Choctaw, Creek, Indian Territory, Nez Percé, Omaha, Osage, Ottawa, Sac and Fox, Seminole, Seneca, State of Sequoyah, Stockbridge and Munsee, and Winnebago. An appendix contains the text of an 1809 talk by Thomas Jefferson to a Cherokee delegation encouraging orderly self-government. There are photographs of title pages of the constitutions and laws.

9 FEDERAL AND STATE INDIAN RELATIONS

Federal policy affecting American Indians has a long history of disastrous, contradictory, and ill-conceived laws, regulations, and reforms. Until recently, the federal government's policy goals have been based on the assumption that Native Americans should and would be assimilated into the American mainstream. Differences over the means of achieving these goals are reflected in the fluctuations in Indian policy.

Historians of federal Indian policy have rarely questioned the assimilationist goals or the means of achieving these goals toward which government officials, missionaries, reformers, and others were working. Some of the histories that contain particularly flagrant statements reflecting uncritical acceptance of proassimilationist ideologies have been excluded from this section.

Several historians in this section discuss Spanish, French, Dutch, British, and colonial programs and their influence in the development of federal policy. Mohr (p. 89) shows how the British machinery for managing American Indian affairs set a precedent for the new American government, which, like the British crown, centralized control of Indian affairs in the hands of superintendents but increased the number of them from two to three. Horsman (p. 87) describes attempts by the government under the Articles of Confederation to confiscate Indian lands while ignoring Indian rights and discusses the failure of this policy. After 1786, he goes on to explain, the United States changed its policy to the British colonial practice of acknowledging Indian rights of soil which had to be purchased by the United States in formal treaties.

Beginning in 1778 and for almost a hundred years, the treaty was the principal instrument of federal Indian policy. During the ninety-three years between 1778 and 1871, the U.S. Senate ratified 372 treaties with Indian tribes. These treaties assumed a contractual relationship between two autonomous parties and were little different from the relationship of power and authority existing between other nations and the United States. According to one writer, the treaties fall into several major categories: treaties of peace and friendship, acknowledgement of U.S. sovereignty, cession, removal, and allotment. "In some cases, treaties provided for more than one of these purposes. Some treaties were negotiated with the Indians on a basis of equality; some were dictated to no longer powerful tribes.

Some treaties followed a successful war; others an unsuccessful war."[1]
Some of the treaties were not negotiated by leaders of tribes, but rather
they were negotiated by one portion of a tribe which presumed to represent
the entire nation. Often, other members of the tribe rejected the treaty or
were ignorant of its being negotiated. Congress ended the practice of
treaty-making with Indians by means of a rider attached to an appropriations bill in 1871. With the abandonment of the treaty process as the legal
link between the tribes and the federal government, acts of Congress took
on the role of treaties. The government subsequently made "agreements"
with tribes which were submitted to both houses of Congress for ratification instead of to the Senate which alone ratified treaties.

The early laws of the U.S. government recognized the largely independent character of Indian tribes but at the same time actively encouraged
Indians to adopt white technology and culture. The earliest laws laid down
detailed rules regulating the intercourse between Indians and whites. Between 1790 and 1834, a series of laws, the Indian Intercourse Acts, were
passed. Prucha (p. 92) discusses the passage of the Trade and Intercourse
Acts of 1790, 1793, 1796, 1798, and 1802 which became the basic law
governing Indian relations until they were replaced by new codes in 1834.
The new codes reorganized the Indian Department and contained a new
Trade and Intercourse Act. All of these laws attempted in particular to
control the trade relationship between the Indians and whites. They specified the geographic boundaries separating "Indian country" from white
settlements and sought to restrain lawless frontier whites who were hostile to Indians and hampered enforcement of federal laws. Other laws
governing Indian-white relations concerned the fur trade and sought to
prevent the use of liquor by traders among Indians.

The federal government made an early effort to compete with the British
and private fur companies by organizing the Indian factory system. The
system was designed to help Indians secure goods at a fair price and to
reduce warfare with tribes. Peake (p. 90) examines the organization of the
factory system created by an act of Congress in 1795, the establishment of
seventeen trade factories between 1795 and 1821, the educational and
religious work of the Indian Trade Office designed to assimilate Indians,
and the failure of the system which was closed down by Congress in 1822.

The management of Indian affairs by the federal government originated
within the War Department where personnel were charged with enforcing
the Intercourse Acts. Beginning in 1806, trade with Indians was managed
by one of the subordinates of the War Secretary, the Superintendent of
Indian Trade, who, in the course of administering the government-
operated trading houses, assumed some of the War Secretary's responsibilities toward the Indians. The Office of Indian Trade was abolished by
Congress in 1822 and the War Secretary again resumed responsibilities for
all Indian-related matters. In 1824, Secretary of War John C. Calhoun
recognized a need for an Indian office to handle Indian affairs and he
established a Bureau of Indian Affairs within the War Department and
appointed Thomas L. McKenney to head the new division. The Bureau's
existence was formalized by Congress in 1834 by the establishment of an

1. Wilcomb Washburn, *The Indian in America* (New York: Harper & Row, 1975), p. 98.

Indian Office headed by a Commissioner of Indian Affairs. Schmeckebier (p. 94) traces the history and activities of the Office of Indian Affairs until 1926. Kvasnicka and Viola (p. 88) provide biographical sketches of the forty-three men who have served as Indian Commissioners from 1824 to 1977 when the office was superseded by that of Assistant Secretary of the Interior for Indian Affairs. Control of the Indian Office was transferred from the War Department to the newly created Department of the Interior in 1849 where it has remained ever since. During the nineteenth century, there was friction between civil and military officials in regard to Indian jurisdiction and differences of opinion arose as to the proper policy to follow. During the 1870s, for example, there was conflict between the two departments over military operations on reservations. Many members of Congress and military people advocated the return of the Bureau of Indian Affairs to the War Department during the 1860s and 1870s but the move was never made.

Between colonial times and 1850, a class of public officers developed whose sole duty was to administer Indian affairs. Gallaher (p. 85) tells of the duties of Indian agents, people who were assigned to live among Indians, from 1789 to 1849. She explains how Congress clearly defined the authority of agents and the administration of Indian affairs in an 1832 act, which created the position of Commissioner of Indian Affairs, and discusses an 1834 law which organized the field service of superintendents, agents, and subagents among American Indians. In a second article, Gallaher (p. 86) considers the increase in the number of agents between the years 1850–71 due to Indians being forced onto reservations and describes the character of agents drawn to the Indian Service. She tells of conflict between civilian agents and army officers over control of reservations. Hill (p. 86) provides historical sketches of field units of the Office of Indian Affairs from 1824 to 1880 which include the names and dates of appointments of superintendents and agents.

The federal government became concerned with educating Indian tribes who lived near frontier settlements and in 1819 Congress passed the Civilization Fund Act to employ "capable" persons willing to teach Indians "the habits and arts of civilization" which meant agriculture for the adults and white language arts and mathematics for the children. Viola (p. 97) discusses the role of Superintendent of Indian Trade McKenney, who was in that position from 1816 to 1822, and his efforts to "civilize" Indians by promoting agriculture and missionary activities among them.

More laws of the United States gradually limited the autonomy of the tribes by restricting their war-making powers, by imposing white legal remedies for crimes committed by Indians, and by forcing Indians to take up white agricultural pursuits.

The policy of removal—moving eastern Native American groups west to get them out of the way—was first suggested by President Jefferson in 1803. The Jeffersonian generation initially believed in a program of "civilizing" Indians through a secular and religious education which would transform them into individual farmers who eventually would be incorporated into white society. It witnessed, however, the disintegration of Indian tribal and personal life as a result of the "civilization" program, warfare with whites, European diseases to which Indians had little resistance, and liquor. Some Jeffersonians began to argue that American Indians in the East should be moved west of the Mississippi River where the "civilizing" program, which had failed in the East, could be carried on. Abel (p. 99) tells of three unsuccessful attempts to remove southeastern tribal groups during the Jeffersonian era.

During the 1820s, government officials and religious and reform organizations who argued for assimilation of Indians into white society merged this philosophy with that of moving Indians west of the Mississippi River where they thought the "civilizing" program could be pursued more successfully. Viola (p. 97) discusses public figures such as Superintendent of Indian Trade McKenney who promoted Indian removal as the Indians' best hope for survival. Between 1820 and 1840 about 100,000 Native Americans were removed either forcibly or voluntarily from their ancestral homes in the Northeast and the Southeast and isolated in enclaves west of the Mississippi River where missionaries and government officials pursued their goals of educating Indians. Abel (p. 99) discusses some voluntary removals in the North and the South between 1820 and 1825.

One of the motivating forces behind the Indian removals of the 1830s was white greed for land, but publicly the policy was masked with arguments that nothing but removal would save the Indians from extinction. Officials, such as President Andrew Jackson, argued that removing Indians from the corrupting influence of white culture would slow the Indians' decline and cause them to gradually lose their "savage" habits and become "civilized," Christianized people. Satz (p. 94) argues that the exigencies of the moment determined components of the removal policy. He discusses removal of the Cherokees and Choctaws—the latter was the first tribe to sign a treaty under the 1830 Removal Act—and other tribes in the Northeast and the Southeast. He examines methods used to obtain removal treaties, such as the government policy of selecting a particular group to represent the entire tribe, promised annuities, and force. He explains why Indian country west of the Mississippi River became an obstacle to continental development and describes how Indian Office agents and missionaries used annuities and education programs to "civilize" and control Indians.

Cherokees, Chickasaws, Choctaws, Creeks, and Seminoles, whose southern lands were coveted by plantation owners, comprised the majority of the people who moved west. Cherokee removal has been the subject of much study, especially because Supreme Court cases arose out of the tribe's resistance to moving. Satz (p. 94) discusses Georgia's power play against the Cherokees and Chief Justice Marshall's decision against the Georgia law.

Tribes in the Northeast were displaced by the expansion of agricultural settlers. Foreman (p. 98) traces the history of the removal of over fifty tribes who lived in Ohio, Michigan, Indiana, Illinois, and New York. He focuses on the 1830s and 1840s when Delawares, Ottawas, Wyandots, Potawatomis, Miamis, Illinois, Kickapoos, Sacs, and Foxes were moved west of the Mississippi.

The removal process was completed around 1840 with the establishment of the large, unorganized "permanent" Indian country west of Arkansas, Missouri, and Iowa. The annexation by the United States of Texas in 1845, Oregon in 1846, plus the addition of the Southwest and California in 1848 created new pressures from European emigrants for ownership of lands west of the Mississippi which had been "permanently" set aside for the Native American groups removed from the East. Several studies discuss the break-up of the "permanent" Indian frontier due to the rapid emigration of non-Indians into the newly acquired territories. Malin (p. 101) looks first at federal Indian policy between 1830 and 1840 and the evolution of a plan to consolidate Indians in a permanent home in the southwest of Indian country to allow for the westward expansion of whites across the northern part of the territory. He examines factors that dictated a change in federal policy between 1840 and 1854 to that of relocating Indian tribes to the north in the Dakotas and to the south in what is now Oklahoma, extinguishing Indian title to the area between the two newly designated Indian countries and opening it to railroads and white settlement. He also considers the Kansas-Nebraska Act of 1854 which established the Kansas and Nebraska Territories and resulted in the removal of many tribes from these areas to Indian Territory, now the state of Oklahoma. Hoopes (p. 101) also explains how Kansas and Nebraska Indians were forced to surrender their lands.

The period after 1848 through the Civil War also saw the formulation of reservation policy as a means of protecting Indian lands from white encroachment and Indians from possible violence. Trennert (p. 96) explores efforts of Indian Office officials between 1846 and 1851 to find an alternative to the extinction of Indians. These efforts produced the rudiments of a reservation system which was to develop fully after the Civil War. He discusses the initial federal policy construct of a line behind which Native American populations would remain racially segregated until "civilized" and describes the end of this barrier philosophy because of the pressures of westward expansion which virtually eliminated the line. Hoopes (p. 101) outlines changes in federal Indian policy in the decade before the Civil War, particularly the development of the California reservations between 1847 and 1860 and details the spread of the reservation system over the entire country. Ellison (p. 104) tells of the federal appropriations for the development and management of a system of small California reservations created by agreement, not treaty, from 1853 to 1860. Coan (p. 103) traces the development of U.S. Indian policy in Oregon and discusses the formation and adoption of Oregon and Washington reservation policy in the mid-1850s. Danziger (p. 99) analyzes the difficulties encountered by Indian Office field officials west of the Mississippi in implementing the government's reservation policy during the Civil War years.

Several books deal with the ordeals of tribes in adapting to reservation life. Berthrong (p. 99), for example, tells of the government policy that was designed to change Cheyennes and Arapahos from mobile hunting societies into sedentary agricultural peoples through instruction in farming, federally operated reservation schools, and Christian education. Hagan (p. 100) discusses the "civilization" (assimilation) programs designed by the government to make Comanches self-sufficient once again through agricultural training and education. Hagan (p. 100), in another book, discusses Indian police and court systems which were in force on most reservations west of the Mississippi River by 1878 and examines the role they played in the "civilization" program until their decline by 1900.

After the Civil War and through the turn of the century, there were movements to reform Indian affairs because of the desperate situation of the Indian people. Native American groups were trying to resist, through wars of increasing violence, encroachments on their lands by settlers, miners, and railroads. Prucha (p. 92) and Mardock (p. 89) deal with the group of humanitarians and their government friends who wanted to help Indians by reforming them. They discuss Grant's peace policy which had two components, the Board of Indian Commissioners and the appointment of different missionary societies to Indian reservations where they were charged with "civilizing" and "evangelizing" Indians. Beaver (p. 82) gives an account of the active partnership between Protestant churches and the government in the maintenance of Christian missions to American Indians from 1641 to 1890, when the alliance dissolved. Prucha describes how organizations such as the Board of Indian Commissioners, the Indian Rights Association, and the Lake Mohonk Conference of Friends of the Indians tried to persuade the government to allot reservations in severalty, assimilate Indians through formal schooling, and dissolve Indian nations of Indian Territory, the lands of which were coveted by farmers. Prucha (p. 92) has put together a collection of writings by these reformers which reflect their views. Historians are still debating whether these humanitarian groups were sincere but misguided in their efforts or venal and underhanded in their motives to change Indians. Mardock explains the conflicts between the army and the antimilitaristic reformers over control of Indian policy and the unsuccessful political efforts to transfer the Indian Bureau back to the War Department. Ellis (p. 100) discusses General John Pope's Indian reform policy, his opposition to civilian control of Indians and to the policy of converting Indians to farmers.

The policy of allotting lands in severalty to Indians was not a new idea. Gates (p. 86) considers the policy of wresting land from Indians through allotments in 1805. He gives examples of allotment policies in the South and explains how the bulk of the allotments passed out of Indian hands into those of whites exploiting them. He examines individual reserves and allotments made north of the Ohio River, first appearing in Indian treaties in 1817. He describes how allotment became a regular feature of treaties with tribes in the Kansas and Nebraska Territories and other areas after 1854 until 1887 and how government officials emphasized allotments as a means of Indians becoming farmers.

The Dawes Act, or the General Allotment Act of 1887, ignoring cultural patterns that were thousands of years old, enshrined in law the idea that American Indians should be assimilated into American civilization, embrace white agrarian values, and become individual land owners. The Act provided for 160-acre allotments of reservation land to Indian heads of family, smaller tracts for single Indians and minors, and protected the land from alienation for twenty-five years. The Act was aimed at dissolving tribes by breaking up Indian reservations, the communal land base of tribal existence. After each Indian had been compelled to take a holding, the remaining lands were often declared surplus and opened for sale to whites by the government. No allowance was made for the lack of farming skills among the Plains Indians. Few people thought far enough ahead to realize that Indians once vested with full title would be divested of the ownership by devious white people. Alienation of Indian land into white ownership proceeded rapidly. The Dawes Act succeeded in depriving Indians of one hundred million acres of land and eventually left one hundred thousand Indians landless. It created tangled legal and economic problems for the future, particularly in Oklahoma.

Federal Indian allotment policy in Oklahoma is a special study. Debo (p. 100) traces the history of the Cherokees, Choctaws, Chickasaws, Creeks, and Seminoles from 1890 until 1936, discusses the work of the Dawes Commission and the effects of the 1898 Curtis Act in extinguishing Indian land titles in Indian Territory, describes the demands of whites in Indian Territory for statehood, and considers the federal government's role in moving the Five Civilized Tribes toward statehood.

There are several works concerning the Dawes Act. One, by Otis (p. 90), contains explanations of the motives of the advocates of the allotment policy and the destructive impact of the Act on Indian societies. Washburn (p. 97) identifies five choices which he believes were actually before legislators in the 1880s and discusses the compromise legislation that finally emerged in 1887 as the Dawes Act. He discusses Indian opposition to severalty legislation and also evaluates the negative impact of the Act.

In the 1920s, another Indian reform movement developed which rejected the reforms of the 1880s and 1890s embodied in the Dawes Act. These reformers demanded that Indians be allowed to keep their cultures. Downes (p. 85) explains how muckraking journals set before the public government mismanagement in tribe after tribe and discusses the Meriam Report of 1928, a government sponsored study criticizing the results of the Dawes Act. He looks at the pre-New Deal phase of the Indian reform movement around 1929 when education and health programs were emphasized under Commissioner of Indian Affairs Rhoads. In 1933, President Roosevelt appointed John Collier as Commissioner of Indian Affairs. Collier instituted the Indian New Deal embodied in the Wheeler-Howard Act or the Indian Reorganization Act of 1934. The Act repealed the Dawes Act and forbade further allotments of Indian lands in severalty and the sale to whites of unallotted lands. Its fundamental aims were development of Indian economic resources and restoration of Indian self-determination through revival of tribal governments. Tribes, at their own option, could incorporate under provisions of the Act and elect tribal governments invested with certain legal powers. A revolving loan fund was created in the amount of $10 million for the purpose of aiding tribal councils in promoting economic development. There were provisions for scholarships for Indians attending vocational and trade schools, for giving preference to Indians for Indian Bureau civil service jobs, and for adding land to reservations. All the tribes of Oklahoma were excluded from important parts of the legislation, some sections did not apply to Alaska, and the enlargement of the Navajo Reservation was prohibited. The Secretary of the Interior was invested with a great deal of power in approving tribal constitutions, vetoing certain tribal council actions, and making rules for managing forests and grazing lands.

The Indian New Deal was not entirely successful. Philp (p. 90) argues that hostility in Congress and misunderstanding of Indian needs by the white community hampered the reform program. He explains John Collier's administrative shortcomings and his flawed assumptions about Indians. G. Taylor (p. 95) argues that tribal reorganization failed because Collier and his coworkers had basic misconceptions about Indian societies and how they functioned. He explains that the reasons the new tribal governments aroused little support among the people they were supposed to represent included the facts that few Indian groups had ever functioned practically on the tribal level, there was intratribal factionalism and rivalry, and the political structures that were established were foreign to Indian societies. Parman (p. 102) shows that New Deal Indian policies on the Navajo Reservation exacerbated Navajo internal conflicts. He also explains how the advent of World War II created problems that negated advances of New Deal programs.

In 1946, the Indian Claims Commission was created by Congress to adjudicate claims against the U.S. government by tribes for compensation for land losses during the treaty period. Before the Commission was created, claims of the tribes, bands, and other groups against the United States could only be brought to court if Congress authorized the action. Smith (p. 95) analyzes more than 220 major cases of Indian claims which had been decided in the U.S. Court of Claims from the 1880s to the establishment of the Indian Claims Commission in 1946. The Indian Claims Commission Series of Clearwater Publishing (p. 87) includes nearly all of the historically relevant materials generated by the ICC litigation including the Commission's findings of fact, opinions, orders, and final awards, written reports prepared by experts and submitted as testimony by plaintiffs, and other materials.

During the years following Collier's resignation in 1945 and his departure from the Indian Service, white misconceptions about Indian needs and aspirations contributed to a return to the policy of rapid assimilation of Indians. After World War II, the policy known as termination, or the elimination of the special relationship between Indians and the federal government, was accelerated. In 1950, the first terminationist Commissioner took office. In 1953, Congress approved House Concurrent Resolution 108. It confirmed termination as official government policy and specified certain tribes and groups from which federal services were to be withdrawn. This was not really a new policy but a return, in effect, to the Dawes program of assimilation and opening up reservation lands to nonwhites.

Between 1954 and 1971, California rancherías, the Poncas of Nebraska, several tribes in Oklahoma, the Klamath tribe and Western Oregon bands of Indians, the Catawbas of South Carolina, the Alabama-Coushattas of Texas, the Southern Paiutes, Uintahs and Ourays of Utah, and the Menominees of Wisconsin were terminated. These groups no longer had trust status with the federal government and were no longer eligible for special services to Indians. Stern (p. 104) describes the 1954 termination of the Klamath Reservation in Oregon.

Another federal policy aimed at hastening assimilation was the relocation program developed in the early 1950s. The Bureau of Indian Affairs offered employment assistance to Indians if they would leave their reservations and relocate in urban communities. Thousands of Indians migrated to Los Angeles, Chicago, Denver, and San Francisco-Oakland and in lesser numbers to other urban centers. Neils (p. 89) examines the development and operation of the Federal Relocation Assistance Program which critics maintain was allied with the forced termination policy.

During the 1960s, there was a historic shift from assimilationist goals and policies, of which termination was a result, toward a policy in which the federal government recognized and respected cultural differences, encouraged self-determination, and financially aided tribes in achieving this goal. In the Kennedy and Johnson administrations, Indian affairs achieved a new place and there was an increasing availability of federal resources to Indian communities, particularly for economic development, housing, and vocational education, health, and revitalizing the arts. President Johnson called for an end to termination and proposed a new goal that stressed self-determination. During the Nixon administration, the goal of self-determination was pursued. Blue Lake was restored to the Taos Pueblo and 21,000 acres to the Yakimas, both significant restorations of land rather than financial awards and important results of the Nixon self-determination policy. In 1971, the Alaska natives were guaranteed title to forty million acres. During the Ford administration, the Havasupais succeeded in their peaceful struggle for trust title to a portion of their ancient homeland along the Grand Canyon's south rim. The 1975 Grand Canyon National Park Enlargement Act authorized the United States to hold in trust for the Havasupai 185,000 acres of the land they have used and occupied for centuries. Also during the Ford administration, one of the most significant pieces of legislation since 1934 was enacted. In 1975, the Indian Self-Determination and Education Assistance Act was enacted. This Act contained language repudiating termination policy, committed the federal government to a continuing relationship with Indians, and obliged it to foster Indian involvement and participation in directing education and service programs. The Act also provided for tribes to contract to administer certain programs such as education. Also in 1975, the Congress enacted legislation that created an American Policy Review Commission to undertake a study of Indian affairs and to make recommendations for revisions in federal policies and programs. In 1977, the Policy Review Commission completed its work and submitted 206 recommendations in the fields of federal Indian trust relations; tribal government; federal, state, and tribal administration of Indian policy; education; health; reservation economic resources; community social services; off-reservation Indians; terminated and nonrecognized Indians; law consolidation, revision, and codification; special problems areas of Alaska, Oklahoma, California, and tribes of the Eastern Seaboard (pp. 80–82).

Currently, some organizations and individuals are marshalling private and public forces to end the federal Indian trust relationship. Costo and Henry (p. 84) examine the center of the struggle for Indian rights in the 1970s in the state of Washington and respond to arguments spelled out in a book that calls for the abrogation of Indian treaties.

There are several standard works that deal with the legal relations of Indians and the federal government. Felix Cohen's *Handbook of Federal Indian Law* and its 1958 revision *Federal Indian Law* (p. 83) are indispensable volumes on the subject. Kappler's *Indian Affairs: Laws and Treaties* (p. 88) provides a record of the relationship between Indians and the U.S. government from 1778 to 1938. He reprints the texts of ratified and unratified treaties from 1778 to 1871, the records of the sale of Indian lands, laws, executive proclamations, and orders, and decisions of the Supreme Court concerning Indian affairs. Washburn (p. 98) provides a legal history of Indian-white relations from the sixteenth through the twentieth centuries. Price (p. 91) surveys the legal context of American Indian history and policy from the nineteenth century to contemporary times, and Rosen (p. 93) surveys the contemporary complexities and contradictions of American Indian law.

AMERICAN INDIAN POLICY REVIEW COMMISSION. *Final Report.* 2 vols. Washington, D.C.: Government Printing Office, 1977. Vol. 1. 624pp. Vol. 2. 923pp. Bibliography.

This final report of the American Indian Policy Review Commission represents two years of intensive investigative work encompassing the entire field of federal-Indian relations. Chapters in the first volume consider the history of United States-Indian relations, contemporary Indian conditions, and distinctive doctrines and concepts of American Indian law. There are 206 recommendations for the following areas of study: federal Indian trust relations; tribal government; federal administration of Indian policy; economic resources of Indian country; community social services; off-reservation Indians; terminated Indians; nonrecognized Indians; special problem areas of Alaska, Oklahoma, California, and the tribes of the Eastern Seaboard; and general problems. This volume concludes with the separate dissenting views of Congressman Lloyd Meeds, vice-chairman of the Commission, the separate views of the Commission chairman, Senator James Abourezk, and five Indian Commissioners. The second volume contains appendixes and an index. The appendixes include an explanation of how the Commission did its work, a bibliography of materials used by the Commission, a format for the proposed annual report on Indian affairs, a discussion of federal programs serving Indians, and comments received on the tentative final draft report.

————. *Final Report. Task Force One on Trust Responsibilities and the Federal-Indian Relationship; Including Treaty Review.* Washington, D.C.: Government Printing Office, 1976. 315pp.

This volume examines the historical and legal basis for the unique relationship between the federal government and the native peoples together with the many interpretations and philosophies of federal trust responsibility including water rights, forestry, tribal government, and the unique difficulties of the Oklahoma tribes. Sections discuss Indian population distributions, tribal land, and economic resources in relation to other populations of the United States and explain the continuing debate among competing interests and influences for controlling the natives' destiny. There is a general history of the origins and application of federal Indian law from its European roots in the 1700s to periods of national expansion. There are brief statements on the general status of current treaty law and problems revolving around application of trust

responsibility. This volume contains proposed recommendations and documents of support. It is based on field studies, hearings, site visits, conferences, and interviews.

————. *Final Report. Task Force Two on Tribal Government.* Washington, D.C.: Government Printing Office, 1976. 365pp.

This volume examines the right of self-government according to the unique cultural and community values of tribes along with the changes in federal law and policy which would improve the quality of tribal relationships with the U.S. government. Chapters discuss the relationship between Indian tribes and the Interior Department, tribes as functioning governments, federal responsibility to provide support for the functions of tribal government, the status of tribal government and federal domestic assistance programs, land consolidation and acquisition, special problems of small tribes, and tribal government accountability. There are proposed recommendations and nineteen supplementary reports covering a full range of problems related to tribal governments. The volume is based on surveys and conferences with all federally recognized tribes.

————. *Final Report. Task Force Three on Federal Administration and Structure of Indian Affairs.* Washington, D.C.: Government Printing Office, 1976. 232pp.

This volume reviews the federal government structure to determine the sources of administering the trust responsibility and looks at past performances including delivery of Indian programs and their effect on self-government and self-determination. Chapters consider federal Indian assistance programs and the delivery of services, the Bureau of Indian Affairs (BIA), and the eligibility of tribes and Indians for federal services. There are proposed recommendations and appendixes including the BIA Management Study, a review of statutes and regulations, and declarations of Native American purposes and sovereignty. The sixty-nine page *Report on Bureau of Indian Affairs Management Practices* reviews the organization's structure, budget, personnel, and management. There are recommendations for changing the BIA structure, management and information systems, and procedures. The volume is based on interviews with tribal governments and joint hearings with other task forces.

———. *Final Report. Task Force Four on Federal, State, and Tribal Jurisdiction.* Washington, D.C.: Government Printing Office, 1976. 258pp.

This volume examines jurisdictional authority and describes the broad legal authority of tribal governments as affected by or specifically removed by Congress. One section examines Public Law 280, its theory and purpose, the current status of implementing it, the Indian and non-Indian perspective in Public Law 280 states, the retrocession movement, and special problem areas regarding recent retrocession experiences, and technical and legal services. The next section looks at the federal role in jurisdiction focusing on the Major Crimes and the General and Assimilative Crimes Acts and the applicability of various federal statutes to Indians. The next section concerns special problem areas including on-reservation and off-reservation aboriginal hunting and fishing rights, child custody, jurisdiction over non-Indians, federal and state taxation of Indians and Indian property, taxation by Indian tribes, land use controls by the federal government, states, tribes, and Oklahoma. The last section looks at tribal jurisdiction over non-Indians and tribal justice systems under the Indian Civil Rights Act. There are proposed recommendations and four supplementary reports on water rights, child welfare, hunting and fishing rights, and a proposal for clarifying the tax status of Indians. The volume is based on the testimony of tribal, state, local, and federal officials, Indians, and non-Indian citizens.

———. *Final Report. Task Force Five: Indian Education.* Washington, D.C.: Government Printing Office, 1976. 382pp.

This volume examines how the education of Indians is disjointed and remote from Indian control. One section looks at the policies and finances affecting Indian education from precolonial times to the 1970s, types of schools educating Indian people, federal appropriations over the years for Indian education, and different federal philosophies governing Indian education over the past thirty years. Other sections concern the U.S. Office of Education and the Bureau of Indian Affairs (BIA), federal agencies involved in Indian education, and state policies and finance. There are special studies on Navajo education, education needs and problems of nonfederally recognized Indians, a survey on primary and secondary education, BIA off-reservation boarding schools, Indian community controlled schools, and higher education. There are proposed recommendations and twenty-six supplementary reports including historical and contemporary financing, enrollment, Indian community-controlled schools, and federal policy. The volume is based on hearings, surveys, conferences, and field studies.

———. *Final Report. Task Force Six on Indian Health.* Washington, D.C.: Government Printing Office, 1976. 264pp.

This volume examines the poor quality of Indian health resulting from insufficient funds, inadequate management, and the absence of an Indian health strategy. Sections deal with the history of federal involvement in health care to Indians, the legal basis of federal health services to Indians, the health status of Indians (nutrition, mental health, and traditional Indian medicine), and the delivery system (the Indian Health Service, contract health care, and community health representatives). The last section deals with special problems such as the health care of urban Oklahoma, California, and Alaska natives and discrimination and civil rights. There are proposed recommendations and four appendixes, the last of which deals with the impact of National Health Insurance on Indian health issues. The volume is based on information from states, the Indian Health Service, public hearings, site visits, and data from questionnaires.

———. *Final Report. Task Force Seven on Reservation and Resource Development and Protection.* Washington, D.C.: Government Printing Office, 1976. 214pp.

This report examines the obstacles to reservation economic development and criticizes federal, state, and local governments for encroaching on and usurping tribal jurisdiction, Indian property and resource rights, and intervening in the tribal development process. One section deals with tribal governments as promoters of economic development; examines the control, use, development, and protection of Indian resources (land, agriculture, livestock, minerals, forests, fishing); and discusses resource protection, Indian capital, and human resources. Other sections deal with federal government policies and programs showing that the Bureau of Indian Affairs, with authority designated by the trust relationship, has not been an advocate of economic development, and that the Economic Development Administration (EDA) has provided planning, technical and management assistance, capital, and infrastructure development with little success. There are proposed recommendations and four supplementary reports on Indian mineral agreements, a case study of the EDA, Indian housing efforts in the United States, and a case study of Project Evaluation. Numerous tables display relevant data.

———. *Final Report. Task Force Eight on Urban and Rural Non-Reservation Indians.* Washington, D.C.: Government Printing Office, 1976. 144pp.

This report examines the unique socioeconomic problems of Indian people who no longer reside on reservations and the functions of Indian centers which have been organized to deal with their difficulties. Sections cover the history of Indian migration to urban or rural areas, the extent of federal trust responsibility to nonreservation Indians, the needs of off-reservation Indians including employment, education, housing, health, legal services, Indian adoption, care for the elderly, alcoholism counseling, transportation, need for facilities, and alternative elective bodies. There are proposed recommendations for seven supplementary reports, including a directory of urban Indian and related groups and organizations, a profile of the urban Indian population and services, an Indian inmate needs assessment, and a California Department of Housing and Community Development statement. The volume is based on site hearings and questionnaires.

―――. *Final Report. Task Force Nine on Law Consolidation, Revision, and Codification.* 2 vols. Washington, D.C.: Government Printing Office, 1976. Vol. 1. 386pp. Vol. 2. 1,044pp.
This report focuses on the laws contained in Title 25, that part of the U.S. code of federal regulations dealing with the Bureau of Indian Affairs (BIA), the Indian Arts and Crafts Board, and the Indian Claims Commission, which are out of date and in conflict with later statutes. The first volume deals with the historical development of the federal statutory and regulatory systems, federal legislation and Indian policy over the past two hundred years, congressional commitment to the permanency of Indian tribes and to the principles of self-determination and self-government. Chapters contain recommendations on revising Title 25 of the U.S. Code that consider the basic principles of the federal trust responsibilities to Indian tribes, federal administration of Indian affairs, the acquisition, consolidation, management, and disposition of Indian lands, natural resources, economic development, financial management of Indian funds by the BIA, descent and distribution, attorney's fees in Indian litigation, jurisdiction and procedure, followed by a section on research memoranda supporting these major recommendations. The last section deals with the BIA manual system, special recommendations on Oklahoma, and other proposed recommendations. Volume two contains appendixes of master charts that do a section-by-section analysis of Title 25, exhibits cited in the Report, cross-reference tables between Code of Federal Regulations provisions and the U.S. Code and Statutes-at-Large, distribution tables on placement of Statutes-at-Large in the U.S. Code, a subject matter breakdown of Title 25, and correspondence. The volumes are based on site visits, intertribal conferences, hearings, and tribal and federal personnel commentary.

―――. *Final Report. Task Force Ten on Terminated and Nonfederally Recognized Indians.* Washington, D.C.: Government Printing Office, 1976. 1,732pp.
This report examines the historical background, status, and needs of terminated and nonfederally recognized Indians, appraises federal programs and census data, tells of the restoration of terminated tribes, and evaluates the question of who is an Indian. There are reviews of federal policy regarding terminated and nonfederally recognized tribes, bands, and groups of Oregon, New England, Long Island, and Arizona. The Commission examines federal policy concerning North Carolina's nonfederally recognized Indian communities, landless tribes of Washington State, and the Tunica Indians of Louisiana. Other sections consider the problem of identifying unrecognized Indians in demographic terms, review the history of termination legislation, cite the advantages of federal recognition, and recount the federal decision in favor of Passamaquoddy recognition. There are recommendations

and a bibliography. The volume is based on hearings and site visits, questionnaires, and a computer analysis of U.S. census tapes.

American Indian Treaty Series. 8 vols. Washington, D.C.: Institute for the Development of Indian Law, 1973–1975.
This series contains treaties and agreements made between the U.S. government and Indian tribes. It is comprised of separate books for the treaties and agreements of the Sioux Nation, the Pacific Northwest, the northern plains, eastern Oklahoma, the Southwest (including western Oklahoma), the Five Civilized Tribes, the Chippewas, and the Great Lakes region. Also included is a chronological list of all the treaties and agreements made by Indian tribes with the United States, including unratified treaties and legal citations.

BARSCH, RUSSEL LAWRENCE, and JAMES YOUNGBLOOD HENDERSON. *The Road: Indian Tribes and Political Liberty.* Berkeley: University of California Press, 1980. 301pp.
See annotation on pages 55, 82.

BEAVER, R. PIERCE. *Church, State and the American Indians: Two and a Half Centuries of Partnership in Missions between Protestant Churches and Government.* St. Louis: Concordia Publishing House, 1966. 230pp. Bibliography.
This book contains an account of the active partnership between Protestant churches and government in the maintenance of missions to natives from 1641, the beginning of missionary work by John Eliot, to about 1890 when the partnership dissolved. The author examines New England Protestant missions, colonial governments, and the belief that native missions were a proper concern of the state. Chapters deal with the early nineteenth-century federal policy of financing missionaries to "civilize and Christianize" natives, conflicts of interest between some missionary forces and government officials over the federal policy of removal in the Northeast and Southeast in the second quarter of the nineteenth century, and President Grant's peace policy including the voluntary Board of Indian Commissioners and missionary societies who were to participate in the peace policy by "civilizing and evangelizing" natives on reservations. Concluding chapters deal with the dissolution of the mission-government partnership as a result of Protestant-Catholic conflicts over native schools; Protestant missionary proassimilation views on federal policy during the Grant and Hayes administrations, and the attitude of churches until the 1950s. The book is chiefly based on religious primary and secondary sources.

BOARD OF INDIAN COMMISSIONERS. *Annual Reports of the Board of Indian Commissioners to the Secretary of the Interior, 1869–1932.* 63 vols. Washington, D.C.: Government Printing Office, 1890–1933.
These annual reports were written by the Board of Indian Commissioners, a group which was selected by the presidents of the United States and

which served without pay. The Board exercised joint control with the Interior Secretary over disbursements of federal funds to "promote civilization" among the Indians. The reports contain information about Indian affairs in all sections of the country, reports of visits made by the Commissioners to Indian reservations, of tribal councils, transcriptions of Indian speeches, letters, financial statements of congressional appropriations, and recommendations for improving the Indian situation.

BROPHY, WILLIAM A. and SOPHIE D. ABERLE. *The Indian: America's Unfinished Business: Report of the Commission on the Rights, Liberties, and Responsibilities of the American Indian.* Norman: University of Oklahoma Press, 1966. 236pp. Illustrated.

This report of investigations conducted by the Commission on the contemporary status of Native Americans deals with those Indians who, primarily through tribal membership, have a constitutional relationship with the federal government. The report, therefore, excludes natives of Alaska and those east of the Mississippi River. The Commission discussed the needs, problems, and politics of Indians with scholars, government officials, and Indians and concluded that assimilation was a worthwhile solution that must be accomplished for Indians. The first chapters give basic information about Indians including their values, attitudes, and legal status, and tell of the role of the Bureau of Indian Affairs (BIA). The report cites landmarks in Indian law, explains tribal governments and their governing powers, discusses current problems in Indian country concerning the administration of justice, and considers the role of courts adjudicating an Indian problem. There is material on present-day reservation economic conditions, future economic development and its costs, the BIA and its purpose and structure, and possible measures for improving its services. The Commission deals with some of the steps needed to raise the present levels of educational achievement among Indian children and to improve the poor health of Indians. The Commission describes the negative effects imposed termination had on the Paiutes, Klamaths, and Menominees in the 1950s, and suggests ways of terminating relations between the federal government and Indian groups in which Indians cooperate. There are tables of trust lands, population, financial assistance statutes relevant to Indians, and infant and death rates. There is one map and there are photographs of contemporary natives and their lifestyles.

CAHN, EDGAR S., ed. *Our Brother's Keeper: The Indian in White America.* Washington, D.C.: Community Center Press, 1970. 206pp. Illustrated. Bibliography.

This is a study of Native Americans in contemporary America and the Bureau of Indian Affairs (BIA), the federal agency which dominates them, as well as a collection of Native American statements that illustrate their historic and present condition. The book begins with anecdotes about the BIA and explanations about its duties, authority, and power

and the reasons that natives defend the agency. The editor looks at education, health, and land, areas in which government policies and practices have eroded native heritage. He argues that federal policy and practice reward Indians who do not assert themselves, who assume a posture of dependency, and who alienate themselves from their land, people, and heritage. Looking at sources of resistance to change including the bureaucratic structure of the BIA, the Bureau's lowly and compromised position within the Interior Department, and the politics of natives versus the politics of resource development, he concludes with a tribute to native cultural beliefs and recounts some better known recommendations made to reform federal policy since 1928. There are photographs of contemporary Indians.

COHEN, FELIX S. *Handbook of Federal Indian Law, with Reference Tables and Index.* Washington, D.C.: Government Printing Office, 1942; reprint ed.: Albuquerque: University of New Mexico Press, 1972. 688pp. Revised ed.: *Federal Indian Law.* Prepared by the Office of the Solicitor, Department of the Interior. Washington, D.C.: Government Printing Office, 1958; reprint ed.: New York: Association on American Indian Affairs and Dobbs Ferry, N.Y.: Oceana Publications, 1966. 1,106pp.

The Handbook of Federal Indian Law and its subsequent revision *Federal Indian Law,* revision of which is underway at the Solicitor's Office, are standard works in Indian legal matters. The first chapters deal with definitions of "Indian," Indian country and title, the scope of federal power including sources of federal power, treaty-making and commerce with Indian tribes, national defense, congressional power over tribal membership, and administrative power over tribal and individual lands and funds. Cohen describes the history of federal Indian legislation from 1789 to 1957 including the history of treaties and Indian agreements from 1532 to 1871. He deals with the development and evolution of the policies of the Bureau of Indian Affairs from 1825 to 1957, and federal services for Indians including education, health, rations, relief and rehabilitation, social security benefits, federal loans, reclamation and irrigation, and legal help. He discusses criminal and civil jurisdiction, Indian trade and liquor laws, the scope of tribal self-government and the legal status of Indian tribes. He explains the scope of state power over Indian affairs; the rights, liberties, and duties of Indians; and spells out in detail the definition and forms of tribal property and the nature of individual rights in tribal and real property and in personalty. Cohen discusses state taxation of tribal and individual Indian lands, personal property and income, state sales and inheritance taxes, and federal and tribal taxation. The concluding chapter deals with the laws of special groups—the Pueblos of New Mexico, Alaska natives, New York Indians, and Oklahoma tribes. The book has a table of cases, and the footnotes throughout are based on cases, treaties, and federal legislation. The University of New Mexico edition has an unannotated bibliography.

COHEN, LUCY KRAMER, ed. *The Legal Conscience: Selected Papers of Felix S. Cohen.* New Haven, Conn.: Yale University Press, 1960; reprint ed.: Hamden, Conn.: Archon, 1970:213–334.

The second part of this book, entitled "The Indians' Quest for Justice," contains nine essays by Felix Cohen on federal Indian policy. The first, "Anthropology and the Problems of Indian Administration," deals with education, problems of administrative areas, economic activities, land tenure, inheritance, health conditions, art, and recreation. The second, "How Long Will Indian Constitutions Last?," concerns the ninety-seven Indian tribes that framed constitutions for self-government between 1935 and 1939, and the third, entitled "The Spanish Origin of Indian Rights in the Law of the United States," shows the basic similarity of principle in the two legal systems. The remaining essays are "Indians as Citizens," "Indian Claims," "Original Indian Title," "Indian Self-Government," "Americanizing the White Man," (explains the impact of Indian cultures on white Americans), and "Indian Wardship: The Twilight of a Myth." The essays are based on federal legislation, judicial opinions, and secondary works.

COSTO, RUPERT, and JEANNETTE HENRY. *Indian Treaties: Two Centuries of Dishonor.* San Francisco: Indian Historian Press, 1977. 242pp. Bibliography.

The authors discuss Indian treaties and the major aspects of contemporary Indian affairs (tribal organization and jurisdiction, economic development, legislation, self-determination, taxation, water and other resource rights) which are affected by issues raised by Indian treaties. They begin with the historic and legal justification for the unique position of tribes since their first contacts with whites, the purposes for which treaties were made, and a brief historical summary of treaty-making with Indians until the method was terminated in 1871. The authors give examples of violations against Indian rights, state discriminatory practices, conflict of interest among agencies in the Interior Department, tribes victimized by corporate interests, and violations of Indian treaties, sovereignty, and land resources. The authors describe congressional attempts in the 1970s to destroy Indian sovereignty by arguing for states' rights in Indian affairs, an issue that began in 1787. They look at the organizations and individuals who are marshalling private and public forces to abrogate Indian treaties, states controlled by corporate powers, and their efforts to end the federal-Indian trust relationship. They tell of the media that misunderstand the Indian-federal government relationship and "Indian renegades" who help states and corporations. The authors examine the center of the struggle for Indian rights in the 1970s in the state of Washington and include excerpts from a book entitled *Indian Treaties: American Nightmare* which calls for the abrogation of Indian treaties and their responses to arguments raised by the book. The authors survey some contemporary representative tribes who hold land in various types of ownership: tribal, allotted, and federal, and summarize economic conditions on reservations. They

explain the American Indian Policy Review Commission's indictments of the Bureau of Indian Affairs, review Indian legislation that has reduced the tribes' capacity for self-government, and cite the mst important Commission recommendations. The authors provide a partial text of the dissent of Lloyd Meeds, the Commission's vice-chairman, and make responses to his ideology which guides opponents of Indian rights. There are appendixes including the text of the Joint Resolution to establish the Commission, a list of its members, a chronology of Indian treaties, 1778–1868, and agreements, 1792–1883, major laws which apply to Indians of all tribes, and a speech supporting Meeds's dissent. There is an unannotated bibliography of books, newspapers, periodicals, federal information sources, organizations, and basic references on Indian affairs.

DELORIA, VINE, JR. *Behind the Trail of Broken Treaties: An Indian Declaration of Independence.* New York: Delacorte, 1974. 263pp.

The author discusses actions brought by American Indians to force the federal government to honor its past treaties, to institute a new treaty relationship with tribes, and to allow a new legal sovereign status to exist as an alternative to present federal policies and programs. He begins with a discussion of different ways the government insured confiscation of Indian lands after the period of treaty-making ended in 1872, particularly the allotment of Indian lands from the late 1880s through the 1950s, the effect of the civil rights movement of the sixties on Indians, and the growing Indian activist movement. He describes the organization of the American Indian Movement (AIM), the planning of the 1972 "Trail of Broken Treaties" caravan and its program of Twenty Points redesigning the status of Indian tribes and the nature of their federal relationship. He discusses in detail the sixth demand that all Indians be governed by treaty relationships. He describes the occupation of the Bureau of Indian Affairs building, gives a brief history of the Oglala Sioux of Pine Ridge Reservation and the 1972 occupation of Wounded Knee on Pine Ridge. The author reviews the basis for the claim to world recognition made by the people at Wounded Knee, summarizes how the settlement of the continent was justified by Europeans with their doctrine of discovery, and how Indian tribes became domestic subjects of the new U.S. government upon its assumption of discovery rights from Great Britain. He argues that the history of Indian treaties and the existence of certain constitutional provisions support the basic theory that Indian tribes are foreign nations with respect to the United States. He discusses the proposal to restore Indian tribes to quasi-international independent status with the United States acting as their protector. He reviews international law and practice regarding concepts of sovereignty which justifies the Indian demand for sovereign status, cites the 1934 Indian Reorganization Act as a far reaching piece of legislation in regard to legal status, and examines Indian claims against the United States. He concludes with a discussion of the pressure for international recognition building up among traditional Indians and the need for the

United States to acknowledge to the world the international status of Indian nations. The book is based on court cases cited throughout the book. See also: Deloria's *Custer Died for Your Sins: An Indian Manifesto* (p. 9).

DIPPIE, BRIAN W. *The Vanishing American: White Attitudes and U.S. Indian Policy.* Middletown, Conn.: Wesleyan University Press, 1982. 464pp. Illustrated. Bibliography.
Dippie provides a history of the ambivalent attitudes of white Americans toward American Indians, centering around the pervasive myth that the Indian was unable to adapt to the aggressive spread of white civilization, and hence doomed to disappear. He traces the twists and turns of U.S. Indian policy and the ideological supports for it, from the early nineteenth century to the Second World War. He explains how the changing moods of pity and of hostility toward the Indians justified at various times white conquest of the tribes, eviction from and seizure of tribal lands, confinement on reservations and paternalistic governmental control of Indian education and mores. There are pictures illustrating the text.

DOWNES, RANDOLPH C. "A Crusade for Indian Reform, 1922–1934." *Mississippi Valley Historical Review* 32, no. 3 (December 1945):331–54.
The author shows how the Wheeler-Howard Act of 1934 was the culmination of over a decade of legislation aimed at stopping Indian landlessness and pauperization resulting from the administration of the allotment system. He looks at the muckraking stage that preceded reform including the 1922–24 fight against the Bursum Pueblo Land Bill which was killed, muckraking journals which set before the public alleged government maladministration in tribe after tribe, and the Meriam Report of 1928. He looks at the pre-New Deal phase of the Indian reform movement around 1929 when education and health programs were emphasized under Commissioner Rhoads until Collier replaced him in 1933. He concludes with the argument that Collier carried on, supplemented, and accelerated what Rhoads had begun which culminated in the enactment of the 1934 Wheeler-Howard Act.

FEY, HAROLD E., and D'ARCY MCNICKLE. *Indians and Other Americans: Two Ways of Life Meet.* New York: Harper & Brothers, 1959: revised ed.: New York: Harper & Row, 1970. 274pp. Illustrated.
The authors discuss the vanishing land base and loss of sovereignty of Indian tribes since their first contacts with Europeans and Americans, explain the opposing philosophies that have governed federal Indian policy, and tell of the organized efforts by Indians since the 1960s to handle their own problems. They begin with the story of the peopling of the Western Hemisphere, explain European-Indian contacts over 400 years and conflicts in traditions of Indians compelled to accept European laws and practices pertaining to land which resulted in a vanishing land base. They discuss the development of U.S. federal Indian policy which

resulted in the Indians' loss of freedom as self-governing communities. They consider the history of the Bureau of Indian Affairs, the government agency responsible for managing Indian affairs, the history and effects of the allotment policy of 1887, the findings and recommendations of the 1928 Meriam survey of the Institute for Government Research regarding the economic and social conditions of Indians, and the adoption of the Indian Reorganization Act and other reform legislation in 1934. The authors consider Indian education policy since the seventeenth century, contemporary education reforms of the federal government, opposition to reform programs in the 1940s and 1950s culminating in the termination policy, and the effects of termination on the Klamath. They discuss the relocation program and administration of Indian affairs in the 1950s, and tell of the Navajo experience in which tribal self-government and property rights have been maintained. They conclude with a discussion of Indians formulating their own action plans in the 1960s for solving their complex problems. There is an appendix of Indian languages and chapter footnotes based on published primary and secondary works.

GALLAHER, RUTH A. "The Indian Agent in the United States Before 1850." *Iowa Journal of History and Politics* 14, no. 1 (January 1916):3–55.
The author deals with the gradual development of a class of public officers whose sole duty was to administer Indian affairs from colonial times to 1850. She gives an account of Indian administration in New York which illustrates the work of agents during the colonial period. She explains the British administration of Indian affairs around 1763 which had centralization of authority represented by the crown superintendent and diffusion of power represented by colonial commissioners and agents. She considers the revolutionary period with its newly organized system of administering Indian affairs by dividing the territory into three departments each supervised by commissioners, the reorganization of Indian affairs in 1786, and Indian agents from 1789 to 1849 who were either frontiersmen, traders, or military officers sent to live among Indians to whom they were assigned by treat provisions. The author considers their duties, especially the work done among the Creeks by Benjamin Hawkins, the chief agent south of the Ohio River, and looks at the number, type, and salary of personnel employed in the Indian agency located within the War Department. She explains how Congress clearly defined the authority of agents and the administration of Indian affairs in an 1832 act by which the office of the Commissioner of Indian Affairs was created and the 1834 law which organized the field service of superintendents, agents, and subagents among Indians. She describes duties of field service officials, their role during the period of westward expansion to persuade Indians to move and to prohibit the use of liquor among them. She concludes by focusing on the establishment of the first government agency, the Sac and Fox, within present-day Iowa, describes its employees and agency life, and tells of the trans-

fer of the Indian office to the Interior Department in 1849. There are some dated language and opinions. There are footnotes based on published primary and secondary works.

————. "The Indian Agent in the United States since 1850." *Iowa Journal of History and Politics* 14, no. 2 (April 1916):173–238.

The author deals with agents who lived among Indians from 1850 to the early 1900s. She considers the increase in the number of agents from 1850 to 1871 due to Indians being forced onto reservations which enlarged the size of agencies and the amount of money and goods which agents had to handle and which increased the political spoils. She describes the character of agents drawn to the Indian service, their duties, their methods, and agency life in the 1860s, and considers the corruption and conflict between civilian agents and army officers over control of the reservations. She tells of reforms in the 1870s which involved substituting religious control for political influence and eliminating superintendencies. She looks at agents during this period of attempted reform, their salaries, the growth in the complexity of administering affairs on reservations, reasons for reducing the number of agents, and the criticisms leveled at them. She describes the dissatisfaction with civilian agents after 1892 under the political spoils system, a time when the government emphasized education, and agents became teachers. She looks at the duties of agents in connection with the allotment of reservations and the elimination of ration distribution and the pass system. She concludes with a summary of the history of the work of Indian agents divided into six periods: the colonial history of English settlements, the Revolutionary War and years under the Articles of Confederation, 1789–1849, 1849–70, 1870–92, and 1892 until the early 1900s. The footnotes are based on published primary and secondary works. Ruth A. Gallaher also wrote "Indian Agents in Iowa: I. Agents Among the Sacs and Foxes." *Iowa Journal of History and Politics* 14, no. 3. (July 1916):348–94, and "Indian Agents in Iowa: II. Agents at the Winnebago, St. Peter's, Council Bluffs, and Tama Agencies." *Iowa Journal of History and Politics* 14, no. 4. (October 1916):559–96.

GATES, PAUL W. "Indian Allotments Preceding the Dawes Act." In *The Frontier Challenge: Responses to the Trans-Mississippi West,* edited by John G. Clark, pp. 141–67. Lawrence: University Press of Kansas, 1971.

The author considers the policy of wresting land from Indians through allotments which began in 1805, long before the Dawes Act of 1887 was passed. He discusses several examples of allotment policies appearing in treaties by 1805 with the southeastern Cherokees, Creeks, Choctaws, and Chickasaws and explains how the bulk of allotments passed out of Indian hands into those of whites exploiting them. He examines individual reserves and allotments north of the Ohio River, which first appears in Indian treaties in 1817, and explains that traders were persuaded to support cessions of Indian land and the removal of Indians

because individual reserves offered chiefs and headmen a means to pay off their debts to traders. He describes how allotment of Indian lands in severalty became a regular feature of treaties with tribes in Kansas and Nebraska Territories and other areas after 1854 until 1887, and how government officials emphasized allotments as a means of Indians becoming farmers and ending tribal ownership. He concludes with a brief mention of the 1887 Dawes Act. The article is based largely on government documents cited in notes.

HARMON, GEORGE DEWEY. *Sixty Years of Indian Affairs: Political, Economic, and Diplomatic 1789–1850.* Chapel Hill: University of North Carolina, 1941. 428pp. Bibliography.

This book examines the economic, political, and diplomatic aspects of federal native policy between 1789 and 1850, focusing on the Northeast, Southeast, and Plains areas. Part 1, which summarizes native policy before 1780, deals with the federal policy of persuasion and negotiation between 1789 and 1825 in dealing with the Iroquois of New York and other Indian nations of the Northeast and Southeast. The author explains the nature of native title to the soil and surveys federal educational and economic policies, especially trading houses which existed from 1795 to 1822. Part 2 is concerned with the federal policy of force and removal between 1825 and 1850. The author describes the Indian Bureau's reorganization, Cherokee removal, and federal economic policy concerning natives in the North, South, and Plains areas. Part 3 deals with the federal government's administration of trust funds and education programs for natives and summarizes federal native land policy of securing cessions by treaties between 1789 and 1850. Seven tables illustrate the expenditures of the Indian Trade Department, education programs, and compensation for lands taken. The book is based on unpublished and published primary and secondary books and articles, laws and treaties, and state and local histories.

HILL, EDWARD E. *The Office of Indian Affairs, 1824–1880: Historical Sketches.* New York: Clearwater Publishing, 1974. 246pp.

This volume contains brief historical sketches of field units of the Office of Indian Affairs from 1824 to 1880. The sketches were originally prepared to enable researchers to locate general correspondence received from superintendents, agents, and other field officials that are reproduced in Microcopy 234, *Letters Received by the Office of Indian Affairs, 1824–1880,* a microfilm publication of the National Archives and Records Service. The sketches provide brief histories of the major field units (superintendencies, agencies, and subagencies) of the Office of Indian Affairs including the dates of their establishment and discontinuance, tribal and geographical areas of responsibility, locations of headquarters, related units, names and dates of the appointment of superintendents and agents, and suggestions for locations of other records of specific tribes. There is an introduction that discusses two principal types of field jurisdiction, superintendencies and agencies, the content of the files and filing system reproduced in Microcopy 234, and the arrangement of letters within each subject heading. There is an index that lists tribes and more important bands under the supervision of the Office of Indian Affairs and a jurisdictional index that lists the names and dates of Indian superintendencies and agencies and the file headings under which correspondence concerning them may be found in Microcopy 234.

————, comp. *Preliminary Inventory of the Records of the Bureau of Indian Affairs*. Vols. 1 and 2, no. 163. Washington, D.C.: National Archives and Records Service, 1965. 459pp.
The records described in this inventory are those of the Bureau of Indian Affairs (BIA) in the National Archives as of March 31, 1965, designated as Record Group 75. Included in the first volume are records of the Secretary of War relating to Indian affairs between 1800 and 1824 that were separated from War Office records and transferred to the Bureau, records of the Indian Trade Office, general records of the Bureau, those relating to Indian removal, land division, land sales and leases, claims, enrollment, and records of most of the divisions of the Bureau that existed before 1940. In addition, the compiler discusses the history, development, and organization of the BIA and the functions of different divisions and related records in other record groups. The second volume contains field office records of superintendencies and agencies, nonreservation schools, cartographic materials maintained separately from textual records, and records of the Board of Indian Commissioners and the Indian Arts and Crafts Board units closely connected with the Bureau.

HORSMAN, REGINALD. *Expansion and American Indian Policy, 1783–1812*. East Lansing: Michigan State University Press, 1967. 209pp. Bibliography.
The author traces the attempts of the new federal government to formulate a coherent Indian policy between the end of the American Revolution and the War of 1812 that balanced the increasing population's desire for territorial expansion with the fair treatment of Indians. He begins by describing the Confederation Government's attempted policy of confiscating Indian lands and ignoring Indian rights and tells why this policy failed. He discusses how the United States began to change its policy to the British after 1786 through the 1790s, as well as the colonial practice of acknowledging Indian rights of soil which had to be purchased by the United States in formal treaties and how this policy of forced purchase failed because it ignored the desires of states, settlers, and Indians. He considers a series of trade and intercourse acts that were passed to regulate the American frontier advance in the North and South. The author explains in detail how Jefferson obtained large tracts of land from Indians both north and south of the Ohio River by 1809, how he attempted to combine an expansionist land policy with a program of "civilizing" Indians, meeting with little success in the North but more success in the South, particularly

among the Cherokees. He also explains the growth of Indian resistance in the North and South by the end of Jefferson's presidency and why many Indians of the Old Northwest became pro-British in the War of 1812. The bibliography lists unpublished and published primary and secondary works.

Indian Claims Commission Series: The Library of American Indian Affairs. New York: Clearwater Publishing, 1973.
The Indian Claims Commission (ICC) was created by an act of Congress in 1946 to adjudicate claims against the U.S. government made by tribes or groups of Indians living within the United States. In the course of the litigation, hundreds of thousands of pages of documents have been created, many of which have anthropological and historical research value. Five collections have been published in microfiche containing nearly all of the historically relevant materials generated by the litigation. The first collection consists of the Commission's findings of fact, opinions, orders, and final awards. The decisions are issued in paper form chronologically and in sequentially numbered volumes. The second set consists of written reports prepared by experts from many fields and submitted as testimony by plaintiffs and by the Justice Department. The third set consists of transcripts of oral expert testimony, and the fourth contains briefs, concise statements of the main legal points, the claimants' original petitions, and the answers by the defendant, along with subsequent submissions. The original papers and subsequent briefs outline the key issues in each case and the crux of the arguments around those issues. This category also includes proposed findings and exhibit digests of both sides. The last collection includes the General Accounting Office reports prepared for the Court of Claims which provides an accounting of the government's disbursements to the tribes under a treaty that has been the basis of a claim before the Commission. Clearwater has also published a booklet entitled *Ethnogeographical Guide to the Indian Claims Commission* which serves as a brief introduction to the literature of the Commission and divides the United States into nine geographical regions listing the Indian tribes within each region.

JOHNSON, STEVEN L. *Guide to American Indian Documents in the Congressional Serial Set: 1817–1899*. New York: Clearwater Publishing, 1977. 503pp.
This volume contains a chronological list of documents from the Congressional Serial Set dealing primarily with Indian-U.S. government relations prior to 1900. Since Indian-federal government relations were chiefly legal and fiscal, the documents mainly relate to the Indians' legal rights and the cost to the government of Indian administration. The largest categories of documents are concerned with claims prosecuted against the government for losses caused by "Indian" depredations and for service in Indian wars. The author begins by discussing the major categories of congressional publications: anything published under the authority of

the whole Congress, of either house, or of any committee of either house. He is concerned with one of the major classes of congressional publications, documents or reports which were ordered to be printed by the fifteenth through the fifty-fifth Congress, or between December 1, 1817 and March 3, 1899. He deals with documents and reports received by the congresses from the executive department, congressional committees, and other sources rather than with the legislative process (debates) or with the products of that process (laws, resolutions). He explains the classification system and indexes for naming the documents and reports published in the Serial Set, and discusses the use of the guide to the chronological section of 10,649 documents concerning Indians, contents of which are briefly described. There are subject indexes of tribes, events, and regions and three appendixes that list other sets of American Indian documents not published in the Serial Set.

KAPPLER, CHARLES J., comp. and ed. *Indian Affairs: Laws and Treaties.* 5 vols. Washington, D.C.: Government Printing Office, 1904–1941; reprint eds., 5 vols.: New York: AMS Press, 1977 and Washington, D.C.: Government Printing Office. Vol. 2: *Indian Treaties, 1778–1883.* New York: Interland Publishing, 1975. 1,110pp. Illustrated.

These five volumes provide a record of the relationships from 1778 to 1938 between Indians and the federal government. They include Indian treaties from 1778 to 1871, when the last one was entered into, the records of the sale of Indian lands, U.S. presidential proclamations, statistics of Indian agencies and tribes, miscellaneous letters and documents relating to executive orders establishing reservations, and decisions of the Supreme Court relating to Indian affairs. The first volume of laws, executive orders, and proclamations relate to Indians from 1871 to 1902. The second volume contains the complete text of every ratified and unratified treaty and agreement made between the U.S. government and Indians, beginning with the Delawares in 1778 until 1883. (Interland's reprint provides annotations, exact dates, locations, and names of signers on both sides for each treaty and a map.) The third volume contains laws annotated with citations and opinions whenever they were found to have been subject to adjudication or other actions until 1913. The fourth volume contains laws, the texts of unratified treaties, and discussions of Indian legal matters such as the power of Congress, federal jurisdiction, citizenship, and Indian rights to land. There is a reprint of Title 25 (Indians) of the United States Code. The fifth volume of laws updates the compilation through 1938. Each volume is indexed.

KVASNICKA, ROBERT M., and HERMAN J. VIOLA. *The Commissioners of Indian Affairs, 1824–1977.* Lincoln: University of Nebraska Press, 1979. 350pp. Bibliography.

This volume contains biographical sketches of forty-three men who served as Indian Commissioners from 1824, when Thomas L. McKenney was appointed, to 1977 when the office was superceded by that of Assistant Secretary of the Interior for Indian Affairs. The Commissioners of Indian Affairs figured in the formulation of policy, negotiation of treaties, adjudication of claims, and other matters that involved the federal government and its relations with Indians. The sketches emphasize their careers as Commissioners, the policies and procedures they favored, their relations with Congress and the president, the achievements and failures of their administrations, and important events during their terms of office. Each sketch is followed by a bibliographical essay describing the important sources relating to the Commissioner in question. The final chapter discusses major primary and secondary sources used in compiling the sketches. There is a list of annual reports of the Commissioners in the Congressional Serial Set. The biographies are based on annual reports of the Commissioners and other documents in the National Archives.

LEVITAN, SAR A., and BARBARA HETRICK. *Big Brother's Indian Programs with Reservations.* New York: McGraw-Hill, 1971. 228pp. Illustrated.

The authors analyze and appraise contemporary federal assistance programs designed to raise the standard of living of Indians on or near reservations and of Alaskan natives under federal jurisdiction. The first chapter considers official and Indian definitions of "Indian," demographic and socioeconomic characteristics, and the legal status of Indians. The authors begin by discussing educational programs which utilize nearly a third of the total funds allocated to Indians on reservations, then consider reservation medical care, community organization, welfare assistance and services, tribal trust funds and follow with a review and analysis of efforts to develop natural, economic, and human resources. The final chapter indicates a direction that federally supported Indian programs might take in the future. Each chapter contains notes based on government documents and secondary works. There are photographs of contemporary Indians and thirty-four tables of data.

———, and WILLIAM B. JOHNSTON. *Indian Giving: Federal Programs for Native Americans.* Baltimore: Johns Hopkins University Press, 1975. 83pp. Illustrated.

This book contains a general study of American Indians on and off reservations in contemporary times and looks at federal programs designed to improve the Indians' conditions. The authors begin with Indian population figures, discuss Indian migrations from reservation to cities, and tell of attempts of urban Indians to adjust to life off reservations, and explain Indians' legal and political status. They consider economic problems of reservation Indians, federal economic development programs designed to alleviate these problems, education levels and performance of Indians, the Indian school system, community control, and federal educational programs. The authors look at Indian health problems, federal health care programs, Indian family problems, and the Indian Health Service. They tell of federal programs that fund indigent families, and describe housing and police protection programs, as well as the development of tribal governments, the establishment of community organizations, and the existence of a federal bureaucracy that manages Indian tribal assets and lands. They conclude with a brief overview of the "Indian question" and suggest directions federal policy might take. There are eighteen tables and nine charts that illustrate the text and chapter footnotes based chiefly on government reports and hearings.

MARDOCK, ROBERT WINSTON. *The Reformers and the American Indian.* Columbia: University of Missouri Press, 1971. 245pp. Bibliography.

This book contains a study of the people who wanted to reform Native American policy with a program based on education, Christianity, and civilization during the post-Civil War years through the 1880s. The author discusses some of the antislavery humanitarians who turned their attention to natives in the 1840s and 1850s, describes the beliefs and objectives of individuals and organizations interested in a Native peace policy and its inauguration under the Grant administration, and explains how the 1873 Modoc War and 1876 Custer catastrophe jeopardized the policy. Chapters consider the reformers' criticisms of the administration's peace policy in the mid-1870s, the conflict between the Army and the antimilitarist reformers over control of the policy, explains the native policy of the Hayes administration in which church participation was gradually eliminated, and explores the unsuccessful political efforts to transfer the Indian Bureau to the War Department. The author explains Ponca resistance to the federal government's removal and reservation policies and the Ute uprising which aroused widespread support for a second wave of native reform that began in 1879. The concluding chapter discusses government and reform efforts to apportion native lands to tribal members, an idea promoted since the early nineteenth century which culminated in the 1887 Dawes Severalty Act.

MOHR, WALTER H. *Federal Indian Relations, 1774–1788.* Philadelphia: University of Pennsylvania Press, 1933. 247pp. Illustrated. Bibliography.

The author traces the attempts of Congress under the Articles of Confederation to evolve a federal system for the management of Indian affairs. He begins with a general view of tribes during the final period of imperial control and shows how the British machinery for managing Indian affairs ceased to function, and notes the early steps taken by the new government based on imperial precedent in centralizing control of Indian affairs in the hands of two superintendents. He describes Indians as a factor in the Revolutionary War noting the American failure to secure Indians as allies, evaluates the military importance of Indian auxiliaries, and tells of the congressional machinery of treaties as a means of controlling Indians. He describes problems of negotiating with northern Indians and their resistance to giving up land in several treaties. He tells of problems encountered with southern Indians involving state-federal conflicts over control of Indian affairs, southern state con-

flicts with Indians, and Spanish influence in southern Indian affairs. The author concludes with a discussion of how the early Indian policy of the central government was challenged by the states and explains the attempts of Congress to develop and regulate Indian trade in the North and South and finance its Indian program. There is some dated language. There is one map and an unannotated bibliography of unpublished and published primary and secondary works.

THE NATIONAL ARCHIVES. *List of Documents Concerning Negotiations of Ratified Indian Treaties, 1801–1869.* Special List no. 6. Washington, D.C.: National Archives, 1949; reprint ed.: Millwood, N.Y.: Kraus Reprint Co., 1975. 175pp.

This work is a select list of documentary materials concerning the negotiations of 374 ratified treaties that are in the records of the Bureau of Indian Affairs and in the Office of the Secretary of Interior. These materials throw light on the policies and purposes of the people who negotiated these treaties. There are three types of documentation that exist in these records: instructions issued to treaty commissioners, records of treaty council proceedings, and correspondence concerning the treaty during and immediately after the negotiation period up to the time of its transmittal to the president for submission to the Senate. This list begins with those documents concerning the 1801 treaty with the Chickasaws and ends with those concerning the 1868 treaty with the Nez Percés. Documents for each treaty are listed chronologically. The list does not include documents pertaining to unratified treaties or other agreements with Indian tribes or bands. Treaties earlier than 1801 are not included as no documents of importance concerning their negotiation have been uncovered among the records searched in preparing this list. There is an appendix that lists officials concerned with negotiating Indian treaties including the U.S. Commissioners of Indian Affairs and Secretaries of the War and Interior.

NEILS, ELAINE M. "Federal Relocation Assistance Program." In *Reservation to City: Indian Migration and Federal Relocation.* University of Chicago Department of Geography Research Paper no. 131, pp. 46–67. Chicago: University of Chicago Department of Geography, 1971. Illustrated. Bibliography.

The author examines the development and operation of the Federal Relocation Assistance Program which began in 1952. She begins with a discussion of the conflicting forces in Indian affairs and national politics that converged in the early 1950s to produce the relocation program including the effects of World War II, postwar years of hunger among Indians, and termination policy. She discusses the choice of the government to relocate surplus population away from reservations as a way to ameliorate the desperate economic situation of tribes rather than to develop the reservations, and recounts the various criticisms of the policy. The author tells of the program's orientation toward permanent urban relocation with stress placed on its voluntary aspect as a major concession to criticisms of its original alliance with forced termination. She describes how the process of "dropping" Indians into big cities has ironically drawn the federal government into a network of personal relationships with Indians. She discusses the evolution of the operation of the relocation program from employment offices established in the 1950s in Denver, Salt Lake City, and Los Angeles to serve Navajo applicants, to the Bureau's expansion of services in the 1960s for relocatees from all reservations with the stress still on permanent urban relocation. There are tables of Menominees relocating from 1952 to 1961 and one that shows the place of the Relocation Assistance Program within the total bureau operations. There is a bibliography of published government and secondary works and papers.

NICHOLS, DAVID A. *Lincoln and the Indians: Civil War Policy and Politics.* Columbia: University of Missouri Press, 1978. 223pp. Bibliography.

The author discusses President Lincoln's Indian policies from 1861 to 1864. He begins with a discussion of the Office of Indian Affairs, arguing it was a corrupt and powerful political machine, and discusses the situation of the Five Civilized Tribes in Indian Territory, some of whom willingly joined the Confederacy but many of whom were driven to the Old South because Lincoln failed to exploit any military advantage in Indian Territory early in the Civil War. He describes Lincoln's indecision to utilize troops in an aborted southern expedition designed to repossess Indian Territory and return destitute Indian refugees living in Kansas to Indian Territory. He argues that Indian refugees in Kansas were subject to Lincoln's policy of exploiting them as pawns in the struggle with the South and that Lincoln exploited Indian troops to aid the Union military effort rather than allowing them to defend their homes. The author discusses the corruption in the Minnesota Indian system which led to the 1862 Sioux uprising against whites. He analyzes Lincoln's refusal to execute more than 300 Indian prisoners by bargaining with Minnesotans for the removal from Minnesota of tribes, including innocent Winnebagos, and for the payment of depredation claims. He describes the incessant arguments of reformers like Bishop Whipple who pushed for reform of the Indian system in 1862 and 1863, and Lincoln's endorsement of the reform movement and the reasons for its failure. He looks at Lincoln's plan to concentrate Indian tribes in an area which merged with militarism, and the fiascos in New Mexico and Colorado where military brutality produced tragedy. He concludes by discussing the attitudes Lincolnians held about Indians as savages and by explaining that the Lincoln era was a time when the seeds of reform were sown. The book is based on unpublished and published primary and secondary sources.

OTIS, D. S. "History of the Allotment Policy." In *Readjustment of Indian Affairs. Hearings before the House Committee on Indian Affairs, on H. R. 7902,* 73rd Congress, 2nd session, 1934. Part 9,

pp. 428–89; reprint ed.: *The Dawes Act and the Allotment of Indian Lands.* Edited and with an Introduction by Francis Paul Prucha. Norman: University of Oklahoma Press, 1973. 197pp.

The author presents a study of the Dawes Act of 1887 and its impact upon Indian societies and cultures. He explains the motives of the advocates of the allotment policy and studies the ways in which the legislation functioned in the crucial early years after its enactment. He shows how the allotment policy fitted well into the dominant views of the age of individualism by considering the policy of Indian education as it worked throughout the allotment period and which furthered Indian subjection. He studies how provisions in the Act for leasing land caused Indians to circumvent responsibilities of private ownership and enabled white settlers and promoters to exploit Indian lands. He concludes with an investigation of the effects of the Dawes Act up to 1900 and shows why the policy failed to fulfill the hopes of its sponsors. In the introduction, Prucha discusses a few corrections he has made in the original 1934 text, explains the policy of allotment, Otis's life, and considers other books dealing with the Dawes Act. The Otis text is based on government reports and debates and reform materials cited in notes.

PEAKE, ORA BROOKS. *A History of the United States Indian Factory System, 1795–1822.* Denver: Sage Books, 1954. 340pp. Illustrated. Bibliography.

This book contains a study of the U.S. Indian factory system, one of the earliest efforts on the part of the federal government to conduct a business in competition with private industry, the purpose of which was to help natives secure goods at their actual cost and restrain them from warfare. Chapters examine the organization of the factory system created by an act of Congress in 1795; the establishment of the trade factories from the first at Colerain, Georgia, in 1795 to the last one established at St. Peter, Minnesota, in 1821; describes the factory buildings and furniture; the agents employed and merchandise they purchased for the factories; transportation of merchandise by boats or wagons; merchandise sold; gifts and annuities distributed to natives at the factories; and the products purchased from natives. The author details the heavy losses suffered by the factory system as a result of the War of 1812, the educational and religious work of the Indian Trade Office, and contemporary criticism of the factory system by Indian agents and representatives of private fur companies. The concluding chapter gives the reasons for the economic failure of the system which was closed down by congressional action. There are thirty-one appendixes illustrating the text, a map showing the location of the factories, and facsimiles of several National Archive records. The book is based on manuscript material in the National Archives, published works, atlases, and maps.

PHILP, KENNETH R. *John Collier's Crusade for Indian Reform.* Tucson: University of Arizona Press, 1977. 304pp. Illustrated. Bibliography.

The author gives an account of John Collier's

philosophy and program, tells of the tensions that existed between him and assimilationists, and analyzes government Indian policy from the 1920s through the 1940s. He begins with Collier's trip to Taos Pueblo in 1920 which began his crusade to protect tribal institutions and property rights, and discusses how he helped Pueblo Indians organize opposition to legislation that threatened their Spanish land grants. He explains how Collier discredited the government's attempts to suppress Indian dances and Indian religious freedom, how he insisted on Indians receiving royalties from water power sites and mineral lands, and how he acted on behalf of Indians while associated with the American Indian Defense Association during the 1920s. He describes Herbert Hoover's administration which was committed to humanitarian programs but which was unable to alter Indian affairs, Franklin D. Roosevelt's appointment of Collier as Indian Commissioner in 1933, and the beginning of the New Deal relief and recovery programs. He discusses the negative reactions of assimilationist Indians and white groups when the Wheeler-Howard Bill was drawn up and describes the Indian Reorganization Act of 1934, a compromise measure which failed to incorporate all of Collier's reforms. He explains how the IRA was based on the concept of cultural pluralism, ended land allotment, and enabled some tribes to secure a measure of political and economic control over their own futures. He describes how several tribes established viable self-governments but indicates how the IRA was flawed in that it imposed rigid political and economic ideas on tribes that varied in their cultural orientation. He argues that hostility in Congress and misunderstanding of Indian needs in the white community hampered the reform program. He discusses Navajo resistance to Collier's policies and problems with Pueblos who were only mildly interested in the IRA. He explains Collier's administrative shortcomings, his flawed assumptions about Indians, the negative impact of World War II on Collier's reforms, and his resignation in 1945. The author discusses how Collier continued to work for the preservation of preindustrial cultures throughout the world and how he opposed termination, and summarizes his achievements and shortcomings. There are photographs of Collier and other influential people of the era, and also of Taos. There is a bibliographical essay of unpublished and published primary and secondary materials.

PRICE, MONROE E. *Law and the American Indian: Readings, Notes, and Cases.* Indianapolis: Bobbs-Merrill, 1973. 807pp. Bibliography.
This book surveys the legal context of American Indian history and policy from the nineteenth century to contemporary times. The author provides a detailed analysis of jurisdictional problems including the power of tribes to tax, jurisdiction of tribes over non-Indians, and commercial transactions. He surveys the expansion of tribal sovereignty, including an assessment of current efforts to provide more power to tribes; traces the history of efforts by the federal and state governments to weaken and destroy tribal governments, looking at various tech-

niques to accomplish this goal. He examines the conflict between states and tribes to control activities on reservations, including a comprehensive study of Public Law 280, the surrender of civil jurisdiction over Indian country from the federal government to the states. The book contains an up-to-date catalog and analysis of the cases interpreting the Indian Bill of Rights, the Civil Rights Act of 1968, and a lengthy study of concepts of property rights, including a discussion of treaty rights, original title, and trust responsibility. Concluding chapters deal with the manner in which the U.S. legal framework weakens, alters, undermines, or strengthens tribal governments by looking at government control of education, subsistence, judicial process, the vote, and the religious beliefs of tribal members. The book contains references to more than 600 cases relating to Indian legal problems and contains a bibliography and law review articles on eighteen selected subjects such as civil and constitutional rights, taxation, and fishing and hunting rights.

PRIEST, LORING BENSON. *Uncle Sam's Stepchildren: The Reformation of United States Indian Policy, 1865–1887.* New Brunswick, N.J.: Rutgers University Press, 1942; reprint ed.: Lincoln: University of Nebraska Press, 1975. 310pp.
This study concerns the changes in American Indian policy between the close of the Civil War and the passage of the Dawes Severalty Act of 1887. The author begins by describing four unsuccessful attempts at reform. The first involved government efforts to concentrate and confine Indian settlement to the Sioux Reservation north of Nebraska and to Indian Territory south of Kansas and the opposition to this plan. The second involved unsuccessful efforts to transfer authority over Indians from the Interior Department to the War Department. The third involved church nominations of Indian officials, interdenominational rivalry, Catholic opposition, and the failure of the policy by 1880. The fourth concerned the appointment of a Board of Indian Commissioners in 1869 to give advice and opposition to it by other government agencies and Congress. The author looks at the reasons for the rise of public interest in Indian reform, individual efforts between 1865 and 1880, and the rise of effective Indian organizations after 1880. He looks at the policies the reformers condemned including the treaty system, tribal autonomy, the annuity, and the reservation systems. He explains the reformers' view of assimilation through education as a solution to the "Indian problem" and tells of the opposition to reforms by supporters who benefited from existing Indian policies. He concludes with a discussion of Canada's Indian policy, the failure of early severalty plans, severalty debates of the 1880s, and Senator Dawes's views. He briefly examines three controversial Indian problems, their legal status, provisions for Indian land distribution, and the question of forcing allotment upon tribes and looks at the ways they were resolved when the Dawes Act was passed in 1887. There are footnotes based chiefly on unpublished and published govern-

ment documents, Board of Indian Commissioners materials, and other primary sources.

————, ed. *New American State Papers: Indian Affairs*. 13 vols. Wilmington, Del.: Scholarly Resources, 1973.

This is one of twelve subject sets covering the major areas of government activity from 1789 to 1860. Each subject set consists of documents drawn from the original American State Papers, the Congressional Serial Set, the National Archives and the Library of Congress. The documents included are arranged chronologically through each subject. An introduction to each subject discusses the documents and their relationship to the subject area. Each volume contains a list of the documents contained in it. The documents in Indian Affairs are arranged in four areas: General, Indians of the Northwest, Indians of the Southeast, and Indians of the Plains. General materials include documents on Indian land cessions, Indian trade and the trading house system, statistical information on trust funds, schools, and Indian education, and all the annual reports of the Commissioner of Indian Affairs from 1825 to 1860 which contain personal accounts of Indian life. The volumes on Indians of the Northwest include documents on the tribes of New York and the Shawnees, Potawatomis, Winnebagos, Chippewas, Sacs, and Foxes among others. Volumes on Indians of the Southeast include documents on the Cherokees, Chickasaws, Choctaws, Creeks, and Seminoles. Many of the documents cover the great Indian removal crisis of the 1820s and the 1830s. The Plains volume includes materials on early contacts between the government and those tribes which figured more prominently in pre-Civil War years such as the Sioux, Comanches, and Pawnees among others.

PRUCHA, FRANCIS PAUL. *American Indian Policy in Crisis: Christian Reformers and the Indian, 1865–1900*. Norman: University of Oklahoma Press, 1976. 456pp. Illustrated. Bibliography.

This book tells the history of federal native policy in the last third of the nineteenth century by focusing on a group of humanitarians and their government friends who wanted to reform native affairs by Christianizing the natives and assimilating them into American society. The author describes the beginnings of reform, defines President Grant's peace policy and its two structural components: the Board of Indian Commissioners and the apportionment of Indian agencies among church groups. Chapters discuss the threat to the civil peace program by advocates of the military management of native affairs and tell of the development of reservation policy to concentrate natives on a few reserves to segregate them from whites. Prucha describes the new Christian reformers, their organizations and beliefs, and native policy reform from 1880 to 1900 considering the reformers' views of reservations, agents, and native police and courts as instruments of civilization. He considers their subsequent efforts to allot reservation lands in severalty and assimilate natives through schools. Concluding chapters discuss the reformers' desire to improve the quality of In-

dian agents and their successful liquidation of Indian Territory coveted by farmers. There are four maps and photographs of Indians and reformers. The book is based chiefly on government sources.

A selection of the writings of these reformers dealing with native policy reform, land in severalty, law, and education can be found in Francis Paul Prucha, ed., *Americanizing the American Indians: Writings by the Friends of the Indian, 1880–1900*. Cambridge, Mass.: Harvard University Press, 1973. 358pp. Bibliography.

————. *American Indian Policy in the Formative Years: The Indian Trade and Intercourse Acts, 1790–1834*. Cambridge, Mass.: Harvard University Press, 1962. 303pp. Bibliography.

The author traces the history of the formative period of federal Indian policy from 1790 to 1834 that was expressed in treaties and in a series of laws, the Indian Intercourse Acts, the first of which was passed in 1790 and the last in 1834. He considers the hostility of frontier people who tried to hamper enforcement of federal laws, describes briefly colonial and imperial Indian policies, and those of the Continental Congress and the early years of the Constitution. He discusses the passage of the Trade and Intercourse Acts of 1790, 1793, 1796, 1799, and 1802 which became the basic law governing Indian relations and which also sought to restrain lawless frontier whites from violating treaties made with Indians until these acts were replaced by a new codification of Indian policy in 1834. He discusses the Indian Department, personnel within the War Department appointed to deal with Indians and enforce the Intercourse Acts, the creation of the Bureau of Indian Affairs within the War Department in 1824, and the establishment of a definitive organization in 1834. He looks at fur trade regulations, an essential element in federal Indian policy, the origin of the factory system in 1796, its purpose, the failure of the trading houses, and the problems of enforcing laws to prevent the use of liquor by traders among Indians. He examines the problems of removing intruders from Indian lands, particularly the settlers' lawless encroachment on Cherokee lands in Tennessee and other areas, provisions in Indian Intercourse Acts for regularizing criminal court procedures in cases arising between natives and white citizens, and tells of the lack of punishment of whites who committed crimes against Indians. The author discusses federal programs of "civilizing" Indians by promoting agricultural pursuits, educating children, and removing Indians beyond contact with whites to a permanent reservation west of the Mississippi, focusing on the Cherokees and their removal from Georgia. He concludes with chapters on the 1834 legislation which included a reorganization of the Indian Department, a new Trade and Intercourse Act, and a proposed organization of a western territory to provide a government for Indians who emigrated west. There is a bibliographical essay discussing the principal sources upon which the study is based grouped into sections including archival materials, federal and territorial papers, congressional and presidential documents, federal and state materials, colonial and imperial Indian policy, the Continental Congress, the Constitution, Indian Department, Indian trade, education and civilization, removal, and the laws of 1834.

————. *Documents of United States Indian Policy.* Lincoln: University of Nebraska Press, 1975. 278pp. Bibliography.

This compilation makes available the essential laws and official and quasi-official statements on federal Indian policy from George Washington's recommendations of 1783 to the Menominee Restoration Act of 1973. Included in the 161 selections arranged chronologically are treaties which illustrate important policies, fundamental laws governing Indian relations, key Supreme Court decisions, messages of presidents of the United States, extracts from the reports of the Commissioner of Indian Affairs and the Secretary of the Interior, reports of special commissions and investigating committees, and recent proposals for Indian self-determination. Brief headnotes explain each document. These documents mark significant formulations of policy in the conduct of Indian affairs by the federal government which, by legislative enactment, administrative decree, or judicial decision, were the vehicles for changes in the course of events, or they indicate fundamental reactions to such policies or actions. There is a bibliography of published reference works and secondary books and articles.

————. *Indian Peace Medals in American History.* Madison: State Historical Society of Wisconsin, 1971. 186pp. Illustrated. Bibliography.

The author gives a history of the production of silver medals, known as Indian peace medals, designed for presentation to Indian chiefs and warriors for the part they played in American Indian policy from 1789 to around 1890, the time the last medals were designed. The first part of the book presents the history of the use of medals by the French, Spanish, and English who set precedents for the Americans. This section includes information on medals as they evolved from symbols of allegiance to the United States and rewards for accepting white ways to rewards for good behavior or for services performed. Prucha discusses George Washington's Indian medals; the Spanish use of medals in the Trans-Mississippi West; medals distributed by Lewis and Clark and Zebulon M. Pike on their expeditions in the early nineteenth century; other distributed before the War of 1812; their use in the Old Northwest, the Missouri River valley, and the South; medals associated with treaty signing; and their use after the Civil War. The second part contains a catalog of the individual medals with a brief history of the design and manufacture of each. The author discusses and illustrates the medals presented by George Washington, Thomas Jefferson, James Madison, James Monroe, John Q. Adams, Andrew Jackson, Martin Van Buren, John Tyler, James Polk, Zachary Taylor, Millard Fillmore, Franklin Pierce, James Buchanan, Abraham Lincoln, Andrew Johnson, Ulysses S. Grant, Rutherford B. Hayes, James Garfield, Chester A. Arthur, Grover Cleveland, and Benjamin

Harrison. He concludes with a discussion of counterfeits and traders' medals. There are sixty-four illustrations of medals in obverse and reverse as well as a list of collections of Indian peace medals. The book is based on unpublished and published primary and secondary materials.

————. *Lewis Cass and American Indian Policy.* Detroit: Detroit Historical Society, 1967. 18pp.

This lecture analyzes the Indian policy of Lewis Cass who, first as governor of Michigan Territory from 1813 to 1831, then as Secretary of War in Jackson's cabinet from 1831 to 1836, was active during the period when guidelines for dealing with Indians were being drawn. The author examines the principles underlying Cass's early Indian policy, including the distribution of presents to counteract the British, the stationing of regular army troops in his territory as a preventive measure, an organized Indian Department, and his friendship with the American Fur Company. The author looks at Cass's low regard of Indians as savages who should be reclaimed by civilization, but notes his honesty in dealing with them and his position that the United States had a responsibility for the Indians. He also tells of Cass's views about how to acquire Indian lands and his positions on removal.

————; WILLIAM T. HAGAN; and ALVIN M. JOSEPHY, JR. *American Indian Policy.* Indianapolis: Indiana Historical Society, 1971. 65pp.

This book contains three essays concerning federal Indian policy from pre-Civil War times to 1970. The first by Prucha, "The Image of the Indian in Pre-Civil War America," considers the views held about Indians by Thomas Jefferson, Lewis Cass, Andrew Jackson, Horace Greeley, and Francis Parkman and the consequences these views had for official American Indian policy aimed at the ultimate assimilation of Indians into American society. Hagan's "Indian Policy after the Civil War: The Reservation Experience," deals with the reservation system designed to "civilize" Indians, explains five elements of the "civilization" formula in theory, and looks at how each element worked out in practice by focusing on Kiowas and Comanches to the turn of the century. Josephy's essay, "Toward Freedom: The American Indian in the Twentieth Century," analyzes the ultimate federal goal of assimilating Indians as expressed in the 1890 Census of the United States, in the 1887 Allotment Act, and in termination and relocation programs of the 1950s. He describes the new era in federal Indian relations beginning in 1970 with the growth of Indian self-determination. Notes follow Prucha's and Josephy's essays.

ROSEN, LAWRENCE. *American Indians and the Law.* New Brunswick, N.J.: Transaction Books, 1978. 223pp.

This symposium surveys the historical, economic, social, and administrative context within which relations between Indians and white Americans have developed, explores a series of specific issues affecting the economic and cultural basis of Indian experiences, and illuminates the complexities and contradictions of the law as it relates to Indian Americans and their place in American society. There is a foreword by Rosen that reviews federal Indian policy and the unique legal position of Indians in American society. The first section includes an essay by Lloyd Means on the Indian Policy Review Commission, created in 1975 to review historical and legal developments underlying the Indians' unique relationship to the federal government in order to determine the nature and scope of necessary revisions in formulating policies and programs for Indians; an essay by Wilcomb E. Washburn on the historical context of American Indian legal problems; and one by Russel L. Barsch and J. Youngsblood on tribal courts, the model code, and police in American Indian policy. There is an essay by Steve Nickeson on the structure of the Bureau of Indian Affairs from 1824 until the present. In the second section, contributors focus on the contest for control of water and mineral resources in Montana, Wyoming, and Arizona; the Alaska Native Claims Settlement Act; tribal taxing power over non-Indians; and funding Indian education.

ROSS, NORMAN A., comp. and ed. *Index to the Decisions of the Indian Claims Commission.* New York: Clearwater Publishing, 1973. 158pp.

This volume provides an alphabetical Table of Cases of the Indian Claims Commission's findings of fact, opinions, orders, and final awards which are issued by the Commission in paper form chronologically and in sequentially numbered volumes. Each case summarizes the progress of the claim, directs the researcher to the volume and page number of each decision in each claim, and alerts the reader to appeals. The volume also contains an index of all the claims according to the docket numbers assigned by the Commission with the names of all claimants in each case, plus an alphabetical index by claimant and tribe. Ross has also prepared an *Index to the Expert Testimony before the Indian Claims Commission* (Clearwater, 1973, 102pp.) which contains a listing of all of the written reports prepared by experts from many fields, indexed by tribe and docket numbers, author, state, and Royce area. An index in preparation is *Index to the Briefs, Transcripts, and GAO Reports before the Indian Claims Commission* (160pp.). It provides a listing for each docket of the witnesses and Indian claimants whose testimony is contained in the transcripts for that docket, together with the dates of the hearings transcribed. It also provides an author index to the transcripts. Also in preparation is Wilkinson, Cragun and Barker, *Index/Digest to the Decisions of the Indian Claims Commission* edited by the American Indian Studies Center of the University of California at Los Angeles (500pp.).

SATZ, RONALD N. *American Indian Policy in the Jacksonian Era.* Lincoln: University of Nebraska Press, 1975. 343pp. Illustrated. Bibliography.

The author analyzes federal Indian policy during the Jacksonian era, the 1830s and 1840s, arguing that exigencies of the moment determined components of the removal policy. He begins with a discussion of Jackson's Indian removal policy, con-

siders the critics and allies of his policy, and tells of the long debate in both houses of Congress over the administration's removal bill until the measure passed into law in 1830. He examines political opposition to the administration and the removal act and the way this opposition was defused, Georgia's extension of state law over Indians, and Chief Justice Marshall's decision declaring the law unconstitutional. He analyzes the successful negotiations with Choctaws in Mississippi, the first tribe to sign a removal treaty under the 1830 Removal Act, and the ensuing removal in 1831–33 under the direction of the War Department reflecting confusion, bureaucratic inefficiency, and hardships that typified the westward emigration of Indians during the Jacksonian era. He explains Choctaw allotments, fraud, and speculation, and looks at the methods used to obtain removal treaties from Creeks, Cherokees, Chickasaws, and Seminoles, including the government policy of selecting a particular group to represent the tribe, and annuities and force. He describes the government's concern for economy, makeshift arrangements, and continuous relocation of Indians in the Old Northwest. He tells of the efforts by some (and opposition by others) to create an Indian territory and the ensuing debate and Congressional defeat of the 1834 territorial bill. He considers the Office of Indian Affairs from 1789, when all matters pertaining to Indians were relegated to the War Department, and describes the Commissioner of Indian Affairs and Indian Field Service who formulated and executed Indian policy. He looks at the reasons why the Indian country created in 1830 became an obstacle to continental development, and tells of Indian Office agents and missionaries who used annuities and educational programs to control and "civilize" Indians. He describes the development of a paternalistic relationship which made Indians dependent on government personnel, annuities, and services and made them subject to but not part of the American political system. The appendix contains the 1830 Removal Act. There are five maps, paintings of removal proponents and Indian leaders, and a bibliography of unpublished and published primary and secondary sources.

SCHMECKEBIER, LAURENCE F. *The Office of Indian Affairs: Its History, Activities, and Organization.* Baltimore: Johns Hopkins University Press, 1927; reprint ed.: New York: AMS Press, 1972. 591pp. Illustrated. Bibliography.

The author traces the history of the establishment and development of the Office of Indian Affairs from the late 1700s until 1926. He considers specific Indian Office activities and the organization for handling them, personnel, laws and regulations governing office operations, and financial statements showing its appropriations and expenditures over the years. He divides the main features of the history of the Indian Office, which coincides with the history of federal Indian policy, into three periods: the treaty period up to 1871, the reservation period from 1871 to 1887, and the allotment and citizenship period, 1887–1927. He gives several reasons why the United States has controlled

Indian affairs, tells of special provisions for the Five Civilized Tribes (Cherokees, Creeks, Choctaws, Chickasaws, and Seminoles) who are usually omitted from general legislation and the removal of Indians from Kansas and Nebraska to lands ceded by the Five Tribes during the 1860s and 1870s. He looks at activities of the Indian Office including allotments of severalty; issuing patents in fee and certificates of competency; supervising real estate; managing Indian monies, education, medical care, industrial advancement, and rations; policing Indian reservations, suppressing the liquor trade, controlling Indian traders, and aiding missions. The author considers the Office's administrative organization including the President, Interior Secretary, Offices of the Commissioner and the Chief Clerk, and the administrative, medical, purchase, probate, finance, land, irrigation, and forestry divisions. He describes the appointment and compensation of personnel, Indian employment, and personnel problems. The appendix contains statistical tables on Indians and Indian Service activities for 1926, an outline of the Office of Indian Affairs organization both of Washington and field units, a compilation of laws relating to Indian rights up to 1927, and statements of several classes of Indian Service appropriations. There are two maps and a bibliography of published primary and secondary works about the Office of Indian Affairs divided into topics such as education and citizenship, natural resources, law, etc.

SHEEHAN, BERNARD W. *Seeds of Extinction: Jeffersonian Philanthrophy and the American Indian.* Chapel Hill: University of North Carolina, 1973; reprint ed.: New York: W. W. Norton, 1974. 301pp. Bibliography.

The author gives an account of the Jeffersonian era's beliefs about Indian peoples in the late eighteenth and early nineteenth centuries and how these attitudes translated into a private and government policy designed to "civilize" the tribes. The first two sections concern the ideas around which the Jeffersonian generation constructed its understanding of Indian-white relationships, including a belief in the unity of mankind, in the inherent quality of Indians, and in environmentalism, which led to a secular and religious program for transforming Indians into individual farmers and ultimately incorporating them into white society. The third part, "Illusions," concerns Indian-white frontier violence, the antithesis of civilization according to Jeffersonians, which precluded the Indians' chance to attain civilization; the Indians' personal and tribal disintegration as a result of the "civilizing" program, which brought stress and anxiety to tribal order; and war, European diseases, and alcohol. The author concludes with a discussion of some humanitarians and government officials who, in the mid-1820s, wanted the policy of removing tribes beyond the Mississippi River where the "civilizing" program which failed in the East could be carried on. The book is based chiefly on government and archival materials and published primary materials which are discussed in an essay and listed as well.

SMITH, E. B., comp. *Indian Tribal Claims.* 2 vols. Washington, D.C.: University Publications of America, 1976. Vol. 1. 480pp. Vol. 2. 508pp.

This author, who originally compiled this work in 1947, provides a documentary and analytical summary of more than 220 major cases of Indian claims which had been decided in the Court of Claims from the 1880s to the establishment of the Indian Claims Commission in 1947. The two volumes depict the history of litigation between the United States and the many tribes and bands of Indians found within the territorial limits of the United States. For each case, the following information is supplied: (1) the jurisdictional act under which the claim was filed; (2) the location and population of the tribe(s) filing the claim; (3) the amount claimed; (4) the nature of the claim; (5) action taken in the judicial system; (6) the judgment; and (7) the amount offset. The author also supplies a history of the facts of each case, a summary of the arguments for each side, and excerpts from the decisions.

SORKIN, ALAN L. *American Indians and Federal Aid.* Washington, D.C.: Brookings Institution, 1971. 231pp. Bibliography.

The author describes and assesses some of the current major federal assistance programs for developing the economic potential of reservations and for aiding those natives who want to relocate and evaluates the impact of these programs on native economic well being. Included are specific proposals for improving the federal programs he describes. Programs described and evaluated are education, vocational instruction, health and family maintenance services, agricultural and industrial development, employment assistance, job training, property and income management, low-cost housing, and welfare services. There are thirty-five tables that illustrate the text, and the appendix contains statistical tables and an evaluation of three recent manpower programs. The book is based chiefly on interviews with natives and unpublished Bureau of Indian Affairs' materials.

TAYLOR, GRAHAM D. *The New Deal and American Indian Tribalism: The Administration of the Indian Reorganization Act, 1935–45.* Lincoln: University of Nebraska Press, 1979. 203pp. Bibliography.

The author provides an assessment of the successes and failures of the Indian New Deal, focusing in part on the failure of the tribal reorganizational effort to produce the lasting changes in Indian administration that John Collier, the reformist Commissioner of Indian Affairs, hoped for. He explains the reasons that new tribal governments aroused little support among the people they were supposed to represent, including the facts that few Indian groups had ever functioned practically on the tribal level, there was intratribal factionalism and rivalry, and the political structures established by the Indian Reorganization Act were foreign to Indian societies. The author reviews in detail the implementation of the reorganization legislation among a wide range of Indian groups challenging the claims of Collier and others that it was largely successful. He analyzes the Navajo experience during the New Deal, the tribe with which the reformers had their most serious setback. He shows that the reasons for the failure of tribal reorganization lay in the basic misconceptions that Collier and his coworkers held about Indian societies and how they functioned. He argues that the reforms of the Indian New Deal failed to endure because they were imposed on some Indians who did not see these proposals as answers to their needs. The study also attempts to demonstrate where and under what conditions a genuine sense of Indian self-determination developed. There is a bibliographical essay discussing the published primary and secondary sources upon which the book is based.

TAYLOR, THEODORE W. *The States and Their Indian Citizens*. Washington, D.C.: Government Printing Office, 1972. 307pp. Illustrated. Bibliography.

This study concerns the relationship of Indians to their own tribal governments, the federal, and local and state governments. The author begins with a brief history of the swings in federal Indian policy from 1783 to the 1960s, and he reviews the increased state involvement in Indian affairs in the 1950s and the development of the concept of state and local government responsibility for Indians. He describes the piecemeal transfer of federal Indian activities to states, including education, social services, roads, agriculture, soil and moisture conservation, health, law and order, inheritance, industrial development, and considers the states' organized efforts to improve native life. The author describes federal moves to terminate special relationships with Indians in the 1950s, and federal policy concerned with Indian economic development and involvement in the 1960s. He looks at the problems of relations between Indian citizens and states today, cites state Indian populations, and explains state and federal government trust responsibilities for Indian lands. He examines education, law and order, and organizational arrangements to indicate the variations of responsibility among tribal, state, and federal governments for Indians, and proposes social programs that would improve their life. The author looks at several areas that should remain federal responsibility stemming from treaty agreements and court decisions including reservation boundaries, water rights, heirship land, and tribal government. He considers policy options in distributing functions between state and federal governments, and concludes that Indian motivation and power, effective tribal government, and Indian culture and adaptive ability will play a role in changing their lives. There are photographs of contemporary Indians. The appendix includes a color map showing federal and state reservations, analyses of special presidential messages on Indians, and a table that shows by state the acres of Indian land, population, and whether Indian children are educated by public or federal schools. There are lists of state reservations, Indian groups without trust lands, terminated tribes and groups, federally recognized tribes, and a copy of the questionnaires sent to states and tribal officers upon which the book is largely based.

TRENNERT, ROBERT A. *Alternative to Extinction: Federal Indian Policy and the Beginnings of the Reservation System, 1846–1851*. Philadelphia: Temple University Press, 1975. 263pp. Bibliography.

This study explores the efforts of Indian Office officials between 1846 and 1851 in finding an alternative to the extinction of natives which, the author argues, resulted in the rudiments of the modern reservation system which developed fully after the Civil War. The author also deals with the various influences that affected formulation of Native American policy. He discusses the federal policy of a line behind which native populations would remain racially segregated until "civilized," and the end of this barrier philosophy which necessitated the formulation of a new policy. Chapters describe policy formulation and political considerations, the reorganization of the Indian Office, and the commencement of a limited reservation system from 1845 to 1851. Chapters discuss the situation of tribal groups in four selected frontier areas: Texas (Comanches, Kiowas, Lipan Apaches, and others); New Mexico (Pueblos, Utes, Navajos, Apaches, and Comanches); the country along the banks of the Lower Missouri River (Pawnees, Otos, Missouris, and Omahas); and the central Plains (Cheyennes, Arapahos, and Sioux) from 1846 to 1851 to see why reservations were required and why local factors impeded their initial success. The book is based on unpublished and published primary and secondary books and articles.

TYLER, S. LYMAN. *A History of Indian Policy*. Washington, D.C.: Department of the Interior, 1973. 328pp. Illustrated. Bibliography.

This government document gives a brief history of the changes in federal Indian policy from the colonial period to the 1970s. Tyler begins by discussing Spanish, French, Dutch, and English Indian programs and colonial precedents which helped establish American Indian policy. He explains the Indian programs of the Continental Congress, the Confederation, and the Constitution, and tells of the creation of the factory system, the civilization fund, and the Office of Indian Affairs. He explains the removal of Indians east of the Mississippi River to western territories, the development of the reservation system when western lands were needed for further expansion, experiments with allotments in the 1850s, reform movements, Grant's peace policy, educational programs, law and order on reservations, and the end of the treaty period in 1871. He discusses the allotment period designed to assimilate and "civilize" Indians, its failure, and reform efforts to improve Indian life; the policy reversal to tribal reorganization under the New Deal in the 1930s, and congressional criticisms of the way Indian affairs were being conducted. He looks at the change in government methods in the late 1940s and 1950s to try to assimilate Indians through relocation and termination, and the reversal in Indian policy in the 1960s to self-determination, employment assistance, and economic and capital development for Indian communities. Concluding chapters look at self-determination through Indian leadership in the late 1960s and early 1970s and government Indian policy goals for the early 1970s. An appendix lists important dates in Indian policy and the administrators of Indian affairs from 1789 to 1969; maps and photographs portray contemporary Indian life and art; and a briefly annotated bibliography lists unpublished and published primary and secondary works.

UNITED STATES. CONGRESS. *American State Papers: Documents, Legislative and Executive of the Congress of the United States.* 38 vols. Washington, D.C.: Gales & Seaton, 1832–61.

The congressional papers are arranged in ten classes. The most important for Indian affairs is Class 2: *Indian Affairs,* 2 vols. (Washington, D.C.: 1832–34) which consists of documents selected from the papers of the first through the nineteenth Congress, March 3, 1789 to March 3, 1827. Other documents relating to Indian affairs can be found in Class 5: *Military Affairs,* 7 vols.; Class 8: *Public Lands,* 8 vols.; and Class 10: *Miscellaneous,* 2 vols.

————. Office of Indian Affairs. *Annual Reports of the Commissioner of Indian Affairs, Reports for the Years 1824 to 1899.* Washington, D.C.: Government Printing Office, 1825–99; reprint ed.: New York: AMS Press, 1974. 65 vols.

This set of annual reports of the Commissioners of Indian Affairs from 1824 to 1899 is a resource for the study of the official history of the federal government's relations with Native Americans, for the changing government policies which affected the attitudes of commissioners, reservation agents, and the army, as well as a resource for the Indian point of view because statements by Indians were often included. The reports contain indictments of government policy and recommendations for change. Federal management of Indian affairs originated within the War Department in 1824 and its existence was formalized in 1834 by the establishment of an Indian Office headed by a Commissioner of Indian Affairs. During the War Department years, 1824–48, annual reports, which were filled with correspondence from agents in the field, were directed to the War Secretary where they became part of the department's annual summaries of activities or were published as parts of Senate and House executive documents. The Office of Indian Affairs was transferred to the Interior Department in 1849 and the reports from 1849 to 1899 were addressed to the Secretary of the Interior. The reports are compiled in sequential order in sixty-five volumes.

VIOLA, HERMAN J. *Thomas L. McKenney: Architect of America's Early Indian Policy, 1816–1830.* Chicago: Swallow Press, 1974. 365pp. Illustrated. Bibliography.

The author traces the career of McKenney between 1816 and 1830 during which time he administered the nation's Indian affairs, first as Superintendent of Indian Trade (1816–22) and then as head of the Office of Indian Affairs in the War Department (1824–30). The author also considers how McKenney was a pioneer in the study of North American ethnology and the major architect of government reform and removal programs that had a major impact on Indians. He discusses events in which McKenney had leading roles, including the factory system and his defense of it, reform to "civilize" Indians by promoting agriculture and missionary activities among them, and passage of the 1819 Indian Civilization Act which provided funds for schooling Indian children. He looks at the period when McKenney was out of office after the factories were abolished, the initial organization of the Office of Indian Affairs in the War Department, McKenney's appointment to head it by Secretary of War Calhoun, and his work there in preparing, negotiating, and implementing treaties and entertaining Indians who visited Washington. He discusses McKenney's 1826–27 tour of Michigan Territory with Governor Lewis Cass where he negotiated treaties; his administration of day to day details in the Indian Office, and his role in promoting Indian removal as the best hope for the Indians. He discusses McKenney's dismissal from the Office, the collection of artifacts McKenney assembled while in office, and describes the publication of the *History of the Indian Tribes of North America,* three volumes of portraits and biographical sketches by McKenney and James Hall, prepared between 1836 and 1844. He concludes by discussing McKenney's years after his dismissal from office until his death in 1859. An appendix summarizes the dates, locations, and factors of seventeen factories operating or established during McKenney's tenure of office. The work includes one map of the factory locations, illustrations of McKenney and government officials, and a bibliography of unpublished and published primary and secondary works.

WASHBURN, WILCOMB E. *The Assault on Indian Tribalism: The General Allotment Law (Dawes Act) of 1887.* Philadelphia: Lippincott, 1975. 79pp. Bibliography.

This volume consists of a narrative and analytical historical essay in which the author identifies five choices which he believes were actually made before the decision makers of federal Indian policy in the 1880s. In the first part he describes the five various alternatives faced by legislators and the compromise legislation that finally emerged in 1887 as the General Allotment Act. He looks at reform organizations of the 1870s, the Indians' opposition to severalty, and the role of the "experts" and humanitarians who demanded forcible allotment of Indian lands and the destruction of tribal organizations. He discusses the decision for compulsory allotment of land as a key plank in the reform plan as well as subsidiary issues, such as the provision for American citizenship, that became part of the Dawes Act. The second part of the volume contains, in whole or in part, the most appropriate source documents that illustrate alternatives described in the first part. The epilogue evaluates the negative impact of the Dawes Act, and the last part contains a bibliographical essay that evaluates basic source documents dealing with the origins of the Dawes Act, manuscript and secondary works, and the roles of Richard H. Pratt, Alice Fletcher, and the Lake Mohonk conferences in the movement culminating in severalty legislation.

———. *Red Man's Land/White Man's Law: A Study of the Past and Present Status of the American Indian.* New York: Scribner's, 1971. 280pp.

This book presents a legal history of native-white relations and the process by which the natives' right to their land was eroded from the period of their first contacts with Europeans down to the present day. Part 1 begins with a chapter on the theoretical and theological roots of European ethnocentrism and imperialism. Part 2 surveys the history of native policy in seventeenth-century New England and Virginia revealing theoretical conflicts that marked the native-white relationships and the history of eighteenth-century relations between natives and British and American governments in the Northeast and Southeast, which ended the power and independence of native nations. This section reviews nineteenth-century native policy which gradually diminished native rights to the land through treaties until 1871, and examines twentieth-century termination policy. Part 3 examines the contemporary land status of natives in light of present-day law and policy, and tells of legislative and judicial injustices, the Indian Claims Commission, the concept of "original Native title" and selected tribal cases involving it. The author looks at land problems of Alaska, Oklahoma, and New Mexico natives, and native land allotments, heirship problems, and legislation. Part four examines contemporary native legal rights, reservations, and relationships to federal institutions and whites. This book is partly based on government documents cited in footnotes.

———, ed. *The American Indian and the United States: A Documentary History.* New York: Random House, 1973. 4 vols.; reprint ed.: Westport, Conn.: Greenwood Press, 1977. 3,119pp. Illustrated.

These volumes contain reprints of selected documents drawn from five principal classes that illustrate the history of the special relationship between Indians and the federal government that has evolved from 1763 until 1973. Two hundred sixteen documents have been selected from reports of the Commissioner of Indian Affairs, congressional debates in Indian affairs, major peace treaties, laws, acts and ordinances of Congress, and judicial decisions affecting Indians. Each of the five sources is treated in a separate section of the collection, and each section is provided with an introduction explaining the significance of the documents that follow. Each document, arranged chronologically within the particular section, is prefaced with a brief interpretative summary placing the document in perspective relative to the overall history. Volume 1 contains forty-four reports of the Commissioners of Indian Affairs from 1826 to 1901; volume 2 contains thirty-three reports from 1902 to 1963 and twelve congressional debates on Indian Affairs from 1830 to 1866; and volume 3 contains eighteen debates from 1866 to 1970, eighteen acts, ordinances, and proclamations from 1763 to 1968, and the 1778 Indian treaty. The fourth volume contains forty-two treaties from 1784 to 1868 and forty-six legal decisions from 1823 to 1973. There is a map of Indian land cessions, 1776–1945.

WEST, MARY BETH, ed. *Manual of Indian Law.* Oakland, Calif.: American Indian Lawyer Training Program, 1976. 300pp. Bibliography.

This work was written to provide an understanding of basic Indian law to practicing and prospective Native American lawyers and other persons involved in Indian affairs. Fourteen sections deal with tribal powers, the Indian Civil Rights Act, civil and criminal jurisdiction, tribal courts, Public Law 280 (state jurisdiction over Indians), Indian hunting and fishing law, water rights, taxation, treaty law, education contracting, the Alaska Native Claims Settlement Act, and Oklahoma Indian legal issues. Each section provides an overview of the subject matter and appendixes provide information on related court cases, case study documents, and bibliographic information.

NORTHEAST

FOREMAN, GRANT. *The Last Trek of the Indians.* Chicago: University of Chicago Press, 1946. 382pp. Illustrated. Bibliography.

The author traces the history of the removal of over fifty Indian tribes who lived in Ohio, Michigan, New York, Indiana, and Illinois to their final homes in Oklahoma from the early eighteenth century until the turn of the nineteenth century. He begins with a discussion of the earliest treaties with tribes from 1778 to 1818 and with the tribes who lived in and were removed from present-day Ohio, Indiana, and Illinois. He briefly reviews the earlier, more or less voluntary, but haphazard westward emigration of Indians to Kansas, and the hostility of western Indians who were forced to make room for the immigrants. He tells of the development of President Monroe's voluntary Indian removal policy, the removal of Indians north of Ohio during Jackson's administration which established Indian removal as a federal policy, and which looked to extinction of all Indian titles in Illinois, Indiana, Ohio, and Michigan Territory. The author focuses on the 1830s and 1840s when the Ottawas, Wyandots, Potawatomis, Miamis, Sacs, and Foxes were removed west of the Mississippi, and considers the brief resistance of eastern Indians in Kansas who were again uprooted, compelled to move, and forced to yield a large part of their reservation to whites. He tells of the state of immigrant Kansas Indians including the Delawares, Ottawas, Wyandots, Miamis, Illinois, Kickapoos, Potawatomis, Sacs, and Foxes from the 1830s to the 1870s. He explores federal legislation designed to set up a common government for Indians in the West, deals with the state of immigrant Indians who came principally from Kansas and Nebraska, the Pawnees, Poncas, Otos, Missourias, and Iowas, from the 1830s to the 1890s. He discusses the Osages, who were removed from Oklahoma to Kansas reservations and then forced to return to Oklahoma; the emigration of several native groups from Texas to western Oklahoma in the late 1850s; and immigrant Cheyennes and Arapahos and other tribal groups, who settled on reservations in Oklahoma. He concludes with a brief discussion of the Catawbas, Natchez, Nez

Percés, and New York Indians who also lived within Oklahoma, and describes the remnants of eight immigrant tribes located in Quapaw Agency in northeastern Oklahoma. There are eight maps. The history is based principally on archival materials and government documents.

HAUPTMAN, LAURENCE M. *The Iroquois and the New Deal.* Syracuse: Syracuse University Press, 1982. 276pp. Illustrated. Bibliography.

The author examines the U.S. government's policy toward the Iroquois from the end of World War I to World War II focusing on the New Deal period. He explains Iroquois concepts of sovereignty, John Collier and his relationships with the Iroquois, describes the policies of the Bureau of Indian Affairs, and the passage of the Indian Reorganization Act of 1934. He examines the Oneida language and folklore project, the Seneca renaissance, New Deal community action programs in New York, and deals with the Senecas and Cayugas of Oklahoma during this period. There is one map, photographs of Iroquois, and a bibliography listing manuscripts, interviews, government publications, court cases, newspapers and articles, books, and pamphlets.

SOUTHEAST

ABEL, ANNIE H. "The History of Events Resulting in Indian Consolidation West of the Mississippi." In *Annual Report of the American Historical Association for the Year, 1906,* vol. 1, pp. 233–450.

This study traces the history of the federal Indian policy of removing Indians from east to west of the Mississippi River from 1803, the origin of the idea, to the time systematic migrations became national policy in 1830. The author considers President Jefferson's ideas on removal in 1803 and looks at three unsuccessful attempts to remove southeastern Chickasaws, Choctaws, and Cherokees. The author studies the War of 1812 and its bearing on native removal, discusses Presidents James Monroe, John Q. Adams, and Andrew Jackson, as well as John C. Calhoun, who all favored removal measures, and the history of voluntary removal in the North and the South from 1820 to 1825. Abel considers state-federal conflicts over removal policies, passage of the Removal Act of 1830, and the development of Jackson's compulsory removal policy.

GREAT PLAINS

BERTHRONG, DONALD J. *The Cheyenne and Arapaho Ordeal: Reservation and Agency Life in the Indian Territory, 1875–1907.* Norman: University of Oklahoma Press, 1976. 402pp. Illustrated. Bibliography.

The author recounts the application of reservation and assimilation policies, the Dawes and Burke Acts, to the Cheyennes and Arapahoes in Oklahoma from 1875 to 1907. He begins with the Southern Cheyennes and Arapahoes, who were restricted to a reservation in Indian Territory, and describes the civil-military bickering over responsibility for providing food to starving Indians. He tells of the transfer of Northern Cheyenne bands to the Cheyenne-Arapaho Agency and their flight back north to lands from which most were eventually removed in 1883. He describes the assimilationist government policy committed to changing Cheyennes from a hunting to an agricultural economy through farming, reservation schools, and Christian education. He examines the reasons for Southern Cheyenne aversion to farming, alternative employment including stock raising and freighting, and the educational curriculum and schools designed to "civilize" Indians. He discusses the occupation of the reservation in the early 1880s by cattlemen, Indian resistance to the licensing program, the removal of herds, the government agents' twofold program of destroying the traditional Indian way of life and introducing changes aimed at self-sufficiency through agriculture, and Cheyenne-Arapaho resistance. He also looks at the application of the allotment system to the two tribes in 1891, the end of the reservation, problems related to leased and inherited lands, the influx of farmers, ranchers, and settlers onto former reservation lands, and their antagonism and discrimination towards Indians. The author concludes with a description of early twentieth-century stagnant economic conditions, federal efforts to eliminate Indian dependence on the government, the application of the 1906 Burke Act by which "competent" Indians could sell their allotments, and the Indians' participation in peyote ceremonies. There are three maps and photographs of Cheyennes, Arapahoes, and agency officials. The book is based on unpublished and published primary and secondary sources.

DANZIGER, EDMUND JEFFERSON, JR. *Indians and Bureaucrats: Administering the Reservation Policy during the Civil War.* Urbana: University of Illinois Press, 1974. 240pp. Illustrated. Bibliography.

The author analyzes the problems faced by Indian Office field officials west of the Mississippi River in implementing the government's reservation policy during the Civil War years, 1861–65, describes the administrative structure of the Indian Office, and surveys its problems in the 1850s. He compares administrative problems of superintendencies in Colorado, Montana, Utah, Nevada, the Southwest, Oklahoma Territory, Kansas, Nebraska, Minnesota, the Dakotas, the Pacific Northwest, and California. Briefly he describes the 1864 Sand Creek Massacre, the Navajos at Bosque Redondo, and the Minnesota Sioux uprising of 1862, which led to the expulsion of the Santee Sioux from the state. He focuses on the Indian Office's management and problems with two representative groups, the Cheyennes, a mobile people, and the Santee Sioux, a reservation tribe, and the impact of the Civil War years on federal-Indian relations. He suggests a program that the government might have implemented during the last half of the nineteenth century to solve the "Indian problem." There is a map and an unannotated bibliography of unpublished and published primary and secondary materials.

DEBO, ANGIE. *And Still the Waters Run.* Princeton: Princeton University Press, 1940; reprint ed.: Princeton: Princeton University Press, 1972. 417pp. Illustrated. Bibliography.

The author traces the history of the Five Civilized Tribes (the Cherokee, Choctaw, Chickasaw, Creek, and Seminole Nations) in Oklahoma from 1890 until 1936. She discusses the white system of private land ownership, the work of the Dawes Commission and the Curtis Act in extinguishing Indians' land titles in Indian Territory, and explains the responses of each of the Five Tribes to the allotment policy. She describes the federal government's ineffective policy of administering the five tribal estates, the subsequent plunder and exploitation of Indians and their land, and speculative development and corruption from 1898 to 1908. The author tells of the demands of white inhabitants of Indian Territory for statehood, the efforts of some Indians who opposed it, and the exploitation of adult and minor allottees after Oklahoma became a state in 1908. She details some of the litigation undertaken by the federal government or prosecuted by state officials on behalf of the Five Tribes' allottees to recover lands, and considers the conflicts between the despoilers and defenders of the Five Tribes' allottees, federal administration of the Five Tribes' undivided tribal property, and supervision of individual restricted allottees within Oklahoma after 1906. Concluding chapters summarize Indian and white acculturation in Oklahoma; the Indians' adjustment to alien economic, political, and social systems; the appearance of a constructive federal Indian policy in the 1930s; and include a brief inventory of the Five Tribes' property holdings, population, and other possessions. A preface in the reprint edition updates the work. There are maps and an unannotated bibliography of unpublished and published primary and secondary works and personal interviews.

ELLIS, RICHARD N. *General Pope and U.S. Indian Policy.* Albuquerque: University of New Mexico Press, 1970. 287pp. Illustrated. Bibliography.

This book tells the story of federal-Indian relations west of the Mississippi River, civil-military squabbles over control of Indians, and the development of Indian policy in the northern and southern Plains and the Southwest as seen from the point of view of General John Pope, U.S. military Commander in the West from the time of the Civil War to his 1886 retirement. The author describes Pope's battles with the Minnesota Sioux in the early 1860s and with the Indian Office over existing federal Indian policy, especially annuity treaties. He explains Pope's Indian reform policy to maintain peace on the frontier from 1862 to 1864 by assimilating Indians into white culture, ending joint jurisdiction over Indians with sole military control of Indian affairs, restricting Indians to reservations by force, and punishing raiders so as to prevent their extermination. The author discusses Pope's command of the Division and Department of Missouri, which included parts of the Plains, his military expeditions against the Sioux and Cheyennes, struggles with the Indian Bureau over treatment of

Indians, protecting lines of travel and settlement, and continuous warfare with several Plains tribes in the southern and central Plains. Briefly he discusses the early 1870s Quaker-style peace policy, Pope's opposition to humanitarian control of Indian affairs, and the ineffectiveness of the peace policy on the southern Plains. The author describes Pope's campaigns against Plains tribes in 1874 and the termination of hostilities on the southern Plains by 1875. He tells of the conflict between the War and Interior Departments over military operations on reservations and over feeding agency Indians in the mid-1870s. He details Pope's efforts toward improvement of the government's treatment of Indians and his opposition to the government policy of converting Indians to farmers. He concludes with Pope's dealings with New Mexico's Apaches and Colorado's Utes, and tells of the debate over transferring control of Indian affairs to the War Department and the inability of the army to please both frontier people and humanitarians. There are photographs of Pope, army officers, and Indians. The book is based on Pope's letters and other unpublished and published primary and secondary works.

HAGAN, WILLIAM T. *Indian Police and Judges: Experiments in Acculturation and Control.* New Haven, Conn.: Yale University Press, 1966. 194pp. Illustrated. Bibliography.

This book considers the evolution and role of the Indian police and court systems inaugurated by the Office of Indian Affairs on most reservations west of the Mississippi River between 1878 and 1900. The author explains the role played by native police and courts in acculturating their people to white legal concepts and helping to eliminate military interference with reservation populations. Chapters describe Plains native law ways and those of the Five Civilized Tribes which resembled white institutions, explain one of the earliest and most successful uses of native police at John P. Clum's Apache San Carlos Agency, and enumerate problems in recruiting natives. The author details various activities of the police, especially the late nineteenth-century policy of serving as agents of the "civilization" program. Briefly he describes the performances of native police forces on several Sioux reservations, discusses the origin and operations of the Courts of Indian Offenses authorized in 1883, particularly that of Judge Quanah Parker of the Kiowa Agency, Oklahoma, and considers several reasons for the decline of native courts and police by 1900. The concluding chapter deals with the argument that native police and courts were valuable as bridges between cultures. Throughout the book, there are accounts of day-to-day life on reservations during the late nineteenth century. There are photographs of agents, native police, and Judge Parker. The book is based on unpublished and published primary and secondary works.

————. *United States-Comanche Relations: The Reservation Years.* New Haven, Conn.: Yale University Press, 1976. 336pp. Illustrated. Bibliography.

The author traces the reservation years of the Comanches in Oklahoma and Texas from 1867 until the turn of the century to demonstrate U.S. Indian policy goals. He begins with the history and negotiations of the 1867 Treaty of Medicine Lodge, which provided the framework of services and supervision that was expected, in thirty years, to transform the Comanche hunters into self-sufficient farmers and cattlemen. Also discussed are the resistance of some Comanche bands to locating on the reservation, the appointment of Lawrie Tatum as a Comanche agent (part of President Grant's Quaker peace policy), the problems concerning the lack of rations and the withholding of annuity goods, and the 1875 surrender by the remaining Comanche bands marking the end of their resistance and free existence. The author examines the "civilization" (assimilation) program of the government, its efforts to break up the band system, and to make Comanches self-sufficient through agriculture, stock raising, and education. He looks at the series of agents who presided over the Comanches, white encroachment and leasing on the reservation, and the role of Quanah Parker after his 1875 surrender. He discusses special interest groups (cattlemen, missionaries, army officers, licensed traders, land-hungry settlers, as well as Comanche factions) who combined and divided to further their own interests on the Comanche Reservation. He concludes by describing the implementation of the allotment in severalty program, which helped to dissolve the old Comanche way of life and strip them of land. There are three maps, photographs of Comanches, and an unannotated bibliography of unpublished and published primary and secondary works.

HOOPES, ALBAN W. *Indian Affairs and Their Administration: With Special Reference to the Far West, 1849–1860*. Philadelphia: University of Pennsylvania Press, 1932. 264pp. Bibliography.

The author outlines important changes in federal Indian policy in the decade before the Civil War, particularly the development of the reservation system in California. He explains the manner in which the old policy of maintaining a large, unorganized, and "permanent" Indian country west of Arkansas, Missouri, and Iowa came to an end due to the rapid emigration to the Pacific following American land acquisitions made between 1845 and 1848, surrounding Indian country with organized territories and states of whites by 1850. He looks at the Office of Indian Affairs, from 1849 to 1860, the administrative structure and daily life of superintendents, and considers the origins and development of the reservation system in California from 1847 to 1860. He looks at Indian affairs and policy from 1849 to 1860 in Oregon and Washington where there was a great deal of Indian-white conflict, focusing on the Oregon Rogue River and Washington Yakima wars, discusses Indian affairs in Utah where the Indian service was inefficient and Indians impoverished, and in New Mexico and Texas. He studies the terms of the Fort Laramie and Fort Atkinson treaties which were related to the 1854 organization of Kansas and Nebraska territories, through which railroads could run and which brought about the final extinction of Indian country north of the area held by the Five Civilized Tribes, and the

removal of many tribes from Kansas and Nebraska to Indian Territory. Finally, he examines how Indian title to much of Nebraska was extinguished from 1854 to 1861 by treaties, discusses the Indian-settler conflict in Kansas where small, weak tribes were forced to surrender most of their Kansas holdings, and considers how the system of reservations, which was established in the midst of white country in California, spread over the entire country. There is some dated language and a bibliography of unpublished and published primary and secondary works.

LAWSON, MICHAEL L. *Dammed Indians: The Pick-Sloan Plan and the Missouri River Sioux, 1944–1980*. Norman: University of Oklahoma Press, 1981. 352pp. Bibliography.

The author uses the Sioux reservations flooded by the Pick-Sloan Plan as examples of federal acquisition of trust land and the application of recent Indian policies. He sketches briefly the history of the Missouri Basin, the Pick-Sloan legislation, and the land and peoples of the reservations. He chronicles the events from the 1940s through the 1960s when the impact of the federal water projects was most keenly felt, and describes in detail the personalities and agencies involved. He tells how the Pick-Sloan Plan in the Missouri River Basin was developed by the U.S. Corps of Engineers and the Bureau of Reclamation in 1944 and argues that the project caused more damage to Indians than any other public works project in America. He describes how three of the dams constructed—the Fort Randall, Oahe, and Big Bend dams—flooded over 202,00 acres of Sioux bottomland on the Standing Rock, Cheyenne River, Lower Brulé, Crow Creek, and Yankton reservations in North and South Dakota.

MALIN, JAMES C. *Indian Policy and Westward Expansion*. Bulletin of the University of Kansas Humanistic Studies, vol. 2, no. 3. Lawrence: University of Kansas, 1921. 108pp. Illustrated. Bibliography.

This book traces the history of Indian policy from 1830 to 1854 in the trans-Mississippi Valley set apart wholly for occupation by Indians and looks at three phases through which Indian policy passed during those years. The first phase, 1830–40, saw the removal of Indians from areas east of the Mississippi River to regions west of it and the formulation of general principles of policy and administration. The second phase brought the evolution of the plan of consolidating Indians in a permanent home in the southwest of Indian country to allow for westward expansion of whites across the northern part. And the third phase, 1840–54, involved the factors that dictated a change in federal policy to that of relocating Indian tribes to the north and south of Indian country so that westward expansion could progress undisturbed through a central route to the Pacific. The author examines the factors contributing to the revision of the old Indian policy, including westward expansion and settlement of the Pacific Coast, the Pacific Railroad, westward expansion and the organization of Nebraska, and the changed living conditions of Indians, which required a change in policy to insure their safety. He concludes with a consideration of the new Indian policy of shifting Indians northward to the Dakotas and southward to the present state of Oklahoma forming two Indian colonies, and extinguishing Indian title to the country between them and opening it to white settlement. He discusses the 1854 Kansas-Nebraska Act, which formed the Kansas and Nebraska territories. There are some dated opinions, three maps, and an unannotated bibliography of unpublished and published primary and secondary materials.

SOUTHWEST

DALE, EDWARD EVERETT. *The Indians of the Southwest: A Century of Development under the United States.* Norman: University of Oklahoma Press, 1949. 283pp. Illustrated. Bibliography.

This book contains a broad survey of several aspects of Native American administration from 1848 to the mid-twentieth century in southern and central California, Nevada, Utah, Arizona, and the western half of New Mexico. The author describes federal policies and regulations used by the government in its efforts to make farmers out of the natives newly brought under its jurisdiction in 1848. Chapters provide a brief overview of southwestern natives and deal with federal relations with natives of California, New Mexico, Arizona, Utah, and Nevada from 1848 to 1868 by focusing on the officials who administered reservations, education, health, and other assimilationist federal programs. The author looks at the poor conditions of southern California Mission natives, 1868–1903; the Army's subduing of Apaches, 1869–86; peaceful relations with Arizona and New Mexico natives; and federal administration in Utah and Nevada, 1869–1900. Concluding chapters survey native-government relations in the Southwest as a whole from 1900 to 1947 considering the poor conditions which led to national investigations, and the adoption of the ideas and policies of John Collier. There are some dated opinions. Included are one map and illustrations of southwestern natives and their way of life.

KELLY, LAWRENCE C. *The Navajo Indians and Federal Indian Policy, 1900–1935.* Tucson: University of Arizona Press, 1968. 221pp. Illustrated. Bibliography.

The author studies federal Indian policy applied to Navajos of New Mexico and Arizona from 1913 to 1935. He begins with a brief history of Navajo-white contact until 1913 and explains the Navajo world view and their reactions to federal Indian policy in the first third of the twentieth century. He looks at several Navajo attempts between 1912 and 1921 to enlarge their reservation boundaries and the success of one measure, the concerted efforts waged by stock and farming interests after 1900 to halt the enlargement of the Navajo reservation, and the battle conducted by western mining interests, who wished to open up the Indian reserves, explained against the background of the conflict between conservationists and exploiters of the public domain. He discusses the oil discovery on the Navajo reservation in 1922 and the attempts to exploit this resource through the 1920 General Leasing Act. He looks at the conflict, proposals, and legislation for dealing with royalty questions relating to oil and gas produced on executive-order reservations, and the Indian Oil Act of 1927, a victory for Indians who possessed executive-order reservations. He describes the overgrazing of the Navajo reservation and the sheep and horse reduction programs of the 1920s, Navajo efforts to obtain more land in the 1920s and 1930s, and opposition to Navajo expansion in New Mexico. He examines efforts in the 1920s to break up the reservation system, tells of criticisms of the Indian administration, surveys the Meriam report, and explains the New Deal in the 1930s, under Commissioner of Indian Affairs John Collier. He tells of the Navajo rejections of the 1934 Wheeler-Howard Bill and the stock reduction program. He concludes with a description of the educational and health problems of Navajos in the 1920s, which the federal government failed to recognize, the Navajo Tribal Council created in 1923 which has become an articulate and sometimes representative organization of the Navajo people, and Navajo adjustment to American life since 1935. There are two maps and a bibliography of unpublished and published primary and secondary works.

OGLE, RALPH HEDRICK. *Federal Control of the Western Apaches, 1848–1886.* Introduction by Oakah L. Jones, Jr. Albuquerque: University of New Mexico, 1970. 259pp. Illustrated. Bibliography. [Originally published in *New Mexico Historical Review* 14 (October 1939):309–65; 15 (January 1940):12–71, (April 1940):188–248, and (July 1940):269–335.]

This book traces the efforts of the federal government to assert control over western Apaches of southeastern Arizona and southwestern New Mexico from 1848 until 1886, focusing on frequent policy changes and lack of harmony among government agencies. Chapters deal with ethnological and geographical factors that had a bearing on managing the Apaches, describe twenty years of chiefly military control over the Apaches, and later years of civilian-military squabbles over their control, and Arizona settlers pressing for Apache annihilation. The author describes how reservation policy was hindered by military-civilian rivalry for control and by the corruption of government officials. Concluding chapters describe the federal policy decision to concentrate all Apaches on one reservation at San Carlos, the work of John P. Clum, San Carlos agent, who tried to eliminate military control, and the end of Apache resistance by 1886. The introduction defines groups constituting the western Apaches, comments on the text originally written in 1939 and 1940, and describes Ogle's life and the importance of this work. There is some dated terminology and one map. The book is based on unpublished and published primary materials and secondary works.

PARMAN, DONALD L. *The Navajos and the New Deal.*

New Haven, Conn.: Yale University Press, 1976. 316pp. Illustrated. Bibliography.

The author gives an account of how New Deal Indian policy operated on the Navajo Reservation, explains Navajo experiences during the period, and assesses the philosophy that Commissioner of Indian Affairs John Collier attempted to implement after he assumed office in 1933. He begins with a brief review of the tribe's history and their socio-political institutions as well as their relationships with successive waves of Spanish, Mexicans, and Americans who claimed the region in which the Navajos lived. He describes the central theme of Collier's policy as uncompromising rejection of past efforts to assimilate Indians into white society and encouragement of Indians to be Indians. He describes how the New Deal launched a variety of major conservation programs on the Navajo Reservation to alleviate poverty and disease in the 1930s, including herd reduction, grazing regulations, medical care, land management, education, and the reshaping of tribal government. He discusses divisions among the Indians between traditional leaders and those favoring assimilation, as well as rivalry between religious and community factions revealing the simplistic nature of Collier's views about Indian cultural homogeneity. He also shows how government efforts to introduce tribal reorganization, herd reduction and range controls, and educational reforms exacerbated these internal conflicts. He tells of the shift of Navajo leaders from support to opposition of the government because much of what was attempted by the federal government policy violated important customs and patterns of Navajo life. He considers the critical reactions of whites to New Deal programs and conflicts between the Collier administration, which wanted to enlarge the Navajo Reservation, and local whites who defeated the legislation. He explains how the advent of World War II created problems that negated advances of New Deal programs, and assesses New Deal policies as either having become fixtures in subsequent administrations or been discarded. One map, photographs of Navajos, and a bibliography of unpublished and published primary and secondary works and interviews are included.

WEAVER, THOMAS, ed. *Indians of Arizona: A Contemporary Perspective.* Tucson: University of Arizona Press, 1974. 169pp. Illustrated.

The author surveys Arizona native cultures and the history of their relationships to Spanish, federal, and state governments from ancestral to current times. He surveys Arizona's ancient tribes, discusses the laws and impact of the Spanish, the first Europeans to explore Arizona, mid-nineteenth century American control of Arizona, reservation assimilation policy, and the impact of the 1887 Dawes Act. He deals with twentieth-century New Deal policy and legislation, termination, House Concurrent Resolution 108, and Public Law 280. He considers contemporary Arizona Indians, their reservations, and urban communities; their relationship to the federal government; and political, economic, and other living conditions. He tells of the legal basis of tribal government; state and federal employment, economic development, and assistance programs; and mission, federal, and public school systems for non-Indians and Indians. There are two maps, photographs of Arizona Indians and their environs, eleven tables that illustrate the text, and a suggested reading list.

GREAT BASIN-PLATEAU

COAN, C. F. "The Adoption of the Reservation Policy in the Pacific Northwest, 1853 to 1855." *Quarterly of the Oregon Historical Society* 23, no. 1 (March 1922):1–37. Illustrated.

The author traces the formation and adoption of Oregon and Washington reservation policy in 1854 and the work of Joel Palmer who succeeded Anson Dart in 1853 as superintendent of Indian affairs in Oregon. He gives details of several treaties made by Palmer with Oregon Indians, looks at Washington's Indian policy, identical to that adopted for Oregon Territory, and the role of Isaac I. Stevens, Washington's governor and superintendent of Indian affairs, who was faced with the problem of increasing numbers of land-hungry settlers who wanted Indian lands. He looks at the common features of the treaties made by Palmer and Stevens which provided for cessions of great parts of the region, furnished reservations as homes, and supplied annual appropriations. He explains the negotiation of treaties made by Palmer and Stevens which extinguished land title west of the Cascade Mountains in Washington and Oregon during 1854 and 1855, discusses treaty-making east of the Cascades which encountered Indian opposition, and concludes with the genesis of the 1855 Yakima Indian War which resulted when settlers moved into the interior and which delayed the ratification of the majority of treaties until 1859. There is one map and Palmer's 1853 Annual Report proposing the reservation system. The article is based largely on correspondence.

——. "The First Stage of the Federal Indian Policy in the Pacific Northwest, 1849–1852." *Quarterly of the Oregon Historical Society* 22, no. 1 (March 1921):46–89. Illustrated.

The author summarizes Indian-white relations from 1774 to 1849 in the Pacific Northwest, and describes the development of U.S. Indian policy in Oregon, organized as a territory in 1849. He looks at the role of Joseph Lane, the first Oregon governor and ex-officio superintendent of Indian affairs, and how he succeeded in establishing amicable relations between the two races. He examines the policies of Samuel Thurston, the Oregon delegate to Congress, who wanted to move Indians living west of the Cascade Mountains to country east of them, the Congressional appointment of commissioners and their instructions to negotiate with Indians west of the Cascades. He gives details of the 1851 treaties made by the commissioners who adopted plans of their own to allow Indians to remain in the Willamette Valley on reservations of tribal lands, and their rejection by the U.S. Senate. He explains the work of Anson Dart, superintendent of Indian affairs in 1850, and the thirteen treaties he made in 1851 with Indians of western Oregon, allowing similar terms as the previous commissioners, and gives the reasons why they were rejected by the government. There is an appendix containing Dart's report on the thirteen treaties he negotiated, copies of four of the treaties, and one map of Indian land cessions provided for in the unratified treaties of 1851 and those eventually ratified in 1859. The article is based largely on government documents and unpublished materials.

STERN, THEODORE. *The Klamath Tribe: A People and Their Reservation.* Seattle: University of Washington Press, 1966. 356pp. Illustrated. Bibliography.

This book contains a case study of federal reform policy as applied to the Klamath tribe of south central Oregon from the 1840s to 1954. Part one briefly describes Klamath and Modoc life before white contact to the signing of the 1864 treaty, which formed the reservation and involved the Klamaths in a program of directed change designed to make them into farmers. Parts two and three consider the twenty-year period of agency domination, government programs designed to transform Klamath economic and political structure, religion and family life; the period of allotments, and the ineffectiveness and decline of agency supervision. The concluding sections deal with modern Klamath demography, economy, social life, local political relations and tribal government, the 1954 termination of the reservation, and an analysis of federal programs of directed change and their effects on the Klamaths in particular. There is an appendix of letters written by Klamaths, four maps, and photographs of Klamath people and their reservation. The book is partly based on unpublished materials.

CALIFORNIA

ANDERSON, GEORGE E.; W. H. ELLISON; and ROBERT F. HEIZER. *Treaty Making and Treaty Rejection by the Federal Government in California, 1850–1852.* Ballena Press Publications in Archaeology, Ethnology, and History, no. 9. Socorro, N. Mex.: Ballena Press, 1978. 124pp. Bibliography.

Four separate papers explain the negotiation of eighteen treaties between California tribes and three U.S. commissioners appointed by President Fillmore between 1850 and 1852, explore problems in identifying so-called tribes which signed the treaties, and discuss the debates in the California State Legislature and U.S. Senate which were effective in causing the latter body to refuse to ratify them. Papers include "Treaty-making by the Federal Government in California, 1851–1852," "Majority and Minority Reports of the Special Committee to Inquire Into the Treaties Made by the United States Commissioners with the Indians of California," "Rejection of California Indian Treaties: A Study in Local Influence on National Policy," and "Senate Committee Debate on Appropriation of Funds for Aid to Indians of California Provided by the Three Treaty Commissioners." There are refer-

ences in each paper based chiefly on government documents.

ELLISON, WILLIAM H. "The Federal Indian Policy in California, 1846–1860." *Mississippi Valley Historical Review* 9, no. 1 (June 1922):37–67.

The author deals with changes in federal Indian policy in California from 1846 to 1860. He begins with sketches of Spanish and Mexican policy in California, discusses the efforts of federal military authorities to maintain peaceful relations after the American occupation of California, and describes the discovery of gold and the rush of immigrants to California. The appointment of three agents in 1850, their work in negotiating eighteen treaties between California tribes and the United States which affected 139 tribes or bands, and the rejection of the treaties by the U.S. Senate in 1852 due to the violent reaction in California to giving Indians valuable areas of land are also covered. The author discusses federal appropriations for the development and management of a system of small military reservations created by agreement, not treaty, from 1853 to 1856, the abandonment of California Indian agents and military reservations because the system failed, and the new method of administering Indian affairs instituted in 1860, dividing the state into southern and northern districts and placing Indians on small reservations, again created by agreement. There are some dated opinions. The article is based on government documents and unpublished and published works.

ALASKA

AMERICAN INDIAN POLICY REVIEW COMMISSION. *Special Joint Task Force Report on Alaskan Native Issues.* Washington, D.C.: Government Printing Office, 1976. 90pp.

This volume gives a historical summary of federal policy in Alaska from 1867 until the Alaskan Native Claims Settlement Act of 1971 and considers the Act's provisions and the current and long term issues related to the Act that have caused conflicts and ambiguities. The Commission explains the kinds of governments under which native villages operate in Alaska today, the status of the villages, and their place within the jurisdictional structure. The volume concludes with six recommendations. The appendix contains long term projects for native ownership and control of lands conveyed under the 1971 Act and Alaskan field visit reports.

BIBLIOGRAPHIES

BUCHANAN, JIM, and FRAN BURKERT. *A Bibliography of Current American Indian Policy.* Public Administration Series Bibliography no. P188. Monticello, Ill.: Vance Bibliographies, 1979. 69pp.

This bibliography lists 750 items that the authors consider a basic collection of materials for examining Indian policies of federal, state, county, local, and tribal governments, whether in the fields of law, education, health, social and economic development, or other fields where Indian policies are created, legislated, and implemented. The items reflect the various Indian policies of different levels of governments: the fifty state governments, municipalities, county governments, and departments of the federal government, some of which come into conflict with each other over Indians. There are various issues discussed in the introduction and for which references are given. These are aboriginal rights and claims; economic development; education; fishing, hunting and trapping rights; jurisdictional questions; self-determination; and water rights. There is a subject index.

PRUCHA, FRANCIS PAUL. "Documents of the Federal Government." In *A Bibliographical Guide to the History of Indian-White Relations in the United States,* pp. 6–12. Chicago: University of Chicago Press, 1977.
This section of the unannotated bibliography lists printed federal government records that are important to the study of all aspects of Indian relations. The author lists over seventy compilations, catalogs, indexes, and guides to help locate material. The subsections include Guides to Government Publications (Proceedings, Debates, Documents and Reports, Bills and Resolutions, Hearings), Federal Laws and Treaties, Materials from the Executive Branch, Court Decisions, and Special Publications.

———. "The Indian Department." In *A Bibliographical Guide to the History of Indian-White Relations in the United States,* pp. 108–18. Chicago: University of Chicago Press, 1977.
This section of the unannotated bibliography lists works that concern the Bureau of Indian Affairs and the personnel of the Indian superintendencies and agencies that make up what has often been called the Indian Department. The people in these offices carried out the Indian policy of the federal government and often helped to formulate it. The subsections include the Bureau of Indian Affairs, Agents and Superintendents, Agencies and Superintendencies, Indian Reservations, Indian Reservations: Grazing, and Indian Police and Judges.

———. "Legal Relations." In *A Bibliographical Guide to the History of Indian-White Relations in the United States,* pp. 229–39. Chicago: University of Chicago Press, 1977.
This section of the unannotated bibliography lists works on the legal status and rights of Indians. The subsections include: Reference Works and Periodicals, Legal Status: General and Miscellaneous Studies, Indian Rights, Civil Rights Act 1968, Jurisdiction, Taxation, Water Rights, Hunting and Fishing Rights, Legal Services, and Tribal Law and Government.

———. *United States Indian Policy: A Critical Bibliography.* Bloomington: Indiana University Press, 1977. 54pp.

This work is one of the volumes in the Newberry Library Center for the History of the American Indian bibliographical series. Sources are critiqued in a twenty-seven page essay which is followed by an alphabetical listing of 175 sources. The author summarizes general and introductory books, as well as U.S. Indian policy and tribal reactions, and he provides a list of works for a beginner and for a basic library collection. The bibliographic essay is divided into sections on preremoval policy, Indian removal, westward expansion, the Civil War period, post-Civil War Indian reform, the Indian New Deal, and recent history. He discusses special topics which include education, legal status, missionary occupation, the Bureau of Indian Affairs, and Indian wars. Selected tribal histories are listed, and a brief section on collections of government documents is included.

SABATINI, JOSEPH D., comp. *American Indian Law: A Bibliography of Books, Law Review Articles, and Indian Periodicals.* Albuquerque: University of New Mexico American Indian Law Center, 1973. 44pp.
This bibliography is intended as a basic guide to materials available in the UNM Law Library collection, which covers many subjects of Indian law, from primitive law to the complex tribal, state, and federal relationships of today. Also included in the collection are materials on related subjects, such as Indian economic and community development, education, history, tribal government and politics, chosen to reflect the major topics of interest in Indian law today. There are sections on books and Indian periodicals that have been selected from the American Indian Law Center holdings and on law review articles that have been selected primarily from entries in the *Index to Legal Periodicals,* which is comprehensive for articles from 1900 through January 1973, and also includes nineteenth-century items.

WEBB, VINCENT J. *Indian Justice: A Research Bibliography.* Council of Planning Librarians Exchange Bibliography no. 1134. Monticello, Ill.: Vance Bibliographies, 1976. 67pp.
This bibliography contains a listing of articles, books, and bibliographies on the subject of Indian justice. Sections deal with socioeconomic and historical situations of Indians in the United States, processes of demographic and social change, social psychology of Native Americans, and social problems, such as alcoholism and urban problems. There are items on operations of criminal justice agencies dealing with Indians (law enforcement, judicial and correctional personnel, prosecution, and defense), and differing jurisdictional limits of federal, state, county, local, and tribal criminal justice agencies. There are items pertaining to tribal law, sovereignty, the civil rights of Indians, Native American property and resource rights, and the nature of federal and state Indian policies.

10   HISTORIES

A staggering number of books and articles about the history of the relations between Native Americans and whites in North America over the past 500 years have been published. This literature is often controversial, partisan, and full of dated terminology and opinions describing the conflicts between American Indians and whites. Readers will discover that social scientists have fundamental disagreements and biases when they interpret data from the past. Some writers emphasize the unjust or unconscionable actions by settlers, missionaries, and the federal government, while others highlight the more honorable dealings on the part of whites.

Most writers spell out the impact of European beliefs and actions on Indian nations and discuss to a limited extent the impact of Indians on white culture. They usually tell of the decades of conflict between two disparate civilizations—different ways of living, different folkways, religions, etc. Because of the seeming incompatibility of these two ways of living, many historians have accepted the idea that Indian societies should have adopted white culture in order to survive peacefully, never questioning the motives or goals of those people in the past who insisted it was desirable to assimilate Indians into the American mainstream. In many cases, the historians were prisoners of the times in which they wrote. Their opinions and language which today may be pejorative were not always intentionally used to cast aspersions, but were common currency of the time. MacLeod (p. 124), who advocated assimilation as a solution to the "Indian problem," wrote in 1928 when there was no notion about the need for cultural pluralism. The historic shift from assimilation to cultural pluralism as a viable goal did not occur until the early 1960s. The fact that so many Native Americans have been so ardently determined to resist white culture and maintain their political and social organization, world views, religions, customs, and languages despite years of federal assimilation programs suggests that Indians consider their ways of life to be as worthy as that of the white Americans. Too many writers, however, implicitly accept the idea that Indian societies are somehow inferior. Jennings (p. 132) argues that, in the case of colonial Indian-white relations, there is an uncritical acceptance among historians of the myth of a master civilization locked in a battle with savagery. One may add that too many historians writing today still accept this myth as valid.

Several historians point out the patterns of white relations with Indians that were established during the colonial era and which were characteristic of relations that were to prevail for centuries. In the first stage, a period of Indian-white equality, friendly relations were maintained in order for whites to survive. The prior right of Indians to soil was recognized and negotiations and treaties were made between equals. DePuy (p. 169) gives brief contents of fifty-four treaties dating from 1677 to 1768 made between Indians and English colonies. When English settlements became stronger and permanent, the white populations larger and armed, the white attitude toward Indians shifted to arrogance. The English forced the Indians to obey their laws and to submit to their demands. Eventually, Indian political sovereignty was eliminated as a result of U.S. Indian policy.

Indians and Blacks. One area that has been generally overlooked in the study of Indian history is the relationship between Indians and blacks. These two groups were associated as fellow slaves in New England, the middle, and southern colonies. Porter (p. 125) points out that their relations depended on circumstances and not on mutually shared feelings that as members of nonwhite races they were natural allies. Blacks mistreated Indians and Indians killed blacks while some runaway slaves were protected by certain tribes in the northern part of the United States. Willis (p. 145) attributes the mutual hostility that existed between Indians and blacks in the colonies in the eighteenth century to a white policy designed to create antagonisms and thereby prevent a coalition between the two groups, each of which outnumbered the white population.

There were slave-holding Indians in the South and in Indian Territory, particularly among the Seminoles where black status, however, was practically equal to that of the owner. Peddue (p. 144) traces the history of slavery among the Cherokees of Tennessee, Georgia, and North Carolina. Many Seminoles and their black allies tried unsuccessfully to resist removal to Indian Territory in two Seminole wars and once removed to Oklahoma Territory were continually raided by slave-hunters until a number of them fled to Mexico. McReynolds (p. 143) tells of the relationship between blacks and Seminoles and Creeks, and Debo (p. 140) discusses Creek and black relations in Oklahoma.

Relations between Indians and blacks in the Old Northwest, Rocky Mountains, Plains, and the Pacific Coast, where slavery never was an important institution, were much the same as that between Indians and whites in terms of trading, intermarrying, and fighting.

European Diseases. Early European explorers came to North America in search of a northwest passage to the Orient, gold, spices, riches, and fame. The explorers and other groups who followed carried with them diseases to which the Indians had no or little resistance. Scholars feel many more Indians died from these catastrophic diseases than from the protracted warfare with whites. Epidemics of smallpox, cholera, measles, and tuberculosis decimated whole peoples or annihilated them altogether. Some tribes lost most of their population within a matter of weeks when illness infected the group. In 1615, an English slave trader, Captain Hunt, made plans to kidnap some Wampanoag Indians on the Massachusetts Coast.

Some of his men were infected with smallpox which rapidly spread to the Wampanoags and wiped out two-thirds of them. The Huron Confederacy and Iroquois Confederacy lost over half of their populations in the 1630s and 1640s due to epidemics. Schlesier (p. 135) argues that the wars of the Iroquois and the destruction or dispersal of many tribes, particularly the Hurons, around the middle of the seventeenth century was the outcome of a set of destructive forces, smallpox emerging as the most significant. Hundreds of years later, in the early nineteenth century, epidemics continued to decimate Indians in the West. In 1837, a smallpox epidemic among the Mandans, Hidatsas, Arikaras, Blackfeet, Sioux, and Pawnees killed about 14,000 people. Meyer (p. 153) tells of the disastrous effects of disease on the Mandans, Hidatsas, and Arikaras, who reorganized after the epidemic into a single village so few were the survivors.

European Treatment of Indians. Dutch, Spanish, French, and English penetration of North America began almost at the same time. There were numerous exploratory expeditions attempted by three of the powers, but permanent settlements, with the exception of St. Augustine, were not made until the first decade of the seventeenth century. Jamestown was begun by the British in 1607, Quebec in Canada by the French in 1608, Santa Fe by the Spanish and New Amsterdam by the Dutch in 1609. The four colonial powers were not always similar in their approach to dealing with Indians, although in every area settled by Europeans "Indians were victims . . . they suffered discrimination, exploitation, and wholesale destruction—by disease and demoralization if not by sword and bullet. But there were differences of degree in treatment and differences of emphasis in attitudes among the colonizing groups."[1] Many of the historians have studied colonial treatments of Indians. MacLeod (p. 124), for example, examines the differences between the Spanish and Anglo-Americans in their treatment of Indians. Peckham and Gibson (p. 135) have collected six essays, each briefly exploring Indian policies and practices of the several European nations. Jaenen (p. 132) discusses various aspects of the nature of French contact with Indian peoples. Lauber (p. 133) explains the enslavement of Indians by the French, Spanish, and English including the methods used to enslave natives, their employment, treatment, and manumission.

The French in Canada were primarily interested in the fur trade and less covetous of land than other Europeans. They developed no permanent settlements in the interior and made no great demands on the Indians for land because they were not interested in settling the land for farming. Intent on the fur trade, which depended on the friendship of Indian trappers and go-betweens, they needed to secure the trust and allegiance of Indian partners. The Spanish were interested in precious metals and forced Indian labor and the Dutch hungered for furs and some land. Trelease (p. 136) explains the beginning of New Netherland and the Dutch interest in the fur trade and Indian land. He tells of warfare between Dutch colonists and Algonquian Indians and discusses Dutch commercial relations with Iroquois Indians. Weslager (p. 138) describes the rivalry between Dutch and Swedes for Indian lands and beaver furs until 1664.

1. Alden T. Vaughan, *New England Frontier: Puritans and Indians, 1620–1675*, revised ed. (New York: Norton, 1979), p. xxxiii.

The English wanted Indian lands because they were primarily farmers although some were interested in the fur trade.

Treatment of Indians varied widely in the British colonies because the imperial government permitted each colony to make its own Indian policy. The crown found it too difficult to enforce uniform policies and regulations on the Indian frontier. English colonies eventually contended with each other as well as the British crown over Indian trade policy and defense. For example, Reid (p. 144) and Crane (p. 140) describe South Carolina's intercolonial problems over control of Indian trade, particularly with Virginia, from 1670 to 1715. In an effort to gain control over all Indian-white relations throughout the colonies, the imperial government formed the Indian superintendency system in the newly created Northern and Southern Departments in the mid-eighteenth century but various colonies interfered with the effectiveness of the Indian superintendents.

Missionaries. The missionary spirit of Christianity was another motivating force in European expansion during the seventeenth century. Colonial charters frequently carried a clause enjoining the grantees to convert and "civilize" the Indians. Puritans formed fourteen "praying towns" among southern New England Algonquians from the late 1640s to the 1670s. Potential converts were removed to and isolated in the towns away from the influences of English settlers and other Indians. Salisbury (p. 135) examines the program and role in English policy of John Eliot, the minister who established the fourteen towns, and the effects of Eliot's program on the "praying" Indians until the defeat of Eliot's missionary program. The Virginia Company appropriated money to educate young Indians, separated from their families by force if necessary, in Virginia homes. The result of Indians' conversion to Christianity was to engender divisiveness within tribes. Berkhofer (p. 128) explains the plight of Indian converts in their own tribes and Trigger (p. 136) argues that the Iroquois were victorious over the Hurons by 1649 in part because the latter were factionalized into traditional and Christian camps and demoralized by French Jesuit activities. The Spanish in the Southwest established missions to which Indians were voluntarily or forcibly drawn to become Christianized and "civilized." Indian life in the missions, which expanded up the California coast in the eighteenth century, was harsh. The missions, which broke up in the early nineteenth century, were outposts of the Spanish empire where Indians were introduced to Spanish material goods and spiritual life. At the end of nearly two centuries of efforts, both the French and English missions had failed to convert and "civilize" the majority of the Indians. Native Americans, by and large, simply did not wish to be converted to Christianity. There was a continuing effort to convert Indians in the eighteenth century but it failed, Berkhofer argues, because the missionaries' prowhite attitudes and their general cultural attitudes and assumptions about Indians prevented them from succeeding. Later, in the mid-nineteenth century Catholic and Protestant missionaries traveled to Oregon and Washington. Their teachings again undermined tribal institutions and created bitter factions within tribes.

Resistance to Settlers. In almost every instance, the first arrivals to North America were received with kindness and hospitality. The Wampanoags' principal chief, Massasoit, and the principal chief of the Virginia Indians, Powhatan, offered food and shelter and instruction in how to survive in the North American environment. Both men maintained peace with the white colonists until they died.

From the beginning, however, English colonists pressured Indians to adopt the supposedly "civilized" and superior European lifestyle and religion and often employed repressive measures to overpower Indians who did not comply. These colonists wanted Indian land as well. They and other settlers who followed used deceitful procedures to extinguish title to Indian lands when the rightful owners refused to sell. Many Indians in New England tried to resist English pressures for their lands. As a result, two major New England wars were fought in the seventeenth century: the 1637 Pequot War and, in 1675–76, King Philip's War in which the Indians were defeated after bitter and violent struggles. Vaughan (p. 137), Leach (p. 133), and Jennings (p. 132) offer differing narrative interpretations of these two wars. Leach assigns Puritan avarice for land and misunderstandings that accompanied land transactions an important role and Jennings considers an ideology of conquest a crucial factor in Puritan land lust. Vaughan, in his 1965 version, argues that Puritans followed humane policies in their relationships with Indians.

In Virginia, there were two fiercely fought wars, in 1622 and 1644, in which Indians were defeated after rejecting demands for more lands and resisting the colonists' encroachments on their lands. These early Indian wars in southern New England and Virginia resulted in the end of organized Indian resistance to English expansion in that region and precipitated the decline of Indian political power.

Before the French and Indian War in 1754, almost every colony was afflicted with Indian-white conflicts. The Tuscarora War of 1711–12, a revolt against white encroachments, resulted in the partial decimation of these North Carolina Indians and saw the retreat northward of the survivors. In the Yamasee War of 1715, a rebellion of southern Indians, prompted by general resentments against English economic exploitation as well as by a fear of English agricultural expansion, resulted in the near extermination of the Yamasees by settlers in South Carolina. Milling (p. 143) and Crane (p. 140) both describe the Tuscarora and Yamasee Wars.

In New York, the Dutch and bands of Algonquians engaged in border warfare until the Indians were defeated. By the end of the seventeenth century, tribes along the Atlantic Seaboard had been destroyed, dispersed, or subjected to the control of the European colonists.

In these colonial wars as well as other battles that were fought throughout the next two hundred years, Indians fought on both sides. As guides and auxiliaries to white troops, Indians were often pitted against Indians.

The Fur Trade. Throughout the colonial period and well into the nineteenth century, the fur trade was one of the principal business enterprises in North America. European fashions demanded furs for use in making hats, coats, dress trimmings, and other articles of clothing. Trading with Indian peoples for furs began immediately in the colonies on the East Coast and gradually, as Indians' lands became depleted of the desired fur-bearing animals, traders moved inland in search of new sources. For a time, trade with Europeans benefited Indians. The goods they received in trade for pelts made life easier. Guns made hunting more bountiful, metal kettles were more practical to cook in, steel tools were more efficient than those made from stone and bone. European cloth replaced clothing made from fur, thus saving hours of preparation. Some scholars argue that Indians soon regarded the traders' goods as necessities as they began to discard their own less efficient equivalent tools and technologies. These scholars point out that once the Indians used needles, scissors, knives, and hundreds of other items, they became irrevocably dependent on these goods and were unable to do without them. This is one theory and arguable. On the basis of present-day observations in South America, some scientists now argue that the affected population becomes dependent on these things because their basic economic systems have been disrupted and their resources diminished with the diminished subsistence area.

The gradual extermination of wildlife, especially of fur-bearing animals, on Indian lands caused starvation, reshaped social organizations, and altered the subsistence patterns of Indians. The Indians became even more dependent on whites for commodities in order to survive.

By the mid-1700s, traders wanted Indian lands as well as pelts. Unscrupulous English and French traders along the northeastern colonial frontier profited by swindling Indians out of furs and large areas of land by using unprincipled tactics. Some traders carried rum with them and encouraged tribal people to become drunk before beginning the bartering for furs and goods. Because some British and French traders persisted in offering liquor, they succeeded in making it a requisite of the fur trade. Some tribes were forced to trade their entire catch of furs to certain traders at the traders' prices under threat of punishment. Some tribes became deeply in debt to certain traders, the latter of whom gained title to immense areas of valuable Indian lands in exchange for cancelling the debt. Although not all traders cheated Indians, eventually the fur trade left the Indian societies greatly weakened. Spanish, English, and French traders contended for furs harvested by the tribes. They manipulated tribal people who supported whichever rival supplied them with the goods they wanted. The Indians were more content with the British traders whose prices were more favorable than those of the French traders and whose goods were superior in quality to French wares.

Anglo-French rivalry in the fur trade was an important element in the struggle over control of North America which climaxed in the Seven Years' War, or the French and Indian War. Indian intertribal conflicts were greatly aggravated by the increasing demand for furs by rival European traders and tribes began to compete for the limited supplies of pelts. The intertribal conflicts were exacerbated by the incessant wars between European powers during which European nations encouraged tribes allied with them to attack tribes allied with other powers.

The Politics of Gift-Giving. During the French and Indian War, the British recruited thousands of Indians as allies through tremendous outlays of gifts. One of the ways Indians and the French or English had been negotiating was by exchanging gifts. Mutually exchanged presents cemented the political relationship between an Indian nation and a European nation.

Political gifts of peace medals were also given to heads of various Indian nations by European powers, a practice which was continued by the American leaders. The medals were designed to suggest either an informal or formal alliance between the Indians and the power that awarded the medal. Jacobs (p. 131) describes the competition between the French and British in giving presents to Indians in order to secure their allegiance and examines the role the presents played in the diplomatic history of Indian politics in the Northeast from 1748 to 1763. Presents and medals for Indians, although they secured diplomatic alliances, represented substantial outlays of sums to colonial governments.

French control of the fur trade was over when they were defeated in the Seven Years' War. England took control of Canada and the Old Northwest by the 1763 Treaty of Paris. The defeat of the French left most of the Indian nations of the interior of Canada and the Old Northwest without a potential ally against the encroaching English colonies.

The British substantially reduced the handing out of presents to Indians, an action which angered tribes who needed the goods to alleviate their suffering after the war. In addition, an extremely high schedule of prices for goods was instituted which outraged Indians who could not go to English trading posts and obtain supplies on credit or as gifts, as had been the custom with the French. The presence of British forts reduced Indian hunting territories and also angered the Indians. The British failure to supply western Indians enabled certain chiefs to mobilize Indian discontent. By 1763, the tribal peoples along the whole northwestern frontier were ready to retaliate against the Euro-Americans, and Pontiac led an angry Indian population against British aggressors in the area north of Ohio. The uprising ended in defeat.

Pre-Revolutionary British Crown Policy. The British crown in an effort to avert further trouble with Indians forbade white settlement in the region west of the Appalachian Mountains. From 1763 to 1775, British measures such as the Proclamation of 1763 and the treaties concluded with western tribes which set boundary lines and regulations concerning land purchases and trade with Indians were ineffectual. Frontier people and land speculators who wanted to invade the Indians' domain ignored British regulations, and the plans of the crown for protecting Indian rights in land broke down. Alden (p. 138) discusses the policy of John Stuart, Superintendent of the Southern Indian District, who tried to maintain the Indian boundaries against American encroachment and settlement before the Revolution. The British government stationed a standing army in the colonies to enforce the Proclamation and then taxed the colonists to help pay for the venture. The colonists protested and revolted against the British government. They resented the closing of the frontier, the British military force, and the taxes levied for its support. These and other grievances led to the American Revolution.

The American Revolution. Indians feared more the land-hungry American colonists than the British, therefore the majority of the Indians allied themselves with the crown. The British could pose as defenders of Indian lands against the avarice of settlers, and the trade goods that Indians depended on were available from English traders. The new Congress which initially tried to secure Indian neutrality later endeavored to engage Indians in the service of the United Colonies. The Indians who supported the American cause were the exception. Graymont (p. 130) and Grinde (p. 130) both trace the events that led to the involvement of the Iroquois Confederacy in the Revolution. They examine how and why some factions of the Oneidas and the Tuscaroras took the American side while most took the British side, which threw the Iroquois into civil war. O'Donnell (p. 143) and Cotterill (p. 140) discuss certain southeastern tribes during the Revolution. Southern tribes, especially the Creeks and Cherokees, were active for the British, but the Catawbas aided the Americans. Corkran (p. 139) discusses Creek alliance with the British, and Brown (p. 138) describes the Catawba alliance with the Americans. The Americans were not able to win the allegiance of most Indians because their goods were no match for the British goods and because the Americans in the Ohio Valley were committing atrocities against the Indians.

In the Treaty of Paris which ended the conflict, the British granted the Americans title to the entire Northwest, disregarding the tribal peoples who lived in this territory and made no provisions for the Indian allies who had supported the British cause. The British remained in possession of frontier posts around the Great Lakes from which they continued to trade English goods for Indian furs.

Post-Revolutionary Conflicts. After the Revolution, there was blatant contempt for Indians both in the Northeast and the Southeast. Settlers poured into the lands north of the Ohio River ignoring Indian rights. There were military clashes in the Ohio country between U.S. troops and Indians as a result of white intrusion on Indian lands. Defeated chiefs were forced to cede a large portion of Ohio and other parts of the Northwest Territory. Blumenthal (p. 121) tells some of the sordid methods by which tribes were exploited and shorn of their lands. Many Indians in the South turned to the Spanish for support in the face of pressure from American settlers and land speculators.

The War of 1812. Tecumseh and his brother, the Prophet, urged Indians to stop alienating land held in common by all the tribes in their area. The British listened to Tecumseh's complaints against the American intruders and led him to believe they would support him in driving the Americans back from the Ohio. A frontier war between some of Tecumseh's followers and American troops began in 1811 and merged with the War of 1812, a war between the Americans and the British. The war was the last in which the Indians allied themselves with a foreign power against the Americans. Again, some Indians were pro-American although the sympathies of most tribes, in the Northeast and the Southeast, were with the British. When the War of 1812 broke out, most tribes in the Old Northwest were hostile to Americans and became auxiliaries, scouts, and raiders for the British forces. Tecumseh and his followers joined the British but were defeated.

In the South, a portion of the Creeks called the Red Sticks were armed against the Americans and the tribe engaged in a civil war and, with their forces split, suffered a defeat by American troops which resulted in the cession of nearly all the Creek lands in Alabama.

After the end of the War of 1812, tribes in the Northwest Territory and in the Southeast, deprived of their British allies, were coerced into signing a series of treaties that extinguished their title to large areas of land. Nearly all the tribes continued to occupy greatly reduced portions of their ancestral lands until Andrew Jackson became president, and eventually the tribes were forcibly removed west of the Mississippi River by the government.

Removal. In 1803 President Jefferson had envisaged plans for the voluntary removal of Indians to unsettled portions of Louisiana Territory that America had acquired from France. Presidents Monroe and Adams were unwilling to use military force to remove tribes, but President Jackson sponsored a removal bill in 1830 which involved forcible removal. In the Southeast, great numbers of settlers demanded that Indians be cleared out of their way. Georgia, Alabama, and Mississippi outlawed tribal governments and placed Indians under state government control. The situation of the tribes deteriorated under these laws. Bribery, threats, intimidation, and force were used to secure some kind of assent to removal treaties, most of which were agreed to by unrepresentative persons of the tribes. A series of fraudulent treaties with the Cherokees, Creeks, Choctaws, Chickasaws, and Seminoles were ratified and they were forced to move west of the Mississippi River during the 1830s under military escort. Debo (p. 148) and DeRosier (p. 141) tell of the Choctaw removal from Mississippi in the early 1830s, the first tribal population to be removed to Indian Territory. Young (p. 145) discusses the removal and allotment treaties affecting the Choctaws, Creeks, and Chickasaws from Mississippi and Alabama during the 1830s and tells how rival land speculators and companies scrambled for tribal allotments. Gibson (p. 142) tells of the Chickasaw removal from Mississippi and Alabama, McReynolds (p. 143) describes the Seminole removal from Florida, Debo (p. 140) tells of the Creek removal from Alabama and Georgia, and Wilkins (p. 145), King (p. 142), and Carter (p. 139) discuss the Cherokee removal from Georgia. Foreman (p. 141) surveys the forcible expulsion of the Five Civilized Tribes from the South, describing the inadequate government preparations, cruel and unnecessary suffering experienced by the emigrants, and discusses the people who profited from removal contracts.

In the North, white homesteaders overran tribal lands driving many Indian peoples from their homelands. In many cases, several Indians in a tribe were coerced into signing away their tribe's lands without the consent of the rest.

Armed resistance came from a few tribes but particularly from the Florida Seminoles, a small number of whom resisted removal in several wars with the U.S. Army and whose descendants still remain in Florida today. Jahoda (p. 132) and Hagan (p. 150) both tell the story of the Sacs and Foxes, led by Black Hawk, who resisted removal from Illinois but were defeated in 1831 and 1832, and forced to move. Jahoda also describes the removals of Senecas, Delawares, Shawnees, and Wyandots from Ohio and Oneidas from New York. Weslager (p. 138) tells the story of the Delaware removals in great detail and Edmunds (p. 129) considers Potawatomi removal.

Intertribal Conflicts in the Western Lands. Most of the Indians from east of the Mississippi River were settled in Nebraska, Kansas, and Oklahoma by 1840. Clashes occurred between the migrating tribes and the Prairie and

Plains tribes who had been persuaded to surrender some of their lands to make room for the displaced peoples. The western Indians resented the new tribes with whom they now had to compete in hunting buffalo, their chief source of food. The government failed to protect the displaced Indians in their new locations and they had to resort to fighting in order to survive. Foreman (p. 141) deals with the problems of the Cherokees, Choctaws, Creeks, and Chickasaws in establishing amicable relations in a strange country in the face of opposition from Osages, Pawnees, Kiowas, Comanches, and other indigenous nations who were required by the government to make room for the newcomers. Foreman also discusses the rehabilitation and reconstruction of the Five Civilized Tribes after the demoralization and impoverishment caused by forcible removal from the Southeast to Indian Territory. Hagan (p. 150) tells of the Sacs and Foxes who were moved to a Kansas reservation where they had to battle Plains tribes in order to survive.

Later Removals. The lands west of the Mississippi River were forever guaranteed to the tribes who were moved there. But white settlers did not stop at the Mississippi River, and the government again had to formulate new policies. In the 1840s, a number of tribes who had been moved to small reservations in eastern Kansas were forced to make new cessions as settlers moved in on them. Almost all these tribes were moved to Oklahoma. Unrau (p. 155) tells of the Kansa forced to leave eastern Kansas and Chapman (p. 148) tells of Otoes and Missourias who were moved from Kansas and Nebraska to Oklahoma. Territorial governments were organized to protect the settlers and in 1854 the Kansas-Nebraska bill completely dispossessed Indians of lands in these regions that had been guaranteed to them forever. Miner and Unrau (p. 153) identify techniques by which Indian removal from Kansas was accomplished and show how the territory evolved from a permanent habitat of thousands of Indians from eastern tribes in 1854 to a state with only a few Indians by 1875.

White Emigrants. In 1846 Texas with its many Indian tribes entered the Union and Oregon was acquired from Britain, and in 1848 the United States acquired the Southwest and California from Mexico. Travel routes running through Indian-owned land to these newly acquired regions were established. Friction developed along the routes as emigrants drove buffalo herds from the Indians' hunting grounds. Government agents who wished to secure the safe passage of these travelers along the Oregon and Santa Fe Trails convinced thousands of Plains Indians representing many different tribes to sign the Fort Laramie Treaty in 1851. The treaty set boundaries between tribes, authorized roads and military posts within their territories, where troops were stationed to protect emigrants and punish Indians, and guaranteed safety to white travelers along the travel routes in return for which Indians were promised annuities.

The Civil War. The Civil War slowed down the westward movement of whites but was disastrous for many Indians. When the war broke out in 1861, tribes and factions of tribes of the Five Civilized Tribes (the Cherokees, Creeks, Chickasaws, Choctaws, and Seminoles) were divided in their support of the Confederacy or the federal cause. The failure of the federal government to protect the Five Tribes in their new environment explains why some Indians supported the Confederacy. The Choctaws and Chickasaws were overwhelmingly pro-South and the Creeks and Cherokees were evenly divided in their allegiance. Abel (p. 146) explains that Indian Territory figured prominently in Confederate designs for the West because of its geographic position and economic importance and explains how Confederate diplomacy secured alliance treaties and assurances of military assistance from the Five Tribes. Abel (p. 146) discusses the instability of the Indian-Confederate alliance, Confederate mismanagement of Indian affairs, and the pitting of Union-allied against Confederate-allied Indians. She attributes war conditions in Indian Territory to its being a pawn between contending forces and considers the growth of unionist sentiment among southern Indians. Abel (p. 146) also deals with the negotiations and provisions of the 1866 Reconstruction treaties with the Five Civilized Tribes which readjusted their relations with the federal government after the war. Bailey (p. 147) tells of the political, economic, social, and educational efforts toward reconstruction by each of the Five Tribes in Indian Territory after the war until 1877. He discusses the development of railroads in Indian Territory and federal goals of securing Indian lands in Indian Territory.

There were violent Indian-white clashes during the Civil War. In 1862, the Santee Sioux attacked whites in Minnesota, their resentments fired, in part, by the failure of the government to deliver needed goods. Meyer (p. 153) describes this conflict. In the Southwest, Navajos were rounded up in 1863 and held in captivity at Bosque Redondo, New Mexico, for five years, and Black Kettle's band of peaceful Cheyennes was massacred at Sand Creek, Colorado, in 1864.

Indian-White Conflicts, 1860–1890. From 1860 to 1890, white settlements continued to expand over Indian lands, wiping out the two great buffalo herds, the principal source of food for Plains Indians, usurping and depleting other resources—game, wood, and water—with government encouragement. The southern buffalo herd was destroyed by 1880 and the northern herd was gone from the Plains by 1885.

There was incessant conflict between white soldiers and settlers on the Plains, in Texas, in the Southwest, the Pacific Northwest, California, and the Basin-Plateau area between 1850 and 1890. Utley (p. 156) examines the relations between the regular and volunteer frontiersmen and Indians from 1848 to 1891. He argues that the frontier army was neither the vanguard of civilization nor a barbaric band of butchers but rather a conventional military force trying to control unconventional enemies with conventional military organization and methods. Another writer (Ellis, p. 148) argues that despite the excesses by which many military men acquired reputations as exterminationists, the military also provided examples of understanding and support for the needs of Indians.

Great Basin–Plateau, 1820s–1850s. In the 1820s and 1830s trappers and traders moved into Indian lands of the Interior and the Rocky Mountains. The Inter-Tribal Council of Nevada (p. 163) describes the influx of fur trappers, traders, Mormon missionaries, miners, and settlers into the Nevada, Utah, Idaho, California, and Oregon lands of the Numa, the Northern

Paiutes; Nuwuvi, Southern Paiutes; Wa She Shu, Washos; and Newe, Western Shoshones.

Johnson (p. 163) discusses the invasion of fur trappers, traders, and miners into Nevada's Walker River Paiute lands. Americans and British competed for furs in the Interior until 1846 when the fur trade declined. From the fur trappers and traders, some tribes learned of Christianity and requested religious instruction for their people. In the 1840s, Catholic and Protestant missionaries traveled to the Interior to open missions among the Cayuses, Nez Percés, Flatheads, and others. The missionaries' efforts ultimately undermined tribal institutions and created bitter factions that weakened tribes. In addition, competition among missionaries for Indian converts caused divisiveness within tribes. Burns (p. 162) examines Jesuit involvement in Indian-white troubles in present-day Oregon, Washington, Idaho, and western Montana from 1840 to 1880. Josephy (p. 164) and Slickpoo (p. 165) tell of Protestant and Catholic missionaries who competed for Nez Percé converts.

The writings of missionaries encouraged more American settlements in Oregon country. Ruby and Brown (p. 164) tell of the influx of miners into Spokane country, particularly after gold was discovered there. Mining towns soon crowded out Indian villages in the Wallowa Valley in the 1860s. Clashes and wars eventually occurred in the 1850s between Oregon and Washington settlers, miners, and troops and Indian tribes. Beckham (p. 161) describes the Rogue River Wars of the 1850s in which Rogue River Indians unsuccessfully tried to resist white settlers and miners who had moved into their lands. Eventually, tribes in Idaho, Oregon, and Washington were defeated by troops and put on reservations. Their lands were opened to settlers.

Texas. In Texas, laws denying Indians all rights resulted in the guerrilla warfare between Texas Rangers and Comanches, Kiowas, and bands of Apaches for several decades until the Indians were defeated. Newcomb (p. 154) tells of the almost complete extermination of Texas Indians by the Spanish, Mexicans, Texans, and Americans in turn.

California. In California, Indians were crushed by whites who poured into California during the gold rush. Indian villages and hunting and gathering grounds were overrun. In the early 1850s, the American government extinguished Indian titles to California land, and reservations were established for the Indians whose population continued to decline between 1850 and 1860 from an estimated 100,000 to 16,000. Heizer (p. 167) and Castillo (p. 165) deal with the life of California Indians under Spanish, Mexican, and American rule and stress the violence, decimation of the Indian population, and restrictive and discriminatory legislation of these three countries. Phillips (p. 167) tells of the Cahuillas, Cupeños, and Luiseños who chose either to resist or cooperate with the Spanish, Mexicans, and Americans in order to preserve their cultures and political sovereignty. Cook (p. 166) investigates the population decline of California Indians under the Spanish mission system from 1770 to 1840. He tells of the Indians' rebellions and fugitivism, their lack of immunity to infections, and their suboptimal diet which probably predisposed them to disease. He examines how factors such as resistance to conversion, confinement, forced labor, punishment, and the missions' overpopulation sapped the Indians' collective strength. Cook (p. 166) studies the population decline of non-Christianized California Indians in the interior from 1800 to 1848 who never came under mission influence but were exposed directly to Spanish civilian and military contact. He concludes that disease and forced removal of large numbers of Indians from their normal habitat as a result of missionization, not warfare, resulted in the large population reduction. Last, Cook (p. 166) investigates the decline of Indian populations from 1848 to 1870 due to conflicts with Americans which involved direct armed conflicts, disease, starvation, depletion of the food supply, and the inability to adjust to new economic conditions. Cook concludes that the greatest population decline and adjustments came under American rule.

The Southwest. The Spanish empire moved into southwestern Indian lands in the late sixteenth century for wealth, converts, and slaves and ruled there until 1821. Hostility developed between the Spanish and the Apaches and their Pueblo allies. The harsh rule of some Spanish governors plus religious and economic oppression led to an allied Pueblo-Apache revolt against the Spanish empire in northern New Spain. The 1680 Pueblo revolt, the most well known, was brought to an end by Spanish counter-offensives in 1692. Jones (p. 159) discusses the period 1692–1704 when the Spanish took advantage of Pueblo disunity to reconquer New Mexico with the assistance of friendly Pueblo forces and examines the growth of the Spanish-Pueblo alliance that lasted until the early nineteenth century. Sando (p. 159), a Jemez Pueblo, covers the same ground in his work. Gunnerson (p. 158) tells of one fundamental characteristic of Spanish conquest and settlement, the reliance on Pueblo, Jicarilla Apache, and other Indian auxiliaries who assisted in the defense of New Spain's northern frontier against other Indians, particularly the Apaches, from 1692 to 1794. Kenner (p. 159) tells of the Spanish use of Plains Comanches in fighting Apache enemies. Terrell (p. 160), Sonnichsen (p. 160), and Thrapp (p. 161) tell of Apache conflicts with the Spanish from the mid-sixteenth century to the late eighteenth century and their conflicts with Comanches, Mexicans, and Americans during the nineteenth century.

Between 1860 and 1885, Apache bands in Arizona and New Mexico waged defensive warfare against large numbers of U.S. troops and other whites. They were defeated and put on reservations where they did not wish to be. By 1886 the army succeeded in ending militant raids by the small, elusive bands of Apaches. Thrapp (p. 161) discusses the unremitting conflict between Apaches and the white population for control of Apacheria from 1860 to 1886, which marked the end of nearly three centuries of Apache-white warfare in the Southwest. Sando (p. 159) reviews the destructive role of the United States in Pueblo Indian affairs after 1848. McNitt (p. 159) argues that the Spanish, Mexicans, and Americans who colonized the Navajo territory in succession were essentially alike in their mistreatment of Navajos. He describes Spanish and Mexican enslavement of Navajos, land encroachment, their denial of human rights, and their warfare with the Navajos. He considers American appropriation of Navajo land, treaties allowing Navajo enslavement to continue, and armed hostilities between the Navajos and the Americans.

Great Plains. Although some warfare had occurred earlier, the period of 1860 to 1877 saw the major assault by the U.S. government on the lands of the Plains Indians and the general defensive warfare waged by the Sioux, Cheyennes, Arapahos, Kiowas, Kiowa Apaches, and Comanches from the Dakotas to Texas. Hyde (p. 151) examines the era of white encroachment on Sioux lands between 1861 and 1870, particularly the invasion of the Black Hills by settlers in the 1870s. He describes Sioux opposition to the invasion of their lands and analyzes the motives of several Sioux leaders including Red Cloud, Spotted Tail, and Crazy Horse.

Reservations. By 1877, the Plains Indians were militarily defeated by powerful white armies and technology. They and other Indians were confined to reservations where tribes were subjected to Bureau of Indian Affairs programs involving economic development, housing, health, education, and law and order designed to "civilize" them and train them to become farmers. Danziger (p. 128) describes federal programs of cultural assimilation forced on the Chippewas, Hyde (p. 151) tells of Sioux confinement to reservations in South Dakota and their resistance to federal farming programs, and Meyer (p. 153) explains government efforts to alter the lifestyle of the Mandans, Hidatsas, and Arikaras on the Fort Berthold Reservation. Sonnichsen (p. 160) tells of government efforts after 1880 to push Apaches into the American mainstream, Spicer (p. 160) discusses the mid-nineteenth century federal policy of isolating Southwestern Indians on reservations, and Ruby and Brown (p. 164) discuss early twentieth-century federal programs of education among Spokanes in Washington. Emmitt (p. 162) describes the plans of government agent Meeker to "civilize" and control the movements of Colorado's Utes and the latters' antagonism to the agent's plan to teach them to farm. Johnson (p. 163) tells of federal programs designed to make farmers out of Nevada Paiutes, and Castillo (p. 165) describes the years from 1880 to 1930 when California Indians were forcibly assimilated into white ways through government education, health programs, and allotments.

The Ghost Dance. Some Indians turned for help to the supernatural. The Ghost Dance promised the return of the buffalo and the disappearance of white people through peaceful means, the dance. The religion spread from Nevada where it originated to Plains reservations in the Dakotas. In 1890, Sioux Ghost Dancers were slaughtered at Wounded Knee in South Dakota thus ending overt resistance to white authority for the time being. Utley (p. 156) and Schuskey (p. 155) tell the story of the Ghost Dance religion and its growth among Sioux tribes, the arrival of army troops at Sioux agencies, the Battle of Wounded Knee Creek, and the end of the Ghost Dance religion.

The Northwest Coast and Alaska. Several books discuss Russian and American penetration into Alaska and the Northwest Coast: Gunther (p. 168), Hayes (p. 168), Oswalt (p. 168). Van Stone (p. 169) tells of the cultural changes caused by Russians and Americans, who bought title to Alaska in 1867. He discusses the activities of the Russian Orthodox and the Moravian churches and Russian fur traders. Ray (p. 169) examines changes brought about by American mining activities in the late nineteenth century, schools with assimilationist programs, and missions. De Laguna (p. 167) describes the effects of Russian and American culture on the Yakutat Tlingit. Hays (p. 168) describes the period of Russian colonization on the Northwest Coast until 1868.

Reformers. In the 1880s, there was a growing interest among individuals in Indian welfare and several reform organizations were formed such as the Indian Rights Organization organized by the Quakers in 1882. A classic example of reform literature was a book written by Helen Hunt Jackson entitled *A Century of Dishonor* (p. 123), which traced the plight of several Indian tribes and called for a more humane federal Indian policy. Her polemic helped to awaken Americans to the wrongs perpetrated against Indians and played a role in generating federal efforts to reform Indian affairs. These reformers believed that breaking up reservations, dissolving tribes, and making individual Indians into property owners was the solution to the problem of assimilating Indians into the American mainstream. The Dawes Act of 1887 enshrined these views into law.

The Meriam Report, the first intensive study of Indian economic and social problems, appeared in 1928. It was prepared by the Institution for Government Research under the direction of Lewis Meriam. It criticized the allotment policy instituted in 1887 to break up tribally owned lands by dividing them up and allotting specified amounts to individuals with the surplus land going to whites. This policy was abandoned under Commissioner of Indian Affairs, John Collier, in the mid-1930s. Policies initiated during Collier's term were intended to strengthen tribes politically and economically and encourage Indian religions and arts and crafts. During World War II, however, the detribalization process accelerated again. During the 1950s, a policy of termination, ending a tribe's special relationship with the federal government, was pursued. Ourada (p. 134) tells the story of the Menominees in Wisconsin, one of the tribes that was terminated and how the tribe succeeded in getting its tribal status restored in 1973.

Native American Self-Determination. Native Americans have rarely been consulted to find out what they want, nor have programs been developed with their input and participation. In the 1960s, Indians began to collaborate in order to take control of their own future. A nationwide Indian conference was held at the University of Chicago in 1961. Seven hundred Indians from sixty-four tribes participated and created a "Declaration of Indian Purpose," which attacked termination and supported the right of a tribal community to maintain itself and develop with government assistance. New organizations with militant programs and a commitment to direct action were developed by Indian groups. They occupied Alcatraz Island in 1969, took over the Bureau of Indian Affairs building in Washington in 1972, and occupied the town of Wounded Knee, South Dakota, in 1973. These groups and many other contemporary Indians are fighting to survive as Indians without being assimilated into the American mainstream.

These activities have certainly captured the romantic imagination of non-Indians and have appealed to their own frustrations. Some Native Americans and others involved with Indian affairs debate, however, whether the activities have actually helped or improved anything in Indian country. The Bureau of Indian Affairs was working for reform but it has never recovered from the takeover; Pine Ridge is still bitter and divided over Wounded Knee; and Alcatraz has become a park.

There are notable tribal activities that have been productive in terms of Indians maintaining their identities. Tribes are running their own elementary schools and community colleges. They are managing health services, and operating hotels, motels, factories, and other businesses. Indians of different tribes have also organized professional organizations such as the American Indian Nurses Association and the Association of American Indian Physicians. These activities, which do not garner the media spotlight, are contributing substantially to Native Americans determining their own futures.

BLUMENTHAL, WALTER HART. *American Indians Dispossessed: Fraud in Land Cessions Forced upon the Tribes.* Philadelphia: George S. MacManus, 1955; reprint ed.: New York: Arno Press, 1975. 200pp.

The author traces the story of how tribes from colonial times through the mid-1950s have been induced or compelled to give up their lands by treaties and other means. He argues that duplicity and fraud pervaded too many of the treaty stipulations and briefly explains how several of the land grabs were achieved by quasi-legal methods and subterfuge, including the 1737 Walking Purchase, the 1784 Treaty of Fort Stanwix, and others. He describes some of the methods by which tribes were exploited and shorn of their lands during the colonial and early national periods. He reviews how white land fever and sordid methods led to the removal of Cherokees from Georgia, Chickasaws and Choctaws from Mississippi, Creeks from Alabama, and Seminoles from Florida. Briefly he explains the occasional protests made by American officials in the early nineteenth century against exploring tribal territory, reviews nineteenth-century government methods used throughout the country to dispossess particular tribes of their lands, and concludes with a discussion of how tribes were dispossessed of land by termination in the 1950s. There are footnotes and a list of sources for studying treaties and land cessions.

BOWDEN, HENRY WARNER. *American Indians and Christian Missions: Studies in Cultural Conflict.* Chicago: University of Chicago Press, 1981. 256pp. Illustrated. Bibliography.

The author presents a history of the encounters between Native Americans and evangelizing whites from the period of exploration and colonization to the present. The book gives both a broad overview of four centuries of cultural history and detailed instances of relations between discrete Indian, European (Spanish, French, and English), and subsequent American groups in concrete historical settings. Chapters deal with pre-Columbian cultures and values, southwestern Indians and Spanish missions, northeastern Indians and French and English missions, and missions in the eighteenth, nineteenth, and twentieth centuries. The author deals

with ancient shamans, modern Sun Dances, Christian evangelism, and the Native American Church among other Indian religious groups. There are three maps and a bibliographical essay that suggests further readings in the areas of general readings, Indians in the American Southwest, Iroquoian-speaking peoples of the Northeast, early French missionary activity, Algonquians of the Northeast, eighteenth-century missions, Indians in the middle colonies, nineteenth-century missions, Plains Indians and federal policy, contemporary federal policy, and new Indian religious expressions.

BRANDON, WILLIAM. *The Last Americans: The Indian in American Culture.* New York: McGraw-Hill, 1974. 553pp. Bibliography.

This book contains a history of North American Indians from ancient times to the present. The author begins with a survey of the latest archaeological data, examines fundamental differences between the Old and the New Worlds and native cultures of North and South America and Mexico. He looks at the reactions of northeastern, southeastern, and southwestern peoples to the battles for empire among the French, English, and Spanish monarchies. He examines the crucial role of the Iroquois in colonial North America; considers the dispossession of southeastern Creeks, Cherokees and Choctaws; the removal of natives from the Old Northwest; and looks at the cultures and conflict with whites of Eskimos, Northwest Coast, California, Plateau, and Plains Indian peoples, particularly the Apaches and their record of hostility to the Spanish and Americans; and surveys federal native policies such as reservations, allotments, termination, and present-day assaults on native communities. The book includes a portfolio of Native American poetry and extensive notes.

COFFER, WILLIAM E. (Koi Hosh). *Phoenix: The Decline and Rebirth of the Indian People.* New York: Van Nostrand Reinhold, 1979. 277pp. Illustrated. Bibliography.

This book traces the history of the Indian peoples' struggle for survival after the European discovery of America. The author begins with a concise historical description of Native American civilizations before the coming of the Europeans, continues with the Spanish conquests in the New World, the depredations of Indian lands and cultures by the early British settlers, and the removal of the Indians from the East as white settlements pushed westward. He explains how the ideas of Christianity and European civilization were continuously used to justify removal, extermination, and enslavement of Indian peoples. In addition, he provides an account of Indian resistance to white expansion until the final subjugation of Indian tribes by government bureaucrats, the unrelenting encroachment on Indian lands in the early decades of the twentieth century, the gradual enlightenment of government policy in the 1930s, and the increasing demands of Indians for self-determination in the 1960s. There are four maps and drawings that illustrate the text. The bibliography lists published primary and secondary sources.

DEBO, ANGIE. *A History of the Indians of the United States.* Norman: University of Oklahoma Press, 1970. 386pp. Illustrated. Bibliography.

This is a survey of the Indians of the United States, including Eskimos and Aleuts of Alaska, from their first contact with Europeans in the fifteenth century until the present. Included are descriptions of the first meetings of Indians with French, British, Dutch, and Spanish explorers; the dispossession of Indian lands by colonial expansion; Indian involvement in imperial rivalries; relations with the new American republic; and the ensuing century of war and encroachment. The author tells of tribes fighting for their homelands across America, the reservation system, the destructive allotment policy, the reform movement of the 1920s to the 1940s, and the terminations policy of the 1950s. She concludes with a review of the more recent aspects of government Indian policy and the good and bad administrative practices and measures to which Indians have been subjected. The author emphasizes the history of Oklahoma Indians, including the effects of removal to Indian Territory, Civil War, and Reconstruction; liquidation of tribal entities; and their present situation. There are several maps and photographs that show diverse scenes of Indian ways of life.

DENNIS, HENRY C., comp. and ed. *The American Indian, 1492–1970: A Chronology and Fact Book.* Dobbs Ferry, N.Y.: Oceana Publications, 1971. 137pp. Bibliography.

This volume contains a chronology of events recorded by historians as significant dates in American Indian history from 1492 to 1970. Each year is accompanied by one or more brief paragraphs describing important events. Following the chronology are sections entitled "Some Prominent Indian Figures of the Past" and "A Random Sampling of Contemporary Indians and Their Activities." The appendixes include population figures and lists of Indian wars and local disturbances, U.S. administrators of federal Indian policy, government appropriations for Indian education from 1877 to 1969, Indian museums, names and addresses of a few Indian organizations, and Indian publications and audiovisual suggestions.

Early American Indian Documents: Treaties and Laws, 1607–1789. 20 vols. Washington, D.C.: University Publications of America, 1978– .

These volumes contain a comprehensive collection of documentary materials on Indian-white relations before 1789 including diplomatic documents, treaties between the early colonial governments and Indian tribes, conference proceedings, and the laws concerning Indians passed by colonial, state, and early national governments. Texts of the treaties are preceded by historical commentary that helps the reader understand the conditions under which the treaties were made. The laws of every colony are preceded by introductions that explain the context of the original documents.

HAGAN, WILLIAM T. *American Indians.* Chicago: University of Chicago Press, 1961; revised ed.: Chicago: University of Chicago Press, 1979. 193pp. Illustrated. Bibliography.

In this volume, the author traces the different stages of the history of the clash between Indians and whites from the mid-seventeenth century to the present time. He begins with a discussion of various colonial Indian land policies and native resistance, British-French rivalry for Indian trade and allies, and British Indian policy after the French were defeated. He describes how the natives were divided over which side to support in the American Revolution, considers early federal Indian policy in the Northeast and Southeast, white settlers' demands for native land, treaties of cession, sporadic native resistance, and the British contest with America for tribal favor until the former were defeated in the War of 1812. He also looks at the way Indian policy changed after the 1812 War when the threat of British intervention was gone, describes voluntary and forced removals from 1816 to 1850, particularly focusing on the experiences of Southeast and Winnebago Indians, and gives reasons for the failure of the government program to "civilize" Indians after 1812. He discusses the period 1840–76 in the Plains, Southwest, California, and Plateau areas when tribes resisted the settlers' demands for land, and looks at military clashes between Indians and whites, natives during the Civil War, Grant's peace policy of the 1870s, and the end of the Indian wars. He examines the growing interest in Indian reform during the 1880s to correct wrongs done against Indians, considers the late nineteenth-century Indian religious movements and federal programs designed to force acculturation, particularly the severalty policy, the Indian Reorganization Act of 1934, and the termination and relocation policies of the 1950s. He explores Indian attempts at political and economic self-determination on reservations starting in the mid-1960s, their dealings with the government, and the philosophies and organizations of the new Red Power movement. There is a list of important dates in Indian-white relations from 1622 to 1958. Included are photographs of Indians.

HERTZBERG, HAZEL W. *The Search for an American Indian Identity: Modern Pan-Indian Move-*

ments. Syracuse: Syracuse University Press, 1971. 362pp. Illustrated. Bibliography.

This study identifies, analyzes, and compares the basic varieties of national Pan-Indianism—religious, reform, and fraternal—and traces their historical development during the formative period, the first third of the twentieth century. The author describes the historical roots, major ideas, leadership, constituency, organizational forms, activities, and connections with each other of the three types of Pan-Indianism. She considers the relationship to basic trends in American life of reform groups such as the Society of American Indians and the National Council of American Indians; urban and fraternal orders such as the Teepee Order of America and the Grand Council Fire of the American Indians; and religious groups such as the peyote cult and the Native American Church. The study also considers the periods preceding and succeeding the formative years of modern Pan-Indianism. A background chapter recounts some of the nineteenth-century tribal and early Pan-Indian responses to encroaching white society and traces the major forces that produced modern Pan-Indianism. There is an outline of Pan-Indian movements since the New Deal which shows their adaptation to new historical contexts, and a concluding chapter examines the significance of the total Pan-Indian experience in its relationship both to Indian life and to the wider society. There are photographs of Pan-Indians.

HORR, DAVID AGEE, comp. and ed. *American Indian Ethnohistory.* New York: Garland Publishing, 1974. 118 vols.

This collection contains the material submitted as evidence in the claims brought by Indian groups against the U.S. government under the provisions of the Indian Claims Act of 1946. In order to settle the questions of Indian land title, use, and occupancy, scholars researched the aboriginal and colonial history, tribal political structure, economy, kinship patterns, technology, and other cultural and historical factors of tribes pressing claims. These reports and findings are organized by tribe and area into 118 volumes, each with a uniform format. Each volume contains a map showing the 1950 location of the tribe(s) in question and its estimated aboriginal range. The preliminary material on a particular tribe or area contains introductory statements on the nature of the claims proceedings, the gathering of the scholarly materials, as well as a brief introduction to the tribe(s). Following the reports on a particular tribe or area, the pertinent opinions and findings of fact of the Indian Claims Commission are included and cross-referenced to findings for related tribes or groups. There are volumes on California, Paiutes, Mohaves, Utes, Shoshones (in the California and Basin-Plateau area), Apaches, Navajos, Pueblos, Hopis, Hualapais, Yavapais, Havasupais, Pima-Maricopas, Papagos, Oregon, Coast Salish and Western Washington, Interior Salish and Eastern Washington, Nez Percés, Blackfeet, Crows, Sioux, Kiowa-Comanches, Arapaho-Cheyennes, Osages, Omahas, Poncas, Pawnees, Kansas, Otos, Missourias, Caddoans, Wichitas, and Creeks, as well as Indians of Ohio, Michigan, Illinois, Indiana, Wisconsin, and Florida.

JACKSON, HELEN HUNT. *A Century of Dishonor: A Sketch of the United States Government's Dealings with Some of the Indian Tribes.* New York: Harper & Brothers, 1881; reprint ed.: Williamstown, Mass.: Corner House Publishers, 1973. 457pp.

This classic, an example of reform literature, deals with the plight of Native Americans and calls for a more humane federal Indian policy. Jackson's intention was to awaken the American conscience to the wrongs perpetrated against natives and her work produced a strong public reaction that a solution was needed and played a role in generating federal efforts to ameliorate the natives' condition. The author surveys to 1880 American relations with the Delawares, Cheyennes, Nez Percés, Sioux, Poncas, Winnebagos, and Cherokees. Also included are accounts of three large-scale massacres of Indians by whites and fourteen appendixes dealing with varied aspects of Indian-white relations.

JOHANSEN, BRUCE, and ROBERTO MAESTAS. *Wasi'chu: The Continuing Indian Wars.* New York: Monthly Review Press, 1979. 268pp.

This book is about Indian resistance to Wasi'chu (literally, "greedy one") or the corporations and individuals who continue to ravage and steal Indian land and resources for private profit and to the economic system that nourishes and rewards them. The authors document the means by which Indians have been subjugated, both as individuals and as a people. They discuss underlying reasons for the subjugation, found in the rich resources still held by Indian Nations and coveted by U.S. corporations who are often supported by the U.S. government. Chapters deal with the struggle over coal and uranium deposits on native land, over strip mining in Montana, and over fishing rights in the state of Washington. Chapters describe the rise of political consciousness among Indians and the development of their resistance movement on local levels and nationwide. Finally, the authors discuss the wider political implications of this movement, linking Indian struggles with that of colonized people all over the world. There are photographs and the book is heavily footnoted.

JOSEPHY, ALVIN M., JR. *The Indian Heritage of America.* New York: Knopf, 1968; reprint ed.: New York: Bantam, 1969. 397pp. Illustrated. Bibliography.

The author surveys what is known about Indians of North, Central, and South America from ancestral times to the present. Introductory chapters discuss misconceptions about Indians, and explain their diversities and similarities and contributions to contemporary life. The author discusses the origins of early people in the Americas, the beginnings of agriculture, and the prehistory, ways of life, and characteristics of natives in various culture areas including the Arctic, Subarctic, Pacific Northwest Coast, Northeast Woodland, Southeast, Plains, Great Basin, Plateau, California, Southwest, Northern Mexico, Central American and Caribbean Areas, Middle and South America. The remaining chapters review the general impact of Europeans on native cultures, the European conquest of Latin America, the United States, and Canada, shifting government policies of the United States and the current situation in which Indians are fighting to survive without being totally assimilated. There are eleven maps and photographs of artifacts, native ways of life, and Indian-white contact. The book is based on published primary and secondary works.

KVASNICKA, ROBERT M., and JANE F. SMITH, eds. *Indian-White Relations: A Persistent Paradox.* National Archives Conference vol. 10. Washington, D.C.: Howard University Press, 1976. 278pp. Illustrated.

This volume contains conference papers from the 1972 National Archives and Records Service conference on Research on the History of Indian-White Relations. The papers focus attention on the resources in the U.S. National Archives for research on North American Indians. The introductory essay considers the problems that arise in writing Indian history and the first several papers assess the history, use, and potential of the records of the National Archives and Records Service for Indian historical research. The next two papers deal with the theme of Indian assimilation in the nineteenth century, one concerning American Indian policy from 1824 to 1830 and the Board of Indian Commissioners, and the other dealing with ethnocentric reform from 1878 to 1893. Several papers consider Indian collections outside the National Archives and Records Service, artifacts and pictures as documents in the history of Indian-white relations, major Oklahoma Indian record collections, and archives of the Duke Project in American Indian history. One paper evaluates the character and role of the frontier army, others concern Indian reservation policy, aspects of twentieth-century federal Indian policy, John Collier and the Indian New Deal, and the Bureau of Indian Affairs in 1972. There are six maps and photographs from the National Archives.

MACLEOD, WILLIAM CHRISTIE. *The American Indian Frontier.* New York: Knopf, 1928. 598pp. Illustrated. Bibliography.

The author traces the history of Indian-white relations and Indian policy in North and South America from the beginning of the sixteenth century to 1927. He first discusses the origins of natives, surveys their cultures, tells of the destructive role of liquor and disease in native life, and examines European discoveries in America. The second section deals with the sixteenth-century Spanish crown's encomienda system and other factors that resulted in the extermination of West Indian natives, seventeenth-century Spanish policy in Brazil, missionary activities in North and South America from 1510 to 1848, native enslavement in Latin America, and colonizing business corporations or joint stock companies in North America. The third part deals with the nature of the fur trade between natives and the French and English, the seventeenth-century practice of purchasing native lands in New England and the southern colonies, early Indian wars of 1637–76 in New England and Virginia which resulted in the decline of native political power and the ascendancy of European power there, the destruction of coastal tribes, and the cultural deterioration of the Iroquois due to their involvement in the British-French rivalry, 1607–1754. The fourth section examines the differences between the Latin- and Anglo-Americans in their treatment of natives, the Catholic mission system in California, the destructive nature of North American intertribal wars, and the use of Indians as auxiliaries in the struggle between rival European powers. He discusses the origin of race prejudice, racial segregation on reservations in North and Latin America, and the nature and development of early colonial North American reservations. The fifth section looks at British Indian policy which destroyed Indian political power in the Old Northwest, native resistance to white settlement, and the rise of reservations in the Appalachian region and westward in the nineteenth century. He tells of the removal of southeastern tribes to west of the Mississippi River, the destruction of California and Oregon Indians, the breakup of Oklahoma Indian country, Plains Indian resistance as a result of the incursion of miners, civil-military conflicts over native policy, and the rise of native prophets. He concludes with a discussion of allotment and argues the desirability of natives assimilating into American society, thus ending the "Indian problem." There are thirteen maps and eleven appendixes.

MANYPENNY, GEORGE W. *Our Indian Wards.* Foreword by Henry E. Fritz. Cincinnati: Robert Clarke, 1880; reprint ed.: New York: De Capo, 1972. 445pp.

This book, an example of reform literature by a Commissioner of Indian Affairs, 1853–57, contains a plea for the just treatment of natives and a recital of military injustices done to them. Manypenny provides a concise history of the relations between the settlers and the natives from their first contacts through the 1870s. He records the broken treaties, successive wars caused by white people's rapacity, and native uprootings throughout the nineteenth century, the dishonesty of government agencies, and the erosion of native cultures. In particular, Manypenny details the removal of southern natives to west of the Mississippi River, the destruction of the buffalo, the expeditions of Generals Hancock, Sherman, and Custer that illustrate the unsuitability of army control of native affairs, and the extermination of unsubmissive tribes. The foreword discusses Manypenny's work and reform efforts on behalf of natives, his antagonism to military management of native affairs, summarizes Grant's peace policy, and Manypenny's views about it.

MARRIOTT, ALICE, and CAROL K. RACHLIN. *American Epic: The Story of the American Indian.* New York: Putman's, 1969; reprint ed.: New York: New American Library, 1970. 254pp. Illustrated. Bibliography.

This book contains a history of some North American native peoples, their cultures from ancient times to the present, and the effects of European events and Euro-American contacts on intertribal relations. Part 1 looks at the origins, migrations, and way of life of native cultures before and as a result of European contact. The authors look at the people of the ancient Mississippi Valley, the Northeast, Southeast, early peoples of the Southwest, people of the pueblos, Plains, Basin-Plateau, California, Northwest, and Subarctic. Part 2 looks at Spanish, French, and English policies of developing North America; European wars affecting the course of North American history; and other political, economic, and social forces that shaped native lives until the present. The authors examine changes in southeastern native cultures as a result of English contact, particularly the Cherokees and their removal, native groups in the North and South who resisted removal, and the Osages of the Mississippi Valley. Part 3 focuses on natives today and their efforts to improve reservation life in the areas of health, education, and religion; examines the work of anthropologists and the patterns of native resistance. There are pictures of artifacts and contemporary natives. The book is based partially on field work.

MCNICKLE, D'ARCY. *Indian Tribes of the United States: Ethnic and Cultural Survival*. New York: Oxford University Press, 1962; revised ed.: *Native American Tribalism: Indian Survivals and Revivals*. New York: Oxford University Press, 1973. 190pp. Illustrated.

The author briefly traces the history of Indian-white relations in the United States and Canada and the ways natives have managed to remain an ethnic and cultural enclave within American and Canadian society from the coming of Europeans to the present. He begins by drawing a generalized picture of the peoples who have survived in numbers, social organization, custom, physical resources, and in their position before the law. He looks at efforts by Spain, England, Holland, and France during the sixteenth through the eighteenth centuries to occupy American land, defend their occupations against indigenous tribes and other European powers, and to devise procedures to get title to Indian lands. He considers the shrinking of the American and Canadian Indian land base due to nineteenth-century government policies, removal of the southeastern Indians, and allotment of Indian lands due to the 1887 Dawes Act. The author tells of reform efforts during the first third of the twentieth century and the termination policy of the 1950s. He describes Indian resistance to termination of federal responsibility, the development of a philosophy of self-determination and of Indian organizations to handle their own problems. He concludes with a discussion of contemporary Canadian Indian problems and Canadian Indian policy; Alaskan native efforts to get aboriginal land titles resulting in the Alaska Settlement Act of 1971 and the 1971 return of Blue Lake to the Taos Indians. The preface in the 1973 edition analyzes the 1972 occupation of the Bureau of Indian Affairs building in Washington and the 1973 seizure of the town of Wounded Knee, South Dakota. There is an appendix of the geographical distribution of principal American tribes and Canadian linguistic groupings, several maps and photographs of contemporary Indians, and chapter notes based largely on government publications.

MERIAM, LEWIS. *The Problem of Indian Administration*. Institute for Government Research. Baltimore: Johns Hopkins University Press, 1928. 872pp.

This study contains the 1928 report of the survey of Indian affairs conducted by the Institute for Government Research made at the request of Hubert Work who was Secretary of the Interior in 1926. Made under the direction of Lewis Meriam of the Institute in cooperation with nine specialists, the survey has been considered an example of reform propaganda, particularly because it was highly critical of American Indian policies. Part 1 contains a summary of the findings indicating that the majority of Indians were impoverished and ill adjusted to American society and prescribes long range recommendations centered primarily around education in its broadest sense and immediate action recommendations. There are discussions of the survey's methodology, recommendations for improving the Indian Service and its personnel and for improving statistics and record-keeping regarding Indians. The second part contains very detailed reports of the Indians' educational, social, health, and economic problems and legal problems involving property rights. There are tables throughout.

PORTER, KENNETH W. "Notes Supplementary to 'Relations between Negroes and Indians.'" *Journal of Negro History* 18, no. 3 (July 1933):282–321.

The author provides supplementary notes to his article "Relations between Negroes and Indians within the Present Limits of the United States" (see below). He discusses Estevanico and other blacks who accompanied Spanish explorers, black ill treatment of Indians, blacks killed by hostile natives, blacks fighting by the side of Indian masters against other blacks, and protective treatment of runaway slaves by certain tribes in the northern part of the United States. He looks at relations between reservation and free blacks illustrated by the Long Island Shinnecock natives, provides new information on the part played by blacks in the Seminole wars, statistics on the numbers of natives and blacks among several slave-holding tribes, the status of blacks among the Seminoles, and discusses the leading Seminole black partisan, Abraham. He describes Negro servitude among the Five Civilized Tribes in Indian Territory at the time of the Civil War, looks at black-Indian relations in Ohio, Illinois, and the Plains which were infrequent, and the admittance of natives to Hampton Normal and Agricultural Institute in 1878. He concludes with a few generalizations about the nature of black-Indian relationships which were occasionally significant in influencing U.S. Indian policy and in modifying the racial makeup of both races.

———. "Relations between Negroes and Indians within the Present Limits of the United States."

Journal of Negro History 17, no. 3 (July 1932): 287–367.

The author examines relations between Indians and blacks within the United States from the 1530s to the end of the nineteenth century. He begins by telling of the casual contacts between natives and African slaves accompanying exploring expeditions, illustrated by Estevanico and his contacts with southwestern Indians in the 1530s, Marcos Lopez's contacts with Northwest Coast Indians in the late 1780s, and York of the Lewis and Clark expedition in the early 1800s who encountered Plains and Plateau peoples. He considers the character of Indian-black relations, when the two groups were associated as fellow slaves, in New England, the Middle colonies, and the South. He points out that relations depended on circumstances and not on mutually shared feelings that as members of nonwhite races they were natural allies, and that there was no evidence of an understanding between African slaves and Indian tribes. He looks at native groups who protected runaway African slaves, intermarriage between freed blacks and reservation Indians, establishment of mixed-blood communities isolated from all three races, and the contributions of a few mixed-bloods. He deals with slave-holding natives in the South and in Indian Territory, particularly the Seminoles where the status of a slave was practically equal to that of the owner, and the parts played during the two Seminole wars by the Seminoles and their black allies who resisted removal to Indian Territory. He tells of the Seminole and black allies in Indian Territory, a number of whom were forced to go to Mexico by raiding Creek and Comanche slavehunters, and, looks at Indian Territory during the post-Civil War period and the kind of treatment accorded emancipated blacks by Creeks, Choctaws, Cherokees, Chickasaws, and Seminoles. He surveys relations between the two races in the Old Northwest, the Rocky Mountain region, and Pacific Coast where slavery never was an important institution and where relations were similar to Indians and whites in terms of trading, intermarrying, and fighting.

SPICER, EDWARD H. *A Short History of the Indians of the United States.* New York: Van Nostrand Reinhold, 1969. 319pp. Bibliography.

Spicer traces the history of intertribal relations, relations with whites, and adaptations Indians had to make in the wake of the growing white military and political dominance from 1540 to 1968. He also provides a selection of fifty-one documents keyed to the text. He begins with the period of 1540–1794 in which Europeans and natives vied for land, trade advantages, and political power and in which no one people were dominant. He describes the adaptive measures employed by Indians in their contacts with whites, the creation of new political organizations such as the Creek and Iroquois Confederacies, federations that failed, tribes that were displaced, Pueblo adaptations, and the 1680 Pueblo Revolt. He considers the period of 1763–1848 when Britain emerged as the dominant power in the East and Indians adapted by reorienting their religious faith

or political organization illustrated by the Handsome Lake religion, the rise of Algonquian prophets, Cherokee secular reorganization, and cultural pluralism in New Mexico. The author looks at the period of 1831–98 in which Indian political rights were eliminated as the result of U.S. Indian policy and several forms of native adaptations emerged including messianism, religious revitalization, political reorganization, military resistance, and passivism illustrated by the Five Civilized Tribes, displaced Algonquians, Plains tribes, Southwestern groups, and California natives. He looks at the colonial period of 1871–1934 and federal programs of cultural assimilation which included the reservation system, allotment, boarding schools, and considers native reactions including the growth of tribal factional strife and the Native American Church. Concluding chapters in the first part deal with the period of 1924–68 and new cultural developments among many emerging native societies and the submergence of other tribes into the larger society. The second part contains fifty-one documents divided into sections entitled "Indian History as seen by Indians," "White Politics," "White Viewpoints," and "Indian Prophets and Spokesmen."

UNDERHILL, RUTH MURRAY. *Red Man's America: A History of Indians in the United States.* Chicago: University of Chicago Press, 1953. 400pp. Illustrated. Bibliography.

The author presents the highlights of Indian history on a regional basis from ancestral times to the present. She begins with the first migrations, the peopling of North and South America, and describes the earliest corn-growers and cultures of Mexico, Central America, and eastern South America. She continues with surveys of the Cherokees, Creeks, Chickasaws, Choctaws, and Seminoles of the Southeast who were removed to Oklahoma; Algonquian tribes of the Atlantic Seaboard; the five New York Iroquois tribes; the tribes of the Great Lakes and Upper Mississippi; early Siouan- and Caddoan-speaking residents of the Plains, Siouan- and Algonquian-speaking peoples who moved into the Plains with the coming of the horse; the Southwestern agriculturalists, the Mogollon, Hohokam, Pueblos, and Pimans; the Navajos and Apaches, late arrivals to the Southwest; the tribes of the Great Basin and the Plateau; the Indians of California; and the tribes of the Pacific Northwest. The last chapter sketches the history of government policy divided into six phases corresponding to stages in the nation's history. Each chapter contains a summary of food, hunting methods, clothing, house types, equipment, war, and games of tribes that lived in each geographic region. There are eleven maps and photographs of artifacts from all the regions. The book is based partly on the author's own field work.

VECSEY, CHRISTOPHER, and ROBERT W. VENABLES, eds. *American Indian Environments: Ecological Issues in Native American History.* Syracuse: Syracuse University Press, 1980. 208pp. Illustrated.

This volume contains ten essays by Indians and

non-Indians that describe and analyze historical and contemporary relations between Native Americans and the natural world. The essays focus on the role of the environment on American Indian religions; on contrasting Indian and white attitudes toward nature, subsistence techniques, and land-based sovereignty; Indian struggles with non-Indians over possession and use of land; white removal of Indians from their land bases; the plight of various uprooted Indians, and the resulting clashes between Indian groups themselves as they competed for scarce resources; and the effects of white ecological practices on the Indian population as well as on the American landscape itself. The chapters attempt to cover a broad range of time, from first contact to contemporary time, as well as space, from the Northeast to the Southwest. There are sixteen illustrations and chapter notes.

WASHBURN, WILCOMB. *The Indian in America.* New York: Harper & Row, 1975. 296pp. Illustrated. Bibliography.

The author synthesizes information about American Indians including their origins, consistent patterns of behavior and beliefs that characterize Indian individuals and groups, descriptions of Indian social structure and world view, and the history of Indian-white relations. He divides the history of Indian-white contact into three parts. The first part deals with Indians when they lived and acted as equals to white people, the second with Indians when their equality was challenged and destroyed by whites, and the third with the Indians' new relationship with American society in the present day. The author includes discussions on trade relationships, political negotiations between Indians and whites, Christian missionary efforts and Indian responses, Indian wars during the colonial period, the American Revolution in the North and South and its aftermath, removal policy, coercion of Indians west of the Mississippi, the Civil War and its aftermath, reservation system and life, the allotment policy, and the social, economic, and political status of Indians in the twentieth century. There are three maps, portraits of Indian people, and photographs of artifacts. The book is based on Indian oral tradition, the study of art and artifacts and unpublished and published sources.

WAX, MURRAY L. *Indian Americans: Unity and Diversity.* Englewood Cliffs, N.J.: Prentice-Hall, 1971. 236pp. Bibliography.

This volume is concerned with the historical and contemporary situations and problems of Native American peoples and also provides a guide to the kinds of information that are available about Indians. The first part, historical developments and comparative relationships, surveys some of the interactions between various invading groups of Europeans and representative bands of native inhabitants of the Americas over several centuries during which Indians declined in military, political, and economic power. There are an analysis and tables of estimated aboriginal populations of Spanish America, the United States, and Canada. In the second part, the author looks at the nature of con-temporary Plains reservation communities and tribal nonreservation life illustrated by the Oklahoma Cherokees. The third part concerns Pan-Indian responses to the invasion of white Europeans, problems of Indians in cities and their modes of adaptation, and the ideologies or conceptual models by which Indians and white groups have related to each other. Appendixes contain lists of reference works, films, maps, periodicals, sources of information, and records; information on federal expenditures for Indian programs, and reference materials on Indian populations, education, and health.

WEBB, GEORGE W. *Chronological List of Engagements between the Regular Army of the United States and Various Tribes of Hostile Indians Which Occurred during the Years 1790 to 1898, Inclusive.* St. Joseph, Mo.: Wing Printing, 1939. 141pp.; reprint ed.: New York: AMS Press, 1974.

This volume contains hundreds of listings of engagements between the U.S. Army and Indian tribes from October, 1790 to May, 1897. The location, names of battles, companies involved, major officers, and Indian leaders are cited as well as the names of army officers killed and the number of Indians involved, killed, or wounded. There is an index of geographic locations, army regulars, Indian leaders, U.S. Army companies, and forts.

NORTHEAST

ANSON, BERT. *The Miami Indians.* Norman: University of Oklahoma Press, 1970. 329pp. Illustrated. Bibliography.

The author traces the history of the Miami Indians of Indiana and Oklahoma from 1658 to the present, emphasizing the few occasions in which the tribe played significant roles in the development of the Old Northwest. The author describes early Miami cultural patterns before 1700 and subsequent changes brought about in tribal life as a result of French domination south of the Great Lakes from 1700 to 1763 and British control from 1763 to 1783. He argues that the Miami emerged as a pivotal tribe during the French-British imperial wars, discusses the Miami Confederacy, its relations with other tribes, and its role in trying to resist American settlement on its lands in the 1780s. He tells of William Henry Harrison who secured title to millions of acres of Indian land through treaties, Indian efforts at alliance to resist American expansion, especially Tecumseh's resistance, and the Miamis during the War of 1812 when they ceased to be a military threat. He describes the treaty-making period during which the Miamis played a role because they owned land important to white expansion and their emigration in 1846–47 which produced two branches, the Indiana and the Kansas-Oklahoma group. The author discusses the small Miami tribe of Oklahoma which has maintained an active tribal organization, the Miamis in Indiana from 1846 to 1968 and their legal positions, and closes with a brief treatment of contemporary Miamis. There are six maps and photographs and paintings of Miamis. The bibliography lists published primary and secondary sources.

BERKHOFER, ROBERT F., JR. *Salvation and the Savage: An Analysis of Protestant Missions and American Indian Response, 1787–1862.* Lexington: University of Kentucky Press, 1965. 186pp. Bibliography.

This volume presents the conclusions derived from a comparative study of Protestant missionary groups' activities and responses to them by the Oneidas, Tuscaroras, and Senecas of New York and Wisconsin, the Cherokees and Choctaws of the South, the Ojibways and Sioux of the Great Lakes, the Ottawas of Kansas, the Nez Percés in the Plateau, and several other tribes. The first several chapters deal with the missionaries' general attitudes and assumptions and how these were a crucial part of their efforts to inculcate education, religion, and farming in their charges. The author covers the relationship between the missionaries and federal government representatives, and with other missionaries, traders, and soldiers in representing American civilization to the natives. He looks at native response to the missionaries, the plight of native converts in their own tribes, and native reaction in the context of acculturation and cultural change theory. The epilogue considers the failure of the missionary enterprise given the participants' cultural assumptions, the persistence of native cultures, and the missionaries' racial attitudes. The book is based on manuscripts, religious and tribal histories, federal Indian policy, and anthropological theory. There is an extensive bibliographical essay of native missionary history from the Revolution to the Civil War organized by denominations and societies: Moravian, Quaker, Congregationalist and Presbyterian, Baptist, Methodist, Episcopalian, and Lutheran.

BRASSER, TED J. *Riding on the Frontier's Crest: Mahican Indian Culture and Culture Change.* National Museum of Man, Mercury Series, Ethnology Division Paper no. 13. Ottawa: National Museum of Canada, 1974. 91pp. Illustrated. Bibliography.

The author summarizes the history and changing culture of the Mahican Indians originally inhabiting the Hudson Valley in New York State. The study gives information on traditional Mahican culture, especially social organization and the Mahican role in the fur trade period during the seventeenth century with special attention given to the Mahican-Iroquois relationship. He tells of the major aspects of culture change caused by Mahican removals which were a result of the colonists' pressures during the fur trade period, and activities of missionaries among the Mahicans who moved to the mission village of Stockbridge, Massachusetts. He tells of culture change in the eighteenth and nineteenth centuries as a result of new socioeconomic conditions and briefly discusses the contemporary Stockbridge-Munsee reservation community. He concludes by drawing similarities between Mahican and Iroquois cultures and corrects, as he does throughout the work, the misleading information about the Mahican tribe. A chronological listing of Mahican locations, a map, and paintings of Mahican Indians are included.

CLIFTON, JAMES A. *The Prairie People: Continuity and Change in Potawatomi Indian Culture, 1665–1965.* Lawrence: Regents Press of Kansas, 1977. 529pp. Illustrated. Bibliography.

This study focuses on the Prairie band of Potawatomis, located today near Topeka, Kansas, over the course of the last three centuries. The author discusses how the Potawatomis constituted a single tribal society until the 1830s, with villages distributed in a four-state area around Lake Michigan until the selling off of Potawatomi lands which caused constituent villages to scatter into many small, culturally disparate communities from the Ontario Peninsula to Mexico. He discusses how, during the three centuries, the Potawatomis were variously entangled with a large number of tribal groups; the colonial empires of France, Britain, and Spain; and the two emergent nation-states of Canada and the United States. The author evaluates the Potawatomis' traditional economy and technology, leadership and government, patterns of feuding and warfare, ideology, and religion. He explains their migrations and resettlement in Indiana, Illinois, Michigan, Wisconsin, Iowa, and Kansas; describes their adaptive strategy of abandoning canoes for horses, fishing for buffalo hunting on the Plains; their service as mercenaries in a series of American colonial wars; and their work as primary producers of goods and brokers in the fur trade. He discusses Potawatomi alliances formed with France and Britain which were forces on the colonial frontier. The author also covers the Potawatomis in the modern world, viewing the Prairie band community against its nonreservation context and revealing a people who have retained traditional cultural forms, who have adopted other cultural elements from Indians and Europeans, and who have resisted enforced culture change and assimilation. There are fifteen maps and more than thirty photographs and sketches of Potawatomis and their lifestyle. The bibliography lists unpublished and published primary and secondary materials.

DANZIGER, EDMUND JEFFERSON, JR. *The Chippewas of Lake Superior.* Norman: University of Oklahoma Press, 1978. 263pp. Illustrated. Bibliography.

The author tells the history of the Chippewa bands of parts of Michigan, Wisconsin, and Minnesota from traditional times to the present. He begins with descriptions of traditional Lake Superior Chippewa culture, the coming of French Jesuit missionaries and fur traders from the mid-seventeenth century, and the advent of British rule in the 1760s, both regimes altering Chippewa life very little because they were solely interested in procuring furs. He describes Chippewa relations, from 1815 to 1854, with the American Fur Company which also wished to preserve the fur trade with the Chippewas and modified life very little, and with white miners, lumbermen, farmers, town builders, Indian agents, and missionaries who warred on Chippewa culture and seized their land for exploitation. He looks at the turning point, the 1854 treaty which extinguished Chippewa title to certain lands and confined Chippewas to reservations in their homeland and which became pivotal to their cultural disintegration and to the end of their sociopolitical independence. He examines life on the Chippewa reservations in Wisconsin, Michigan, and Minnesota from 1854 to 1900 where Indians were vulnerable to the Bureau of Indian Affairs' programs involving economic development, housing, health, education, and law and order designed to "civilize" them and train them to become farmers. He tells of the period from 1900 to 1934 when Chippewas were impoverished and maladjusted due to the assault on their culture, the period from 1934 to 1964 when Chippewas achieved some cultural independence and limited self-government due to the Indian Reorganization Act, and the period from 1964 to 1975 when they began to administer their own programs to try and solve their many problems. There are two maps and photographs of Chippewas and their traditional and contemporary life. The book is based on personal interviews and unpublished and published primary and secondary accounts.

DOWNES, RANDOLPH C. *Council Fires on the Upper Ohio: A Narrative of Indian Affairs in the Upper Ohio Valley until 1795.* Pittsburgh: University of Pittsburgh Press, 1940. 367pp. Illustrated. Bibliography.

This work traces the history of the arrival of Indians in the upper Ohio Valley and their struggle with white people for control of the region from 1775 to 1795. The author treats the settlement of the Shawnee in western Pennsylvania from 1720 to 1745, their departure, and Iroquois supremacy in western Pennsylvania from 1745 to 1754 when they returned to New York. He discusses western Pennsylvania tribes alternating in their support of French and British rivals who competed for Indian trade and support, the Ohio Valley Indians' support of French occupation and revolt against British occupation, and European trade policies from 1753 to 1765. He tells of the maneuverings of Loyalists and Patriots to gain the allegiance of Ohio Valley Indians in the American Revolution, the establishment and abandonment of forts in Indian country which were part of the Continental government policy to protect Americans from Indians. He examines warfare between Americans and tribes of the Old Northwest from 1779 until 1782 when conflict between Britain and America ceased in the Northeast. He examines the American policy of modified aggression into Indian lands of Ohio, Pennsylvania, and New York from 1782 to 1789, the war for the Ohio River boundary, 1789–95, and the Greenville Treaty which ended the Indian contest for control of the Ohio. There is one map and a bibliography of unpublished and published primary and secondary works.

EDMUNDS, R. DAVID. *The Potawatomis: Keepers of the Fire.* Norman: University of Oklahoma Press, 1978. 362pp. Illustrated. Bibliography.

The author presents the history of the Potawatomis, a tribe living in Wisconsin, Illinois, Indiana, and Michigan from the mid-seventeenth to the mid-nineteenth century when they were removed to Kansas. He describes the close Potawatomi-French relationship, beginning in the mid-seventeenth century, lasting through the colonial period, and continuing after the French withdrew from the Midwest. He explains the Potawatomis' active participation in the fur trade, friendship with French fur traders and government leaders, and faithful fighting alongside French allies against the English in Pennsylvania and New York during the colonial wars. He describes how French technology both enriched and destroyed traditional Potawatomi culture, tells of the Potawatomi-French alliance which concentrated its efforts on defeating the Foxes. Explaining that tribal divisions grew as French fortunes declined, he tells why many Potawatomis shifted their allegiance to the British while others preferred to attack them in the 1763 Pontiac Rebellion. He discusses the Potawatomi-British alliance which tried to oppose American attempts to occupy the Ohio during the American Revolution, during Tecumseh's uprising, and during the War of 1812. The author discusses changes in Potawatomi life after 1815 with the advancing tide of white settlement, forced land cessions in Illinois, Wisconsin, Indiana, and Michigan in exchange for government annuities, Potawatomi political fragmentation, resistance to conversion into farmers, population shifts westward, and forced removal west of the Mississippi by 1840. There are five maps and photographs of Potawatomis and their environment. The book is based on unpublished and published primary and secondary sources.

FENTON, WILLIAM N. "Problems Arising from the Historic Northeastern Position of the Iroquois." In *Essays in Historical Anthropology of North America*, pp. 159–251. Smithsonian Miscellaneous Collections, vol. 100. Washington, D.C.: Smithsonian Institution, 1940. Bibliography.

Fenton locates the known Iroquois groups of New York and Ontario, Canada, at various points from the seventeenth to the twentieth centuries and traces their known historic movements to help explain their intrusive linguistic and cultural origins in the Northeast. He begins with Cartier's 1534 discovery of the Laurentian Iroquois and accounts for their disappearance by suggesting several hypotheses; locates the Hurons and traces their village movements until 1650 when they were dispersed; and briefly looks at locations of the Tobacco, Neutral, and Erie villages until they were all dispersed during the seventeenth century. He considers trading relations between Algonquians and Hurons, indicating an early cultural assimilation between them, and suggests that when the Iroquois conquered the Hurons they benefited by the adjustments the Hurons had made to Algonquian economy. He gives the sites of Mohawk, Onondaga, Oneida, Cayuga, and Seneca villages from the seventeenth through the nineteenth centuries. He shows that at the turn of the eighteenth century the stream of cultural infusion shifted from the Huron-Ottawas south to the Delaware, Shawnee, and Siouan tribes and to southeastern patterns from those in historic times. There are six maps and tables of Iroquois peoples and their locality. The article is based on published primary and secondary works.

GRAYMONT, BARBARA. *The Iroquois in the American Revolution.* Syracuse: Syracuse University Press, 1972. 359pp. Illustrated. Bibliography.

In this study, the author traces the events during the 1770s that led to the involvement of the Iroquois Confederacy of New York in the American Revolution, despite the Confederacy's efforts to remain neutral. She examines why some factions took the American side and most took the British side which threw the Iroquois into civil war. The first chapter describes the social and hunting patterns, language, warfare, and religion of various Iroquoian-speaking peoples, before the Revolution, including the five tribes of New York state who formed the original Iroquois Confederacy. Her cultural analysis of the role of Iroquois women in political life, of the perennial clash between young warriors and older peace chiefs, and of the inter- and intratribal League factionalism explains why it was not possible for the Iroquois to remain neutral. The author explains the involvement of the Iroquois in imperial rivalries between the English and the French until the latter were defeated and considers the use of religion as a branch of diplomacy in bringing Indian tribes under French or British influence. The author discusses how the Confederacy was caught in the middle of the struggle between England and her colonies and examines the diplomatic negotiations of the Six Nations with either the British or American antagonists who all wished to secure the tribes' loyalty during the early years of the Revolution. She reveals the severe pressures placed upon the Indians who were inevitably drawn into the war in battles which pitted British-allied Iroquois against American-allied Iroquois and turned the Revolution into an Iroquois civil war as well. The author describes the battles, campaigns, and border raids of the war and discusses the roles of Colonel Guy Johnson, Sir William Johnson, General Philip Schuyler, Joseph and Mary Brant, Cornplanter, Red Jacket, and others. The author analyzes the fate of the Iroquois in the immediate postwar period, concluding that the pro-American Oneidas and Tuscaroras were no better off than the pro-British tribes because the Treaty of Fort Stanwix forced the Iroquois, who were abandoned by the British, to give away large tracts of land. The appendix contains the text of the Treaty and the Haldimand Grants. There are three maps and illustrations of Indian and white participants. A lengthy bibliographical essay cites notable collections of primary sources for the study of the Iroquois participation in the American Revolution and lists and evaluates unpublished and published materials for each of the ten chapters.

GRINDE, DONALD A., JR. *The Iroquois and the Founding of the American Nation.* San Francisco: Indian Historian Press, 1977. 175pp. Illustrated. Bibliography.

The author discusses the impact and extent of the influence of Iroquoian concepts upon the American people from the late seventeenth century to the end of the American Revolution. He begins with a brief discussion of the philosophy and cultural and historical background of the Iroquois of New York, compares seventeenth- and eighteenth-century European political concepts of freedom and democracy with Iroquois ideas, describes the impact of the European economic system on Iroquois economic organization, and the impact of Iroquois ideas about government and freedom upon Americans. The author describes Iroquois diplomacy with rival powers Britain and France during the last half of the seventeenth and the first half of the eighteenth century and diplomatic maneuvers with white colonists up to the American Revolution. He explains Iroquois neutrality and eventual embroilment in the American war for independence, alliances either with Americans or the British, and civil war within the Iroquois Confederacy. He describes major battles in which the Iroquois were involved, Iroquois raids against white people along the American frontier, and the British and American abandonment of the Iroquois in treaty negotiations at the end of the Revolution. He concludes with a chapter on the legacy of the ideals of the Iroquois Confederacy for past and contemporary societies. The Constitution of the Five Nations and the 1754 Albany Plan of Government are reprinted. There are three maps, several paintings of Iroquois, and a bibliography of unpublished and published primary and secondary materials.

HAVILAND, WILLIAM A., and MARJORY W. POWER. *The Original Vermonters: Native Inhabitants Past and Present.* Hanover, N.H.: University Press of New England, 1981. 324pp. Illustrated. Bibliography.

The authors discuss Vermont's native inhabitants from the time of the region's first settlement 10,000 years ago down to the present. They tell how people lived in Vermont before Europeans arrived, focusing on the Paleo-Indians, the first Vermonters, and the Archaic culture and the Woodland period in Vermont. The authors explain why the Vermont Indians lived the way they did and what has been their fate as a result of European intrusion and domination. They tell of epidemics and plague, the fur trade, the Abenaki-Iroquoian wars, the Abenaki-British wars, and usurpation by the new United States. Particular attention is paid to Vermont's Abenakis who have recently reasserted their ethnic and cultural identity in the face of pressure to renounce their cultural heritage. The authors describe Western Abenaki social and political organization, life cycle, world view, and social control. There is a chapter on Native Americans in Vermont today. There are maps, numerous illustrations of artifacts and the Vermont Indians' way of life. The bibliography lists the unpublished manuscripts, archaeological reports, artifact collections, and published works which the authors utilized for research. There are four appendixes dealing with contemporary Vermont Indian affairs.

HICKERSON, HAROLD. *The Chippewa and Their Neighbors: A Study in Ethnohistory.* New York: Holt, Rinehart & Winston, 1970. 133pp. Illustrated. Bibliography.

This book examines the culture and history of aboriginal Chippewas who lived in present-day

Wisconsin and Minnesota and the factors which caused them to change between the seventeenth and nineteenth centuries. The author first discusses ethnohistorical methods and their application to Chippewas and surveys a number of historical techniques employed by cultural anthropologists in reconstructing past cultures and the dynamics of culture change. He pieces together important features of Chippewa social organization and its reorganization from 1640 to 1670 in a period of both direct and indirect contact with Europeans and their economic systems. He discusses the functions and history of Midewiwin (natavistic ceremonials), a reaction to European contact which began at the turn of the eighteenth century. He discusses the dynamics of territorial relations between the Chippewas and Siouan Dakotas in terms of occupancy, contested areas, and fur trade competition, and examines the nature of and the effects of Chippewa-Dakota warfare on their subsistence patterns and political organization. The epilogue discusses the use of documentary materials in reconstructing past cultures. There are several maps and photographs of Chippewa artifacts.

HYDE, GEORGE E. *Indians of the Woodlands: From Prehistoric Times to 1725.* Norman: University of Oklahoma Press, 1962. 295pp. Illustrated. Bibliography.

Hyde discusses the prehistoric and early historic periods of Indian tribes situated between the Ohio Valley and the Great Lakes and the Hudson and the Mississippi rivers. The first two-thirds of the book deal with the archaeology of the area and the last third concerns French trading, missionary, and exploring activities in the Upper Great Lakes and the Mississippi Valley in the late seventeenth century and the disunity and war among the resident tribes themselves. He traces the movements of half of the Indian population driven out of the Ohio Valley by Iroquois attacks and who fled into lands beyond the Mississippi River before the beginning of the historic period. For example, he gives evidence of the flight of the Osage-Omaha and Quapaw groups from the Ohio Valley around 1650 and the migration of Omahas from the lower Mississippi northward through Iowa around 1673. He discusses Indian trade, the source of wealth and power for the French, and analyzes French maps and documents to ascertain the group of tribes living in northwestern Iowa between 1670 and 1683. He discusses the Pawnees who held both banks of the Mississippi River before the Sioux arrived and describes the situation of Indians living in South Dakota after 1690 who were fugitive groups raided by enemies armed with European weapons. He concludes by considering how, by the close of the seventeenth century, the tribes of the North-Central Woodlands were facing destruction from petty feuds, disunity, and European intrusions into their lands. There are five maps and sketches of Hopewell (prehistoric) women, men, and artifacts. The book is based on published primary and secondary works.

JACOBS, WILBUR R. *Dispossessing the American Indian: Indians and Whites on the Colonial Frontier.* New York: Scribner's, 1972. 240pp. Illustrated.

This collection of essays focuses on the confrontation between Eastern Woodland Indians and Anglo-American pioneers of the eighteenth century and the essays fall into three general groups. The first few sketch the background of Indian-white contacts, the impact of the fur trade on the aboriginal way of life and lands, the use of wampum in diplomacy, and white gift-giving by which Britain and France controlled native populations. The second group of essays considers aspects of Indian-white relations including Edmund Atkin's scheme for British imperial Indian control, the killing of prisoners by Indians at Fort William Henry in 1757, Pontiac's conspiracy to remove Britain from North America, and the 1763 Appalachian Indian Boundary line. The third group gives an overview of early native-white relations on a worldwide scale, which includes the attitudes and policies of British colonials towards Woodland Indians and a comparative analysis of experiences shared by natives of North America, Australia, and New Guinea. An epilogue summarizes the contributions of Woodland Indians and two appendixes provide the chronological highlights of early American Indian-white relations and early native-white contacts in Australia and New Guinea. There are six maps and historical photographs of native peoples from North America, Australia, and New Guinea. Also included are an essay evaluating secondary works in the field of Indian-white relations and extensive footnotes of manuscript collections and published primary and secondary works.

———. *Wilderness Politics and Indian Gifts: The Northern Colonial Frontier, 1748–1763.* Stanford, Calif.: Stanford University Press, 1950; reprint ed.: Lincoln: University of Nebraska Press, 1966. 208pp. Illustrated. Bibliography. (Formerly entitled *Diplomacy and Indian Gifts: Anglo-French Rivalry Along the Ohio and Northwest Frontiers, 1748–1763.*)

The author traces the competition between the French and English in giving presents to natives in order to secure their alliance which was part of their struggle for empire in North America and evaluates the role the presents played in the diplomatic history of native politics in the Northeast from 1748 to 1763. He begins with a discussion of the established Indian custom of giving and receiving presents and then compares the systems of distributing presents used by the French and British. He describes the types of presents given by the French and British, the "civilizing" influence of such gifts, and the financial expense of gift-giving to individual colonies and the British government. He tells of the distribution of presents by Colonel William Johnson to the Iroquois Confederacy which became a bulwark against the French in North America. He looks at the use of French force and English gift-giving to secure warriors for the eventual contest for control of North America between 1752 and 1754 and the use of presents by the British in 1755 to secure native auxiliaries in frontier campaigns against the French. He describes how presents to the Iroquois and their allies became an important issue in controlling the Indians during the last phases of struggle for empire and how the Cherokee proved to be an important English ally on the Ohio frontier during the French-Indian attacks. He suggests reasons for the 1763 Indian rebellion under Pontiac, especially the British failure to supply western Indians with goods. The book is based on unpublished and published primary and secondary works.

JAENEN, CORNELIUS J. *Friend and Foe: Aspects of French-Amerindian Cultural Contact in the Sixteenth and Seventeenth Centuries.* Toronto: McClelland & Stewart, 1976. 207pp. Illustrated. Bibliography.

In this study, the author considers the various aspects of the nature of French contact with American Indian peoples in the Northeast during the sixteenth and seventeenth centuries. The author discusses Cartier's initial expedition in 1534, contemporary French views of Indian character and cultures, and examines early Jesuit and Recollet missionary efforts to convert Indians to Catholicism as well as the many obstacles to evangelizing them. The author deals with the similarities, differences, and accommodations in value systems as a result of culture contact, the complex of social problems such as alcoholism and epidemics resulting from culture contact and clash, and the disruption of traditional native cultures. He examines sixteenth- and seventeenth-century barbarism and cruelty tolerated in French and native societies and the differences in their warfare and torture practices. He discusses how French policy towards American Indians from the time of the initial contact was based on assimilation through conversion, education, integration, and segregation on reservations, first introduced in 1637, to force Indians into becoming sedentary agriculturalists like the French. In the conclusion, the author surveys French and Indian beliefs about each other as a result of cultural contact and the effects of contact on both the French and Indians. There are several prints illustrating sixteenth- and seventeenth-century Indian life. The bibliography is based chiefly on unpublished and published primary sources.

JAHODA, GLORIA. *The Trail of Tears: The Story of the American Indian Removals 1813–1855.* New York: Holt, Rinehart & Winston, 1975. 356pp. Illustrated. Bibliography.

This book chronicles the story of the removal and forced migration of more than fifty tribes from their ancestral homelands in the Northeast and Southeast to Oklahoma Territory during the first half of the nineteenth century. The author begins with a summary of the evolution of federal Indian removal policy from 1813 to 1830, the year the Indian Removal Bill passed, and describes the 1830 removals of Oneidas, Senecas, Delawares, and Shawnees from the Northeast. She tells of the resistance of Sacs led by Black Hawk to removal from Illinois and their defeat, and discusses the removal of Creeks, Chickasaws, and Choctaws from the Southeast. Chapters discuss the smallpox epidemic that killed upper Missouri River Mandans; the work of Catholic priest

Benjamin Petit among the Potawatomis in northern Indiana; Cherokee removal from Tennessee, North Carolina, and Georgia; and the Wyandot removal from Ohio. She describes the war between Florida's Seminoles and the American Army resulting in the removal of a portion of the tribe to Oklahoma Territory and the resistance of other Seminoles who still remain in Florida. The concluding chapter concerns the treaties that were negotiated in the 1850s by George W. Manypenny that diminished reservation sizes. There are photographs of various native people. The book is based partly on native statements and government documents.

JENNINGS, FRANCIS. *The Invasion of America: Indians, Colonialism, and the Cant of Conquest.* Chapel Hill: University of North Carolina Press, 1975; reprint ed.: New York: Norton, 1976. 369pp. Illustrated. Bibliography.

The author reexamines the records of Indian-European relations in colonial America, concentrating on New England from 1634 to 1675 as an illustrative case study. The first chapter describes the book's ethnological method and terminology. The author argues at the outset that the European colonial leaders who led the assault on native land, sovereignty, and life consciously created an ideology of conquest to justify their actions using distortion, prevarication, and propaganda as a cover. He dissects the misleading implications of the terminology the English used about Indians, such as America being a wilderness inhabited by savages, a still current assumption contributing to the maintenance of the conqueror mythology and the uncritical acceptance of colonial writings. He examines dramatic demographic changes that counter the fallacy that Indians were savages with limited populations; and examines the reciprocity of discovery between Indians and Europeans, European conceptions of Indian religions, economic relations and the fur trade, tribal political organization, treaty relations, and the natives' loss of sovereignty and property through peaceful purchase of their territory. He concludes this section with a discussion of the myth of a master civilization locked in battle with savagery in which the motives for aboriginal war and European influence on Indian warfare are described. The second part of the book offers a narrative reinterpretation of Indian-white relations in southern New England from the 1637 Pequot War to the 1675 King Philip's War and exposes the distortions of key Puritan sources. The author discusses Connecticut and Massachusetts struggling over the Pequot Indians and the Puritan conquest of the Pequots. He examines two major Puritan institutions, the missionary reservations and the federation of Puritan governments called the United Colonies of New England, and explains how these two institutions contributed to the conquest of the Narragansetts in 1675. In the appendix, Jennings makes a comparison between colonial America and medieval Europe as examples of the formative period of a large society and argues that there is a need for more comparative studies to show the basic relationships and growth of institutions. There are four maps and engravings which illustrate the text. The bibliography consists of official records listed by governments and anthropological materials written before and after 1800.

KAWASHIMA, YASU. "Legal Origins of the Indian Reservation in Colonial Massachusetts." *American Journal of Legal History* 13, no. 1 (January 1969):42–56.

The author examines the origins and objectives of the Indian reservation system in colonial Massachusetts by analyzing colonial legislation. He concludes that the reservation was not an integral part in the colony's political system because it was administered directly by the colonial government through guardians and few reservations attained the status of the English township. The legislation indicated it was a temporary system designed to rule natives in an orderly manner until the latter were assimilated into white society. He looks at the 1677 policy of confining natives to specific areas which included a scheme for four, and later three, native reservations where the people were required to live. He considers the 1694 act by which reservation natives came under the jurisdiction of white commissioners who regulated Indian conduct and examines several mid-eighteenth-century acts which provided the legal framework but no special judicial system for the reservation in colonial Massachusetts. He tells of the policy shift of the colonial government from that of providing natives with autonomy to that of controlling their activities on reservations. He looks at reservation officials and the governmental structure and regulations directed toward protecting the system, preventing white encroachment on reservation land, and the experiments of the Stockbridge and Mashpee Indian villages where the Indians had some autonomy as well as internal improvements. The author studies the special restrictive regulations applied to natives and the reservation's lack of township status, concluding with a discussion of the deterioration of the Massachusetts reservation system during the 1750s and 1760s. There are footnotes based on unpublished and published primary and secondary works.

KEESING, FELIX M. *The Menominee Indians of Wisconsin: A Study of Three Centuries of Cultural Contact and Change.* Introduction by Frank C. Miller. Memoirs of the American Philosophical Society, vol. 10. Philadelphia: American Philosophical Society, 1939; reprint ed.: New York: Johnson Reprint, 1971. 261pp. Illustrated. Bibliography.

This book analyzes the impact of whites on the Menominees of northern Wisconsin from the 1630s to 1929. Chapters discuss ancestral Menominee culture and migrations; the impact of French explorers, traders, Jesuit missionaries, soldiers, and political leaders upon Menominee culture and other tribes of the region until 1760. The author looks at British and American relations with Menominee people, analyzing the influence of the fur trade and its decline on Menominee economic and social life. Chapters deal with white pressure for the tribe's lands, subjection to government control, and removal to a reservation by the 1850s where economic activities largely centered on lumbering. The author considers government efforts designed to make Menominees into farmers and the rapid disintegration of the old culture by the turn of the twentieth century. The concluding chapter deals with early twentieth-century Menominee reservation life and the ecological, economic, and social changes and disorganization resulting from white influences and briefly criticizes federal assimilation policies. In the introduction, Miller analyzes Keesing's study and tells about his life, updates Menominee history through the 1950s, and cites other Menominee studies. There are four maps and photographs of Menominees and their way of life. The book is partly based on museum artifacts and field work.

LAUBER, ALMON W. *Indian Slavery in Colonial Times within the Present Limits of the United States.* Columbia University Studies in History, Economics, and Public Law, vol. 54, no. 3. New York: Columbia University Press, 1913. 352pp. Bibliography.

This is a study of the slavery of North American Indians in the North and South during the colonial period. The author treats in detail the enslavement of Indians by other Indians, the French, and the Spanish including information on processes of enslavement, employment of slaves, their treatment, and manumission, giving comparative numbers of slaves in different colonies. In addition, he examines English methods of enslavement including warfare, kidnapping, slave trade and other processes; looks at the economic basis of enslavement, methods of employing slaves, their treatment, and the eventual decline of native slavery. The book is based on manuscripts and published accounts listed in an extensive, unannotated bibliography.

LEACH, DOUGLAS EDWARD. *Flintlock and Tomahawk: New England in King Philip's War.* New York: Norton, 1958. 304pp. Illustrated. Bibliography.

The author provides a history of King Philip's War in 1675 and 1676 in southern New England (Massachusetts Bay, Plymouth, Connecticut, and Rhode Island colonies). He finds the basic causes of the conflict in Puritan land avarice and the misunderstandings that accompanied land transactions between Europeans and Indians. He discusses the Narragansetts, Nipmucks, Wampanoags, Mohegans, and Pequots who lived in southern New England and the role of Metacomet, the Wampanoag sachem who was called King Philip by the English, in starting the war against the New England colonists. The background of the struggle and the Puritan and Indian ways of life are described as well as the developing dominance of the white culture which provoked the rebellion that gradually spread among tribes in southern New England. The battles, massacres, stratagems, and logistics of the war are all described as are leaders on both sides—Philip, Uncas, Ninigret, Canonchet, Roger Williams, Benjamin Church, Governor Winslow, Samuel Mosely—figuring prominently in the story. The author considers all the factors contributing to the defeat of the

Indians and surveys the effects of the war on the lives of both Indians and colonists. He discusses ways the colonial governments handled recruiting, supply, finance of their effort, and persecution of friendly Indians. The author uses some terms which have pejorative meanings and offers some opinions that are dated. There are five maps that illustrate the history and portraits of colony leaders and one Indian. The bibliography includes unpublished and published primary materials and secondary accounts of the war.

NAMMACK, GEORGIANA C. *Fraud, Politics and the Dispossession of the Indians: The Iroquois Land Frontier in the Colonial Period.* Norman: University of Oklahoma Press, 1969. 128pp. Illustrated. Bibliography.

The author studies conflict, politics, and rivalries over Indian lands on the Iroquois frontier during the era of British control from 1664 to the 1770s. She selects representative case studies to illustrate various aspects of land problems along the frontier: the Mohawk Flatts, the Canajohary Patent, the Kayaderosseras grant, and the Philipse Patent. In addition, she looks at the development of imperial Indian land policy. The book contains illustrations of old maps and of the principal Indians and colonial officials who figured in the land problems.

NASH, GARY B. *Red, White, and Black: The Peoples of Early America.* Englewood Cliffs, N.J.: Prentice-Hall, 1974. 350pp. Illustrated. Bibliography.

The author gives the history of Native Americans, Europeans, and Africans of eastern North America during the seventeenth and eighteenth centuries and how their cultures were changed by the complex process of cultural interaction. After a survey of the early native cultures of the New World with special attention given the Iroquois, Cherokees, and Creeks, Nash introduces the competing European cultures and describes and analyzes demographic factors, missions, wars, Indian and African enslavement, trade, disease, miscegenation, diplomacy, and other facets of European-Indian contact on the eastern seaboard. He compares Spanish, French, and Dutch policies toward the Indians and Africans and shows that English-Indian relations differed from region to region. He concludes with a summary of cultural interaction among the three groups on the eve of the American Revolution. Nash provides a brief section devoted to "African-Indian contact," a summary of studies on Indian slaves, racial attitudes of blacks and Indians, intermarriage, etc. There are a map and reproductions of artwork.

NEWCOMB, WILLIAM W., JR. *The Culture and Acculturation of the Delaware Indians.* University of Michigan Museum of Anthropology, Anthropological Papers, no. 10. Ann Arbor: University of Michigan Press, 1956. 141pp. Illustrated. Bibliography.

This is a study of the Delawares who lived in parts of present-day Delaware, and how and why their culture changed under the impact of Euro-

American civilization from the early sixteenth to the mid-nineteenth century. The first part of the book deals with early historic Delaware culture including its location, origins, linguistic affiliations, population, subsistence patterns, economy, material culture, social and political organization, warfare, religion, magic, and folklore. The second part deals with Delaware acculturation as a result of contact with European and American cultures. The author begins with the period from 1524 to 1690 when Delawares borrowed many technological traits directly from Europeans, continues with the period from 1690 to 1750 when the political entity known as the Delaware tribe emerged, looks at the period from 1750 to 1814 when Delawares became militaristic and underwent a second acculturation, and ends during 1814–67 when the Delawares were politically and militarily dominated by the United States and culturally deteriorating. He discusses Delaware assimilation after 1867 in terms of technology, economy, social organization, religion, and language and briefly describes Delaware participation in Cherokee-Delaware Pan-Indianism, evidence of their not being fully assimilated into white society. He concludes with an analysis of the reasons for acculturation in some parts of Delaware culture before it appeared in others throughout the various time periods. An appendix discusses the eyewitness accounts the author used. There are a map and figures on Delaware kinship terminology and linguistics. The work is partly based on the author's field work.

OURADA, PATRICIA K. *The Menominee Indians: A History.* Norman: University of Oklahoma, 1979. 274pp. Illustrated. Bibliography.

The author narrates the history of the Menominees of Wisconsin from ancestral times to the present time. She begins with a description of Menominee culture before contact and tells of their relationship with French explorers, fur traders, and missionaries beginning in the mid-seventeenth century, and their loyalty to the French in the latter's war with the English until France lost its empire in 1763. She explains Menominee relations with the British whom the tribe supported throughout the American Revolution and the War of 1812. She considers U.S. treaties in the 1830s by which the Menominees ceded portions of their land to tribes of the Six Nations and to Wisconsin lumbermen, attempts by people of Wisconsin to wrest the remainder of Menominee land, and the role of Chief Oshkosh who was determined that the Menominees remain in the land of their origins. The author studies reservation life from the 1860s to the 1890s, discussing the Menominees' support of the Union cause in the Civil War and looks at the first half of the twentieth century. She examines the termination policy applied to the Menominees in the 1950s by the federal government, who decided the tribe was ready to end all special relationships and treaty guarantees, and the disastrous results for the tribe in the 1960s. She describes the role of the grassroots movement called DRUMS (Determination of Rights and Unity for Menominee Shareholders), which led the Menominees to seek reversal of Menominee termination, and the restoration of tribal status in 1973. There are two maps and photographs of Menominees and their environment. The book is based on unpublished and published primary and secondary materials. See also Peroff, *Menominee DRUMS* (below).

PARKER, ARTHUR C. "Analytical History of the Seneca Indians." *Researches and Transactions of the New York State Archaeological Association,* vol. 6, no. 1–5. Rochester: Lewis H. Morgan Chapter, 1926. 162pp. Illustrated.

The author traces the history of the Seneca tribe of New York from ancestral times to the mid-nineteenth century. He begins by discussing the inhabitants of the Genesee country in New York State before the Senecas arrived, briefly describes several Iroquois-speaking tribes and salient features of the Iroquois political organization, and tells of the Algonquian enemies of the Iroquois. He surveys Seneca wars with the Hurons, French, Algonquian Indians, and other tribes from 1630 to around 1685 and describes the material culture and social organization of the Senecas. He outlines eighteenth-century events leading the Senecas to choose the English as allies over the French, tells of Seneca factionalism, highlights the roles of Joseph Brant, William Johnson, Pontiac, and others, and discusses the effects of pre-Revolutionary events and the American Revolution on the Senecas. He concludes by discussing how Iroquois title to land was extinguished after the Revolution and how the Senecas were defrauded of land promised to them. The author, a Seneca, maintains that the Senecas preserved themselves after resisting both European and American encroachments and argues that Indians were a constructive factor in American history in that they kept Europeans in a zone where they developed an American national consciousness. One map and illustrations of Iroquois people and artifacts are included. The work is based on manuscript files and personal field work conducted by the author.

PECKHAM, HOWARD, and CHARLES GIBSON, eds. *Attitudes of Colonial Powers toward the American Indian.* Salt Lake City: University of Utah Press, 1969. 139pp.

This book contains a collection of six essays, each briefly exploring the separate Indian policies and practices of several European nations during the sixteenth, seventeenth, and eighteenth centuries. The six include: (1) "Indians and Spaniards in the New World: A Personal View" by Lewis Hanke; (2) "Black Robes Versus White Settlers: The Struggle for 'Freedom of the Indians' in Colonial Brazil" by David Alden (the struggle between Society of Jesus and white settlers over Indians); (3) "Dutch Treatment of the American Indian, with Particular Reference to New Netherland" by Allen W. Trelease; (4) "The French and the Indians" by Mason Wade; (5) "British-Colonial Attitudes and Policies toward the Indian in the American Colonies" by Wilbur R. Jacobs; and (6) "Political Incorporation and Culture Change in New Spain: A Study in Spanish-Indian Relations" by Edward H. Spicer. Each essay contains footnotes based on unpublished and published primary and secondary sources.

PEROFF, NICHOLAS C. *Menominee DRUMS: Tribal Termination and Restoration, 1954–1974.* Norman: University of Oklahoma Press, 1981. 368pp. Illustrated. Bibliography.

This is a history of the organized campaign called DRUMS (Determination of Rights and Unity for Menominee Shareholders) that was established to achieve restoration of the Menominees' reservation and federally protected tribal status.

RONDA, JAMES P. "We Are All Well As We Are: An Indian Critique of Seventeenth Century Christian Missions." *William and Mary Quarterly,* Third Series, 34, no. 1 (January 1977):66–82.

This article concentrates on several Native American reactions to Christian missionary activity rather than on the missionaries' programs. The author reconstructs Native American criticisms of the missions by examining their responses to Christian theological ideas of sin, guilt, heaven, hell, and baptism. He examines the words of Huron and Montagnais natives in New France in particular.

SALISBURY, NEAL. "Red Puritans: The Praying Indians of Massachusetts Bay and John Eliot." *William and Mary Quarterly,* Third Series 31, no. 1 (January 1974):27–54.

This essay, focusing on Massachusetts Bay, examines the program and role in English policy of John Eliot, the minister who established fourteen "praying towns" among southern New England Algonquians from the late 1640s through the 1670s as well as the effects of the policy on the "praying" Indians. Salisbury describes how Eliot set out to "civilize" natives, by regrouping them into specially constructed "praying towns" where they were isolated from settlers and other Indians and where legal codes were designed to uproot Indian cultures, a prerequisite to conversion. He explains that natives who responded to the missionaries were those whose ways were already disappearing under the impact of the European invasion and briefly looks at the Massachusetts Indians who demonstrate the sequence through which a tribe passed before receiving the missionaries. The tactics Eliot and other missionaries used to undermine the loyalty of tribal members to sachems, intratribal conflicts between converts and those loyal to traditional ways, and opposition from the white population, especially those in immediate contact with the towns, are also examined. Further, the author tells of the education program of inculcating Puritan cultural and religious values in Indian adults and children and explains their conversion experiences. He concludes with the outbreak of King Philip's War and the Nipmuck defection which brought the defeat of Eliot's missionary program and the plan to convert the four remaining "praying towns" into reservations for natives. There are footnotes based on published primary and secondary works. See also Ronda, above.

SCHLESIER, KARL H. "Epidemics and Indian Middlemen: Rethinking the Wars of the Iroquois, 1609–1653." *Ethnohistory* 23, no. 2 (Spring 1976):129–45. Bibliography.

In this paper, the author reexamines events in

northeastern North America during the first half of the seventeenth century and argues that the Iroquois did not fight the French colonials and French-dominated tribes for economic reasons or for territorial gains. He also argues that the destruction or dispersal of many tribes around the middle of the seventeenth century was not a result of the fur trade but rather an outcome of a set of destructive forces, smallpox emerging as the most significant. The paper refutes the central theory advanced by George T. Hunt in his book, *The Wars of the Iroquois: A Study in Intertribal Relations* (Madison: University of Wisconsin Press, 1940, 1967). The author begins by examining Hunt's thesis that Iroquois wars from 1642 to 1688 were fought for economic reasons and argues that the Iroquois never attempted to become middlemen of the fur trade and were not after territory. He explains the treaty policy of Champlain and successive New France governors that divided the Huron and caused their political demise and dispersion by 1650. He describes how, between 1634 and 1640, the Huron and other tribes in direct or indirect contact with French people were also struck by smallpox epidemics and how, after the disease declined (1642–53), the Iroquois retaliated for their loss of life through small raiding parties on the French.

SEGAL, CHARLES M., and DAVID C. STINEBACK. *Puritans, Indians, and Manifest Destiny.* New York: Putnam's, 1977. 257pp. Illustrated.

This book combines a history of Puritan-Indian relations and an anthology of fifty-five seventeenth-century primary documents dealing with aspects of that relationship. The introduction treats colonial interracial relations and analyzes the impact of European settlements on Indian cultures during the seventeenth and eighteenth centuries. The authors argue that the history of Puritan and Indian relations is best seen as a cultural conflict with a theological basis. The documents, excerpted or in their entirety, deal with five aspects of Puritan-Indian contact labeled land and trade, government relations, the Pequot War, the conversion of Indians to Christianity, and King Philip's War. They are arranged chronologically according to their inception as important concerns in Puritan-Indian relations. The authors maintain that economic dealings between Puritans and Indians preceded the first political arrangements, which came before the onset of the Pequot War, the missionary effort to the Indians initiated after the war, and before King Philip's War. Each topic includes an introduction to the issues raised by seventeenth-century events and a selection of key documents. In the conclusion, the authors state that the dynamic of Puritan-Indian conflict in New England provides a model for understanding the later conflict between white Americans and other Indian tribes during the westward movement in America. There are a map, a chronology of events of Puritan-Indian relations, and suggested readings.

TRELEASE, ALLEN W. *Indian Affairs in Colonial New York: The Seventeenth Century.* Ithaca: Cornell University Press, 1960; reprint ed.: Port Washington, N.Y.: Kennikat Press, 1971. 397pp. Illustrated. Bibliography.

In this book, the author traces the history of Indian-white contacts in seventeenth-century New York dividing it into two phases, the first corresponding roughly with the period of Dutch rule before 1664 (when New Amsterdam became New York) which was concerned with the Algonquian bands, and the second, the English period after 1664 which was chiefly concerned with the Iroquois. The first chapter gives descriptions of the social organization, economy, population, kinship, and settlement patterns of Algonquian Indians in present-day New Jersey and New York and the five Iroquois Nations of present-day New York. The author details the beginnings of New Netherland and the Dutch interest in the fur trade and Indian land, describes the governors of the province, warfare between Dutch colonists and Algonquian Indians, the liquor and firearms traffic, and Dutch commercial relations with the Iroquois. Trelease discusses New York's relations with seaboard Algonquian bands, its management of the fur trade, French-English rivalries for North American furs and Iroquois allegiance, the Iroquois' established policy of neutrality in regard to the English-French contest, and appraises Governor Thomas Dongan's Indian policies in the 1680s. In this work, the author reinterprets George Hunt's economic thesis regarding the origins of the Iroquois wars (in *The Wars of the Iroquois: A Study in Intertribal Relations.* Madison: University of Wisconsin Press, 1940, 1967). He argues that the wars were motivated by the Iroquois' search for new beaver supplies which led to armed resistance by enemies and for other reasons that predated the arrival of whites. There are maps that illustrate the history and pictures of persons important to colonial New York. The bibliography includes unpublished and published primary sources and secondary works.

TRIGGER, BRUCE. *The Children of Aataentsic: A History of the Huron People to 1660.* 2 vols. Montreal: McGill-Queen's University Press, 1976. 913pp. Illustrated. Bibliography.

The author provides the history of the Huron of southern Ontario, Canada, whom he traces from aboriginal times until they ceased to exist as a distinct people around 1649. Although he focuses on the French occupation of the St. Lawrence Valley and on the Huron, his story takes in the whole northeastern portion of North America. In the first volume, Trigger discusses in detail his aims, methods, and assumptions in writing the book. He describes the main patterns of Huron culture as they evolved in Ontario, briefly compares Hurons with other Iroquoian-speaking peoples, reviews Iroquoian archaeology, and surveys the indirect influence of Europeans on Hurons before 1609, the year of their first direct contact with French people. The author presents a detailed analysis of Huron interaction with the French in which he identifies two phases, the first from 1609 to 1634 in which the basic pattern of Huron economic and social relations remained essentially the same as it had before contact. He explains how the Hurons developed a trading relationship with the Europeans and adjusted to their trading goods. In the second volume, Trigger discusses the second phase of contact, after 1634, when the Hurons lost half of their population to epidemics, the Jesuits made inroads among them, and they became economically dependent on the French fur trade. He argues that in the 1630s and 1640s the Iroquois shifted from traditional, small-scale raids for revenge to larger attacks for economic gain and that the Iroquois were victorious over the Hurons by 1649 because the latter were factionalized into traditional and Christian camps, demoralized by Jesuit activities and by disease, and insufficiently supplied with guns by the French. The author also deals with the end of the Huron Confederacy and the Hurons' dispersal and discusses the early years of struggle for individual and collective survival by remnants of the Confederacy. The conclusion summarizes certain aspects of the Huron experience that may be useful for interpreting phases of interaction between Europeans and other Indian peoples. There are thirty-seven maps and over fifty illustrations that pertain to Huron history and intertribal relations in the sixteenth and seventeenth centuries. The extensive unannotated bibliography contains unpublished and published primary and secondary works.

VAUGHAN, ALDEN T. *New England Frontier: Puritans and Indians, 1620–1675.* Boston: Little, Brown, 1965; revised ed.: New York: Norton, 1979. 430pp. Illustrated. Bibliography.

In his 1965 study, Vaughan examines how Puritan settlers of New England viewed Indians, how their perceptions shaped their conduct toward them, and gauges the impact of Puritan colonization on Indians from 1620 to 1675. He argues that New England Puritans followed a humane, peaceful, and just policy in their commercial, religious, and financial dealings with Indians during the period under study. Briefly he surveys encounters between early explorers and New England natives and surveys the economy, politics, religion, warfare, subsistence patterns, and customs of Abenakis, Massachusetts, Narragansetts, Wampanoags, Pennacooks, and Pequots, focusing on the way Puritans conceived of native character and society. He describes the Pilgrims' settlement at New Plymouth, the Plymouth-Wampanoag alliance and cordial relations with other tribes, and their Indian policy from 1620 to 1630, characterized as just and tolerant. He examines the growth of the Massachusetts Bay Colony, its relations with New England Indians and its Indian policy from 1630 to 1636, and argues there was a similarity in English and native concepts of land tenure and sale of land. The author treats the Puritan expansion into Rhode Island and Connecticut and the attitudes and actions of Roger Williams towards the Indians. Discussing the Puritan-Pequot War of 1637, he argues that the Pequot must bear most of the blame for the war and he considers the effects of the war on the balance of power which shifted from the natives to the English colonies. He examines the Puritan policy of colonial confederation between 1638 and 1675 due to English politics, threats from certain tribes, and intertribal clashes. In dealing with Puritan justice, laws, and litigation from 1620 to 1675, Vaughan argues that the Puritans were orderly and just in controlling interracial affairs in the New England colonies. He discusses Puritan-Indian commercial relations with furs at the heart of the economy and the lack of success of Puritan missionary efforts, particularly its "praying towns." The epilogue focuses on King Philip's War and its relationship to earlier Puritan-Indian affairs, particularly on "praying" Indians, and stresses that when the clashes came the divisions were over issues, not race. The author concludes by reevaluating the traditional assumptions about Puritan-Indian relations and lauds Puritan conduct of Indian affairs by describing six things they did not do to Indians. In the introduction to the 1979 edition, Vaughan reconsiders various facets of the Puritans' Indian policies and attitudes and discusses several major themes and episodes that have spurred scholarly debate during the intervening fifteen years. He compares the treatment of Indians by the Spanish, Portuguese, French, and Dutch and also compares Puritan policy with that of other English colonies. There are other revisions in the text, appendixes of legal documents illustrating Puritan-Indian relations, two maps, and pictures of New England Indians and Puritans. The book is based on unpublished and published seventeenth-century records and contemporary secondary works.

WALLACE, ANTHONY F. C. *The Death and Rebirth of the Seneca: The History and Culture of the Great Iroquois Nation, Their Destruction and Demoralization, and Their Cultural Revival at the Hands of the Indian Visionary, Handsome Lake.* New York: Knopf, 1970. 384pp. Illustrated. Bibliography.

This book contains an account of the decline of the Senecas of New York throughout the eighteenth century followed by a description of their renaissance induced by Handsome Lake's teaching in the early nineteenth century. In the first part, Wallace describes Seneca cultural life in the first half of the eighteenth century and explains in psychosocial terms what it meant to be a Seneca child, clan matriarch, warrior, or statesman. He gives a picture of Seneca policy, economy, social structure, and military institutions, and emphasizes the centrality of religion in Seneca life. In the second part of the book, Wallace describes and analyzes French destruction of the diplomatic "play-off" system, the disastrous effects of the American Revolution, the collapse of the native confederation, the establishment of American sovereignty over the Iroquois, and the post-Revolutionary growth of reservations. He dissects Iroquois social pathology caused by depopulation, disease, factionalism, and loss of confidence. The third part is an account of Handsome Lake's life, the moral reformation and social reconstruction of the Iroquois made possible by his leadership, his theory of religion as revitalization, and the message he preached from 1799 until 1815. There are paintings and drawings of Oneidas and Senecas. The book is based on unpublished and published primary and secondary sources.

―――. *King of the Delawares: Teedyuscung, 1700–1763.* Philadelphia: University of Pennsylvania Press, 1949. 305pp. Illustrated. Bibliography.

In this book about Indian-white relations in eighteenth-century Pennsylvania, the author argues that Teedyuscung had wanted to make Englishmen out of Indians, but was killed by the English for refusing to allow white people to steal Indian lands.

WALLACE, PAUL A. *Indians in Pennsylvania.* Harrisburg: Pennsylvania Historical and Museum Commission, 1961. 194pp. Illustrated.

The author gives an account of various Indian groups resident in Pennsylvania at the time of the first European explorations, at the beginning of the seventeenth century, through the eighteenth century. The first sections are devoted to brief general statements concerning the origins of native culture, with specific reference to the Susquehannocks, Monongahelas, and Eries in Pennsylvania and several sections treat aspects of Delaware life as recorded in historical accounts. Wallace describes the Iroquois Confederacy and its military organization as it laid claim after 1675 to extensive territories of which Pennsylvania lands were a part. He discusses the intertribal wars the Iroquois were involved in to survive in the beaver trade, their success in dispersing rivals, and their policy of armed neutrality as a means of holding the balance of power between the French and the English. The role of the Iroquois in populating Pennsylvania from 1675 until 1755 with native refugee groups such as the Nanticokes, Tuscaroras, and Shawnees who moved there after pressures from whites and other Indians dislodged them from their original homes is also examined. The author describes and lists thirty-three land transactions that extinguished Indian rights to Pennsylvania lands, causing the withdrawal of Delawares from Pennsylvania from the late seventeenth to the late eighteenth century. Also included is an account of the policy by which Pennsylvania conducted nonviolent Indian relations until 1755 and the colony's involvement in several wars that ended Indian occupancy in Pennsylvania. There are thirty-six biographical sketches and several illustrations of famous Pennsylvania Indians as well as notes on the current location of descendants of Pennsylvania Indians.

WESLAGER, CLINTON ALFRED. *The Delaware Indians: A History.* New Brunswick, N.J.: Rutgers University Press, 1972. 546pp. Illustrated.

Weslager traces three centuries of the Delawares, a people who originally lived in New Jersey, Delaware, Pennsylvania, and New York and who now live in Oklahoma, Wisconsin, Kansas, and Ontario, Canada. He begins by discussing the modern descendants of Delawares, describes the ways Delawares lived before European contact, and tells the story of the *Walam Olum,* a pictographic history of the Delawares. Early seventeenth-century fur trade relations between the Dutch and the Delawares which wrought changes in Indian culture is discussed, as is the enmity existing between the Dutch and the Delaware and Susquehannock nations. He treats the rivalry between Dutch and Swedes for Indian lands and beaver furs until 1664, tells of Delaware life under English rulers after 1664, discusses William Penn's humanitarian Indian policy which continued from 1682 to 1715 when James Logan instituted Pennsylvania's new Indian policy strengthening the Iroquois, former enemies of the Delawares. Chapters describe English-French imperial rivalries in the Ohio River valley, explain how both countries courted alliance with the Delawares, and examine Delaware diplomacy and warfare against these two European rivals and the United States after 1775. Weslager briefly focuses on the role of Delaware Teedyuscung, Moravian missionary efforts, Delaware intertribal relations, and the Delawares' forced migration to western Pennsylvania, Ohio, Indiana, Missouri, Kansas, Oklahoma, and Texas as a result of pressures from white settlers. The book concludes with a brief survey of the current litigation involving millions of dollars which the Delawares claim the U.S. government owes them for Indiana and Kansas land. There are maps, illustrations of Delawares and their housing, and extensive footnoting based on unpublished and published materials.

SOUTHEAST

ALDEN, JOHN RICHARD. *John Stuart and the Southern Colonial Frontier: A Study of Indian Relations, War, Trade, and Land Problems in the Southern Wilderness, 1754–1775.* Ann Arbor: University of Michigan Press, 1944; reprint ed.: New York: Gordian Press, 1966. 384pp. Illustrated. Bibliography.

This book presents a history of the struggle for empire between France and England in the South from 1754 to 1775, the development and execution of British Indian policy, and the career of John Stuart and his conduct of native affairs. Part 1 deals with the Cherokees, Creeks, Choctaws, Chickasaws, and Seminoles during the Seven Years' War, 1754–61. Alden discusses Anglo-Indian trade relations, trade rivalry between the English and French, South Carolina's Indian policy, the Anglo-Cherokee alliance and war, and Anglo-French rivalry in Creek country. Part 2 deals with the imperial management of Indian relations under Stuart from 1763 to 1775 and explains the evolution of the Office of the Superintendent and Stuart's manipulation before the American Revolution. The author explains Stuart's policy of trying to maintain native boundaries against American encroachment and settlement, his efforts at trying to regulate Indian trade, and details his other problems arising from the presence of the French and later the Spanish west of the Mississippi River. There are appendixes of Stuart's trade regulations and his attitudes about British missionaries as well as four maps. The book is based on unpublished and published primary documents and maps.

BROWN, DOUGLAS SUMMERS. *The Catawba Indians: The People of the River.* Columbia: University of

South Carolina Press, 1966. 400pp. Illustrated. Bibliography.

Brown traces the history of the Catawbas of South Carolina from their origins to the mid-twentieth century, beginning with a discussion of the Siouan-speaking tribes who make up what in historic times has been called the Catawba Nation, their origins and prehistory, contacts with the Spanish, French, and English colonial settlers, and trade with Virginians. He examines the Catawba alliance with the English against the Spanish from 1670 to 1742, with colonists in the 1711 Tuscarora War, with other southeastern tribes in an attempt to wipe out South Carolina settlements in the Yamasee War of 1715, and with the Americans in the Revolution. Accounts are given about other Indians with whom the Catawba fought in historic times. Also covered are the leasing of Catawba lands to whites, the Treaty of 1840 by which Catawbas sold their lands to South Carolina, and the dispersion of the Nation, some to the North Carolina Cherokees, others to the West and Southwest, some to return to the old South Carolina reservation until land was obtained for another. The book concludes with a discussion of the Catawbas who severed their relationship with the federal government in 1959. There are nine maps and paintings of colonial officials, Catawbas, and their lands. The book is based on unpublished and published primary and secondary sources.

BURT, JESSE, and ROBERT B. FERGUSON. *Indians of the Southeast: Then and Now.* Nashville: Abingdon Press, 1973. 304pp. Illustrated. Bibliography.

The authors provide a general treatment of the histories and cultures of southeastern tribes from their origins to the present time. A brief survey of the earlier peoples who lived in the Southeast is followed by a description of the languages, subsistence patterns, religious beliefs, rituals, ceremonies, games, dances, music, and childhood of the Cherokees, Chickasaws, Choctaws, Creeks, Seminoles, and other groups who lived in Alabama, Florida, Georgia, Louisiana, Mississippi, North and South Carolina, and Tennessee. The authors tell of the arrival of the Spanish, French, and English and their rivalry for Indian trading rights and allies, and the prevalence of disease and warfare in southeastern tribes as a result of European contacts. They briefly discuss Indian tribes allied with either the French or the British, tribal factionalism, U.S. Indian policy, the removal of five southeastern tribes, and tell of those groups that resisted moving to the West. A survey of the history of the five southeastern tribes removed to Oklahoma and those tribes remaining in the Southeast from the mid-nineteenth century until the early 1970s is included. There are maps and many drawings and photographs of artifacts, historic and present-day southeastern Indians, Indian paintings, baskets, and lifeways.

CARTER, SAMUEL, III. *Cherokee Sunset: A Nation Betrayed; A Narrative of Travail and Triumph, Persecution and Exile.* Garden City, N.Y.: Doubleday, 1976. 318pp. Illustrated. Bibliography.

Carter traces the history of the Cherokees of Georgia, Tennessee, and North Carolina from the early 1800s to the Civil War. He covers the Cherokee way of life before European contact, Cherokee religious training and schools, the prolonged dispute with Georgia, the rise of the *Cherokee Phoenix,* the first Indian language newspaper and its suppression from 1828 to 1834, federal Indian removal policy, and the removal Treaty of New Echota. He cites rival Cherokee parties, the pro-Treaty, headed by John Ridge and Elias Boudinet, and the anti-Treaty, headed by John Ross, then discusses the 1837 voluntary removal of Treaty Party Cherokees, the 1838 enforced removal via the Trail of Tears to Oklahoma, and the subsequent political assassinations of Ridge and Boudinet in Oklahoma. There are maps and photographs of Cherokees, their lifestyle, and the *Cherokee Phoenix.* The book is based partly on material from the *Cherokee Phoenix* and Cherokee writings.

CORKRAN, DAVID H. *The Cherokee Frontier: Conflict and Survival, 1740–1762.* Norman: University of Oklahoma Press, 1962. 302pp. Illustrated. Bibliography.

Corkran traces the history of the Cherokees of North and South Carolina and Georgia, their culture, motives, objectives, policies, intratribal problems, and international situation during the colonial period. He discusses the rivalry of interests among the three regional Cherokee communities (the Lower Towns, Middle settlements, and Overhill) with their semiautonomous governing councils of headmen, particularly focusing on the struggle of Chota, capital of the Overhills, to assert its ascendancy over the centrifugal forces in the nation. Chapters describe intercolonial rivalry for Cherokee auxiliaries, and the demand of Cherokees for trade and presents from British allies. The rivalry between England and France for Cherokee allegiance, pro- and anti-English Cherokee factions, the 1760 Cherokee war on Carolina, the successful British campaigns of 1760–61, and the provisions of the peace treaty are also covered. There are two maps and reproductions of drawings of Cherokees, colonials, forts, and documents as well as a bibliographical essay that explains the principal sources used from colonial South Carolina, Virginia, and Georgia. The book is based on unpublished and published primary and secondary materials.

———. *The Creek Frontier, 1540–1783.* Norman: University of Oklahoma Press, 1967. 343pp. Illustrated. Bibliography.

This book contains a history of the Creeks who lived in Alabama, Georgia, and much of northern Florida from 1540 to 1783. The introduction gives a brief ethnographic account focusing on Creek social and political institutions. Chapters survey mid-sixteenth century Spanish explorations by De Soto and De Luna of Creek country, the rise of the Creeks to power over neighboring tribes (1670–1715), and Creek diplomatic policy with the Spanish, British, and French focusing on its national policy of neutralism until the American Revolution when the Creeks allied with the British against the American patriots. Corkran explains French and British conflict and machinations for southeastern native alliances and wars with Cherokees and Choctaws as well as the Yamasee War, the English war with Spain, 1739–48, and the American Revolution in which the Creeks were involved. He also discusses Creek trade with the English, political factionalism and treaty-making, land cessions, and pressures resulting from English settlement. Throughout the book, the author focuses on Creek personalities such as "Emperor" Brims, "Queen" Mary, the anti-English Mortar, and the rise to leadership of pro-British Alexander McGillivray. There are two maps and pictures of Creek people. The book is based on unpublished and published primary and secondary works.

COTTERILL, R. S. *The Southern Indians: The Story of the Civilized Tribes before Removal.* Norman: University of Oklahoma Press, 1954. 255pp. Illustrated. Bibliography.

This book traces the history of southeastern Indians, particularly the Cherokees, Creeks, Choctaws, and Chickasaws, from ancestral times to 1830. The author presents a general sketch of southeastern Indian culture, trade relationships of the four tribes with colonial governments, and English-French rivalry for Indian allies. He describes the pro-American and pro-British activities of the four tribes during the American Revolution and postwar tensions among southeastern tribes. Also considered are the political tactics of Creek Alexander McGillivray from 1783 to 1793, efforts of Americans to enlist southern Indians in campaigns against northern tribes, trade alliances between the four tribes and Spain, intertribal warfare, and the successive pressures put on the southeastern tribes by federal and state governments to cede tribal lands. Cotterill discusses the Shawnee Tecumseh's visit in 1811 to the Creeks and Choctaws to unite them with him in a league of peace; the Creek War of 1813–14, a result of tension between two Creek factions, which involved neighboring tribes and the American government; postwar conflicts over tribal boundaries; land cessions; and the removal of some Cherokees to west of the Mississippi. He concludes by summarizing changes in southeastern tribal life from the 1780s to the 1830s and events leading to the acceptance of the removal of several southeastern tribes. There are five maps, portraits of southeastern Indians, and a bibliography of unpublished manuscripts and secondary works.

CRANE, VERNER W. *The Southern Frontier, 1670– 1732.* Ann Arbor: University of Michigan Press, 1929. 391pp. Illustrated. Bibliography.

Crane tells of English colonial expansion in South Carolina from 1670 to 1732, Britain's conflicts with the French and Spanish for control of North America, and competition among the three for Indian trade and alliances. Beginning with a discussion of Britain's contacts with the Spanish in Florida and with South Carolina Indians involving clashes, enslavement, and trade, he then examines the development of a western Indian trading expansion in the seventeenth century, French-English collision over

trade with trans-Appalachian western Indians, the southern frontier in Queen Anne's War, and French-English rivalry for Indian alliances. He analyzes the structure and workings of the Charles Town Indian trade in skins and leathers; South Carolina's intercolonial problems over control of Indian trade, particularly with Virginia, 1670–1715; the Yamasee War, 1715–16, a revolt against the Carolina trading regime by the Yamasees, Creeks, Choctaws, and Cherokees as well as tribes of the Piedmont and others; and looks at the new South Carolina system of Indian defense. Crane also describes the beginnings of the British western policy, 1715–21, and the establishment of royal government in Carolina, programs formulated to challenge French progress in the West. He looks at the three-sided rivalries and intrigues of the English, French, and Spanish for Indian allegiance from 1715 to 1735; new advances of English colonization on the southern frontier from 1721 to 1730; and the philanthropic and strategic movements resulting in the establishment of Georgia. There is one map and several tables on trade statistics. The book is based on unpublished and published primary and secondary sources and maps.

CRAVEN, WESLEY FRANK. "Indian Policy in Early Virginia." *William and Mary Quarterly,* Third Series, 1, no. 1 (January 1944):65–82.

This article examines the deviating course of Indian policy in early Virginia from 1608 until 1662. The author considers the English settlers' initial guiding principles to share resources with Indians and convert them to Christianity, European intrusion, enmity between the two peoples, and the 1622 massacre and 1646 peace treaty which resulted in Virginia's unsuccessful effort to set aside a reservation where Indians would be free of white people's intrusion. He concludes with a discussion of policy after 1650 directed toward equitable division of the land, conversion of Indian economy, and the Revisal of 1662, a comprehensive statute which was Virginia's decision to deal more justly with Indians and was the main body of Virginia law for twenty-five years. There is some dated language. The article is footnoted with unpublished and published works.

DEBO, ANGIE. *The Road to Disappearance.* Norman: University of Oklahoma Press, 1941. 399pp. Illustrated. Bibliography.

Debo traces the history of the Creeks of Alabama and Georgia from the time just before contact with whites through their removal to Oklahoma. She summarizes the political, social, and economic organization of the Creeks, especially their Confederacy, Creek contacts with the Spanish and French, and trade with colonial Georgians. Following are discussions on Alexander McGillivray's rise to power and his foreign policy dedicated to preserving Creek independence and territorial integrity with Spain and the United States, white settlers' encroachment, Creek land cessions from 1790 to 1805, Creek-Georgia border conflicts, the 1812–14 Red Stick War against the United States, and the Creeks' immense cessions of land in Alabama and

Georgia which destroyed the old way of life. She looks at the removal of Georgia and Alabama Creeks to Oklahoma after the remainder of their lands were ceded and describes how shattered Creek remnants rebuilt a nation politically, economically, and educationally in Oklahoma from the 1830s to the 1850s, explaining their relations with other Oklahoma tribes and their survival through accepting white ways. She discusses how the Civil War divided the Creeks into Confederate and Federal factions and disrupted Creek development and tells of the punitive Reconstruction Treaty of 1866 by which the Creeks resumed relations with the United States. The author tells how the Creeks tried to heal their postwar internal divisions, achieve economic recovery and adjust themselves to changing conditions forced upon them by postwar railroad development, land grabbers, and white immigrants who threatened the tribe's existence but were hindered by their own spiritual disintegration and the growing black power in their midst. The author discusses the black slaves owned by Creeks, black adoption and intermarriage with Creeks, the Creek-Seminole controversy over blacks, their role in the Civil War, and their alliance with full-bloods and political power. The author describes how the Creek's political development was complicated by external influence, factional control of law enforcement, and disorganization of their government. She looks at Creek social, economic, educational, and religious life and intertribal relations in the 1880s, and the Creek factions' long struggle over the constitution. The conclusion discusses the creation of Indian Territory courts, occupation of Creek country by cattlemen, the Dawes Severalty Act, Creek financial troubles, factionalism, and surrender of tribal institutions. There are four maps and photographs of Creek people. The book is based on Creek informants and writings, as well as unpublished and published primary and secondary materials.

DeRosier, Arthur H. *The Removal of the Choctaw Indians*. Knoxville: University of Tennessee Press, 1970. 208pp. Illustrated. Bibliography.

This book contains a history of the removal of the Choctaw Nation from Mississippi lands to Indian Territory in the early 1830s, the first tribal population to be removed to the West under removal treaties. DeRosier begins with a description of the Choctaws when they first met Europeans after 1500 and details how they were a powerful community in lower Mississippi Valley diplomacy with Spain, France, Great Britain, and the United States. He describes the importance of native politics in American government affairs before 1830 and summarizes native policies of early presidents from Washington through Jackson. Also treated are the 1820 Doak's Stand Treaty, a reflection of John C. Calhoun's moderate policy embodying steps toward voluntary removal of natives to the West, the 1830 Dancing Rabbit Creek Treaty forcibly removing Choctaws to Indian Territory, and three formal Choctaw removals completed by 1833. The appendixes include the text of the two treaties and removal regulations and there are three maps as well as photographs of Choctaws and federal removal agents. The book is based on unpublished and published primary and secondary materials.

DeVorsey, Louis, Jr. *The Indian Boundary in the Southern Colonies, 1763–1775*. Chapel Hill: University of North Carolina Press, 1966. 267pp. Illustrated. Bibliography.

DeVorsey gives an account of the evolution of the Indian Boundary in the southern colonies from 1763 to 1775 and analyzes the British problems of colonial expansion in the southeastern quarter of North America as it confronted opposing interests of native tribes and the French and Spanish powers. He discusses the evolution of a boundary line which emerged on the map from the Ohio River south to the Florida peninsula and west to the Mississippi River and explains that the line was designed to separate lands reserved for Indian use from those available for occupation and exploitation by settlers of European origin and their African slaves. The book begins with a description of the contest for control of southeastern North America among the British, French, and Spanish and the people who lived there, the Cherokees, Catawbas, Creeks, Chickasaws, and Choctaws. Chapters examine the evolution of different sections of the Southern Indian Boundary line including the Virginia-Cherokee boundary, the North Carolina-Cherokee boundary, the South Carolina-Cherokee boundary, two Georgia-Indian boundaries, the East Florida-Creek boundary, and the West Florida-Indian boundary. The concluding chapter discusses John Stuart's efforts in 1775 to produce a reliable map of the Boundary line. There are twenty-nine maps that illustrate stages in the evolution of the Indian Boundary and are derived from the analysis of many contemporaneous sources such as manuscripts, printed maps, surveyor sketches, and treaty articles. The work is based on American and British archival records and eighteenth-century maps and published primary and secondary works.

Foreman, Grant. *Indian Removal: Emigration of the Five Civilized Tribes of Indians*. Norman: University of Oklahoma Press, 1932. 415pp. Illustrated. Bibliography.

This book tells of the forcible removal and expulsion of the Cherokees, Choctaws, Creeks, Chickasaws, and Seminoles from the South during the 1830s. The first section tells of the Choctaw removal from Mississippi in which Foreman examines the first treaty ratified under the 1830 Removal Act, the Choctaw Treaty of Dancing Rabbit Creek, Choctaw exploration of new western lands, their removals and suffering during 1831–33, and their arrival and living conditions in Indian Territory. The second section examines Creek removal from Alabama, their 1834 emigration, land frauds against the Creeks, a long military journal of events, and Creek suffering. Section 3 concerns Chickasaw removal from Mississippi and Alabama, their migrations, and settlement in the West. Section 4 deals with the Cherokee removal from Georgia, state oppression against the Cherokees, their defense of their tribal existence, and forcible removal and suffering. The fifth section considers Seminole removal from Florida, the Second Seminole War, some Seminole resistance to removal, the capture of Osceola, deportation of Seminole captives, and the surrender of Pascofa. Throughout the five sections, the author describes the inadequate government preparations for removal including the appointments of political incompetents to posts of authority and their mismanagement; the cruel and unnecessary suffering experienced by the emigrants; the work of regular army officers and soldiers who removed Indians with as much comfort as possible within the provisions made by Washington; and the people who profited from removal contracts. There are six maps and illustrations of removal scenes. The book is based on unpublished materials and secondary sources.

GIBSON, ARRELL MORGAN. *The Chickasaws.* Norman: University of Oklahoma Press, 1963. 312pp. Illustrated. Bibliography.

This book traces the history of the Chickasaws who lived in parts of Mississippi, Alabama, Tennessee, and Kentucky from 1540 to the early twentieth century. Briefly Gibson reconstructs the tribe's traditional way of life, looking at its relations with European nations from 1540 to 1763, emphasizing its attachment to the English, and warfare with the French. He treats the period 1763–86 when English, Spanish, and Americans competed for control of the Chickasaws and describes subsequent tribal factionalism and societal and institutional disorganization brought about by the intrusion of these alien forces. He discusses the years 1786–1837 in which Chickasaw independence eroded and traditional lifeways were corrupted by federal government policies, Protestant missionaries, and the state governments of Alabama and Mississippi. Also covered are the liquidation of the Chickasaw homeland by 1837, their forced migration to Indian Territory, and the emergence by 1850 of a new Chickasaw society containing old and new elements; the Chickasaw alliance with the Confederacy; the disruptive influence of the Civil War and its aftermath on tribal life; and the absorption of Chickasaws into the emerging state of Oklahoma in 1906, signaling the end of their existence as a semiautonomous Indian republic. Finally, the author treats traditional Chickasaw governmental apparatus, politics, factions, and leadership and the new forms and processes that were adopted by the tribe in the postremoval period until 1906 when the tribal government was extinguished. There are maps and photographs of Chickasaw people. The book is based on unpublished and published primary and secondary works.

HUDSON, CHARLES M. *The Catawba Nation.* University of Georgia Monographs, no. 18. Athens: University of Georgia Press, 1970. 142pp. Illustrated. Bibliography.

In this book, Hudson reconstructs the history of the Catawba Indians of South Carolina from ancestral times to the present. Beginning with a cultural account of the Catawbas until the early eighteenth century, he explains how, during the eighteenth century, Charleston traders came to control the Catawbas and the latter became of little military importance. He shows that most of the Catawba aboriginal cultural patterns were gone in the nineteenth century, incorporated into the plural structure of South Carolina society, while the twentieth century saw the Catawbas become a highly assimilated ethnic group in a modern industrial society and terminating their status as Indians with the Bureau of Indian Affairs. Hudson considers Catawba folk history as it is remembered today and describes the different version the local whites have of Catawba history. There is one map. The book is based on field work and published primary and secondary sources.

————, ed. *Four Centuries of Southern Indians.* Athens: University of Georgia Press, 1975. 173pp.

This book contains a collection of nine essays, each with its own bibliography. The first by James Covington, entitled "Relations between the Eastern Timucuan Indians and the French and Spanish, 1564–1567," is concerned with entanglements of the natives in French and Spanish colonial rivalry. The second by Douglas W. Boyce, entitled "Did a Tuscarora Confederacy Exist?" shows that the Tuscaroras were a collection of autonomous villages with a dependency on European trade goods. The third by James H. O'Donnell III, entitled "The Southern Indians in the War for American Independence, 1775–1783," discusses alliances with the Loyalists. The fourth by Jack D. L. Holmes, entitled "Spanish Policy toward the Southern Indians in the 1790s," describes Spanish policy aimed at alliances with southern natives to check American settler expansionism and land speculation. The fifth by Arthur H. DeRosier, Jr., entitled "Myths and Realities in Indian Westward Removal: The Choctaw Example," clears up misconceptions regarding Choctaw removal. The sixth by John H. Peterson, Jr. is entitled "Louisiana Choctaw Life at the End of the Nineteenth Century"; the seventh by Raymond D. Fogelson is entitled "An Analysis of Cherokee Sorcery and Witchcraft"; the eighth by Albert L. Wahrhaftig is entitled "Institution Building among Oklahoma's Traditional Cherokees"; and the last by Charles Crowe is entitled "Indians and Blacks in White America."

KING, DUANE H. *The Cherokee Indian Nation: A Troubled History.* Knoxville: University of Tennessee Press, 1979. 256pp. Illustrated.

This volume of twelve essays traces the history and changing culture of the Cherokees who have lived in North and South Carolina, Georgia, and Tennessee from ancestral to contemporary times. The introduction summarizes three hundred years of Cherokee-white relations and the following essays consider the origins and development of Cherokee culture and law, the distribution of eighteenth-century Cherokee settlements, pseudo-Cherokee charlatan William A. Bowles and Cherokee involvement in international diplomacy during the last decade of the eighteenth century, early nineteenth-century Cherokee political organization, the development of plantation slavery before Cherokee removal, the removal of 1828–35, and postremoval factionalism. Other essays consider the origin of the Eastern Cherokees as a social and political entity, the role of Tsali in early nineteenth-century Cherokee history, and William H. Thomas who devoted years to lobbying in Washington in the mid-nineteenth century on behalf of the Cherokees' financial claims. Concluding chapters deal with contemporary problems among the Eastern and Western Cherokees who are taking steps to improve their life, and the Oklahoma Cherokee men who have banded together in a revival of their ancient tribal government structure. There are five maps, photographs of archaeological finds, and tables of eighteenth-century Cherokee Lower, Middle Valley, and Overhill towns. There are chapter notes from manuscript materials, primary and secondary accounts.

LURIE, NANCY OESTREICH. "Indian Cultural Adjustments to European Civilization." In *Seventeenth-Century America: Essays in Colonial History,* edited by James Morton Smith, pp. 33–60. Chapel Hill: University of North Carolina Press, 1959.

Lurie explains seventeenth-century contacts between Algonquian-speaking tribes of the Powhatan Confederacy along the Virginia Coast and Europeans in terms of the Indians' cultural patterns that predated the arrival of the Jamestown settlers. First the author describes the similarities in the economic, political, and social life of the Powhatan Confederacy and Europeans. After explaining the initial Indian-European contacts, in which the former were interested in obtaining material goods, her study focuses on the Powhatan Confederacy's primary method of adjusting to the changes wrought by European society in Virginia. She also looks at the Indians' rigid resistance to alien ways and their cultural annihilation in the 1622 and 1644 uprisings rather than adapting to the settlers' foreign culture until the cultural disorganization of the Confederacy at the end of the seventeenth century. The article is based partly on seventeenth-century primary documents.

McREYNOLDS, EDWIN C. *The Seminoles.* Norman: University of Oklahoma Press, 1957. 394pp. Illustrated. Bibliography.

This book traces the history of the Seminoles of Florida from their first contacts with whites until the first third of the twentieth century. McReynolds discusses how the Seminoles and Creeks were diplomatic factors in U.S.-Spanish relations after the Spanish recovery of Florida in 1783, explains the alignment of Creeks and Seminoles on the British side in the War of 1812, and tells of the American acquisition of Florida from the Spanish in 1819. He looks at Seminole restriction to reservations in the southern part of Florida, white agitation for Seminole removal to the West from 1826 to 1834, three Seminole wars against the United States to resist dispossession of their homeland, removal by force of some Seminoles, and their struggle to adjust in the West as well as their difficult relationship with the Creeks. Further, he tells of the destructive impact of the Civil War on the Seminoles, reconstruction, recovery, events leading to the abolishment of the Seminole tribal government in 1906, and briefly considers the history of Seminole-U.S. relations through the first third of the twentieth century. Throughout, the author considers the status, treatment, and relationship of blacks to Seminoles and Creeks and tells of important persons in Seminole history such as Osceola and his role in resisting removal, Billy Bowlegs, John F. Brown, and others. There are three maps and photographs of Seminoles and their lands. The book is based on unpublished and published primary and secondary works.

MILLING, CHAPMAN J. *Red Carolinians.* Chapel Hill: University of North Carolina Press, 1940. 438pp. Illustrated. Bibliography.

The history of each tribe which occupied South Carolina for any period and their relations with other tribes in South Carolina, Florida, Mississippi, Illinois, and New York during the eighteenth century is covered in this book. Milling begins by reconstructing the general way of life of colonial South Carolina Indians, describes Cusabos and their relations with the Spanish, French, and British from the sixteenth to the eighteenth centuries and their decline. He gives brief historical accounts of the Creeks, Westos, Shawnees (Savannah), Yamasees, and Apalachees and their relations with Spain, France, and Britain or colonists. He describes the Tuscarora War of 1711 in North Carolina against the colonists and the Yamasee War of 1715 in South Carolina, discussing the allies and enemies of each. Briefly he considers the Apalachicolas, Yuchis, and Chickasaws and their intertribal relations; the Siouan river tribes of eastern Carolina; and provides more detail on the Catawabas, their intertribal relations, wars, and relations with North and South Carolina. The author describes eighteenth-century Cherokee alliances, enemies, intertribal relations and warfare with whites of South Carolina and Tennessee; describes U.S. efforts to dispossess Indians of land; and outlines the 1838 Cherokee removal, Cherokee factionalism during this period, and Cherokee efforts to resist dispossession into the twentieth century. He also examines the history and present-day situation of Eastern Cherokees who resisted removal. There are photographs that illustrate the history. Some language and generalizations are dated. The book is based on unpublished and published primary and secondary works and maps.

O'DONNELL, JAMES H., III. *Southern Indians in the American Revolution.* Knoxville: University of Tennessee Press, 1973. 171pp. Illustrated. Bibliography.

This book focuses on the Cherokees, Chickasaws, Creeks, and Choctaws of the South during the years from 1775 to 1783; the impact of the American Revolution on these tribes, and their influence in affecting the course of the war. The author discusses tribal factionalism over loyalties to French, British, or Spanish governments and the approaches developed by the British whose native policy was one of friendship with limited Indian military action and the Americans whose policy was one of friendship with Indian neutrality as its goal. Chapters describe the effects on other tribes of the southern states' successful war against the Cherokees in 1776, the southern tribes' ineffectual support of the British, military successes of the Spanish in the South after 1781, and the decline and end of the British Southern Indian Department. There are three maps. The book is based on unpublished British and American primary materials, and published and microfilmed secondary materials.

PEDDUE, THEDA. *Slavery and the Evolution of Cherokee Society, 1540–1866.* Knoxville: University of Tennessee Press, 1979. 207pp. Illustrated. Bibliography.

Peddue examines the history of slavery among the Cherokees of Tennessee, Georgia, and North Carolina as it evolved from 1540 to 1866, indicating not only how the institution changed but how it affected the Cherokees and their total tribal structure. Beginning with a description of aboriginal Cherokee slaves, traditionally acquired through warfare, and the system as it existed in the context of Cherokee social, economic, and political institutions, she discusses how the European economic system and version of slavery gradually undermined and transformed Cherokee slavery from one where slaves contributed nothing to Cherokee economy to one where forced labor increased agricultural production. Looking at the traffic in Indian slaves, the author explains the various contacts between African slaves and Cherokees and southern colonial efforts to keep the two groups apart. She also looks at the alteration of Cherokee social, economic, and political systems which preceded the development of plantation slavery, the latter of which helped to create two distinct economic and cultural divisions within Cherokee society before removal. The author considers how postremoval chaos in Indian Territory resulted in a hardening of the Cherokee planters' attitudes towards blacks, who were resisting slavery, and a strengthening of the slave code. And, describing the treatment and use of slaves by Cherokee masters and Cherokee factionalism inflamed by the Civil War, Peddue argues that contemporary Cherokee factions have roots in the institution of slavery. There are five maps.

REID, JOHN PHILLIP. *A Better Kind of Hatchet: Law, Trade, and Diplomacy in the Cherokee Nation during the Early Years of European Contact.* University Park: Pennsylvania State University Press, 1976. 249pp.

This book deals with trade, law, and diplomatic relations between eighteenth-century Cherokees of South Carolina and Europeans. Beginning with a discussion of Cherokee government, law, and kinship patterns and the strategic Cherokee geographical position, Reid tells of slave and other trade contacts between Cherokees and South Carolina, trade competition from Virginia, Cherokee contacts with eighteenth-century English common law which governed trade and trade goods, and the tribe's growing dependence on European manufactured goods. He discusses the 1715 Yamasee War, conflict between the British and most of the southern tribal nations who were against the Carolina trading system in which most Cherokees sided with the British, Cherokee-Creek hostile relations, and Cherokee factionalism. The author also examines Cherokee efforts to undermine the 1716 trade monopoly statute, the end of South Carolina's control over regulating Indian trade, and the restoration of private trade. He considers Cherokee relations with Carolina traders and the need to regulate the latter which brought European law into the Cherokee nation. Comparing the British and Cherokee law ways, Reid concludes with a summary of the ways eighteenth-century British law accommodated itself to southern Indian customs and practices while Cherokee law refused to adjust to British ways.

RIGHTS, DOUGLAS LETELL. *The American Indian in North Carolina.* Durham, N.C.: Duke University Press, 1947; reprint ed.: Winston-Salem, N.C.: John F. Blair, 1957. 298pp. Illustrated. Bibliography.

This book identifies the tribes of North Carolina and describes their cultures and movements from their first contacts with explorers to contemporary times. Briefly summarizing contacts between Spanish explorers and North Carolina Indians in the mid-sixteenth century and English explorers during the late sixteenth century, Rights discusses the decline of coastal Algonquian tribes (Hatteras, Chowan, Weapomeiok, Machapunga, Bay River, Pamlico, Coranine, Neuse, Woccon, and Cape Fear) after contact with white settlers who pushed into North Carolina in the middle to late seventeenth century. He looks at the Tuscaroras and their resistance to white encroachment in their territory and the outbreak of the Tuscarora War in the early eighteenth century; tells of John Lawson, a traveler, who furnished a great deal of information about North Carolina Indians; Colonel William Bird's survey of the dividing line between North Carolina and Virginia; and the disintegration during the eighteenth century of the Piedmont tribes—Saponi, Tutelo, Saura, Keyauwee, Eno, and others. He briefly looks at Catawba history and culture and the Indians of Robeson County. The author provides lengthy descriptions of Cherokee culture, their friendly relations with North Carolinians in the early to mid-eighteenth century, white encroachment on Cherokee lands, warfare, federal government-Cherokee relations and the removal of a portion of the Cherokees from North Carolina to Oklahoma. He looks at the Eastern Cherokees who resisted removal; examines Cherokee sacred formulas, the property of shamans; and Cherokee theology, myths, and games. He concludes with notes on native life in general, North Carolina archaeology, and provides a detailed account of North Carolina artifacts. There are maps and photographs of artifacts and historic and contemporary North Carolina Indians.

SATZ, RONALD N. *Tennessee's Indian Peoples.* Knoxville: University of Tennessee Press, 1976. 109pp. Illustrated. Bibliography.

Satz describes the cultures of Tennessee's Indians and traces the history of Indian-white relations from 1540 when Hernando De Soto's invasion of Indian lands marked the onslaught of great change in Tennessee's Indians. He explains how Cherokees, Chickasaws, Creeks, Shawnees, and other Indian people lived, reared families, farmed and hunted, worshipped, played, fought, and governed themselves. Describing the eventual destruction of these societies due to the external pressures for Indian lands and by the internal changes wrought by the increasing dependence on white trade goods, Satz focuses in particular on Cherokee-white relations. There are five maps and photographs of Tennessee's Indian peoples and scenes that reflect their life.

STURTEVANT, WILLIAM C. "Spanish-Indian Relations in Southeastern North America." *Ethnohistory* 9, no. 1 (Winter 1962):41–94. Illustrated. Bibliography.

This paper analyzes the processes and results of contact between native cultures and Spanish colonial institutions in different areas from 1513 to 1821: the Carolina-Virginia coast, the Georgia-North Carolina coast, the St. Augustine region, northeast Florida, Apalachee, westernmost Florida, south Florida, and the Georgia-Alabama interior. The author identifies and and describes five phases during which the nature of European-Indian relations was distinctly different from the preceding and following phases. He describes briefly for all eight areas the exploration phase beginning in 1513, the period of coexistence, the mission period, depopulation of native populations, and diplomacy. The appendix discusses how historians could better assist anthropologists by locating, describing, and publishing primary documentary materials. A map and a figure of the phases of Spanish-Indian relations are included. The paper is based on Spanish and English materials.

WETMORE, RUTH Y. *First on the Land: The North Carolina Indians.* Winston-Salem, N.C.: John F. Blair, 1975. 196pp. Illustrated. Bibliography.

This book presents brief descriptions of the history and cultures of North Carolina's Indians from ancestral times to the present. The author looks at Indian life in general and in North Carolina thousands of years ago, reviews primary sources to describe briefly the contacts of twenty-eight different tribes with whites from the mid-sixteenth century, their linguistic families, clashes between natives and whites in the seventeenth century, and the eighteenth-century Tuscarora, Yamasee, and Cherokee Wars which diminished North Carolina's native populations by 1730. She also lists the twenty-eight tribes living in North Carolina and briefly traces their histories and populations from the time of contact with Europeans to one of three conclusions: dissolution of the tribes, removal to a reservation, or departure from the state. Briefly considered is the daily and spiritual and ceremonial life of Indians before or immediately after white

contact. The concluding chapter details the population and brief history since 1730 of contemporary North Carolina natives. There are tables of population figures, four maps, and photographs of contemporary Indian life.

WILKINS, THURMAN. *Cherokee Tragedy: The Story of the Ridge Family and the Decimation of a People.* New York: Macmillan, 1970. 398pp. Illustrated. Bibliography.

Wilkins traces the history of the Cherokees of southern Appalachia and their forced removal to Oklahoma from 1771 to 1839 while focusing on the lives of Cherokees, Major Ridge, his son John, and his nephew Elias Boudinet. He begins by examining the life of Major Ridge, one of those Cherokees who had adopted white culture and who brought "civilization" to the tribe in the form of new schools and the English language, and looks at John Ridge's education, political factionalism within the tribe, futile efforts of the two Ridges to negotiate promises of fair treatment from Washington, federal Indian removal policy, and events culminating in the 1835 Treaty of New Echota. He discusses the struggle between John Ross, one of the leaders of the anti-Treaty faction and pro-Treaty Ridge, the forced removal of the Cherokees from their ancestral homeland, and their journey west to Oklahoma Territory. He tells of the years of violence among the Ross and Ridge factions, resulting in the 1839 murders of Major and John Ridge and Elias Boudinet by the Ross faction. There are photographs of Cherokees.

WILLIS, WILLIAM S., JR. "Divide and Rule: Red, White, and Black in the Southeast." *Journal of Negro History* 48, no. 3 (July 1963):157–76; reprint ed.: In *Red, White and Black: Symposium on Indians in the Old South,* edited by Charles M. Hudson, pp. 99–115. Southern Anthropological Society Proceedings, no. 5. Athens: University of Georgia Press, 1971.

Willis tries to explain the mutual hostility existing between Indians and blacks in the eighteenth-century southeastern colonies, especially South Carolina, as a result of white policy designed to create antagonism and prevent alliances between the two groups, each of which outnumbered the white minority. He explains how and why South Carolina tried to keep Indians, primarily Creeks and Cherokees, and blacks socially apart, as well as citing the ways whites created antagonisms between the two groups by encouraging Indians to behave as enemies of free blacks, by slave-catching, betraying runaway slaves, stealing and trading them themselves, and crushing slave insurrections. There are footnotes based on unpublished and published materials.

YOUNG, MARY ELIZABETH. *Redskins, Ruffleshirts, and Rednecks: Indian Allotments in Alabama and Mississippi, 1830–1860.* Norman: University of Oklahoma Press, 1961. 213pp. Illustrated. Bibliography.

In this study, the author tells how the allotment policy (allotting portions of ceded lands to individual natives and opening the remaining lands to white settlement) first employed on a large scale in the 1830 Choctaw, 1832 Creek, and 1834 Chickasaw Treaties resulted in speculation in Indian lands which delayed tribal emigration west of the Mississippi River and confused land titles over large areas of Alabama and Mississippi. Briefly giving a general summary of Indian removal policies, she also examines the removal of the Choctaws, Creeks, and Chickasaws from Mississippi and Alabama during the 1830s. She discusses the contradictory intentions of the allotment treaties—both trying to assimilate and remove natives from white society; federal government assistance to agents of assimilation; the crisis in relations between the southern tribes and federal and state governments over Indian resistance to cessions and emigration; and the passage of the 1830 Indian removal bill. The author examines the progress of "civilization" among the Choctaws and the growth, composition, and role of tribal factionalism in the negotiation of a Choctaw removal treaty, and the contest among rival speculators which delayed removal. She also looks at the Creek allotment treaty and the scramble of individual land speculators and land companies for Creek allotments. Chapters examine the Chickasaw treaty and the cooperation among speculators in adjusting disputes among themselves and the abundance of capital available for investment in Chickasaw lands. Concluding chapters look at land company policy (illustrated by the New York and Mississippi Land Companies), the role of the speculator in the community, public land sales in the 1830s, and the native allotment policy of the Jacksonian administration. The author reveals the means by which settlers and speculators acquired those lands allotted to Indians who chose to remain in their homeland instead of removing to Indian Territory. There are seventeen maps, two graphs, and six tables that illustrate the text as well as photographs of Indians and federal officials. There is a bibliography of unpublished and published primary and secondary sources.

GREAT PLAINS

ABEL, ANNIE HELOISE. *The Slaveholding Indians.* Vol. 1, *The American Indian as Slaveholder and Secessionist: An Omitted Chapter in the Diplomatic History of the Southern Confederacy.* Cleveland: Arthur H. Clark, 1919; reprint ed.: St. Clair Shores, Mich.: Scholarly Press, 1972. 394pp. Illustrated. Bibliography.

The first volume of a three-volume work deals with the general situation of the Cherokees, Chickasaws, Creeks, Choctaws, and Seminoles in the present states of Oklahoma and Kansas from 1830 to 1860, the year antedating the Civil War. The federal Indian policy of compulsory removal and reservations, and tribal cleavages into secessionist and unionist elements are explained as well as the role of Texas and Arkansas in persuading southern natives to participate in the Civil War. Chapters describe how Indian Territory figured prominently

in Confederate designs for the West due to its geographic position and economic importance and detail the history of Confederate diplomacy in securing alliance treaties and assurances of military assistance from the five Nations. The author argues that the failure of the federal government to afford southern natives protection guaranteed by treaty was the main cause of Indians entering into alliance with the Confederacy. There is some dated terminology. The appendix contains miscellaneous manuscript materials illustrating the text. There are maps and Cherokee portraits. The volume is based on official records of the "War of Rebellion," unpublished manuscript records from the U.S. Indian Office, and published primary and secondary works.

———. *The Slaveholding Indians.* Vol. 2, *The Indian as Participant in the Civil War.* Cleveland: Arthur H. Clark, 1919; reprint ed.: New York: Johnson Reprint, 1970. 403pp. Illustrated. Bibliography.

The second volume of a three-volume work covers the actions of the Cherokees, Chickasaws, Creeks, Choctaws, and Seminoles during the Civil War years, 1861–65. The author discusses the instability of the alliance between the Indians and Confederates, the conflicts within the U.S. military over Union enlistment of loyal Indians, the misfortunes of native refugees in southern Kansas and their removal to the Sac and Fox Agency. Chapters cover the role of Indians in the guerilla border warfare in the West between contending white governments, the Confederacy's attempts to organize a western superintendency of Indian Affairs and its mismanagement of Indian affairs. The author considers tribal dissensions and the pitting of federally-allied against Confederate-allied natives, war conditions in Indian Territory in 1863 as a result of its being a pawn between contending forces, and the wavering alliance and the growth of a unionist sentiment among southern natives. Certain Confederate and federal generals and native people who played important roles in Indian Territory affairs are highlighted. There are an appendix, facsimiles of documents, and one map. The book is based on documentary materials and published primary and secondary works.

———. *The Slaveholding Indians.* Vol. 3, *The American Indian under Reconstruction.* Cleveland: Arthur H. Clark, 1925; reprint ed.: New York: Johnson Reprint, 1970. 419pp. Bibliography.

The third volume of a three-volume work deals with the negotiation of reconstruction treaties the American government made with southern tribes of Indian Territory in 1866. The author discusses the return of refugees to Indian Territory; the cattle-stealing business during the mid-1860s in Indian Territory, a product of the federal government's lack of military protection of natives; the dismissal of Indians in federal employ; and the attempts of Cherokees and other tribes to reunite their nations. Chapters expose the motives behind territorial organization of Indian country and the miserable conditions of freed people there, and describe the peace council at Fort Smith in 1865, composed of unionist and secessionist natives, which established the formal peace between the federal government and several Indian nations in Indian Territory. The concluding chapters discuss the negotiations and provisions of the 1866 treaties with the Cherokees, Chickasaws, Creeks, Choctaws, and Seminoles which concluded formal reconstruction and accomplished the readjustment of their relations with the federal government. The book is based on documentary materials and published primary and secondary works.

BAILEY, M. THOMAS. *Reconstruction in Indian Territory: A Story of Avarice, Discrimination, and Opportunism.* Port Washington, N.Y.: Kennikat Press, 1972. 225pp. Illustrated. Bibliography.

This book gives an account of the political, economic, and educational efforts toward reconstruction by the Cherokees, Chickasaws, Creeks, Choctaws, and Seminoles in Indian Territory, the present state of Oklahoma, from 1865 to 1877. Bailey begins with a review of the removal of the Five Civilized Tribes from their ancestral homeland east of the Mississippi River, the process of reconstructing life in Indian Territory prior to the Civil War, tribal factions, and the alliance of the tribes with the Confederate states. Chapters look at the problems of the second reconstruction period, particularly the loyal factions of the Creek, Seminole, and Cherokee Nations who had been destitute refugees in Kansas during the Civil War, the 1865 Fort Smith Conference in which a peace treaty was signed, and the negotiations of the 1866 reconstruction treaties to reestablish Indian relations with the federal government. The author examines federal goals of securing native lands, native population concentration, and consolidated territorial government. The reconstruction of each of the Five Tribes is treated separately, including topics such as agricultural adjustments, finances, intertribal relations, reorganization of political and social institutions, freed slaves, education, religion, and railroad development in native territory. There are five maps. The book is based on unpublished and published secondary works.

BAIRD, W. DAVID. *The Quapaw Indians: A History of the Downstream People.* Norman: University of Oklahoma Press, 1979. 320pp. Illustrated. Bibliography.

Baird traces the history of the Quapaws, who originally lived in Arkansas and who now live in Oklahoma, from the mid-seventeenth century into the 1970s. He describes how during the eighteenth century both the French and Spanish tried to use the Quapaws in their imperial ambitions west of the Mississippi River, how the tribe became allied to the U.S. government after 1803, and how later the tribe was judged an impediment to agricultural exploitation of the Arkansas River valley and in time was removed to Indian Territory. He also relates the trauma of reservation life when major changes were made in traditional lifeways to accommodate alien cultural patterns and how, in

1893, the Quapaws unilaterally allotted their reservation and all but abandoned their tribal life. Observing that great wealth accrued to individual members of the tribe following the discovery of lead and zinc ore on the reservation and the mining boom of the 1920s, Baird comments that the mines and wealth are gone today. The book concludes with a discussion of how an award of the Indian Claims Commission in 1954 encouraged some members of the tribe to reclaim and preserve a number of the distinctive traditions of their ancestors. There are maps and photographs of Quapaws and their way of life. The bibliography lists unpublished and published primary and secondary sources.

BERTHRONG, DONALD J. *The Southern Cheyennes.* Norman: University of Oklahoma Press, 1963. 446pp. Illustrated. Bibliography.

Berthrong provides a history of the Southern Cheyennes who occupied the central and southern Plains from their origins until 1875. First he summarizes the early migrations of the Cheyennes, their way of life, religion, and government in the early nineteenth century, their removal to the Arkansas River in the middle nineteenth century, and intertribal wars on the central and southern Plains. He also considers the history of Cheyenne contact with federal government agents, treaty-making, punitive army expeditions, and problems with emigrants and settlers. Describing in detail events leading to the massacre of Arapahoes and Cheyennes at Sand Creek in 1864, native reprisals, and the alternating years of hostilities and treaty-making between the Cheyennes and the government until the Indians were put on an Oklahoma reservation in 1869, Berthrong concludes by describing the first few years of reservation life and unrest among the Cheyennes. There are three maps and photographs of Cheyennes and their way of life. The book is based on Cheyenne tradition, archival material, and published primary and secondary works.

BLAINE, MARTHA ROYCE. *The Ioway Indians.* Norman: University of Oklahoma Press, 1978. 384pp. Illustrated. Bibliography.

The author traces the history of the Ioway Indians who lived in Iowa, Missouri, Nebraska, Kansas, and Oklahoma from ancient times to the early twentieth century. She identifies archaeological sites in northeastern Iowa inhabited by Ioway groups before recorded times and traces their relations with the Sioux, Winnebagos, Foxes, Sacs, Pawnees, and others. She discusses the seventeenth and eighteenth centuries when French, Spanish, and English traders vied for the tribe's favor and for permission to cross Ioway lands. The author explains how the Ioways maintained their position as trading middlemen as long as possible and maintained relations with the colonial governments of all three countries. She discusses how the Ioways fought in the French and Indian War in New York, the War of 1812, and the Civil War. She tells how, by the end of the nineteenth century, the tribe had lost its economic base and cultural integrity through land cession treaties and, through voluntary and forced removals, left lands in Iowa and Missouri and was placed on small reservations in Nebraska and Kansas, and how a part of the tribe was removed to Oklahoma Territory in the 1880s where descendants live today. The author adds the Ioways' comments on the European society they visited and descriptions of tribal culture by missionaries and travelers. There are four maps and photographs of Ioway Indians and their way of life. The book is based on field work and unpublished and published primary and secondary sources.

CHAPMAN, BERLIN B. *The Otoes and Missourias: A Study of Indian Removal and the Legal Aftermath.* Oklahoma City: Times Journal Publishing, 1965. 405pp. Illustrated.

This book gives the history of the Otoes and Missourias, two confederated tribes, through three centuries during which they possessed tribal lands in present-day Iowa, Nebraska, Kansas, and Oklahoma. The author begins with a description of the migration of the Otoes to a permanent village in Nebraska in the early eighteenth century where the Missourias joined with them. He considers the various land relinquishments and acquisitions of the two tribes in Nebraska in the treaties of 1825, 1830, and 1833 which were designed to maintain peace, establish boundaries among tribes, and recognize Indian title within fixed boundaries. He looks at the 1854 treaty in which the Otoes relinquished all claim to land on the east side of the Missouri River, which provided for allotments to tribal individuals or families, and established the tribe on the Big Blue River Reservation in Nebraska and Kansas. The author tells of the allotment of the Nemaha Half-Breed Reservation, the Otoes' dispossession of the Big Blue River Reservation by white settlers, politics, and railroad interests during the 1860s and 1870s, and their removal to Indian Territory by 1881 after the tribe consented to the sale of their Kansas-Nebraska lands. He explains how the Otoes and Missourias acquired their last reservation near Red Rock, Oklahoma, looks at the federal government's 1882–83 sale to settlers of the Otoe-Missouria lands in Kansas and Nebraska, and tells of the two tribes' acceptance of a lesser sum due them for the land sales. The author relates how the reservation lands were allotted under the Dawes Act and eventually dissolved by 1907. He tells of the case the Otoe and Missouria tribes brought to federal courts in which they pioneered in demonstrating that the Indian Claims Commission (ICC) jurisdiction extended to awarding compensation for Indian title to tribal lands taken by the United States. He considers twentieth-century pressures put on the Otoes and Missourias to assimilate and tribal resistance; pressures put on them to receive patents in fee for their lands in which oil and gas were discovered; and their fractionated heirship land problems. There are three appendixes of allotment rolls, maps, and illustrations of Otoes, documents, and ICC people. The book is based on manuscript materials, federal court cases, and testimony of tribal members.

DEBO, ANGIE. *The Five Civilized Tribes of Oklahoma: Report on Social and Economic Conditions.* Philadelphia: Indian Rights Assn., 1951. 35pp. Illustrated.

This pamphlet contains the results of the author's survey of social and economic conditions in full-blood settlements of Cherokees, Creeks, Choctaws, Chickasaws, and Seminoles in Oklahoma in the 1940s. She describes the impoverishment of the Five Tribes and their loss of land and explains the constructive economic rehabilitation programs enacted through provisions of the Oklahoma Indian Welfare Act of 1936 illustrated by the establishment of the Cherokee strawberry industry and farm loans. She describes land purchased under the Welfare Act for the Five Tribes, Muskogee supervision of individual Indian property, and programs of social and educational rehabilitation. The author examines agencies that she argues should be responsible for helping to improve the economic situation, the Muskogee Agency, church, and tribal organizations. The pamphlet is based on the author's field work and includes a map and notes.

————. *The Rise and Fall of the Choctaw Republic.* Norman: University of Oklahoma Press, 1934, 1961. 314pp. Illustrated. Bibliography.

The author traces the history of the Choctaws in Oklahoma after the Civil War until the close of the nineteenth century. She begins with a discussion of Choctaw aboriginal institutions in Mississippi, the early historic period when Choctaws were subjected to the imperial contest among England, France, and Spain for control of North America, and the series of land treaties with the United States that gradually absorbed the Choctaw territory and finally removed the tribe in the early 1830s to Oklahoma. The author describes the changes in the tribe's law, religion, schools, and economy as a result of three centuries of contact with whites and considers the first generation of orderly development of Choctaw political, economic, and social institutions in the lands to which they had been driven. She explains how the Choctaws allied with the Confederacy and participated in the Civil War, which disrupted their society and caused social and economic problems, resumed relations with the federal government, and adjusted to the changed status of their former slaves. She describes the new era of railroad, coal, and timber enterprises after the Civil War, white immigration, and the evolution of Choctaw government machinery to manage the corporations and other complicated economic interests. The concluding chapters deal with the contest between the Choctaws and the United States for the maintenance of tribal autonomy, the liquidation of their tribal estate in the late 1890s and early 1900s, and the final dissolution of Choctaw national government when it passed out of existence as a separate political entity in 1907 when Oklahoma became a state. There are six maps and photographs of Choctaws. The book is based on Choctaw materials and unpublished and published works.

ELLIS, RICHARD N. *The Western American Indian: Case Studies in Tribal History.* Lincoln: University of Nebraska Press, 1972. 203pp. Bibliography.

This book provides case studies on major topics which illuminate the impact of white settlement and federal policy and actions on western tribes in the post-1850 period. The articles provide in-depth treatment of specific issues such as federal treaty-making techniques in a discussion about the 1855 Walla Walla council with Plateau tribes in Washington Territory and the 1866 negotiations with the Sioux at Fort Laramie; Plains warfare illustrated by the 1868 Battle of the Washita against the Cheyenne; the peacetime role of the military on the Plains; President Grant's Indian peace policy on the Yakima Reservation; the end of Apache resistance in the Southwest; Sioux reservation life in the 1880s; and allotment theory and practice on the Southern Cheyenne and Arapaho Reservation from 1887 to 1907. The remaining articles deal with the principles underlying the 1934 Indian New Deal; Santee Sioux relations with the federal government after 1934, the 1946 Indian Claims Commission, and a survey of cases litigated in the Court of Claims; and the Menominee experience of termination in the 1950s.

EWERS, JOHN C. *The Blackfeet: Raiders on the Northwestern Plains.* Norman: University of Oklahoma Press, 1958. 348pp. Illustrated. Bibliography.

This book contains a history of the tribe located in present-day Montana and its relations with whites in the eighteenth and nineteenth centuries. The author describes traditional Blackfeet culture before contact with white culture and at the middle of the nineteenth century. Chapters discuss the conditions and events which altered habits and customs from 1850 to the mid-1940s, considering Blackfeet relations with white trappers and traders, a growing dependence on their wares, Catholic and Protestant missionaries competing for converts, and the arrival of settlers, government agents, and the army. The author looks at cessions of Blackfeet hunting grounds, confinement to reservations and division into the American and Canadian Blackfeet, extermination of the buffalo, which impoverished the Blackfeet and made them dependent on government assistance, and twentieth-century efforts to preserve their cultural heritage and economic independence under changed conditions. There are three maps, drawings, and photographs of Blackfeet and their lifestyle. Blackfeet informants provide part of the basis for the book.

FEHRENBACH, T. R. *Comanches: The Destruction of a People.* New York: Knopf, 1974. 557pp. Illustrated. Bibliography.

This book contains the story of the Comanches who controlled parts of present-day Texas, New Mexico, Oklahoma, Kansas, and Colorado from the sixteenth century to their destruction as an independent people in the 1870s. The author begins with a description of sixteenth-century Comanche way of life, especially their war ethos, in the eastern Rockies of present-day Wyoming before they acquired Spanish horses which helped them seize control of the southern Plains and describes late

seventeenth- and early eighteenth-century upheavals and warfare between natives due to their access to European firearms. Chapters describe how Comanches destroyed Spanish dreams of empire in North America, blocked the French advance into the Southwest, fought the Mexican Republic, and became for more than sixty years an obstacle to Anglo-American conquest of the continent until they were finally conquered by U.S. Army units and Texas rangers in raids and battles from the mid-nineteenth century and were virtually annihilated as a society in the 1870s. The concluding chapters describe the vast internecine tribal wars among continental Indians in the mid-nineteenth century, the different modes of warfare between soldiers and frontier people, and the failure of post-Civil War peace and reservation policies. There are maps and photographs of Comanche people and artifacts.

FOREMAN, GRANT. *Advancing the Frontier, 1830– 1860.* Norman: University of Oklahoma Press, 1933. 363pp. Illustrated. Bibliography.

Foreman records the era from 1830 to 1860 when thousands of Indians were forcibly removed from southern states east of the Mississippi River and had to find new homes in the future state of Oklahoma, which was the home of numerous Plains natives. Chapters deal with the problems of immigrant Cherokees, Chickasaws, Creeks, and Choctaws in adjusting to a strange country and establishing amicable relations in the face of opposition from Osages, Pawnees, Kiowas, Comanches, and other indigenous people who were required by the federal government to make room for the newcomers. The author describes the erection of frontier army posts designed to protect immigrant Indians from indigenous Indians, the features of native hostilities, international tribal councils organized to establish rules of conduct and friendship between immigrant and other tribes in Indian Territory, and examines the federal government's attempts to organize the natives into an Indian state. There is one map, as well as illustrations of buildings, Plains life, treaty councils, and ground plans of forts. The book is based on unpublished federal archival materials, U.S. Senate document no. 512, and published works.

―――. *The Five Civilized Tribes: Cherokee, Chickasaw, Choctaw, Creek, Seminole.* Norman: University of Oklahoma Press, 1934. 455pp. Illustrated. Bibliography.

This is an account of the rehabilitation and reconstruction of the Five Civilized Tribes after the demoralization and impoverishment caused by their forcible removal from the Southeast to Indian Territory from 1830 to 1860. The book deals respectively with the efforts of Choctaws, Chickasaws, Creeks, Seminoles, and Cherokees to maintain their cultures while adapting to alien influences and altered conditions. The author describes tribal factions, personalities, and relations among the five removed Nations and efforts to organize their governments, schools, and other institutions. He examines relations with missionaries and the army, the federal government and its inadequate, unjust, and inept policies, white contractors, and hostile, indigenous tribes. There are eyewitness accounts of the five removed tribes, and the longest section deals with the Cherokees and their educational pursuits, particularly literacy, and the achievement of Sequoyah. There are one map and pictures of people from the five tribes. There is some dated terminology. The book is based on unpublished and published primary and secondary works.

————. *Indians and Pioneers: The Story of the American Southwest before 1830.* Norman: University of Oklahoma Press, 1930. 300pp. Illustrated. Bibliography.

The author traces the history of Indian-white relations in Oklahoma from the late seventeenth century until 1830. He discusses the French and Spanish explorations of Oklahoma Territory before the Louisiana Purchase, the Cherokee immigration from the Southeast to west of the Mississippi River between 1796 and 1817, and Cherokee-Osage warfare over Osage lands in eastern Oklahoma during the first quarter of the nineteenth century. He describes the missionaries and their schools located among the Osages and Cherokees, considers the intrusion of white settlers, hunters, and traders on Osage lands and their retaliation against them, and U.S. military invasion of Osage country. He analyzes pressures put on immigrant eastern Indians by western Indians and Cherokee plans for organized defensive and offensive alliances with other immigrant tribes. He discusses the destitution of immigrant tribes driven to Osage country where they were all compelled to hunt for food and the bloody contest between immigrant Indians and Osage that made Oklahoma a battleground during the late 1820s. He concludes with a discussion of white-Cherokee contests over land, Indian raids against white settlements, government removal by treaty of a portion of the Creek Nation to west of the Mississippi, and the efforts of the federal and state governments east of the Mississippi to remove other Indians westward. There are one map and paintings of Osages. There is a brief essay on the archival materials used, and the bibliography lists published primary and secondary books and newspapers.

GIBSON, ARRELL MORGAN. *The Kickapoos: Lords of the Middle Border.* Norman: University of Oklahoma Press, 1963. 391pp. Illustrated. Bibliography.

The author traces the history of the Kickapoos (who have been located at times in Wisconsin, Illinois, Indiana, Ohio, Michigan, New York, Pennsylvania, Iowa, Missouri, Kansas, Oklahoma, Texas, and northern Mexico) from their first contacts with Europeans in the early seventeenth century to the 1920s. He discusses relations with the French, Spanish, and English whom the Kickapoos esteemed and their fierce resistance to American settlement, U.S. Indian policy, and reservation life. He discusses Kickapoo friendly and hostile relations with other tribes, the tribe's role as mercaries for the Spanish, French, British, and Mexicans, and northern and southern tribal factions. He describes treaties signed, Kickapoo removal west of the Mississippi in the early nineteenth century, the manner in which the Kickapoos were divested of lands, dominance of Kickapoo power in the middle border extending from the Missouri River southward into Coahuilla, Mexico, in the nineteenth century, and Kickapoo-Mexican warfare with Texas in the nineteenth century. He concludes with descriptions of Kickapoo behavior during the Civil War, the southern Kickapoo reservation period from 1874 to 1895, forced allotment, and the recovery of Kickapoo allotments lost in a land conspiracy. There are seven maps and photographs of Kickapoos and their way of life. The book is based on unpublished and published primary and secondary works.

HAGAN, WILLIAM T. *The Sac and Fox Indians.* Norman: University of Oklahoma Press, 1958. 287pp. Illustrated. Bibliography.

This book presents a history of the relations between the Sacs and Foxes (considered as two tribes throughout the book) who were successively located in Iowa, Kansas, and Oklahoma and their relations with the American government during the nineteenth century. The author describes the treaties made with the federal government in which tribal lands were ceded, as well as relations with other tribes, intertribal wars, and the contest between the British and Americans to win Sac and Fox favor. The discussion of the two tribes in the War of 1812 focuses on the roles of Keokuk and Black Hawk (both Sacs). Chapters look at the events of 1832, Black Hawk's War, and the subsequent history of the Sacs and Foxes as they were shuttled from one reservation to another as a result of white greed for land. The author examines Sac and Fox factionalism, removal in 1845 to a Kansas reservation where they battled Plains tribes, and removal in 1867 to Indian Territory. He concludes with a brief history of the Oklahoma Sacs and Foxes through the 1950s. There are maps and pictures of Sac and Fox people. The book is based on unpublished and published primary and secondary works.

HAINES, FRANCIS. *The Plains Indians.* New York: Thomas Y. Crowell, 1976. 213pp. Illustrated. Bibliography.

This study reexamines and reevaluates the history and culture of Plains tribes who lived in an area that reaches from central Texas northward into Canada and from the Rocky Mountains eastward to near the Mississippi River from 1200 to the mid-nineteenth century. The author first discusses how the Great Plains were virtually unpopulated until 1200 and how scattered migrations during the next four centuries brought twenty-seven peoples (Pawnee, Wichita, Kiowa, Apache, Dakota, Mandan, Cheyenne, Blackfeet, and others) there from the Eastern Woodlands, Canadian Plains, and the Southwest. Chapters discuss the changes horses and Dutch, French, and English trade in guns brought about in the tribes' lifestyle. The author summarizes the movements of each tribe, its location and population for the year 1780, and then follows separate bands through intertribal warfare, smallpox epidemics, and European contacts and confrontations. The concluding chapters look at the constant reshuffling of tribes and tribal boundaries from 1680 to 1850, consider the growth and spread of a general Plains culture that gives buffalo-hunting tribes a uniform appearance by the mid-nineteenth century, and describe the Dog Soldier system, encampment police, war activities, and the Sun Dance. The introduction discusses the origins of the Plains stereotype. The book is based on unpublished and published primary and secondary sources.

HYDE, GEORGE E. *Indians of the High Plains: From the Prehistoric Period to the Coming of Europeans.* Norman: University of Oklahoma Press, 1959. 228pp. Illustrated. Bibliography.

The author traces the history of several Plains tribes who lived in an area extending from the plains of western Canada to Texas and northern Mexico from 1300 to 1800. He begins with a discussion of the early Apaches from ancestral times until the decline of their power after 1700 and their relationship with Navajos, Pueblos, and Spanish; sets forth the history, achievements, and locations of the Plains Apaches known before 1800 as the Padoucas, confused, the author argues, with the Comanches. He describes the coming of the Utes and Comanches who drove the Apaches from the Plains by 1750, their relations with Spain and France, the Comanche war against the Utes, their former allies, and how they made themselves masters of the southern Plains. The author tells the story of the rise and fall of the Snakes who dominated the northern plains from before 1700 to about 1770, until they were swept aside by other Plains tribes, notably the Blackfeet. He concludes with a discussion of the confusion that has existed over who the Padoucas and Ietans were, groups that vanished after 1822. There are three maps, photographs of Plains peoples and settlements, and a bibliography of published primary and secondary sources.

————. *The Pawnee Indians.* Norman: University of Oklahoma Press, 1951; reprint ed.: 1974. 372pp. Illustrated.

This book contains the history of the Pawnees and kindred Caddoan Nations located in an area extending from Nebraska to Mexico from their origins until the turn of the twentieth century. The author begins with an overview of the principal Caddoan tribes, examining archaeological evidence concerning their early movements, especially those of the Pawnee tribes in Nebraska and the plains south of the Arkansas River. He details late seventeenth-century Pawnee-Apache warfare in the southwestern plains, eighteenth-century Pawnee-French trade relations, and fighting and disunity among the four Nebraska Pawnee groups; and considers the lives of some Pawnee chiefs and missionary work among the tribe. He discusses how permanent Pawnee villages and the social, political, and religious organization made them fixed targets for the enemies who threatened their tribal existence in the mid-nineteenth century, examines the union of Pawnee groups in the mid-nineteenth century for survival, and their alliance with whites against

their Plains enemies. The concluding chapters discuss shifting federal Indian policies, Pawnee removal to a reservation in Indian Territory in 1875, government neglect, and mistakes in the policies of Quaker agents. There are appendixes with descriptions of Pawnee culture, fourteen maps, and photographs of Pawnees and their customs. The book is partly based on Pawnee oral history and archaeological evidence.

————. *Red Cloud's Folk: A History of the Oglala Sioux Indians.* Norman: University of Oklahoma Press, 1937. 331pp. Illustrated. Bibliography.

This volume presents the history of one of the Teton Sioux tribes from the time of its origins until it was forced onto its present South Dakota reservation. The first part of the book, 1650–1860, tells the story of the migrations and early history of the Oglalas and other Tetons when they developed from small bands who originally lived in Minnesota to powerful Nations living in the South Dakota Black Hills. Part 2 deals with the era of white encroachment on Sioux lands, 1861–70, native opposition to it, and Red Cloud's role in averting war. The third part tells of the establishment of the Red Cloud Agency and early years on the reservation, 1870–79. The author discusses the government's seizure of the Black Hills and the attitudes and conduct of the friendly agency Sioux who tried to keep out of the war led by Sitting Bull and Crazy Horse in the late 1870s. There are appendixes of Oglala social organization and population and two maps. The book is based partly on personal interviews. *See also* James C. Olson, *Red Cloud and the Sioux Problem,* page 154.

————. *A Sioux Chronicle.* Norman: University of Oklahoma Press, 1956. 334pp. Illustrated.

This volume contains the history of the South Dakota Teton Sioux from 1877 to 1891. The author describes Sioux confinement to a reservation in South Dakota, control by American government agents, and Sioux struggles to resist federal farming programs and land purchase commissions. The author considers yearly conflicts between the Sioux and the government, especially the Ghost Dance troubles of 1890 that led to a disaster for the Sioux at Wounded Knee. Biographical details of the lives of Spotted Tail, Red Cloud, and other chiefs are included; there are two maps. *See also* James C. Olson, *Red Cloud and the Sioux Problem,* page 154.

————. *Spotted Tail's Folk: A History of the Brule Sioux.* Norman: University of Oklahoma Press, 1961. 325pp. Illustrated. Bibliography.

The author gives an account of the Brulé Sioux of South Dakota from 1800 until 1881 and tells about the life of Spotted Tail (Sinte Galeska) and his role from 1850 to 1880. He begins with a description of Brulé relations with other Sioux camps and Plains tribes, particularly the Pawnees whom they disliked immensely. The author describes armed conflict with the army in the 1850s, Spotted Tail's lead in the killing of Lieutenant Grattan and his men, his military imprisonment at Fort Leavenworth,

Kansas, where he came to believe that Brulés would be destroyed in war with Americans, and his subsequent stand for peace with whites from that time on. The author examines the split in the Brulé tribe and other Sioux bands between those friendly to whites and those unfriendly, warfare between the Sioux and the army, the 1866 Fort Laramie Treaty Council signed by Spotted Tail and other friendly Sioux but not by Red Cloud and other leaders hostile to the United States. He describes the removal of Brulés to a Missouri reservation in 1868, where the government controlled them and interfered in their life. He explains the government's Sioux appeasement policy, Spotted Tail's efforts to protect his people from being rushed into white people's ways by the government, white invasion of the Black Hills in the 1870s, and warfare with the army. He analyzes factions and motives of Sioux leaders Red Cloud, Crazy Horse, and others. He discusses opposition among Brulés to Spotted Tail's leadership and the latter's murder in 1881. Throughout, the author analyzes ongoing criticism of Spotted Tail's behavior as weak, wicked, pacific, etc. The epilogue brings the story about the Brulés and Spotted Tail's family to the present. There are four maps and photographs of Spotted Tail and other Sioux leaders. The book is based on unpublished and published primary and secondary works. *See also* James C. Olson, *Red Cloud and the Sioux Problem*, page 154.

LEWIS, OSCAR. *The Effects of White Contact upon Blackfeet Culture with Special Reference to the Role of the Fur Trade*. American Ethnological Society Monograph no. 6. Seattle: University of Washington Press, 1942. 73pp. Illustrated. Bibliography.

Lewis tells of the changes which occurred in Blackfeet institutions (economy, social organization, and warfare) following their contacts with fur companies in Canada and the United States from 1754 to the 1870s. He begins with a discussion of Blackfeet origins, early locations, and movements, and looks at the history of the Blackfeet's direct contact with whites as a result of the expansion of the fur trade in the Canadian Northwest from 1754 to 1830 when the heyday of the Canadian fur trade ended. He examines the history of the American fur trade relations with the Blackfeet from 1808 to the 1870s, initially marked by hostility, but much improved after the American Fur Company began extensive trade in buffalo hides. The author discusses the reasons for greater harmony between Blackfeet and Canadian fur traders as compared with Americans and describes the differences among three Blackfeet tribes that have caused divergences in their relations with other tribes and whites. He looks at the effects of the fur trade on Blackfeet material culture, marriage, social organization, and religion; and the methods, motives, and organization of Blackfeet warfare. He concludes with a discussion of the fur trade, together with the horse and gun, as mainsprings of Blackfeet culture change in the nineteenth century. The appendix compares prereservation Blackfeet relations with American and Canadian governments. There are

three maps and the study is based largely on fur trade records.

MATHEWS, JOHN JOSEPH. *The Osages: Children of the Middle Waters*. Norman: University of Oklahoma Press, 1961. 823pp. Illustrated. Bibliography.

This book contains a history of the Osage people who lived in Missouri and Kansas in ancestral times until their removal to Oklahoma through the 1940s. The author divides the book into five parts, the first of which details Osage origin myths, pre-European lifeways, allies, and enemies. The second part concerns initial and subsequent contacts of Osages with French missionaries, traders, explorers, and trappers from the latter part of the seventeenth century which affected economic organization and warfare as well as the Osages' use of horses and guns, intertribal relations, and slave trading. The author explains the important geographic position of the Osages which made them a factor in the struggle for power among France, Spain, and England for control of America; analyzes the policy behind French alliance with the Osages; discusses Osage involvement in the English-Spanish power conflict after 1770; and describes pre-nineteenth-century social organization, customs, and manners. Part 3 considers these lifeways and their disruption as well as Osage tribal disorganization which was closely interwoven with the story of American Indian policies through the mid-nineteenth century. The author examines American exploration of Osage lands and east-of-the-Mississippi Indians driven from their ancient domains and settled on Osage lands. He discusses American acquisition of Osage land, Osage forced movement westward, Cherokee-Osage conflicts, and missionary efforts among the Osage. Part 4 describes new Osage alliances, Plains intertribal warfare, epidemics, buffalo slaughter, settlers' encroachment on the Osage reserve, Osage removal from Kansas, and reservation life in Oklahoma. Part 5 deals with the new Osage religion of peyotism, dissolution of the Osage Nation, and incorporation into the state of Oklahoma in 1907. There are four maps. The book is based on Osage oral history and informants in addition to unpublished and published primary and secondary books.

MAYHALL, MILDRED P. *The Kiowas*. Norman: University of Oklahoma Press, 1962. 315pp. Illustrated. Bibliography.

This is the history of the Kiowas of Oklahoma and Texas from their origins in the northern Rocky Mountains to the 1960s. The author begins with early Kiowa alliances with other Plains tribes in the 1700s and cites descriptions of Kiowas made by the French from the late seventeenth to the early eighteenth century and by Lewis and Clark and other nineteenth-century Americans. She discusses the evolution of Plains culture, with the horse as its basis, describes Kiowa culture in detail, and reprints the Anko and Sett'an pictographic calendars that record Kiowa events from 1832 to 1892. She tells of Kiowa history after 1840 when social forces began to change this people, and describes how the Kiowas allied with Comanches, Southern Cheyennes, and Arapahoes who harrassed traders, trappers, the military, and peaceful Indians. She describes how, in the wars of the 1860s and 1870s, the Kiowas and the U.S. Army fought for control over the Plains until the buffalo were gone and the Kiowas were defeated. Kiowa reservation life with its cultural disintegration is described and, in the concluding discussion, the author argues that Kiowas need to acculturate to white ways. There is some dated terminology. There is an appendix that discusses Plains archaeology, one map, photographs of Kiowas and their calendars, and a bibliography of published primary and secondary sources.

MEYER, ROY W. *History of the Santee Sioux: United States Indian Policy on Trial.* Lincoln: University of Nebraska Press, 1967. 434pp. Illustrated. Bibliography.

This book contains the history of the four eastern bands of Santee Sioux from the mid-seventeenth century when they lived in Minnesota through the twentieth century. Bands are now located in North and South Dakota, Nebraska, and Minnesota. The first six chapters consider the effects of a century and a half of European contact (1650–1800) on the Santee Sioux bands, relations with the American government and missionaries since 1805, treaties and cessions of Santee land, reservation life, the 1862 Sioux Uprising which resulted in the expulsion of Santee bands from Minnesota, and the resultant dispersal and shattering of Santee unity. The author discusses identity and dependency of the Mdewakanton and Wahpekutes on the Nebraska Santee Reservation in the late nineteenth century. He looks at the Sissetons and Wahpetons who were placed on the Sisseton Reservation in South Dakota and on the Devil's Lake Reservation in North Dakota, discusses those Santees who fled to Flandreau, South Dakota, to establish a colony, and tells of those who never left Minnesota and established a permanent community there in the early twentieth century. The concluding chapters describe how the various fragments of Santee Sioux have been affected by the general course of twentieth-century federal policy, describe the divergent courses they have followed in reaction to frequent policy reversals, and analyze the roots of the Indian "problem" as it exists today, adding suggestions for its solution. There is an appendix of treaties made with the Santee Sioux, seven maps, and photographs of Santee Sioux reservation life.

————. *The Village Indians of the Upper Missouri: The Mandans, Hidatsas, and Arikaras.* Lincoln: University of Nebraska Press, 1977. 354pp. Illustrated. Bibliography.

Meyer provides a history of the Mandans, Hidatsas, and Arikaras, the Three Affiliated Tribes, from their first appearances in the upper Missouri River valley in North and South Dakota to the 1970s. He briefly surveys Mandan culture around 1700, examines the Three Tribes as they were seen by early nineteenth-century white visitors, sketches upper Missouri village culture in the early 1830s, looks at the role of disease, the collapse of the Three Tribes, and their reorganization and revival in a single village. Chapters consider relations with

the Sioux, the impact of American agents, army, missionaries, and fur traders; conditions at Fort Berthold Reservation from the 1860s to the end of the century, and government efforts to alter the Three Tribes' lifestyle. The remaining chapters deal with the impact of drought, depression, and war on Berthold; the disruption and social dislocation caused by the construction of the Garrison Dam in the late 1940s which inundated portions of the reservation where most of the people lived; and recovery from economic decline in the 1960s and 1970s. There are five maps and paintings and photographs of the Three Tribes' culture. The book is partly based on manuscript material.

MINER, H. CRAIG. *The Corporation and the Indian: Tribal Sovereignty and Industrial Civilization in Indian Territory, 1865–1907.* Columbia: University of Missouri Press, 1976. 236pp. Illustrated. Bibliography.

This is an account of the dealings of corporations with tribes in Indian Territory, particularly the Cherokees, Choctaws, and Osages, between the Civil War and Oklahoma statehood, in which the author argues that the most important force in destroying tribal sovereignty was corporate industrialization. He begins with 1865, which marked the beginning of corporate activities in America and the decline of Indian sovereignty. He explains how railroad corporations entered Indian Territory in the late 1870s and tells how some Indians accommodated themselves to corporations for profit while others repudiated them. He describes how coal corporations were established upon tribal lands and threatened traditional tribal institutions and sovereignty. He considers the Territorial Ring, a corporate lobby pressing for creation of a U.S. territorial government in Indian Territory which would eliminate dual sovereignty and open the region to white settlement. He looks at the alliance between railroad corporations and settler organizations, cattle corporations and their role in the economic exploitation of Indian Territory in the 1880s, and exploitation of petroleum resources in the 1890s, the last major type of corporate activity with which sovereign Indian governments of Indian Territory had to deal. He focuses on the Osages and how they dealt with corporate pressures and concludes with a description of clerks in Indian Territory who represented both government and corporations, their role in protecting Indian rights, and their bureaucratic tangles. The book is largely based on manuscript sources from tribal governments and federal agencies.

————, and WILL E. UNRAU. *The End of Indian Kansas: A Study of Cultural Revolution, 1854–1871.* Lawrence: Regents Press of Kansas, 1978. 179pp. Illustrated. Bibliography.

The authors identify techniques by which the removal of Indians from Kansas was accomplished and show how the territory evolved from a "permanent" habitat of thousands of Indians from eastern tribes in 1854 to a state with only a few Indians by 1875. They look at territorial Kansas from 1854 to 1861, military inaction in expelling intruders, speculators, and illegal squatters, the exploitation of Indians, and the role of territorial leadership in promoting removal. The authors consider the appeal of white assumptions concerning the proper uses of nature as a psychological basis for dissolving tribal hegemony over the Kansas, region and look at the groundwork for the exploitation of Kansas' natural resources established in treaties of the 1850s and 1860s. They look at case studies which document that once treaties were signed, railroad people, land speculators, and timber operations entrenched themselves on Indian lands, and tribal destruction among the Delawares, Sacs and Foxes, Potawatomis, Kickapoos, and Shawnees began. They examine Indian Rings and circumstances by which they succeeded in diverting large amounts of Indian capital to their own use and explore reasons for certain leaders helping the rings. They conclude by discussing the pressure of white settlers, which was central to the removal of Kansas tribes in the 1870s. One map, photographs of Kansas Indians, and a bibliography of unpublished and published primary and secondary materials are included.

NEWCOMB, W. W., JR. *The Indians of Texas: From Prehistoric to Modern Times.* Austin: University of Texas Press, 1961. 404pp. Illustrated. Bibliography.

This author describes Texas Indian cultures prior to the time they were greatly changed by contacts with whites, arranged, according to him, in an ascending order of technological productivity. Parts 1 and 2 outline ancestral Texas Indian history and describe the origins, history, and culture of the Coahuiltecan of south Texas and the Karankawa of the Gulf Coast. Part 3 considers the problem of how and when natives acquired horses and the cultural changes wrought in the Texas southern plains peoples and describes the origins, history, and culture of Lipan Apaches, Tonkawas of central Texas, Comanches, Kiowas, and Kiowa Apaches. Part 4 deals with the Jumanos of southwest Texas, the Wichitas in the north, the Caddo Confederacies in east Texas, and Texas Atakapan-speaking natives. Section five provides an overall view of the almost complete extermination of Texas Indians by the Spanish, Mexicans, Texans, and Americans with whom they came into contact and conflict. There are four maps and photographs and sketches of Texas natives and their way of life. There is some dated terminology.

OLSON, JAMES C. *Red Cloud and the Sioux Problem.* Lincoln: University of Nebraska Press, 1965. 375pp. Illustrated. Bibliography.

This book covers the same ground as Hyde's *Red Cloud's Folk, Spotted Tail's Folk,* and *A Sioux Chronicle* and is intended as a supplement, not a revision of these works.

ORTIZ, ROXANNE DUNBAR. *The Great Sioux Nation: Sitting in Judgment on America.* New York: American Indian Treaty Council Information Center, Berkeley, Calif.: Moon Books, 1977. 224pp. Illustrated. Bibliography.

This book is based on and contains testimony heard at the Sioux Treaty Hearing held December, 1974, in Federal District Court, Lincoln, Nebraska, in which approximately sixty-five defendants charged with criminal acts allegedly done on the Pine Ridge Sioux Reservation during the 1973 Wounded Knee siege moved for dismissal. The Wounded Knee siege occurred when certain Sioux asserted sovereignty based on the 1868 Fort Laramie Treaty. Testimony by traditional Indians, historians, attorneys, and anthropologists is presented topically and chronologically (not in the order presented at the hearing) and deals with past and present-day Sioux culture, Sioux-U.S. relations, and Sioux oral history. The first part of the book contains unedited testimony of spiritual leader Leonard Crow Dog, attorneys' direct examination of him, and testimony related to the 1890 Wounded Knee massacre and the 1973 Wounded Knee siege. Other parts deal with Native American cultures, Indian-U.S. relations, the 1868 Fort Laramie Treaty between the Sioux and the United States, the oral history of the treaty and its validity compared to written history, the period after 1868 when the Sioux were put on reservations, and the present situation and Sioux goals. The conclusion includes excerpts of Judge Urbom's negative decision and the document entitled "Declaration of Continuing Independence" outlining the international direction native peoples are taking. The introduction contains pieces on oral history, sovereignty, and a concise history of U.S.-Sioux relations. There are photographs of the witnesses and an unannotated, topical bibliography including sections on North American colonialism, Indian cultures, oral history, legal studies, cases and statutes, bibliographies, and periodicals.

POWELL, PETER JOHN. *People of the Sacred Mountain: A History of the Northern Cheyenne Chiefs and Warrior Societies, 1830–1879.* 2 vols. San Francisco: Harper & Row, 1981. 1,441pp. Illustrated. Bibliography.

The author presents a visual and narrative history of the Northern Cheyenne. The two-volume book describes, in the voices of the Cheyennes themselves, the historical, social, and religious roles of the Council chiefs, the peace chiefs, and warrior societies. The story begins in the days of freedom in the 1830s, moves through the intertribal battles of the 1840s and 1850s, and continues on through the wars to save the tribal lands, buffalo, and sacred way of life from the white invaders of the 1860s and the 1870s. The history concludes with the march of Little Wolf, Morning Star, and their people as they fled the Indian Territory in 1878 to return home. The first volume covers 1830–68, and the second covers 1868–79 and contains an epilogue entitled "The Return to the Sacred Mountains, 1969–1974." There are notes, maps, a bibliography, and a list of Cheyennes whose knowledge helped to make the volumes possible. The work is illustrated with seventy-seven full-color, full-page reproductions of ledger art and 136 photographs that document the history. The drawings portray real events as painted by the warriors who actually took part in them or by artist friends who recreated the battle scenes as they were described to them. There are paintings of the Battles of the Little Bighorn, Rosebud, and the fight with MacKenzie's troopers in the Bighorn Mountains, of warrior society parades, and hunting and courting scenes. The photographs spanning the years 1851 to 1974 represent every major historical photographer of the Plains Indian tribes. Most of the portraits are accompanied with short biographical sketches. *People of the Sacred Mountain* makes up the third and fourth volumes of a five-volume work on Cheyenne culture. The first two volumes were published in 1969 as *Sweet Medicine: The Continued History of the Sacred Arrows, the Sun Dance and the Sacred Buffalo Hat in Northern Cheyenne History.*

ROE, FRANK GILBERT. *The Indian and the Horse.* Norman: University of Oklahoma Press, 1955. 434pp. Illustrated. Bibliography.

This book summarizes existing evidence concerning the appearance and impact of horses upon the Plains Indians, the principal horse-using tribes of North America, focusing on aspects of chronology, geography, and tribal reactions. The author argues that the horse extended and developed long existent customs and characteristics among natives and exerted profound influences in the spiritual realm. Part 1 considers the dog culture of various tribes, discards the "stray" theory of the acquisition of Indian horses, and argues that natives acquired them by direct action. He looks at the wide adoption of the horse after its first appearance in territories on either side of the Mississippi River. The author discusses estimates of time when horses were acquired by the Utes, Apaches, Pawnees, Comanches, Kiowas, and the Caddoans of the southern Plains, by the Sioux, Blackfeet, Cheyennes, Plains Crees, and Assiniboins of the northern Plains, by the Flatheads and other nations of the Plateau region, and concludes this section with a treatment of horse coloration. In part 2, the author argues the lack of influence of the horse in regard to migrations and warring among native societies which prevailed from remote times, treats the methods by which natives acquired skill in caring for horses, discusses them as economic and social assets, and roughly estimates tribal resources in horses. He concludes with a discussion of the influence of horses upon native psychology, especially the status of women in postequestrian tribal life, and the influence of horses upon buffalo hunting. There are one map, three appendixes, paintings and photographs of horses and native riders. The book is based on primary and secondary sources, especially monographs dealing with individual tribes and their relationship with horses.

SCHUSKEY, ERNEST L. *The Forgotten Sioux: An Ethnohistory of the Lower Brule Reservation.* Chicago: Nelson-Hall, 1975. 269pp. Illustrated. Bibliography.

The author provides a history of the Lower Brulé band of Teton Dakotas, who settled in eastern South Dakota, from their origins to the mid-1970s. He begins with a brief description of Teton Dakota culture emphasizing its adaptability and describes the variability in the Teton individual's way of life. He discusses the relationships of Brulés with fur traders, explorers, government agents, and settlers, treaty-making, the establishment of the Lower Brulé Reservation in 1868, and the growing economic dependency on whites. The author tells of Teton armed resistance to the federal government from 1868 to 1876 which overshadowed the Lower Brulés' history of attempting peaceful cooperation with whites rather than warfare. He describes the years of 1877 to 1890 when reformers pursued the goal of totally assimilating Indians, looks at the federal government policy of allotment, and summarizes the Ghost Dance and events of Wounded Knee in 1890. He concludes by explaining Brulé political, economic, and legal problems in the twentieth century, contemporary social organization, the Brulés' request for termination, and their future outlook. There are two maps and photographs of Lower Brulé people. The book is based on the author's field work and published primary and secondary works.

TRENHOLM, VIRGINIA COLE. *The Arapahoes: Our People.* Norman: University of Oklahoma Press, 1970. 372pp. Illustrated. Bibliography.

Trenholm traces the history of the Arapahoes from their ancestral homes in Minnesota and Canada to the beginning of the twentieth century when they lived in Wyoming, Montana, and Oklahoma. She discusses Arapaho political, economic, and social organization and law ways before contact with Europeans, relations with other Plains tribes and fur traders, intertribal warfare, treaties, battles with whites, religious acculturation fostered by church schools, religious revivalism, and reservation life. There are detailed accounts of the Ghost Dance and peyote cult. The author studies the geographic separation of the Arapahoes, who were divided into two branches, and the effects of acculturation on them. She tells of the southern Arapahoes who lost their ceremonies and tribal lands in Oklahoma and the northern Arapahoes on the Wyoming Wind River Reservation who have maintained more of their culture. There is one map plus photographs of historic Arapahoes and their way of life. The book is based on unpublished and published primary and secondary works.

UNRAU, WILLIAM E. *The Kansa Indians: A History of the Wind People, 1673–1873.* Norman: University of Oklahoma Press, 1971. 244pp. Illustrated. Bibliography.

This book presents the history of the Kansa natives who lived in eastern Kansas from the late seventeenth century to their forced removal to Indian Territory in 1873. The author discusses Kansa migrations, their semisedentary way of life, the impact on the Kansa of eighteenth-century Spanish, English, and French fur traders and nineteenth-century American merchants and land speculators who undermined their subsistence economy. The author describes the destruction of the buffalo supply; the federal government's plan to force the Kansa into becoming farmers after the 1825 treaties and its failure to provide economic assistance; cessions of land that diminished the Kansa domain, diseases that accounted for a high mortality rate, and government agents, Methodist missionaries, white settlers, and intertribal relations that caused problems for the Kansa and altered their way of life. The concluding chapter deals with the last forced migration to Indian Territory in 1873. There are four maps and photographs of Kansa people, artifacts, and buildings. The book is based on unpublished and published primary and secondary works.

UTLEY, ROBERT M. *Frontier Regulars: The United States Army and the Indian, 1866–1891.* New York: Macmillan, 1973. 462pp. Illustrated. Bibliography.

This book examines the conflicts between the U.S. Army and Native American tribes which started after the Civil War and concluded with the massacre at Wounded Knee. The author considers the frontier army neither as the vanguard of civilization nor a barbaric band of butchers but rather as a conventional military force trying to control unconventional enemies with conventional military organization and methods. He describes the conditions of army life, the overall strategy that was used to secure the West, and bureaucratic infighting between the War Department and Indian Bureau which hampered U.S. Indian policy. Most of the study gives year-by-year, campaign-by-campaign accounts of how the cavalry and infantry subjugated the Indians in the Plains, Texas and the Mexican border, the Southwest, Pacific Northwest, California, and Basin-Plateau areas. There are fourteen maps and an unannotated bibliography of government manuscript sources upon which the book is largely based and other published primary and secondary works.

———. *Frontiersmen in Blue: The United States Army and the Indian, 1848–1865.* New York: Macmillan, 1967. 384pp. Illustrated. Bibliography.

This book examines the relations between regular and volunteer frontiersmen, between the Mexican War and the Civil War. The author recounts the evolution of the nation's military and civil policies towards the Indians and the army's skirmishes with nearly all the tribes from 1848 to 1865. He considers how the army protected settlements, policed travel routes, and succeeded or failed in warring with Indians. He describes the struggles of the frontier army to survive in the western environment and the problems in differentiating the numerous western Indian nations. He discusses the divisions, departments, and districts which underwent continuous geographical redefinition and describes the basic framework of forts erected in the 1850s and 1860s in six geographical commands (Departments of the West, Texas, New Mexico, Utah, California, and Oregon). The author considers the transcontinental thoroughfares (Oregon, Santa Fe, and Bozeman Trails) that provided the skeleton for the distribution of troops, the basic pattern of defensive systems created in the Southwest and in Texas, and the military strategy of a fixed post (forts and bases) system that prevailed over roving columns on the Indian frontier. He discusses two precedents set by the U.S. Army in conducting offensive operations, winter campaigns and the practice of "total war," deliberately killing women and children. There are seven maps and photographs and paintings of American soldiers, native warriors, and forts. There is a bibliography of government manuscripts and published primary and secondary works.

———. *The Last Days of the Sioux Nation.* New Haven, Conn.: Yale University Press, 1963. 314pp. Illustrated. Bibliography.

This book deals with the Ghost Dance religion and reservation life among the Teton Dakotas of South Dakota during the 1880s, culminating in the Wounded Knee Massacre of 1890 and the subsequent surrender of the Sioux in 1891. The author begins with a description of nineteenth-century Teton culture on the Great Sioux Reservation where the traditional way of life deteriorated as a result of federal policies designed to "civilize" the Dakotas. He looks at Sioux opposition to the allotment policy, the selling of surplus lands to white settlers, and the Dakotas' eventual acceptance of the 1890 land agreement which opened ceded territory to settlement. He examines the rise of Paiute Wovoka, a Messiah, and the Ghost Dance religion he preached in 1890 to rid Indians of their alien oppressor and to restore the traditional way of life, as well as the growth of religion among Dakota tribes. He describes the negative reaction of Sioux agents to adherents of the Ghost Dance religion, the arrival of army troops at Rosebud and Pine Ridge agencies, the contest between Interior and War Departments for control of native affairs, Sitting Bull's role in the Ghost Dance, military plans for his arrest, and his death. Utley describes the decision of Big Foot, who was controlled by younger band members, to go to Pine Ridge Agency, the troops' opposition, the Battle of Wounded Knee Creek, December 29, 1890, and the subsequent court of inquiry that investigated Colonel James Forsyth's role in the slaughter. He discusses the military conquest and surrender of thousands of "hostiles" to the U.S. Army, the end of the Ghost Dance uprising, and briefly describes General Miles's program to save the Sioux. There are five maps and photographs of Sioux, Ghost Dancers, U.S. troops, and Wounded Knee Creek. The book is based on unpublished and published primary and secondary works.

WEIST, TOM. *A History of the Cheyenne People.* Billings: Montana Council for Indian Education, 1977. 227pp. Illustrated. Bibliography.

This book presents the history of the Northern Cheyenne of present-day Montana from ancient to contemporary times. The basic outline of the history follows the generalized time periods recognized by older Cheyennes. The author gives brief descriptions of "ancient times" based on legends when the Cheyennes were hunters and fishermen in the northern woodlands. He describes "the time of the dogs" when Cheyennes were planters living in earth lodge villages on the Minnesota, Cheyenne, and Missouri Rivers. He discusses "the time of the buffalo" when the Cheyennes migrated westward onto the Plains from 1600 to 1780, by which time they had horses and were hunting buffalo. The author describes the nineteenth-century Cheyenne mounted way of life and culture, treaties, and warfare with whites following the course of both Northern and Southern Cheyenne history until 1865 when the Southern Cheyennes and Southern Arapahoes were settled on an Oklahoma reservation. He describes Northern Cheyenne battles after 1865, their defeat, removal of a Northern Cheyenne group in 1877 to the Southern Cheyenne reservation, and the group's march back to Montana. The author describes "the time of the horse" and Cheyenne adjustment to life on the Montana Tongue River Reservation, conflict with neighboring white ranchers, the rise of the Ghost Dance religion, the Native American Church, and Mennonite Church among the Northern Cheyennes, and early twentieth-century reservation development. He concludes with the period of self-government after 1934 and describes the work of the Northern Cheyenne Tribal Council to improve Cheyenne life. There are thirteen maps and numerous photographs of Cheyenne life. The bibliography lists published primary and secondary accounts.

SOUTHWEST

DOZIER, EDWARD P. *The Pueblo Indians of North America.* New York: Holt, Rinehart, & Winston, 1970. 224pp. Illustrated. Bibliography.

This study considers the Pueblo peoples of New Mexico and Arizona from ancestral times until the present and their adaption to changing physical, socioeconomic, and political environments. In part 1, the author describes the Pueblos today and the sources of change in Pueblo government, education, health, and community life. Part 2 surveys prehistoric Pueblo cultures until the early sixteenth century, and then focuses on Spanish colonization and the changes in Pueblo culture as a result of Spanish contacts. After the decline of Spanish power in the eighteenth century came the period of Anglo-American dominance and the problems associated with federal government control and supervision from 1900 to 1968. The third part discusses traditional Pueblo society, particularly the dichotomy between Western Pueblos (Hopi, Hano, Zuñi, Laguna, and Acoma) and the Eastern Rio Grande Pueblos (Santa Ana, San Felipe, Santo Domingo, Cochiti, Zia, Jemez, Sandia, Isleta, Tesque, Nambe, Pojoaque, San Ildefonso, Santa Clara, and San Juan). The last section provides information about general Pueblo cultural characteristics. There are tables illustrating Pueblo-Euro-American relations, population figures, and Pueblo ceremonial organization and symbolism. There are maps and pictures of Pueblo peoples. The book is based on primary and secondary sources.

FORBES, JACK D. *Apache, Navajo, and Spaniard.*

Norman: University of Oklahoma Press, 1960. 304pp. Illustrated. Bibliography.

Forbes traces the history of southern Athapaskans of New Mexico and Arizona and their relations with other natives and with the Spanish empire from the first written records of 1540 until 1698 showing that the Athapaskans served as a barrier to the westward expansion of the Spanish empire. He begins by challenging the theories of the origins of southern Athapaskans and of the Apaches as savage bandits. He studies the Spanish empire in Mexico, trends of native relations established in northern New Spain from 1542 to 1600 such as the mission system, and the northward advance of the Spanish into Pueblo and Apache lands in the late sixteenth century for wealth, converts, and slaves. He examines the essentially peaceful, commercial relations between Pueblo and Athapaskan peoples and shows that Spanish interference in the Southwest broke up peaceful Indian relations and led to an increase of warfare. Chapters consider the development of hostility between the Spanish and the Athapaskans and their Pueblo allies in the early seventeenth century, the harsh rule of some of New Mexico's Spanish governors, and the conflict between Franciscans and secular officials over native affairs throughout these administrations. The author focuses on different phases of twenty years of native revolt against the Spanish empire in northern New Spain, especially the 1680 Pueblo revolt followed by Spanish counteroffensives which brought the revolt to an end by 1698 in New Mexico. There are four maps. The book is based on unpublished and published Spanish sources.

―――. *Warriors of the Colorado: The Yumas of the Quechan Nation and Their Neighbors.* Norman: University of Oklahoma Press, 1965. 378pp. Illustrated. Bibliography.

Containing a history of the Quechan, a Colorado River people of Arizona, from their origins until 1852 when their lands were occupied by U.S. military forces, this book looks at the development of many groups which bordered upon the Quechan including the Kamias, Cocopas, Halchidhomas, Mohaneos, Maricopas, Pimas, and Papagos. The author surveys archaeology, folklore, and Yuman linguistics to help reconstruct pre-1540 Quechan and Yuma history. He describes their way of life, relations with neighboring Yumans, and intertribal warfare. Chapters consider Spanish expansion and conquest in the Southwest, seventeenth-century native revolts against the Spanish, Spanish missionary work among Colorado River natives in the late eighteenth century, Spanish explorations of the Colorado River delta, and the late eighteenth-century Quechan revolt against the Spanish Empire. He tells of Anglo-American expansion in the Colorado River area from the 1820s, friction between Quechan and Mexicans, and the American conquest of the Quechan in the mid-nineteenth century. There is an appendix of Quechan population, leadership, and land ownership, three maps, and pictures of Yuman people and missions. The book is based on unpublished and published primary and secondary sources.

GUNNERSON, DOLORES A. *The Jicarilla Apaches: A Study in Survival*. DeKalb: Northern Illinois University Press, 1974. 326pp. Illustrated. Bibliography.

The author reconstructs the origins and history of the Jicarilla Apaches of New Mexico from the early sixteenth to the end of the nineteenth century. The first part deals with the history of Apacheans before 1700, particularly the Jicarillas, known in the Southwest before 1700 by other names. The author argues that the history of the Apaches began in the early 1500s in the north as Plains nomads who became the ancestors of the Jicarillas who settled in the mountains of New Mexico. She considers Spanish, Pueblo, and Apache relations from 1609 to 1680 and the Apache-Pueblo alliance in the 1680 Pueblo rebellion against the Spanish which lasted until 1692 when the Spanish reconquered New Mexico. The author concludes the first part with speculations about proto-Apachean migrations and their buffalo culture. The second part contains post-1700 linguistic, archaeological, and ethnographic data about the Jicarilla Apaches, who were the last tribe to be permanently settled on a reservation in 1887, reviews their relations with Pueblos, Utes, and other tribes, and looks at the use of Jicarillas as scouts and auxiliaries on Spanish military campaigns. She traces the Cuartelejo and Paloma Apaches from 1700 to 1800 until they joined other Apaches in Colorado for protection against enemy bands. She explains how the three allied bands drifted southward becoming known as Llaneros and finally returned to New Mexico where by 1801 they explicitly claimed to be part of the Jicarillas. These bands are known as the Llanero band of the present Jicarilla tribe. There are eight maps and a bibliography of unpublished and published Spanish and English works.

HALEY, JAMES L. *Apaches: A History and Culture Portrait*. Garden City, N.Y.: Doubleday, 1981. 453pp. Illustrated. Bibliography.

The author gives an in-depth cultural portrait of Apaches, presenting religious beliefs that suffused every aspect of their daily lives, their subsistence techniques, rites, customs, myths, and medicines as a backdrop to the decades that precede the Apaches' final defeat in 1886. The author argues that it is not possible to understand the Apaches' history except through their complicated lifeway and how it shaped their perception of outsiders. He focuses on army officers, Indian agents, and charismatic Apache chiefs who play decisive roles. There are three maps and photographs of Apache people, culture, country, and army officers. See Worcester, *The Apaches*, page 161.

HIRST, STEPHEN. *Life in a Narrow Place: The Havasupai in the Grand Canyon*. New York: McKay, 1976. 302pp. Illustrated. Bibliography.

Hirst traces the history of the Havasupai Indians who have lived at the bottom of Arizona's Havasu Canyon in the summer and along the Grand Canyon's south rim in winter since ancestral times, describes their confinement to the Canyon in the late nineteenth century, and considers their nearly century long campaign to regain title to their winter homeland on the plateau lands above their canyon. He begins with a description of contemporary Havasupai culture and briefly traces the tribe's history and culture until the 1850s when their lands were invaded by surveyors and settlers. He discusses the 1882 creation of the Havasupai Reservation which restricted the Havasupais to Havasu Canyon and turned their winter plateau homeland into public property, although the Havasupais were promised use of their old plateau lands outside the canyon. The author describes the efforts of the Forest and the National Parks Service in the twentieth century to make the tribe vacate their plateau lands. He briefly considers the 1941 Hualapai right to possess forfeited railroad lands within their territory and the implications for the Havasupais. He describes Havasupai attempts in the early 1940s to regain some of their plateau lands within their winter range, the Parks Service opposition, social deterioration, and other disruptive effects on the Havasupais stemming from the termination policy of the 1950s. He concludes by treating the Havasupai battles in the 1970s with the Parks and Forest Service officials, certain environmentalists, and Congress and the successful passage in 1975 of legislation that restored title to a portion of their ancient homeland. There are two maps, over one hundred photographs taken by Terry and Lyntha Scott Eiler, and archival photographs that illustrate Havasupai life over the past century. The book is based on unpublished and published materials and Havasupai testimony.

JOHN, ELIZABETH A. H. *Storms Brewed in Other Men's Worlds; The Confrontation of Indians, Spanish, and French in the Southwest, 1540–1795*. College Station: Texas A & M University Press, 1975. 805pp. Illustrated. Bibliography.

This volume concerns the history of the Indian peoples whose lands fell within the Spanish provinces of New Mexico and Texas and within French Louisiana, and the impact of the Europeans on the Indians from the earliest contacts in the 1540s to the crumbling of Spanish power in the 1790s. The author begins with the earliest documentation of each people, examining how Indian societies coped with the experience of revolutionary change, and views the interplay among diverse Indian peoples and European intruders. The author illuminates varying dimensions of Indian experience which include Navajos and Comanches forging distinct cultural revolutions from the Spanish encounter; Apaches, Utes, Wichitas, and Tonkawas preserving and intensifying old patterns while assimilating profound changes; Hopis defending old ways through resistance to change; Pueblos conserving basic values through subtle accommodations to imposed change; and Caddos all but destroyed by change. She details population movements, territoriality, intergroup relations, tribal factionalism, culture change, political processes in various Indian societies, and Indian statesmanship. She also looks at the experience of Hispanic communities of New Mexico and Texas and their relations with Indians. There are four maps and reproductions of sixteen paintings that record the ancestral southwestern experience. The book is based on archival sources in New Mexico, Texas, Mexico, and Spain, as well as collections of published documents.

JONES, OAKAH L., JR. *Pueblo Warriors and Spanish Conquest*. Norman: University of Oklahoma Press, 1966. 225pp. Illustrated. Bibliography.

This book examines the Spanish policy, practices, organization, and significance of Pueblo auxiliaries who assisted in the defense of New Spain's northern frontier against other Indians, particularly the Apaches, from 1692 to 1794. The author summarizes the information about a fundamental characteristic of Spanish conquest and settlement from the sixteenth to the eighteenth century—the reliance on native allies. Chapters discuss the period from 1692 to 1704 when the Spanish took advantage of Pueblo disunity to conquer New Mexico with the assistance of friendly Pueblo forces and examines the growth of the Spanish-Pueblo alliance. The author describes the pacification of New Mexico's resisting tribes in the later half of the eighteenth century by using the locally developed policy of enlisting Pueblos, Utes, and Navajos in the Spanish-Pueblo alliance against certain Apache bands. He reconstructs a hypothetical campaign in which Pueblo auxiliaries are enlisted, and summarizes, in the epilogue, Pueblo assistance in the nineteenth century. There are four maps and photographs of Pueblos. The book is based on unpublished and published Spanish and English materials.

KENNER, CHARLES L. *A History of New Mexico-Plains Indian Relations*. Norman: University of Oklahoma Press, 1969. 250pp. Illustrated. Bibliography.

Kenner studies the economic, social, and cultural effects of interchange which the period of 1598 to 1874 produced upon New Mexicans and Pueblo and Plains Indians. He begins by discussing alternating periods of peace, war, and trade between upper Rio Grande valley Pueblos and southern Plains peoples during the fifteenth and sixteenth centuries, describes Pueblo-Apache resistance to Spanish settlement in New Mexico after 1598 and Pueblo-Apache trade during the seventeenth century. The author examines Spanish trade relations with Plains Indians, Comanche raids beginning in the 1740s against the Spanish, and Pueblos challenging the New Mexico frontier until 1786 when peace was negotiated. He discusses peaceful Comanche-New Mexico relations from 1786 to 1846 characterized by stability, the Spanish use of Comanches to fight against certain Apaches, and the American challenge to the Spanish for the loyalty of Plains Indians from the early 1800s. He looks at the era of the Comancheros, New Mexican traders who were allied with and traded with the Comanches from 1786 to 1860, their competition with American traders, and American attempts to break up their commerce. Chapters examine American control of the New Mexican territory from 1848 to 1861, Comanche resentment of Anglo ranchers, New Mexican military force offensives in the 1860s against Comanches and Kiowas, and Comanche reprisals.

He explains how the Comancheros encouraged Comanches and Kiowas to steal Texas cattle in the early 1860s, tells of the suppression of the Comanchero cattle trade by New Mexican ranchers and military officials, and looks at the end of Comanche control of the southern Plains in the Red River War of 1874. There are three maps and photographs of New Mexico Indians. The book is based on unpublished and published primary and secondary works.

McNITT, FRANK. *Navajo Wars: Military Campaigns, Slave Raids, and Reprisals*. Albuquerque: University of New Mexico Press, 1972. 477pp. Illustrated. Bibliography.

The author traces the history of the Navajo wars with white colonizers of New Mexico Territory from the time of Coronado's arrival on the plains of New Mexico to the 1861 Fort Fauntleroy massacre, arguing that the Spanish, Mexicans, and Americans who colonized the Navajo Territory in succession were essentially alike in their mistreatment of Navajos and that all the quarrels followed a pattern first established by the Spanish in the seventeenth century. He considers Spanish and Mexican rule, enslavement of Navajos, land encroachment and denial of human rights by both, and the resultant warfare with the two nations until 1846. He next discusses American appropriation of Navajo land, treaties allowing Navajo enslavement to continue, and armed hostilities, concluding with a discussion of the attack on the Navajos at Fort Fauntleroy by the U.S. cavalry. There are documents in the appendix concerning traffic in slaves, the Navajos' origin, warfare, and the 1855 treaty. There are photographs of Navajos and army officers. The bibliography lists unpublished and published Spanish as well as English works.

MINGE, WARD ALAN. *Acoma: Pueblo in the Sky*. Albuquerque: University of New Mexico Press, 1976. 180pp. Illustrated. Bibliography.

Minge examines the social, economic, and political history of the Acoma pueblo located in western New Mexico from the sixteenth century to the present. He begins with archaeological evidence and historic references to Acoma, describes the Acoma under Spanish rule, 1598–1821, under Mexican rule, 1821–46, and under United States rule after 1848. He explains Acoma assimilation and adaptation of Spanish, Mexican, and American institutions and the relationship between the pueblo and the Bureau of Indian Affairs (BIA). The final chapter discusses the problems Acoma faces in the twentieth century, with emphasis on the threatened destruction of their traditional way of life. There are seven appendixes, ten tables, and photographs of Acoma pueblo people, lands, and arts. There is a bibliographical essay discussing Spanish primary sources and BIA records upon which the book is largely based.

SANDO, JOE S. *The Pueblo Indians*. San Francisco: Indian Historian Press, 1976. 247pp. Illustrated. Bibliography.

The author, a Jemez Pueblo, traces the history of New Mexico's nineteen Pueblo tribes from ancestral times to the present. He begins with a discussion of Pueblo people today: their geographic locations, language, government, traditional history, religion, and economy. He turns to the Spanish conquest of the Pueblos in the seventeenth century, the 1680 Pueblo revolt against Spanish religious and economic slavery, the return of the Spanish in 1692, the growth of the Pueblo-Spanish political-cultural alliance that lasted until the early nineteenth century, and the death of the Spanish regime. Briefly he examines Pueblo life under the Mexicans and the destructive role of the United States after 1848, looking at specific aspects of the Pueblo struggle with the U.S. government over land, water rights, education, economy, and religion. The concluding chapter includes nine biographies of men who have shaped recent Pueblo history. The appendix contains a historical outline of the Pueblo Indians, the Constitution of the All-Indian Pueblo Council, and demographic figures. There are eight maps and photographs of Pueblo people and places. The book is partly based on oral interviews.

SONNICHSEN, C. L. *The Mescalero Apaches*. Norman: University of Oklahoma Press, 1958. 303pp. Illustrated. Bibliography.

This is a history of the Mescalero subdivision of the eastern Apaches who lived in present-day New Mexico from their origins to the 1950s. The author surveys Apache culture, describes hostile relations between the Spanish and eastern Apaches from their first contacts in the mid-sixteenth to the late eighteenth century, and tells of hostile relations between Apaches and Comanches since the late seventeenth century and hostile relations between Apaches and Mexicans beginning in 1824. Chapters consider the warfare between U.S. Army units and Apaches in the mid-nineteenth century; their captivity at Bosque Redondo, and escape; federal reservation policy in the 1870s; military campaigns against Victorio and the Mescalero Apaches; and the end of the wars and the imprisonment of Apaches in the late nineteenth century. The author describes seventy years of shifting federal policy after 1880 "to push Apaches into the mainstream of American life" and looks at life on the Mescalero Reservation in the 1950s. There is some dated terminology. There are two maps and pictures of Apaches and their way of life. The book is based on interviews with Apaches and unpublished and published primary and secondary works.

SPICER, EDWARD H. *Cycles of Conquest: The Impact of Spain, Mexico, and the United States on the Indians of the Southwest, 1533–1960*. Tucson: University of Arizona Press, 1962. 609pp. Illustrated. Bibliography.

Spicer's study concerns the ways the southwestern native cultures responded to the civilizations of Spain, Mexico, and the United States and the results of this culture contact from 1600 to 1960. The introduction briefly describes the general characteristics of Indians of northwestern New Spain around 1600. In the first part, the author considers the contacts of the Tarahumaras, Mayos, Yaquis, Lower Pimas,

Opatas, Seris, Upper Pimas, Eastern and Western Pueblos, Navajos, Western Apaches, and Yumas with Spanish and Anglo-Americans from the last decade of the sixteenth to the twentieth century. Part 2 summarizes some of the major features of successive Spanish, Mexican, and Anglo-American programs for "civilizing" the Indians, especially the mid-nineteenth century Anglo policy of isolating them on reservations. Part 3 discusses native political systems and contrasts them with Spanish government from the time of their first contacts. The author considers the uneven political integration of Indians into the three nations; the uneven adoption of the official languages of the three nations; the diffusion of Spanish and English; the persistence and modification of native languages; native community reorientation, religious diversification, and economic integration. The last part concerns theoretical discussions of culture change processes. There are twenty maps.

TERRELL, JOHN UPTON. *Apache Chronicle*. New York: World Publishing, 1972. 411pp. Illustrated. Bibliography.

Tracing the history of the Apache bands largely located in Arizona, New Mexico, and Texas from their first contacts with the Spanish in 1535 to the surrender of Geronomo in 1886, the author also gives a picture of the diverse ways of life of the various tribes and of the personalities of some of their leaders, including Mangas Coloradas, Cochise, and Geronimo. The book is organized by centuries and covers the Spanish Conquest, the Mexican War of Independence in 1821, the Mexican-American War, the American occupancy of the Southwest in 1846, and the effects of the Civil War. The author looks at the corruption of the Indian Bureau; the conflicts between it and the U.S. Army; and Spanish and Mexican atrocities against Apaches. Throughout the book, the author discusses the myriad incidents culminating in the surrender of the last Apaches to the army and documents the role of the whites in the creation of the myth of the bloodthirsty Apaches. There are maps and photographs of Apaches. The bibliography lists published primary and secondary materials.

———. *The Arrow and the Cross: A History of the American Indian and the Missionaries*. Santa Barbara, Calif.: Capra Press, 1979. 253pp. Illustrated. Bibliography.

Terrell describes the missionary penetrations in the Southwest, California, the Rocky Mountains, and Oregon from the mid-sixteenth to the mid-nineteenth century. He describes how Protestant and Catholic missionaries strove to crush the Indians' resistance to Christianity through mental and physical pressures. He tells of the excursions of Coronado through present-day Arizona, New Mexico, and Texas which brought Christianity to the southwestern Indians and discusses the missionaries who were stationed in the Southwest, the Indians' suffering as a result of the laws and tenets of Christianity forced on them, and their resistance to the missionaries. He cites some of the governors and missionaries who served in New Mexico and their internecine conflict which victimized the Indians during the seventeenth century until the Pueblos revolted against their oppressors in 1680. The author discusses Serra and the nine missions he founded in California during the 1770s and the one in 1782, explains the founding of twelve other missions built along the California coast during the late 1700s and the first quarter of the eighteenth century which, he argues, comprised a penal system for the Mission Indians. He explains how Christianity reached the Indians of Oregon, discusses the subsequent struggle among Protestants and the conflict between Protestants and Catholics to capture Indian souls, concluding with a retelling and analysis of the killing of the Whitmans, who were missionaries, and others by the Cayuse people in 1847. There are two pictures and a bibliography of published sources.

THRAPP, DAN L. *The Conquest of Apacheria.* Norman: University of Oklahoma Press, 1967. 405pp. Illustrated. Bibliography.

This book contains the story of the unremitting conflict between Apaches and the white population for control of Apacheria, extending from the Colorado River to the Rio Grande and from the canyons southward into Mexico, from 1860 to 1886. The author briefly traces the origins of the conflict of the Apaches with Spanish, Mexicans, and Americans; describes expeditions by volunteers against the Apaches; the mid-1860s war between the Walapai and the military in northwest Apacheria; and highlights the life of soldiering and the careers of various soldiers and Apaches who fought each other. Chapters discuss the Camp Grant Massacre of 1871 in which Apache people were murdered; General Crook's offensive campaigns against western Apache bands; Apache agent John Clum's career and his difficulties in supervising the San Carlos reservation; and bickering between the Indian Service and army officials in Apacheria. The author discusses the raids and warfare started by Victorio, Nana, Juh, and Geronimo in the 1880s and the army campaigns against them which lasted until 1886 when Geronimo surrendered, marking the end of nearly three centuries of Apache-white warfare in the Southwest. There is some dated terminology. There are six maps and photographs of Apacheria, Apaches, and army officers. The book is based on unpublished materials and published primary and secondary sources.

————. *Victorio and the Mimbres Apaches.* Norman: University of Oklahoma Press, 1974. 393pp. Illustrated. Bibliography.

Thrapp examines the history of the Mimbres Apaches of New Mexico, their relations with the Spanish in the late eighteenth century and the Americans in the nineteenth century, and Victorio's guerrilla warfare against white Americans until his 1880 death in Mexico. He briefly describes the Apaches' culture, treaties signed with the Spanish and Americans, the evolution of Victorio's leadership, the flood of white settlers that poured into Mimbres lands after reports of the 1859 gold discovery, and constant clashes between Apaches and white settlers and soldiers. He highlights the civil and military obstacles to peaceful management of Indian affairs and discusses the actions of several Apaches including Mangas Coloradas, Juh, and Cochise. He discusses several Apache removals to different reservations in the 1870s, hunger and rationing problems, and Victorio's flight from the San Carlos Reservation to Mexico. He concludes with a discussion of Victorio's guerrilla war against the whites who sought to take over his homeland, U.S. military operations against him, and Victorio's death at Mexican hands. There are photographs of Apache peoples and their homeland. The book is based on unpublished and published primary and secondary works.

UNDERHILL, RUTH M. *The Navajos.* Norman: University of Oklahoma Press, 1956. 299pp. Illustrated. Bibliography.

This is a history of the Navajos from the time of their appearance in the Southwest (New Mexico, Arizona, Colorado, and Utah) to the 1950s, focusing on their change from food collectors to gardeners and pastoralists to wage earners. Examining complex myths and facts, the author describes the ancestors of the present Navajo people and the latter's arrival and early years in the Southwest. Chapters look at the close cultural contacts with agricultural Pueblos and cultural borrowing from them in the late seventeenth to late eighteenth century, the arrival of Spanish sheep and horses, and expansion after 1690 into the area which eventually became their reservation. The author discusses Navajo raids against the Spanish in New Mexico, first contacts with and raids against the United States after 1846, the American war against the Navajo in 1864, removal to the Fort Sumner reservation, their return to their original homeland, and reservation years of dependency after 1868. The author considers Navajo-government relations, twentieth-century social, economic, and medical problems confronting Navajos as well as permanent cultural changes in their life and efforts to govern themselves. There are two maps and photographs of Navajos and their way of life. The book is based largely on Navajo informants and reservation records.

WORCESTER, DONALD. *The Apaches: Eagles of the Southwest.* Norman: University of Oklahoma Press, 1980. 400pp. Illustrated.

This volume contains a full history of the Apaches, from early battles with the Spanish to present-day life on southwestern reservations.

GREAT BASIN–PLATEAU

BECKHAM, STEPHEN DOW. *Requiem for a People: The Rogue River Indians and the Frontiersmen.* Norman: University of Oklahoma Press, 1971. 214pp. Illustrated. Bibliography.

Beckham examines the history of the Rogue River Indians in southwestern Oregon from their first contacts with white people in the late eighteenth century to the removal of their survivors in 1856 to the Siletz Reservation in northern Oregon.

He sketches the origins of the three linguistic groups who made up the Rogue River Indians, and discusses their habits, rituals, and skills. He tells of their encounters with British and American fur trappers and traders, American settlers, cattle drivers, and gold seekers from the late eighteenth century to the mid-nineteenth century, and of intermittent hostilities by Rogues in reaction to white settlers and miners encroaching on their territory. He describes the Rogue River Wars of the 1850s in which the U.S. Army took part, the final struggles of 1855–56, and the forced removal of Rogue River bands to reservations in the north of Oregon. There are two maps, photographs, and sketches of Rogue River Indians and their lands. The book is based on unpublished and published primary and secondary accounts.

BURNS, ROBERT IGNATIUS, S. J. *The Jesuits and the Indian Wars of the Northwest.* New Haven, Conn.: Yale University Press, 1966. 512pp. Illustrated. Bibliography.

The focus of this study is Jesuit involvement in native-white troubles in the upper interior of American Oregon country which included the future states of Oregon, Washington, Idaho, and Montana from 1840 to 1880. Nations dwelling in the Interior were the Flatheads, Kutenais, Kalispels, Pend d'Oreilles, Coeur d'Alenes, Nez Percés, Lakes, San Poils, Kettles, Spokanes, Palouses, Walla Wallas, Cayuses, Okanogans, Columbias, Yakimas, and Umatillas. The author describes the arrival of the Jesuit Order in the late 1830s, considers their beliefs and missionary activities, and focuses on their work in creating, preserving, and restoring the peace among the Interior tribes, their tribal allies, and failures. He cites the role of Jesuits in several episodes: the 1855 Treaty troubles, especially with the Flatheads, the 1855–56 war between Interior tribes and American troops over the seizure of Indian domains; the 1858–59 expeditions of Colonels Steptoe and Wright against several Interior tribes, and the Nez Percé War of 1877. The author describes the beliefs and activities of Palouse Tilcoax, Spokane Polatkin, Kettle Denis, and Jesuit leaders Joset, Hoecken, and DeSmet. There are nine maps and renderings and photographs of missions, Jesuits, and tribal leaders. The book is based on manuscripts in some fifty American and European depositories, Jesuit materials, and published primary and secondary books and articles.

EMMITT, ROBERT. *The Last War Trail: The Utes and the Settlement of Colorado.* Norman: University of Oklahoma Press, 1954. 333pp. Illustrated. Bibliography.

This book presents a history of the Utes who lived in the Rocky Mountains of western Colorado, focusing on events in the late 1870s. The author discusses Ute culture and their friendly relations with the state of Colorado in the 1860s and early 1870s. He describes the life of Nathan C. Meeker, an agent assigned to the White River Agency on the Ute Reservation in 1878, his plan for "civilizing" and controlling the movements of the Ute people, and their antagonism to Meeker's plan to teach them to farm. He relates the Ute version of the 1879 battle at Milk River with Major Thornburgh's troops and the 1879 killings of Meeker and others. The concluding chapter discusses the way the government seized the Ute mountain reservation and removed most of the people to Utah territory and a few to southwestern Colorado. There are three maps. The book is based on Ute and white informants as well as additional sources.

FAHEY, JOHN. *The Flathead Indians.* Norman: University of Oklahoma Press, 1974. 366pp. Illustrated. Bibliography.

The author traces the history of the Flathead (Salish) Indians of western Montana from their origins until the opening of their reservation to white settlement in 1910. The author briefly summarizes Flathead prehistory, notes the 1805 Lewis and Clark discovery of Flatheads, and surveys the political, economic, and social forces that altered their lives from 1805 to 1910. These include the rise and decline of fur trading, Jesuit missionaries, U.S. government agents, President Grant's peace policy, the decimation of buffalo herds, dispossession of their lands by an Indian policy designed to dismantle tribal unity, removal to a reservation, allotment of lands in severalty to Indians, and the constricting of the reservation. He tells of the resistance of Charlot, an aging chief, to the federal government and the opening of Flathead agricultural lands to settlers in 1910. There are maps and photographs of Flatheads. The book is based on unpublished and published materials.

HAINES, FRANCIS. *The Nez Percés: Tribesmen of the Columbia Plateau.* Norman: University of Oklahoma Press, 1955. 326pp. Illustrated. Bibliography.

Haines traces the history of the Nez Percés who lived in parts of Idaho, Oregon, and Washington from ancestral times to the end of the nineteenth century. He begins with a physical description of Nez Percé land, their ancestral culture in sedentary fishing villages, their transformation into a Plains hunting tribe with a buffalo culture after acquiring horses, and their traditional enemies and allies. He discusses early nineteenth-century contacts with Lewis and Clark, fur trappers and traders, the Nez Percé delegation that traveled to St. Louis to ask for Christian teachers, the arrival of the first missionaries in the middle 1830s, and the missions' decline in the 1840s. He examines Washington Territory's policy of intertribal peace, reservations established to open up Basin land to white settlement, the 1855 treaty and creation of a Nez Percé reservation, tribal division into treaty and antitreaty factions, and gold discovery on Nez Percé lands which brought miners, and the 1863 treaty which reduced the reservation size. He describes the reform program of government agents to "civilize" the Nez Percés, white encroachment on the reservation, and Indian resistance leading to the Nez Percé War of 1877. In that war a small band of Nez Percés strategically retreated from the U.S. Army, General O. O. Howard narrowly won, and Chief Joseph became a hero due to his military skill. The author concludes with the exile of the Nez Percés to Indian Territory, postwar Nez Percé reservation life, allotment of tribal lands, and the breakup of the reservation by 1895. There are four maps, photographs, and paintings of the Nez Percé way of life and lands. There is a bibliographical essay discussing the materials used, including manuscripts and published primary and secondary works.

INTER-TRIBAL COUNCIL OF NEVADA. *Newe: A Western Shoshone History*. Reno: Inter-Tribal Council, 1976. 143pp. Illustrated. Bibliography.

This book contains an account of the Western Shoshones (Newe) who lived in parts of Nevada, Utah, Idaho, and California from ancestral times to the mid-twentieth century. The Council describes the Newe way of life before contact, the arrival of trappers and emigrants from 1827 to 1846, the arrival of forty-niners and settlers such as Mormons and government agents between 1847 and 1854, the depletion of Newe land and resources by white intrusions, and the creation of reservations and colonies to keep Indians away from lands whites had stolen from them. The Council describes the creation of the Duck Valley Reservation in 1877 and the creation in the twentieth century of the Goshute Reservation, the Battle Mountain, Elko and Elk Colonies, the Yomba, Duckwater, and South Fork Reservations, the Wells Indian Village, and the Death Valley Newe. The appendixes contain the treaties of 1855 and 1863. There are seven maps and photographs of Shoshones and their way of life. The book is based on interviews, government documents, and unpublished and published primary and secondary materials.

———. *Numa: A Northern Paiute History*. Reno: Inter-Tribal Council, 1976. 132pp. Illustrated. Bibliography.

This book contains an account of the Northern Paiute (Numa) who lived in parts of Nevada, Oregon, Idaho, and California from ancestral times to the present. The first chapter describes the patterns of life common to different northern Paiute bands before contact with white people who began to explore the Great Basin in the 1820s. The following chapters chronicle the influx of fur traders, emigrants, miners, and settlers, and the problems they created for the Numa, the 1860 Pyramid Lake War, Numa displacement, and establishment of reservations. The concluding chapters tell the history and present situation of each reservation and colony formed in the twentieth century and the problems they have all faced. The following are discussed: Lovelock Colony, McDermitt Reservation, Mason and Smith Valleys Reservation, Pyramid Lake Reservation, Reno Sparks Colony, Stillwater Reservation, Fallon Colony, Summit Lake Reservation, and Walker River Reservation. There are eight maps of Numa land and photographs and sketches of Numa people. The book is based on interviews and unpublished and published primary materials and secondary works.

———. *Nuwuvi: A Southern Paiute History*. Reno: Inter-Tribal Council, 1976. 177pp. Illustrated. Bibliography.

This book contains an account of the Southern Paiutes (Nuwuvi) who lived in parts of Nevada, Utah, and Arizona from ancestral times to the present. The history begins with a description of Nuwuvi bands, their lands, subsistence, and way of life. There are chapters on the first intrusions of explorers in the late eighteenth century, American traders in the first quarter of the nineteenth century, and the Spanish and Mexican slave trade. The Council describes the coming of the Mormons in 1847 who settled and expanded into Nuwuvi lands, hostilities between whites and Paiutes, white expropriation of Nuwuvi lands, and disruption of the Nuwuvi independent lifestyle by 1869. There are chapters on four Nuwuvi reservations—the Moapi, Shivwits, Las Vegas, and Cedar City—which alternate with chapters on their legends. There are four maps, photographs of the people and land, and a Nuwuvi chronology. The book is based on unpublished and published primary and secondary materials.

———. *Wa She Shu: A Washo Tribal History*. Reno: Inter-Tribal Council, 1976. 120pp. Illustrated. Bibliography.

This book contains an account of the Washos (Wa She Shu) of Nevada from ancestral times to the twentieth century. The Council describes Washo lands, especially Lake Tahoe (Da ow a ga), subsistence patterns, and the way of life before white contact. There are discussions of the arrival of white fur traders and explorers in the early nineteenth century and emigrant groups in the middle nineteenth century, white exploitation of Washo lands and resources, displacement from ancient homes, and Washo allotments. The Council tells of the Washos's difficulties in the early twentieth century with their unclear political status, lack of treaties, and little government assistance. The Council describes the Washos's organization as a tribal entity in 1937 with a reservation for the first time and their new plans to develop land. There are four maps and photographs of Washos and their way of life. The book is based on interviews, government documents, and unpublished and published primary and secondary sources.

JOHNSON, EDWARD C. *Walker River Paiutes: A Tribal History*. Schurz, Nevada: Walker River Paiute Tribe, 1975. 200pp. Illustrated.

Johnson gives an account of the Walker River Paiutes who have lived around Walker Lake, Nevada, from ancestral times to 1974. He begins with a description of the Northern Paiute Great Basin culture before white contact and tells of the movement of fur trappers and traders into the area by the early 1820s, altering the balance of nature. He discusses the 1848 discovery of gold in California and gold and silver in western Nevada, which brought more settlers into the area by the 1850s, further disrupting the environment. He examines the formation of the reservation at Pyramid and Walker Lake in the late 1850s and early 1860s, the formation of the Nevada Territory in 1861, and the state government in 1864. He tells of the influx of white miners, farmers, and ranchers who clashed with the Paiutes, and explains the importance of two prophets, Wodziwob and Wovoka, the Ghost Dances of the 1860s and 1870s, federal policy designed to make farmers out of Paiutes, and problems with water rights and irrigation and with the Carson and Colorado Railroad which was built through the reservation in 1880–81. In addition, he looks at the factors (schools, Indian police and law, the Chinese, and white doctors) that caused great changes in the Paiute lifestyle beginning in the late nineteenth century. He describes the allotment of the reservation and its opening to white settlement, the treatment of Paiutes during the Walker River Agency period, 1909–35, the development of tribal government from 1935 to 1974, and the ways the Paiutes have tried to preserve their remaining resources. The author concludes with a survey of Paiute sports and recreation from 1880 to 1974 and tells of the Walker Lake sea serpents. There are two appendixes of Walker River tribal leaders, 1850–1974, and a chronology of events, 1776–1974. There are maps and photographs of historic and contemporary Paiutes and their lands. The book is based on taped interviews and unpublished and published materials cited in footnotes.

JOSEPHY, ALVIN M., JR. *The Nez Percé Indians and the Opening of the Northwest.* New Haven, Conn.: Yale University Press, 1965. 705pp. Illustrated. Bibliography. Abridged ed.: New Haven, Conn.: Yale University Press, 1971.

Josephy provides a history of the Nez Percés from 1805, the time Lewis and Clark entered their homeland in parts of present-day Washington, Oregon, Idaho, and Montana, to the 1877 Nez Percé retreat from U.S. Army troops. In the first part of the book, he gives a brief cultural description of the Nez Percé people and details three decades of their embroilment in the white fur trade as well as their becoming armed and enriched with manufactured goods. The second part describes the missionary period after 1834 when Protestant and Catholic missionaries competed for converts and caused division within the Nez Percé tribe until 1847 when the Protestant Whitmans were murdered by Cayuse Indians who had been filled with lies about the missionaries. The author describes the warring between Cayuse and American soldiers in 1848, the role of Isaac Stevens in opening up Indian lands to settlers in the early 1850s, the Walla Walla Council of 1855 in which Indians were forced to sell part of their lands and settle on a reservation, and the wars between Indian Nations and white troops in Oregon and Washington territories during the 1850s. He describes how one Nez Percé faction signed a treaty extinguishing title to an enormous portion of the reservation and alienated antitreaty Nez Percé bands. In the third part, the author describes the events leading up to the 1877 war, discusses Joseph and his nontreaty band, the conflict over the Wallowa Valley where Joseph wished to live, despite the government's proclaiming it open to white settlement, and federal efforts to drive him to the reservation. The author gives an account of the 1877 struggle between the troops led by General Oliver O. Howard and Colonel Nelson Miles and the Nez Percés led by Joseph, Looking Glass, White Bird, and others. He recounts the 1,700-mile retreat of the Indians who fought with outstanding strategy until Joseph surrendered to save the surviving Nez Percés from starving and freezing. The book concludes with an epilogue about Joseph which explains the latter's growth in the public's mind as the symbol of Nez Percé heroism and his efforts to get his exiled people returned to Idaho. There are eleven maps, sketches, and photographs of Nez Percés that illustrate the text. The bibliography includes manuscript and published primary and secondary sources.

RUBY, ROBERT H., and JOHN A. BROWN. *The Cayuse Indians: Imperial Tribesmen of Old Oregon.* Norman: University of Oklahoma Press, 1972. 340pp. Illustrated. Bibliography.

The authors trace the history of the Cayuse, a small nation situated in parts of present-day Oregon and Washington, from ancestral times through the nineteenth century. They describe Cayuse culture before white contact, alliances and enemies, and mobility and wealth due to the acquisition of horses. They discuss the impact of fur traders, contacts with missionaries, the reasons some Cayuses killed several missionaries in 1847, and the subsequent open warfare between the Cayuses and allied tribes and Oregon troops. They describe federal policies imposed on the Cayuses after the Oregon Territory was established in 1848, including the 1855 treaty extinguishing Cayuse title to their land, removal to the Umatilla reservation, and programs of pacification and subjection. The authors tell of those Cayuses who refused to go and joined bands of Nez Percés and other tribes until they were driven to the Umatilla Reservation by soldiers, and discuss further reductions in reservation size at the end of the nineteenth century. There are several appendixes concerning the Whitman Massacre and 1855 treaty. There are eight maps, paintings, photographs, and sketches of Cayuses, their land, and territorial officials. The book is based on personal interviews and unpublished and published primary and secondary works.

————. *Indians of the Pacific Northwest: A History.* Norman: University of Oklahoma Press, 1981. 294pp. Illustrated. Bibliography.

The authors survey the entire Pacific Northwest including more than 100 tribes in fifteen language groups and focusing on Indian-white contact and conflict between 1775 and 1900. There is a narrative of intertribal fighting, skirmishes, battles, and broader wars with the whites, of rivalry among religious groups who came to "civilize" the Indians, and of some attempts at outright extermination. The authors show how the conflict in the Northwest followed a similar pattern that resulted in forcible confinement to reservations and destruction of native cultures. There are eight maps and numerous photographs of Indian people.

————. *The Spokane Indians: Children of the Sun.*

Norman: University of Oklahoma Press, 1970. 346pp. Illustrated. Bibliography.

This book covers the history of the Lower, Middle, and Upper divisions of the Spokane people of the central Columbia Plateau in Washington and parts of Idaho and Montana from ancestral times to the 1960s. The authors describe precontact life, alliances and enemies; the arrival of fur traders and Protestant and Catholic missionaries at the end of the eighteenth century; and the influx of miners in the mid-nineteenth century after gold was discovered in Spokane country. They discuss the warfare between Spokane bands and neighboring tribes who tried to resist white encroachment and the army, detailing Spokane social deterioration after the army's victory, increasing immigration into Spokane country resulting in native-white conflicts, railroad development, and removal from one reservation to another in the late 1800s. The concluding chapters deal with early twentieth-century federal administration of the Spokanes, emphasizing allotment, education, and contemporary Spokane claims against the government for lands lost. There are five maps and illustrations of Spokane people, environments, and missionaries. The book is based on Spokane informants and unpublished and published primary and secondary works.

SLICKPOO, ALLEN P. *Noon Nee-Me-Poo (We, The Nez Percés)*, vol. 1. Lapwai, Idaho: Nez Percé Tribe of Idaho, 1973. 316pp. Illustrated. Bibliography.

In this volume, the author relates the history of the Nez Percé people whose aboriginal domain was located in parts of Idaho, Washington, and Oregon from ancestral times until the present time. He begins with the explanation of the origin of the Nez Percé, describes their culture, and then tells of the Lewis and Clark expedition, which came into contact with the Nation in 1805, and the arrival of missionaries who demoralized the Nez Percés. The author provides an excerpted version of the official proceedings of the 1855 treaty council held at Walla Walla between the U.S. government, Nez Percés, and other tribes, and discusses subsequent treaties that were instruments designed to gain land. He discusses the Nez Percé reservations, the 1877 war, exile into Oklahoma, allotment and the opening of the reservation, the development of tribal government from 1927 to 1935, and the efforts of the Nez Percé Tribal Business Committee to modernize the 1927 Constitution and political structure. There is an appendix of the 1855, 1863, and 1868 treaties. There are two maps and numerous photographs and sketches of Nez Percé country, people, and artifacts. The book is based on interviews with elderly Nez Percés and published primary and secondary works.

TRENHOLM, VIRGINIA COLE, and MAURINE CARLEY. *The Shoshonis: Sentinels of the Rockies.* Norman: University of Oklahoma Press, 1964. 367pp. Illustrated. Bibliography.

The authors trace the history of the Shoshones who all originated in the Great Basin and whose territory stretched across parts of California, Nevada, Utah, Idaho, Wyoming, Colorado, and Oregon

from their origins until 1960. They describe the major cultural division of the Shoshone Nation into the Western groups who clung to their original way of life and the Northern ones who show the influence of the Plains and Plateau peoples. They describe the culture of the Western Shoshones, the Panamints of California, Snakes of Oregon, Shoshones of Nevada and Utah, Goshutes, Webers, and Utes of Utah, and the Snake River Indians of Idaho and tell of the three groups of Northern Shoshones who moved out on the Plains as early as the 1500s. The authors tell of nineteenth-century contacts with explorers and fur traders, troublesome relations with Plains tribes, Mormon missionary efforts, and the life of Washakie. They consider Shoshone resistance to white encroachment and federal Indian policy establishing Shoshone reservations in the last quarter of the nineteenth century. They conclude with the treatment of three religious trends among the Shoshones—the Sun and Ghost Dances and the peyote cult—and Shoshone land cases against the government. There are two maps and photographs of Shoshones. The book is based on unpublished and published primary and secondary materials.

CALIFORNIA

CASTILLO, EDWARD D. "Impact of Euro-American Exploration and Settlement." *Handbook of North American Indians: California,* edited by Robert F. Heizer, pp. 99–127. Vol. 8 *Handbook of North American Indians,* William C. Sturtevant, gen. ed. Washington, D.C.: Smithsonian Institution, 1978.

This chapter reassesses the history of California Indian-white relations from 1769 to the 1970s. The author first considers the Spanish period, 1769–1821, with its Indian policies and establishment of twenty-one missions of the "reduccion" type designed to control Indian peoples and territories which they resisted in both passive and violent ways. He considers how the Spanish invasion and occupation was catastrophic for the coastal Mission natives causing a decline in their population chiefly due to disease. After a look at the Mexican period, 1821–36, and warfare between non-Christianized tribes of the California interior and Mexican colonists, he describes the American period after 1848 with its land hunger, intense exploitation of natural resources, and warfare between Indian peoples and Anglo-Americans commencing almost at once. He explains the destruction of the native economy, new labor conditions forcing accommodation, discriminatory legislation against Indians, and steady loss of life due to disease. The author discusses the negotiation of eighteen treaties by three U.S. treaty commissioners which were rejected by the U.S. Senate; the confusion of authority among federal, state, and local governments in regard to Indian policy; the plan to establish reservations in conjunction with military posts, and the abandonment of this plan. He looks at the disintegration of the colonial system during the 1860s, dwindling populations, the failure of the reservation system due to the hostile frontier society bordering the reserves, and government abandonment of reservations and aid. The author examines the application of the "Quaker Policy" to California natives which added the church as yet another hostile factor to the situation and tells of the social upheaval despite Indian Service attempts at reform. He tells of the 1880s to the 1930s when Indians were forcibly assimilated into white ways through government education, health programs, and allotments. Finally, he views the 1930s to the 1960s when opposing Indian philosophies governed Indian policy, and considers Indian Reorganization Act reform legislation, termination, relocation, and the organized efforts of California Indians in the 1960s and 1970s to solve their own problems. There are one map and several photographs. The article is based on published primary and secondary works. See also Edward D. Castillo, "Twentieth-Century Movements," in *Handbook of North American Indians: California,* pp. 713–17.

COOK, SHERBURNE F. *The Conflict between the California Indian and White Civilization.* Vol. 1. *The Indian Versus the Spanish Mission.* Ibero-Americana 21. Berkeley: University of California Press, 1943. 194pp.
This study investigates the disintegration of California Indians under the influence of Spanish missions from 1770 to 1840. The author assesses and evaluates forces in the mission environment which contributed to the population decline of California Indians. He tells of the Indians' lack of immunity to infection and suboptimal diet, factors which predisposed them to disease. He considers the Indians' fugitivism and physical rebellions and negative individual and group responses to the mission environment. He examines how resistance to conversion and confinement, labor, punishment, sex anomalies, homesickness for the ancestral environment, the mission's overpopulation, and other forces sapped the Indians' collective strength. The author considers the Indians' resistance to the forced labor system and mission curtailment of sex functions, and relates the character and extent of physical disciplinary measures employed under the mission system. He looks at several Indian cultural factors (property rights, language, customs, religious beliefs) and how these were modified by the missions. There are an appendix of the aboriginal population of California and five tables with estimates of population decline, food supply, fugitives, and those punished during the Spanish period. The work is based on unpublished manuscripts and published primary and secondary works. There is some dated terminology.

————. *The Conflict between the California Indian and White Civilization.* Vol. 2, *The Physical and Demographic Reaction of the Non-mission Indians in Colonial and Provincial California.* Ibero-Americana 22. Berkeley: University of California Press, 1943. 56pp.
This study investigates the decline of the population of the interior California Indians who were never under mission influence but were exposed directly to Spanish civilian and military contact

from 1800 to 1848. The author begins by examining the small number of casualties due to recorded Spanish expeditions into the interior and concludes that warfare was a minor factor in the disintegration of the Indian population up to 1848. He looks at the large reduction in population of Pomos, Wappos, Wintuns, Maidus, Sierra Miwoks, and Yokuts due to disease and forced removal of large numbers of Indians from their normal habitat as a result of missionization. He points out aspects of the disintegration of Indian society including the destruction of property, desertion of villages, captivity and removal of Indians, and internecine struggle. Finally, he looks at the interior tribes' active resistance to the Spanish which was powerful enough to minimize the effects of warfare, disease, and forced removal and compares the difference in behavior between Mission Indians and Indians in the interior. There are three tables, two of which list recorded expeditions against interior Indians. The work is based on unpublished manuscripts and published primary and secondary works.

————. *The Conflict between the California Indian and White Civilization.* Vol. 3, *The American Invasion, 1848–1870.* Ibero-Americana 23. Berkeley: University of California Press, 1943. 115pp.
This study investigates the decline of Indian populations from 1848 to 1870 due to conflict with Americans. The author discusses the different modes of colonization and considers the differences in economic and social attitudes towards Indians of Anglo-Americans and Spanish Americans. He looks at the constant losses suffered through direct armed conflict during the early years of American occupation in central and northern California (1848–65) as well as the number of Indian social homicides during the same period due to quarrels, liquor, revenge for injury, and internecine fighting arising from social conditions imposed by the whites. He views the decline in the Indian population due to disease and the serious depletion of the food supply caused by the Americans. He discusses the Indian reactions and adaptions to the white free labor system of the 1850s and 1860s and the force of cultural backgrounds that prevented Indians from readjusting to new economic conditions. He tells of the disintegration of Indian sexual customs, a response by individuals to unfavorable living conditions created through racial conflict. The author concludes with a comparison of Indian response (decline in population) in missions, six tribes in contact with Spanish civilian-military civilization, and contact with Anglo-American settlers. Through his comparison of the effects of war, disease, and starvation for the three periods he concludes that the greatest population decline and adjustments came under the Americans. There are five tables showing Indian population figures 'and declines by tribes. The work is based on unpublished manuscripts and published primary and secondary works.

FORBES, JACK D. *Native Americans of California and Nevada.* Healdsburg, Calif.: Naturegraph, 1969. 202pp. Illustrated. Bibliography.
This book is designed to provide an introduction

to the evolution of Native American peoples, particularly in California and Nevada, to native-white relations that have contributed to present-day conditions of native communities and individuals, and to basic concepts relating to native studies. Forbes begins with the significance of the Native American legacy to American society, considers the origins of Indians, and discusses the earliest Americans and their cultures, particularly those of the California-Great Basin area. He tells of contacts with Europeans, the Spanish invasion of 1769, native resistance and other responses, the Mexican-Indian period of 1822–48 when the Indian population was reduced, and the Anglo-American invasion from 1848 to 1873 during which the California natives were conquered militarily. He deals with conditions faced by Native Americans in the first decades of conquest, 1850–80, and the period of 1880–1900 when Indians resisted federal policies. He examines the twentieth-century native struggles for equality of citizenship, land and compensation, better education, and the end of discrimination and poverty. Concluding chapters discuss the basic concepts for understanding native history and culture and suggest a community responsive, multicultural approach to native education. The author provides a bibliography of selected materials on American Indians, books on California and Nevada Indian history and culture, and lists other source materials for studying California-Nevada Indians. The appendix contains linguistic classifications of California and Nevada Indians. There are seven maps, sketches of artifacts, and photographs of California and Nevada Indians.

HEIZER, ROBERT F., and ALAN J. ALMQUIST. *The Other Californians: Prejudice and Discrimination under Spain, Mexico, and the United States to 1920.* Berkeley: University of California Press, 1971. 278pp. Illustrated. Bibliography.

This is a history of the prejudice and discriminatory acts directed against Native Americans, Mexicans, Chinese, Japanese, and blacks in California from 1770 to 1920. The first chapter, which deals with Indians under Spanish and Mexican rule between 1769 and 1846, stresses the increasingly violent relationships between Indians and Spanish overlords, the Spanish mission system, and Mexican rule from 1821 to 1846. The second chapter, which deals with Indians and white Californians from the 1850s to the 1870s, outlines their violent relationships and tells of native population decimation, slavery, and white restrictive or discriminatory legislation. Several chapters concern the federal government's attempt in the 1850s to make treaties with California natives, the opposition of California legislators to these eighteen treaties, U.S. Senate rejection, and congressional establishment of California reservations, California state constitutional debates on race and rights in 1849, and court decisions involving natives and their lands. The remaining chapters concern "other California," and a chapter at the end contains lengthy documents which illustrate the text. There are one map and etchings of nonwhite minorities.

PHILLIPS, GEORGE HARWOOD. *Chiefs and Challengers: Indian Resistance and Cooperation in Southern California.* Berkeley: University of California Press, 1975. 225pp. Illustrated. Bibliography.

This study focuses on three southern California peoples, the Cahuillas, Cupeños, and Luiseños, their cultures and interrelations, the impact of the Spanish which forced the three groups into making adjustments to preserve their cultures and political sovereignty, and their responses to Spanish, Mexicans, and Americans from the late 1760s to the early 1860s. The author examines the diplomatic, military, and political activities of three territorial chiefs, Cahuilla Juan Antonio, Cupeño Antonio Garra, and Luiseño Manuelito Cota who, from the mid-1840s to the early 1860s, implemented policies of resistance or cooperation toward the Mexicans and Anglo-Americans which helped to determine the general direction of history in the interior of southern California. The conclusion contains an analysis of historical developments between the 1850s and the 1860s. There are four maps and illustrations of missions, natives, and white people relevant to the history of southern California. The book is based on unpublished and published primary and secondary works.

SHIPEK, FLORENCE C. "History of Southern California Mission Indians." In *Handbook of North American Indians: California,* edited by Robert F. Heizer, pp. 610–18. Vol. 8 *Handbook of North American Indians,* William C. Sturtevant, gen. ed. Washington, D.C.: Smithsonian Institution, 1978.

This author discusses twentieth-century socio-political developments among Mission Indians of southern California. She first considers the economic status of Mission Indians since the turn of the century and the continuity of land ownership concepts among various Mission Indian nations. She looks at the political activity of California natives which has involved the use of advocates to plead their causes until the 1960s when the Indians began developing effective organizations to handle their problems within the framework of twentieth-century institutions, modern contractual forms of government, business relationships, and voluntary organizations. There are one map, photographs of California natives, and a table of California Indian trust lands. The article is based on published primary and secondary works.

NORTHWEST COAST

DE LAGUNA, FREDERICA. "Through Alien Eyes: A History of the Yakutat." In *Under Mount Saint Elias: The History and Culture of the Yakutat Tlingit.* Part 1, pp. 107–207. Smithsonian Contributions to Anthropology, vol. 7. Washington, D.C.: Smithsonian Institution Press, 1972. Illustrated. Bibliography.

The author discusses the history of the Yakutat Tlingit from the visit of the first Europeans to the Gulf Coast of Alaska in the mid-eighteenth century until 1900. She describes the late eighteenth-century explorations to Alaska by the Russians, Spanish, English, and French; Russian expeditions to the mainland during the 1780s; and the first known explorations of Yakutat Bay in 1787 which included descriptions of the Tlingits made by English Captain George Dixon. She tells of other voyages of exploration to the Gulf of Alaska by English Captain James Colnett, the Russians Ismailov and Bocharov, and Captain William Douglas all in 1788, by the Spanish in 1791, and by the English Captain George Vancouver in 1794. She describes the plans of the Russian Shelikhov to expand his trading company in Alaska in the 1790s, tells of another Russian expedition to the Yakutats in 1794 by Purtov and Kulikalov, and discusses the establishment of posts at Yakutat and Sitka from 1795 to 1801 by Russians. In addition to describing the destruction of the Russian fort at Sitka by Aleuts in 1802 and the revolt of the Tlingit against the Yakutat fort in 1805, she also tells of epidemics that killed many Yakutats in the early nineteenth century, trade with Russians, and life under American rule after 1867 during which changes were not immediately felt. She discusses the period, beginning in 1880, when white Americans began to study Tlingit culture seriously and also surveys the writings of several scholars which give information about Yakutat culture and their relations to whites. In the conclusion she discusses the effects of gold miners on Yakutat culture, gives the impressions of a missionary, and describes a village at the turn of the century. The history is based on field work and published primary and secondary works.

GUNTHER, ERNA. *Indian Life on the Northwest Coast of North America as Seen by the Early Explorers and Fur Traders during the Last Decades of the Eighteenth Century.* Chicago: University of Chicago Press, 1972. 277pp. Illustrated. Bibliography.

Gunther has assembled all the information available on Northwest Coast Indian life from eighteenth-century travel accounts that relate the character of Indian life before more extensive white settlement began to bring great changes. She begins with the Russians' exploration of Alaska and the first visits by Europeans to the Northwest Coast, the Spanish expedition of 1774 and subsequent Spanish expeditions in 1775 and 1779 which conveyed information about the Indians. She tells of Captain Cook's third voyage to the Pacific Ocean arriving at Nootka Sound in 1778 and summarizes eighteenth-century ethnography of the Nootkas which illustrates native life of the central region of the Northwest Coast. The author discusses major expeditions by eighteenth-century European navigators who gained knowledge about the Strait of Juan de Fuca and the Columbia River and provided detailed information about Northwest Coast natives, particularly the Chinook. She continues with the Spanish and British expeditions through the Inside Passage in the early 1790s and the contacts between Indians and explorers of southeast Alaska, particularly Vancouver who secured information about the Tlingits. She discusses the Haida of the Queen Charlotte Islands and the changes which

had taken place among them, concluding with descriptions of the Chugach of Prince William Sound, the Athapaskans of Cook Inlet, and the Aleuts of Unalaska. The appendix contains a catalog of all known eighteenth-century Northwest Coast objects in European museums and explanations of technological processes of the eighteenth century. There are a map and over fifty photographs and sketches, chiefly of artifacts. The book is largely based on every available eighteenth-century travel account written about the Northwest Coast by European explorers and fur traders as well as the author's examination of artifacts collected on expeditions but now in museums.

HAYS, H. R. *Children of the Raven: The Seven Indian Nations of the Northwest Coast.* New York: McGraw-Hill, 1975. 314pp. Illustrated. Bibliography.

The author describes the history and culture of seven native groups that live along the Pacific coast from the Alaskan Panhandle to northern Washington—The Tlingits, Haidas, Tsimshians, Kwakiutls, Bella Coolas, Nootkas, and Coast Salish—from the eighteenth century to the present. He briefly treats the contacts of Russian, Spanish, English, and French explorers and fur traders with Northwest Coast groups. He discusses the era of fur company control, the period of Russian colonization on the Northwest Coast until 1868, describes the attitudes and intervention of missionaries and Canadian government agents in the lives of Indians during the second half of the nineteenth century, especially noting the Indian-white struggle over the potlatch. He cites the Alaskan Native Brotherhood, organized at the beginning of the twentieth century, and describes the cultural concepts and activities shared by the seven native groups before they were acculturated. The last section of the book deals with the present efforts of Canadian native people to defend their interests, administrative changes which have improved the Indians' condition in some areas, the status of Indians as wards, and a cultural revival among the seven Northwest Coast Nations. There is one map, as well as historic and contemporary photographs of Northwest Coast daily life, housing, carvings, etc. The book is based on recorded interviews and published primary and secondary accounts.

ALASKA

OSWALT, WENDELL H. *Eskimos and Explorers.* Novato, Calif.: Chandler & Sharp, 1979. 368pp. Illustrated. Bibliography.

This book is a history of western contact with Eskimos from about A.D. 1000 to the present over the territory that extends from Alaska to Greenland. The author discusses the Norse experience, early northern encounters, western and eastern Greenlanders, and Polar and Canadian Eskimos. He also describes Eskimos of southwestern Alaska before contact with explorers, Russian penetration into Alaska, and Eskimo culture after discovery. There are discussions of regional material culture and trade, missionaries, health conditions, economic development, and political domination. There is an appendix on aboriginal population and the distribution of tribes and the Eskimo culture area. There are over seventy drawings of Eskimos, their artifacts, way of life, and contact with Europeans as well as two foldout maps. The book is based upon explorers' accounts about Eskimos.

RAY, DOROTHY JEAN. *The Eskimos of Bering Strait, 1650–1898.* Seattle: University of Washington Press, 1975. 305pp. Illustrated. Bibliography.

Ray describes and analyzes changes that took place in the Bering Strait Eskimo culture from 1650 to 1898. First she describes the Bering Strait geography, then deals with the area's history divided into four broad time periods based on the character and scope of European activities that began in Russian Siberia and continued in Russian America, later Alaska. She discusses the first period, 1650–1732, a time in which all information about Alaska came through Russian Cossacks; the second period, 1778–1833, a time of European and Russian explorations; the period of 1833–67 and coastal commerce; and the last period, 1867–98, which found the Americans at Bering Strait. She includes observations of the Bering Strait Eskimos by James Cook, Ivan Kobelev, Joseph Billings, Otto Von Kotzebue, and other Russian explorers; a summary of the Bering Strait culture based on these observations; and an explanation of tribal distribution, population, political organization, and utilization of land by twenty or so Eskimo tribes during the period 1778–1833. The author discusses the diaries and publications of telegraph men which contain material about Bering Strait Eskimo culture from 1848 to 1867, the American purchase of Alaska in 1867, and the changes brought about in late nineteenth-century Eskimo life by mining activities, schools, missions, and the reindeer industry. She concludes with a summary of Bering Strait culture from 1867 to 1898 and the voluntary acculturation of the Eskimos. There are five maps and photography and drawings of Eskimos and their culture. The book is based on Eskimo informants and unpublished and published primary sources.

VAN STONE, JAMES W. *Eskimos of the Nushagak River: An Ethnographic History.* University of Washington Publications in Anthropology, vol. 15. Seattle: University of Washington Press, 1967. 192pp. Illustrated. Bibliography.

The author examines the cultural changes of Nushagak Eskimos of southwestern Alaska after contact with Russians and Americans from the late eighteenth century to contemporary times. The introduction gives a geographical and ethnological background of the Nushagak region. In the first part, the author outlines the history of Russian and American exploration of the Nushagak River region from 1778 to 1935. He examines the activities of agents of culture change, the Russian Orthodox and Moravian churches, and fur traders, particularly the Russian-American Company, and surveys the commercial fishing industry that developed during the 1890s, mining and reindeer herding, educational

programs of the missions, and twentieth-century medical services. The second part reconstructs Eskimo population groupings, settlement patterns, and the yearly subsistence cycle activities in the nineteenth and early twentieth century and describes present-day subsistence activities and settlement patterns. The author concludes by comparing problems peculiar to the Nushagak with those of Eskimos of other areas and considers the general problems of cultural change characteristic of Alaska. There are four maps. The book is based on the author's field work and Russian and English archival materials.

BIBLIOGRAPHIES

BEAN, LOWELL JOHN, and SYLVIA BRAKKE VANE. *California Indians: Primary Resources—A Guide to Manuscripts, Artifacts, Documents, Serials, Music and Illustrations.* Ramona, Calif.: Ballena Press, 1977. 227pp.

This bibliography, which is a guide to locating institutions that hold primary resource materials on California Indians, begins with a discussion on the location and use of published and archival government documents as a resource for both ethnography and ethnohistory of California's indigenous peoples. The main body of the book is organized alphabetically by geographical areas of California, states other than California, and other countries. For each area institutions are named which hold manuscripts, archival material, photographs, maps, newspapers, periodicals, pamphlets, artifacts, recordings, special collections, and other resources, and the holdings are described. There are resources arranged by type rather than area including serial publications, audiovisual materials, and sources of out-of-print but commercially available materials, and a bibliography of reference and other pertinent volumes.

CUTHBERTSON, STUART, and JOHN C. EWERS. *A Preliminary Bibliography on the American Fur Trade.* St. Louis: U.S. Dept. of the Interior, National Park Service, 1939. 191pp.

This bibliography lists published materials on Indians and the American fur trade divided into areas of New France, New England, New Netherland, New Sweden and New York, Virginia and Maryland, the Carolinas and the Southeast, Pennsylvania and the Ohio Valley, the Great Lakes region, Mississippi Valley, Missouri and Platte Valleys, the Rockies north of the Arkansas, the Arkansas and the Southwest, Hudson Bay and western Canada, the Pacific Slope and Alaska. There are sources covering broader areas such as colonial America, histories, commerce, and material about the buffalo.

DEPUY, HENRY F. *A Bibliography of the English Colonial Treaties with the American Indians Including a Synopsis of Each Treaty.* New York: Lenox Club, 1917; reprint ed.: New York: AMS Press, 1971. 50pp. Illustrated.

This monograph includes fifty-four treaties dating from 1677 to 1768 that were made between

Indians and the English colonies. A very brief synopsis of the contents of each treaty is given, intended to hint at the main subjects discussed in the treaty, and to indicate where copies of the treaty may be located in principal libraries and private collections. The author gives the date of when and where each treaty was signed and published. There are fifty facsimiles of title pages of the printed treaties.

DONNELLY, JOSEPH P. *A Tentative Bibliography for the Colonial Fur Trade in the American Colonies: 1608–1800.* Saint Louis University Studies Monograph Series, Social Sciences no. 2. St. Louis: Saint Louis University Press, 1947. 48pp.

This bibliography includes works on the colonial fur trade from 1608 to 1800 listed under six sections: general bibliographical aids, colonial New England, the middle colonies, the southern colonies, imperial control of the fur trade, and Anglo-Spanish rivalry. Each section, except the first, is divided into four types of works—general, primary sources, secondary sources, and periodical literature.

FENTON, WILLIAM N. *American Indian and White Relations to 1830: Needs and Opportunities for Study.* Chapel Hill: University of North Carolina Press, 1957. 139pp.

The book begins with an essay entitled "Indian and White Relations in Eastern North America: A Common Ground for History and Ethnology" by Fenton which discusses Indian ethnography for historians, historical materials on Indian and white relations, particularly the Iroquois, the method of ethnohistory, and common tasks which history and ethnology can undertake for the common enrichment of both disciplines. He discusses general ethnographic works of importance to historians and cites those works about tribes that come from four language families: Algonquian, Iroquoian, Siouan, and Muskogean. The bibliography that follows the essay is divided into seven categories: (1) reference and bibliographical aids; (2) ethnological literature; (3) historical literature written before and after 1850; (4) selected serials; (5) manuscript sources in New England, the Middle Atlantic, District of Columbia, South, Middle West, Far West, Canada, and on microfilm; (6) documentary publications; and (7) works on special topics: portraiture, literature, songs, art, biography, autobiography, captivities, missions and education, government policy, and the Indian in literature and thought.

HEIZER, ROBERT F.; KAREN M. NISSEN; and EDWARD D. CASTILLO. *California Indian History: A Classified and Annotated Guide to Source Materials.* Ramona, Calif.: Ballena Press, 1975. 90pp.

This topical and chronological bibliography provides a guide to most of the important and generally available sources on California Indian history from ancient to contemporary times. There are 685 citations, many of which are annotated, classified under seven headings with each subdivided into specific subjects. The first chapter, "The Period of Native History (?B.C.–1542A.D.)" is divided into Archaeology: Prehistoric and Historic; Linguistics;

Physical Anthropology; Demography; Ethnography; Tribal Ethnographies, General Surveys, Social-Political Organization, War, Religion, Material Culture, Economy, and World View; and Folklore and Music. The second chapter, "Period of Spanish and Mexican Contact (1542–1846)" is divided into Exploration, Settlement, and Indian Response. The third chapter, "Period of Anglo Conquest (1846–1873)" is divided into Legal Status of Indians, Gold Rush, Treaty-Making, Land Titles, Reservations, and Social Conditions. The fourth chapter "Aftermath of Conquest (1873–1920)" is divided into Reservation Affairs, Condition of Indians, Acculturation, Condition of Mission Indians of Southern California, Education, Religious Movements, Legal Status of Indians, and Claims Cases. The fifth chapter, "Period of Indian Nationalism (1920–1974)" is divided into Indian Welfare Organizations, Political Organizations of Indians, and Recent Indian Nationalism. The sixth chapter contains works written by Indians and the seventh, source materials, includes museum collections, documentary archives, films, pictorial archives, and bibliographies. There are indexes of tribes and authors.

KLUCKHOHN, CLYDE A., and KATHERINE SPENCER. *A Bibliography of Navajo Indians.* New York: J. J. Augustin, 1940. 93pp.

This annotated bibliography on Navajos from ancestral to contemporary times is divided into six sections. The first deals with bibliographies, reference works, catalogs, and collections of documents pertaining to the Southwest; the second deals with primary and secondary historical works on Navajos; and the third contains materials which give information on physical geography, topography, climate, and the use of flora and fauna by Navajos. The fourth section lists anthropological materials including works on archaeology and origins, physical anthropology (including articles on medical work and on population), linguistics and vocabularies, and ethnological works on material culture, economy and technology, social organization, ceremonialism and mythology, music and poetry, witchcraft, and accounts of other tribes which have notes on the Navajo. The fifth section deals with Navajo-white relations, and the last contains materials on Navajos in nonfiction, fiction, plays, poetry, songs, and juvenile literature. There is an index of authors.

PRUCHA, FRANCIS PAUL. *A Bibliographical Guide to the History of Indian-White Relations in the United States.* Chicago: University of Chicago Press, 1977. 454pp.

This bibliographic guide is intended as a tool for persons primarily interested in the history of Indian-white relations from colonial days to the present in the United States. British colonial Indian affairs have been included, but Canadian items have generally been excluded as well as materials dealing with Spanish-Indian relations in what is now the United States. This bibliography lists 9,705 items published through 1974, but a few items published later have been included. Part 1 lists the important guides and other reference works that will direct readers to materials on Indian affairs in government archives and publications, in manuscript collections, in newspapers and periodicals, and in other categories of sources not limited to Indian-white relations, only. Part 2 gives lists of books, articles, and other published works dealing with a wide variety of Indian-white relations. The bibliography is organized by subjects that cut across the whole continuum of Indian-white relations, and there are introductions which provide a schematic overview of each section on the history of Indian-white relationships. Since each work is entered in the bibliography only once, there is an extensive index to help locate items that touch on given topics. The chapters are entitled "Materials in the National Archives," "Documents of the Federal Government," "Guides to Manuscripts," "Guides to Other Sources," "Indian Affairs/Indian Policy," "The Indian Department," "Treaties and Councils," "Land and the Indians," "Military Relations," "Trade and Traders," "Missions and Missionaries," "Legal Relations," "Indian Educations," "Indian Health," "Social and Economic Developments," and "Indians and Indian Groups." The last chapter entitled "Special Topics" includes Indian Captivities, Peace Medals, Delegations, Concepts and Images of the Indian, Ideas on Race, Contributions of Indians to American Life, Indian Place-Names, Persons Influential in Indian Affairs, Indian Writings, and On the Writing of Indian History.

———. *Indian-White Relations in the United States: A Bibliography of Works Published 1975–1980.* Lincoln: University of Nebraska Press, 1982. 180pp.
This supplement to *A Bibliographical Guide to the History of Indian-White Relations in the United States* lists 3,400 items for the period 1975–80. Topics include federal Indian policy, treaties, education, legal relations, health, land and other resources, trade relations, missions and missionaries, agents and the Bureau of Indian Affairs, reservations, and Indian wars. Special topics include demography, white images of Indians, Indians in literature and art, and the writing of Indian history. There is a new subheading entitled "Indian Women," and popular interest in Indians is covered in sections devoted to current comments on Indian affairs. There is a large section which lists works that focus on tribes or regional groups of Indians.

REBER, BRUCE. *The United States Army and the Indian Wars in the Trans-Mississippi West, 1860–1898.* Special Bibliography 17. Carlisle Barracks, Pa.: U.S. Army Military History Institute, 1978. 186pp.
This bibliography of books and journal articles makes available the holdings of the U.S. Army Military History Institute on the Indian wars in the trans-Mississippi West from 1860 to 1898, materials pertaining to the Carlisle Indian School from 1879 to 1918, and descriptions of the Institute's photographic collections depicting the military history of the American West, 1880–98. The first part contains general references, materials categorized under twenty-three geographical regions, twenty-

four tribes, forts, military units, personal reminiscences, memoirs, biographies, and miscellaneous topics including bibliographies. The second part lists manuscript holdings on the Indian wars, and the third contains holdings on the Carlisle Indian School.

ROUSE, IRVING, and JOHN M. GOGGIN. *An Anthropological Bibliography of the Eastern Seaboard.* Eastern States Archaeological Federation Research Publication no. 1. New Haven, Conn.: By the Federation, 1947. 174pp.
This unannotated bibliography contains three sections of materials ("Archaeology," "Ethnology," and "Indian History") dealing only with the states on the Atlantic Seaboard from the seventeenth to the twentieth century. Items have not been eliminated from this listing because of poor quality. The third section, "Indian History," contains items which are narrative rather than analytical and which deal primarily with events and personalities rather than with customs, or racial or linguistic categories. The majority of items are concerned wholly or in part with relations between Indians and European settlers. Others include tribal histories, travel accounts, biographies of Indian or white persons who have figured prominently in relations between Indians and whites, and studies of Indian place-names or trails. The historical section is divided into geographic regions. Following an introduction in which items dealing with the whole or major part of the eastern seaboard can be found, there are sections on eastern Canada divided into general, Labrador, New Brunswick, Newfoundland, Nova Scotia, Quebec, and southeastern Ontario; New England states divided into general, Connecticut, Maine, Massachusetts, New Hampshire, and Vermont; Mid-Atlantic states divided into general, Delaware, Maryland, New Jersey, New York, Pennsylvania, and West Virginia; and southeastern states divided into general, Florida, Georgia, North and South Carolina, and Virginia.

SMITH, DWIGHT L. *Indians of the United States and Canada: A Bibliography.* Santa Barbara, Calif.: American Bibliographical Center-CLIO Press, 1973. 450pp.
This bibliography contains 1,771 selected abstracts gathered from *America: History and Life,* an abstracts publication. The articles constitute a bibliographical report on Native American scholarship which has appeared in historical and social science periodic literature of the world from 1954 to 1972. The first section includes pre-Columbian Indian history divided into general and ten geographical regions. The second section, tribal history, 1492–1900, is divided into ten regions and further divided by tribes. The third section deals with materials on general Indian history from 1492 to 1900, with no regional breakdown, and the last section on Indians in the twentieth century deals with general, urban, and regional areas further divided by tribes. There is an index with subject, author, biographical, and geographical entries.

TYLER, S. LYMAN. *The Ute People: A Bibliographical*

Checklist. Indian Studies No. 3. Provo, Utah: Brigham Young University, 1964. 120pp.

This unannotated bibliography lists 1,234 materials pertinent to the history of the Ute Indians who frequented western Colorado, northern New Mexico and Arizona, and most of Utah, their linguistic relatives, and other neighboring Indian groups from 1538 to contemporary times. The work is divided into bibliographies and guides; Spanish and English manuscript materials for the Spanish and Mexican periods, 1538–1845; U.S. government documents; Utah territorial documents; contemporary newspapers and periodicals; and the longest section which contains hundreds of published primary and secondary books, articles, and theses.

WEIMAN, PAUL L. *A Bibliography of the Iroquoian Literature: Partially Annotated.* New York State Museum and Science Service, Bulletin no. 411.

Albany: University of the State of New York, 1969. 254pp.

This bibliography lists works concerned mainly with the Five Iroquois Nations although materials on other Iroquoian groups are included. The annotations of certain books and articles briefly summarize the contents, are seldom critical, and are included because they are readily available. Categories include archaeology, bibliography, biography, ceremonialism and religion, contemporary movements, folklore and mythology, general ethnology and history, geographic place-names, herbalism, foods, medicinal lore, and tobacco. There is a section on history and culture contacts subdivided into Dutch, English, and American; French and Canadian; state and federal relations; and twentieth-century acculturation and conservatism. The concluding categories include language, material culture, physical anthropology, and social and political organization.

11 POPULATION AND DEMOGRAPHY

Demography, the study of population statistics, is a changing science and current controversies in the field over North American aboriginal population are providing opportunities for demographers to develop new methods. One of the earliest estimates of the aboriginal population of North America was done by Mooney in 1928 (p. 175). He used dead reckoning and projected straight back from current census records to produce his estimate. Recently demographers have challenged Mooney's techniques. For example, in 1966 Dobyns (p. 174), in order to estimate an aboriginal population, postulated a twenty to one reduction in the aboriginal population over the last five hundred years, accounting for that population reduction by disease, particularly disease brought by whites. As a consequence, a discussion of disease dynamics is an important part of Dobyns's demographic work. This approach is quite different from any of the methods Mooney used thirty-eight years before. For further discussions of current demographic theory and technique Denevan (p. 174) has compiled eight essays which give an overview of the controversial past estimates of aboriginal populations and an indication of new approaches to the question. Jacobs (p. 175) also reviews the work of current and past demographers. These works in addition to Dobyns's study vividly illustrate the way an important controversy produces change in an entire field of inquiry.

The question that is producing so much controversy in current demographic circles is what was the population of Native Americans at the time of the arrival of Europeans? Mooney's dead reckoning and projecting straight back from current census records yielded an estimate of 1,152,950. However, Dobyns's methods suggest a hemispheric contact population of 90 million. Other estimates in Jacobs place the Western Hemisphere population at between 50 and 100 million. Most current demographers are estimating such large contact populations.

These large estimates of the aboriginal population at contact with the Europeans raise the question of why there was such a dramatic change in population over the past few hundred years. Many demographers suggest that diseases introduced by whites account for much of the change. Crosby (p. 174) discusses the disastrous consequences of Old World diseases in two chapters. Dobyns (p. 174) studies disease at length in his work on aboriginal population figures. Stearn and Stearn (p. 175) document the effect of smallpox, reporting a fatality rate of 55 to 90 percent in some tribes while among whites the rate was 10 to 15 percent. Further, they suggest that the disease was used as a tool for genocide by the European invaders. Cook (p. 175) also discusses smallpox and several other Old World diseases such as tuberculosis and dysentery in his article on disease among New England Indians. Martin (p. 175) suggests that wildlife diseases played a part in the depopulation of the Native Americans. He advances evidence of seventeenth- and eighteenth-century wildlife epidemics which had never occurred before contact, maintaining that there was a causal relationship between animal epidemics and human epidemics. Various demographers suggest that alcohol, reservation life, and warfare also took a large toll on the native population.

Though disease, war, and hardship obliterated the American Indian population in the last three centuries, the twentieth century seems to have brought an upswing in population. The 1970 U.S. Census (p. 175) documents the current Indian population as well as its social condition. In addition, Wissler's study (p. 175) of Plains Indians cites an increase in population after 1905. The demographic history of a southwestern Indian community by Aberle et al. (p. 176) also documents a certain amount of population recovery in the twentieth century. However, an increase in population does not necessarily indicate a return to prosperity. The 1970 Census presents a grim picture of the social and economic status of most Indians in the United States today.

CROSBY, ALFRED W. JR. *The Columbian Exchange: Biological and Cultural Consequences of 1492.* Westport, Conn.: Greenwood Press, 1972. 268pp. Illustrated. Bibliography.

Crosby's book deals with all aspects of European/Native American historical contact, beginning with a contrast of Old and New World flora, fauna, and human societies. Two chapters deal with the disastrous consequences of the introduction of Old World diseases, which, when coupled with warfare, decimated so many Native American societies. One of the disease chapters reappraises the controversial early history of syphilis. Other sections deal with the exchange of edible and nonedible plants and animals, and the effects of New World foods on Old World demography. A final chapter describes the ongoing nature of the Old/New World exchanges. The author concludes with an evaluation of the exchange: "The Columbian Exchange has left us [humanity] with not a richer but a more impoverished genetic pool. We, all of the life on this planet, are the less for Columbus, and the impoverishment will increase." Three maps depict the world distribution of blood types and there are reproductions of "New World prints."

DENEVAN, WILLIAM M., ed. *The Native Population of the Americas in 1492.* Madison: University of Wisconsin Press, 1976. 353pp. Illustrated. Bibliography.

This is a collection of eight essays on the native population of North and South America at the time of first European contact. Chapters are divided geo- graphically (Caribbean, Central America, and Yucatán; Mexico; South America; and North America); the particular regions considered are Hispaniola, Nicaragua, central Mexico, the central Andes, Argentina, and Amazonia. One essay dealing with North America, "The Sources and Methodology for Mooney's Estimates of North American Indian Populations" by Douglas H. Ubelaker, provides some overview of controversial past estimates and indications of new approaches. There are tables of population statistics, graphs of population history, and a 600-entry bibliography.

DOBYNS, HENRY F. "Estimating Aboriginal American Population: An Appraisal of Techniques with a New Hemispheric Estimate." *Current Anthropology* 7 (1966):395–416.

The author analyzes "methodological reasons why most prior estimates of aboriginal American population imply small scale preconquest societies and concludes that the population was far larger than has been thought." He notes the great range in estimates, finds projecting backward from current Indian census figures and dead reckoning particularly poor techniques, and ethnohistorical methods less deficient. Dobyns postulates a twenty to one reduction in aboriginal population over the past 500 years, which suggests a hemispheric contact population of 90 million. He devotes considerable time to the discussion of disease dynamics as they affected Native Americans. There are two tables: one illustrates initial Indian mortality in Mexico and Central America and one the estimated aboriginal population by region—North America, Mexico, Central America, Caribbean islands, Andean civilization, and marginal South America.

JACOBS, WILBUR R. "The Tip of an Iceberg: Pre-Columbian Indian Demography and Some Implications for Revisionism." *William and Mary Quarterly* 31 (1974):123–32.

This work reviews the efforts of contemporary demographers to more accurately estimate the aboriginal population of the Americas. The earlier population figures of James Mooney, Alfred L. Kroeber, and Ángel Rosenblat are subjected to criticism. New estimates place the Western Hemisphere population at between 50 and 100 million. "Thus we have an invasion of Europeans into areas that were even more densely settled than parts of Europe." The works of Sherburne Cook, Woodrow Borah, and Henry Dobyns are favorably reviewed.

MARTIN, CALVIN. "Wildlife Diseases as a Factor in the Depopulation of the North American Indian." *The Western Historical Quarterly* 7 (1976):47–62.

Martin provides a general account of the destructive spread of European diseases through the aboriginal communities of the New World and notes the variety in research into the role zoonotic diseases may have played in the depopulation of Native Americans. He reviews evidence of epizootics (wildlife epidemics) in the seventeenth and eighteenth centuries which appear never to have occurred prior to contact, arguing that the evidence suggests causal relationships between epizootics and human epidemics in some instances. The tribes referenced include Blackfeet, Cree, Ottawa, and Chippewa.

MOONEY, JAMES. *The Aboriginal Population of America North of Mexico.* Smithsonian Miscellaneous Collections 80, no. 7. Washington, D.C.: Government Printing Office, 1928. 40pp. Bibliography.

Mooney's work is the first widely known attempt to assess the aboriginal population of North America above the Rio Grande. His actual figures for early contact population are generally low; by current demographic theory they are off by a factor of about ten. Figures are arranged by geographic region and, within regions, by tribe. Regions include North Atlantic states, South Atlantic states, Gulf states, Central states, the Plains, the Columbia region, California, central Rocky Mountain region, New Mexico and Arizona, Greenland, eastern Canada, central Canada, British Columbia, and Alaska. Mooney provides an "early" (usually 1600) figure (later for western Canadian and Alaskan groups) and an estimate of the 1900 or 1906 population. The total "early" estimate is 1,152,950; the 1900/1906 figure is 406,506.

STEARN, E. WAGNER, and ALLEN E. STEARN. *The Effect of Smallpox on the Density of the Amerindian.* Boston: Bruce Humphries, 1945. 153pp. Bibliography.

This work documents the history of smallpox, the most feared and destructive Old World disease responsible for more Native American deaths during the first centuries of European contact than any other single cause, and its use as a tool for genocide by the European invaders of the Western Hemisphere. Case fatality among certain tribes during isolated epidemics of 55 to over 90 percent has been reported, while case fatality of New England Europeans during epidemics was more on the order of 10 to 15 percent. Dense populations in Central and Meso-America and Massachusetts promoted the rapid spread of all contagious diseases. Sections deal with the disease in Mexico and Central America in the sixteenth century, in New England and eastern Canada in the seventeenth century, its general spread in the eighteenth century, immunization of native peoples, the disease in the nineteenth and twentieth centuries, and the effect and control of smallpox among Native Americans. Two tables depict the population and mortality of selected tribes in the mid-nineteenth century and case statistics for the period 1898–1903.

U.S. DEPARTMENT OF COMMERCE. *1970 Census of Population Subject Reports: American Indians.* Washington, D.C.: Department of Commerce, 1973. 192pp. Illustrated.

The first special report of the Bureau of the Census on Native Americans in this century includes a brief discussion of methodology and sections on Indian population by age, sex, urban or rural residence, social and economic characteristics, family income and housing characteristics, employment characteristics, population by tribe, reservation population, and first language of Indians. Two maps depict the 1970 U.S. standard metropolitan statistical areas and U.S. regions and geographic divisions. The population statistics of the work are based on a 20 percent sampling of the population and depended upon self-identification of American Indian background.

NORTHEAST

COOK, SHERBURNE F. "The Significance of Disease in the Extinction of the New England Indians." *Human Biology* 45 (1973):485–508. Bibliography.

This article focuses on the decline in population of New England tribes after contact with whites. The relatively dense population of the Massachusetts Bay area promoted the onslaught of extremely lethal epidemics, two of the worst being the plague in 1617 and smallpox in 1633. Chronic maladies such as tuberculosis and dysentery also promoted population decline. Two tables document the population decline of the Wampanoag people on Martha's Vineyard and Nantucket between 1640 and 1800.

GREAT PLAINS

WISSLER, CLARK. *Population Changes among the Northern Plains Indians.* Yale University Publications in Anthropology no. 1. New Haven, Conn.: Yale University Press, 1936. 20pp. Bibliography.

Here the author attempts to determine the relative sizes of Northern Plains tribes during the fur trade period, defined as 1670 to 1870, and to document population trends during the reservation period, 1870 to the time of publication. Tribes considered include Blackfeet, Blood, Piegan, Gros Ventre, Sarsi, Assiniboin, and Western Cree. Later investigators have found many of the sources controversial. General references are made to particular smallpox epidemics. Statistics for the reservation period, taken from U.S. and Canadian government records, reveal declining populations until about 1905 and the subsequent recovery of populations for all tribes.

SOUTHWEST

ABERLE, S. D.; J. H. WATKINS; and E. H. PITNEY. "The Vital History of San Juan Pueblo." *Human Biology* 12 (1940):141–87. Illustrated. Bibliography.

This work concerns the historical demography of the San Juan Pueblo since 1790, over 200 years after initial white contact which resulted in substantial population decline. However, the population history illustrates a substantial recovery in the twentieth century. Sections deal with population trends, characteristics of family size, age and sex, natality, total birth trends, multiple birth trends, fertility, mortality, and epidemics. Included, is a map of San Juan pueblo lands as well as numerous tables and graphs of demographic statistics. The bibliography includes primary accounts, genealogies, and Spanish, Mexican, and U.S. government documents.

CALIFORNIA

ASCHMANN, HOMER. *The Central Desert of Baja California: Demography and Ecology.* Ibero-Americana, vol. 42. Berkeley: University of California Press, 1959. 315pp. Illustrated. Bibliography.

Aschmann deals with the historical demography of Baja California in detail. Sections include the physical character of the Central Desert, European-Native American contact, aboriginal peoples, ecology of the Central Desert Indians, aboriginal demographic equilibrium, size of the aboriginal population, Mission Indian history, and causes for Mission Indian population decline. Tribes of the Central Desert and nearby region include the Nakipa, Cochimi Alcwa'ala, (Paipai), and Koliwa. Ten figures depict demographic statistics and nine maps illustrate plant and precipitation distributions, regions of Baja California, European expansion, and native languages and Spanish missions. Plates show plants and views of human activities.

BIBLIOGRAPHY

DOBYNS, HENRY F. *Native American Historical Demography: A Critical Bibliography.* Bloomington: Indiana University Press, 1976. 95pp.

This is the sixth volume in the Newberry Library series of critical bibliographies. The author reviews sources dealing with the demography of natives in North and South America, discussing the reasons why scholars have traditionally underestimated the aboriginal population of the New World. The effects of European diseases, warfare, the fur trade, and alcohol are summarized. Two hundred and seventeen sources are reviewed. The discussion is divided into sections on aboriginal population; history of epidemics; endemic diseases, warfare, and famine; depopulation trends; population recovery; demographic case studies; and published federal sources on Native American populations. The vast majority of sources cited are fairly recent (post-1950); the oldest work mentioned dates to 1822. Dobyns recommends works for the beginner and for a basic library collection.

12   HEALTH, MEDICINE, AND DISEASE

To American Indians of the past and to many in the present, medicine means more than treating diseases and healing injuries.

> All these things which we speak of as medicine the Indian calls mysterious, and when he calls them mysterious this only means that they are beyond his power to account for... All Indian languages have words which are the equivalent of our word medicine, sometimes with curative properties; but the Indian's translation of "medicine," used in the sense of magical or supernatural, would be mysterious, inexplicable, unaccountable.[1]

Another author, Levy (p. 179), states that the Indian concept of medicine goes far beyond the white notion of either healing through drugs or the healing arts in general to embrace the notion of supernatural power for the benefit of the whole tribe. To many Native Americans, medicine is intimately connected with religion, they are aspects of the same thing. Medicine has formalized religious aspects, ceremonial rituals that are not aimed at treating the injury or disease but rather are performed in order to discover why a particular injury or disease has occurred; these ceremonials are aimed at healing the whole person. Native American medicine therefore has combined two systems of healing, the practical alleviation of symptoms and the religious ceremony which cures the whole person. The tribes of North America have had a wide range of religious and healing systems ranging from one religious-medical specialist, often called a shaman, who performs all the healing tasks in groups such as the Eskimos, to healing societies such as the Midewiwin of the Ojibways (Chippewas). The works by Crockett (p. 179), Jilek (p. 181), Levy (p. 179), and Vogel (p. 180) look at these aspects of Indian culture.

The Native American concept of medicine also embraces some of the principles of modern psychiatry. Bahr (p. 180) discusses several of the reasons why Indian curing shares more with psychiatry than with any other branch of Western medicine. For example, the commitment to explore "How does it feel" defines a large area common to psychiatry and Indian curing. Jilek (p. 181) describes how the mental health problems of Coast Salish Indians were treated through combining psychiatric management with indigenous procedures.

---

1. Virgil J. Vogel, *American Indian Medicine* (Norman: University of Oklahoma Press, 1970), p. 22.

The works in this section by Bahr (p. 180), Bergman (p. 181), Levy (p. 179), and Vogel (p. 180) contain information on the traditional native theories of disease and medicine and descriptions of healing ceremonies and medicine men who have power beyond that of physical healing. There are works that contain accounts of the Native Americans' practical knowledge. Their knowledge and use of plants was extensive. It has been estimated that well over 200 drugs of the official U.S. drug compendia had been used by Indians.[2] Some works discuss the medical practices of individual tribes (Andros, p. 180; Ashburn, below; Bergman, p. 181; Hrdlička, p. 179; Whiting, p. 181) as well as native contributions to medicine and pharmacology (Vogel, p. 180; Brooks, p. 179). There are descriptions of bleeding techniques, sweat baths, rubbing and sucking, bone setting, suturing, dressing fractures, herbs for treating diseases, heat treatments, purgatives, enemas, cauterization, poultices, and many other techniques all known to a degree by various tribes.

Some of the works in the field also describe the incidence and destructive effects of Old World diseases on Indian populations which had little immunity to them (Andros, Ashburn, Major, p. 179). The diseases of smallpox, measles, scarlet fever, typhus fever, malaria, yellow fever, tuberculosis, meningitis, diptheria, influenza, syphilis, dysentery, and others played leading roles in shaping the course of North American Indian history. Some of the indigenous afflictions are reviewed such as digestive disorders, pneumonia, and arthritis (Hrdlička). Some works discuss the medical use of peyote (La Barre, p. 179) and the use of magic in treating mental disease in contact societies largely caused by the cataclysmic effects of diseases which decimated communities (Major).

There are several articles that describe contemporary mental health problems of Native Americans (Crockett, p. 179; National Institute of Mental Health, p. 180; Westermeyer, p. 180). The writers examine the incidence and severity of Indian alcoholism and the suicide problem of the American Indian population which has a suicide rate about twice the national average.

Vogel's *American Indian Medicine* (p. 180) contains a forty-four page unannotated bibliography listing hundreds of unpublished and published materials concerning all aspects of Native American health, disease, medicine, pharmacology, theories of disease, etc. The Barrow bibliography (p. 181) focuses on sources that deal with contemporary native health, medicine, and disease.

Most of the works in this section were written without the input of native peoples, particularly traditional medicine people. The information has come from early missionary accounts, notes of travelers, U.S. army surgeons and other medical practitioners, and the reports of physicians on reservations. Consequently, some of the materials contain Euro-American misconceptions about traditional native medical beliefs and practices.

ASHBURN, P. M. *The Ranks of Death: A Medical History of the Conquest of America.* Edited by Frank Ashburn. New York: Coward McCann, 1947. 298pp. Bibliography.

This is a medical history of the conquest of America, told in the language of a military historian. The author brings together materials on the role a variety of diseases played in the invasion of the

2. Michael A. Weiner, *Earth Medicine—Earth Food: Plant Remedies, Drugs, and Natural Foods by the North American Indians* (New York: Collier, 1980), p. 7.

Western Hemisphere: smallpox/measles/scarlet fever/typhus fever/malaria/yellow fever/tuberculosis/pleurisy/pneumonia/diphtheria/influenza/modorra/meningitis/intestinal infections and parasitic worms (dysentery, hookworm, etc.)/syphilis, skin diseases, and other miscellaneous diseases. Chapters also deal with the black migration to the Americas, European and Native American medical techniques at the time of contact, and famine and scurvy as afflictions of the invaders.

BROOKS, HARLOW. "The Medicine of the American Indian." *Journal of Laboratory and Clinical Medicine* 19, no. 1 (October 1933):1–23.

Brooks notes that Western medicine, and all other medicines, are evolutionary in nature, building upon what has been discovered before. He also writes that Westerners appreciate the history of Native America less than that of any other world area, and that "American Indian" is a misnomer for hundreds of distinct cultures. Remarks about traditional medicine are generally restricted to the Ojibway, Sioux, Blackfeet, Apache, Navajo, and Puebloan peoples. Some Native American contributions to Euro-America including architecture and artistic influence, corn, cocoa, quinine, tobacco, potatoes, beans, squash, melons, tomatoes, and irrigation techniques are briefly mentioned. The author expresses great respect and admiration for native medicine systems and writes "pioneer medicine in this country has been almost entirely derived from Indian methods" and "there are few methods of modern medicine which were not represented in kind, if not in precise technic by Indian methods." He discusses how some of the world's most important drugs and medicinal substances are Native American, reviews early sources of observation of medical practices, as well as medical practices themselves, and briefly summarizes important herbal contributions.

CROCKETT, DAVID C. "Medicine among the American Indians." *HSMHA Health Reports* 85, no. 5 (May 1971):399–407. Illustrated.

Crockett reviews cultural, religious, and other practices among American Indians. He looks at the functions of the medicine men and briefly describes the medicinal and health practices of seven distinct cultural groups, both in the past and in the present. The seven groups considered are the people of the eastern forests, pueblo farmers, desert dwellers, Navajo shepherds, hunters of the Plains, northern fishermen, and seed gatherers. The author concludes by describing the current health status of Indians. There is a map showing the locations of the seven cultural groups.

HRDLIČKA, ALEŠ. "Disease, Medicine, and Surgery among the American Aborigines." *Journal of the American Medical Association* 99, no. 20 (1932): 1661–66.

This article considers physiological differences in blood types, pulse rates, metabolism, and muscular strength between Native Americans and Europeans. The author reviews the destructive effects of Old World diseases along with indigenous afflic-tions such as digestive disorders, pneumonia, and arthritis. He describes the treatment of disease, medicine men, surgery, obstetrics, medicines, sweat baths, mechanical cures (rubbing, sucking, etc.), and shamans' procedures. The author reflects the "evolution of culture" theory of anthropology of his time. The article is based on primary accounts.

LA BARRE, WESTON. "Primitive Psychotherapy in Native American Cultures: Peyotism and Confessions." *Journal of Abnormal and Social Psychology* 43, no. 3 (July 1947):294–309. Bibliography.

La Barre examines the pre-Columbian use of peyote by Aztec, Huichol, Cora, and other Mexican tribes and considers the spread of the peyote cult since 1870 to the Indians of the United States, particularly the societies of the Great Basin and Great Plains. He describes the early pan-tribal Native American Church which uses peyote as part of its ceremony, the physical effects of it, along with a typical peyote ceremony. The author notes that while the ceremony may be similar for some fifty tribes, cultural and individual differences endow the ceremony with differing psychological meanings for members of different societies. He mentions the medicinal use and controversy surrounding peyote use in communities like Taos pueblo, but his emphasis is on the practice and psychological value of confession in association with the ceremony. Tribes mentioned include Osaji, Lenape, Oto, Taos, Mescalero Apache, Tonkawa, Kiowa, Comanche, Caddo, Yuchi, Shawnee, Kickapoo, Creek, Kiowa Apache, Quapaw, Cheyenne, Winnebago, Tarahumare, Arapaho, Inca, Maya, Chichimeca Aztec, Huichol, Tahltan, Cree, Slave, Ojibway, Salteaux, Blackfeet, Sioux, Crow, Iowa, Iroquois, and Inuit.

LEVY, JERROLD E. "Indian Healing Arts." *The American Way* 4, no. 9 (September 1971):24–31.

Briefly the author discusses the practical knowledge Indians had of drugs and medical techniques, arguing that they are not the key to understanding Indian medicine as a total healing system. He describes the formalized aspects of the healing system, ceremonial rituals that were aimed at finding out why a person was injured or diseased, considers the traditional ritualistic practices of the Navajos, and explores the question of whether these ceremonies actually cured or did anything to benefit the people practicing them.

MAJOR, ROBERT C. "Aboriginal American Medicine North of Mexico." *Annals of Medical History* 10, no. 6 (November 1938):534–49. Illustrated. Bibliography.

This work does not deal with the detailed medical practices of a single tribe, but postulates that "the identity of all forms of primitive medicine . . . is now so well established as to be axiomatic." The author attempts to indicate how native North American medicines can fit into his general "scheme of primitive medicine." While his basic hypothesis is not necessarily valid, he does provide interesting descriptions of medical practices. Early English observations and the ethnocentrism which colored them are described along with the impact of Old World diseases on Indian populations which had little immunity to their destructive spread. Specific tribes mentioned include Iroquois, Hupa, Maidu, Neotka, Apache, Seneca, Ten'a, Choctaw, Eskimo, Hopi, Lenape, Algonquians, Cherokee, Ottawa, Sioux, Carolina Algonquians, Omaha, Ponca, general Mexican peoples, and the Chippewa whose medical practices he emphasizes. The author concludes that functional mental disease in contact societies was much more widespread than early observers suspected (largely due to the cataclysmic effects of diseases which sometimes killed the majority of members of some communities). He describes magical practices that were increasingly used for treating mental illness where they probably had substantial value and explains how societies relied more on herbalism and its realistic accessories in treating organic disease.

NATIONAL INSTITUTE OF MENTAL HEALTH. *Suicide, Homicide, and Alcoholism among American Indians: Guidelines for Help.* Washington, D.C.: Government Printing Office, 1973. 36pp. Bibliography.
This publication contains "how-to" guidelines which describe ways for recognizing, handling, and preventing possible suicides among American Indians as well as providing survey data and literature for use as a planning guide in the development of crisis intervention and suicide prevention programs. The work begins with a discussion of contemporary health problems of Indians, surveys the current status of Indian suicide and alcoholism, and considers the problems of transition of those Indians who choose to leave the reservation. One section discusses ways to identify potential suicides, lists and describes over twenty preventive steps as well as ingredients of an Indian suicide prevention program and ways to prevent suicide in jail. There is a discussion of Indian homicide, the incidence and severity of Indian alcoholism, reasons the dependency on alcohol develops, group resources for rehabilitation, causes of suicides related to alcoholism, and recommendations for the future. There are seven tables of data, two appendixes, and a list of references.
See also Philip A. May and Larry H. Dizmang. "Suicide and the American Indian." *Psychiatric Annals* 4, no. 11 (November 1974):22–28. Bibliography.

VOGEL, VIRGIL J. *American Indian Medicine.* Norman: University of Oklahoma Press, 1970. 584pp. Illustrated. Bibliography.
The author explains that to American Indians the term medicine embraced much more than the cure of disease and the healing of injuries. The focus in this book is on these aspects, and particularly those that Euro-Americans have borrowed. Vogel reviews the more widely known Native American contributions to medicine (cocaine, curare, and the inspiration for insulin and birth control pills) in an introductory chapter. Other sections include native theories of disease and shamanistic practices, early European observations of Indian medicine, Indian health and disease, therapeutic

methods, and a lengthy appendix of Indian contributions to pharmacology. Twenty-four illustrations depict medical practices and medicinal plants. The bibliography includes unpublished material, books and pamphlets, articles, dispensatories, formularies, pharmacopoeias and related sources, bibliographical aids, reference books, and guides to information sources. There is also an index of botanical names.

WESTERMEYER, JOSEPH. " 'The Drunken Indian': Myths and Realities." *Psychiatric Annals* 4, no. 11 (November 1974):29–36. Bibliography.
Westermeyer looks at the misconceptions and associated political strategies that flow from the nonlogical stereotype of the drunken Indian, reviewing the data on the alcohol usage and alcohol-related problems of Indian people. He first considers common misconceptions regarding Indians and liquor, then reviews the research findings on Indians and alcohol, and concludes that with regard to alcohol usage and alcohol-related problems an extremely wide variation exists among Indian tribes, among subgroups within tribes, and among individual Indians.

NORTHEAST

ANDROS, F. "The Medicine and Surgery of the Winnebago and Dakota Indians." *Journal of the American Medical Association* 1, no. 4 (August 4, 1883):116–18.
The author, a doctor, spent considerable time with the Winnebagos and Sioux and here records his personal observations. He discusses common diseases and the incidence of Old World diseases among the tribes, describes bleeding techniques, sweat baths, and herbal remedies. He also discusses the knowledge the Winnebago and Dakota lacked with regard to anatomy, amputation, and removing gunshot from wounds. He explains their lack of a general remedy for snake bite or hydrophobia, how they secured large wounds with sutures of animal sinew, and how they did "dress a fracture very neatly."

SOUTHWEST

BAHR, DONALD M. "Psychiatry and Indian Curing." *Indian Programs* 2, no. 4 (Fall 1973):1, 4–9. Bibliography.
This article presents several reasons why American Indian curing shares more with psychiatry than with any other branch of Western medicine. The author examines some anthropological writings on southwestern Indian ethnopsychiatry which make negative judgments on Navajo theory as self-deceptive and Apache theory as faith healing. He argues that judgments as to which system (Western or Indian) is more insightful or achieves more lasting cures must be qualified "from the theoretical perspective of the other system" so as to clearly separate the statement from matters of personal belief, emphasizing that it is necessary to meet

each system on its own terms. He analyzes the Piman (Pima-Papago) curing technique of "blowing" in terms of Piman theory and experience, concluding that theory is a special sort of verbalizing while subjective experience encompasses data of a much broader scope.

BERGMAN, ROBERT L. "A School for Medicine Men." *American Journal of Psychiatry* 30 (1973):663–66. Bibliography.
The author discusses the establishment and training program of a Navajo school for medicine men (and women) and his involvement in it. From a psychiatrist's point of view, he describes the nature of the curative ceremonies and a few of what he perceives as their effects. He also discusses his role in teaching the medicine men and trainees something about Western medicine and psychiatry and their reactions. A brief general background of Navajo medicine and rituals is provided along with a history of the school. Traditional Navajo criticisms of the Gallup Indian Medical Center provide insights into the Navajo world view.

GORMAN, CARL N. *Navajo Theory of Disease and Healing Practices.* Window Rock, Ariz.: Navajo Health Authority, 1973. 19pp.
The work presents common Euro-American feelings and misconceptions about the Navajo world view and medicine. A doctor with the Indian Health Service who has some understanding of traditional belief is quoted as saying that Navajo medicine men reunite the three learned professions of theology, law, and medicine. The dimensions of the Navajo concept of harmony are explained, along with the power of pure, or good, thought, and the psychic dimensions of healing are discussed, along with herbal science. The author draws parallels (where possible) between Navajo and Euro-American medical practices, and describes the typical Navajo reliance on both systems of medical care.

SANDNER, DONALD F. "Navajo Medicine." *Human Nature* 1, no. 7 (1978):54–62. Illustrated. Bibliography.
This is a review of many aspects of Navajo healing. The author feels that "as symbolic healing it has much in common with contemporary or 'Western' psychiatry." He reviews the dependence of the average Navajo person on both Navajo and Euro-American medical practices, along with the educational process which leads an individual to become a medicine man or woman. The concept of harmony, central to the Navajo world view, is presented; several of the ten major ways, or healing ceremonies, are discussed; and translations of a number of chants are included. The bibliography includes sources which are at least thirty years old. There are photographs of ceremonies and drawings based on sand paintings.

WADDELL, JACK O., and MICHAEL W. EVERETT. *Drinking among Southwestern Indians: An Anthropological Perspective.* Tucson: University of Arizona Press, 1980. 248pp. Illustrated.
This is a collection of ethnographic studies on American Indians and drinking. They examine the drinking behavior of four contemporary American Indian cultures of the southwestern United States: Papagos, Taos Pueblos, Navajos, and White Mountain Apaches. Contributing anthropologists and health workers discuss historical antecedents, alcohol and mental health programs, social drinking contexts, and native perceptions of the problem. There are maps, tables, and figures that illustrate the book.

WHITING, ALFRED F. "Leaves from a Hopi Doctor's Casebook." *Bulletin of the New York Academy of Medicine* 47 (1971):125–46. Illustrated.
A summary of Hopi history and culture and curative ceremonies, this work includes a biography of the principle informant, Edmund Nequatewa, a traditional Hopi doctor, along with a rendition of the "First Bonesetter" which embodies the Hopi method of bonesetting. The author describes the modern Hopi doctor as "essentially a herbalist" with about 100 medicinal plants in his or her geographic area with which to work. Remedies for a variety of afflictions and conditions are mentioned. Nineteen case histories of the Hopi doctor are included that deal with stomach, eye, and throat ailments, pus, hiccups, inducing vomiting, constipation, cramps, sore muscles, rheumatism, skin ulcers, syphilis, tumors, wounds and cuts, measles, and birth control. There is a photograph of the Hopi doctor-informant.

NORTHWEST

JILEK, W. G. "Indian Healing Power: Indigenous Therapeutic Practices in the Pacific Northwest." *Psychiatric Annals* 4, no. 11 (November 1974):13, 17, 20–21. Bibliography.
Jilek discusses how a two-pronged approach, combining modified psychiatric management with indigenous procedures, was used to treat the mental health problems of Coast Salish Indians of British Columbia and Washington. He describes the native therapeutic activities that were used in doctoring the patients and concludes by arguing that a comprehensive mental health program for Native Americans should strive to combine Western with traditional American Indian approaches.

BIBLIOGRAPHIES

BARROW, MARK V.; JERRY D. NISWANDER; and ROBERT FORTUINE. *Health and Disease of American Indians North of Mexico: A Bibliography 1800–1969.* Gainesville: University of Florida Press, 1972. 147pp.
This work deals only with North American Indians; Inuit peoples are covered in Robert Fortuine's *Health of Eskimos: A Bibliography, 1857–1967* (Hanover, N.H.: Dartmouth College Library, 1968). Sources dealing with indigenous theories of disease and medicine are excluded. Nearly 1,500 sources are included, most of them taken from U.S. and Canadian public health journals and reports. The sources deal with medical literature; biological ab-

stracts; annual reports of general bibliography; and studies of healthy individuals, Indian health and disease, health programs for Indian people, infectious agents and diseases, diseases transmitted from person to person, diseases transmitted from animals and/or soil to people, neoplasms, mental health and psychiatric disorders, pregnancy, childbirth and gynecological conditions, congenital malformations, child health, diseases of specific body systems, and dental health. The work includes author, subject, and tribal indexes.

THE NAVAJO ETHNO-MEDICAL ENCYCLOPEDIA PROJ-ECT STAFF. *Available Literature on Native Healing Science.* Shiprock, N. Mex.: Navajo Health Authority, 1976. 38pp.

A partially annotated bibliography of sources on traditional Navajo medicine, sections of this work include Navajo mythologies and legends, Navajo ceremonies, Navajo sand paintings, Navajo language and culture (including works dealing specifically with medicine, defined as the Western cultural category), microfilms, and ethnobotany papers. Some of the works deal with Apache subjects. None of the twenty-five ethnobotany papers listed deal specifically with Navajo subjects.

13   SUBSISTENCE PATTERNS

The main interest of every human society lies in the acquisition of a dependable and adequate food supply as well as the other necessities of life. The physical environment of North Amerca with its sharp differences in topography, soil, and climate, coupled with a rich variety of flora and fauna, afforded Native Americans a number of ways of obtaining food. While the geographical environment played an important role in terms of the raw materials it offered, North American Indian groups used geographical circumstances according to their own beliefs, customs, and ingenuity to invent different methods of obtaining and preparing food. These methods principally included the systematic harvesting of wild plants and wild plant products, the cultivation of domesticated plants, hunting, and fishing.

Although most aboriginal cultures relied on more than one source of food, Indian groups have nevertheless been classified in terms of the method employed in obtaining the food that dominated their economy, i.e., fishing, hunting, gathering (wild plants), or farming. For example, fish was the staple food of Indians on the Northwest Coast and in parts of Alaska; game predominated in the Plains area and most of the Arctic; wild plants were the principal food of Indians in most of California and the Great Basin area; and cultivated plants predominated in the Northeast, the Southwest, and sporadically in the Plains region. Consequently, books and articles written on the subject of food economies of Indian tribes generally concentrate on the manner in which a major or some portion of the food was obtained rather than on the entire range of methods used by a group.

All the works in this section contain descriptions of the geographic environment (topography, soil, flora, fauna, climate, boundaries) of the tribe under consideration. The authors of some of the studies, written in the early part of this century, argued that the physical environment largely determined the cultural landscape. Gilmore (p. 189) supported the idea that "The dominant character of the vegetation of a region is always an important factor in shaping the culture of that region. . . ." This concept of environmental determinism, the control of the physical environment over people's activities, came under fire around 1920, with the eventual result that more recent studies involving geographical dimensions now examine all variables, physical and cultural, of a problem. For example, in his study of the Ten'a Indians, Sullivan (p. 195) found that although the people did not practice agriculture, it was not due to the fact that it is impossible to raise domestic plants a few degrees this side of the Arctic Circle. On the contrary, non-Indians have attempted agriculture on a small scale with some success. Rather, the author found a reluctance on the part of the Ten'a to depart from their traditional way of life. Although some of these works are of the determinist persuasion, this does not detract from the valuable information they contain about subsistence patterns.

Indian corn or maize (Zea mays) was the most important and widespread cultivated food plant in North America, as shown in the works of Butler (p. 187), Parker (p. 187), and Will and Hyde (p. 190). At the time of the first European contact, this plant, discovered, utilized, and cultivated by people in North America more than 2,000 years ago, was grown all the way from the Great Lakes and the Lower St. Lawrence Valley to Chile and Argentina. It constituted more of the food supply than all other cultivated plants combined. Other plants, including beans and squash, were also cultivated by Indians long before there was any contact with European farmers.

Much of the material written about Indian subsistence patterns concerns the agricultural food economies of certain tribal groups in the Northeast, Southwest, and the Plains region. These accounts include information on the ways tribes planted and harvested corn and other plants for food and nonfood products. They describe the different kinds of digging tools used in planting as well as the field practices including natural irrigation, particularly in the Southwest, the clearing of farm land, the gender division of labor for farming activities, and ownership of property.

For thousands of years before European contact, American Indians knew an extraordinary number of uses for the wild plants that grew throughout North America. There plants survived and reproduced without human interference although their products were collected and utilized. For almost every plant Indians found some practical use, either for food, drink, medicine, or other purposes. Wild plants dominated subsistence in California, the Great Basin, and a small part of the Southwest. In these areas, some Indian groups satisfied virtually all their needs from the wild plants that grew in their environment. Before the time of agriculture, wild plants were probably much more important in the areas which later relied on cultivated plants. Although agricultural Indians commonly depended upon a relatively few species of plants and animals, they still were familiar with and occasionally used many wild plants.

Certain people in every tribe acquired a fund of knowledge concerning the utilization of wild plants for food and nonfood purposes. They knew the habitats of plants, their characteristics and habits, ecologic relations, geographic distribution, the time for harvesting them, and methods of using them for preparing medicines. They knew how to prepare wild plants as ceremonial or practical objects, and they were conversant with the way the plants figured in the folklore of their tribe. Supplementing this body of special plant lore, other members of the tribe also knew a great deal about plants in general, their common uses, structure, functions, habits, and habitat. Of necessity, a discriminating knowledge of many plants was required for all people within any tribe in order to be assured of the basic essentials of life.

Over seventy years ago, some anthropologists and botanists recognized the value of studying the uses to which wild plants were put by a given people. Ethnobotanical investigations were undertaken to learn the relationship between the floral environment and the lives, practices, thought, and outlook upon life of particular tribal groups. These studies contain information on aboriginal uses of plants for food and medicine, in material culture, for ceremonial purposes, and, in some cases, tribal nomenclature associated with wild plants.

In over half of the area of aboriginal America at the time of European contact, the Indians did not farm but lived exclusively by gathering wild plants, hunting, or fishing. Indians had a tremendous knowledge of the habits of animals and fish; both hunting and fishing developed into complex systems with physical and intellectual components. An important means of subsistence in aboriginal America, animal life in regions covering nearly all of Canada and Alaska and the middle half of the United States was hunted for food, clothing, shelter, and other materials. Nelson (p. 195) cites the Eskimo hunters of Alaska who, because of their ingenuity and the variety of implements, weapons, and methods they developed, raised the art of hunting to a high state of differentiation and remain supreme among hunting peoples of the world.

Fishing as a dominant subsistence activity and an important source of food in several areas of North America is covered in works by Kroeber (p. 194), Nelson (p. 195), and Rostlund (p. 186). Northwest Coast fishing tribes developed fishing skills, equipment, and knowledge that in conjunction with an ample food supply permitted them to create a relatively sedentary way of life.

The techniques and utensils used in preparing, cooking, preserving, and storing food are described for the food economies dependent on domesticated and wild plants as well as for those food economies primarily dependent on game and fish. Since harvesting and preparing foods often required small portable receptacles, many of the studies contain information and illustrations of carrying baskets and other similar utensils which were made with great technical skill and patience by women of the tribes.

Food is interrelated with religion in Indian cultures. Since natural forces are thought to determine one's success in food gathering whether it is by hunting, fishing, gathering wild plants, or farming, these forces must be controlled through ritual. Studies concerning Indian food economies contain notes on the vital role ritual plays in various stages of cultivating plants, harvesting wild species, and preparing them for food or nonfood purposes, as well as information on the religious ceremonies, rituals, and taboos associated with hunting and fishing.

All the studies, whether of cultivated or wild plants, provide the botanical, common English, and tribal names.

Much of the information in these books and articles was furnished by informants, usually elderly members of the tribes, who, fearing that their knowledge would die with them, gave their accounts in order to preserve the information for their own people as well as for others. Some of the words, expressions, and opinions used in these books and articles, many of which are over sixty years old, represent the biases of the time in which they were written but do not materially affect the value of the works. Many of the accounts also contain information about medicinal and other nonfood uses of plants and linguistic aspects of tribal plant terminology. Both medicine and language are topics treated separately in other parts of this volume.

BENGT, ANELL. *Running Down and Driving of Game in North America.* Lund, Sweden: Berlingska Boktryckeriet, 1969. 129pp. Illustrated.

This book gives a general description of the methods used in driving and running down game by Indians of North America (including Canada) before and after contact with Europeans. The first part of the book describes different methods used by various Eskimo and tribal groups of the Northwest Coast and western Plateau; in southern Washington, Oregon, and California; in the Great Basin, Southwest, and Great Lakes regions; in the Plains, Northeast, and Southeast areas; and discusses methods used among the northern Algonquian and northern Athapaskan tribes to hunt land game. The second part of the study examines the cultural, economical, biological, and ecological factors which determine the particular driving methods and their geographic distribution. Eight maps show the distribution of hunting methods in North America. The author uses accounts of modern ethnographers for most of his study except for information relating to tribes in the northeastern United States and eastern Canada where he relies on accounts over one hundred years old.

HARVARD, VALERY. "Drink Plants of the North American Indians." *Bulletin of the Torrey Botanical Club* 23, no. 2 (February 1896):33–46.

The drink plants used by Indians north of Mexico before contact with Europeans are considered under three heads: those yielding alcoholic beverages, those resulting in stimulating or exhilarating effects, and those furnishing palatable juices, and by infusion, beverages that quench thirst. The study excludes medicinal uses of plants. The botanical names are given along with descriptions of the plants and the environments in which they grow, the parts used, methods of preparing them as drinks, and the tribes who used them.

HOLMES, GEORGE K. "Aboriginal Agriculture: The American Indians." In *Cyclopedia of American Agriculture: A Popular Survey of Agricultural Conditions, Practices, and Ideals in the United States and Canada.* 2nd ed. Edited by Liberty H. Bailey. 4 vols. Vol. 4: *Farm and Community,* pp. 24–39. New York: Macmillan, 1910. Illustrated. Bibliography.

This article briefly describes the agricultural history of American Indians north of Mexico, concentrating on regions where agriculture had been developed to such a degree that subsistence was chiefly derived from cultivated plants. The agricul-

ture and diet of the peoples of Virginia, New England, the Southeast, the Omahas of the Plains, the Southwest (the Hopis in particular), the Pacific Coast, and Canada are discussed. A series of general statements about agricultural methods and plants used, and a list of plants utilized before contact with Europeans, selected from the writings of travelers and investigators, are included. Plants are listed according to whether they were cultivated or harvested without cultivation. The uses of each plant and parts used are given. Also listed are plants utilized by the peoples of Mendocino County, California, including the uses of each plant and parts used. The article is illustrated throughout with sketches of agricultural implements.

ROSTLUND, ERHARD. *Freshwater Fish and Fishing in Native North America.* University of California Publications in Geography, vol. 9. Berkeley: University of California Press, 1952; reprint ed.: New York: Johnson Reprint, 1968. 313pp. Illustrated. Bibliography.

Rostlund explores the economic and cultural significance of freshwater fish as food (including anadromous forms which ascend rivers from the sea to spawn—salmon and shad) and of fishing to North American Indian tribes, his inquiry dealing primarily with aboriginal times before contact with whites. Part 1 includes chapters on the food value of freshwater fish, the principal species in the fish resource and its quantitative aspects, productivity of fresh waters, and a resume by region of the resource in the United States and Canada. Part 2 deals with aboriginal fishery and fishing methods including fish nets, weirs, and traps; fish spears, hooks, poisons, and other minor methods; fish preservation and the attitudes of tribes toward fish as food. In the last chapter the author concludes that there were different geographical origins of aboriginal fishery in North America. There are extensive historical and anthropological references organized by regions given for the chapter on fishing methods. Over forty maps represent continental patterns of range or distribution of freshwater fish, aboriginal fishing methods, fish provinces, and show the location of major Indian tribes in early historic times. There are tables of estimated productivity of fish in inland waters and a bibliography that includes many accounts of early explorers and travelers.

YANOVSKY, ELIAS. *Food Plants of the North American Indians.* Department of Agriculture, Miscellaneous Publication, no. 237. Washington,

D.C.: Government Printing Office, 1936. 83pp. Bibliography.

This publication contains a summary of the records of food plants used by Indians of the United States and Canada which appeared in ethnobotanical publications. The list contains 1,112 species belonging to 444 genera of plants distributed among 120 families. Brief information is supplied for each item including the way tribes used the plant and the names of the original authorities who secured the information. Example: "FUNGI. *Agaricaceae. Agaricus campestris L.* Eaten in California and by Iroquois Indians, although some Indians are superstitious about it. Chestnut (8, p. 301), Waugh (72, p. 121)." A table summarizing food plant families with number of genera and species is included.

NORTHEAST

BUTLER, EVA L. "Algonkian Culture and Use of Maize in Southern New England." *Bulletin of the Archaeological Society of Connecticut,* no. 22 (December 1948):3–39. Bibliography.

Butler's article investigates the significant part played by maize (corn) in the economic, religious, and social life of seventeenth- and eighteenth-century Algonquian Indians (Abenakis, Massachusetts, Mohegans, Narragansetts, Nipmucks, and Pequots) of southern New England, the material organized according to topics. The author discusses the traditional Indian and modern theories of the origins of maize; clearing of the land, planting times, implements, fertilization; the care and protection of crops; harvesting, preservation, and storage of corn; the uses of corn and the utensils used in cooking, preparing, and serving it. Customs, beliefs, and ceremonies involving maize and the roles of men and women are briefly discussed. The bibliography lists narrative accounts of early explorers and settlers as well as little-known manuscripts upon which the information regarding corn is based.

DENSMORE, FRANCES. *Uses of Plants by the Chippewa Indians.* Bureau of American Ethnology 44th Annual Report, 1926–27, pp. 275–397. Washington, D.C.: Government Printing Office, 1928. Illustrated. Reprint ed.: New York: Dover, 1974.

This study was done during the 1920s among women and men from five Chippewa reservations in Minnesota, one reservation in Wisconsin, and one in Ontario, Canada, who were able to describe former methods of preparing vegetal foods. Information includes a physical description of the White Earth Reservation, where the majority of the plants were obtained, the types of vegetal foods with botanical and common English names provided, and the plant parts used. There are descriptions of obtaining maple sugar and harvesting wild rice, important vegetal foods, and the preparation of beverages, seasonings, cereals, vegetables, fruits, and berries. There are brief chapters on plants used in dyes and as charms, plants used in the decorative arts, and a list of articles made of birch bark. Two

reports are included in this study, one about the medicinal properties of sixty-nine plants used by the Chippewa and the other a list of the principal active medicinal constituents of these plants. There is also a long chapter on plants as medicine. There is an extensive list of plants according to botanical names with the common English and native name for each plant plus Chippewa and other tribes' uses of the plant. Plants are also listed according to their common English names with botanical equivalents and native names with common English equivalents.

JENKS, ALBERT ERNEST. *The Wild Rice Gatherers of the Upper Lakes: A Study in American Primitive Economics.* Bureau of American Ethnology 19th Annual Report, part 2, 1897–98, pp. 1091–1137. Washington, D.C.: Government Printing Office, 1900. Illustrated. Bibliography.

The author deals with the wild rice producing Indians of two linguistic stocks, the Algonquian Chippewas, Menominees, Sacs, Foxes, Ottawas, Potawatomis, Mascoutens, and Kickapoos; and the Siouan Dakotas, Winnebagos, and Assiniboines of the Upper Great Lakes region, from the seventeenth to the nineteenth centuries. Chapters include botanical information about wild rice, its habitat by states; historical background and population figures for the peoples involved in wild rice production; describe processes of harvesting and preparing the grain; discuss community reaction and adjustments to the availability of an ample food supply; examine property rights in rice beds and the division of labor; give information on nutrition and ways of preparing wild rice as food, wild rice in ceremony and mythology, Indian populations of the wild rice district (northeastern and northern parts of Wisconsin and part of Minnesota east of the Mississippi River), and the influence of wild rice on geographic nomenclature. The study throws light on the 250-year conflict between Dakota and Chippewa Indians and on the fur trade in that area. Photographs show wild rice beds and kernels, wigwams, implements, and canoes; a map shows the wild rice population, value per bushel, composition of cereals and other foods, and Indian populations in the wild rice district in 1764, 1778, 1806, and 1822. The bibliography includes numerous early narratives and anthropological studies.

PARKER, ARTHUR C. *Iroquois Uses of Maize and Other Food Plants.* New York State Museum Bulletin 144. Albany: University of the State of New York, 1910; reprint ed.: *Parker on the Iroquois,* edited by William N. Fenton. Syracuse: Syracuse University Press, 1968. 119pp. Illustrated. Bibliography.

This data about Iroquois preparation and uses of maize and other vegetal foods was collected from Cayuga, Mohawk, Oneida, Onondaga, Seneca, and Tuscarora Indians in New York State and the Grand River Reservation, Six Nations, Canada. Part 1 includes information about the origins of maize and its importance to the English colonist, early records of corn cultivation among Iroquois and cognate tribes, Iroquois customs of corn cultivation (division of labor, land clearing, preparing the soil, planting, communal customs, harvesting, and storage), corn ceremonials and legends, varieties of maize used by Iroquois and other eastern Indians, Seneca corn cultivation terminology, utensils employed in the preparation of corn for food, cooking and eating customs, foods prepared from corn, and other uses of corn plants. Part 2 contains notes on other kinds of food plants used by the Iroquois including beans, squash, other vine vegetals, fruit, nuts, sap, bark, and roots. There are photographs and drawings of utensils used in planting, harvesting, preparing, and for eating food; baskets; storage pits; longhouses; varieties of corn and their nonfood products. The bibliography includes many accounts of early explorers and travelers. Arthur C. Parker was a member of the Seneca tribe.

SMITH, HURON H. *Ethnobotany of the Menomini Indians.* Bulletin of the Public Museum of the City of Milwaukee, 4, no. 1, pp. 1–174. Milwaukee: Public Museum Board of Directors, 1923. Illustrated.

The data in this study was collected on the Menominee Reservation in northeastern Wisconsin during 1921 and 1922 from people well versed in aboriginal uses of plants for foods, textiles, medicines, and other items. Sections include a history of medicine in Menominee religion and lore as well as a list of medicinal plants which gives the common English, botanical, and Menominee names for each plant, followed by information on its uses, properties, use by non-Indians, and any known myths connected with the plant. The same procedure is followed for uncultivated vegetal plants used as foods, fibers, dyes, and for miscellaneous purposes—tanning, love charms, sacred or ceremonial functions. At the end plants are listed by their botanical and English names and there are 125 photographs of Menominee people, the Menominee Reservation, and vegetal plants. This volume includes two other ethnobotanical studies organized in the same manner by Huron H. Smith: (1) *Ethnobotany of the Meskwaki Indians,* Bulletin of the Public Museum of the City of Milwaukee, 4, no. 2 (1928):175–326. Illustrated. (Tama, Iowa), and (2) *Ethnobotany of the Ojibwe Indians,* Bulletin of the Public Museum of the City of Milwaukee, 4, no. 3 (1932):327–525. Illustrated. (Wisconsin, Minnesota). The same author published another study, *Ethnobotany of the Forest Potawatomi Indians,* Bulletin of the Public Museum of the City of Milwaukee, 7, no. 1 (1933):1–230. Illustrated. (Wisconsin).

WAUGH, FREDERICK WILKERSON. *Iroquois Foods and Food Preparation.* Canada Department of Mines, Geological Survey Memoir 86, no. 12, Anthropological Series. Ottawa: Government Printing Bureau, 1916. 235pp. Illustrated. Bibliography.

This investigation was done between 1912 and 1915 among the Iroquois of Ontario and Quebec provinces in Canada and in New York State who were well versed in Iroquois food culture. There is specific information on the agricultural methods and customs of five Iroquoian tribes—Cayuga, Mohawk, Onondaga, Oneida, and Seneca—concerning the division of labor and communal customs; the planting, harvesting, and storage of corn; ceremonials; customs; and the implements used in gathering, preparing, and eating food. A section on food materials includes recipes for corn, beans, pumpkins, squash, cucumbers, and melons. There is a section on the use of leaves, stems, bark, roots, edible fungi, nuts, fruit, fish, and animals as food. There is information about saccharine foods, beverages, and salt as a food material. There are photographs of wooden bowls; baskets; longhouses; corn cribs; utensils used in gathering, preparing, and eating foods; corn and bean varieties; and women preparing corn for food.

WITTHOFT, JOHN. "The American Indian as Hunter." *Pennsylvania Game News* 24, nos. 2, 3, 4 (February, March, April 1953):12–16, 16–22, 8–13. Rev. ed.: *Reprints in Anthropology from the Pennsylvania Historical and Museum Commission,* no. 6. Harrisburg: Pennsylvania Historical and Museum Commission, 1967. Illustrated.

Witthoft presents a generalized sketch of Native American hunting culture during the late prehistoric and early colonial times based on information drawn from many sources including peoples of the Northeast (Seneca and Delaware) and Southeast (Cherokee). Part 1, which contains a historical background of the differences between American Indians and Europeans in their attitudes toward land, game, and hunting, maintains that in Europe hunting was considered a sport that was the prerogative of the upper class and was not looked upon as a significant source of food, whereas for American Indians hunting was an essential economic activity—a necessary and significant food source. There are explanations of the division of labor between the sexes which involved equal responsibility for women, the agriculturalists, and men, the hunters. The religious aspects of both roles and the lot of American Indian women compared with that of colonial Euro-American women are discussed. Part 2 deals with supernaturalism, ritual, religious beliefs, and practices of hunters in the Northeast in aboriginal times. Part 3 deals with hunting and trapping deer, the most valuable animal to the Northeast Indian economy, elk, bear, small animals and birds, and describes weapons and traps used.

YARNELL, RICHARD ASA. *Aboriginal Relationships between Culture and Plant Life in the Upper Great Lakes Region.* Anthropological Papers of the Museum of Anthropology, University of Michigan, no. 23. Ann Arbor: University of Michigan Press, 1964. 218pp. Bibliography.

In this report, the author deals with the interrelationships between cultures of three language families (Iroquoian Hurons, Tobaccos, and Neutrals; Siouan Winnebagos; and Algonquian Ottawas, Chippewas, Menominees, Potawatomis, Mascoutens, Miamis, Sacs, and Foxes and plant life in the Upper Great Lakes region from the Archaic period (A.D. 500–700) to contact with non-Indians. Chapters include a physical description of the area, its vegetation, prehistory and paleoecology, ethnogeography, ethnohistory, and paleoethnobotany; information on the use of plants as food before contact with whites; and the use of plants as beverages, for flavoring, medicine, ceremonial purposes, smoking, dyeing, and in technology. There are chapters on the effects of human activities on the plant ecology of the region and a history of the cultivation of plants. Several appendixes give botanical data on the plants used for various purposes; tables provide information about archaeological plant sites and remains; and maps show prehistoric sites of cultivated plants.

SOUTHEAST

SWANTON, JOHN R. *The Indians of the Southeastern United States.* Bureau of American Ethnology Bulletin 137, pp. 1–11, 242–381. Washington, D.C.: Government Printing Office, 1946; reprint ed.: Westport, Conn: Greenwood Press, 1969. Illustrated. Bibliography.

Sections of this comprehensive book on southeastern Indians deal with subsistence patterns in aboriginal and historic times. General information is given for peoples living in the territory now embraced by Georgia, Florida, Alabama, Mississippi, Louisiana, northeastern Texas, southern Arkansas, southern and western South Carolina,.the westernmost section of North Carolina, and nearly all of Tennessee. There is information about the geographic environment, mineral, vegetal, and animal materials used; annual economic cycles, geographic distribution of raw materials; food economies (horticulture, hunting, and fishing); domestication of animals in pre-Columbian and historic times; and the preparation and preservation of vegetable and animal foods. Tables give geographic and tribal distributions of vegetable and animal foods, a map shows the distribution of certain natural resources used by Southeast Indians, and a large selection of pictures at the end of the book illustrates subsistence patterns. An extensive bibliography of historical and anthropological sources is prefaced by a long essay on source materials.

GREAT PLAINS

GILMORE, MELVIN RANDOLPH. *Uses of Plants by the Indians of the Missouri River Region.* Bureau of American Ethnology 33rd Annual Report, 1911–12, pp. 43–154. Washington, D.C.: Government Printing Office, 1919. Illustrated. Bibliography.

This study was done among elderly people of the Dakota, Omaha, Pawnee, Ponca, and Winnebago tribes inhabiting the region that is now the state of Nebraska. There are brief notes on ethnobotany, the influence of human populations on flora. A long taxonomic list of cultivated and uncultivated plants used by the peoples of the Missouri River region includes botanical, common English, and tribal names; parts used for food or for nonfood products; and methods of preparation. Religious songs, beliefs, and customs pertinent to individual plants are described. A glossary of the plant names mentioned in the monograph is arranged alphabetically under botanical names, followed by corresponding common English, Dakota, Omaha, Winnebago, and

Pawnee names; other glossaries present plant names arranged under the tribal and common English names. There are illustrations of plants.

HOLDER, PRESTON. *The Hoe and the Horse on the Plains: A Study of Cultural Development among North American Indians.* Lincoln: University of Nebraska Press, 1970. 176pp. Illustrated. Bibliography.

Holder examines two ways of life representing fundamentally different accommodations to the Plains environment resulting from distinctive traditions of the people involved and the related socioeconomic structures: horticultural, hoe farming villages with roots deep in the prehistory of the Mississippi Valley, represented in this study by central and northern Caddoan-speaking peoples, and the equestrian bison hunting societies represented by the Siouan-speaking people. The examination covers Plains prehistory through the nineteenth century. The first chapter describes the nature of Plains geography, European efforts to penetrate the Great Plains area and exploit its resources from the sixteenth to the eighteenth century, the U.S. government's acquisition of the Louisiana Territory, and intertribal conflict during the eighteenth and nineteenth centuries, a response to social change. Other chapters compare the horticultural and mobile ways of life including ethnographic information on Caddoan-, Algonquian-, and Siouan-speaking peoples; describe the relationship between hoe farmers and equestrian hunters; discuss the severe pressures on the farmers and hunters by Europeans; and examine the collapse of village economy and rise of nomadism. There is a map of Plains tribes, photographs of equestrian hunting encampments and horticultural villages, and a bibliography listing many archaeological, ethnographic, and historical source materials.

VESTAL, PAUL A., and RICHARD EVANS SCHULTES. *The Economic Botany of the Kiowa Indians As It Relates to the History of the Tribe.* Cambridge, Mass.: Botanical Museum, 1939. 110pp. Illustrated. Bibliography.

The data in this study was collected from people on the Kiowa Reservation near Anadarko, Oklahoma, who were still well versed about plant uses, and from ethnological sources. There are brief notes on the history of the movements of the Kiowa tribe from early times to the end of the nineteenth century. A section on plants gives their botanical, common English, and Kiowa names; parts used for food or beverages and nonfood purposes; methods of preparation; and the geographic distribution of each species. There is a discussion in which the authors maintain that there is a correlation between the tribe's knowledge of plants and the history of its warfare and migrations, that Kiowa knowledge of plants was expanded by the acquisition of horses which enabled them to travel great distances and come into contact with other tribes who used unfamiliar plants. Horses and an abundant, easily obtainable food supply (buffalo) also seem to have made the tribe less dependent on the plant kingdom. Another section of the study concerns plants known to and used by the Kiowa, the plants divided into five groups corresponding to the five areas most prominently associated with the journey of the tribe from its original home to its final settlement on the Oklahoma reservation: plants known to the Kiowa in their traditional home and in their Black Hills residence, plants known after expulsion from the Black Hills, plants found on the reservation, plants introduced by American settlers, and those brought from the Southwest. The authors conclude that relatively few plants were borrowed by the Kiowa and that plants of vital importance to the basic economy of the tribe were known before their settlement on the Oklahoma reservation, the exception being peyote, which has played a dominant part in the Kiowa Reservation economy. There are photographs of plants, plant materials used in the peyote ceremony, and a map of Kiowa migrations.

WILL, GEORGE FRANCIS, and GEORGE E. HYDE. *Corn among the Indians of the Upper Missouri.* St. Louis: William Harvey Miner, 1917; reprint ed.: Lincoln: University of Nebraska Press, 1964. 323pp. Illustrated.

Will and Hyde deal with the agricultural-sedentary societies of the Upper Missouri area (a region along the Missouri River from the mouth of the Platte River north to the Rocky Mountains, embracing a large area of country on both sides of the river). Tribes representing two linguistic stocks are discussed: the Caddoan-speaking Pawnees and Arikaras and the Siouan-speaking Mandans, Hidatsas, Crows, Omahas, Poncas, Otos, and Iowas. The authors use eighteenth- and nineteenth-century accounts of explorers and travelers to present brief discussions of early intertribal trade in corn and of later trade with non-Indians as well as tribal migrations and early histories. Fifty varieties of native corn discovered in the Missouri Valley are described in detail and there are accounts of the agricultural methods of Upper Missouri tribes, their techniques in harvesting and storing corn, ways of preparing it for food, myths about the origin of corn, and various ceremonies, beliefs, and practices involving corn. Photographs of the varieties of Upper Missouri corn and other vegetables carry the information through the early twentieth century.

WILSON, GILBERT LIVINGSTONE. *Agriculture of the Hidatsa Indians: An Indian Interpretation.* University of Minnesota Studies in the Social Sciences, no. 9. Minneapolis: University of Minnesota, 1917. 129pp. Illustrated.

Wilson's study of the economic life of the Hidatsas is based largely on data obtained from Maxi'diwac, or Buffalobird-woman, an expert agriculturalist of the Hidatsa tribe who was born about 1839. The material, collected by the author during the summers of 1912 to 1915 at the Fort Berthold Reservation in North Dakota, presents Maxi'diwac's interpretation of Hidatsa agricultural economics and the philosophy behind her labors. Through an interpreter, her son Edward Goodbird, Maxi'diwac describes the agricultural practices of the Hidatsas in the middle nineteenth century, including infor-

mation on the clearing of fields, tools used, the planting, harvesting, drying, storing, and use of corn, sunflower seeds, squash, beans, tobacco, and government allotted plants. Corn, its varieties and the customs and traditions surrounding it, is discussed in more detail than the other plants. Photographs and sketches illustrate plants, fields, models of tools, a drying frame, and other objects pertaining to agriculture.

SOUTHWEST

BRADFIELD, MAITLAND. *The Changing Pattern of Hopi Agriculture.* Occasional Paper of the Royal Anthropological Institute of Great Britain and Ireland, no. 30. London: Royal Anthropological Institute, 1971. 66pp. Illustrated.

Based on field work done in the late 1960s, this is an ecological study concerned with the relationship of the Hopi pueblo in the southwestern United States to its physical and plant environment. The account includes information on the physiography of Black Mesa, and the controlling factors of Hopi agriculture: snowfall, frost, summer rains, vegetation, and soils; the geological structure and land forms of the Oraibi Valley; and the social correlations of land in and out of use before and after 1906. The author discusses the choice of field sites as related to the availability of surface runoff water, describes the effects on Hopi agriculture of the loss of one-third of the best farm land, and considers the introduction, first, of draft animals, and then pickup trucks. Climatic events of 1866–1905 are related to the splitting of the village of Oraibi in 1906. On the basis of new evidence, events prior to and subsequent to the split of the village are reinterpreted in a postscript. Maps of Oraibi Valley show the Hopi field system in 1966 and the geological formations across the main valley; diagrams show Black Mesa and Hopi villages, geological structures, land forms, and vegetational zones of Oraibi Valley; photographs show Oraibi Valley land forms, plants, terrain, cornfields, and gullying. Tables list snow and rainfall for parts of the Hopi pueblo and show the changes in land use in the Oraibi Valley from 1851 to 1965.

CASTETTER, EDWARD F. *Uncultivated Plants Used as Sources of Food.* University of New Mexico Bulletin, Ethnobiological Studies in the American Southwest, no. 1. Biological Series 4, no. 1. Albuquerque: University of New Mexico Press, 1935. 62pp. Bibliography.

This study discusses 210 uncultivated plants used by Indians of the Southwest (Pueblos, Apaches, Papago-Pimas, Navajos, Yumas, Paiutes, and others) before contact with the Spanish. The plants are listed alphabetically according to botanical names, each one followed by the abbreviated name of the person who first described the species, the common English name of the plant, and the Spanish and/or Indian name when available. There is an index of common English and Spanish names to help locate plants known only under such names. The plants and their specific parts are grouped according to use, especially as foods, by the different tribal groups mentioned.

————, and WILLIS H. BELL. *Pima and Papago Indian Agriculture.* Albuquerque: University of New Mexico Press, 1942. 245pp. Illustrated. Bibliography.

This book on Piman agriculture is based on studies made between 1938 and 1940 among the Pimas on the Gila River Indian Reservation, centered at Sacaton, Arizona, the Papagos on reservations with headquarters at Sells and San Xavier, Arizona, and a few Papagos on the so-called Maricopa Indian Reservation at Maricopa, Arizona. The account of Pima and Papago agriculture presents a composite picture of information gathered from numerous informants and supplemented by written data. Initial chapters include the history of the Piman people (i.e., the Pimas and Papagos living in both the United States and Mexico); a description of the land, climate, and vegetation of Piman territory, most of which lies within an area known as the Sonoran Desert; and a discussion of ancient Piman agriculture and early food gathering. Later chapters discuss the utilization of wild plants and animals; Piman cultivated crops including maize, beans, pumpkins, cotton, gourds, tobacco, martynia, wheat, barley, melons, peas, and chilis; the selection, development, and ownership of land; agricultural implements; the planting, irrigation, and cultivation of crops; and the techniques employed in harvesting, storing, seed selection, and crop utilization. Tobacco growing as a ceremonial agriculture and smoking as a ceremonial practice are discussed along with the general ceremonial aspects of Piman agriculture. Illustrations include agricultural implements, Papago fields, and the Rain Dance. There is a bibliography of archaeological, ethnographical, and historical materials.

————, and WILLIS H. BELL. *Yuman Indian Agriculture: Primitive Subsistence on the Lower Colorado and Gila Rivers.* Albuquerque: University of New Mexico Press, 1951. 274pp. Illustrated. Bibliography.

This investigation of Yuman agriculture is based on studies made between 1937 and 1941 among the Mohaves, Yumas, and Cocopas living on the lower Colorado River, as well as the Maricopas living on the Gila River. This account of agricultural activities and practices of the tribes under consideration is a composite picture drawn from numerous informants. Chapters include a description of the Lower Colorado River valley and environs and information on the peoples living along the River during prehistoric and historic times; a discussion of the general basis of a subsistence pattern which combined agricultural crop cultivation with the gathering of wild food plants; agricultural implements and cultivated crops including maize, pumpkins, gourds, cotton, tobacco, melons, beans, and sunflowers; an account of agricultural techniques employed including water utilization, land ownership, planting, harvesting, semicultivation of seed plants, a unique fea-

ture of the Yuman tribes on the Gila River, and utilization of wild plants and animal products. Final chapters discuss ritualism and group activities and compare the cultures of the Gila River Pima-Papago peoples and the Lower Colorado River Yuman tribes regarding agricultural methods. Maps show the location of Lower and Middle Colorado River Yuman tribes at various periods in time and distribution of Cocopa Indians on the Colorado River in 1905 and 1940. There is an extensive bibliography of biological, historical, ethnographical, and archaeological materials.

————, and RUTH M. UNDERHILL. *The Ethnobotany of the Papago Indians.* University of New Mexico Bulletin, Ethnobiological Studies in the American Southwest, no. 2. Biological Series 4, no. 2. Albuquerque: University of New Mexico Press, 1935. 84pp. Bibliography.

This study done between 1931 and 1934 with the Piman-speaking Papagos who live in southern Arizona shows that the tribe depended on both wild and cultivated plants for their food supply in aboriginal times. Part 1 includes information on uncultivated plants used for food, beverages, smoking, and chewing. Botanical, Papago, and common English names, harvest season, and parts used are given for small succulent and large coarse green plants; root, tuber, and bulk crops; fruit bearing plants and seeds; beverage and wild tobacco plants. Other sections of the study include information on the growing and utilization of cultivated plants such as legumes, corn, wheat, and cotton; a brief history of Papago agriculture showing that the tribe has had at times a well-developed agriculture; hunting and utilization of large and small game, reptiles, and worms as food; domestication of animals; and the Papago diet. There are descriptions of animals and plants used as sources of clothing, ornament, cosmetics, rope, and medicine and plants used in basketry and weaving. The authors end with a brief cultural discussion of the Papagos. There are lists of plants and animals with common English, Spanish, and botanical names.

CUSHING, FRANK HAMILTON. *Zuñi Breadstuff.* Indian Notes and Monographs, vol. 8. New York: Museum of the American Indian, 1920; reprint ed.: New York: Museum of the American Indian, 1974. 673pp. Illustrated.

Cushing, who lived with and observed the Zuñi from 1879 to 1884, examines the interrelationships between Zuñi ceremonial life, folk history, everyday customs, and the role of corn in all of these activities. There is a survey of the food plants of this desert pueblo located in the extreme western part of New Mexico. Chapters include an outline of Zuñi mythology, pueblo philosophy, and folklore connected with corn; a discussion of land laws, farming customs, and methods; and a description of food preparation, eating customs, corn dances, and festivals. There are footnotes throughout the book plus illustrations of Zuñi cornfields, plants, gardens, and implements. The reprint edition contains a brief biography of Cushing's life and activities.

ELMORE, FRANCES H. *Ethnobotany of the Navajo.* University of New Mexico and the School of American Research Monograph Series 1, no. 7, pp. 1–136. Albuquerque: University of New Mexico Press, 1943. Bibliography.

Elmore collected the data in this study from 1936 to 1943 in the Chaco Canyon National Monument, New Mexico, among older Navajo people who were well versed in aboriginal plant names and uses. There is a physical description of Navajo country and its vegetation, brief information on food, ceremonial and medicinal plants, and medicine men, especially in connection with their use of plants. The plants are grouped into eighty-two families, with the botanical, common English, and Navajo names, and literary translations given for all members of each family along with literature references. The parts of plants; their uses as foods, dyes, utensils, and medicine; the methods of preparation; and ceremonial significance, if any, follow the various names for each plant. A group of tables at the end of the study lists medicinal plants used to treat internal and external disorders; plants used as food, dyes, or beverages; and plants used in ceremonials and basketry. Appendixes list plant products and by-products and general Navajo terms for plants.

FORDE, CYRIL DARYLL. *Hopi Agriculture and Land Ownership.* Journal of the Royal Anthropological Institute of Great Britain and Ireland, vol. 61, pp. 357–405. London: Royal Anthropological Institute, 1931. Illustrated.

Field work done during the summer of 1929 with informants from six villages located on the First and Second Mesas of the Hopi pueblo, the westernmost pueblo located in Arizona in the desert region of the Upper Colorado Basin, is the basis for this study. (First Mesa villages: Walpi, Sichomovi, and Hano. Second Mesa villages: Mishongnovi, Shipaulovi, and Shimopovi [*sic*].) The account demonstrates that the Hopi, by adapting to local conditions and by using ingenious devices, successfully cultivated plants of the maize-squash complex. It also includes information on the physical conditions of the pueblo, village, and clan lands and boundaries; crop and garden distribution; theory of land distribution and disposition of family fields within particular clans; Zuñi land holding and inheritance; agricultural seasons and calendars; cultivation of crops including corn, beans, melons, squash, sunflower, and cotton; magic, ritual, and social organizations integrated with agricultural practice. The roles of men and women and the function of maternal clans in determining the distribution and acquisition of fields are briefly mentioned. Photographs show planted fields and irrigated gardens; diagrams show topographic and sociological conditions of Hopi agriculture; and tables list clans and their lands, lineage, and irrigated gardens.

HENDERSON, JUNIUS, and JOHN PEABODY HARRINGTON. *Ethnozoology of the Tewa Indians.* Bureau of American Ethnology Bulletin 56. Washington, D.C.: Government Printing Office, 1914. 76pp. Bibliography.

Informants provide material on the Tewa use of

mammals, birds, reptiles, amphibians, fish, insects, crustaceans, myriapods, arachnids, mollusks, and lower invertebrates. Zoological, common English, and Tewa names are also provided.

HILL, WILLARD WILLIAMS. *The Agricultural and Hunting Methods of the Navajo Indians.* Yale University Publications in Anthropology, no. 18. New Haven, Conn.: Yale University Press, 1938. 193pp. Illustrated. Bibliography.

The material in this book, gathered between 1933 and 1935 from over forty Navajo men and women living on the Navajo Reservation, includes descriptions of Navajo agricultural and hunting methods, provides historic documentation relating to these phases of Navajo life, and discusses the cultural variations due to geography or influences of other cultures. Other sections of the book show the integration of agricultural ritual into agricultural processes; describe ritual and nonritual forms of hunting; and show the unusual amount of ritual integrated into the various activities of everyday life. The book closes with a brief section comparing Navajo agricultural and hunting methods with the peoples of the Plains, Great Basin, the Southwest, and Mexico. Photographs and drawings include a map of Navajo territory, Navajo fields, ceremonial objects, and traps used in hunting.

ROBBINS, WILFRED WILLIAM; JOHN PEABODY HARRINGTON; and BARBARA FREIRE-MARRECO. *Ethnobotany of the Tewa Indians.* Bureau of American Ethnology Bulletin 55. Washington, D.C.: Government Printing Office, 1916. 118pp. Illustrated. Bibliography.

This study was done between 1910 and 1911 among the Tewa of New Mexico in the pueblos of Nambe, Pojoaque, San Ildefonso, San Juan, Santa Clara, and Tesuque, and the Tewa among the Hopi at Hano, Arizona, who were still knowledgeable about aboriginal plant use. The first part of the book groups plant names and words in the Tewa language and gives information on words the Tewa use to distinguish plants from animals and minerals. A list of descriptive plant names of Tewa or Spanish origin is included along with the Tewa names designating parts and functions of plants (flowers, leaves, seeds, and fruit); Tewa terminology for the growth of plants, their condition, dead or alive, their color, and their qualities such as size, taste, odor, texture, wetness or dryness are also given. There is an annotated list of wild plants used by the Tewa (trees, shrubs, herbs, cacti, vines, grasses, and plants outside Tewa country); plants cultivated by the Tewa before Spanish intrusion, especially corn, beans, squash, cotton, and tobacco; food plants acquired and cultivated by the Tewa; plants and fruits harvested but not cultivated, and fruits cultivated. The botanical, common English, Tewa, and Spanish names for the plants are given as well as the parts used, and the method of preparing them for use. There are photographs and sketches of cultivated and wild plants used by the Tewa and an index of botanical names with corresponding common English names.

STEVENSON, MATILDA COXE. *Ethnobotany of the Zuni Indians.* Bureau of American Ethnology 30th Annual Report, 1908–1909, pp. 31–102. Washington, D.C.: Government Printing Office, 1915. Illustrated.

Stevenson's work was done between 1879 and 1908 at Zuñi pueblo, located in the arid country of the extreme western part of New Mexico, with several Zuñi people well versed in the uses of wild plants. Information is given on medical practices and medicinal plants as well as botanical, common English, and Zuñi names, the parts used, and method of preparation for these as well as for edible plants, plants used in weaving, dyeing, basketry, and pottery decoration. Folklore about plants and their use in ceremonials is also included. There are illustrations of plants and a list of plants by their botanical names only.

STEWART, GUY R. "Conservatism in Pueblo Agriculture: Present Day Flood Water Irrigation." In *The Scientific Monthly* (October 1940):329–40. Illustrated.

This examination of the agricultural practices of twentieth-century Hopi and Zuni cultivators sheds light on ancient ways of cultivating corn, beans, and squash through a study of the Hopis and Zuñis, who maintained their way of life after contact with the non-Indian system of planting corn and minor crops. Floodwater farming which enables the Hopis, located at the southern end of the high upland known as Black Mesa, to live in a rigorous environment is described. The author discusses methods of preparing the land for planting, the risks inherent in this agricultural system, and the system the Hopis have devised to minimize those risks through their land holding arrangements. Brief notes on the religious aspects of Hopi farming are included. The irrigation of corn crops by the Zuñis, located in the arid environment of central New Mexico, is described to a lesser degree. The article closes with a brief discussion of the abandonment of many early agricultural communities of the Southwest. There are photographs of different aspects of Hopi and Zuñi floodwater irrigation.

WHITE, LESLIE A. *Notes on the Ethnobotany of the Keres.* Papers of the Michigan Academy of Science, Arts and Letters, vol. 30, pp. 557–68. Ann Arbor: University of Michigan Press, 1945. Bibliography.

This study was done between 1926 and 1941 among the people of the eastern Keresan pueblos of New Mexico: Acoma, Santa Ana, Zia, Santo Domingo, and Cochiti. The information includes the Keresan names of cultivated and wild plants, their botanical and common English names; parts used, method of preparation, data on their uses (food, medicine, and magic); and some Keresan beliefs concerning plants.

WHITING, ALFRED F. *Ethnobotany of the Hopi.* Museum of Northern Arizona Bulletin, no. 15. Flagstaff: Northern Arizona Society of Science and Art, 1939. 120pp. Bibliography.

Whiting's data was collected between 1935 and 1937 in two Hopi villages on the Second Mesa— Mishongnovi and Shipaulovi—and in the village of Oraibi on the Third Mesa. The author discusses the Hopi, their physical environment, and attitudes toward nature and gives a brief history of agriculture in the Southwest. He describes Hopi crops cultivated since prehistoric times, plants acquired and cultivated after the Spanish and Mormon invasions, agricultural methodology, the preparation of corn dishes, and the cultivation and use of wild plants as sustenance. This book includes information on plants used in house construction, hunting, and war; for implements and personal decoration; in firemaking; as musical instruments; for household utensils; and in arts and crafts. Also included is a description of the herbs used as medicine; plants of ceremonial and magical importance; plant symbols in social and ceremonial life; and the Hopis' adjustments to environmental change. A chapter on plant terminology includes the botanical and Hopi names. An annotated list of cultivated and uncultivated plants that are harvested is arranged in families with botanical, common English, and Hopi names, plant availability, and use within the Hopi cultural context included. There is an alphabetical index by Hopi name followed by common English and botanical names.

GREAT BASIN–PLATEAU

CHAMBERLIN, RALPH V. *The Ethnobotany of the Gosiute Indians of Utah.* Memoirs of the American Anthropological Association, vol. 2, pp. 331–405. Menasha, Wis.: American Anthropological Assn., 1907–1915; reprint ed.: Mamaroneck, N.Y.: Kraus Reprint Co., 1964.

Information concerning traditional Goshute use of vegetal foods at the turn of the century is presented in this article. The information was obtained from older men and women of the tribe. A description of the Goshute geographic environment in Utah includes the plants and animals of the area. There are general discussions of the uses of vegetal products as food, beverages, chewing gum, and for smoking, domestic objects, shelter, and curative purposes. The parts of the plants used, methods of preparation, and the botanical, Indian, and common English names are given. A long discussion of word formation in the Goshute language is included. There is a list of plants according to botanical names with tribal and common English equivalents and a list of Goshute names with botanical and common English equivalents.

COLVILLE, FREDERICK V. *Notes on the Plants Used by the Klamath Indians of Oregon.* Contributions from the U.S. National Herbarium, vol. 5, pp. 87–110. Washington, D.C.: Government Printing Office, 1897–1901.

This study was done in 1896 with Klamath Indians of southeastern Oregon who were knowledgeable about the principal plants used in former times by the tribe. The botanical, Klamath, and common English names are given for each plant as well as a description of the plant, the parts used, and method of preparation as food, dye, as wood, in basketry, and for medicine. The use of the plant by other tribes in the area is also given. There is an alphabetical list of Indian plant names with their botanical name equivalents and an index of common English names.

CALIFORNIA

BARROWS, DAVID PRESCOTT. *The Ethnobotany of the Coahuilla Indians of Southern California.* Chicago: University of Chicago Press, 1900; reprint ed.: Banning, Calif.: Malki Museum Press, 1967. 133pp. Bibliography.

Done in the 1890s among Cahuilla Indians of southern California, this book deals with plants used by the Cahuilla in earlier times. Chapters include information on Cahuilla tribal relations and history; a discussion of the linguistic affinities of the Cahuilla with other tribes; a description of the arid geographic environment; information about Cahuilla houses and house building; a description of baskets and basket-making; and the gathering, preparation, and storage of foods. The author includes plant materials used to make various articles, their botanical and Cahuilla names, parts used, and the method of preparing the products. Sixty uncultivated food plants and twenty-eight more utilized for drinks, narcotics, stimulants, or medicines—all indigenous to the desert or semidesert localities—are described along with their botanical, Cahuilla, and common English names, parts used, and how they are prepared. In the reprint edition there are two introductory essays about David Prescott Barrows by Harry W. Lawton and Lowell John Bean; an essay about the Cahuilla language by William Bright; and an unannotated bibliography of the Cahuilla Indians by Lawton and Bean.

CHESTNUT, V. K. *Plants Used by the Indians of Mendocino County, California.* Contributions from the U.S. National Herbarium, vol. 7, pp. 295–422. Washington, D.C.: Government Printing Office, 1900–1902. Illustrated.

This study of the traditional uses of plants in Mendocino County on the Round Valley Indian Reservation, home of the Yuki Indians, and at the town of Ukiah, near the Yokaia and Pomo Indians, was done in 1897–98. The information, which was obtained from Yuki, Yokaia, and Pomo informants, details a subsistence pattern in which virtually every kind of plant was used as food, medicine, and beverages in former times as well as in the nineteenth century. The organization of the economic plants is by families. The botanical, common English, and Indian plant names are given as well as a description of the plant, the parts used, and the various methods of preparation. A long section discusses acorns (oak family) as a vegetal food used by the peoples of the interior part of the county. The manner of collecting and preparing acorns is described as well as their food value. There is a long classified list of economic plants according to their

uses: food, clothing, house and furnishings, heating, cooking and lighting, manufacture, field industries, travel and transportation, extractions from plants used in language and communication, war, amusement, ceremonies and religion, medicine, poisons, and art. There is a glossary of Indian names with botanical equivalents in addition to photographs and sketches of whole plants, their relevant parts, and baskets.

KROEBER, ALFRED LEWIS. *Fishing among the Indians of Northwestern California.* University of California Anthropological Records 21, no. 1, pp. 1–210. Berkeley: University of California Press, 1960. Illustrated. Bibliography.

Kroeber's work primarily concerns the Yuroks, Hupas, and Karoks living on the Lower Klamath, Trinity, and Salmon rivers and the Tolowas, Coastal Yuroks, and Wiyots living along the ocean in northwestern California, with comparisons throughout of central California groups from aboriginal times to the middle of the twentieth century. This account of fishing as a major source of food, based on historical and anthropological sources, includes chapters on fishing rights; varieties of fish utilized; fishing methods; weirs and nets; net making and netting implements; basketry traps; fish harpoons and spears; fish poisons and other methods of catching fish; transporting, preserving, storing, and cooking fish; beliefs, restrictions, and ceremonies; shellfish and the hunting of sea mammals. Seventy-four maps graphically summarize the known distribution of traits concerned with fishing and other related elements of the material culture, each map showing the territorial and tribal limits of a single trait. There are also thirty-two photographs of fish weirs, fishing implements, and nets.

NORTHWEST COAST

GUNTHER, ERNA. *Ethnobotany of Western Washington.* University of Washington Publications in Anthropology 10, no. 1. Seattle: University of Washington Press, 1945; rev. ed.: 1971, pp. 1–62. Illustrated. Bibliography.

This study of the traditional uses of more than 150 indigenous vegetal plants by eighteen small tribes of western Washington was based on information given by men and women of the tribes. The cultures and geographic environments of the eighteen tribes—Chehalis, Cowlitz, Green River, Klallam, Lower Chinook, Lummi, Makah, Nisqually, Puyallup, Quileute, Quinault, Samish, Skagit, Skokomish, Snohomish, Snuqualmie, Squaxin, and Swinomish—are described briefly. The plants are organized into over forty families. Within each plant species a list of corresponding tribal names is followed by information arranged according to the use of the plant as food, as medicine, and in making clothes and other objects. A chart shows which kinds of plants were used by each tribe. An index lists the plants in the article by common English names and a map of western Washington shows the location of the tribes concerned.

SUBARCTIC

NELSON, RICHARD K. *Hunters of the Northern Forest: Designs for Survival among the Alaskan Kutchin.* Chicago: University of Chicago Press, 1973. 339pp. Illustrated. Bibliography.

The major portion of this research was done among the Kutchin Indians of interior subarctic Alaska from 1967 to 1971 in the village of Chalkyitsik where the author observed and participated in the activities described. The study is concerned with the modern and traditional knowledge and techniques associated with hunting, fishing, trapping, and general survival among the Athapaskan-speaking Kutchin. Sections of the book describe Kutchin environment and summarize the annual life cycle; hunting and fishing techniques, knowledge of important game species, uses of vegetation, methods of summer travel and navigation by boats, and camping procedures; the importance of trapping in Kutchin lifeways, techniques of winter travel (dog teams and snowmobiles) and survival; and methods of trapping, snaring, and hunting fur animals. The last section deals with the history and ecological factors influencing Kutchin settlement patterns (from a nomadic lifestyle to trapline settlements to villages), culture change, and its effects on environmental adaptation. There are comparisons of environmental adaptation between the Kutchin and North Alaskan Eskimos. Photographs, diagrams, and drawings show aspects of hunting, fishing, and trapping.

ALASKA

NELSON, RICHARD K. *Hunters of the Northern Ice.* Chicago: University of Chicago Press, 1969. 429pp. Illustrated. Bibliography.

The research for this book was done between 1964 and 1966 among Eskimos of northwestern arctic Alaska. The author presents a detailed study of the traditional and modern Eskimo methods of hunting, traveling, and surviving on sea ice. The complicated body of knowledge, techniques, and equipment employed by the Eskimos in their adaptation to one of the most extreme environments on earth us discussed. Part 1 includes a geographic description of the eastern and western sections of the Arctic Coast and the three villages of Barrow, Point Hope, and Wainwright where the author observed and participated in the activities described. Sea ice in its early stages of development, in winter and in summer, in its movements and fragmentation is described as are drift ice survival methods and astronomical phenomena. Part 2 discusses the food resources of the sea-ice environment: invertebrates, fish, birds, arctic fox, polar bear, white whale, harbor seal, and walrus; hunting behavior and methods for dealing with each aspect of sea-ice environment, and the effect of hunting on the total ecology of northwestern Alaska Eskimos. There is a brief discussion of some of the personality characteristics of the Eskimo hunter, and the last chapter discusses the decline of hunting skills and knowledge. There are photographs of hunting scenes, maps of northwestern Alaska, and appendixes which include the method of the author's study, Eskimo sea-ice terminology, and climatic information.

OSWALT, WENDELL H. "A Western Eskimo Ethnobotany." *Anthropological Papers of the University of Alaska* 6, no. 1 (December 1957):17–36. Illustrated. Bibliography.

This article concerns the botanical knowledge and plant uses among the residents of Napaskiak, a western Eskimo village, provides brief notes on the ethnobotanical knowledge among Alaskan Eskimos in general, and shows that plant products have played a role in Eskimo subsistence patterns. The information was obtained from several informants and by direct observation by the author. The study contains descriptions of over sixty plants, grouped by their use as food, manufactures and fuels, medicines, ceremonial equipment, tobacco, and perfumes. Included for each species are the botanical, common English, and Eskimo names plus a translation into English of the Eskimo term, uses of the plant, and information on whether the plant is still used or not. Following this data on plants used at Napaskiak are comparisons with reported uses of the same or similar plants among other Alaska Eskimos. There is a map of western Alaskan areas referred to in the article.

SULLIVAN, ROBERT J. *The Ten'a Food Quest.* Catholic University of America, Anthropological Series, no. 11. Washington, D.C.: Catholic University of America Press, 1942. 142pp. Illustrated.

Sullivan's work was done among Ten'a groups living in three villages, Koyukuk, Nulato, and Kaltog, along the Yukon River in western Alaska from 1936 to 1937. In addition to informants, the author studied the manuscripts of a missionary who lived among the Ten'a. Concerned primarily with the role which the food quest (acquiring food, preparing, eating, and storing it) plays in the culture of the Ten'a, an Athapaskan-speaking people, the material is divided into two sections corresponding to the two main seasons recognized in the Ten'a annual cycle: the summer food quest and the winter food quest. The author shows how each of the food quests is characterized by a dominant food-getting activity, the summer devoted primarily to fishing and the winter to hunting and trapping. He gives a brief survey of the natural environment, showing that there are only a few kinds of food available, and provides a list of the fish, mammals, birds, plants, and trees with their scientific and common English names. The section on the summer food quest describes the preparation of equipment, the fish camps, religious beliefs, customs, ceremonies, duck hunting, and the annual summer feast. The section on the winter food quest describes the equipment, the winter hunting camps, fish traps, hunting of large game, trapping, mid-winter celebrations, and struggles to survive. There are photographs of a fish wheel, fish drying racks, winter fish traps, and the wolverine ceremony.

BIBLIOGRAPHY

EDWARDS, EVERETT E., and WAYNE D. RASMUSSEN. *A Bibliography on the Agriculture of the American Indians*. Department of Agriculture, Miscellaneous Publication no. 447. Washington, D.C.: Government Printing Office, 1942. 107pp.

The authors, in a brief introduction keyed to entries in the bibliography, give the history of agriculture in the Americas from its beginnings and summarize the contributions of Native Americans to agriculture. Annotated entries in the bibliography are presented in sections entitled: comprehensive histories; comprehensive references (pre-Columbian Native American agriculture); agriculture of particular regions and tribes with emphasis on the methods used in terrace farming, irrigation, conservation (the Aztec; in California, the Caribbean Sea islands and Central America; the Inca, Iroquois, and Maya; in Michigan, Minnesota, the Missouri River region, and New England; the southeastern and southwestern United States; in Virginia and Wisconsin); animals and crops domesticated and raised by Native Americans (bees, corn, cotton, maple sugar, potatoes, tobacco, and wild rice; dogs, wild turkeys and, later, horses). The following section on agriculture of Indian reservations in the United States includes references on problems of irrigation, conservation, forestry, and land use. The listing concludes with a detailed section on uncultivated plants used (food, industrial, medicinal) and a subject-author index. This bibliography includes all references cited by Edwards in *Agriculture of the American Indians: A Classified List of Annotated Historical References, with an Introduction*. Department of Agriculture Library. Bibliographical Contributions, no. 23. Washington, D.C.: Government Printing Office, 1932, edition 1; 1933, edition 2.

STURTEVANT, WILLIAM C. "Preliminary Bibliography on Eastern North American Agriculture." *Southeastern Archaeological Conference Bulletin 3*, Proceedings of the 21st Southeastern Archaeological Conference, pp. 1–24. Cambridge, Mass.: The Conference, 1965.

This is an annotated bibliography of articles and books on aboriginal North American agriculture east of the Plains, including ethnological, archaeological, historical, and botanical sources. The coverage is limited to accounts of the characteristics and history of agricultural techniques and tools, lists and discussions of cultigens, and some of the principal botanical sources of the cultigens. Only items which specifically refer to Indian maize east of the Plains were chosen from the extensive botanical literature covering maize. Material on uses of cultivated plants, on agricultural ceremonies and mythology, and on nonagricultural ethnobotany was excluded from this bibliography.

14   ECONOMIC ASPECTS

The Native Americans' approach to economics provides both insight into their culture as well as another area of conflict with white society. Traditional Indian approaches to wealth, distribution of wealth, trading, and so on are all very characteristic of their culture. Students of Native American culture can learn a great deal through the traditional Indian approach to economics. However, because native culture does have its very own approach to economics, that sphere is almost necessarily an area of conflict between whites and Indians.

Traditional tribal economics were subsistence economics, with generally no wage earners, no cash, and no accumulation of wealth. The works by Driver and Massey (p. 199) and Forde (p. 199) treat general Indian economy. Although tribal economies were not working with capital, there was a good deal of trading which seems to have been practiced for thousands of years. Driver (p. 199) provides an overview of exchange and trade. Hodge (p. 199) and Terrell (p. 200) both discuss widespread prehistoric trading; they identify ancient trade routes and describe items of exchange. Davis's work (p. 203) studies the trade routes and items of exchange for the California area.

However, as often as Indians traded, they seem also to have given away their overabundance of goods. Grobsmith (p. 201) describes the Lakota Giveaway, a type of feast common to Plains tribes. At this ceremony a complex process of gift exchange fostered social alliance, interdependence, and a redistribution of wealth. Vayda (p. 203) and Drucker (p. 203) study Pomo trade feasts and the potlatch respectively, both ritual feasts and gift exchange ceremonies. Ford (p. 202) notes that some Pueblo societies use ritual ceremonies to redistribute wealth so that unfortunate families can survive temporary difficulties. Another form of mutual aid is the Cherokee economic cooperative called the Gadugi. Fogleson and Kutsche (p. 200) describe in detail this mutual aid society formed for economic and social reciprocity. These cooperatives developed among aboriginal Cherokee towns making them an ancient tradition among this Nation.

From the perspective of a basically capitalist economy this Native American tradition of generosity and reciprocity is surprising. However, Brockman (p. 202) suggests that generosity and reciprocal exchange are common in situations where income is low and unpredictable. Thus, if traditional Indian economies were subsistence economies with incomes that were low and unpredictable, as hunting and agriculture tend to be, reciprocal gift exchange and mutual aid are natural elements of them.

Of course in the confrontation between the Indian and white cultures, economic attitudes and practices became an area of confusion, tension, and conflict. The horse and the fur trade brought the first large changes to the traditional economy. McManus (p. 200) studies the Algonquian's response to the fur trade and Jablow (p. 201) discusses the effects of horses on the Plains Indians' economy. The horse and fur trade brought changes to a subsistence economy, a new system of values and changing authority patterns. Lange (p. 202) evaluates the changes in the Cochiti pueblo as the residents moved from a subsistence to a cash economy. Lange notes, along with the other scholars mentioned here, that changes in the traditional economic system confused moral codes and weakened the usual arrangements of authority and activity.

Two interesting studies analyze in detail the changes in authority and activity of women brought about by economic shifts. Brown (p. 200) finds that Iroquois women in a traditional subsistence economy community controlled agricultural production and distributed food and their authority over these two activities accorded them a high status in the community. In contrast, Hamamsy (p. 202) notes that in a Navajo community shifting from subsistence farming and herding to a dependence on wage work and a cash economy, women lose considerable status and security because their function within the community and the family accords them less power.

Many documents here examine the current economic status of Native Americans and reservations. The American Indian Policy Review Commission (below) paints a grim picture of widespread deprivation among Indians which is unequal to that affecting any other U.S. group. The same Commission as well as Ortiz (p. 199), Sorkin (p. 200), and Gilbreath (p. 202) examine federal programs on reservations, the development of natural resources and industry on reservations, and community responses. The Commission and Sorkin both see the development of natural resources as an important factor in the future of Native American communities. However, studies done by the U.S. Senate Committee on Interior and Insular Affairs (p. 200) notes that the federal government has failed to manage those resources well or to help the Native Americans to develop and manage them. Several Native American authors included in Stanley's collection of essays (p. 200) conclude that all projects to develop reservation resources must respect existing social relationships and values. How to do that, to retain a traditional approach to economics within a larger national and world economy, each based on a different set of ideas, is a very difficult question which must now face the Native American community.

AMERICAN INDIAN POLICY REVIEW COMMISSION. "Contemporary Indian Conditions." In *Final Report,* vol. 1, pp. 83–94. Washington, D.C.: Government Printing Office, 1977.
The available statistics on Native Americans in the United States are examined in this study. Population distribution, income, employment, health, housing, and education statistics are analyzed and the profile that emerges is grim: Native Americans, whether men or women living in the city or country, suffer from inadequate education, relatively poor health, low incomes, poor housing, and water and sanitary conditions generally regarded as unacceptable. The statistics paint a picture of widespread

deprivation unequaled by any other group in the United States.

———. "The Economics of Indian Country." In *Final Report,* vol. 1, pp. 301–65. Washington, D.C.: Government Printing Office, 1977. Bibliography, "Economic Development," vol. 2, pp. 60–65.
The structure of differing tribal economies and the use of reservation resources are the focus of this paper. Subjects covered include: natural resources protection and recovery, land, agriculture, timber, water, mineral and human resources; transport, power, water and communications systems; investment capital; investment of trust funds; and enterprise development efforts. The Commission's recommendations for each subject are included. General recommendations suggest the establishment of development goals which reflect the long-term interests of all tribal members as the first and most basic step, to be followed by an evaluation of possible strategies. The essential theme throughout is that tribes must reclaim control over their resources and must be responsible for all decisions as to their use and development.

———. *Final Report. Task Force Seven on Reservation and Resource Development and Protection.* Washington, D.C.: Government Printing Office, 1976. 214pp.
The Commission's report considers a number of issues relating to the development and protection of American Indian-owned natural resources. Among the issues are: the ability of tribal governments to control and promote economic development; the scope and quality of tribal planning; the current control, use and development of reservation resources including land, minerals, timber, and water; and the insufficiency of capital and manpower training. Also examined are federal policies and programs relating to resource development. Appendixes discuss mineral agreements, summarizing new agreements in developing countries and discussing the determinants of bargaining strengths, and analyze the Economic Development Administration. In addition, they examine Indian housing efforts in the United States and present a case study of a project evaluation for an Indian reservation.

BOISE CASCADE CENTER FOR COMMUNITY DEVELOPMENT. *Indian Economic Development,* vol. 1, 81pp.; vol. 2, 54pp. Washington, D.C.: Economic Development Administration, Department of Commerce, 1972.
This report presents the 1971–72 findings of an evaluation team that investigated sixteen projects which had been part of the Selected Indian Reservation Program undertaken by the Economic Development Administration (EDA). Evaluators examined program records, interviewed EDA personnel and Native American people involved in the programs, managers of EDA-funded projects, and others involved with economic development. Volume 1 outlines the aims of the study and presents a summary report of the findings, with recommendations. Volume 2 contains the individual reservation reports with conclusions and recommendations, setting, background, and project analysis for each.

DRIVER, HAROLD E. "Exchange and Trade." In *Indians of North America.* 2nd ed., rev., pp. 208–21. Chicago: University of Chicago Press, 1969. Bibliography.
This chapter describes gift and ceremonial exchange of economic goods and discusses trade, trade items, and trade routes. See also: "Property and Inheritance," (pp. 269–86). References receive full citation in a bibliography at the end of the book.

———, and WILLIAM C. MASSEY. "Economics." In *Comparative Studies of North American Indians.* Transactions of the American Philosophical Society, n.s., 47, part 2, pp. 363–94. Philadelphia: American Philosophical Society, 1957. Illustrated. Bibliography.
The authors utilize data accumulated since 1939 to reconstruct prehistoric practices of Native Americans regarding the division and specialization of labor, exchange and distribution of goods, property and inheritance, eagle-catching sites, wild plant tracts and farm land, and ownership and inheritance of chattels. Maps show the distribution of traits.

FORDE, C. DARYLL. *Habitat, Economy and Society.* New York: Dutton, 1964. 500pp. Illustrated. Bibliography.
This book, originally published in 1934, deals with the economic and social life of a number of non-European peoples in different regions of the world. The author considers the broad aspects of economic patterns and discusses their relation to the physical environment, to social organization, and to major factors in the growth of society. The Native American studies include: "The Paiute: Collectors of the Great Basin," "The Blackfoot: Buffalo Hunters of the North American Plains," "The Nootka, Kwakiutl and Other Fishing Peoples (Tlinget and Haida are included) of British Columbia," "The Eskimo: Seal and Caribou Hunters in Arctic America," and "The Hopi and Yuma: Flood Farmers in the North American Desert."

HODGE, FREDERICK W., ed. "Commerce." In *Handbook of American Indians North of Mexico.* Bureau of American Ethnology Bulletin 30, part 1, pp. 330–32. Washington, D.C.: Government Printing Office, 1907–10.
Evidences of widespread prehistoric commerce in North America are examined for the Arctic area, Canada, the Atlantic slope from Labrador to Georgia, the Mississippi River area, the Gulf area, and the Southwest. See also: "Boats," "Exchange," "Fur Trade," "Horse," (part 1); "Trails and Traderoutes," "Travel," and "Travois" (part 2); and bibliographies under each of these.

ORTIZ, ROXANNE DUNBAR, ed. *Economic Development in American Indian Reservations.* Native American Studies, Development Series No. 1. Albuquerque: University of New Mexico Press, 1979. 156pp.
The articles and essays in this collection are organized into four parts. Part 1 presents a narrative poem regarding the feelings and values of Native

Americans and includes an essay on sovereignty and self-determination. Part 2 provides the historical background for the economic underdevelopment of American Indian societies. Part 3 contains a case study of the Navajo Reservation, and Part 4 deals with the politics and underdevelopment, economic development, and contemporary strategy of a transnational energy corporation.

SORKIN, ALAN L. "The Economic Basis of Indian Life." In *The Annals of the American Academy of Political and Social Science* vol. 436, pp. 1–12. Philadelphia: American Academy of Political and Social Science, 1978.

Sorkin's paper focuses on trends in the economic position of Native Americans. He discusses income, occupational status, task assignments, various programs designed to foster reservation development, agriculture, minerals, and urban programs.

STANLEY, SAM, ed. *American Indian Economic Development.* Chicago: Aldine, 1978. 609pp.

This collection of essays examines economic development efforts in seven widely scattered Native American communities which vary in size both in terms of population and land area. Groups studied include: Navajo (Arizona, New Mexico), Lummis (Washington), Morongo (California), Oglala Sioux (South Dakota), Passamaquoddy (Maine), Cherokees (Oklahoma), and Papagos (Arizona). Economic development is considered from an anthropological perspective in most of the articles. The authors present the historical and cultural background of the people, discuss efforts and attitudes toward economic development, and speculate as to why projects succeeded or failed. Most of the articles are coauthored or authored by Native Americans. There is general agreement among the authors that development projects which ignore the existing systems of social relationships and land-use ideas are doomed to failure. A concluding chapter offers general suggestions to improve the situation.

TERRELL, JOHN UPTON. *Traders of the Western Morning.* Los Angeles: Southwest Museum, 1967. 129pp. Bibliography.

Relying on published sources, Terrell discusses the channels of trade that were established thousands of years ago and utilized for centuries by Native Americans. Geographically, the book covers the area that is now the United States, Mexico, and Central America. Items of trade and barter are described, and trade routes for both prehistoric and early historic times are identified.

U.S. CONGRESS. HOUSE COMMITTEE ON INTERIOR AND INSULAR AFFAIRS, HOUSE OF REPRESENTATIVES. *Indian Economic Development Programs,* part 1, 382pp.; part 2, 233pp.; part 2a, 97pp. Washington, D.C.: Government Printing Office, 1979. Serial No. 96–7.

This Committee report of oversight hearings presents verbal and written testimony from a wide range of representatives of governmental, tribal, and private agencies regarding the economic status of American Indian reservations, on efforts to improve the status, and on problems encountered.

Part 1 contains statements by federal officials from relevant governmental agencies. Part 2 contains statements by representatives of Native American organizations and private agencies active in the field of American Indian affairs. Part 2a presents case studies of certain selected tribal enterprises.

U.S. CONGRESS. SENATE COMMITTEE ON INTERIOR AND INSULAR AFFAIRS. *Management of Indian Natural Resources,* parts 1 and 2. Washington, D.C.: Government Printing Office, 1975–76. 117pp.

This report by the General Accounting Office reviews the management by the Bureau of Indian Affairs of natural resources on selected American Indian reservations, and presents comments, evaluations, and recommendations. The report underscores the importance of Indian-owned natural resources to the future of affected tribes and highlights the federal government's failure to manage those resources properly. Part 1 covers forestland, rangeland, and cropland. Part 2 deals with coal, oil, and gas. The report includes inventory and income data, such as it is, for all the resources studied.

NORTHEAST

BROWN, JUDITH K. "Economic Organization and the Position of Women among the Iroquois." *Ethnology* 17 (1970):151–67. Bibliography.

The relationship between the position of women and their economic role is examined through a comparative consideration of ethnohistoric and ethnographic data relating to the Iroquois of North America and the Bemba of northern Rhodesia. The article discusses the economic organization of subsistence activities of the two groups, the factors of food production and distribution. On the basis of the evidence, the author finds that Iroquois women were accorded a high status because they controlled the factors of agricultural production and maintained the right to distribute food.

MCMANUS, JOHN. "An Economic Analysis of Indian Behavior in the North American Fur Trade." *Journal of Economic History* no. 32 (1972):36–53.

The economic behavior of Algonquian bands in northern Ontario and Quebec is examined in the context of the institutions by which they coordinated their actions or allocated their productive resources. The author seeks an institutional explanation for the depletion of beaver resources and searches for enforced constraints on behavior that would be consistent with the establishment of exclusive territories. He concludes that the institutional characteristics of the groups can be analyzed as an equilibrium set of behavioral constraints serving to maximize the income of the members of the band, subject to the costs of enforcing exclusive rights.

SOUTHEAST

FOGELSON, RAYMOND D., and PAUL KUTSCHE. "Cherokee Economic Cooperatives: The Gadugi." In *Symposium on Cherokee and Iroquois Culture,* edited by William N. Fenton and John Gulick, pp. 87–123. Bureau of American Ethnology Bulletin 180. Washington, D.C.: Government Printing Office, 1961.

This paper is based on information gathered among the Cherokees in western North Carolina. The authors describe the Gadugi, a mutual aid society—or company—formed by a group of men for continued economic and social reciprocity, an economic institution of considerable age. The authors document the origin of the Gadugi in the aboriginal Cherokee town organization, trace the forces responsible for the dissolution of the older town organization, and present background to, and a description of, the Gadugi as it has persisted in one community.

GREAT PLAINS

GROBSMITH, ELIZABETH S. "The Lakota Giveaway: A System of Social Reciprocity." *Plains Anthropologist* 24, no. 84, part 1 (May 1979):123–31.

Grobsmith explores the complex economic and social roles which gift-exchange plays among the people of the Rosebud Sioux Reservation in South Dakota, as illustrated in the Giveaway Ceremony, or Feast, common to the tribes of the Central Plains. Reciprocal gift-giving is examined as a tradition promoting social alliance, interdependence, and the redistribution of wealth.

JABLOW, JOSEPH. *The Cheyenne in Plains Indian Trade Relations 1795–1840.* Monographs of the American Ethnological Society, no. 19. New York: J. J. Augustin, 1951. 100pp. Bibliography.

This study examines the economic relationship among Native American groups of the Great Plains in the United States and southern Canada from 1795 until 1840. Inter- and extratribal trade is looked at. The author discusses the influence of the horse and the fur trade on the structure and function of intertribal trade in the Great Plains and summarizes the changes in basic subsistence, values and attitudes, and patterns of authority engendered by the Cheyenne role in the trade. Groups studied include the Sioux (Dakota), Arikara, Cheyenne, Kiowa, and Comanche.

MEKEEL, H. SCUDDER. "The Economy of a Modern Teton Dakota Community." *Yale University Publications in Anthropology,* no. 6, pp. 3–14. New Haven, Conn.: Human Relations Area Files Press, 1970.

Information for this study was collected in the White Clay District of the Pine Ridge Reservation in South Dakota. The economic behavior of the people of the community is considered in the light of prime values (or master ideals) expressed in the traditional Dakota economy and the force they exert. The author contrasts Teton ideals (bravery, generosity, fortitude, and moral integrity) with those of American society and finds little room for compromise between such diametrically opposed viewpoints on the symbolic use of wealth. This is a reprint of the 1936 edition.

MISHKIN, BERNARD. *Rank and Warfare among the Plains Indians.* Monographs of the American Ethnological Society, no. 3. Seattle: University of Washington Press, 1940, 1966. 65pp. Bibliography.

Based mainly on information gathered among the Kiowa Indians in Oklahoma in 1935, this study examines the influence of the horse in Plains culture and discusses its economic implications among other Plains tribes. The author describes the structure of Kiowa warfare and its role in creating wealth and rank, discusses the various categories and privileges of Kiowa society, and identifies new prerequisites of rank that evolved by the middle of the last century as wealth became separated from warfare. The author finds that the horse, rank, and warfare were inextricably interwoven in the Plains economy and society. This is a reprint of the 1940 edition.

SOUTHWEST

ABERLE, SOPHIE D. "The Pueblo Indians of New Mexico: Their Land, Economy and Civil Organization." *American Anthropologist* 50, no. 4, part 2 (1948):1–93; reprinted in *Memoirs of the American Anthropological Association,* vol. 70. Menasha, Wis.: The Association, 1948.

Aberle considers external and internal forces that have had an impact on Pueblo economy and civil organizations, and explores the response of Pueblo society in terms of adjustments effected in reaction to both. The first part of the article deals with outside pressures engendered by the Spanish and Anglo-American presence, which provoked years of contention over boundaries, titles to grants, and legislation regarding land ownership; the rest of the article examines forces within Pueblo society, explores Pueblo economy and civil organization, and discusses the relation between Pueblo economy and the contemporary civil organizations. The author, federal "superintendent" at the All Pueblos Agency from 1934 to 1943, concludes that through their adaptive strategies the Pueblo civil organizations have maintained their vitality throughout and cautions the federal government to limit its authority.

ADAMS, WILLIAM Y., and LORAINE T. RUFFING. "Shonto Revisited: Measures of Social and Economic Change in a Navajo Community, 1955–1971." *American Anthropologist* 79, no. 1 (1977): 58–83. Bibliography.

Data obtained in studies done sixteen years apart provide a measure of social and economic change and persistence in a Navajo community during a period of unprecedented growth and modernization on the Navajo Reservation. The authors find that "Shonto" exhibits growth without change, in terms of social development, and growth without progress, in terms of economic development. The initial study, with the primary focus on the role of the non-Indian trader, is *Shonto: A Study of the Role of the Trader in a Modern Navajo Community,* by William Y. Adams. Bureau of American Ethnology

Bulletin 188. Washington, D.C.: Government Printing Office, 1963.

BEAGLEHOLE, ERNEST. *Notes on Hopi Economic Life.* Yale University Publications in Anthropology, no. 15. New Haven, Conn.: Yale University Press, 1937. 88pp. Bibliography.
Field work done in 1932 and 1934 in the two Second Mesa Hopi villages of Mishongnovi and Shipaulovi is the basis for this study. Hopi economic processes and values are discussed in the context of basic social institutions. The author explores the economic aspects of the organization of the Hopi household and kin and clan units; presents an inventory of the main types of Hopi wealth; describes patterns of ownership, division of labor, education, and work psychology; and examines the nature and extent of the control of property. In addition, he also tells of agriculture, secondary productive activities, and foods and their preparation. The distribution of wealth through ceremony, exchange of gifts, forfeits, and trade is also discussed.

FORD, RICHARD I. "An Ecological Perspective on the Eastern Pueblos." In *New Perspectives on the Pueblos,* edited by Alfonso Ortiz, pp. 1–18. Albuquerque: University of New Mexico Press, 1972. Bibliography.
This paper examines the role of ritual for assisting the survival of a population through the regulation of the redistribution of foods and other economic goods. The author discusses the environmental variables that affect household productivity of some Pueblo societies in the southwestern United States and describes the regulatory mechanisms that have operated there within the historic period to accommodate families whose food stores are exhausted. The information is considered in light of the hypothesis that in an egalitarian society living in an effective environment with unpredictable and potentially disastrous fluctuations of biotic and abiotic variables, reciprocity and ritual will regulate the circulation of nutrients for the survival of the human population.

GILBREATH, KENT. *Red Capitalism: An Analysis of the Navajo Economy.* Norman: University of Oklahoma Press, 1973. 157pp. Bibliography.
Gilbreath deals with the development of the small business sector of the economy on the largest reservation (some 22,000 square miles) in the United States, which also has the largest population (over 120,000). He analyzes the Navajo business community, focusing on institutional and cultural hindrances to reservation business development. Sections deal with legal and political problems, financing Navajo businesses, cultural influences on business development, and education. There is a summary with recommendations. The author finds that the underdeveloped state of the business community on the Navajo reservation permits the income generated by primary industries to flow off-reservation without creating secondary jobs and incomes on-reservation, and concludes that the development of Navajo small businesses would result in immediate economic benefits, given the

limitations of the reservation's capital and entrepreneurial resources.

HAMAMSY, LAILA SHUKRY. "The Role of Women in a Changing Navajo Society." *American Anthropologist* 59, no. 1 (1957):101–11.
Woman's role in traditional Navajo economic and social systems is discussed and contrasted to role changes brought about during the early 1950s by drastic changes introduced into the Navajo community of Fruitland, New Mexico, by directed social change, in the form of government programs designed to counteract the results of other government programs, and by an increased dependence on wage work in a cash economy, as opposed to a farming and herding-based subsistence. The information suggests that the Navajo women of Fruitland were affected adversely by the changes, in terms of their economic position, the significance of their function within the family, in their sense of security, and their bargaining position in family interaction. (A broader-based account of the changes imposed on this small Navajo community by external forces can be found in *Fruitland, New Mexico: A Navaho Community in Transition* by Tom T. Sasaki. Ithaca: Cornell University Press, 1960.)

LANGE, CHARLES H. "The Role of Economics in Cochiti Pueblo Culture Change." *American Anthropologist* 55, no. 5, part 5 (1953):674–94.
Based on the author's field research in the early 1950s and on information in historical documents, this article studies the effects of economic change tn the social, ceremonial, and political patterns of Cochiti pueblo, a village some thirty miles southwest of Santa Fe, New Mexico. Cochiti property and ownership, agricultural and non-agricultural economy, and social, ceremonial and political organizations and changes are examined. The author finds that up until 1930 economic changes affecting Cochiti had been absorbed for the most part within existing systems, but that as of 1930, when a shift toward a cash economy occurred, the complex of social controls began to weaken. Based on his evaluation of Cochiti culture up to and including 1952, the author makes predictions about possible future developments. The author also wrote *Cochiti: A New Mexico Pueblo, Past and Present.* Austin: University of Texas Press, 1959.

GREAT BASIN–PLATEAU

BROCKMAN, C. THOMAS. "Reciprocity and Market Exchange on the Flathead Reservation." *Northwest Anthropological Research Notes* 5, no. 1 (1971):77–86.
This paper examines the linkage between social class and economic marginality on the Flathead Reservation in western Montana. The author reviews Flathead economic history and cultural environment and analyzes data on occupation, income, and households. He identifies two economic orientations within the community: (1) reciprocal exchanges (a traditional practice) as an adjustment to low, unpredictable income; and (2) the amassing of

goods where incomes are relatively high and secure.

STERN, THEODORE, and JAMES P. BOGGS. "White and Indian Farmers on the Umatilla Indian Reservation." *Northwest Anthropological Research Notes* 5, no. 1 (1971):37–76.

Stern and Boggs study generations-long leasing relationships between Umatilla land owners and white farmers in northeastern Oregon. They describe a dual economy dominated progressively by non-Indian farmers who have better access to capital, expertise, and power, in which the Umatillas suffer progressive economic deprivation through many separate exchanges rather than through an organized program administered by the government, and assert that this process of gradual deprivation tends to occur wherever native-owned resources are exploited by non-Indians in North America.

CALIFORNIA

DAVIS, JAMES T. "Trade Routes and Economic Exchange among the Indians of California." In *Aboriginal California: Three Studies in Culture History,* pp. 1–75. The University of California Research Facility. Berkeley: University of California Press, 1963. Bibliography. (Also in Reports of the University of California Archaeological Survey, no. 54, 1961.)

This study presents detailed information on items exchanged by barter among various Native American groups in California. A map shows the known trails over which commodities were carried and a table lists trade items, including the number of times each item is mentioned in the literature as being imported or exported. Different aboriginal ethnographic groups are listed and items traded to and received from other groups are identified for each listing. The trails of aboriginal California are correlated with modern thoroughfares.

KING, CHESTER. "The Chumash Inter-Village Economic Exchange." In *The American Indian Reader: Anthropology,* pp. 125–51. San Francisco: Indian Historian Press, 1972.

King asserts that the Chumash Indians, who occupied areas on the coast of southern California, on the Santa Barbara Channel Islands, and in the inland valleys adjacent to the coast, maintained a market economy with standardized, portable mediums of exchange which frequently were used to purchase subsistence materials, most manufactured goods, and some services.

KROEBER, A. L. "Yurok Law and Custom." In *The California Indians: A Source Book,* edited by Robert F. Heizer and M. A. Whipple, pp. 394–99. Berkeley: University of California Press, 1971.

The author discusses the use of dentalium shells by the Yurok Indians in northwestern California as a medium of exchange. Dollar equivalencies (early 1900s) are assigned, the use of articles other than shells is examined, and a list of Yurok valuations

provides information on various kinds of economic exchanges. See subsections: "Money," "Treasure," and "Valuations."

VAYDA, ANDREW P. "Pomo Trade Feasts." In *Tribal and Peasant Economies,* edited by George Dalton, pp. 494–500. Garden City, N.Y.: Natural History Press, 1967.

This article, based on data from ethnographic accounts of intervillage trade among the Pomo Indians of central California, examines Pomo-sponsored feasts at which food was exchanged for shell beads, which also had other economic uses. The author considers the evidence and finds that the trade feasts apparently served to augment the capacity of people from differing areas to postpone the consumption of subsistence goods.

NORTHWEST COAST

DRUCKER, PHILIP. "The Potlatch." In *Tribal and Peasant Economies,* edited by George Dalton, pp. 481–93. Garden City, N.Y.: Natural History Press, 1967.

Drucker examines the ceremonial exchange of economic goods, the potlatch, as practiced by the Kwakiutl Indians of the Northwest Coast. He shows that the notorious case of the aggressive, ostentatious nature of the Kwakiutl potlatch was a very late development, evolving after the Kwakiutl became importantly enmeshed in cash-earning.

OBERG, KALFERO. *The Social Economy of the Tlingit Indians.* Foreword by Wilson Duff. Seattle: University of Washington Press, 1973. 146pp. Bibliography.

This discussion of the traditional Tlingit economic and social system is based on research done in 1931 in the southeastern Alaska villages of Klukwan, Sitka, and Wrangell. The author presents background information on Tlingit history, physical type, technology, culture, and social organization; discusses property, the rights of individuals to the disposal of objects of social value, and the annual cycle of production; examines the organization of labor, trade, and consumption of wealth; and considers the economic system of the Tlingit and its relation to their social structure and belief system. An appendix lists natural resources, medicinal herbs, and clans.

BIBLIOGRAPHIES

GAGALA, KENNETH. *The Economics of Minorities: A Guide to Information Sources.* Economic Information Guide Series No. 2, pp. 167–74. Detroit: Gale Research, 1976.

This bibliography covers many periodicals, books, and some government documents published between 1965 and 1974. Citations with annotations are arranged alphabetically by author. Items include material on modern economics and social and political economy.

HODGE, WILLIAM H. "Economics." In *A Bibliography of North American Indians: Selected and Partially Annotated with Study Guides,* pp. 28–29. New York: Interland Publishing, 1975.

Thirty-two items in this category are concerned with the various ways that Native Americans use money and other units of value within traditional and nontraditional milieus. See also: *Anthropology of Development* (pp. 136–47). Most of the material in this category is concerned with the use of government funds to improve Native American communities. Several articles deal with the economic position of Alaska natives, others discuss community and economic development. Citations in each category are annotated when the title is not self-explanatory.

SNODGRASS, MARJORIE P. *Economic Development of American Indians and Eskimos, 1930 through 1967: A Bibliography.* Washington, D.C.: Department of the Interior, 1968. 263pp.

This unannotated bibliography lists 1,595 published and unpublished materials dealing with the economic development efforts of Native American and Eskimo communities and individuals. For the purpose of this listing, economic development is defined as individual or collective efforts, on- or off-reservation, designed to produce tangible income. Works are listed under: arts and crafts development; economic development of natural resources; farming, ranching, range resources, and related industries; fish and wildlife development; forests and related industries; human resources; industrial and commercial development; irrigation, dams, and reclamation projects; minerals and mining; overall economic development plans; socioeconomic studies and plans; soil and moisture conservation, and water resources; ten-year plans; and tourism and recreation development. The index lists sources by reservation and by Bureau of Indian Affairs field office for native villages in Alaska.

THORNTON, RUSSELL, and MARY K. GRASMICK. *Bibliography of Social Science Research and Writings on American Indians.* Center for Urban and Regional Affairs, Publication No. 79-1. Minneapolis: University of Minnesota Press, 1979. 160pp.

A section in this unannotated bibliography lists articles about American Indians published through 1976 in scholarly economics journals. Articles on anthropology have been excluded. Titles are grouped under genre of journal, in this case economics, with an alphabetical list of authors.

U.S. DEPARTMENT OF HOUSING AND URBAN DEVELOPMENT. *The North American Indian: A Bibliography of Community Development.* Washington, D.C.: Department of Housing and Urban Development, 1975. 65pp.

This work lists 403 items with one-line descriptions accompanying each citation. Sources are listed under ten headings: "Background," "Government Relations," "Legal Aspects," "Demographic Distribution," "Cultural and Social Indicators," "Community Development and Economic Conditions," "Education," "Health," "Housing," and "Urbanization." Sub-bibliographies appear in each of the ten divisions. In addition, a roster entitled "Comprehensive Planning Reports on Indian Tribal Bodies Sponsored by HUD" is also included.

15   ARCHITECTURE AND HOUSING

North America had its own indigenous original architecture long before
Europeans arrived. It has always had an enormous and varied landscape
with multifarious materials and climates, and has provided almost every
kind of material for building: hard and soft woods for timber, dirt for
adobe, grass for thatch, bark for shingling, poles for framework. Every
Indian tribe constructed some form of dwelling out of these materials and
many tribes used more than one structure depending on the season of the
year and other circumstances. There were the bark houses of the Penobscots; the longhouses of the Iroquoian tribes; the domed houses of the
Chippewas; the tipis of the Crows, Cheyennes, Sioux, and Blackfeet; the
earth lodges of the Mandans, Hidatsas, and Pawnees; the stone and adobe
pueblos of the southwestern Indians; the hogans of the Navajos; the log
dwellings of Puget Sound Indians; the grass houses of the Wichitas and
Caddos as well as other types.

Over the past ninety years, anthropologists, geographers and other social
scientists have been intrigued with the various kinds of Indian dwellings.
Some have explored the relationship between Indian habitations and their
immediate environment, while others have analyzed the cultures of Indian
tribes and related social customs to the Indian structures.

There are a number of scholars who are studying the tribal cosmology
and world view built into native houses and religious structures, village
ground plans, and human movements during ceremonial and domestic occasions. The forthcoming study by Nabokov and Easton (p. 208), which
contains a comprehensive treatment of the structural variety and cultural
interpretations of the full range of North American Indian dwelling types,
explores the religious/philosophical dimension of each native house type
and cites unpublished and published studies that contain information on
house symbolism.

Numbers of anthropologists writing over fifty years ago put forward the
theory that the forms of Indian habitations were determined by regional
environmental conditions. Writers including Bushnell (p. 209), Fewkes
(p. 212), Geare (p. 207), Mindeleff (p. 213), and Waterman (p. 208) describe
the flora of a region, stressing that the local materials affected the style
and materials of dwellings. They held that an abundance of timber in the
eastern woodlands resulted in tribal habitations of logs or frames covered

with bark; that limited forest growth on the plains resulted in lodges with a frame of timber thatched with prairie grass and covered with earth; or that the arid environment of the Southwest resulted in pueblos made of adobe, sun-dried bricks of earth, or flat stones. Other anthropologists have rejected this theory of environmental determinism, contending that the environment does not determine people's cultures, but merely sets the outer limits and offers opportunities which influence cultures only in the most general ways. These writers have studied the social structures and customs as well as the economic life of Indian tribes and theorize that these cultural configurations determine the shape, size, and materials used in their habitations. Goddard (p. 207) and Morgan (p. 207) argue that the size and shape of dwellings depended in many instances on the social organization of a tribe. There were tribes whose members built structures for single families, such as the Penobscots and Navajos, and there were other groups whose members lived communally and built houses large enough to accommodate several families, such as the Iroquois and Indians of Puget Sound. Writers argue that large households composed of several families resulted from efforts to procure food, the commanding concern of their life. Therefore, subsistence patterns which greatly influenced social forms were reflected in certain kinds of dwellings.

Lately, writers such as Scully and Current (p. 213) are incorporating elements from both the environmental and the cultural theories by viewing Indian habitations as ecologically adapted to the environment as well as centrally tied to a particular way of life. They stress that Indian habitations vary with climate, geographic location, the form of the society, and the relationship of clans and families.

Anthropologists have studied the form, methods of construction, and materials used in the different habitations and other structures that Native Americans have constructed such as kivas, ceremonial chambers, and sweat houses. They describe houses with round ground plans, either of conical or dome shape, which were almost universal in North America; houses with rectangular ground plans, more limited in distribution in the United States to the Northwest Coast, the Southwest, and east of the Mississippi River; semisubterranean houses, with or without tunnel entrances; and houses erected over pits located throughout the entire western half of the country. Swanton's study (p. 209) focuses on tribes that constructed two or more types of dwellings which were used either for summer or winter lodging, and Bushnell (p. 209) describes how some tribes erected temporary shelters during long journeys in search of buffalo and other game.

Among many Indian tribes of North America, women were the architects of their communities. Most notably, in the Plains area, women working together designed, fabricated, and constructed the dwelling units which have provoked the imaginations of people throughout the world, the tipis. Indian women not only manufactured and constructed these houses and decorated the interiors, they also chose the location of the village sites. The studies by Campbell (p. 210), the Laubins (p. 210), and McClintock (p. 211) report the important role of women regarding tipis and explain the two possible types of tipi pole arrangement, either a three-pole or four-pole foundation.

Some anthropologists who study Indian habitations are of the opinion that only the Indian pueblos of the Southwest, especially those built in the twelfth and the thirteenth centuries, called by some the "golden age" of the pueblos, merit the label "architecture." These structures, from one to four stories high, made of durable materials, adobe and stone, have been studied extensively by archaeologists, social-cultural anthropologists, architects, photographers, and others. The interrelationships between the ancient Pueblo peoples, their physical environment, and their architecture have been studied as well as the details of the structures they built: size, construction materials, masonry, and fittings such as doors, fireplaces, and ceilings. In addition, scholars study contemporary pueblos because traditional and architectural evidence indicate that some of the pueblo ruins and cliff dwellings were built and occupied by ancestors of southwest Pueblo Indians.

DENVER ART MUSEUM. Department of Indian Art. Indian Leaflet Series, vol. 1, 1930–32. 3pp. Illustrated. Bibliography.

no. 9	(1930)	Southwestern Indian Dwellings
no. 12	(1930)	The Iroquois Long House
no. 19	(1931)	The Plains Indian Tipi
no. 20	(1931)	The Plains Indian Earth Lodge: Historic Period
no. 34	(1931)	Puget Sound Indian Houses
no. 39	(1932)	New England Indian Houses, Forts, and Villages
no. 42	(1932)	The Grass House of the Wichita and Caddo

Each three-page leaflet gives a brief description of the Native American groups under consideration and their geographic location. Descriptions of dwellings include construction, interior arrangement, basic structured framework, furniture, firemaking, and other ethnographic information. Photographs or drawings of each dwelling are included, and there are brief bibliographies in each leaflet giving the historical and anthropological sources from which the information is drawn.

GEARE, R. I. "Typical Homes of American Indians." *Out West: A Magazine of the Old Pacific and the New* 27, no. 2 (August 1907):98–114. Illustrated.

Dwellings of representative Native American groups throughout the American continent are described, which the author contends reflect adaption to regional environmental conditions, both in ancient and historic times. Based on other written studies, the article covers the principal house types which evolved through variations in climatic conditions and the needs of people in the following regions: the Arctic area inhabited by Greenland and Alaskan Eskimos, the former living in snow houses and the latter in log-and-earth dwellings; the North Pacific area with Haida Indians living in timber houses with totem poles; eastern Canadian Algonquian-speaking Montagnais Indians living in hide dwellings; the California, Utah, and Nevada area, with people living in houses of board-and-shingle; the Great Plains area with people living in buffalo hide tents; the Missouri Valley region with people

in earth-covered houses; Arizona and New Mexico with the ancient multistory dwellings of the pueblos; the Sonoran region in Arizona and Mexico with Papagos living in grass-covered, dome-shaped houses; Venezuelan Indians living in dwellings built over water; and Patagonia, with the Tehuelche people living in tall houses made of sticks and skins. There are photographs of eleven models of different house styles in North and South America including models of ancient cliff dwellings.

GODDARD, PLINY E. "Native Dwellings of North America." *Natural History* 28, no. 2 (March–April 1928):191–203. Illustrated.

Goddard describes the variety of house styles utilized in North America in pre-European times maintaining that the materials, shapes, and sizes of dwellings were determined chiefly by the economic lifestyles of the people rather than by geographical and climatic conditions. The study, based on written sources, shows that the size of a dwelling in many instances also depended on the social customs and family structure of any given group. The survey begins with a discussion of Eskimo summer and winter habitations and continues with descriptions of hide tipis in Canada east of the Rocky Mountains and in the United States between the Rockies and the Mississippi River, conical bark-covered houses of Algonquian Indians in the New England states and in the eastern provinces of Canada, longhouses in New York (Iroquois) and in Virginia, earth lodges of some groups in the Plains area, plank houses along the Pacific Coast from northern California to the Alaskan peninsula, and the cave dwellings and multistoried houses of the pueblos in the Southwest. There are photographs of scenes in an Apache house, in the pueblos, in a Navajo hogan and summer house, in an Eskimo winter snow house, in a Micmac wigwam, in Haida and Hupa houses, and in Plains earth lodges and tipis.

MORGAN, LEWIS H. *Houses and House-Life of the American Aborigines*. Contributions to North American Ethnology, vol. 4. Washington, D.C.:

Government Printing Office, 1881; reprint ed: Introduction by Paul Bohannan'. Chicago: University of Chicago Press, 1965. 319pp. Illustrated.

This study discusses the architecture of the peoples of North and Central America and its relations to social structure. Morgan contends that subsistence was a preoccupation which greatly influenced social organization and resulted in dwellings of large households composed of several families. The information is based on data from the author's field work, material supplied by informants, correspondence with other scholars, and a study of early narrative accounts, plus anthropological and historical literature. Chapters explain the social and governmental organization of Indians in North, Central, and South America into gentes, phratries, tribes, and confederacies of tribes and the functions of each in the social system; discuss the common practice of hospitality among Indian tribes including the Iroquois of New York, tribes in the Southeast, Northeast, the Plains region, the Northwest, Great Lakes region, Southwest, and Indians of Mexico, Central, and South America; describe the cohesive local communities that were basic units of consumption among tribal groups all over the Americas; and examine tribal customs with regard to land and food throughout the Americas. Chapter 5 contains a description of house styles north of New Mexico in which the author proposes that the tribes' social organization and customs were incorporated into their architecture. The various lodges of California Indians and tribes in the Columbia River valley are considered, as are Chippewa houses in the Great Lakes region, Sioux hide tents on the Plains, villages in Virginia, Nyack Indian houses on Long Island, Iroquois longhouses in New York, Mandan houses in the Upper Missouri region, and houses of Maricopa and Mohaves of the Lower Colorado River. The remaining chapters discuss pueblo houses and the lifestyles of Santo Domingo, Zuñi, Hopi, Taos, Jemez, and Zia Indians in New Mexico which Morgan believes were determined by social organization and the need for defense; house ruins of Indians of the San Juan River valley and its tributaries; earthworks of the Ohio Valley Moundbuilders; houses of the Aztecs; and ruins in Yucatán and Central America. There are footnotes throughout the book citing the sources the author studied. Drawings include California lodges, a Chippewa wigwam, a Dakota skin tent, Virginia Indian villages, an Iroquois longhouse, the ground plans of a longhouse and a Mandan house. There are sketches of pueblo ruins and ground plans in the Southwest, Yucatán, and Central America, and photographs of pueblos in the Southwest. The introduction discusses Morgan, his work, his influence on other scholars and the field of anthropology, and misinterpretations in *Houses and House-Life*.

NABOKOV, PETER, and ROBERT EASTON. *Native American Architecture*. New York: Oxford University Press, forthcoming. ca. 225pp. Illustrated. Bibliography.

The authors present a comprehensive survey of the structural variety and cultural interpretations of the full range of North American Indian domestic and ceremonial dwellings from ancestral to current times. The introduction explains four primary themes that organize the study of each house type. The first theme concerns ecosystems and landscapes out of which the structures evolved, the climate to which they had to respond, and the available materials which also determined their design, shape, and size. The second theme involves the ethnohistorical chronicle of the dwelling's evolution in relation to its' role in the social/political life of a tribal community. The third theme involves the architectural analysis of house design and construction, and the last explores the tribal cosmology and world view built into the house structure, its setting, village layout, and human movements during ceremonial and domestic occasions. The structures that are discussed are encampments, snow houses, wickiups, Wichita grass houses, sweat houses, northern and southern style Plains tipis, other kinds of tipis, longhouses, thatched houses, food shelters, desert dwellings such as hogans, California houses, earth lodges, communal spaces, Northwest Coast houses, houses for the dead, pueblos, kivas, houses of reservation years, and traditional houses today. There are hundreds of photographs and drawings that illustrate the dwellings and village settlement patterns. The book is based on field work, Indian accounts, and unpublished and published primary and secondary accounts listed in the bibliography.

WATERMAN, THOMAS TALBOT. "North American Indian Dwellings." *The Geographical Review* 14, no. 1 (January 1924):1–25. Illustrated. Bibliography. Reprint ed.: *Annual Report of the Board of Regents of The Smithsonian Institution 1924,* pp. 46–455. Washington, D.C.: Government Printing Office, 1925.

This study deals with the ways in which geographic forces operated in shaping or modifying aboriginal dwellings in North America. The author contends that the forms of Indian habitations were affected by climate and were modified according to the materials available. House types discussed include: the wigwam of Algonquian-speaking agricultural peoples who lived over a large part of eastern North America; the tipi of the Great Plains; the underground or pit dwellings of the Plateau, Northwest, and Plains areas of western North America which varied in size, shape, and materials according to local conditions; the subterranean lodges of the Plateau, a modified form of the pit dwelling, the earth lodge of some of the Plains peoples; the ancient underground structures in the Southwest; the plank houses of the tribes of the Pacific Northwest; and the houses of the Eskimos. A brief discussion of puzzling types of habitations is also included. A map of the distribution of pit structures in western North America and photographs of ancient and historic dwellings in different regions of North America illustrating marked contrasts in form and materials are included. There is a bibliography of early narrative accounts and archaeological, historical, and anthropological source materials.

NORTHEAST

BUSHNELL, DAVID I., JR. *Native Villages and Village Sites East of the Mississippi.* Bureau of American Ethnology Bulletin 69. Washington, D.C.: Government Printing Office, 1919. 111pp. Illustrated. Bibliography.

This is a study of the family dwellings, other structures, and villages of Native American groups in the eastern United States (the area extending eastward from the Mississippi River to the Atlantic) who, with a diversity of language and influenced by a great range of environmental conditions, had developed distinct house forms. Section 1 describes the principal groups in the East belonging to seven linguistic families (Algonquian, Iroquoian, Muskogean, Siouan, Timucuan, Tunican, and Uchean) as they were when first encountered by Europeans. In section 2 there are descriptions of Algonquian wigwams of various materials and shapes and their interiors, particularly in New England states, the South and the Great Lakes region; longhouses for communal living and other dwellings typical of Iroquoian tribes in the southern and northern sections of the eastern United States; multiple family dwellings of Muskogean tribes in the southeastern section, particularly the Creek, Natchez, and Seminole villages, and of the Timucuan tribes. The description of settlements of Siouan, Tunican, and Uchean tribes are based on meager references. The references chosen report the differences in appearance of villages as well as individual structures and describe some of the forms of temporary shelters constructed by every tribe. There are pictures of southeastern terrain, typical Algonquian structures, Choctaw, Creek, and Seminole habitations, ground plans of longhouses, Creek towns, and other structures. The bibliography includes many accounts of French explorers, colonists, travelers, traders, and missionaries.

———. "Ojibway Habitations and Other Structures." *Annual Report of the Board of Regents, Smithsonian Institution 1916/1917,* pp. 609–17. Washington, D.C.: Government Printing Office, 1919. Illustrated.

Bushnell's discussion of the dome-shaped wigwams of the northern and central Algonquian tribes, as they once existed in the Upper Mississippi River valley in the vicinity of the Great Lakes and the valley of the Ohio River and eastward to the Atlantic Coast, is based on a study of the last remaining villages and camps of the Chippewa tribe in northern and central Minnesota at the turn of the century. This work contains references to these habitations taken from early narrative accounts and an account of the author's visit to the Chippewa camp in Minnesota from 1899 to 1900, where he studied wigwams. He describes the materials used, the method by which the structures were built including variations, and presents other ethnographic information about the tribe. There are photographs taken by the author of Chippewa wigwams and other structures of various shapes and materials.

PARKER, ELY S. "The Long House." In Lewis H. Morgan, *League of the Ho-de'-no-sau-nee or Iroquois,* edited by Herbert H. Lloyd, vol. 2, pp. 287–302. New York: Dodd, Mead, 1901. Illustrated.

Parker provides physical descriptions, construction methods, and uses of the longhouse until the end of the eighteenth century, based on quotations from Jacques Lafitau, William Bartram, Lewis H. Morgan, and other observers who felt that the longhouse represented Iroquois social and political organization. There are sketches of the ground plans of a Seneca and an Onondaga longhouse and a five-fire longhouse.

WILLOUGHBY, CHARLES C. "Houses and Gardens of the New England Indians." *American Anthropologist* 8, no. 1 (January–March 1906):115–32. Illustrated.

This article discusses the three general types of habitations of New England Indians (Penobscots and Pequots): the round and longhouse, occurring throughout the area, and the conical house, more common in Maine. Brief notes are given for the round and longhouses which were used for dwelling, council, or ceremonial purposes; for the conical houses, the traditional lodge of the Penobscot Indians of Maine; and for other structures, lodge coverings, and house furnishings. There are small sketches of house types and gardens. The notes are based on seventeenth-century historical records.

SOUTHEAST

SWANTON, JOHN R. "Housing." In *The Indians of the Southeastern United States.* Bureau of American Ethnology Bulletin 137. Washington, D.C.: Government Printing Office, 1946; reprint ed.: Westport, Conn.: Greenwood Press, 1969, pp. 387–439. Illustrated. Bibliography.

This chapter contains information about the habitations of tribes of Muskhogean, Tunican, Uchean, Siouan, Iroquoian, Caddoan, and Algonquian linguistic families living in the Southeast. The author shows that there were two principal types of dwellings that existed in aboriginal and historic times, circular winter houses and rectangular summer houses. There are long descriptions of winter and summer houses of the Chickasaws, Creeks, Seminoles, Yuchis, Choctaws, Cherokees, Siouan-speaking peoples, Virginia Algonquians, Natchez, and other tribes. The dimensions of and materials used in house building, the beds, methods of making fires, smoke holes, windows, doors, awnings, sunshades, flags, cushions, towels, soap, and stockades are described for various southeastern tribes. There are drawings of structural details, ceremonial and house ground plans of Creek, Seminole, and Cherokee Indians. The work is based on early accounts and historical and anthropological studies listed in the bibliography which is prefaced by a long essay on southeastern source materials.

GREAT PLAINS

BUSHNELL, DAVID I., JR. *Villages of the Algonquian, Siouan, and Caddoan Tribes West of the Missis-*

sippi. Bureau of American Ethnology Bulletin 77. Washington, D.C.: Government Printing Office, 1922. 211pp. Illustrated. Bibliography.

Tribes belonging to three linguistic groups, Algonquian, Siouan, and Caddoan, whose villages in aboriginal times extended from Arkansas northward to and beyond the Canadian boundary and from the Mississippi River across the Plains to the Rocky Mountains, are the focus of this study. The author briefly describes the importance of the buffalo to tribes west of the Mississippi and discusses the Algonquian tribes (Chippewas, Cheyennes, Arapahoes, Crees, Blackfeet, Illinois, Sacs and Foxes) who lived in timber country, principally in mat-and-bark covered wigwams, and explains that certain members of this linguistic family also used skin tipis typical of the Siouan tribes. He discusses the Siouan tribes (Dakotas, Assiniboines, Omahas, Poncas, Quapaws, Hidatsas, Osages, Kansas, Iowas, Otoes, Missourias, Winnebagos, Crows, and Mandans) who lived primarily in conical skin tipis on the plains, although some members of this linguistic family also constructed earth lodges and mat- or bark-covered dwellings. The author cites Caddoan tribes (Pawnees, Arikaras, Wacos, Wichitas, and Caddos) who generally lived in earth-covered lodges although the Wichitas lived in high, circular, thatched structures. Bushnell asserts that the environment influenced the form of dwellings erected by the various tribes and also discusses how nearly all the tribes had two or more types of dwellings constructed under different conditions, either permanent villages or temporary shelters used during long journeys in search of buffalo. There are numerous illustrations of different kinds of tribal dwellings, other structures, artifacts, and buffalo hunt scenes, each illustration accompanied by extensive notes.

CAMPBELL, WALTER STANLEY. "The Cheyenne Tipi." *American Anthropologist* 17, no. 4 (October–December 1915):685–94. Illustrated.

This study of southern Cheyenne tipi-making in Oklahoma, an art controlled and perpetuated by certain societies or guilds of women, is based on other studies, an examination of old photographs, and on observations of Cheyenne tipis. The author describes the three-pole arrangement in use early in the twentieth century on the Plains and discusses the importance of the poles themselves—either cedar or pine, considered by the Cheyenne to be the most essential part of the tipi—and the distances Cheyenne people travel to get them. The making of the tipi, its cover, and the method of pitching the lodge are described as well as the inside linings and furnishings. The Cheyenne tipi is compared with those of other tribes. The author also compares the early twentieth-century Cheyenne tipis with old photographs of nineteenth-century tipis and discusses the substitution of canvas for buffalo hides, and describes how the notching of the edges of the cover is different as well as the door shape and the presence of windbreaks around the canvas tipis. There are sketches of Cheyenne tipis, a canvas tipi cover pattern, the method of tying three poles, and a ground plan of a Cheyenne tipi.

———. "The Tipis of the Crow Indians." *American Anthropologist* 29, no. 1 (January–March 1927): 87–104. Reprint ed.: Mamaroneck, N.Y.: Kraus Reprint Co., 1962. Illustrated.

This study of Crow tipis in Montana is based on other studies, examination of old photographs, and observations of three- and four-pole tipis. The author discusses the four-pole arrangement of the Crow tipi, as well as three-pole arrangements of other Plains tribes, and shows how the difference in structure affects the cut of the canvas and the tipi's serviceability as a dwelling. He gives notes on how the Crows obtain their poles, how they prepare the canvas, pitch the tipi, and lash on the canvas, all done by women. The ornamentation on Crow tipi covers is described and compared with the tipi covers of other tribes. There are sketches and photographs of a Crow tipi framework, a canvas cover laid flat, the Crow tie (of poles), the ground plan of a Crow tipi, the raising of foundation poles (with and without canvas), and examples of painted Crow tipis.

GRINNELL, GEORGE BIRD. "Early Cheyenne Villages." *American Anthropologist* 20, no. 4 (October–December 1918):pp. 359–80.

This article deals with the Cheyenne in the days before they moved onto the Plains. It is based primarily on traditional Sioux and Cheyenne stories and archeological findings which point back to times when the Cheyenne occupied permanent earth-lodge villages and depended on cultivated crops for subsistence.

LAUBIN, REGINALD, and GLADYS LAUBIN. *The Indian Tipi: Its History, Construction, and Use.* Norman: University of Oklahoma Press, 1957; reprint ed.: New York: Ballantine, 1971. 270pp. Illustrated. Bibliography.

The Laubins' book, based in part on information obtained from Sioux, Crow, and Blackfeet informants in the Plains region (North and South Dakota, and Montana), begins with the history of the tipi from the earliest mention of it in European records around 1540–42, until the first decades of the twentieth century when tipis went out of everyday use. Much of the information in the chapters, while designed to impart information on traditional tipi life and the old ways, is at the same time a technical guide to constructing and living in tipis. There are chapters on the tipi's utility and beauty, the three-pole Sioux tipi, the materials needed to make a cover, how to pitch a tipi, the division of labor, and living in a tipi (linings, furnishings, cooking, fire-making, fuel, tipi etiquette, and year-round camping). Other chapters give information on the sweat lodge; tribal types of tipis including the Cheyenne, Crow, Blackfeet, and Yakima; tipis of children, chiefs, and warrior societies; and those used for councils, burial, ceremonial, and other purposes. The symbolic paintings on Sioux and Cheyenne tipi covers are discussed as well as methods of transporting a tipi. Traditional and modern camp circles, and encampments are described, based on early records and the authors' observations. There is a map of the distribution of tipis and drawings of

Sioux tipi parts, furnishings, living designs; parfleches, boxes, and beaded bags; tools and implements used to make or live in tipis; patterns for Sioux, Crow, Blackfeet, and Yakima tipis; drawings comparing three-pole and four-pole tipis and different tribal smoke-flap styles; drawings of erecting Sioux, Crow, and Blackfeet tipis; drawings of different tribal tipi designs; and contemporary photographs of pole framework and pitching tipis. There is a bibliography of early narrative accounts and anthropological and historical works.

McCLINTOCK, WALTER. *The Blackfoot Tipi.* Southwest Museum Leaflets no. 5. Highland Park, Los Angeles: Southwest Museum, 1936. 11pp. Illustrated.

The information in this study of Blackfeet tipis is based on firsthand observation by the author who lived in Blackfeet camps in Montana. His information about site selection, the preparation of poles and manufacture of tipi covers, setting up the tipi, interior furnishings, and the care of four-pole tipis was obtained from women, the industrialists of the tribe, and authorities in these matters. The decorative painting of Blackfeet tipi covers is also touched on in this leaflet.

————. *Painted Tipis and Picture-Writing of the Blackfoot Indians.* Southwest Museum Leaflets no. 6. Highland Park, Los Angeles: Southwest Museum, 1936. 26pp. Illustrated.

This study, based on McClintock's firsthand observations, discusses the tipi cover decorations and ritual associated with this religious art. Symbols, color, ritual, origin myths, and taboos are explained in detail for specific tipis. Symbols and picture writing on tipi covers, which are the property of the lodge owner, are explained for the author's own tipis as well as picture writing on two war tipis. There are photographs of painted tipis showing symbols and pictographs. Also see: George Bird Grinnell, "The Lodges of the Blackfeet." *American Anthropologist* 3, no. 4 (October–December 1901):650–68. Illustrated.

REID, RUSSELL. "The Earth Lodge." *North Dakota Historical Quarterly* 4, no. 3 (April 1930):174–85. Illustrated.

Reid deals with the earth lodges of village-dwelling, agricultural Mandans and Hidatsas (Siouan) and Arikaras (Caddoan) of the Upper Missouri River region from the time of white contact until the 1870s when earth lodges were replaced by log structures. (The Cheyenne [Algonquian] were known to have lived in earth lodges also, but there are no known written accounts containing descriptions of them.) The information is based on material found in the journals of travelers to what is now the state of North Dakota. Descriptive accounts of Mandan earth lodges (which also apply to Hidatsa lodges) are excerpted from the writings of Lewis and Clark (1804–05), Alexander Henry (1806), George Catlin (1832), Maximilian, Prince of Wied (1833), and J. J. Audubon (1843). Descriptive accounts of Arikara earth lodges are taken from the journals of Lewis and Clark (1804), Henry Bracken-

ridge (1811), and Thaddeus Culbertson (1850). There are illustrations of a Mandan lodge interior and the plan of a Hidatsa village.

WATERMAN, THOMAS TALBOT and Collaborators. *Native Houses of Western North America.* Indian Notes and Monographs Miscellaneous Series, no. 11. New York: Museum of the American Indian, 1921. 97pp. Bibliography.

This study examines houses erected over pits, or pit-houses, throughout the entire western half of the North American continent to determine which tribes in America had houses resembling underground structures found in northeastern Asia. The authors contend that pit-houses, at least of the extreme western area of North America, may have been ultimately derived from Asia. The nature and extent of such structures are discussed for nine areas: the Aleutian Islands and western Alaska; inland from the Stikine River to San Francisco Bay; the Pacific Coast from southern Alaska to northern California which is divided into three areas; the Southwest; southern California; and the Plains region. Pit-dwellings found east of the Mississippi River are also included. The authors discuss the possible relations of rectangular plank-houses built over pits to conical pit-dwellings and describe other structures with pits found in the Plains region, the Southwest, and southern California, (structures of masonry; temporary shelters; houses with a permanent framework of poles covered with bark, thatch, mats, or other materials; houses consisting of a pit, roofed with beams, and covered with earth; and rectangular plank-houses) and indicate the people who use these structures. The facts concerning the houses of each area are presented in a long table entitled "Tabulations" at the end of the paper including the person who observed the structure, the dates when the observations were made, the features of the structure, the geographic region(s) or tribe the description applies to, and a number referring to an accompanying map which shows the occurrence of each structure mentioned by the authorities. There is a bibliography consisting of anthropological and historical literature that was scanned for passages concerning habitation types and a photograph of an earth-covered lodge on Unalaska Island.

SOUTHWEST

CORBETT, JOHN M. "Navajo House Types." *El Palacio* 67, no. 5 (May 1940):97–107. Illustrated. Bibliography.

This article, based on the author's 1937 investigation of 150 hogans in the Chaco Canyon area of San Juan County, New Mexico, and on other written studies of hogans, groups Navajo house types under seven classifications (two square types, three round types, one summer type, and one type that is unclassifiable), all of which are described. Corbett maintains that the Navajo house type was changing rapidly because not a single hogan of the old conventional three-pole tipi type was found in the area investigated and briefly reviews works by earlier writers on Navajo house types in order to correlate the information with that obtained in the late 1930s to determine what changes have taken place in form and materials, attributing the change to Navajo adaptation of an agricultural and more sedentary way of life. There are drawings of five Navajo house types in the Chaco Canyon area and a photograph of a Navajo house in 1940.

FEWKES, JESSE WALTER. "The Sun's Influence on the Form of Hopi Pueblos." *American Anthropologist* 8, no. 1 (January–March 1906):88–100. Illustrated.

In this study, the author argues that the uniform arrangement (parallel rows) and orientation of houses in Hopi villages are largely due to attempts to secure sunny exposures and for protection from the cold and wind. The discussion, based on legends recounted by present inhabitants and observations by the author, is limited to three villages on First Mesa in Arizona: Walpi, Sichomovi, and Hano. Fewkes considers the influence of the arrangement of houses on clan localization; historic modifications of the villages produced by the accession of new clans as recounted in legends; and modifications in architectural features of Hopi villages since contact with Europeans. By examining ground plans and studying legends, he concludes that the evolution of the physical arrangement of all three villages was due mainly to the influence of environmental conditions (to obtain the maximum amount of heat through heliotropic exposure). The author also contends that another factor influencing Hopi architecture was the grouping of clans into composite villages with united rooms as a defensive measure. There are diagrams of the ground plans of the three villages showing the placement of clans.

JUDD, NEIL M. *The Architecture of Pueblo Bonito.* Smithsonian Miscellaneous Collections 147, no. 1. Washington, D.C.: Smithsonian Institution, 1964. 349pp. Illustrated. Bibliography.

Judd's book concerns the houses and house-building of a single prehistoric village, Pueblo Bonito, the oldest and largest ruin of an Indian apartment home. It is located in Chaco Canyon in northwestern New Mexico and was built and occupied around A.D. 900–1100. The study begins with a physical description of Chaco Canyon and a brief history of the discovery and exploration of Pueblo Bonito. The pueblo is a compact structure containing 651 rooms which range in level from one to four stories. One hundred and fifty two of the rooms have been designated by Judd as Old Bonitian and the remainder Late Bonitian, reflecting the fact that the pueblo was the creation of two distinct peoples, each with its own cultural heritage. He considers the four distinct kinds of masonry of the pueblo, the constructional timbers, and the similarities and dissimilarities between Old and Late Bonitian homes as to ceilings, doors, ventilators, storage shelves and clothes racks, granaries, milling rooms, fireplaces, and defensive measures. Detailed information is given on Old Bonitian house construction and kivas, a Pueblo II settlement (A.D. 900–1050),

and Late Bonitian, a Pueblo III settlement (A.D. 1050–1300), and reconstruction activities of Old Bonito. The author also explains how Late Bonitian methods of house construction differed from Old Bonitian ones by describing the former's three construction programs at Pueblo Bonito. Finally, Judd discusses the Northeast Foundation Complex, a large addition to the pueblo that was abandoned by the Late Bonitian architects; the pueblo's thirty-seven kivas; the refuse mounds in front of the pueblo, important for throwing more light on the lives of the Bonitians; and concludes with a brief look at alluviation and agriculture in Chaco Canyon. The appendix contains a table of the dimensions of 351 rooms in the pueblo, excavation notes regarding these rooms, and a partial list of the wall repairs made by Pueblo Bonito expeditions. There are hundreds of photographs of Pueblo Bonito rooms, kivas, ceilings, doors, walls, masonry, Late Bonitian additions, the terrain surrounding the pueblo, and different views of the entire pueblo; the Northeast Foundation Complex; and the refuse mounds. There are ground plans of Pueblo Bonito, Old Bonito and its masonry, the three additions made by the Late Bonitians showing their masonry, profiles of the refuse mounds, kivas, and the Northeast Foundation Complex. There are sketches showing the relationship between Old and Late Bonitian rooms, cross-sections of Old and Late Bonitian rooms, the different kinds of masonry, and kivas. There is a map of the northwest quarter of New Mexico showing the location of the pueblo, a table giving pertinent information on the thirty-seven kivas, and a bibliography.

MAUZY, WAYNE. "Architecture of the Pueblos." *El Palacio* 42, nos. 4–5–6 (January–February–March 1937):21–30. Illustrated.

This nontechnical description discusses how, long before the Spanish came in 1540, Pueblo Indians of the Southwest practiced the art of building shelters of adobe, sun dried bricks, near water courses and principally in the valley of the Rio Grande. The author considers both multiple-story construction built for defense still seen at Taos Pueblo and one and two storied types which have evolved as the need for protection diminished. The ancient Pueblo method of preparing adobe, the methods used after the introduction of wheat by the Spanish, and the process nor building a simple house of adobe are described. Mauzy focuses on the architecture of Taos Pueblo in northern New Mexico which is divided into two main house groups, the north and the south which represent the division of clans, a construction common to most pueblos, asserting that Taos offers a clear view of how these Indian villages looked when the Spanish first came. He briefly discusses how the influence of Indian building has created in the modern Southwest a distinct type of architecture called the Sante Fe or Spanish-Pueblo style, in general use in homes, schools, churches, businesses, and public buildings. Also considered are the building methods of the Spanish Franciscans who embellished the pueblo type in the building of their mission churches.

MINDELEFF, COSMOS. *Navajo Houses.* Bureau of American Ethnology 17th Annual Report, Part 2, 1895–96, pp. 469–517. Washington, D.C.: Government Printing Office, 1898. Illustrated.

This account of Navajo habitations, or hogans, discusses four types: the winter and summer hogans, the sweat house, and the hogan for the Yébïtcai ceremony. Based on material collected by A. M. Stephen who lived among the Navajo for years and on other authoritative sources, the study includes a brief geographic description of the Navajo Reservation and ethnographic information about the Navajo people. The author describes the process of erecting a conventional forked three-pole winter tipi which was the characteristic type of Navajo dwelling around 1895 and details the accompanying ceremony. Navajo construction nomenclature and the rules and precedents governing the form and construction of winter hogans to insure their adherence to ancient models are discussed. The construction of summer shelters, sweat houses, and fire-making are also described as well as the construction, erection, elaborate ceremonies, and songs associated with the Yébïtcai hogan, a special type erected to house the sand painting essential to the Yébïtcai ceremony. Also included are a long list of nomenclature of hogan parts, a map of the Navajo Reservation, sketches showing hogan timber framework, winter and summer hogans, a Yébïtcai house, ground plans of summer shelters, and a photograph of the house of a wealthy Navajo.

———. *A Study of Pueblo Architecture in Tusayan and Cibola.* Bureau of American Ethnology 8th Annual Report, 1886–87, pp. 3–228. Washington, D.C.: Government Printing Office, 1891. Illustrated.

This is a study of architectural ruins and inhabited towns in the ancient provinces of Tusayan and Cibola situated in New Mexico and Arizona within the drainage of the Little Colorado River in the arid Southwest. The material is based on the observations of the author who surveyed and investigated ruins and studied inhabited pueblos from 1881 to 1888, on material collected by A. M. Stephen who lived in Tusayan, and on Tusayan traditional information collected from the elders. Chapter 1 contains an account of the Tusayan pueblos which includes the traditional prehistory, history, religion, and mythology of the people and gives a classification and account of pueblo phratries and gentes. Chapter 2 includes the plans and descriptions of fourteen ruins in the province of Tusayan and eight inhabited villages (Hano, Sichomovi, Walpi, Mishongnovi, Shipaulovi, Shumopavi, Oraibi, and Moenkopi). Chapter 3 includes the plans and descriptions of ten ruins and four inhabited villages of Cibola (Zuñi, Nutria, Pescado, Ojo Caliente). Chapter 4 gives construction details of inhabited Tusayan and Cibolan houses and compares their details with those of well-preserved ruins; discusses kivas (ceremonial chambers) in Tusayan, their use, origin, antiquity, excavation, access, masonry, orientation, ancient form, general construct, furniture, ornaments, and the religious activities connected with these ceremonial chambers; and gives a long list of Tusayan architectural nomenclature. Concluding that some of the village ruins and cliff dwellings were built and occupied by ancestors of late nineteenth-century Pueblo Indians, the author also maintains that the principal characteristics of pueblo architecture (multistoried, terraced houses of rectangular rooms) are the product of adjustments to an arid environment that furnished abundant and suitable building materials and a compelling need for security against raids or attacks. There are over one hundred illustrations including maps of the groups discussed and the topography of the country as well as ground plans of houses and apartments.

SCULLY, VINCENT, and WILLIAM CURRENT. *Pueblo Architecture of the Southwest.* Austin: University of Texas Press, 1971. 98pp. Illustrated.

This photographic essay consists of sixty-five black-and-white full page photographs by Current of the ruins of prehistoric pueblo architecture in Arizona, Colorado, and New Mexico. An essay is keyed to the photographs and captions by Scully outline the principals of pueblo architecture and explain their relation to the lifestyle of the Pueblo people. There are pictures of the cliff dwellings and kivas (ceremonial chambers) in Mesa Verde, Colorado; Pueblo Bonito, the Great Kiva, and Chaco Canyon in New Mexico; dwelling units and kivas in Canyon de Chelly, now the heart of the Navajo Reservation in Arizona; Betatakin, Keet Seel, other ruins, and Navajo National Monument in New Mexico; and the ruins in Three-Turkey Canyon and Canyon del Muerto, Arizona. Current's photographs emphasize spectacular natural formations in which some of the pueblos were built; dramatize the contrast in scale and explore the relationship between human building and natural forms; highlight individual structural units and other major elements of structure; and illustrate the urban patterns and prefigurations of contemporary pueblos. The detailed captions by Scully illuminate pueblo architectural methods, discuss natural formations and architecture in relation to them, and suggest the magnitude of the communal tasks in building the ancient dwellings and kivas.

NORTHWEST COAST

BOAS, FRANZ. "The Houses of the Kwakiutl Indians, British Columbia." *Proceedings of the United States National Museum, 1888* vol. 11, pp. 197–213. Washington, D.C.: Government Printing Office, 1889. Illustrated.

Based on the author's observations at Fort Rupert, British Columbia, from 1886 to 1887, this article describes the plan of a model Kwakiutl house, with sides forty to sixty feet long, and explains the meaning of the carved posts characteristic of these houses. The construction of a Kwakiutl house and the arrangement of space for family life within such a structure is described and compared to other habitations of Northwest Coast Indians. The traditions which correlate Kwakiutl house carvings and masks with the legends referring to ancestors of the gentes, social divisions of Northwest Coast tribes, are related. The author describes the emblems of several gentes, showing that every single carving in the houses of the Kwakiutl tribes has some connection with the traditions of the gentes, several figures occurring frequently in the carvings. There are sketches by the author of the ground plan, front elevation construction, and a longitudinal section of a Kwakiutl house. Sketches of a carved settee, the rear part of a house, carved uprights, carved heraldic columns, house gables, painted house fronts, and house posts of Kwakiutl houses are also included. There is a photograph of the model of a Kwakiutl house with comments by the author, as well as a view of a village in British Columbia.

DE LAGUNA, FREDERICA. "Yakutat Houses." In *Under Mount Saint Elias: The History and Culture of the Yakutat Tlingit.* Part 1. Smithsonian Contributions to Anthropology, vol. 7, pp. 294–327. Washington, D.C.: Smithsonian Institution Press, 1972. Illustrated.

De Laguna examines aboriginal dwellings and other structures of the Yakutat Tlingits, explains the symbolic meaning of the houses, and describes aboriginal winter houses, several old houses, smokehouses, camp cabins, caches, bathhouses, and house furnishings. There are accounts by early explorers of late eighteenth-century houses and camps in Lituya and Yakutat Bay, and houses and camps of the nineteenth-century Khantaak Island, Kayak, Controller and Disenchantment Bay. The author gives a history of a number of the Yakutat houses, discussing when they were built, by whom, the

names given the houses, and their inhabitants from 1880 to 1918. She concludes with a discussion of the demise of the old houses. There are sketches of house plans and smokehouses. The chapter is based on informants and published primary works.

WATERMAN, THOMAS TALBOT, and RUTH GREINER. *Indian Houses of Puget Sound.* Indian Notes and Monographs Miscellaneous Series, no. 9. New York: Museum of the American Indian, 1921. 61pp. Illustrated. Bibliography.

This study outlines the principal features and distribution of three house forms formerly used in the Puget Sound area of Washington State. The features of gabled, shed, and gambrel or lean-to structures are described including the tribes that used them, the Northern Salish and Suquamish, their construction and size, whether or not they were constructed over pits, and comparisons with houses of adjacent and nearby regions. There is a discussion of tribal words for various types of houses, details on constructing a house, interior arrangements, tribal terms for the structural and interior parts of the house, house life, and the regional distribution of the various house forms. Photographs of shed and gabled houses of the Northern Salish and of the site of the Old Man House (Suquamish) are included. The study is based on primary and secondary works as well as field work.

BIBLIOGRAPHY

See PETER NABOKOV and ROBERT EASTON, *Native American Architecture,* p. 208.

16   WARFARE PATTERNS

Much of the anthropological and historical literature on the warfare patterns of American Indians is concerned with the causes of Indian warfare and the kinds of weapons and tactics they used before and after contact with Europeans.

Throughout much of the literature, there is disagreement as to the primary causes of Indian warfare. Some writers argue that the economic factor was the most important motivation while others call attention to the game aspect, revenge, the prestige factor, the religious factor, or the need to replace deceased members of the tribe as reasons for going to war.

In the Northeast there were well-developed warfare patterns according to Driver (p. 216), and Snyderman (p. 217) explains several reasons why the Iroquois went to war. These included the desire for revenge, the necessity of replacing a deceased person in the maternal family, and the desire for prestige. Hadlock (p. 217), who compares the motives for war between the Algonquian hunting tribes of the Northeast and the agricultural tribes of southern New England, contends that the hunting tribes went to war for personal glory or to avenge a wrong rather than to acquire new territory or material wealth.

Some anthropologists who have described the warfare of the Plains Indians regard it as little more than a game. This kind of interpretation not only neglects other explanations but it confuses the causes of war with the reasons why individual warriors fought. Mishkin (p. 218) and Newcomb (p. 218) both feel that the causes of war, economic ones for example, were distinct from the reasons individual men fought, such as to achieve high rank. Newcomb examines the great motivations of individual warriors to go to war because their cultures obliged them to do so and explains that this was not a causal factor in tribal warfare, that the ceaseless warfare on the Plains from the seventeenth to the nineteenth century was the result of a complex of economic and historic factors including migrations and displacements of tribes, competition for good hunting grounds, horses, and weapons, and the machinations of traders and European powers. Mishkin points out that while Plains warfare was principally economic in nature, this did not obviate the game aspect of war. Smith (p. 219), on the other hand, maintains that there is no reason to believe warfare was an integral part of the Plains economy. She also suggests that warfare and acts related to it permeated the aboriginal Plains tribal culture.

In the Southwest, among the Mohave Indians of the Colorado River valley, Fathauer points to the primary cause of tribal warfare as having been inextricably bound with the magico-religious system of that society. Ellis (p. 219) explains that interpueblo warfare in New Mexico was due to transgressions of social prohibitions. McCorkle (p. 220) argues that socio-economic functions of war cannot be applied to the conflicts of California Indian groups where punitive wars prevailed. Codere (p. 220) discusses Kwakiutl warfare and headhunting which was designed to be terrifying and which provided opportunities for acquiring social prestige. Swadesh (p. 220) explains that Nootkas went to war for revenge, retaliation, slaves, material goods, and territorial rights.

Before contact with Europeans, Indians fashioned their own weapons out of the natural materials at hand in their environments. Effective weapons such as bows and arrows, tomahawks, warclubs, lances, and spears were made and used with great skill. After contact with Europeans, either directly or indirectly through trading, Indians east and west of the Mississippi River acquired guns, which eventually replaced their own weapons.

Snyderman (p. 217) and Otterbein (p. 217) both examine Iroquois fighting methods and weapons. Otterbein, using concepts and theories derived from an analysis of Western military history, argues that the Iroquois were a military success during the seventeenth century because they used firearms extensively, abandoned body armor, and deployed their warriors on a scattered basis, all of which gave them an advantage over their enemies.

Secoy (p. 218) deals with changes in military techniques of the Plains Indians from 1630 to 1830, after two centuries of contact with Europeans. He explains the evolution and spread of the horse-and-gun complex and other military techniques on the northern and southern Plains by the mid-nineteenth century. Hanson (p. 217) identifies typical nineteenth-century Teton metal weapons, including firearms, arrowheads, knives, clubs, tomahawks, and swords, and describes how they were used.

De Laguna (p. 220) describes different kinds of weapons used by Yakutat Tlingits, and Farmer (p. 219) surveys six defensive systems used by tribes of the Southwest.

DRIVER, HAROLD E. "Violence, Feuds, Raids, and War." In *Indians of North America*. 2nd ed., rev., pp. 309–29. Chicago: University of Chicago Press, 1969. Bibliography.

Driver surveys patterns of violence, feuds, raids, or war (defined as a military clash between territorial units with true political organization) that prevailed in different parts of aboriginal North America before European contact and maintains that patterns of warfare in particular regions were partly determined by contacts with peoples on the outside. First he considers violence, raids, and feuds that occurred among native peoples of the Arctic, Great Basin, northeast Mexico, and Baja California who lacked true warfare before contact and then among the native peoples of the Subarctic, Northwest Coast, Plateau, California, and the Southwest who possessed a more definite form of warlike behavior. He tells of peoples of the Plains, Prairies, and the East whose warfare was a more integral part of the total culture than in any other region of equal size north of Mexico. He cites distinctive features of warfare patterns in the Plains and the East and examines the multiple motives behind violence, raids, and wars, claiming that economic aspects have more importance than some anthropologists have given them. In addition, he discusses human sacrifice on the southeastern coastal plains and economic conquest and human sacrifice in Meso-America. There is a list of secondary works keyed to a lengthy bibliography in the back of the volume.

VANGEN, ROLAND DEAN. *Indian Weapons*. Palmer Lake, Colo.: Filter Press, 1972. 41pp. Illustrated.

In this work, the author describes the different types of native and imported weapons Indians east and west of the Mississippi River have used in their conflicts with white people. He begins with a general survey of the nature of Indian warfare and how it changed after contact with Europeans. He describes different types of weapons including bows and arrows, tomahawks, war clubs, lances, and spears and the materials they were made from. He discusses the ways Indians east and west of the Mississippi River acquired guns and concludes with a discussion of the miscellaneous weapons Indians used, including several methods of signaling over distances, warpaint, knives, and shields. Throughout the work, the author compares Indian weapons to those of ancient societies and to those of remote areas of the world where weapons similar to those of the Indians are still being used.

NORTHEAST

HADLOCK, WENDELL S. "War among the Northeastern Woodland Indians." *American Anthropologist* 49, no. 2 (April–June 1947):204–21. Bibliography.

This article is an account of warfare of northeastern Algonquian hunting tribes of Maine, New Brunswick, Nova Scotia, and the Lower St. Lawrence and how it differed from warfare of agricultural tribes in the period prior to the development of the fur trade and the struggle for supremacy between France and England. The author analyzes the hunting territories of families, their motives of personal glory, the character of their conflicts, and wars of retaliation and revenge carried on with agricultural tribes of southern New England who desired territorial expansion and who had more time for war than the hunting tribes further north. He explains how the coming of Europeans caused Indians to enter a new phase of warfare. He maintains that hunting Indians of the Northeast Woodlands were not belligerent but would go to war to avenge a wrong committed against them and not for new territory or economic reasons; that the non-belligerent attitude was a result of their concept of property vested in the tribal family and individual hunting families which they could not preempt at will. The article is based largely on published primary accounts.

OTTERBEIN, KEITH F. "Why the Iroquois Won: An Analysis of Iroquois Military Tactics." *Ethnohistory* 11, no. 1 (Winter 1964):56–63. Bibliography.

The author explains why the Iroquois were a military success during the seventeenth century by stressing that they possessed superior weapons and fighting tactics at various times in their intertribal conflicts. His analysis of tactics in terms of weapons, armor, and mobility pertains primarily to the Mohawks, the easternmost Iroquois Nation. He discusses how the extensive use of firearms resulted in the abandonment of body armor and scattered deployment of warriors and how the Iroquois, an agricultural people well supplied with food, were able to put larger "armies" into the field. He analyzes how the Iroquois were often several years more advanced in the use of weapons and tactics than their Algonquian enemies and indicates three peri-

ods when the discrepancy between weapons and tactics gave an advantage to the Iroquois: in the armored phase of the 1630s, in the transitional phase of the 1640s, and in the unarmored phase of the 1660s lasting for several decades. Throughout the paper, the author uses concepts, variables, and theories derived from an analysis of Western military history to understand Iroquois military success. The work is based on published secondary works.

SNYDERMAN, GEORGE. "Behind the Tree of Peace: A Sociological Analysis of Iroquois Warfare." *Pennsylvania Archaeologist* 18, no. 3–4 (Fall 1948):3–93. Illustrated. Bibliography. Reprint ed.: New York: AMS Press, 1976.

Snyderman is concerned with the patterns of war among the Five Nations of Iroquois Indians of New York before and after white contact. He discusses the basic Iroquois unit of social organization, the maternal family, the practice and importance of adoption into the family and army, the powerful role of Iroquois women, the conflicting roles of civil and military authorities, and the establishment of the Iroquois League to keep peace among its members. He looks at the reasons the Iroquois went to war, the desire for revenge, the necessity of replacing a deceased person in the maternal family, and the desire for prestige. He cites army manpower estimates made by students, travelers, missionaries, and Indian agents of the time, all pointing to the small war potential of the Iroquois. He examines Iroquois military training, recruiting of war parties, fighting methods, and weapons and fortification. He concludes that Iroquois war patterns, including the lack of formal armies, military training, and traditional fighting methods, were similar to those of their enemies and determined by their environment, not by social and political organization. There is a chart listing Iroquois population data by tribe from 1250 to 1763, as well as a graph of the Seneca war potential. The work is based on published primary and secondary works.

GREAT PLAINS

HANSON, JAMES AUSTIN. "Metal Weapons." In *Metal Weapons, Tools, and Ornaments of the Teton Dakota Indians*, pp. 14–48. Lincoln: University of Nebraska Press, 1975. Illustrated. Bibliography.

The author identifies typical nineteenth-century Teton metal weapons and how they were used. He also studies the transition of the Teton Sioux from stone age people in the eighteenth century to a nation almost totally dependent on white people's goods obtained from traders and other channels by 1880. He describes firearms (northwest guns: trade, breechloading, repeating, and single-shot rifles; pistols; and double-barreled shotguns), arrowheads, lance heads, knives, clubs, tomahawks, and swords. There are numerous drawings and photographs of the weapons. The work is based on the examination of thousands of artifacts and unpublished and published materials.

MISHKIN, BERNARD. *Rank and Warfare among the Plains Indians.* American Ethnological Society Monograph 3. Seattle: University of Washington Press, 1940. 65pp. Bibliography.

Mishkin reexamines the interrelationships of horse culture, rank, and warfare, and their place in Plains culture, particularly in the Kiowa society, arguing that warfare was principally economic in nature. He begins with a discussion of the characteristic pattern of Plains warfare, raids and revenge parties, and the ways in which men achieved status in terms of their war exploits. He cites the general processes at work following the introduction of the horse into the Coeur d'Alene, Pawnee, and Kiowa societies, who all realized a new standard of wealth as a result. He outlines Kiowa economic-social organization and then describes Kiowa horse raids or revenge war parties, recruitment, return of the party, and the nature of the authority of war party leaders; examines the formal hierarchical rank of military deeds of the Kiowa, how they were publicized, and efforts made to achieve higher rank; describes the place of captives in Kiowa society; and the loss of rank. He concludes with a discussion of the importance of economic motivation in warfare, illustrated by the Osage, Kiowa, and other Plains tribes, which does not imply total rejection of the game aspect in Plains warfare. Maintaining that within the economic framework of war a system of war honors functioned, the successful performance of which was essential to rank, and that the causes for war were distinct from the reasons individual men fought as well as from warpath patterning, the author concludes with an analysis of class and caste differences in Plains society. The work is based on published primary and secondary works.

NEWCOMB, W. W., JR. "A Reexamination of the Causes of Plains Warfare." *American Anthropologist* 52, no. 3 (July–September 1950):317–30. Bibliography.

Newcomb asserts that the ceaseless warfare of the Plains Indians from the seventeenth to the nineteenth century was the result of a complex of economic and historic forces including the migrations and displacements of tribes, competition for good hunting grounds, the need for horses and weapons, and the machinations of traders and European powers. First he examines traditional explanations of Plains warfare that suggest it was little more than a game and which neglect the economic motives in warfare. He feels that the causes of war have been confused with the reasons individual men fight, that traditional explanations consider only individual motivations in warfare. He discusses the major causes of Plains warfare looking first at the migrations of Indian peoples pushing onto the Plains from the East, and the various other migrations, displacements, and amalgamations caused by the invasions of nineteenth-century European traders and settlers. Then he examines competition over horses; struggles over decreasing buffalo hunting grounds and shrinking herds; decreases in game; competition between Plains peoples for European weapons, particularly guns; competition of traders for Indian hides and furs; and the policy of various European nations to play the tribes off against one another and against rival colonial powers. In conclusion he cites individual warriors and their great motivation to go to war because their cultures obliged them to fight, but which was not the causal factor in Plains warfare. The work is based on published primary and secondary works.

SECOY, FRANK RAYMOND. *Changing Military Patterns on the Great Plains: Seventeenth Century through the Early Nineteenth Century.* American Ethnological Society Monograph 21. Seattle: University of Washington Press, 1953. 112pp. Illustrated. Bibliography.

This book focuses on the changes occurring in the military techniques of the Plains Indians during two centuries of contact with Europeans (1630–1830), citing two cultural influences, the Spanish tradition versus the English-French tradition, each of which introduced a different complex of institutions and culture traits, particularly the horse and gun, into three geographic regions of the Plains. Secoy begins with the Apaches of the southwestern Plains who developed a posthorse, pregun military technique pattern in the seventeenth century; describes Spanish armament and Apache armored cavalry, modeled after that of the Spanish; and considers the effects of the Apache military complex on trade, political organization, and neighboring groups such as the Caddoans, Utes, and Comanches who, adopting the military complex in order to survive, subsequently conquered the northern part of the Apache territory in the first third of the eighteenth century. This posthorse, pregun military pattern spread from the Southwest over the Plains in the eighteenth century, while the postgun, prehorse military pattern developed to the east and north of the Plains due to the English-French fur trade which made a regular supply of guns and ammunition available and spread into the northwestern forest area. A transitional state resulted in which the posthorse, pregun and postgun, prehorse patterns met in the northwestern Plains and eventually fused into the horse-and-gun complex of the mid-nineteenth century. Secoy also describes the reorganization of the fur trade after the fall of New France and the extension of British posts in the northwestern plains during the last quarter of the eighteenth and first quarter of the nineteenth century which increased contacts between Indians of the area and European traders with guns. He cites the interdependence between trade and war, maintaining that the implementation of certain military patterns in the Plains was only possible through trading and raiding relations. Finally, the author analyzes Sioux warfare in the northeastern Plains where the horse-and-gun pattern was completely synthesized, traces the advance of the gun to the southern Plains and the development of the full horse-and-gun pattern there, and concludes with a discussion of the development and spread of Plains military techniques within the framework of Plains culture change. There are five maps of the horse-and-gun frontiers from 1630 to 1790 and information on the use of the flintlock muzzle-loader on horseback. The work is based on published Spanish and English primary and secondary materials.

SMITH, MARIAN W. "The War Complex of the Plains Indians." *Proceedings of the American Philosophical Society* 78, no. 3. (1938):425–64. Abridged ed.: In *The American Indian: Past and Present*, edited by Roger L. Nicols and George R. Adams, pp. 146–55. Lexington, Mass.: Xerox College Publishing, 1971.

Smith deals with the various components of the Plains war complex, demonstrating how warfare and acts related to it permeated the aboriginal tribal culture. She discusses war honors such as the coup and taking something from an enemy, explaining that they were acts of bravery developed prior to the horse and gun that did not alter the war system in any fundamental manner. Further, she considers the motivations for combat, the set of rites associated with it, and the benefits which Indians thought they derived from battle; the system of graded war honors and its relation to the life of the individual, the effect of this system upon the fighting situation; the warpath and its ceremonial significance; the organization of warfare around the war party for defense or offense; military leaders; the warpath and war dances, the contacts between each of these and society; and the significance of scalping to the emotional life of the culture. The author maintains that there is no reason to believe warfare was an integral part of the Plains economy or that the prevalence of horse stealing rested upon a purely economic motive. The work is based on published primary and secondary literature.

SOUTHWEST

ELLIS, FLORENCE HAWLEY. "Patterns of Aggression and the War Cult in Southwestern Pueblos." *Southwestern Journal of Anthropology* 7, no. 2 (Summer 1951):177–201.

Ellis considers the existence of historic and contemporary interpueblo warfare in New Mexico. Briefly she explains the structure of warfare in each New Mexico village (Acoma, Laguna, Santa Ana, San Felipe, Santo Domingo, Tewa, Tiwa, Taos, Isleta, Hopi, Cochiti, Zia, and Jemez) except Zuñi, discusses the village and war chiefs, dual leaders, then summarizes the Zuñi war complex in more detail, noting especially how it differs from that of the eastern villages. She asserts that the reasons for interpueblo disunity were due to transgressions of social prohibition and the appearance of nonconformity or competition decried by all and arising from accidental matters such as unusual success in hunting. The work is based largely on A. F. Bandelier's *Final Report of Investigations among the Indians of the Southwestern United States*, Part I (Cambridge, Mass.: Archaeological Institute of America, 1890–92) and other published works cited in footnotes.

FARMER, MALCOLM F. "A Suggested Typology of Defensive Systems of the Southwest." *Southwestern Journal of Anthropology* 13, no. 3 (Autumn 1957):249–66. Illustrated. Bibliography.

This is a survey of six defensive systems and their distribution in the southwestern United States from ancient times to the historic period around 1540. The systems briefly described are palisades, towers, forts, hill slope retreats, fortified villages, and guard villages. Also included are their geographic locations, tribes who used the systems, and when. The author briefly examines the distribution of the six systems outside the Southwest. There is a map as well as a bibliography of archaeological literature.

FATHAUER, GEORGE H. "The Structure and Causation of Mohave Warfare." *Southwestern Journal of Anthropology* 10, no. 1 (Spring 1954):97–118.

This paper supplements Kenneth M. Stewart's report (p. 220) and elaborates on the connections between warfare and other aspects of Mohave culture. The author asserts that the primary cause of Mohave warfare was the magico-religious system of the society, not any economic motivations.

GOODWIN, GRENVILLE. *Western Apache Raiding and Warfare*. Edited by Keith H. Basso. Tucson: University of Arizona Press, 1971. 330pp. Illustrated. Bibliography.

The first part of this book contains personal narratives of six Apaches. The second part contains statements of Western Apaches which spell out aspects of raiding and warfare including weapons, war dances, leadership, preparations and conduct, taboos and warpath language, taboos for women, the use of "power," scalping, the victory celebration, captives, and the novice complex.

HILL, W. W. *Navajo Warfare*. Yale University Publications in Anthropology, no. 5. New Haven, Conn.: Yale University Press, 1936. 19pp. Illustrated.

The author describes the formalized pattern of warfare and war rituals of the Navajos. He discusses two types of offensive warfare, the raid and the reprisal; the formation and personnel of war parties; preparations and equipment; the departure and journey; the attack; and the return observances. There is a photograph of a Navajo warrior. The work is based on field work and published secondary works.

OPLER, MORRIS EDWARD, and HARRY HOIJER. "The Raid and Warpath Language of the Chiricahua Apache." *American Anthropologist* 42, no. 4, part 1 (October–December 1940):617–34.

This article considers the training for raiding and the warpath which began at puberty for Chiricahua boys, the tests to develop them physically, and the behavioral patterns, food restrictions, and ceremonial objects to be mastered on their first four raids or warpath expeditions. The authors' emphasis is on the special language, or vocabulary, which every

Apache boy was obliged to use while he was out on any one of his first four raids or war parties. The ethnological, linguistic, and analytical aspects of seventy-eight Chiricahua raid and warpath words, all nouns, are discussed. The work is based on field work.

STEWART, KENNETH M. "Mohave Warfare." *Southwestern Journal of Anthropology* 3, no. 3 (Autumn 1947):257–78. Bibliography.

This report examines warfare of the Mohave Indians of the Colorado River valley. Stewart discusses the existence of a prestigious warrior class, the Kwanamis, who received dreams for power in war, describes the dreams, way of life, series of tests that boys were subjected to determine their fortitude, the clothing, and weapons of the warriors. He relates how, in late adolescence, boys joined warring expeditions in which Mohaves were allied with Yumas against the Maricopas and Cocopas; describes the makeup of war parties, less frequent than raiding parties, because they were tribal undertakings that had elaborate preparations; battle formations according to weapons; rites associated with warring; the existence of a special scalper; and the taking of captives. In addition, he tells of the Mohave belief in the dangerous potency of the enemy; purification of warriors and captives; postbattle activities; and lists forty-seven warfare traits shared by Mohaves, Yumas, Cocopas, and Maricopas attesting to the homogeneity of the warfare complex among River Yumans. He concludes with an analysis of the River Yuman warfare complex. The work is based on field work and published secondary works. See also: Fathauer, "The Structure and Causation of Mohave Warfare," p. 219.

CALIFORNIA

McCORKLE, THOMAS. "Intergroup Conflict." In *Handbook of North American Indians: California,* edited by Robert F. Heizer, pp. 694–700. Vol. 8 *Handbook of North American Indians,* William C. Sturtevant, gen. ed. Washington, D.C.: Smithsonian Institution, 1978.

The author summarizes conflict in four geographical areas and assesses punitive war in California. He explains the organized, armed conflict among members of California's small Indian societies during the nineteenth century in the northwest Coastal Yurok area, in the Pomo-Wappo region north of San Francisco Bay, in the San Joaquin Valley where Yokuts, Western Mono, and Tubatulabal lived, and in the Lower Colorado River where Quechans and Mohaves lived. He looks at levels of group responsibility, causes of conflicts, types of engagements, casualties, captives and booty, settlement procedures, and functions of war, concluding that Indian societies of California display a wide variety of attitudes toward armed conflict ranging from antiwar to belligerent. He also discusses socioeconomic functions of war and concludes that most cannot be applied to California Indian groups. There are photographs of California Indians with weapons. The work is based on published secondary works.

NORTHWEST COAST

CODERE, HELEN. *Fighting with Property: A Study of Kwakiutl Potlatching and Warfare, 1792–1930.* American Ethnological Society Monograph 18. New York: J. J. Augustin, 1950. 135pp. Illustrated. Bibliography.

Codere examines many interrelated factors that caused an increase in the vigor of the potlatch, or distribution of property, out of a limitless pursuit of social prestige which required continual maintenance against rivals. She tells of the coexistent decrease and final extinction of warfare and physical violence from 1792, the first known contact of the Kwakiutls of Vancouver Island, Canada, with Europeans, until 1930 when potlatches gave out. Beginning with an introduction to Kwakiutl culture, she then describes the various aspects of adjustment to new economic conditions in production and business methods, occupations, income, and population brought about by contact with Europeans. She analyzes Kwakiutl social structure, rivalry, and potlatching, the public distribution of property by individuals, and provides eyewitness accounts of potlatches from 1872 to 1930, discussing changes in them over the centuries until 1930. Citing the methods of Kwakiutl warfare, designed to be terrifying, the opportunities warfare provided for acquiring social prestige, its complex relationship to the winter dance ceremonial and the social organization associated with it, she also includes a history of Kwakiutl warfare which ceased to exist after 1865, and the shift in importance from success in warfare and headhunting to success in potlatching, or fighting with property. She concludes with a summary of historical developments in various areas of life which strengthened the potlatch and weakened and inhibited warfare. There are maps, nineteen tables, and sketches of artifacts. The work is based on published primary and secondary sources.

DE LAGUNA, FREDERICA. "War and Peace." In *Under Mount Saint Elias: The History and Culture of the Yakutat Tlingit.* Part 2, pp. 580–604. Washington, D.C.: Smithsonian Institution Press, 1972. Illustrated. Bibliography.

The author discusses war and peace ways of the Tlingit Indians of Yakutat, Alaska, including types of wars, particularly major ones, military alliances, causes and preparations for war, war parties, and victory and defeat. In addition to descriptions of various kinds of weapons and warrior clothing, she also discusses peace-making after war, especially noting who was authorized to make peace, restitution, retribution, and peace ceremonies. There are sketches of weapons. The work is based on field work and published secondary works.

SWADESH, MORRIS. "Motivations in Nootka Warfare." *Southwestern Journal of Anthropology* 4, no. 1 (Spring 1948):76–93.

Swadesh focuses on the motivations to go to war among the Nootkas who lived along the west coast of Vancouver Island and around Cape Flattery in Washington State from 1785 to 1880. Beginning with brief summaries of the nine war texts on which the article is based, he discusses the taking of heads which were trophies and not a reason for going to war. He cites the reasons most frequently given for going to war including the taking of slaves, women, and children, for which raids were explicitly made; plunder of portable goods; conflicts over territorial rights; revenge; and retaliation. Passages also reflect bonds and internal conflicts of kinship and the caste system. Each motivation for war is illustrated by passages from the nine narratives that bear on it.

17   SOCIAL ORGANIZATION

The social organization of Native American societies has particular as well as universal human aspects. Eggan's article "Kinship, Introduction" (p. 224) suggests that one can study kinship as one of the universals of human society. This same article by Eggan outlines the nature and role of kinship systems in the regulation of behavior. He also includes arguments against the theory that kinship is a universal of human social organization. In "Larger Kin Groups, Kin Terms" (p. 223), Driver describes six kinds of Indian kinship groups in addition to family units and the kinship terminology and its use. For treatment of specific examinations of particular kinship patterns, Queen et al. (p. 225) describe the Hopi family structure and Witherspoon (p. 225) examines Navajo kinship systems.

Kinship ties must of course be founded first in men and women going through the day-after-day routine of having and raising children. Driver studies marriage and the family in his article of the same name (p. 223) and discusses customs and ceremonies connected with birth, maturity, and death in "Life Cycle" (p. 223). Underhill (p. 226) also looks at the largest milestones in life, birth, growing up, marriage, and death, as she describes the home life of Indians in the northwestern part of the United States.

Although the routine and necessary aspects of human life such as kinship and life cycles help to form the social organization of a community, the abstract ideals and archetypes held by a group will also contribute to forming the social structure. Witherspoon (p. 225) explains that the Navajo social relations are ideally symbolized in the mother-child bond and the exchange in husband-wife bonds. In "Personality and Culture" (p. 223) Driver discusses several model personality types in the course of which he concludes that American Indians reveal no strong cases of the Oedipus complex anywhere.

Aside from kinship ties and ideal types, the organization and distribution of power is an important aspect of the social organization of any group. Social power originates in many places but especially in the political and religious spheres. Swanton (p. 224) examines the directly political in his assessment of the status of chiefs among southeastern tribes. In "Social Anthropology of North American Tribes" (p. 224) Eggan notes the political in his study of the social organization and also the influence of religion in the social organization of communities and of sodalities within those communities. Another source of social power which influences the structure of societies is the influence of age. Simmons (p. 224) studies the role of the aged in Native American societies and their influence on the social structure of communities.

Necessity in the form of economic and environmental conditions can exert a strong influence on the structure of society. A farming community would of course be organized differently from a trading community. Or, a community suffering from frequent environmental hardship might organize itself differently from a society which has a fairly consistently bountiful environment. In "Indians, North American" (p. 223), Eggan perceives a dynamic interaction between society and the environment. Bean's essay (p. 225) on the social organization of native groups in California includes a close analysis of the economic aspect of their communities, leading him to suggest that the economic activity of a group profoundly influences the social organization of that group.

DRIVER, HAROLD E. "Larger Kin Groups, Kin Terms." In *Indians of North America*. 2nd ed., rev., pp. 242–68. Chicago: University of Chicago Press, 1969.
Driver describes six kinds of Native American kinship groups that existed in addition to family units, and discusses kinship terminology, the use of kin terms between relations, and the origin of unilateral descent.

———. "Life Cycle." In *Indians of North America*. 2nd ed., rev., pp. 363–78. Chicago: University of Chicago Press, 1969.
This article discusses customs and ceremonies connected with birth, maturity, childbirth, and death.

———. "Marriage and the Family." In *Indians of North America*. 2nd ed., rev., pp. 222–41. Chicago: University of Chicago Press, 1969.
The author presents a generalized account of some marriage customs and practices among Native American groups and describes the different family units of aboriginal North America.

———. "Personality and Culture." In *Indians of North America*. 2nd ed., rev., pp. 431–55. Chicago: University of Chicago Press, 1969.
This article discusses some Native American modal personality types in restricted areas, examining different reports, descriptions, and theories of personality formation. Based on the information, Driver concludes that American Indians reveal no strong cases of the Oedipus complex anywhere.

———. "Rank and Social Class." In *Indians of North America*. 2nd ed., rev., pp. 330–45. Chicago: University of Chicago Press, 1969.
The development and patterns of status, rank, and social classes are discussed for all sections of North America and for Middle America. "Status" and "social class" are defined by the author for the purposes of this study.

———. "Sodalities and Their Ceremonies." In *Indians of North America*. 2nd ed., rev., pp. 345–62. Chicago: University of Chicago Press, 1969.
This chapter discusses societal subgroups not primarily determined by kinship or by co-residence. Sodalities (social, professional, political, religious, etc., associations or clubs) are described for different geographic areas. Their ceremonies and activities, restrictions, and requirements are outlined.

———, and WILLIAM C. MASSEY. "Social Organization." In *Comparative Studies of North American Indians*. Transactions of the American Philosophical Society. New Series. Vol. 47, part 2, pp. 394–421. Philadelphia: American Philosophical Society, 1957.
The authors synthesize data to reconstruct prehistoric Native American social structures on a comparative basis. Marriage and the family, larger kin groups and kinship terminology, infant and child betrothal, incest taboos, cousin marriage, sibs and clans are discussed.

EGGAN, FRED. *The American Indian: Perspectives for the Study of Social Change*. Chicago: Aldine, 1966. 193pp.
In a theoretical approach, Eggan discusses social and kinship changes in Native American societies in instances of European cultural contact and alterations in ecological adaptations. Four analytical chapters demonstrate his method of controlled comparison within a single culture area, such as the Great Plains. He details a wider variety of the established types of kinship and demonstrates that surviving kinship systems are highly sensitive to the changes in ecology and social environment induced by the presence of non-Indian society. The exact nature of the shifts in kinship that have been detected by a number of American ethnologists is elucidated in a synthesis of the data.

———. "Indians, North American." In *International Encyclopedia of the Social Sciences*, vol. 7, edited by David L. Sills, pp. 180–200. New York: Free Press, 1968. Bibliography.

This article outlines the development of the study of Native American social systems and presents a survey of cultural patterns and social organizations in the various regions of North America, with some attention to historical developments. Regions covered are: the Arctic, Plateau, Great Basin, California, Southwest, Plains, Prairie Plains, the eastern Subarctic, the Northeast, and Southeast. The author utilizes the archaeological record, linguistic relationships, historical accounts, and ethnographic data to evaluate the similarities and differences which are found by comparison and to isolate the factors, ecological or social, which may be involved. Ecology is perceived as the dynamic interaction of society, technology, and the environment.

————. "Kinship, Introduction." In *International Encyclopedia of the Social Sciences,* vol. 8, edited by David L. Sills, pp. 390–401. New York: Free Press, 1968. Bibliography.

The nature and role of kinship and kinship systems in the regulation of behavior and the formation of social groups are discussed. The author outlines the historical development of the study of kinship as one of the universals of human society, discusses major contributions to and disagreements about the theory, and describes Native American kinship systems on a comparative basis.

————, ed. *Social Anthropology of North American Tribes: Essays in Social Organization, Law and Religion.* 2nd ed. Chicago: University of Chicago Press, 1955. 456pp. Bibliography.

Articles in this collection describe social behavior in seven Native American groups and discuss some problems in analyzing social organizations. Papers explore the Cheyenne-Arapaho kinship system and behavior (marriage, birth, naming, training, death, mourning); Kiowa Apache behavior patterns and life cycle; Chiricahua Apache social organization; Fox (Mesquakie) kinship, social structure, customs, and life cycle; and Eastern Cherokee social organization. The underlying sanctions of Plains Indian culture are examined, and the place of religious revivalism in the formation of the intercultural community on the Klamath Reservation is considered. A concluding essay is on methodology and results in social anthropology.

SIMMONS, LEO W. *The Role of the Aged in Primitive Society.* New Haven, Conn.: Yale University Press, 1945. 317pp. Bibliography.

Ethnographic and historical data concerning sixteen Native American groups are included in this world-wide study of the position of the aged in native societies. A cross-cultural analysis of selected traits is tested against correlations drawn from a listing of special characteristics which were found to be related to the status and treatment of older people. Based on information drawn from the analysis, the author discusses the ways in which the various societies have ascribed positions of security and prestige to the aged and examines how the elders have been able to achieve such status

and safeguard their interests through personal initiative.

NORTHEAST

GOLDENWEISER, ALEXANDER A. "Iroquois Social Organization." In *The North American Indians: A Sourcebook.* Edited by Roger C. Owen, J. J. F. Deetz, and A. D. Fisher, pp. 565–76. New York: Macmillan, 1967.

This article describes the social organization of the five original members of the Iroquois Confederacy: the Oneida, Onondaga, Cayuga, Mohawk, and Seneca. Family organization, kinship structure, clans, etc., are discussed. (Abridged from "On Iroquois Work, 1912," by A. A. Goldenweiser, in *Summary Report of the Canada Geological Survey,* Seasonal Paper 26 [1913]: pp. 464–65.)

RITZENTHALER, ROBERT E., and PAT RITZENTHALER. "Social Organization." *The Woodland Indians,* pp. 47–54. Garden City, N.Y.: Natural History Press, 1970.

Settlement patterns, kinship, social stratification, social units, clans, dual division, government, and war are discussed for the Central Algonquian groups, including the Chippewa, Ottawa, Potawatomi, Menominee, Cree, Miami, Peoria, Illinois, Shawnee, Piankashaw, Prairie Potawatomi (Mascouten), and Winnebago.

SOUTHEAST

HUDSON, CHARLES M. "Social Organization." *The Southeastern Indians,* pp. 184–257. Knoxville: University of Tennessee Press, 1976.

The kinship system that prevailed among the Native American groups of the Southeast is described. The author discusses kinship categories and terminology, clans, marriage, the chiefdoms, dual organization, households, and politics and law.

SWANTON, JOHN R. "Social Organization." *The Indians of the Southeastern United States.* Bureau of American Ethnology Bulletin 137, pp. 641–736. Washington, D.C.: Smithsonian Institution, 1946; reprint ed.: St. Clair Shores, Mich.: Scholarly Press, 1969. Bibliography.

The status of chiefs among southeastern tribes is examined in this work. Clans; castes; moieties; terms of relationship; names; games; war; marriage customs; customs relating to birth, education, and the division of labor between the sexes; burial customs; and means of communication are discussed by the author with quotes from early writings interspersed throughout the text. References receive full citation in a unified list at the end of the book.

GREAT PLAINS

LOWIE, ROBERT H. "Social Organization." *Indians of the Plains,* pp. 79–130. Garden City, N.Y.: Natural History Press, 1963.

Lowie concentrates on the social organization of

the Native American groups of the Great Plains. Marriage and the family, the life cycle, bands, clans, phratries, moieties, kinship terms, clubs and societies, warfare, rank, law and government, and trade and economic values are discussed.

MIRSKY, JEANETTE. "The Dakota." *Cooperation and Competition among Primitive Peoples.* Edited by Margaret Mead, pp. 382–427. New York: McGraw-Hill, 1937; reprint ed.: Boston: Beacon, 1961.
In this article Mirsky discusses the Teton Dakota social structure. She examines the bands, encampments, structure of the encampment (chief, council, herald, soldier societies, etc.), the extended bilateral family or *tiyospaye;* describes the makeup of the extended family; and gives the kinship terms for various members of the family. The division of labor, values, birth of a male, death of a child, a giveaway, the types of gifts, and etiquette for each are also discussed.

SOUTHWEST

DOZIER, EDWARD P. "Southwestern Social Units and Archaeology." *American Antiquity* 31 (1965–66): 38–47.
This article provides a summary of the present or recent types of social, political, and ceremonial organizations reported in the ethnographic literature from 1908 to 1962 for Native American groups in New Mexico and Arizona. Sociopolitical groups are presented first in terms of a "simple to complex" scheme, followed by an outline of ceremonial units and associated architectural structures. A final section calls attention to certain kinds of material items which may provide leads for the identification of social and ceremonial units in prehistoric sites.

QUEEN, STUART A.; ROBERT W. HABENSTEIN; and JOHN B. ADAMS. "The Matrilineal Hopi Family." In *The Family in Various Cultures,* pp. 45–65. New York: Lippincott, 1961.
This chapter contains a concise description of Hopi family structure (terminology and kinship orientation), family cycle (mate selection, birth, childhood, adolescence, adulthood), family controls, and a discussion of the extended family and matrilineal descent.

WITHERSPOOON, GARY. *Navajo Kinship and Marriage.* Chicago: University of Chicago Press, 1975. 137pp. Bibliography.
This study examines the Navajo kinship system against the background of Navajo cultural values and social structure. Witherspoon distinguishes the cultural system from the social system holding that culture consists of the ideal, conceptual vision of the universe while the social system consists of the actual events and behavior of daily life. Part 1 of the book describes the cultural dimensions of Navajo kinship relations, ideally symbolized in the mother-child bond, and nonkin relationships, ideally based on exchange as exemplified by the husband-wife

bond. Part 2 describes the social organization and daily activities of some 400 people in the Rough Rock-Black Mountain area in the middle of the Navajo Reservation and part 3 presents the author's conclusions.

GREAT BASIN–PLATEAU AND CALIFORNIA

BEAN, LOWELL JOHN. "Social Organization." In *Handbook of North American Indians: California,* edited by Robert F. Heizer, pp. 673–82. Vol. 8 *Handbook of North American Indians,* William C. Sturtevant, gen. ed. Washington, D.C.: Smithsonian Institution, 1978.
This essay discusses the nature of social organization in native California. Refuting the view that California Indian societies were simple, Bean presents a picture of hunters and gatherers whose peculiarly complex social systems were similar to those of horticulturists and some agriculturists with presumably greater technological advantages. He describes basic social units, interface centers (centers of ritual or trade feasts), and levels of organization as well as social mechanisms and specific social institutions which served to increase productive resources and redistributive energy, allowing for maximum use of resources across ecological and political boundaries. The basic features of California aboriginal social organization are summarized.

FOWLER, DON D. "Great Basin Social Organization." In *The Current Status of Anthropological Research in the Great Basin, 1964.* Edited by W. L. D'Azeudo, W. W. Davis, et al., pp. 57–74. Social Sciences and the Humanities Publications No. 1. Reno: Desert Research Institute, 1966. Bibliography.
The author surveys the literature, reviews Great Basin kinship and social organization, discusses various interpretations, and suggests needed field research. Groups discussed include the Paiute, Ute, Shoshone, Washo, and Bannock. Works cited in the text are listed in a unified bibliography at the end of the volume.

STEWARD, JULIAN H. *Basin-Plateau Aboriginal Sociopolitical Groups.* Bureau of American Ethnology Bulletin 120. Washington, D.C.: Government Printing Office, 1938. 335pp. Illustrated. Bibliography.
The author analyzes the ecological and social determinants which in complex interaction produced different kinds of sociopolitical groups in the Basin-Plateau area which includes Nevada, Utah, and parts of Oregon, Idaho, California, Wyoming, and Colorado. Devices for exploiting the environment, density and distribution of populations, roles of the sexes, family, communal groups, marriage, political organization, and settlement patterns are examined. Appendixes provide a tribal distribution chart, vocabularies, kinship terms, native names of and uses of plants, and status terms. Groups studied include the Northern Paiute, Western

Shoshone, Southern Paiute, Northern Shoshone, and some Western Ute bands.

STRONG, WILLIAM DUNCAN. *Aboriginal Society in Southern California*. University of California Publications in Archaeology and Ethnology, vol. 26. Berkeley: University of California Press, 1929; reprint ed.: Mamaroneck, N.Y.: Kraus Reprint Co., 1965. 349pp.

This volume presents information gathered during 1924–25 from Serrano, Cahuilla, Cupeño, and Luiseño informants. Based on the information, the author describes kinship, marriage customs, ceremonial life, villages and clans in order to reconstruct aboriginal social structure, the movements of people, and settlement patterns. Comparative material illustrating the relationship of the groups studied to the general pattern of Native American society in California is also included.

NORTHWEST COAST

MCFEAT, TOM, ed. "Social Organization." *Indians of the North Pacific Coast*, pp. 28–71. Seattle: University of Washington Press, 1966.

Three articles in this section discuss the social organization of groups living along the coast north of Washington State. The social organization of the West Coast tribes, the social organization of the Haida, and the ancestral family of the Bella Coola are the subjects covered.

UNDERHILL, RUTH. "What Was Their Home Life?" *Indians of the Pacific Northwest*, pp. 128–56. Riverside, Calif.: Sherman Institute Press, 1945.

Groups living along the coast of Washington and Oregon are treated. The author describes the beginning of life, growing up, marriage, and the completion of life.

ALASKA

GRABURN, NELSON H. H., and B. STEPHEN STRONG. "Social Structure and Kinship Terminology of North Pacific Groups." *Circumpolar Peoples: An Anthropological Perspective*, pp. 82–93. Pacific Palisades, Calif.: Goodyear Publishing, 1973. Bibliography.

This paper looks at the relationship between the social structure and kin terminology systems of the Yukagirs, Kutchin, Tanaina, and Ingalik, which are organized at the level of ranking societies. A bibliographic essay gives major sources. See also "The Eskimos" (pp. 137–77) for descriptions of the social structure of these two groups.

18   URBAN LIFE

To even the casual observer the lifestyle of American Indians is so intimately connected with their identity that lifestyle almost is their identity. The dramatic change involved in a move from a "traditional" or even reservation setting to an American urban setting almost necessarily creates suffering and difficulty for the Native American. In a broad, general treatment of these difficulties, Sorkin (p. 229) covers many topics relating to the roughly fifty percent of the Native American population living in urban areas.

Several works in this section describe the response of Native Americans to urban life. The Native American Research Group (p. 229), a group of Native Americans themselves, gives a report of their study of 120 American Indian families in the San Francisco Bay area. They focus on family life and child rearing as they affect socialization. Neils (p. 229) explores the effect of physical relocation to the city, the effect of government assistance programs, methods for handling the urban structure, and offers conclusions. Tax (p. 229) was frustrated by Indians who maintain traditional cultures in the urban setting despite a highly individualized culture surrounding them. The author found that such groups thwarted his attempts to study their response to urban life. Waddell and Watson (p. 229) outline federal policies toward urbanizing Indians and also study groups of urban Indians in several areas and types of settings.

The American Indian Policy Review Commission (p. 228) reports on the needs, both social and economic, of Native Americans in urban environments. They also recommend legislative and administrative action to cope with these needs. However, a couple of other works in this section detail solutions and methods for coping in urban settings. The Minnesota Advisory Committee to the U.S. Commission on Civil Rights (p. 228) reports on the responsiveness of Minneapolis-St. Paul institutions to Native Americans. The fact of one instance where urban institutions did respond to the needs of Native Americans suggests that all cities have the capacity to absorb and respond supportively. An additional article about urban ethnic institutions by Price (p. 229) identifies four stages of acculturation and examines the formation of urban institutions by Native Americans themselves. However, of particular interest, Price sees the pressures and difficulties of urban life producing a new pan-Indian culture. Although the transition to urban life produces innumerable problems for the Native American it does appear that it is possible for urban institutions to help with that transition. Further, Price's observation of a new pan-Indian culture suggests that the Native American peoples are resilient enough to respond to difficult situations with life and new growth.

Although most evidence suggests that urban life is primarily fraught with difficulties and suffering for the Native American people, a few groups seem to have coped successfully with modern urban living. Guillemin (p. 228) calls the Micmac urban renegades. They appear to have adapted since the seventeenth century to the urbanization brought by white culture. Thus, their tribal organization encompasses both reservation and city. Hodge (p. 228) finds that the Navajo are as capable of successful urban living as the non-Navajo. Although few choose to stay in an urban setting, the ones who do live quiet, productive lives. Stull (p. 229) observes another group's adaptation to urban settings. He studies the Papago families living in Tucson, Arizona, and notes the differences in rates of adaptation between those engaged in modern and traditional occupations.

Urban life is a phenomenon that is generally not at all natural to Native American culture. Modern urban life is especially foreign to Indians because it is a way of life brought here by Europeans. In no way did the American city develop out of the aboriginal peoples of America. Thus, urban life is difficult for the Native Americans not only because it is so radically different from their traditional lifestyle but also because it is a lifestyle with no connection to their social and cultural structure. That Native Americans have coped at all successfully with modern urban life is a tribute to basic human adaptability.

AMERICAN INDIAN POLICY REVIEW COMMISSION. *Final Report. Task Force Eight on Urban and Rural Non-Reservation Indians.* Washington, D.C.: Government Printing Office, 1976. 144pp.
This report deals with the social and economic needs of Native Americans living in cities, towns, and rural areas, and provides recommendations for legislative and administrative action. There is a listing of urban and related groups and organizations.

GUILLEMIN, JEANNE. *Urban Renegades: The Cultural Strategy of American Indians.* New York: Columbia University Press, 1975. 336pp.
The Micmac community in Boston, Massachusetts, and the customs by which it maintains itself are studied. Discussed are: Micmac social organization as described in the seventeenth century, the fur trade (rise and decline), and the establishment of reservations; Micmac tribal organization as a system encompassing reservation and city; the kind of urban life many Micmacs live from their midteens until they are forced out of the job market by age or illness, the relationships between men and women who live in and around the city; the moral responsibility due Native Americans given their particular situation; and the author's personal reflections on field work.

HODGE, WILLIAM H. *The Albuquerque Navajos.* An-thropological Papers of the University of Arizona, no. 4. Tucson: University of Arizona Press, 1969. 76pp. Bibliography.
This study explores the reasons why some Navajos living in Albuquerque, New Mexico, intended to remain there permanently, and others who intended to, or did, return to the reservation. The author found that while few want to stay in the city permanently, Navajos are as capable of successful urban adaptations as are non-Navajos, and that the large majority lead quiet, productive lives.

MINNESOTA ADVISORY COMMITTEE TO THE U.S. COMMISSION ON CIVIL RIGHTS. *Bridging the Gap: The Twin Cities' Native American Community.* Washington, D.C.: Commission on Civil Rights, 1975. 102pp. Illustrated.
The responsiveness of Minneapolis-St. Paul, Minnesota, institutions to Native Americans in the areas of employment, education, administration of justice, and health care are investigated. An introductory section discusses the legal and political status of American Indians in Minnesota and provides a historical and demographic profile of the Indian population. Subsequent sections present the Committee's findings in the fields investigated and report conclusions, findings, and recommendations. There are figures and tables that illustrate the text.

NATIVE AMERICAN RESEARCH GROUP. *American Indian Socialization to Urban Life: Final Report.* San Francisco: Scientific Analysis Corp., 1975. 110pp. Bibliography.

Researched and written by Native Americans, this report details the results of a study of 120 American Indian families living in the San Francisco Bay area of California. The focus is on family life, child rearing, and socialization practices. Topics include: sociodemographic background of the families; the urban Indian child; Indian identity; the experiences of Native American parents and children in the city; and the urbanization process. Social policy recommendations are included.

NEILS, ELAINE M. *Reservation to City: Indian Migration and Federal Relocation.* Department of Geography Research Paper No. 131. Chicago: University of Chicago Press, 1971. 198pp. Illustrated. Bibliography.

This study explores two facets of the urbanization of Native Americans: their physical location from country to city; and the effect of the government relocation assistance program on migration and on urban experiences of Indians. The author examines census data, describes the federal relocation assistance program and its operation, explores the effects of out-migration on reservation conditions, describes methods of dealing with the urban structure, and offers conclusions. There are tables and maps.

PRICE, JOHN A. "U.S. and Canadian Indian Urban Ethnic Institutions." *Urban Anthropology* 4 (1975):35–52.

This article examines the process of the formation of urban institutions by Native Americans in Los Angeles, San Francisco, Vancouver, and Toronto. The author identifies four stages of acculturation, sees the emergence of a new, urban-based, pan-Indian ethnic culture, and finds that most cities lack organizational means to cope in a creative way with a unique and proud cultural heritage.

SORKIN, ALAN L. *The Urban American Indian.* Lexington, Mass.: Lexington Books, 1978. 158pp.

This book is concerned with the roughly fifty percent of the Native American population living in urban areas. Topics covered include: principal events and legislation affecting Indians; economic and social progress of urban as opposed to reservation populations; human resources and relocation programs; health; housing and social services; education; Indian centers and community development; problems of adjustment; a summary of earlier findings; and suggestions for the future with proposed changes in federal policy.

STULL, DONALD D. "Native American Adaptation to an Urban Environment: The Papago of Tucson, Arizona." *Urban Anthropology* 7 (1978):117–35.

Papago families who have maintained long-term urban residence in Tucson, Arizona, are studied. This article examines demographic changes that took place between 1960 and 1972, and analyzes the differences between persons engaged in modern and traditional occupations to illustrate the kinds and differential rates of adaptation.

TAX, SOL. "The Impact of Urbanization on American Indians." In *American Indians Today,* edited by J. Milton Yinger and George E. Simpson. *The Annals of the American Academy of Political and Social Science* vol. 436, pp. 121–36. Philadelphia: American Academy of Political and Social Science, 1978.

This paper suggests that Native Americans, who maintain kinship and share cultures which contrast greatly with the individualized, impersonal urban societies, somehow frustrate attempts even to research the question of what effect the urbanizing society is having on them. The author holds that American Indians themselves will supply the answers by methods which they determine, when they are given the means to find their own ways in the new environment.

WADDELL, JACK O., and O. MICHAEL WATSON, eds. *American Indian Urbanization.* Institute for the Study of Social Change, Monograph Series No. 4. West Lafayette, Ind.: Purdue Research Foundation, Purdue University, 1973. 139pp.

Papers in this collection outline federal policy regarding the urbanization of Native American populations in the United States; discuss the influence of urbanism on the Hopi of Moenkopi, Arizona; analyze events in the "company town" of Ajo, Arizona; and examine variations in adaptional behavior and social networks among Chippewas in a small city in Minnesota. The papers discuss the Chicago American Indian Center; study Indians in New York City, with the focus on the Mohawks; study Kiowas and Navajos in the San Francisco Bay area; and examine the social networks of Navajos in Denver and their relation to the Bureau of Indian Affairs.

BIBLIOGRAPHIES

BRAMSTEDY, WAYNE G. *North American Indians in Towns and Cities: A Bibliography.* Public Administration Series, Bibliography P. 234. Monticello, Ill.: Vance Bibliographies, 1979. 74pp.

This bibliography lists over 800 sources including books, chapters in books, periodicals, masters theses, doctoral dissertations, and newspaper articles. Citations are listed alphabetically. Section 4 lists guides to documentary searches (abstracts, indexes, etc.).

HODGE, WILLIAM H. "City Living." *A Bibliography of North American Indians: Selected and Partially Annotated with Study Guides,* pp. 28, 127–35. New York: Interland Publishing, 1975.

There are 109 items listed and some have brief annotations.

19   PHYSICAL CHARACTERISTICS

In general, scholars agree that America was populated from Asia, but, given the considerable physical diversity that exists within Native American groups, differ as to how and when. Gordon R. Willey summarizes the two major arguments that seek to explain this diversity: "American Indian populations, both of the ethnographic horizon and from archaeological levels, display a considerable diversity in stature, head form, facial contours, and skin color. This diversity may have resulted from a series of migrations lasting through several millennia following the Pleistocene. On the other hand, these physical variations may have been produced by selective adaptations to a number of environmental circumstances and by genetic drift."[1]

Entries in this section consider Native American peoples in biological or classifactory (taxonomic) contexts. Biocultural adaptation is the theme of Blakely's volume (below) while Jamison et al. (below) and Szathmary and Ossenberg (p. 231) study Eskimos (Inuits). Laughlin (p. 231) has compiled a collection of papers on physical anthropology that explores various related subjects, Newman (p. 231) considers evolutionary changes, and Stewart investigates the stage of evolution reached by aboriginal Native Americans in "A Physical Anthropologist's View . . ." (p. 231). Eight varieties, or subspecies, of early Americans are identified by Neumann (p. 231) and the social aspects of the study of race are discussed by Washburn (p. 231).

BLAKELEY, ROBERT L., ed. *Biocultural Adaptation in Prehistoric America.* Southern Anthropological Society Proceedings, no. 11. Athens: University of Georgia Press, 1976. 144pp. Illustrated.

The premise of this book is that humans survive through biocultural adaptation rather than through either cultural or biological adaptation alone. Papers presented before the eleventh annual meeting of the Southern Anthropological Society, reprinted in this volume, explore various aspects of biocultural adaptation in prehistoric America. The geographic area under consideration ranges from Arkansas on the southwest, to South Dakota on the northwest; from the Central and Lower Illinois River valleys in the midwest, to coastal Georgia. Topics discussed include: cultural information that can be deduced from the analysis of skeletal remains, a biological perspective on a prehistoric cultural system, sociocultural implications of demographic data, a regional perspective on the biocultural dimensions of archaeological study, and the utilization of trace elements and teeth in research.

JAMISON, PAUL L.; STEPHEN L. ZEGURA; FREDERICK A. MILAN, eds. *Eskimos of Northwestern Alaska: A*

1. Gordon R. Willey, *An Introduction to American Archaeology,* vol. 1. (Englewood Cliffs, N.J.: Prentice-Hall, 1966), p. 16.

Biological Perspective. Stroudsburg, Pa.: Dowden, Hutchinson & Ross, 1978. 319 pp.

This volume reports on work done by U.S. scientists participating in an international biological program. In an interdisciplinary approach, twenty-two papers focus on biological variations of the northwestern Alaska Eskimos (Inuits) with particular emphasis given to the relationship between genetic and environmental factors in producing this variation. Topics include: demography, morphology, biochemistry, biomedical parameters, nutrition, physiology, genetics, and behavior. An extensive summary coordinates and integrates the information.

LAUGHLIN, WILLIAM S., ed. *Papers on the Physical Anthropology of the American Indian.* New York: The Viking Fund, Inc., 1951. 202pp. Illustrated. Bibliography.

These papers were presented at a 1948 summer seminar on physical anthropology at the Viking Fund. Topics include: clarification in conceptual approach; new information regarding the presence of white elements; critical analysis of information regarding South American physical types; the affiliation between Aleuts and Eskimos; the pattern of distribution of blood groups, types and factors; use of dentition (dental traits described and illustrated); and genetic characteristics.

NEUMANN, GEORG K. "Archeology and Race in the American Indian." In *Archeology of the Eastern United States,* edited by James B. Griffin, pp. 13–34. Chicago: University of Chicago Press, 1952.

This article, based on archaeologically documented skeletal material from the earliest times to the period of first contact, offers a framework for the reconstruction of the racial history of Native Americans north of Mexico. The author identifies eight subspecies, or varieties, of Homo sapiens and holds that all but one represent separate migrations from northeast Asia.

NEWMAN, MARSHALL T. "Evolutionary Changes in Body Size and Head Form in American Indians." *American Anthropologist* 64 (1962):237–57. Bibliography.

The author examines archaeologically documented sequences of Native American skeletal material and argues that changes in body size and head form of a largely evolutionary nature occurred through time in the Americas, implying few major migrations.

STEWART, T. D. *The People of America.* New York: Scribner's, 1973. 261pp. Illustrated. Bibliography.

The biological aspects of the indigenous human populations of America are emphasized. The author discusses: population figures, physical appearance and dimensions, attempts to modify physical structure, physiological processes, diseases and inheritance patterns, and looks at theories and misconceptions about the origins of American populations. North America, Central America, the West Indies, and South America are included in this discussion.

———. "A Physical Anthropologist's View of the Peopling of the New World." *Southwestern Journal of Anthropology* 16, no. 3 (1960):259–73.

The author considers the problem of the identification of the evolutionary stage reached by the people who first successfully established a beachhead in America. Direct and indirect evidence is examined and the author concludes that skeletal material recovered to date shows the presence of modern human beings over a period of some 20,000 years.

SZATHMARY, EMÖKE, and NANCY S. OSSENBERG. "Are the Biological Differences Between North American Indians and Eskimos Truly Profound?" *Current Anthropology* 19, no. 4 (1978): 673–701. Bibliography.

The authors challenge the prevailing view on the relationship between North American Indians and Eskimos—that the two groups are biologically distinct, although both are branches of the same family tree. The assertion of great divergence is considered in light of genetic and cranial data. Based on their findings, the authors propose a different conceptual framework as a means of resolving conflicting interpretations of the known cultural sequences in Alaska and demonstrate a much closer relationship between Indians and Eskimos than between either group and Asiatic Eskimos and Siberian peoples. The conclusion includes comments upon the work by nineteen scholars and the authors' responses.

WASHBURN, S. L. "The Study of Race." *American Anthropologist* 65, no. 3 (1963):521–31. (Also in Jennings, Jesse D., and Hoebel, E. Adamson, eds. *Readings in Anthropology,* New York: McGraw-Hill, 1972. pp. 123–28.)

The modern concept of race, the interpretation of racial differences, and the social significance of race are discussed. The author maintains that human beings constitute a species and that the important thing is the evolution of this whole group, not the minor differences between its parts. He concludes that the genetic potential of a population is realized only in a social system, for it is that system which gives life or death to its members.

WILLEY, GORDON R. "The New World Peoples." In *An Introduction to American Archaeology,* vol. 1, pp. 12–16. Englewood Cliffs, N.J.: Prentice-Hall, 1966.

In this article Willey surveys the main theories about the racial origins and physical diversity of North American Indians.

BIBLIOGRAPHY

U.S. DEPARTMENT OF THE INTERIOR, BUREAU OF INDIAN AFFAIRS. *Indians: Origins.* Washington, D.C.: Department of the Interior, 1966. 3pp.

Twenty-three sources are suggested in this bibliography.

20   LANGUAGE

Native Americans have never spoken "Indian." Driver states that "Estimates of the total number of American Indian languages on both continents at first contact with Europeans vary from 1,000 . . .   to 2,000. . . . This means that there were between 1,000 and 2,000 distinct forms of speech, each mutually unintelligible with every other."[1] Other scholars estimate that there were at least 500 to 600 mutually unintelligible languages belonging to over ten language families among Native Americans north of Mexico and that over one hundred of these native languages are still spoken today. Forbes (p. 233) discusses how approximately thirty million persons in the Western Hemisphere speak native languages with nearly twenty-five million of them speaking one of ten to fifteen "major" languages. Some of the languages are related and others are as different as English and Chinese. These languages have complex and precise systems of pronunciation and grammar and vocabularies of thousands of words.

Indian languages have been grouped into three great geographical classifications: the languages of America north of Mexico, the languages of Mexico and Central America, and those of South America and the West Indies. Within each geographical area, the languages are classed into genetically related groups or linguistic stocks. The works selected for this chapter largely concern those languages spoken north of Mexico.

Driver (p. 233), Parks (p. 235), Sherzer (p. 234), and Williams (p. 234) deal with phonology, while Couro et al. (p. 235), Driver (p. 233), Einaudi (p. 234), Gorbet (p. 236), Hymes and Bittle (p. 235), Munro (p. 235), Parks (p. 235), Rood (p. 235), Young and Morgan (p. 235), and Williams (p. 234) examine grammatical structures, and Boas (p. 233), Driver (p. 233), Hoijer (p. 234), Hymes and Bittle (p. 235), Sherzer (p. 234), and the Voegelins (p. 234) consider different systems of classifying languages.

Tomkins (p. 235) discusses how the Plains Indians, members of over thirty different tribes speaking several different languages, were nevertheless able to communicate facts and feelings of considerable complexity when they met by using sign language. Forbes (p. 233) considers the "Chinook Jargon," an intertribal trading language developed in the Pacific Northwest before 1800 and still spoken. Boas (p. 233) focuses on the rela-

1. Harold E. Driver, *Indians of North America*. 2nd ed., rev. (Chicago: University of Chicago Press, 1969), p. 25.

tionship between language and culture, while Driver (p. 233) examines culture areas and language areas.

In the Arctic, the correlation between language family and culture area is nearly perfect. The Eskimo-Aleut family coincides exactly with the Arctic culture areas. No other language areas and culture areas match as closely as this Arctic example. Tribes in the same family are usually distant in culture and/or geographical area. For example, the Penobscots of Maine and the Cheyennes of the Plains speak Algonquian languages and the Crow of the Plains and the Catawbas of the Carolinas speak Siouan languages. On the other hand, the Crows and the Cheyennes, who both shared the same lifestyle in the Plains, did not speak the same language.

There are several bibliographies dealing with different aspects of language studies. Loriot (p. 236) deals with comparative American Indian linguistics, Marken (p. 236) lists sources dealing with American Indian languages and literatures, Pilling (p. 236) lists word lists, dictionaries, grammars, translations into Indian languages, and original writings from those tribes that had been first to adopt a written language and Wolff's work (p. 236) concerns bibliographical references on native languages still spoken.

BOAS, FRANZ, ed. *Handbook of American Indian Languages.* 3 vols. Bureau of American Ethnology Bulletin 40. Washington, D.C.: Government Printing Office, 1911. 2,679pp. Reprint ed.: New York: Humanities Press, 1969.

This work features an introductory section and studies of nineteen Native American languages. Boas provides a synopsis of early twentieth-century linguistic theory and sections in his introduction include race and language, the characteristics of language, classification of languages, linguistics and ethnology, and characteristics of Native American languages. The nineteen languages included in the work are Hupa, Tlingit, Haida, Tsimshian, Kwakiutl, Chinook, Maidu, Fox, Dakota, Eskimo, Takelma, Coos, Siuslawan, Chukchee, Tonkawa, Quileute, Yuchi, Zuñi, and Coeur d'Alene. Most of the monographs include sample texts. Boas divides the native languages spoken north of Mexico into fifty-five major families.

DRIVER, HAROLD E. "Language." In *Indians of North America.* 2nd ed., rev., pp. 25–52. Chicago: University of Chicago Press, 1969. Bibliography.

Driver summarizes various aspects of language studies including phonology, the science of speech sounds; grammatical structures; relations of language and culture; classification of languages into universal, convergent, diffusional, and genetic; and geographical relations between language family areas and culture areas. He discusses the first modern genetic classification of North American Indian languages by J. W. Powell in 1891, Swadesh's new method of classifying languages developed around 1950, and concludes with a discussion of the development of forms of true writing. There is a lengthy table entitled "Genetic Classification of North American Indian Languages" and references which are keyed to a lengthy bibliography at the end of the volume.

FORBES, JACK D. *Native American Languages: Preservation and Self-Development.* Davis, Calif.: Native American Studies, Tecumseh Center. University of California, Davis, 1979. 57pp. Illustrated.

Forbes reviews the relationship between community language and ethnic identity, and the current vitality of Native American languages. He discusses how approximately thirty million persons in the Western Hemisphere speak native languages with nearly twenty-five million of them speaking one of ten to fifteen "major" languages, including Quechua, Aymara, Guarani, Maya, Nahuatl, Otomi, Zapotec, Cree, Mixteca, and Navajo. The author promotes the development of an Indian lingua franca (he favors something based on Quechua) to replace the lingua francas, English, Spanish, and Portuguese. Writing systems are also reviewed, including Cherokee, Cree, Inuit, Slave (Tinnéh), Creek, Luiseño, Cupeño, Sioux, and Navajo. A section is devoted to the "Chinook Jargon," an intertribal trading language developed in the Pacific Northwest before 1800 and still spoken.

HALE, KENNETH. "Theoretical Linguistics in Relation to American Indian Communities." In *American Indian Languages and American Linguistics,* edited by Wallace Chafe, pp. 35–50. Lisse, Belgium: Peter de Ridder Press, 1976. Bibliography.

This work reviews the shortage of native linguists and suggests ways in which theoretical linguistics may be used in Indian education particularly in bilingual programs. The bulk of the paper consists of a discussion of a conceivable program for the study of Navajo by Navajo-speaking students in elementary and secondary schools. The bibliography is followed by a discussion by Margaret Langdon.

HOIJER, HARRY. "Indian Languages of North America." In *The North American Indians: A Source Book,* edited by Roger C. Owen, James J. F. Deetz, and Anthony D. Fisher, pp. 76–91. New York: Macmillan, 1967.

In this work, Hoijer presents the 1891 language classification scheme of J. W. Powell and his associates, A. S. Gatschet and J. Owen Dorsey, along with comments of more contemporary linguists who suggest that revisions of Powell's work are required. Major language families and relevant languages are described, including the geographic area in which each language is (or was) spoken. Major families and language isolates include Eskimo-Aleut, Athapaskan, Eyak, Tlingit, Haida, Beothukan, Algonquian, Kutenai, Salishan, Wakashan, Chimakuan, Yurok, Wiyot, Miwok, Costanoan, Yokut, Maidu, Wintun, Takelma, Coos, Siuslaw-Yakonan, Kalapuya, Chinook, Tsimshian, Shanaptian, Waiilatpuan, Lutuamian, Karok, Chimariko, Shasta-Achamaui, Yanan, Pomo, Washoan, Esselenian, Yuman, Salinan, Chumashan, Tonkawa, Coahuiltecan, Karankawa, Yuki, Keresan, Tunican, Atakapa, Chitimachan, Iroquoian, Caddoan, Siouan, Yuchi, Natchez-Muskogean, Timucuan, Uto-Aztecan, Tansan, and Kiowa.

———, et al. *Linguistic Structures of Native America.* Viking Fund Publications in Anthropology, no. 6. New York: Viking Fund, Inc., 1946. 423pp.

This volume contains descriptive sketches of linguistic structures. The first essay, an introduction, includes a classification of the languages north of Mexico, of Mexico itself, and Central and South America. There are also essays on the language of the South Greenlandic Eskimos, Chiricahua Apaches, Algonquians, Delawares, Hopis, Taos, Yokuts, Yumas, Tonkawas, Chitimachas, Tunicas, Aztecs, and Canadian Chipewyans.

SEBEOK, THOMAS A., ed. *Native Languages of the Americas.* 2 vols. New York: Plenum Press, 1976. 1,165pp. Illustrated. Bibliography.

This comprehensive work includes twenty-five sections by twenty-one authors. Among the contributors in volume 1 are Harry Hoijer, Mary Haas, William Bright, Ives Goddard, Herbert Landar, Michael Krauss, Joel Sherzer, and C. F. and F. M. Voegelin. Sections include a history of American linguistics, linguistic prehistory, North American Indian language contact, documents and documentation, general sources on Native North American linguistics, and thirteen areal groupings articles (general, Eskimo, Aleut, Na-Déné, the Northwest, California, Southwestern, Great Basin, Algonquian, Siouan, Iroquoian, Caddoan, and Southeastern) which are simultaneously bibliographic essays. Volume 2 includes works on Central and South American linguistics; detailed checklists of North American Indian languages and South and Central American Indian languages; and statistics on numbers of speakers at a given date, which in many cases may be too low. Each section in both volumes

contains a bibliography and numerous maps depict the geographical extent of particular indigenous languages.

SHERZER, JOEL. *An Areal-Typological Study of American Indian Languages North of Mexico.* Amsterdam: North-Holland Publishing Co., 1976. 284pp. Illustrated. Bibliography.

This study deals with: (1) the history of areal-typographical linguistic studies in North America; (2) a framework for the presentation of areal linguistic phenomena in America; (3) a presentation and discussion of the distribution of phonological and morphological traits of the Arctic, western Subarctic, eastern Subarctic, Northwest Coast, Plateau, California, Southwest, Great Basin, Plains, Northeast, and Southeast; (4) a determination of the linguistic areas north of Mexico together with a discussion of the types of sociolinguistic or communicative conditions which gave rise to the various linguistic areas; and (5) some applications of North American Indian linguistic data for the study of linguistic universals. There are thirteen maps.

VOEGELIN, C. F., and F. M. VOEGELIN. *Map of North America Indian Languages.* Revised Publication, no. 20. New York: American Ethnological Society, 1966.

This oversized map reflects the classificatory consensus reached by scholars. Three kinds of information are included in marginal lists: agreed-upon labels for nine phyla, the language names under the language family names, and the language isolates which have the status of being separate languages and linguistic language families. The map shows national and state boundaries.

NORTHEAST

WILLIAMS, MARIANNE MITHUN. *A Grammar of Tuscarora.* New York: Garland Publishing, 1975. 326pp.

This study provides a description of the phonology, morphology, and syntax of Tuscarora, a northern Iroquoian language now spoken by people living near Niagara Falls, New York, and Brantford, Ontario. The grammar begins by discussing methods of semantic representation. Basic underlying and superficial orders of constituents are examined, along with the relationship between semantic and syntactic case. The author describes three types of Iroquoian words: verbs, nouns, and particles. She discusses the formation of sentences and adverbial constructions; describes complex sentences containing sentential subjects and complements, indirect questions, and relative clauses; and concludes with the basic phonology of the language.

SOUTHEAST

EINAUDI, PAULA F. *A Grammar of Biloxi.* New York: Garland Publishing, 1975. 197pp.

Biloxi, an extinct language since the 1930s, was a member of the southeastern branch of the Siouan language family. In 1892–93 James O. Dorsey did field work with some of the few surviving members of the tribe. This book contains an extensive analysis of Dorsey's work as well as of the few other Biloxi sources available.

GREAT PLAINS

PARKS, DOUGLAS R. *A Grammar of Pawnee*. New York: Garland Publishing, 1975. 369pp.
This study contains a description of the phonology and morphology of the South Band dialect of Pawnee. The author presents a detailed account of the sound system and the inflectional and derivational processes found in the language. Pawnee is a member of the Caddoan family, a group of languages noted for their complex structures. This grammar is one of the first modern, comprehensive descriptions of Pawnee, one of three living Caddoan languages.

ROOD, DAVID S. *Wichita Grammar*. New York: Garland Publishing, 1975. 326pp.
This study is a formal grammatical description of the structure of Wichita, a language currently spoken in central Oklahoma. Wichita is, along with Pawnee and Caddo, one of three living Caddoan languages. This study is one of the first publications describing an entire language using the model developed by Wallace Chafe that describes semantic structures and then progresses through transformations to morphology and finally to phonology.

TOMKINS, WILLIAM. *Universal Indian Sign Language of the Plains Indians of North America*. 5th ed. San Diego: privately printed, 1931; reprint ed., *Indian Sign Language*. New York: Dover, 1969. 106pp. Illustrated.
Tomkins explains how Plains Indians from different tribes and speaking different languages were nevertheless able to communicate facts and feelings of considerable complexity when they met, how they used a language composed of gestures made almost entirely with the hands and fingers. He provides a dictionary of Indian sign language which he learned in the late nineteenth and early twentieth centuries, principally from Sioux Indians in Wyoming. Drawings and short descriptions make clear the proper positions and motions of the hands to convey the meaning of over 870 alphabetically arranged common words which are used in sample sentences. There are also brief sections on the pictography and ideography of Sioux and Ojibway tribes, on sentence formations, and on co-relating sign language and pictography. A brief history of sign language, suggestions for exercises, and several photographs of the author are included.

SOUTHWEST

HYMES, DELL H., and WILLIAM E. BITTLE, eds. *Studies in Southwestern Ethnolinguistics: Meaning and History in the Languages of the American Southwest*. The Hague: Mouton, 1967. 464pp. Illustrated. Bibliography.
This volume contains a series of articles dealing with southwestern Indian languages. The introduction briefly describes the historical and linguistic backgrounds for studies in the book. The articles represent the main currents of continuing research. Topics include "Meaning in Cultural Forms," "Meaning in Lexical Systems," "Meaning in Grammatical Categories," "History in Classifications," "History in Histories and Reconstructions," and "History in Acculturation and Area." Each article has a bibliography and the book itself concludes with a bibliography of the "Southwest Project in Comparative Psycho-linguistics." There are two maps.

MUNRO, PAMELA ELIZABETH LANG. *Topics in Mojave Syntax*. New York: Garland Publishing, 1975. 343pp.
This work is a study of the syntax of Mojave, a language of the Yuman family of Hokan stock, which is spoken on the Colorado River near Parker, Arizona. The basic sentence structure of Mojave is described, including information on case, word order, demonstratives, pronouns, tense, negation, questions, con- and disjunction, and modals. The remainder of the grammar is concerned with sentence structures for which nominalization is important.

YOUNG, ROBERT W., and WILLIAM MORGAN. *The Navaho Language*. Salt Lake City: Deseret Book Co., 1967. 473pp.
This work is an introductory grammar to the most widely spoken Native American language in the United States, Navajo (Dine Bizaad) which is spoken by over 100,000 persons. Included are sample texts, an English-Navajo dictionary, and a Navajo-English dictionary.

CALIFORNIA

BRIGHT, WILLIAM, ed. *Studies in Californian Linguistics*. University of California Publications in Linguistics, vol. 34. Berkeley: University of California Press, 1964. 238pp. Illustrated. Bibliography.
This volume contains nineteen papers on aspects of California Indian linguistics, some of which focus on particular tribes and some which compare two California Indian languages. There is a map of the tribes and languages and a bibliography of all known works concerned primarily with California Indian linguistic data as well as works not primarily concerned with California languages.

COURO, TED; MARGARET LANGDON; et al. *Let's Talk 'Iipay Aa: An Introduction to the Mesa Grande Diegueño Language*. Socorro, N. Mex.: Ballena Press, 1975. 262pp. Illustrated.
This grammar of a southern California Yuman language is a nontechnical introduction to the Diegueño language, the native language of San Diego County and northern Baja California. The grammar is presented in the form of lessons contain-

ing grammatical explanations, sample sentences, and exercises, many of them in the form of cartoons and comic strips. There are also stories, songs, and poems. The book is illustrated with drawings.

GORBET, LARRY PAUL. *A Grammar of Diegueño Nominals.* New York: Garland Publishing, 1975. 250pp.

Diegueño is a language of the Yuman family of the Hokan stock, spoken today in much of San Diego County, California, and in the northern part of Baja California, Mexico. This study describes the subordinate clause constructions of Diegueño, especially those of the Imperial Valley dialect, and explores the relation of subordination to Diegueño grammar as a whole. It also compares these facets of Diegueño to structures of unrelated languages, including English, and to linguistic theory. Beginning with a general outline of Diegueño grammar and a discussion of the nominal case system, Gorbet proceeds to a detailed discussion of clause and complement constructions. Some similar constructions of unrelated languages are noted and discussed in light of the previous analysis. The author concludes by discussing the relation between complementation and relativization in Diegueño and how both are related to other aspects of Diegueño grammar.

BIBLIOGRAPHIES

LORIOT, JAMES. "A Selected Bibliography of Comparative American Indian Linguistics." *International Journal of American Linguistics* 30 (1964): 62–80.

This bibliography contains sources dealing with comparative linguistics. The author states that an attempt has been made to select entries dealing with phonological comparisons. The sources for the selections were the *Bibliographic Linguistique* for 1939–59 and indexes to the *International Journal of American Linguistics and Language* for 1960–61. Entries are divided by linguistic phyla: general, Eskimo-Aleut, Athapaskan, Algonquian-Mosan, Macro-Penutian, Tunican, Mayan, Hokan, Keresan, Iroquois-Caddoan, Siouan, Natchez-Muskhogean, Otomanguean, Arawak, Quechumaran, Tupí-Guaran, and miscellaneous South American. There is nominal annotation.

MARKEN, JACK W. *The American Indian: Language and Literature.* Arlington Heights, Ill.: AHM Publishing, 1978. 205pp.

This work presents, without annotation, sources dealing with American Indian languages and literatures. Works by Native American authors about subjects other than language or literature are included; Inuits and native peoples south of the Rio Grande are not represented. Sections include bibliography, autobiography, general literature, general language, and geographic divisions with literature and language subdivisions by tribe. The author cites sources that include books and articles in approximately 400 journals.

PILLING, JAMES C. *Bibliographies of the Languages of the North American Indians.* 9 parts in 3 vols. Washington, D.C.: Government Printing Office, 1887–94; reprint ed.: New York: AMS Press, 1973. Illustrated.

Pilling's bibliographies of Indian languages are classified into nine parts. They are part 1: Eskimo; part 2: Siouan; part 3: Iroquoian; part 4: Muskhogean; part 5: Algonquian; part 6: Athapaskan; part 7: Chinookan; part 8: Salishan; and part 9: Wakashan. Each bibliography is extensively annotated, some including illustrations of sample texts and alphabets. Each report includes a chronological index. Sources are listed by tribal language. In addition to word lists, dictionaries, and grammars, the bibliography lists all known biblical and other translations into each Indian language and original writings from those tribes that had been first to adopt a written language.

WOLFF, HANS. "Bibliography of Bibliographies of North American Indian Languages Still Spoken." *International Journal of American Linguistics* 13, no. 4 (October 1947):268–73.

This list of bibliographical references includes texts, word lists, complete articles on the languages still spoken, and an alphabetic list of languages and language families. Where no data are available for a language, reference is made to the language family. The paper omits names of extinct languages and tribal designations which frequently enter into the historical sources and in anthropological literature, such as Erie under Iroquoian.

PART IV *Religion, Arts, and Literature*

21 RELIGION AND PHILOSOPHY

The many studies of North American Indians reveal the high degree of religious involvement by both individuals and groups. Whether studying social and political organization or language and picture-writing, material culture or art, economy or even warfare, we must always take into consideration the pervasive influence of religious rituals, ceremonialism, and symbolism on tribal life. Indeed, the religiosity underlying the life of the American Indian shaped a human figure singularly complete, whose dignity, fierceness, generosity, and heroism inspire respect and denote a spirituality often ignored or not properly understood.

The heading "Religion and Philosophy" includes a wide range of activities and cultural expressions. For the purposes of this section, religion includes cults, rituals, and witchcraft as well as what people might easily recognize as religion. Philosophy includes not only fairly abstract approaches to Native American thought but also myths and their interpretation. Driver, in his general work on Native American religion (p. 239), includes a section on religious terms and their definitions.

Driver's article is one of several surveys of Native American religion. Alexander (p. 238) explores common philosophical and religious traits among native religions. Spencer et al. (p. 240) also survey common themes of native religion in a continental survey. Hultkrantz (p. 239) divides his survey between the religions of tribes and the religion of the "high" cultures, particularly the Incas, Maya, and Aztecs. Marriott and Rachlin (p. 239) study mythology and divide Indian myths into four categories: creation stories, supernatural help to the tribe, recent past events, and the world after death.

In addition to the common mythological themes which Marriott and Rachlin point out, Alexander also discusses another common aspect of most Indian religions, the special and intimate relation between the spiritual and the material, particularly between the Indian people and the spiritual sphere. The native people see themselves as specially and closely linked to the spiritual elements of the universe. Benedict (p. 239) points out the common occurrence of a belief in a guardian spirit among a wide range of tribal cultures. Although Native American culture really includes a multitude of different cultures and so, one would think, a multitude of religions, there do seem to be aspects which are common to many or all native religions.

Europeans brought with them Christianity, a new religious influence. They also prompted extremely dramatic historical events in Native American history. As a consequence, native religion has been somewhat influenced by Christianity. Deloria (p. 239) charges that Christianity failed the Native Americans in their social and ethical needs. Underhill (p. 240) also examines the influence of Christianity on native religions.

However, Underhill also notices that postcontact time saw much revitalization of traditional Indian religion. Several other scholars argue that the suffering of the native people under the Europeans produced either a revival in traditional spirituality and religious practice or the development of new practices and cults. Powell (p. 241) describes three central rituals and the teachings surrounding them among the Northern Cheyenne. He stresses that the Cheyenne have consistently maintained these traditions because in them lies the source of their ethnic identity and consequently their strength. Deardorff (p. 240) traces the development of the religion of Handsome Lake, the Iroquois prophet. Apparently, Handsome Lake's teachings were inspired by Quaker ideas which he combined with traditional Iroquois teaching. Wovoka, a Paiute Messiah, predicted the elimination of whites and the return of a time of plenty. These ideas provoked fear of an uprising by the Indians who were starving and confined to reservations. The federal government reacted by sending the cavalry, and Wovoka's mission ended in the bloody massacre at Wounded Knee.

One of the most prominent recent developments in native religion is the peyote cult. Marriott and Rachlin (p. 239) recount the diffusion of this cult from its origin among Mexican Indians to the southern and northern Plains Indians and to some southwestern groups. Aberle (p. 242) discusses the diffusion and opposition to the peyote cult among the Navajo, and Slotkin (p. 240), an official of the Native American Church of North America, gives a current account of the peyote religion and of the church.

One might assume that if people were chased from their land, relentlessly pursued, reduced dramatically in population, and cruelly oppressed, that the last response one would see was an interest in religion. However, the vigor today of traditional native religion denies this assumption. In fact, several of these studies suggest that religion is one of the most important aspects of Native Americans' struggle to survive. Both Powell (p. 241) and Powers (p. 241) show that a native community's religion helps to pass on culture and to maintain identity. Further, Jorgensen (p. 239) argues that the Sun Dance religion developed as an actively defensive response to the oppression by whites, calling the Sun Dance power for the powerless. In other words, a religion which strongly expresses a community's identity and ideals can have the power to support that community even through fearful hardship.

ALEXANDER, HARTLEY BURR. *The World's Rim: Great Mysteries of the North American Indians.* Lincoln: University of Nebraska Press, 1953. 259pp.

This book considers the religious and philosophical aspects of the Native American world view, each chapter focusing on a central theme underlying ceremonies, rituals, and myths. The author identifies a series of common philosophical and religious traits and attempts to define the salient characteristics of the Native American mind. He notes that the world's rim encircles both Indians and non-Indians who, because of the nature of human beings, share some basic concepts about life, but contends that American Indians have developed a sense of partnership between matter and spirit which echoes throughout the great mysteries of the Pipe of Peace, the Tree of Life, the Sun Dance, and of Life and Death.

BENEDICT, RUTH. *The Concept of the Guardian Spirit in North America.* Memoirs of the American Anthropological Association, no. 29. Menasha, Wis.: American Anthropological Assn., 1923. 97pp. Bibliography.

This article investigates the cultural and religious significance of the belief in guardian spirits among the American Indians, also with reference to other aboriginal peoples. Benedict, in the historical-anthropological style of the 1920s, offers a comprehensive survey of how much a widespread concept is reflected in tribal mythologies, puberty rites, social organization, totemism, and shamanism. As a result, while describing the variety of tutelary beings and the tribal differences which are related to them, she also identifies the common elements of "vision and dream" as having continental recurrence and central importance within the concept of the guardian spirit of the Native Americans.

CAPPS, WALTER HOLDEN, ed. *Seeing with a Native Eye: Essays on Native American Religion.* New York: Harper & Row, 1976. 132pp. Illustrated. Bibliography.

Scholars contribute short essays presenting the religious thought of the American Indians. The thesis of this book is that Native American religion today needs to be recognized as a source for insight and guidance for all Americans. The authors investigate the native perspective in relation to everyday life, to concepts of time and place, to the environment, etc. A panel discussion with Åke Hultkrantz, renowned Scandinavian professor of religions, and other scholars emphazises the uniqueness and contemporary importance of Native American religion.

DELORIA, VINE, JR., *God Is Red.* New York: Dell, 1973. 376pp.

This is a contemporary philosophical treatment of the whole religious question in North America in which Deloria asserts that Christianity has failed to address ethical and social needs and therefore God must be sought within the context of Native American religions which allow a qualitative understanding of human existence. Each chapter is a challenge to Western concepts and practices. The author discusses the resurgence of Native American militancy and describes efforts to counteract century-old stereotypes of American Indian cultures and religions.

DRIVER, HAROLD E. "Religion, Magic, Medicine." In *Indians of North America.* 2nd ed., rev., pp. 396–430. Chicago: University of Chicago Press, 1969. Bibliography.

An introductory section discusses terms associated with the anthropological definition of religion, describes some general and social aspects of Native American religions, and explores the functions of magic and medicine. Specifically treated

are: the gods and priests of the Aztecs (Mexico); the magic and medicine men of the Navajo (Southwest); the forgiving aspects of Creek religion (Southeast); the vision quest of the Sanpoil (Northwest-Plateau); and shamanism of the Eskimo (Arctic).

HULTKRANTZ, ÅKE. *The Religions of the American Indians.* Los Angeles: University of California Press, 1979. 335pp. Illustrated. Bibliography.

Hultkrantz presents a detailed and informative overview of the basic religious concepts and beliefs of the American Indians. The book is divided into two sections. Part 1 discusses the contents of tribal religions as expressed in belief in the supernatural, gods and spirits, totemism and shamanism, and reflected in tribal mythology. The author analyzes the significance of traditional tribal ceremonies, cult organizations, and the series of messianic religions. Part 2 looks at the religions of American "high cultures," namely, the Incas of Peru and the Maya and Aztecs of Meso-America, discussing similarities and differences in cultural-historical contexts.

JORGENSEN, JOSEPH G. *The Sun Dance Religion: Power for the Powerless.* Chicago: University of Chicago Press, 1972. 360pp. Illustrated. Bibliography.

The Sun Dance among historical and contemporary Ute and Shoshone tribes is the subject of an indepth analysis which shows how the reservation system, political-economic deprivation, and hence the need for power motivated the diffusion and practice of the Sun Dance religion among these tribes. The author maintains that the modern expression of the Sun Dance, through its ritual and ideology, helps to counteract the pressure of white society and serves to keep alive traditional practices and beliefs of reciprocity and social solidarity, as well as the whole complex of Native American cultural traits. Jorgensen's prediction that the Sun Dance will keep flourishing appears correct, although the redemptive connotations he suggests may be the subject of some disagreement.

LA BARRE, WESTON. *The Peyote Cult.* Hamden, Conn.: Shoe String Press, 1970. 260pp. Illustrated. Bibliography.

Originally published in 1938, the present edition incorporates two recent articles, "Twenty Years of Peyote Studies' and "The Last Five Years of Peyote Studies." Given the amount of information contained and the time span covered, this volume represents the most comprehensive and authoritative study of peyotism in North America. In addition to tracing the history of the diffusion of the peyote religion, the author investigates the botanical, psychological, and physiological characteristics of peyote. Careful attention is given to the ethics, ritual, and ceremonialism of peyotism as expressed by different tribes. The two recent articles summarize and update the current literature.

MARRIOTT, ALICE, and CAROL K. RACHLIN. *American Indian Mythology.* New York: Thomas Y. Crowell, 1968. 252pp. Illustrated. Bibliography.

This book contains a collection of myths and tales

of Native Americans which captures the philosophy and poetry underlying American Indian lore. This knowledge has survived thanks to the oral tradition of aboriginal cultures, and the authors have recorded it directly from informants. The myths, of primary importance in tribal religions, are grouped around four major themes: creation, supernatural help to the tribe, tales of a recent past, and the world after death. The introduction and the opening comments preceding each narration are very informative.

————. *Peyote.* New York: Thomas Y. Crowell, 1971. 128pp. Illustrated. Bibliography.

This is an introductory study to the controversial peyote religion in which the authors trace the history of peyote following its diffusion from the Mexican Indians to the southern and northern Plains and to some Pueblo groups and Navajos. Included is a profile of Quanah Parker, the Comanche chief who was a strong proponent of the peyote religion. Peyote rituals and symbolism, its effects as a drug, and its meaning as a sacrament are looked at from a cultural-historical perspective which allows the identification of both the good and bad aspects of the use of peyote. The authors stress that if suppression occurs, it will drive peyote underground, but will not eradicate it.

NATIVE AMERICAN RIGHTS FUND. *Announcements Winter 1979.* Boulder, Colo.: Native American Rights Fund, Inc. 200pp. Illustrated.

This publication of the Native American Rights Fund treats the recent legal and cultural issues raised by the signing into law of the American Indian Religious Freedom Act (P.L. 95–341) of 1978. In addition to discussing past and contemporary federal repression of Native American religious practices, this issue contains the full Act of 1978, which constitutes a turning point in the legal history of Indian-white relations. An important document, this issue can be purchased by sending 50 cents to NARF, 1506 Broadway, Boulder, CO 80302.

RADIN, PAUL. *Primitive Man as Philosopher.* New York: Dover, 1957. 456pp.

Originally published in 1927, this book was one of the first systematic attempts to free aboriginal peoples of their alleged primitiveness of body and mind. Radin demonstrates that "primitive" people make complex philosophical speculations about the supernatural and the material world. Using various sources on Native American (and other) cultures, he shows how concepts of right and wrong, fate, death and resignation, and the relationship between men and women are treated in philosophical terms which have nothing primitive about them.

SLOTKIN, JAMES SYDNEY. *The Peyote Religion.* Glencoe, Ill.: Free Press, 1956. 195pp. Illustrated. Bibliography.

The peyote religion is presented and defended by an anthropologist who is an elected official of the Native American Church of North America. Slotkin explains the diffusion and success of peyotism

among the North American Indians in terms of culture accommodation and syncretic ethics. The book is the major source on the Native American Church, its personnel, and its local organizations in the United States and Canada. The doctrine, ethics, and rituals of the peyote religion are carefully analyzed and the study also provides detailed information on the legal controversies surrounding the past and present status of the religion.

SPENCER, ROBERT F.; JESSE D. JENNINGS; et al. *The Native Americans.* New York: Harper & Row, 1977. 584pp. Illustrated. Bibliography.

This text treats the major culture areas of North America. For each area, one or more Native American tribes are thoroughly described in terms of their history, social organization, and overall culture, including religion. The sections on tribal religions illustrate the basic beliefs, ceremonies, mythology, shamanism, life cycles, and funerary practices of the tribe described, thus providing a continental survey of Native American religions and cultures. The concluding chapters also discuss the series of nativistic movements, the Ghost Dance, the peyote religion (cult), and the religious and political activism of today's Native Americans.

UNDERHILL, RUTH M. *Red Man's Religion.* Chicago: University of Chicago Press, 1965. 301pp. Illustrated. Bibliography.

This study of the religious beliefs and practices of the North American Indians is a continental survey in which the author discusses the supernatural, impersonal powers, attitudes toward the dead, and shamanism. Chapters look at ceremonies and rituals in terms of culture areas, the Sun Dance of the Plains hunters and gatherers, the planting ceremonies of the peoples of the eastern Woodlands, Great Lakes and Mississippi, and the Southwest. Attention is given to the series of revitalization movements of postcontact times and the author also explores the influence of Christianity on tribal religions, suggesting that Native Americans will contribute to the growth of Christianity.

WALKER, DEWARD E., JR., ed. *Systems of North American Witchcraft and Sorcery.* Anthropological Monographs of the University of Idaho, no. 1. Moscow: University of Idaho, 1970. 295pp. Bibliography.

For purposes of this study, the definition of witchcraft and sorcery is "the aggressive use of supernatural techniques," where supernatural refers to empirically nondemonstrable causation. An introductory essay presents comparative material on witchcraft and sorcery among Native American groups of North America. Articles by areal scholars discuss the functions and practice of witchcraft and sorcery among the Iroquois, Menominee, Nez Percé, Western Apache, Pueblos, Kaska, and Skokomish.

NORTHEAST

DEARDORFF, MERLE H. *The Religion of Handsome Lake: Its Origin and Development.* Bureau of

American Ethnology Bulletin 149, pp. 77–107. Washington, D.C.: Government Printing Office, 1951. Bibliography.

As part of a symposium on selected aspects of Iroquois culture, this article investigates the cultural and historical context in which the Good Message of Handsome Lake, the Seneca Prophet, originated and was diffused among the Iroquois. The author notes that although much of the new religion had been inspired by the Quakers, Handsome Lake maintained traditional Iroquois teachings and ceremonies. The inherent adaptability of the Good Message, which condemns alcohol, witchcraft, and everything "evil," accounts for its continuity through time.

GREAT PLAINS

BROWN, JOSEPH EPES. *The Sacred Pipe: Black Elk's Account of the Seven Rites of the Oglala Sioux.* Norman: University of Oklahoma Press, 1953. 144pp. Illustrated.

Brown has recorded the knowledge, wisdom, and poetry of Black Elk, holy man of the Oglala Sioux, in which he carefully explains the teachings, symbolism, and meaning of the sacred pipe, which represents the alliance between human beings and the Wakan-Tanka. He explains how life is sacred, how it is maintained as such through the observance of funerary practices, the rite of purification, the vision quest, the Sun Dance, the making of relatives, girls' puberty ritual, and the throwing of the ball (i.e., traditional knowledge).

LOWIE, ROBERT H."The Religion of the Crow Indians." *Anthropological Papers of the American Museum of Natural History* 25 (1922):309–444. Illustrated.

This monograph is a detailed account of the major components of Crow religion which penetrate every aspect of individual and tribal life. The Crow believe in an indefinite number of supernatural beings and, lacking a caste of priests, their religious concepts and beliefs have not been standardized. Their rituals center around the interpretation of dreams, the vision quest, purification, offering rites, and the practice of medicine. Shamans are central figures in Crow religion and to them are attributed special powers. This study is a good example of early anthropological research, and it is one of the many analyses of tribal religions, myths, and traditions available in the Anthropological Papers of the American Museum of Natural History.

MOONEY, JAMES. *The Ghost-Dance Religion and the Sioux Outbreak of 1890.* Abridged ed. Introduction by Anthony F.C. Wallace. Chicago: University of Chicago Press, 1965. 359pp. Illustrated. Bibliography.

Originally published in 1896, Mooney's classic study of the origin, diffusion, and end of the Ghost Dance offers detailed information about a very dark era of Indian-white relations. Confined to reservations and made dependent on an insufficient rationing system, the few remaining Plains Indians favorably received the message of Wovoka, the Paiute Messiah. The doctrine of the Ghost Dance predicted the elimination of the whites, the resurrection of the Native American dead, and the return of a time of plenty and freedom for the people. Ferment, hope, and the strenuous dances performed by the Indians alarmed the government which reacted by sending U.S. cavalry to the Sioux reservation. The subsequent massacre at Wounded Knee brought an end to the Ghost Dance religion. To obtain the material for this study, Mooney went among the reservation Indians to record the diffusion and acceptance of the Ghost Dance among the various tribes.

POWELL, PETER J. *Sweet Medicine: The Continuing Role of the Sacred Arrows, the Sun Dance, and the Sacred Buffalo Hat in Northern Cheyenne History.* 2 vols. Norman: University of Oklahoma Press, 1969. 935pp. Illustrated. Bibliography.

Sweet Medicine is the story of the Northern Cheyenne of Montana, caught between two worlds, and their struggle for cultural, religious, and ethnic survival which is possible only through the perpetuation of their sacred tribal traditions and ceremonies. In his attempt to present the theology, rituals, beliefs, and great mysteries of the Cheyenne, Powell has compiled a testimony of the historical and contemporary life of the tribe in which he describes the ceremonies of the Sacred Arrows, the Sun Dance, and the Sacred Buffalo Hat, and their loss and return to the Cheyenne. Given the content, which is sacred to the Northern Cheyenne, the book should be approached with great respect. Drawings and rare photographs are included.

POWERS, WILLIAM K. *Oglala Religion.* Lincoln: University of Nebraska Press, 1977. 233pp. Illustrated. Bibliography.

This is a treatment of Oglala religion and culture in the context of culture contact. Continuity and change represent the two poles of a continuum in which Oglala culture occupies a midrange area. Powers notes that despite changes in their social structure the Oglala have maintained the central themes, beliefs, and practices of their aboriginal religion, which is an indicator of the tribe's ethnic identity. He carefully analyzes the historical background of the Oglala, their contemporary status, and their religious exegesis: the supernatural, the ritual specialists, the myths, and the seven rites with attention to the Sun Dance.

SPIER, LESLIE. "The Sun Dance of the Plains Indians: Its Development and Diffusion." *Anthropological Papers of the American Museum of Natural History* 16, part 7 (1921):451–521. Illustrated. Bibliography.

This is part of a collection of studies on the Sun Dance religion among the Crows, Oglalas, Blackfeet, and other Plains groups; Spier traces the cultural and historical context of the origins and diffusion of the religion among the tribes. The monograph is based on the anthropological theory of diffusion and assimilation of cultural traits, thus Spier shows how different tribes borrowed the

Sun Dance and modified it according to each tribe's cultural, social, and religious needs.

SOUTHWEST

ABERLE, DAVID F. *The Peyote Religion among the Navaho.* Chicago: Aldine, 1966. 454pp. Illustrated. Bibliography.

This book contains a classic study of the diffusion of, and opposition to, the peyote religion among the largest Native American group in the United States. The book, a result of extensive field work in Navajo country (1949–53), is an indepth analysis of the historical, cultural, and psychological factors that have prompted an increasing number of Navajos to join the Native American Church of North America. The ritual, symbolism, beliefs, and values of Navajo peyotism are presented and compared to the elements of traditional Navajo religion. The author reports the views of peyotists and nonpeyotists, pointing out that many allegations against peyotism have not been or cannot be proved.

BODINE, JOHN J. "Taos Blue Lake Controversy." *The Journal of Ethnic Studies* 6, no. 1 (1978):42–48.

Blue Lake is an integral part of the culture and religion of the Taos Pueblo Indians of New Mexico. In addition to providing water to the pueblo, the lake plays a major role in the social, cultural, and religious traditions of the Taos people. Bodine traces the history of the pueblo's sixty-four year struggle to regain possession of their sacred Blue Lake, which in 1906 had been incorporated into the Carson National Forest. He discusses how, for more than half a century, the Taos Indians pressed for the return of Blue Lake, rejecting offers of monetary compensation, and how finally, on December 15, 1970, title to Blue Lake was returned to the pueblo by an Act of Congress, setting an important precedent for Native American claims to land based on the practice of aboriginal religion.

ORTIZ, ALFONSO. *The Tewa World: Space, Time, Being and Becoming in a Pueblo Society.* Chicago: University of Chicago Press, 1969. 197pp. Illustrated. Bibliography.

This book contains one of the most complete descriptions and interpretations of the world view of an American Indian tribe, a penetrating analysis of the belief systems of the Tewa as they relate to their social institutions. The study concentrates on San Juan pueblo, the largest of the surviving Tewa villages in New Mexico. In an analysis of the relationship between symbolic and social dualism, the author focuses on the ideas, rules, and principles of Tewa society as they are reflected in mythology, world view, and ritual. Tewa concepts of space, time, color, number, and existence are examined to determine how cosmological and ritual belief systems reflect, reinforce, and lend continuity to social institutions. The author, born and raised in San Juan pueblo, combines scholarship and traditional knowledge in this pioneering work.

TYLER, HAMILTON A. *Pueblo Gods and Myths.* Norman: University of Oklahoma Press, 1964. 313pp. Bibliography.

Noting the persistence of traditional religions among the Pueblos, the author discusses the theology, gods, and deities of three Pueblo groups, the Zuñis, Keres, and Hopis. The author discussses how the pantheon of these Pueblos is populated by gods and goddesses among whom the sun occupies a place of primary importance and explains that seasonal ceremonies such as the winter solstice celebrate and perpetuate the alliance between people and the supernatural. Cross-references to Greek and Christian religion are valuable tools for a thorough understanding of Pueblo gods and mythical figures. Tyler rejects the evolutionary theory of religion and the stereotype of a child-like mentality attributed to Native Americans.

22   MUSIC AND DANCE

Music and dance play important and varied roles in native culture. As a consequence, exactly how one studies these art forms is not entirely clear. Comstock's book (below) is a collection of essays by scholars in dance, anthropology, and native culture in which they discuss new aspects of research and various instruments for the study of dance. Frisbie (p. 244) examines the history of music and dance research among southwestern Indians, concluding with suggestions for future research. Stevenson's article (p. 245) reviews written sources for Indian music before 1882, giving a picture of the methods used to study early native music.

The role that music, and particularly dance, play in native culture is complex. The Laubins (p. 245) distinguish three types of dance: religious, social, and ceremonial. Kurath, in her article "Dance, Music and Daily Bread" (p. 244), looks at Indian culture in which dance serves to invest the struggle for subsistence with an aura, becoming directly involved in the pursuit of the daily bread.

A few of the works listed here are collections of records of music and dance. Densmore (p. 244) has recorded songs from a wide range of native groups and geographical areas. All the songs are carefully transcribed, translated, and commented on. Risner (p. 245), primarily interested in providing a data base, has compiled material on six North American dance cultures.

Several scholars provide detailed analyses of various dances and musical pieces. In "Native Choreographic Areas of North America" (p. 245), Kurath compares dance patterns and styles of movement. She identifies major areas of dance and discusses two types of circles. Merriam (p. 245) studies the music of the Flathead Indians. In a detailed account he describes all aspects of Flathead music and analyzes its relation to the rest of Flathead culture. Roberts (p. 245) surveys North American aboriginal music, in the process, finding evidence of part-singing and refuting popular notions that Indian music is simple.

Because most of the titles selected treat music and dance in a general way, there is no regional breakdown of titles in this chapter.

COMSTOCK, TAMARA. *New Dimensions in Dance Research: Anthropology and Dance—the American Indian*. Proceedings of the Third Conference on Research in Dance, Council on Research in Dance. New York: CORD, 1974. 353pp. Illustrated. Bibliography.

In this book, scholars of anthropology, dance, and Native American cultures examine the role of dance in a society. Various anthropological research instruments applicable to the study of dance are reviewed and the significance of the dance in nonliterate societies is explored. The values and function of Native American dance are discussed, with a review of the literature. Other subjects include dance in ritual, a dance data check list, evidence for dance in the prehistoric Southwest, dance as an indicator of social class, and a Native American view. Order from CORD, c/o New York University, Education 675, 35 West 4th St., New York, NY 10003.

"Dance" and "Music." In *The New Encyclopaedia Britannica.* Vol. I, Music: pp. 663–69; Dance: pp. 669–76. London: Encyclopaedia Britannica, 1974. Illustrated. Bibliography.
The article on music outlines dominant features of musical styles native to the American continent and describes instruments for all areas. The article on dance examines regional dance styles of: the Arctic (Eskimo or Inuit), eastern Woodlands, Great Plains, Northwest Coast, Northern Desert and California, and the Southwest. Kinds of dance, organization, relations of dancer and diety, extent of dance forms, stylistic considerations, and foreign influence are some of the subjects discussed.

DENSMORE, FRANCES. *The American Indians and Their Music.* New York: Johnson Reprint, 1970. 143pp.
This book, originally published in 1926, briefly discusses the history and customs of Native Americans, then examines Native American music in its various phases. This author recorded and transcribed songs of a wide range of Native American groups. Generally, the informants, singers, and interpreters are identified; a brief history of the group under consideration is given; songs are transcribed, translated, commented on, and listed by class; and instruments are described. Some of the works provide an analysis of tonality, progressions, and adaptations.
Other major studies by Densmore include:
Cheyenne and Arapaho Music. Southwest Museum Papers no. 10. Los Angeles: Southwest Museum, 1936. 111pp.
Chippewa Music. 2 vols. Bureau of American Ethnology Bulletins 45 and 53. Washington, D.C.: Government Printing Office, 1910 and 1913. 264pp.
Mandan and Hidatsa Music. Bureau of American Ethnology Bulletin 80, 1923. 192pp.
Music of Acoma, Isleta, Cochiti and Zuñi Pueblos. Bureau of American Ethnology Bulletin 165, 1957. 117pp.
Music of the Maidu Indians of California. Los Angeles: Southwest Museum, 1958. 67pp.
Papago Music. Bureau of American Ethnology Bulletin 90, 1929. 229pp.
Pawnee Music. Bureau of American Ethnology Bulletin 93, 1929. 129pp.
Seminole Music. Bureau of American Ethnology Bulletin 161, 1956. 223pp.
There are also studies of the music of the Choctaws, the Nootka and Quileute, the Northern Ute,

Teton Sioux and Yuma and Yaqui. For full citations consult "Bibliography: Frances Densmore" (p. 245).

DRIVER, WILHELMINE. "Music and Dance." In Driver, Harold E. *Indians of North America.* 2nd ed., rev., pp. 194–207. Chicago: University of Chicago Press, 1969. Bibliography.
A general discussion of Native American music, dance, and instruments is followed by areal treatments for the Arctic, the Northwest Coast, the Great Basin, California, the Plains-Prairie, the Southwest, the eastern United States, and Meso-America. References receive full citation in a bibliography at the end of the book.

FRISBIE, CHARLOTTE J. *Music and Dance Research of Southwestern United States Indians, Past Trends, Present Activities and Suggestions for Future Research.* Detroit: Information Coordinators, 1977. 109pp. Bibliography.
Major research on Native American music and dance is reviewed. The author describes the orientations, methodologies, and concerns of past research, identifies present research interests and approaches, and offers suggestions for further research. Beginning with the late 1880s, work is summarized by decades to 1969, then research during 1970–77 is discussed. Each section consists of summary statements followed by an outline of each scholar's work. An appendix lists discographies, photorecording companies, and catalogs of southwestern materials in the Archives of Traditional Music at Indiana University, the Archives of Folksong in the Library of Congress, the Lowie Museum of Anthropology at the University of California in Berkeley, and the Southwest Museum in Los Angeles. Reference sources codify extensive information.

HIGHWATER, JAMAKE (JAY MARKS). *Ritual of the Wind: North American Indian Ceremonies, Music, and Dances.* New York: Viking, 1977. 192pp. Illustrated. Bibliography.
Dance, ceremony, and music are presented as reflections of various aspects of Native American life, with bits of information from many cultures included. More than 100 photographs accompany discussions of the Plains Sun Dance, the Cherokee Booger Dance, the Hako ceremony of the Pawnee, the Rain-Power ceremony at San Juan pueblo, and a Navajo Night Chant. A discography of Native American music and a national calendar of ceremonial events are included.

KURATH, GERTRUDE PROKOSCH. "Dance, Music and Daily Bread." *Ethnomusicology* 4 (1960):1–9. Bibliography.
The author looks at the functions of dance and music in cultures where the arts, religion, and economy interact to the extent that dance and music, as ornaments on the universal theme of making a living, invest the struggle for subsistence with an aura. Topics discussed are: the functions of dance

and music in the pursuit of the daily bread; forms, reflection of cultural pattern; process of change; and an evaluation.

———. "Native Choreographic Areas of North America." *American Anthropologist* 55, no. 1 (1953):60–73. Bibliography.

Dance patterns based on consistent features—ground plans, circle or straight line, the typical style of steps and body movement—are compared in this article. The distribution of geometric patterns, style of movement, and cultural implications of forms and motions are discussed. The author identifies two major areas (north and south) and two types of circles. This author has an extensive list of studies. Among them are: "An Analysis of the Iroquois Eagle Dance and Songs." In William N. Fenton, *The Iroquois Eagle Dance: An Offshoot of the Calumet Dance,* pp. 223–306. Bureau of American Ethnology Bulletin 156, 1953; *Michigan Indian Festivals.* Ann Arbor, Mich.: Ann Arbor Publishers, 1966. See also: "Special Bibliography: Gertrude Prokosch Kurath," *Ethnomusicology* 14 (1970): 114–28 (p. 246).

LAUBIN, REGINALD, and GLADYS LAUBIN. *Indian Dances of North America: Their Importance to Indian Life.* Norman: University of Oklahoma Press, 1976. 538pp. Illustrated. Bibliography.

The first part of this book surveys the historical literature on Native American dance, beginning with Jacques Cartier in 1534, and discusses Indian dance in general. Part 2 covers music, masks, paints, and body decoration. Part 3 describes a variety of dances—religious, social, and ceremonial—for the eastern and western United States. Part 4 treats dances of the Pacific Coast, the Southwest, and contemporary dances. The last section of the book is a retrospective and a discussion of concert dancing, the Laubins' metier. The text reflects a purist attitude.

MERRIAM, ALAN P. *Ethnomusicology of the Flathead Indians.* Chicago: Aldine, 1967. 403pp. Illustrated. Bibliography.

Merriam studies music as an aspect of human experience and a part of social life focusing on the Flathead, a Salishan tribe in Montana, from 1805 to the 1950s. Part 1 discusses the sources of music, Flathead ideas of music and musicianship, sound instruments, the uses of music, acculturation, and culture change. Part 2 discusses problems of interpretation, examines Flathead song structure in terms of use categories, and presents generalizations applicable to Flathead music as a whole.

NETTL, BRUNO. *North American Indian Musical Styles.* Memoirs of the American Folklore Society, vol. 45. Philadelphia: American Folklore Society, 1954. 51pp.

The study of North American Indian music is reviewed. The author discusses the distribution of musical style traits in Native American music north of Mexico, stylistic traits common to all areas studied, geographical distribution of most important traits, musical areas, and culture and linguistic areas. Areas treated are: the Arctic (Eskimo or Inuit), Northwest Coast, Great Basin, California, Yuman area, Athapaskan, Plains-Pueblo, and the East. A summary and conclusions are included. An appendix offers musical examples. See also: "American Indian Music." In *The North American Indians: A Sourcebook,* edited by Roger C. Owen, James J. F. Deetz, and Anthony D. Fisher, pp. 109–19. New York: Macmillan, 1967.

RISNER, VICKY J. *Dance Ethnography Data Inventory: A Repository of Dance Research Information on Six North American Indian Dance Cultures: Yurok, Yokut, Havasupai, Tarahumara, Crow and Ojibwa.* Dance Ethnography Data Inventory Project, Department of Dance. Los Angeles: University of California, 1973. 97pp. Bibliography.

The primary purpose of this study is to provide a data base. Anthropological sources and data for the six groups were gathered from the Human Relations Area Files according to culture area and organized into twelve dance categories. Part 2 presents an inventory of the data .

ROBERTS, HELEN N. *Musical Areas in Aboriginal North America.* Yale University Publications in Anthropology, no. 12. New Haven, Conn.: Human Relations Area Files Press, 1936, 1970. 41pp. Illustrated. Bibliography.

Native American instrumental and vocal music are studied regionally on a comparative basis. Vocal and instrumental music are considered separately. The author refutes popular beliefs about Native American music, finds evidence of part-singing, and contends that the music is not as simple as had been believed. There are maps.

STEVENSON, ROBERT. "Written Sources for Indian Music until 1882." *Ethnomusicology* 17 (1973):1–40. Bibliography.

Sources in Theodore Baker's *Uber die musik der nordameridanischen wilden* (1882) are reassessed and new material evaluated in an ethnomusicological context. The author examined rare materials, printed and manuscript, from the British Museum, Bibliotheque Nationale, Newberry Library, Yale University Library, and Bancroft Library for this study. "English Sources for Indian Music until 1882," a continuation of the discussion, is in *Ethnomusicology* 17 (1973):399–442. (Baker's book is available in English in a volume that includes the German text: *On Music of the North American Indians,* translated by Ann Buckley. Source Materials and Studies in Ethnomusicology 9. Buren, Netherlands: Frits Knuf, 1976. 152pp.)

BIBLIOGRAPHIES

"Bibliography: Frances Densmore." *Ethnomusicology Newsletter* 1, part 7 (1956):14–29; part 10 (1957):15; *Ethnomusicology* 2 (1958):28, 131–32.

This bibliography lists articles and books about the music of various Native American groups.

CAVANAGH, BEVERLY. "Annotated Bibliography of

Eskimo Music." *Ethnomusicology* 16 (1972):479–87.

This bibliography includes items on music and musical traditions of the Eskimos (Inuits) of Greenland, the Canadian Arctic, and Alaska.

HICKERSON, JOE. *Annotated Bibliography of North American Indian Music North of Mexico.* Master of Arts thesis, Indiana University, May 1961. 464pp.

An introductory section presents a historical survey of the investigation of North American Indian music and discusses the various types of works included in the bibliography. About 1,000 articles and monographs from over 250 periodicals and publication series, in more than eight languages, and spanning a period of 350 years are listed and annotated. Items are arranged alphabetically by author and indexed according to group or area.

HODGE, WILLIAM H. "Music-Dance." In *A Bibliography of North American Indians: Selected and Partially Annotated with Study Guides*, pp. 193–97. New York: Interland Publishing, 1975.

This bibliography lists fifty-four references. There are brief annotations with some entries.

KEALUNOHOMOKE, JOAN W., and FRANK GILLIS. "Special Bibliography: Gertrude Prokosch Kurath." *Ethnomusicology* 14 (1970):114–28.

This bibliography lists Kurath's studies of ritual and folk dance and music, including audiovisual materials prepared by the authors.

LEE, DOROTHY SARA. *Native American Music and Oral Data: A Catalogue of Sound Recordings 1893–1976.* Bloomington: Indiana University Press, 1979. 463pp.

This catalog is designed to serve as a guide to Native American music and oral data holdings at the Indiana University Archives of Traditional Music, a collection considered to be one of the largest and most complete in existence to date. The first section lists some 500 accessions contained in field, commercial, and broadcast recordings beginning with James Mooney's field recordings of Plains Indians in 1893; an index of cultural and tribal groups is followed by a list of more than 2,500 subject headings (Acorn dance, bear dance, etc.). Each entry gives collector, year, medium, record company, depositor, culture group, culture area, subject heading, length, sound quality, and documentation available.

MERRIAM, ALAN P. "An Annotated Bibliography of Theses and Dissertations in Ethnomusicology and Folk Music Accepted at American Universities." *Ethnomusicology* 4 (1960):21–39.

This bibliography includes titles of theses and dissertations in the field of Native American music, arranged by subject and institution. See also: Frank J. Gillis, "Special Bibliography: An Annotated Bibliography of Theses and Dissertations in Ethnomusicology and Folk Music Accepted at American and Foreign Universities," Supplement I, *Ethnomusicology* 4 (1962):191–219.

23   EDUCATION

Indian society, like every human society, devised a process by which to transmit its culture to the young. Traditionally, the children were informally educated by parents, other relations, the community, daily activities, and through psychological incentives. The amount of formal instruction given Indian children was minimal or nonexistent compared to the kind of schooling that was prevalent in the contemporaneous European world. Pettitt (p. 254) describes several institutions in Indian societies that had educational roles. These include the mother's brother who acted as mentor and disciplinarian and the reliance on the supernatural as the ultimate reference of discipline. He discusses psychologically effective incentives to learning including the use of praise, ridicule, reward, and privilege. He explains how naming practices were a fundamental aid in educating children and in passing on to them certain acceptable social behaviors and intangible cultural values and discusses the educational value of first-food rites, vision quests, and story telling. Morey and Gilliam (p. 254) present the transcript of a conference at which Indians informally discuss the methods used to teach and instill values in children from the time of their birth to early adolescence. The discussion explores the role of grand-parents, legends, family and clan structure, naming practices, and nature. Ten American Indian doctoral students describe what traditional Indian education used to be like in Bryde's work (p. 253), and Knepler (p. 257) tells of Cherokee education before contact with Europeans, describing the methods used including the roles of legend, precept, example, and sanctions.

The formal education of Indians, in the European sense, was instituted shortly after white people came to North America and was dominated and intertwined with the churches for almost three hundred years. French, Spanish, and English missionaries were the first groups to use formal education as a means of changing American Indians into white people. All of the missionaries, regardless of their affiliations or methods of converting Indians to Christianity, tried to influence them to wear European clothing, to learn farming and mechanical skills, to cut their hair, and to adopt other white customs and ways of living. This process became known as "converting" Indians. Jesuits tried to teach Christianity and French manners, customs, and language to potential Indian converts. Several authors in previous chapters tell of Jesuit activities among the tribes of the Great

Lakes and Canada. The Jesuits made inroads among the Indians but their activities demoralized the tribes dividing them into traditional and Christian camps. Spanish Franciscans introduced educational institutions in the seventeenth century to Indian peoples of Arizona, New Mexico, Texas, and California. They gathered Indian families into villages and missions, either voluntarily or forcibly, where they attempted to force them to convert to Catholicism and become "civilized" according to Spanish standards. Pueblo Indians who converted to Catholicism became estranged from their ceremonials which led to factional strife within the pueblos. The missionary system spread up the California coast in the eighteenth century and enveloped tribes in the same forced conversion and "civilization" program. English Protestant missionaries in the Northeast followed the same course. They tried to Anglicize Indians and "civilize" and Christianize Indian children by sending them to schools far from home where they were given an education that was irrelevant to Indian life. Here, as in the Southwest and around the Great Lakes and in Canada, the result of Indians converting to Christianity was divisiveness within the tribes. Tanis (p. 256) discusses one of the missionary attempts carried on by John Eliot, a Puritan cleric of the mid-1600s, who tried to formally educate the Indians of the Massachusetts Bay Colony. He describes the education the Indians received in fourteen "praying villages" that Eliot founded complete with their own civil government and educational system. Robinson (p. 257) surveys efforts in colonial Virginia to educate and convert Indians to Christianity. None of the schools that were started were completely successful in changing Indians into white people.

From the beginning, and until recently, the goal of the federal government regarding American Indians has been to culturally assimilate them into white society either by persuasive or forcible means. The government, like the missionary, has viewed the school as the tool of assimilation.

> Education was the means whereby we emancipated the Indian child from his home, his parents, his extended family, and his cultural heritage. It was in effect an attempt to wash the "savage habits" and "tribal ethic" out of a child's mind and substitute a white middle-class value system in its place.[1]

Education policy has also been interrelated with federal Indian land policy from the beginning. Between 1778 and 1871, when Congress halted treaty making with Indian tribes, over 389 treaties were negotiated by which Indian tribes ceded almost a billion acres to the United States. Provisions for education were common elements in these treaties.

> Government leaders recognized that if Indians could be converted from hunters into farmers, the Indians would require less land and would be easier to contain. Such a policy would naturally mean more land available for settlement by white men. Education of Indians was seen as the means of accomplishing the conversion.[2]

1. U.S. Congress. Senate. Committee on Labor and Public Welfare, Special Subcommittee on Indian Education. *Indian Education: A National Tragedy—A National Challenge.* S. Rept. 501, 91st Cong., 1st sess., 1969. p. 9.

2. Ibid., p. 177.

For a long time, the federal government was uneasy about running schools itself so it subsidized various religious groups to operate them. The basis for most Indian education programs was an act passed by Congress in 1819 entitled the Civilization Fund Act which appropriated an annual "civilizing" fund. The monies were apportioned among various religious denominations who were prominent in their efforts to convert Indians from hunters to agriculturalists. The Act was in effect until 1873, by which time public protests against federal aid to mission schools and the unconstitutional nature of the practice led the government to discontinue it. As a result, a system of federally operated Indian schools developed under the Bureau of Indian Affairs jurisdiction in the late nineteenth century.

Initially, responsibility for educating Indians was in the hands of the Commissioner, a position created by Congress in 1832 and located in the War Department until 1849 when the Indian office was transferred to the Interior Department. The early Commissioners, who viewed Indians as savages, funded and established extensive educational programs of manual training in agriculture and the mechanical arts in order to "civilize" Indians. No attempt was made to incorporate Indian languages, cultures, and histories into the curriculum because the schools and curriculum were designed to be agents for transmitting white "civilization" and spreading Christianity. A representative statement of the early Commissioners' views can be found in the 1851 annual report of the Commissioner of Indian Affairs: "The civilization of the Indians within the territory of the United States is a cherished object of the government. It undoubtedly merits . . . all the means necessary for its accomplishments."[3] In 1889, another commissioner wrote: "The Indians must conform to the white man's ways, peaceably if they will, forcibly if they must."[4]

Knepler (p. 257) tells of general educational policy designed to discourage perpetuation of Indian cultures and encourage substitution of Euro-American culture. He tells of provisions in a 1791 treaty with the Cherokees that provided for their instruction in a number of vocational skills by missionaries who were funded by the government to Christianize and "civilize" the Cherokees and discourage them from perpetuating their culture.

Missionaries also established boarding schools for boys and girls, institutions that were designed to separate children from their family and reservation, strip them of tribal lore and mores, force abandonment of their native languages, and prepare them for life away from their people. In three articles, Foreman (pp. 256–57) tells of the Choctaw Academy for boys founded in 1825 in Kentucky and run by a Baptist teacher. Mitchell and Renken (p. 258) discuss the Bloomfield Academy for girls founded in 1852 in Oklahoma and run by Methodist missionaries. La Flesche, an Omaha, describes his life as a student in a Presbyterian missionary boarding school in Nebraska (p. 258). Kutzleb (p. 257) discusses the founding of the Carlisle Indian School in Pennsylvania in 1879 and Hampton Normal and Agricultural Institute in Virginia whose procedures, activities, and

3. Francis Paul Prucha, ed. *Documents of United States Indian Policy* (Lincoln: University of Nebraska Press, 1975), pp. 85–86.
4. Ibid., p. 177.

emphasis on industrial education were emulated by boarding schools elsewhere. He tells of problems encountered by graduates of these two institutions when they tried to return to tribal life.

In the 1890s, Indian policy changed to that of bringing Indian education completely under federal control and cutting off funds for support of religious schools. The Catholics' Indian school system was the principal beneficiary of federal funds for mission schools when the drive for a public school system for Indians began. Prucha (p. 255) discusses the end of direct federal appropriations to mission schools, the reactions of the Catholics, who battled with the government over the policy change, and examines the tension and conflicts between the Bureau of Catholic Indian missions and the mission boards of the Protestant denominations over the policy change.

The Bureau of Indian Affairs began building its boarding school system in abandoned army posts in the 1870s, emphasizing vocational education. The system was based on the model established by General R. H. Pratt who founded Carlisle Indian School, also in an abandoned army barracks.

During the last three decades of the nineteenth century, the government pursued a policy of dissolving the Indian land base legislatively. The Dawes Act of 1887 provided for land allotments to individual Indians as a means of breaking up the tribal structure and ostensibly giving Indians an opportunity for a more "civilized" life. The result was to reduce the Indian tribal economic base from 140 to 50 million acres. Land policy was again directly related to the government's Indian education policy because the proceeds from the destruction of the Indian land base were used to pay the costs of taking Indian children from their homes and placing them in federal boarding schools, a system designed to dissolve Indian social structure. There were serious strains on Indian family life when small children were taken from their parents and kept until the parents and children became strangers to each other.

Many Indian families resisted the federal government's assault on their lives by refusing to send their children to school. Congress allowed the Secretary of the Interior to withhold food from Indian families who resisted compulsory education.

Conditions at boarding schools, where children were often used as a labor force, received attention with the publication in 1928 of the Meriam Report (p. 253) which was highly critical of the inadequate facilities and operations of boarding schools and condemned the practice of taking children from their homes and placing them in off-reservation boarding schools. The report recommended that substantially improved day schools replace boarding schools, suggested mission schools be continued for Indian parents who preferred them, and suggested that Indians participate in deciding the direction of their schools.

Demands for reform led to a creative and innovative period in Indian education. John Collier became Commissioner of Indian Affairs in the 1930s and initiated cross-cultural educational policy and programs which included closing some boarding schools, opening day schools, introducing bilingual education, adult education, and recruiting and training Indian teachers. Szasz (p. 255) discusses some of Collier's successful efforts and some of his failures, tells of the passage of the 1934 Johnson-O'Malley Act by which the Bureau of Indian Affairs provided funding to state public school districts for the special needs of Indian enrollment, and discusses its weak points.

World War II, the lack of funds, and Congress's attitudes toward Indians caused a shift in federal policy in the mid-1940s from cross-cultural education to coercive assimilation of Indians. After several years, House Concurrent Resolution 108 passed Congress in 1953 and provided the impetus to turn federal policy in the direction of terminating federal recognition, services, and protection to Indians. During the termination period, federal policy encouraged relocation of Indians into cities away from reservations. A number of federal day schools and boarding schools were closed and students transferred to public schools. Those boarding schools that continued to operate used a forced assimilation approach to educate children far from home so they would forget their families and way of life. Indians who were terminated or who lived in states which assumed responsibility for educating Indian children lost eligibility for Johnson-O'Malley funds. Under Williard Beatty, Chief of the Branch of Education of the Bureau of Indian Affairs, education policy was reflected in a statement printed in *Indian Education,* a newsletter of the agency: "The Indian schools must identify the cultural elements of white society and consciously and deliberately teach them within the school."[5]

Termination slowed down by the end of the 1950s and the Bureau of Indian Affairs changed its policy after 1960 from that of trying to assimilate Indians into the mainstream of American culture to a policy of reinforcing Indian cultures and encouraging Indian self-determination. This meant that Indian parents, tribes, and communities were to have a voice in defining goals and educating their children at the national and local levels.

From late 1967 until late 1969, there were major Congressional hearings on Indian education conducted by a special Senate subcommittee on Indian education. The conclusion was reached that the policies and programs for educating Indians were a national tragedy. The subcommittee made sixty recommendations, but the basic national policy was stated at the first: "The subcommittee recommends ... maximum participation and control by Indians in establishing Indian education programs."[6]

There has been growth in the number of on-reservation schools operated by local Indian school boards with government funds. One of the most important of these is the Rough Rock Demonstration School, established in 1966, on the Navajo Reservation in Arizona as a private, nonprofit organization run by a five-member Navajo school board. The Rough Rock school is committed to the involvement of Indians in their school and to the use of culturally sensitive bilingual curricular materials. The school has become a symbol of Indian participation and control and educational innovation. Johnson (p. 258) tells the story of the pioneering effort in Navajo education, community development, and local control at Rough Rock.

A different kind of example of Indian people trying to gain some measure of influence over their own destinies and the destinies of their children

---

5. Williard W. Beatty, *Education for Culture Change: Selected Articles from Indian Education, 1944–1951* (Washington, D.C.: Bureau of Indian Affairs, 1953), p. 11.

6. U.S. Congress. Senate. Committee on Labor and Public Welfare, p. 106.

was the 1967 Northfolk, California All-Indian Statewide Conference on California Indian Education planned and organized by a group of California Indians. The purpose of the conference was to interest a representative cross-section of the California adult Indian population in planning the improvement of the education of their children.

The federal government has passed legislation that provides funds for Indians who wish to reform, control, and participate in establishing their own programs. The Indian Education Act of 1972, the Indian Self-Determination and Educational Assistance Act of 1975, and the Bilingual Education Act, part of the Elementary and Secondary Education Act since 1967, strengthen the concept of Indian self-determination.

The problems experienced by Indian students in elementary and high schools and in boarding schools away from home have generated interest and many studies. Rosalie Wax (p. 258) studies the problems of high school dropouts among Oglala Sioux boys on the Pine Ridge Reservation in South Dakota in the 1960s; Wax, Wax, and Dumont (p. 258) cite teachers, isolation, and social distance as problems of Bureau of Indian Affairs elementary day schools on the Pine Ridge Reservation. Dumont (p. 257) discusses how South Dakota Sioux children and Oklahoma Cherokee children have developed a tactic of silence that excludes teachers from almost all student activities and functions as a medium of communication either to promote or defeat instruction. Philips (p. 259) discusses the reasons for the reluctance of Indian children on the Warm Springs Indian Reservation in Oregon to participate in classroom verbal interactions. Parmee (p. 259) shows how formal education was used to induce cultural change in the San Carlos Apache children of Arizona and how it created serious social and psychological conflicts within their society. He considers the situation of Apache and other Indian students who share problems of social conflict, economic deprivation, cultural instability, and low scholastic achievement. Kleinfeld (p. 260) reports on three away-from-home high school boarding school programs in Alaska and contends that they have created serious social and emotional problems among village students who attend them. Orvik and Barnhardt (p. 260) explain what frustrates the educational process in Alaskan Indian and Eskimo schools, particularly their ethnocentric nature and ineffective teachers.

AXTELL, JAMES. "The White Indians of Colonial America." *William and Mary Quarterly,* Third Series, 32, no. 1 (January 1975):55–88.
Axtell discusses English colonists taken captive by Indians who needed new members for their families and clans, the educational process by which the colonists were adopted into Indian families and acculturated into Indian life, becoming "white" Indians, and several problems colonists had in readjusting to English colonial life after their release by the Indians. Describing the extraordinary drawing power of Indian culture including Indian technology and the civility and kindness to women and children, he also discusses the means by which Indians transformed whites including certain rites, ceremonies, and gifts to purge whiteness, and the daily example and instruction designed to make the captives into Indians. He cites captives who earned the trust of their Indian families being free from compulsion, socially equal, and sharing in leadership and affairs of peace and war, the ways colonists were instructed in language, and how captive boys were physically trained. He looks at the ways colonists acted as Indians in daily community, social, and economic life, and how they acquired the ability to share unconsciously in the values, beliefs, and standards of Indian life.

BEATTY, WILLIARD W. *Education for Cultural Change: Selected Articles from Indian Education, 1944–1953.* Washington, D.C.: Bureau of Indian Affairs, 1953. 512pp.
This volume contains reprints of 192 articles drawn from 125 issues of *Indian Education,* a field

letter of the Education Division of Indian Service designed to inform members of the education staff about the philosophy, policy, and procedures of Indian education. These articles, which reflect the assimilationist principles of Indian education, are grouped under the following topics: administration at the federal and local levels, understanding cultural differences, law and the Indian, Indian children in public schools, teaching methods for the elementary and high schools, art, music, recreation, guidance, improving rural living, language instruction, health and health education, job placement, a special Navajo program, and goals and measurement. An example of an *Indian Education* statement is "an Indian child . . . must be taught all those elements in cultural behavior that will permit . . . easy transition from life among reservation Indians to life among urban non-Indians . . . The Indian school must identify the cultural elements of white society and consciously and deliberately teach them within the school."

BRYDE, JOHN F., ed. *An Indian Philosophy of Education.* Vermillion: University of South Dakota Institute of Indian Studies, 1974. 51pp.
Ten American Indian doctoral students define their philosophies of Indian education in this volume. They discuss their recommendations about what they would like to see schools and curricula do for Indian students, describe various periods in the history of Indian education, tell of Indian values and their own schooling experiences, and non-Indian perceptions of Indians. The majority of the writers describe traditional Indian education in which there was no formal, separate institution in which to learn. Most of the papers have bibliographies and footnotes.

FUCHS, ESTELLE, and ROBERT J. HAVIGHURST. *To Live on This Earth: American Indian Education.* Garden City, N.Y.: Anchor Press, 1973. 390pp. Illustrated. Bibliography.
This book presents the conclusions of a major 1971 national study on the education of tribal and urban Indian children and what Indians think of the process. The authors begin with a summary of the history of Indian education from the seventeenth century to the early 1970s, give contemporary sociodemographic statistics, and describe how the Bureau of Indian Affairs (BIA) meets its legal responsibility for educating two out of every three Indian school-age children. They cite communities where Indian children live and the schools they attend, including BIA day and boarding schools, rural and small city public day schools, and large public city school systems. They discuss the low achievement of Indian children in school—attributed to poverty, language difficulties, problems of self-image, and social adjustments—and explain that while most Indian students and their parents approve of schools, many community leaders disapprove of schools serving Indians. Also covered are the history of the federal boarding school system, the criticisms leveled at it, the curricula, school life, and problems of contemporary elementary and secondary boarding schools, examples of innova-

tions in Indian education, post-high school education for Indians, and Indians in big city schools. The authors provide an evaluation of Indian education, describe programs to improve it, and conclude with a discussion on the need for local control of schools by Indians. The appendix contains a description of the National Study of American Indian Education that the authors directed in 1971 and a summary of their research methods. One map, twelve figures, and twenty-six tables illustrate the text. The book is based on the 1971 study and published secondary research.

HAVIGHURST, ROBERT J. "Indian Education Since 1960." In *American Indians Today,* edited by J. Milton Yinger and George Eaton Simpson, pp. 13–26. The Annals of the American Academy of Political and Social Science, vol. 436. Philadelphia: American Academy of Political and Social Science, 1978.
Havighurst examines the policy of local self-determination for Indian tribes and communities that has evolved since 1960 when the official government policy of assimilating Indians into the mainstream of American culture was changed to one of tolerating cultural pluralism. He discusses the rapid expansion of the number of Indian students in schools and colleges, the growth of reservation schools operated by local Indian school boards with government funds, and the Alaska Native Land Claims Settlement Act which gives Alaskan natives a large amount of money and land as members of native corporations or regional resident groups. He explains how the federal government provided funds in the 1970s to assist Indians in reforming and directing their educational systems, citing in addition the Indian Self-Determination and Educational Assistance Act of 1975, which provides money and requires Indian participation in designing programs, and the Bilingual Education Act of 1967, which provides funds for employing a teaching staff that speaks native languages.

MERIAM, LEWIS, and Associates. "Education." In *The Problem of Indian Administration,* pp. 346–428. Brookings Institution, Institute for Government Research. Baltimore: Johns Hopkins Press, 1928.
The section entitled "Education" deals with some of the findings of the Meriam Report that concludes "the whole Indian problem is essentially an educational one." Topics considered in this chapter are enrollment problems, the need for better trained educational personnel in the Indian Service, curriculum revision, reorganization of the school day, the need for improved teaching methods, reexamination of industrial and agricultural education, and the need for new health, religious, and adult education programs. The study questions the need for nonreservation boarding schools, particularly at the elementary level, and suggests that mission schools continue for Indian parents who prefer them. The advantages of government day and public schools, the need for upgrading secondary schools and school plants and equipment, the need for improving the administration of Indian education, and for increasing the financing of Indian edu-

cation programs are also covered. In the section on family relations, researchers examine the strains on family life due to the government policy of educating children in boarding schools far away from their homes, taking children from their parents when small, and keeping them until the parents and children have become strangers to each other. They discuss the government goal of disrupting family life and the terrible effects of this system on parents and children. There are quotations from Indian children and adults that document the tragedies of children dying at school or parents dying at home. Although some of the language and concepts are dated, the basic criticisms of the harmful effects of boarding schools remain valid.

MITCHELL, FREDRIC. "Church-State Conflict: A Little-Known Part of the Continuing Church-State Conflict Found in Early Indian Education." *Journal of American Indian Education* 2, no. 3 (May 1963):7–14.

Mitchell gives a brief history of federal support of religious Indian schools which started in 1819 when the U.S. Congress appropriated money to the War Department to be used as a "civilizing" fund and which lasted eighty years. The 1890s brought changes in Indian education policy which resulted in federal control of Indian education and the end of government support of religious schools. Non-Catholic churches cooperated with the new policy while Catholics battled with the government over the policy change until relations were severed by the government. The author describes the philosophy of the Catholic church and the important position it occupied in Indian education since 1803, commanding three-quarters of the funds appropriated by Congress and dominating sectarian education under government auspices. He looks briefly at cases involving the right of parents to obtain religious training for their children at their own expense. The article is based largely on government sources cited in footnotes. See also: Fredric Mitchell and James W. Skelton. "The Church-State Conflict in Early Indian Education." *History of Education Quarterly* 6, no. 1 (Spring 1966):41–51.

MOREY, SYLVESTER M., and OLIVIA L. GILLIAM. *Respect for Life: The Traditional Upbringing of American Indian Children.* Garden City, N.Y.: Waldorf Press, 1974. 202pp. Illustrated.

This book reports the discussions that took place at a conference on traditional methods used to teach and instill values in Indian children from the time of their birth to early adolescence. The conference was attended by several Indians from widely separated tribes and officials of the New York Myrin Institute for Adult Education. The book organizes the data on child rearing into the following categories: the discipline of the cradle board, legends, instilling the wish to obey, the role of grandparents, family and clan structure, the home, and nature. Final chapters explore the pressures on Indians today which are counter to traditional methods of upbringing, suggest what Indian education should be in the future, and look at the kinds of contributions American Indian children could make

to modern culture. The appendix lists information about conferees. There are photographs of conferees and drawings that illustrate traditional methods of upbringing.

NATIONAL ADVISORY COUNCIL ON INDIAN EDUCATION. *First Annual Report to the Congress of the United States.* 2 vols. Washington, D.C.: Government Printing Office, 1974.

The first volume of this work includes discussions on Council recommendations concerning self-determination, key education management positions staffed by Native Americans, proper language development, modernization of Indian affairs agencies, Title IV—The Indian Education Act of 1972, and the Bureau of Indian Affairs management practices. There are copies of President Nixon's and Caspar W. Weinberger's Indian policy statements and a report on who are American Indians. The second volume contains the Council's advice, opinions, and comments on recommendations made in two federal reports on Indian education, *Indian Education: A National Tragedy—A National Challenge* and *Between Two Milestones,* and the texts of both reports. The recommendations concern self-determination, Indian policies and goals, legislation, federal funding, the Indian education system, Johnson-O'Malley, Indian culture, local control and accountability, civil rights, health, and information dissemination. The second volume also contains texts of "A Statistical Profile of the Indian," "Title IV—The Indian Education Act of 1972," President Nixon's 1970 message to Congress, and cases illustrating the positive impact of Title IV funds on natives.

PETTITT, GEORGE A. *Primitive Education in North America.* University of California Publications in American Archaeology and Ethnology 43, no. 1, pp. 1–182. Berkeley: University of California Press, 1943. Bibliography.

Pettitt analyzes the educational practices of selected North American Indian cultures north of Mexico before white contact to discover familial and community activities which contribute to conditioning personalities and integrating individuals into social patterns. He suggests that there are several institutions in Indian societies that have educational roles and indicates not only how these institutions discharge their responsibilities but also how this educational function influences character. The first three chapters of the work indicate that the generalization on the lack of discipline in Indian societies is not true. Pettitt cites parental disciplinary practices and the high degree of child indulgence, which he maintains are in balance with the societies' objectives of referring discipline, or authority for it, to an agent outside the immediate parent-child groups. He looks at the role of the mother's brother as mentor and disciplinarian and the reliance upon the supernatural as the ultimate reference of discipline, also stressing that Indian societies use a wide variety of psychologically effective incentives to learning including the use of praise, ridicule, reward, and privilege and that spontaneous imitation was not the basic motive for learning. He describes how Indians have developed naming practices which are a fundamental aid in educating children and in passing on to them certain acceptable social behaviors as well as intangible cultural values and explains that the first-food rites for boys and girls were carefully directed practices designed to help children acquire economic activities such as food gathering. Analyzing the vision quest and the acquisition of the guardian spirit as a general stimulus to the development of the culturally ideal character and personality, the author also describes the professional training of "extramundane intercessors"—shamans, medicine men, conjurors, prophets, seers, and priests—and the importance of story telling as a pedagogical device. The work is based on published sources.

PRUCHA, FRANCIS PAUL. *Churches and the Indian Schools, 1888–1912.* Lincoln: University of Nebraska Press, 1979. 305pp. Illustrated. Bibliography.

The author traces the tension and conflict between Protestants and Catholics over Indian schools at the end of the nineteenth and beginning of the twentieth centuries. The study begins in 1888 when the Catholic Indian school system was the principal beneficiary of federal funds for mission schools and the drive for a public school system for Indians began. Prucha explains the end of direct federal appropriations for mission schools, the fights waged by Catholics for the right of Indian children to attend Catholic schools, for the restoration of rations to Indian children who attended mission schools, for the use of Indian trust and treaty funds to support Catholic Indian schools, and for the right of nuns to wear their religious habits when teaching in schools taken over by the federal government. He discusses how the conflicts were directed by the Bureau of Catholic Indian missions on one side and by the Indian Rights Association allied with the Protestant mission boards on the other. He also tells of the contract schools on Indian reservations, the Lacey Act of 1907, the Supreme Court case of *Quick Bear* v. *Leupp,* and the success of the Catholics in the struggles after 1900, indicating the decline of Protestant-dominated reform groups in directing U.S. Indian policy. There are three appendixes and illustrations of officials, Catholics, and Protestants who figured in the conflicts.

ROSS, RICHARD M. "Cultural Integrity and American Indian Education." *Arizona Law Review* 11 (Winter 1969):641–75.

This article is primarily concerned with the problems of American Indian education but also deals with the more general problem of maintaining the cultural integrity of ethnic minorities and preserving cultural pluralism in the face of pressures for cultural homogeneity. The author analyzes possible constitutional theories (the first, thirteenth, and fourteenth amendments) upon which claims for preservation of cultural integrity could be built using the Amish and Indians as examples. He discusses the history of the Indians' relationship to the federal government including the wars, treaties, statutes, and creation of bureaus and agencies, and

the attempt to end that relationship. He reviews the history of government control of Indian education beginning with the missionaries, the first educators among Indians who were supported by federal aid, educational provisions in treaties aimed at compulsory education, boarding and day schools, integration of Indian children into state public school systems, and signs of change in Bureau of Indian Affairs practices aimed at preserving cultural integrity. Finally, Ross tries to demonstrate that even in the absence of constitutional arguments for preservation of cultural integrity, the federal government has a special responsibility to Indians to supply them with a special kind of education. The article is based on legal citations and secondary sources.

SZASZ, MARGARET CONNELL. *Education and the American Indians: The Road to Self-Determination Since 1928.* Albuquerque: University of New Mexico Press, 1974; revised ed.: 1977. 252pp. Illustrated. Bibliography.

This book traces the history of the conditions in the Bureau of Indian Affairs (BIA) and public schools that shaped Indian education between 1928, the year of the Meriam Report, and 1976. Szasz begins with the background of federal Indian education from 1870 to 1926 with its stress on assimilation, tells of the Meriam Report with its criticisms concentrated on the boarding school system, and new perspectives introduced by anthropologists and progressive educators who helped shape the cross-cultural education policy and program of the thirties and forties advocated by Ryan, Beatty, and Collier and brought to an end by World War II. She describes some of the successful efforts and failures to develop cross-cultural education programs in federal boarding schools during this period. Discussing the 1934 passage of the Johnson-O'Malley (JOM) Act by which the federal government provided funding to public school districts for their Indian enrollment, she tells of the weaknesses of the JOM program. She describes Beatty's World War II and postwar programs and his shift from cross-cultural to assimilation education, illustrated by the Navajo Special Education program which prepared Navajo youths for urban employment. The limited education goals of Hildegard Thompson during the fifties are cited as well as the new directions in federal Indian policy in the late 1960s, including new roles for Indian people in administration and involvement in federal legislation on education. Szasz tells of the beginning of self-determination, especially new Indian political activity, organizations, and experiments in Indian-controlled schools from the elementary to college levels. She concludes with a review of the BIA's failure to develop educational programs geared to meet Indian needs between 1928 and the early 1970s, except for two intervals when its educational policy was oriented to Indians, the 1930s and 1965 to the present, and explains how funding for public schooling has consistently ignored benefits for Indians. The epilogue updates the revised edition by discussing three laws passed by Congress between 1972 and 1975 that promote Indian self-determination. There are two maps and photographs that illustrate the text. The book is based on interviews, archival, and published works.

THOMPSON, THOMAS, ed. *The Schooling of Native Americans*. Washington, D.C.: American Association of Colleges for Teacher Education and Teacher Corps, U.S. Office of Education, 1978. 191pp. Illustrated. Bibliography.

Ten essays by Native Americans who are involved in contemporary Indian education are included in this book. The preface gives a brief account of how Native American schooling has gotten into a deplorable state. There are essays on the inadequacies of white education for Indians, on the problems of a Shoshone-Bannock woman throughout her primary and secondary schooling, a discussion about the multicultural education center at Rough Rock Demonstration School on the Navajo Reservation, and the political realities which face Indian communities as they move toward control of their own schools. Additional essays consider the reasons why Indian students drop out of college, Indian Head Start programs, university Native American studies programs, a hypothetical construct of an ideal school program for Indians, a discussion of Indian autonomy and implications of this concept for Indian control of education, and a discussion of teachers for Indian children. There are four appendixes including a chronology of pivotal dates in Indian education from 1568 to 1975, Indian education organizations, American Indian community colleges, and treaties dealing with Indian education. There are photographs of Indian children. The book is based on personal testimony.

U.S. CONGRESS. Senate. Committee on Labor and Public Welfare. Special Subcommittee on Indian Education. *Indian Education: A National Tragedy—A National Challenge*. S. Rept. 501, 91st Cong., 1st sess., 1969. 220pp.

This report is a distillate of the Senate Subcommittee's work which fills 4,777 pages in seven volumes of hearings and 450 pages in five volumes of committee prints. This collection of articles, reports, testimony, and commentary on the current status of Indian education concludes that the policies and programs for educating Indians are a national tragedy. The first part presents the Subcommittee findings including a historical narrative that concludes the dominant Indian policy of the federal government has been one of assimilation, vacillating between the two extremes of coercion and persuasion, the roots of which have been to exploit and expropriate Indian land and physical resources. The report has analysis on the failure of public schools to provide Indians with an adequate education, the Bureau of Indian Affairs (BIA) policy of transferring Indians into public schools, and the lack of funding to meet the educational needs of Indian students. The Subcommittee analyzes the inadequate budget of the federal schools, deficient academic performance of students, assimilationist goals, poor instruction, rigid environments, minimal parental and community participation, poor BIA organization and administration, and the deficient personnel system. The Subcommittee examines the destructive elementary and off-reservation boarding schools and inadequate vocational and adult education programs. The second part presents the Subcommittee's sixty recommendations which fall into several categories: policy and goals, administration, the role and future of federal schools, and the government role and nonfederal schools. The basic national policy recommendation is that there be maximum participation and control by Indians in establishing Indian education programs and that there be sufficient federal funds to finance these programs. This report is based on hearings held in Washington, D.C. in 1967; in California, Oklahoma, Arizona, South Dakota, Oregon, and Washington, D.C. in 1968; and Washington, D.C. and Alaska in 1969. The five committee prints, all published in 1969, are entitled "A Survey of Research Literature," "Field Investigations and Research Reports," "Compendium of Federal Boarding School Evaluations," "Compilation of Statutes," and "Organization Question."

NORTHEAST

TANIS, NORMAN EARL. "Education in John Eliot's Indian Utopias, 1646–1675." *History of Education Quarterly* 10, no. 3 (Fall 1970):308–23.

Tanis discusses one of the missionary attempts carried on in 1646 by John Eliot, a Puritan cleric, who tried to educate the Indians inhabiting the Massachusetts Bay Colony. He gives a brief biography of Eliot, explains the contents of his preaching, and his founding of the first Indian village, Nonantum, which was one of fourteen villages all of which had their own forms of government and education systems. The founding in 1651 of Natick, the largest of Eliot's villages, and its scheme of civil government is considered, as is the education the Indians received in the villages and the Corporation of the Gospel which provided aid to educate and "civilize" Indians of Massachusetts. The author concludes with a discussion of the dissolution of the villages with the advent of King Philip's War in 1675. The book is largely based on published primary works.

SOUTHEAST

FOREMAN, CAROLYN THOMAS. "The Choctaw Academy." *Chronicles of Oklahoma* 6, no. 4 (December 1928):453–80. Illustrated.

The author describes the establishment of the Choctaw Academy for boys by Colonel Richard Johnson in 1825, first located at Blue Springs, Kentucky, and later moved to White Sulphur Springs in 1831. She explains how the Choctaw Academy was essentially a school for Choctaws although representatives from many other tribes attended it later. She lists names, ages, and tribal affiliations of the boys who attended the school in the 1820s, and tells of reports by Reverend Thomas Henderson, a Baptist teacher, that describe the physical setup and life of the young boys far from their homes and parents. In addition to discussing the excitement over charges against the Academy made in a report by Peter P. Pitchlyn and the responses by Henderson and Johnson which give accounts of life at the school, Foreman also provides two school attendance lists by tribe and considers the effects of the 1833 cholera epidemic which had a role in the eventual closing of the Academy. There is a photograph of Johnson.

——. "The Choctaw Academy." *Chronicles of Oklahoma* 9, no. 4 (December 1931):382–411. Illustrated.
In this article, the author supplements her earlier one to give a more complete history of the Choctaw Academy. She discusses the financial support of the school and tuition and recounts Henderson's letters and reports which convey a picture of school life, the curriculum, health of the students, and physical layout of the Academy. She also provides the 1833 "Choctaw Academy Cholera Report" by the attending physician and describes improved conditions at the school after the epidemic. Lists of youths at the school in 1834 and their tribal affiliations are included and there is a photograph of Henderson.

——. "The Choctaw Academy." *Chronicles of Oklahoma* 10, no. 1 (March 1932):77–114. Illustrated.
This article supplements Foreman's two earlier ones about the history of the Choctaw Academy. She provides a long list of students and their ages as of 1836, several medical reports of students' ill health, and a list of additional rules for the Academy. She recounts the "Annual Report" of the Commissioner of Indian Affairs from 1838 to 1839 which lists 152 students, describes the unwillingness of tribes to send boys to the Academy after 1839, and reprints the 1839 complaint against the Choctaw Academy prepared by thirty-three of its pupils. The contents spread to the tribes and contributed to the end of the school. Reprints of documents discussing conditions at the school in the early 1840s and photographs of two documents from the Academy are included.

KNEPLER, ABRAHAM ELEAZER. "Education in the Cherokee Nation." *Chronicles of Oklahoma* 21, no. 4 (December 1943):378–401.
Knepler describes Cherokee education before contact with Europeans and formal education from the 1790s to the 1890s. He begins with an examination of Cherokee education methods involving legend, precept, example, and sanctions and the absence of restraint. Then he discusses federal Indian policy designed to discourage perpetuation of Indian cultures and encourage substitution of Western culture. Detailing the 1791 treaty provisions that provided for the instruction of Cherokees in a number of vocational skills by missionaries who were encouraged and funded by the federal government to Christianize and "civilize" the Cherokees, he also cites the missionaries' later role in obstructing the government's attempts to remove the Cherokees from the Southeast. He explains Cherokee treaty education funds appropriated through 1805, Cherokee removal to the West, and Cherokee education

until the turn of the century when the government began to assume control over schooling. The article is based on published sources.

ROBINSON, W. STITT, JR. "Indian Education and Missions in Colonial Virginia." *Journal of Southern History* 18, no. 2 (May 1952):152–68.
This is a survey of efforts made in colonial Virginia from 1609 to the 1760s to educate and convert Indians to Christianity. The author discusses plans that were promoted including private instruction of Indian boys, bringing whole families into English settlements to live, education of Indian boys at the College of William and Mary with income from a fund, instruction by schoolmaster Griffin, and missionary work among tribes outside Virginia in the 1750s and 1760s. He concludes that the value of these efforts was difficult to ascertain, but that educating Indian boys cultivated friendly relations between whites and Indians.

GREAT PLAINS

DUMONT, ROBERT V., JR. "Learning English and How to be Silent: Studies in Sioux and Cherokee Classrooms." In *Functions of Language in the Classroom,* edited by Courtney B. Cazden, Vera P. John, and Dell Hymes, pp. 344–69. New York: Teachers College Press, 1972. Bibliography.
Dumont looks at how contemporary Sioux children of South Dakota and Cherokee children of Oklahoma have developed a complex system of communication and control within the classroom, one part of it nonverbal, one part verbal, and how silence governs teaching and learning experiences, representing a student-centered and controlled tactic that excludes teachers from almost all student activities. He explains how silence functions as a medium of communication to both promote and defeat instruction and how it serves as a strategy in student defenses needed to deal with the conflict resulting from cultural differences. He describes two Cherokee classroom discussions and the teachers of the Harris School in Oklahoma where in one environment English serves as a medium of conflict and in the other as a medium of cooperation. The article is based largely on field work.

KUTZLEB, CHARLES R. "Educating Dakota Sioux, 1876–1890." *North Dakota History* 32, no. 4 (October 1965):197–211.
This is a summary of attempts made by the federal government to educate Indians between 1876 and 1890, particularly the Indians in North and South Dakota. The author examines general federal education policy of the period dedicated to assimilating Indian youth into American life by destroying Indian cultures and describes several different types of schools that emerged within the Indian school system such as day, reservation boarding, nonreservation boarding, training schools, public education, and others. He cites the Carlisle Indian School in Pennsylvania founded in 1879 and Hampton Normal and Agricultural Institute in Virginia whose procedures, activities, and emphasis on industrial

education were emulated by reservation schools. Discussing the opposition to educating Indians which came from Indians themselves and from educators who argued over which types of schools were best, he also mentions the problems faced by graduates of Hampton and Carlisle who tried to return to the reservation way of life. He concludes with an analysis of why the efforts to educate the Sioux failed between 1876 and 1890, arguing that they were compulsive and repressive and showing that the numbers educated were small compared to the school-age population. The article is based on published primary and secondary sources.

LA FLESCHE, FRANCIS. *The Middle Five: Indian Schoolboys of the Omaha Tribe.* Madison: University of Wisconsin Press, 1963. 152pp. Illustrated.

This book contains an account of La Flesche's life as a student in a Presbyterian mission school in Nebraska during the mid-1860s. In a series of sketches, he tells of young Indian boys reluctant to abandon Omaha ways and puzzled in their new roles of "make-believe white men." He discusses the English names given the boys by the missionaries, describes ambitions of Indian parents for their children, struggles of the teachers to teach white ways, and the problems met by both parents and teachers in controlling the young students. A map and photographs of La Flesche and the mission school are included.

MITCHELL, IRENE B., and IDA BELLE RENKEN. "The Golden Age of Bloomfield Academy in the Chickasaw Nation." *Chronicles of Oklahoma* 49, no. 4 (Winter 1971–1972):412–23.

The authors discuss the development of the Bloomfield Academy in the Chickasaw district of Indian Territory, a school for girls which began as a boarding school founded by Reverend John H. Carr in 1852, and the role of the Methodist missionaries in educating Chickasaws. They examine the arts curriculum of the Academy, requirements for graduation, and focus on Helen Birdie Smith, a member of the 1904 graduating class, whose speeches on dating and graduating are reprinted.

WAX, MURRAY; ROSALIE WAX; and ROBERT V. DUMONT, JR. *Formal Education in an American Indian Community.* Social Problems Monograph no. 1. Kalamazoo: The Society for the Study of Social Problems, 1964. 126pp.

This paper focuses on the elementary day schools of Pine Ridge Reservation, South Dakota, where "country" Indians, send their children. Citing teachers, isolation, and social distance as the fundamental problems of Indian education, the authors begin with a historical background and a review of ethnographic studies of Dakota peoples and describe three theories under consideration. They describe contemporary Pine Ridge economy, ecology, and educational achievement and explain the confusing situation that exists about the definitions of Indian country. Relating that the conservative "country" Indians feel that school is "good," the authors tell of their complaints, Indian parents' attempts to deal with misbehavior, and their care in dressing their children. They describe the Bureau of Indian Affairs (BIA) school system and ideologies, kinds of teachers in the bureaucracy, their teaching practices, and their negative attitudes toward Indian parents and children, and they consider the struggle between teachers and the peer society of school children. The last chapter looks at conditions in BIA elementary day schools. The authors recommend that Indians be involved in the formulation of policies and the schooling of their children, that control of the elementary school system be transferred to a board selected by Indians, and that organizational changes be made at the secondary level. Last, the authors revise their original theories that oriented their research efforts. There is an appendix of research procedures. There are thirteen tables, largely demographic, and footnotes citing the field work and secondary sources upon which the study is based.

WAX, ROSALIE. "The Warrior Dropouts." *Transaction,* 4 (May 1967):40–46; reprinted in John R. Howard, *Awakening Minorities: American Indians, Mexican Americans, Puerto Ricans,* pp. 27–42. Chicago: Aldine, 1970.

Wax studies the problems of the high school dropouts among Oglala Sioux boys on the Pine Ridge Reservation in South Dakota in the 1960s. She describes traditional Sioux culture where boys are encouraged to be physically reckless and impetuous and to belong to peer groups with intense loyalties. Explaining how these traits were not diminished in day schools where devices were developed by Indian children to frustrate formal learning, she describes the difficulties of "country" Indians (those Indians raised and living out on the reservation and participating in social-ceremonial activities of local, rural Indian communities), entering the alien environment of the Oglala Community High School that values regulations, routine, and diligence. She cites the reasons given by Indians for dropping out, particularly their feeling that they are too vital and independent to submit to a dehumanizing situation. The work is based on field work.

SOUTHWEST

JOHNSON, BRODERICK H. *Navaho Education at Rough Rock.* Rough Rock, Ariz.: Rough Rock Demonstration School, 1968. 212pp. Illustrated.

This book tells the story of the contemporary pioneering effort in Navajo education, community development, and local control. The author begins with the establishment of the Rough Rock school in 1966 with its two governing premises of biculturalism and local control by the Navajo people. He discusses the creation of DINE (Demonstration in Navajo Education), the private, nonprofit organization of Navajo leaders who receive funds and direct the school, and describes the school's physical setting, leadership by the five member all-Navajo school board, later increased to seven, and describes opinions of individual board directors of DINE Johnson also recounts a day with the school board, discusses the establishment of the Navajo Curriculum Center, and training for medicine men apprentices, a project of the school board. Finally, he discusses significant decisions of the board and their disagreements with the administration. There are chapters by Gary Witherspoon on the conclusions of a study of Rough Rock area Navajos concerning their knowledge of the school, a philosophical discussion of the school's background, together with a detailed description of the school board's decisions, activities, and policies. There are many photographs of the Rough Rock school community and drawings of Navajo people.

PARMEE, EDWARD A. *Formal Education and Culture Change: A Modern Apache Indian Community and Government Education Programs.* Tucson: University of Arizona Press, 1968. 132pp. Illustrated.
Parmee shows how formal education can be used to induce cultural change, illustrated by the San Carlos children of Arizona, and how it creates serious social and psychological conflicts within a society, inhibiting adjustment. Beginning with an examination of the growth and refinement of formal education as a technique for inducing culture change in the Indian population since 1776, he continues with a look at the problems of Indian students from other reservations shared by Apache students in the areas of social conflict, economic deprivation, and cultural instability, and also describes academic and social problems of Apache teens in some detail. He reviews the major components of the three major types of school systems (federal, public, and mission) that Apaches have been exposed to, analyzes the reasons for absenteeism, and notes the criteria used to measure the low scholastic achievement of teenage Apache students. He describes factors affecting the education of Apache youth, problems stemming from community, family, and education programs and provides four case histories that illustrate some of the more significant problems and underlying causes. The concluding chapter analyzes why the Apache education program of 1959 and 1961, represented by federal and public education agencies, failed to educate and integrate Apache children into the American mainstream because it failed to accept family, peer, and community influences and include them as part of the formal education process. The author suggests actions that might be taken and reviews developments taken by local education officials since 1961. There are nine tables of Apache education statistics. The book is based on interviews, field work, school records, and published studies and secondary works.

GREAT BASIN–PLATEAU

PHILIPS, SUSAN U. "Participant Structures and Communicative Competence: Warm Springs Children in Community and Classroom." In *Functions of Language in the Classroom,* edited by Courtney B. Cazden, Vera P. John, and Dell Hymes, pp. 370–94. New York: Teachers College Press, 1972. Bibliography.

This article presents reasons for the reluctance of contemporary Indian children of the Warm Springs Indian Reservation in Oregon to participate in classroom verbal interactions because there is a lack of social conditions for participating to which they have been accustomed in the Indian community. Defining school classroom situations in which Indian students' verbal participation is minimal, the author also compares Indian and non-Indian students' verbal participation under classroom and group conditions, and provides educational background information on the Warm Springs Indian Reservation where the research was conducted. She examines learning processes in the home which require minimal verbal performance from children, learning experiences outside the home in social and ritual activities involving community members, and compares the differences between social conditions for verbal participation in classrooms with conditions underlying many Indian events in which children participate. The paper is based on comparative observations in all-Indian and non-Indian classes and there is a bibliography listing published secondary works on Indian education.

CALIFORNIA

AD HOC COMMITTEE ON CALIFORNIA INDIAN EDUCATION. *California Indian Education: Report of the First All-Indian Statewide Conference on California Indian Education.* Modesto, Calif.: California Indian Education Association, 1968. 80pp.
Containing a discussion on the purposes ("To involve our people in planning the improvement of the education of their children") and the background of how the first statewide conference came about, the Ad Hoc Committee report also gives an overview of the Northfolk, California, conference findings, and cites the Conference recommendations for parents of Indian children, for the Indian community, for school administrators and Board members, for colleges and universities, and for teachers and counselors. There are recommendations on the Indian heritage, on textbooks and the mass media, to the state of California, and to the federal government. There are reports of seminar groups and the future plans of the Ad Hoc Committee. The appendix contains documents that relate to the planning of the conference including recommendations from the 1967 Stanislaus Conference held several months before the All-Indian one. "This report . . . represents a significant step in the California Indian people's struggle for psychological liberation . . . The California Indian people are attempting . . . to gain some measure of influence over their own destiny and of the destiny of their children."

NORTHWEST COAST

WOLCOTT, HARRY F. *A Kwakiutl Village and School.* New York: Holt, Rinehart, & Winston, 1967. 132pp. Illustrated. Bibliography.
This book is a case study of contemporary Kwaki-

utl village life along the British Columbia Coast and of a school located within that village. In it are described the social environment from which the school draws its pupils, the interaction of these pupils with the teachers, and the learning tasks and the curriculum set by the latter. The author, a teacher in the school, deals with the frustrations issuing from miscommunications inherent in the cultural differences and the failures issuing from cultural disintegration. The introduction contains a description of the village and of the region and includes information about gathering the data. The first part of the study focuses on the village way of life, the social environment in which the village children learn to become village adults, the annual economic cycle, and social activities of the villagers. The second part deals with the separate educational system operating within the village, one that is formal, directed, and highly focused. The teachers, village school, pupils, classroom program, and parent and pupil attitudes toward formal education are described. There are photographs of the children and tables of pupil and adult activities. The study is based on field work and published secondary works.

ALASKA

KLEINFELD, JUDITH. *A Long Way From Home: Effects of Public High Schools on Village Children Away from Home.* Fairbanks: Center for Northern Educational Research and Institute for Social, Economic, and Government Research, University of Alaska, 1973. 119pp.

Kleinfeld examines the problems of rural secondary education which requires that most Alaskan Eskimo village children attend high schools away from home. The report asserts that three high school programs (the Bethel rural boarding home program, the Nome boarding school program, and the Anchorage urban boarding program) created serious social and emotional problems among village students. Chapters describe curricula, student populations, and their problems in the three high schools, as well as the decrease in dropouts and social and emotional problems of village high school students. The author discusses how high schools away from home make it difficult for village students to solve adolescent problems of forming a strong identity. She reviews the history of secondary school policy in Alaska where decisions are based primarily on economics and politics rather than on educational considerations. She concludes with recommendations that village high schools should be established for the majority of village students and that other away-from-home programs should be closed. There are nine appendixes including the methodology of evaluating high schools, social and emotional problems of away-from-home village students, dropouts and transfers, achievement test scores, courses, grade point averages, attitudes, the background of village students in alternative high school programs, follow-up studies of graduates from these programs, and projected high school enrollment.

ORVIK, JAMES, and RAY BARNHARDT, eds. *Cultural Influences in Alaskan Native Education.* Fairbanks: Center for Northern Educational Research, University of Alaska, 1974. 94pp.

This is a collection of readings that describe educational perspectives and programs in contemporary Alaskan native education. The first two papers help educators understand what frustrates the educational process in a multicultural setting, especially the ethnocentric nature of schools, and explain the different cultural perspectives of the school and community. The following readings treat the characteristics of effective and ineffective teachers of Indian and Eskimo high school students, the impact of village factionalism on Alaskan bush teachers, the training of native teachers, and the adaptation of native learning processes to the classroom. Other papers deal with bilingual education in Alaska, educational program development, the politics of educational control, and the last paper analyzes the potential contributions of anthropology to cross-cultural understanding.

BIBLIOGRAPHIES

BERRY, BREWTON. *The Education of American Indians: A Survey of the Literature.* Washington, D.C.: Government Printing Office, 1969. 121pp.

This volume (one of the five committee prints of the Special Subcommittee on Indian Education) contains a critical discussion and survey of the literature concerning American Indian education keyed to a bibliography of 708 items of varying quality on Indian education that covers a wide range of topics over a considerable period of time. The author begins with a discussion of the unpublished and published literature on the history of Indian education divided into five categories: general histories, missions, institutional, tribal, and regional histories. He discusses the assimilationist objective underlying the introduction of formal education of Indians, examines the evidence in the literature that formal education has failed to meet the Indians' needs including achievement tests, follow-up studies after graduation, urban migrants, absenteeism, and dropouts. He examines the causes discussed in the literature of the failure of Indian students to profit from their schooling under eight categories: debates over Indian intellect, teachers, parents, cultural deprivation, cultural and language barriers, schools, and the Indians' self-concept. The concluding chapter deals with the literature on Indian college students.

BROOKS, I. R., and A. M. MARCHALL. *Native Education in Canada and the United States: A Bibliography.* Calgary, Alberta, Canada: The University of Calgary, Office of Educational Development, 1978. 298pp.

This bibliography includes only works which deal with the pedagogy, sociology, and politics of Indian education from 1900 to 1975. Nearly 3,000 books, articles, papers, and speeches have been organized into nine major parts with each part further subdivided into sections. There is a reader's guide describing the divisions, their contents, and possible usage. Each of the thirty-eight sections has an introduction explaining its contents. The first part, North America, contains sections on the history of Indian education, U.S. and Canadian government reports and studies, general views of U.S. and Canadian education after 1945, reports on the Arctic, Great Lakes, East, Plains, West Coast, and Southwest Indian and non-Indian viewpoints. The second part deals with integration and local control of schools; the third part with curriculum and instruction; the fourth part with reading and language (English, native, bilingualism); and the fifth with programs (adult, vocational, teacher-training, preschool, and Headstart), research, educational and cultural centers, and projects. The sixth part deals with achievements, aspirations, and dropouts; the seventh with sociological factors which influence the environment within which Indian education must operate; and the eighth with psychological factors which influence the behavior of students including attitudes, identity and self-concept, guidance and counseling. The last part treats the psychological (cognitive) factors related to Indians including tests and testing, studies of learning, intellectual ability, and perception. There is a selected bibliography of bibliographies and an author index.

MARTINEZ, CECILIA J., and JAMES E. HEATHMAN, comps. *American Indian Education: A Selected Bibliography.* Las Cruces, N. Mex.: Educational Resources Information Center Clearinghouse on Rural Education and Small Schools, 1969. Supplements issued in 1970, 1971, 1973, 1975, 1976, 1977, and 1979.
The initial bibliography and nine supplements include some of the latest research findings and newest developments in the education of American Indian children. Abstracts follow each citation and a subject index is included at the end of the bibliography and each supplement. The majority of documents cited are available from the ERIC Document Reproduction Service in microfiche and hard cover. The abstracts of documents are from *Research in Education,* a monthly publication from the U.S. Office of Education, and *Current Index to Journals in Education.* Topics cover areas such as American Indian history, culture, language, educational development, educational programs, legal status, acculturation, adjustment problems, adult education, testing, counseling, curriculum, dropouts, early childhood, boarding schools, teachers, and many others.

NATIONAL INDIAN EDUCATION ASSOCIATION. *Native American Evaluations of Media Materials.* 2 vols. Minneapolis: N.I.E.A., Project Media, 1975. 3 supplements issued.

This work presents evaluations of print and nonprint media materials by Native Americans. Works reviewed are materials by, about, and/or for Native Americans. NIEA reviews several hundred items in this work and plans to evaluate up to 19,000 in future years. Each annotation includes the price, tribes covered, general subject, contents, evaluation rating, and the tribal affiliation of the evaluator. The works are listed alphabetically by title and by author.

PRUCHA, FRANCIS PAUL. "Indian Education." In *A Bibliographical Guide to the History of Indian-White Relations in the United States,* pp. 240–73. Chicago: University of Chicago Press, 1977.
This section of the unannotated bibliographical guide contains key reference guides and periodicals and selected works on the history of Indian education and modern Indian education. The topic entitled "History of Indian Education" is subdivided into works on General Historical Studies, Schools and Teachers, Hampton and Carlisle Institutes, the Church-State Controversy, Writings on Indian Education to 1900, and 1901 to 1920. "Modern Indian Education" is subdivided into works on General and Miscellaneous Studies, Language and Communication Skills, Testing and Achievement Studies, Comparative Studies (with non-Indians), Vocational Training, Counseling, Higher Education, Teacher Training, Writings on Indian Education from 1921 to 1932, 1933 to 1945, 1946 to 1960, 1961 to 1970, and from 1970 until the publication of the bibliographical guide in 1977, and Teaching about Indians.

————. "Missions and Missionaries." In *A Bibliographical Guide to the History of Indian-White Relations in the United States,* pp. 202–28. Chicago: University of Chicago Press, 1977.
This section of the unannotated bibliographical guide contains material on the educational work of the various denominations as well as those that deal strictly with religious work and biographical accounts of missionaries and their enterprises. The listing begins with general studies, those works that treat missionary activity in a theoretical or analytical way, and studies that cover more than one denomination. Works dealing with the efforts of colonies to convert Indians are listed next followed by works on Baptist, Catholic, Episcopal, Lutheran, Mennonite, Methodist, Moravian, Mormon, Presbyterian, Congregational, and Quaker Missions, and the American Board of Commissioners for Foreign Missions, an organization made up largely of members of those denominations who had numerous missions among the Indians.

24 ARTS

The artistic achievements of Native Americans reveal a rich variety of techniques and styles that have evolved from many art traditions. Most of the works in this section offer an introduction to the art of North American Indians in its many forms.

General treatments that cover the full range of art forms from all areas of the United States, including Alaska, can be found in "American Indian Peoples, Arts of" (below), Driver (p. 263), Dockstader's *Indian Art in America* (p. 263), and Whiteford (p. 265).

Subjects of individual works include: silverwork, Adair (p. 266); basketry, James (p. 264), Miles and Bovis (p. 264), and Robinson (p. 266); weaving, Amsden (p. 266); beadwork, Orchard (p. 264); porcupine quill decoration, Orchard (p. 264); rawhide, Morrow (p. 264); rock art, Grant (p. 263); clothing, Conn (p. 263); and contemporary crafts, Mary Schneider (p. 264).

Catalogs of major exhibitions provide historical and cultural information and present outstanding examples of artistic accomplishment. This section includes Coe (p. 263), Collins et al. (p. 263), Conn's *Native American Art in the Denver Art Museum* (p. 263), and Walker Art Center et al. (p. 265).

Brody (below), Dunn (p. 266), and Highwater (p. 264) treat the development of American Indian painting; the Monthans (p. 264) profile seventeen contemporary artists working in various media; and Snodgrass's biographical "dictionary" (p. 265) provides information on over 1,000 artists. In addition a number of works deal with Southwestern art traditions and other studies examine art forms characteristic of several other geographical regions. The bibliographies suggest additional sources.

"American Indian Peoples, Arts of." In *The New Encyclopaedia Britannica,* vol. 1, pp. 658–94. London: Encyclopaedia Britannica, 1974. Illustrated. Bibliography.

The literature, music, dance, and visual arts of Native American peoples of North, Central, and South America are discussed in the context of their social, religious, and political milieus and in relation to the Western world. Eskimos, or Inuits, are also included.

BRODY, J. J. *Indian Painters and White Patrons.*

Albuquerque: University of New Mexico Press, 1971. 238pp. Illustrated. Bibliography.

The author considers two opposing interpretations of modern Native American painting: modern painting as an integrated and essentially aboriginal form of expression, and modern painting as nothing more than a commercial art form produced by American Indian painters for non-Indians. He also surveys archaeology throughout the United States, traces early contacts between Indians and Europeans, and analyzes the development of modern American Indian painting.

COE, RALPH T. *Sacred Circles: Two Thousand Years of North American Indian Art.* Kansas City, Mo.: Nelson Gallery of Art, 1977. 252pp. Illustrated.

This catalog includes pictures of over 700 objects of Native American art gathered from six countries for an exhibition. A preface discusses the purposes of the exhibition, describes some of the items in the show, explores the "Indianness" aspect of Native American art, and explains the meaning of the sacred circles. Objects are arranged topically under: "Archaeology," "Woodlands and Athabasca," "Arctic," "Plains," "Southwest," and "California." A concluding section contains photographs by Edward Curtis and other historical material. Captions give the background of each object pictured and identify tribal origin.

COLLINS, HENRY B.; FREDERICA DE LAGUNA; EDMUND CARPENTER; and PETER STONE. *The Far North: 2000 Years of American Eskimo and Indian Art.* Bloomington: Indiana University Press, 1977. 289pp. Illustrated.

This volume features more than 350 items in an exhibition mounted at the National Gallery of Art in Washington, D.C. in 1973. The material was drawn from numerous collections and much of it was displayed in an art museum context for the first time. There are introductory essays for the three groups represented—Eskimos (Inuit), Athapaskans, and Tlingits. Captions identify the objects pictured, giving size, location, and/or owner. Each essay lists references.

CONN, RICHARD. *Native American Art in the Denver Art Museum.* Colorado: Denver Art Museum, 1979. 351pp. Illustrated. Bibliography.

This volume contains 500 examples of Native American art selected first for esthetic quality and then by breadth of chronological and geographic distribution and generic type. A map shows locations of the groups represented and an introductory essay discusses Native American art as art. Geographic areas include: Southeast, Northeast, Subarctic, Woodlands-Midwest, Plains, Southwest, Intermontane, California, Northwest Coast, and the Arctic. Media best represented are pottery, basketry, beadwork, and traditional clothing. Areas best represented are the Southwest, Great Plains, and Northwest Coast. A descriptive caption accompanies each illustration.

————. *Robes of Shell and Sunrise: Personal Decorative Arts of the Native American.* Colorado: Denver Art Museum, 1974. 150pp. Illustrated. Bibliography.

This book, the catalog of an exhibition, displays the richness and diversity of Native American design concepts. Innovations in clothing design and the complex social and religious symbolism in clothing decoration are illustrated. A limited amount of jewelry is included. An essay discusses clothing design and ornamentation as a symbolic means of communication. Items are grouped under: "Body Decoration," "Wrapped and Folded Clothing," "Binary Clothing," "Fitted Clothing (includes moccasins)," and "The Crowning Touch." Each section includes a discussion plus examples and, for some items, patterns. A brief section presents examples that demonstrate a European influence.

DENVER ART MUSEUM, DEPARTMENT OF INDIAN ART. Indian Leaflet Series, nos. 1–171. Denver, Colo.: The Museum, 1930–32. Illustrated. Bibliography.

These three-page reference guides deal with all aspects of Native American arts (design, symbolism, etc.). Each gives a brief historical and ethnographic description of group under consideration. Bibliographies in each leaflet identify sources.

DOCKSTADER, FREDERICK J. *Indian Art in America: The Arts and Crafts of the North American Indian.* Greenwich, Conn.: New York Graphic Society, 1966. 224pp. Illustrated. Bibliography.

This is a representative selection of Native American art including examples of everyday craftsmanship which possess unusual aesthetic values. Every important region and all major techniques are covered. Topics discussed are: visual arts, the Indian as artist, characteristics of Indian art, regionalism, functionalism, religion in art, environment, techniques and expression, folk art and fine art, tribal identity, realism, symbolism, commonality of art, the "primitive art" concept, dating Indian art, non-Indian and Indian (influences), living with nature, areal sketches, new materials, and new palette.

————. *Weaving Arts of the North American Indian.* New York: Thomas Y. Crowell, 1978. 223pp. Illustrated. Bibliography.

Dockstader traces the development of textiles and clothing and discusses the materials used by the Indians. He explores the technical, social, and economic influences on the development of weaving in North America, breaking the area into geographic regions and citing the distinguishing characteristics of the woven works of the groups in each region. A chapter on contemporary weaving is followed by the basic criteria for judging the quality of a woven piece, suggested ways of detecting imitations, and care instructions. While this is not a "how to" book, types of looms, tools, weaving techniques, designs, and materials are described.

DRIVER, HAROLD E. "Art." In *Indians of North America.* 2nd ed., rev., pp. 176–93. Chicago: University of Chicago Press, 1969. Illustrated. Bibliography.

This chapter surveys Native American art techniques and styles of expression in the Arctic, Northwest Coast, Plains, Southwest, East, and Meso-America. The references receive full citation in a bibliography at the end of the book.

GRANT, CAMPBELL. *Rock Art of the American Indian.* New York: Thomas Y. Crowell, 1967. 178pp. Illustrated. Bibliography.

In this survey of Native American rock carvings and paintings, the author reviews other writings and ties the subject together, discussing the purposes, techniques, dating, preservation, and location of the approximately 15,000 sites where rock art may be found. Color and black-and-white photos and drawings point up the similarities, differences, and ritual meaning of examples of rock art.

HIGHWATER, JAMAKE (JAY MARKS). *Song from the Earth: American Indian Painting.* Greenwich, Conn.: New York Graphic Society, 1976. 212pp. Illustrated. Bibliography.

Native American art is surveyed from pre-Columbian times, through eighteenth-century ledger drawings by men held as prisoners in Florida, to the twentieth century. The author offers a political analysis of Native American art in the context of a dominant white society. The achievements of individual artists are presented along with the advances of over-all trends. The controversy surrounding contemporary Indian painting—whether or not such art, through its apparent acceptance of Western views, betrays Native American values and ideals—is highlighted through interviews with Native American artists of varied training and principles. An appendix lists places with important holdings.

JAMES, GEORGE WHARTON. *Indian Basketry* and *How to Make Indian and Other Baskets.* Glorieta, N. Mex.: Rio Grande Press, 1970. (Two volumes bound together.) 271pp. and 136pp. Illustrated. Bibliography.

Indian Basketry, originally published in 1901, discusses basketry in legend, ceremony, basket-making people, materials, colors, forms, symbolism, designs, and uses and offers hints for collectors. The second volume in this edition, originally published in 1904, discusses choice of materials, preparation, dyes, tools and terms, techniques, fancy borders, and finishing.

MILES, CHARLES, and PIERRE BOVIS. *American Indian and Eskimo Basketry: A Key to Identification.* San Francisco: privately printed, 1969. 143pp. Illustrated.

This guide to the nature and identity of the basketry artifacts produced by Native Americans omits all but the essentials. There is a brief description of basketry techniques and a summary of the major distinctive basketry areas. The authors describe the kinds of items made, illustrate four major methods of constructing baskets, and discuss methods of ornamentation. Most of the book is devoted to examples of regional baskets, with an identifying caption for each picture. Order from Pierre Bovis, P.O. Box 26443, San Francisco, 94126.

MONTHAN, GUY, and DORIS MONTHAN. *Art and Indian Individualists.* Flagstaff, Ariz.: Northland Press, 1975. 197pp. Illustrated.

This volume showcases seventeen contemporary Native American artists. Biographical information and photographs and color plates of the work of each artist are included. Media include oil painting, printmaking, silverwork, ceramics, and sculpture. The artists are: Cordero, Da, Golsh, Gorman, Haozous, Hinds, Houser, Hyde, Ingram, Charles and Otellie Loloma, Lovato, Medicine Flower, Monongye, Naranjo, Scholder, and White.

MORROW, MABLE. *Indian Rawhide: An American Folk Art.* Norman: University of Oklahoma Press, 1975. 243pp. Illustrated. Bibliography.

This study describes how animal skins were prepared, worked, decorated, and used by Native American groups, with emphasis on those in the Plains area who used untanned hides extensively. With major attention paid to the painted decorations on parfleches, rawhide envelopes of all sizes used for carrying food and as luggage, the author analyzes geometric designs to demonstrate that specific patterns and styles were typical of particular groups.

ORCHARD, WILLIAM C. *Beads and Beadwork of the American Indians.* Museum of the American Indian, Contributions vol. 2. New York: Museum of the American Indian, 1929; 2nd ed., 1975. 168pp. Illustrated.

Various techniques employed by Native Americans in producing numerous forms of bead ornamentation are described. The author discusses the manufacture and use of shell, pearl, bone, stone, and metal beads, and also wampum. Also covered are beads of "odd forms and materials" (basketry, wood, gum, clay), trade beads, woven bead work, sewing techniques, edgings, bead inlays, and beaded baskets.

————. *The Technique of Porcupine Decoration among the Indians of North America.* Museum of the American Indian, Contributions vol. 4, no. 1. New York: Museum of the American Indian, 1916; 2nd ed., 1971. 82pp. Illustrated.

This volume studies the use of dyed porcupine quills as a decorative material, an art unique among North American Indians. A commentary discusses the techniques and styles developed by the various Native American groups who practiced the art.

SCHNEIDER, MARY JANE. *Contemporary Indian Crafts.* A Special Exhibit Sponsored by the Museum of Anthropology, University of Missouri. Columbia: University of Missouri Press, 1972. 51pp. Illustrated. Bibliography.

This booklet offers a general introduction to contemporary Native American crafts from all areas of North America. There are sections on basketry, beadwork, pottery, metalwork, painting, carving, ribbon applique, featherwork, quillwork, and weaving. Examples illustrating traditional techniques used in new combinations and new techniques used in traditional manners are included, each section giving a brief description of traditional techniques for objects under consideration and then showing the modern products. A reprint of *Source Directory 1,* published by the Indian Arts and Crafts Board of the Department of the Interior, listing Native American organizations marketing arts and crafts, is appended.

SCHNEIDER, RICHARD C. *Crafts of the North American Indians: A Craftsman's Manual.* New York: Van Nostrand Reinhold, 1972. 325pp. Illustrated.

Schneider describes the process of making items of skin and leather, beadwork, bark, basketry, ceramics, fiber, and corn husks. Also included are instructions for making one's own tools and for processing materials to be used. The author stresses the quality and experience of producing an item, urges noncompetition with Native American craftworkers, and discourages the manufacture of artifacts that carry religious overtones and spiritual significance (drums, pipes, masks, etc.). Articles are limited mostly to those of northeastern groups.

SNODGRASS, JEANNE. *American Indian Painters: A Biographical Dictionary.* Museum of the American Indian, Contributions vol. 21, part 1. New York: Museum of the American Indian, 1968. 269pp. Bibliography.

Biographical information on over 1,000 artists includes tribal affiliation (when known), significant dates, education, honors, and public and private exhibitions and collections in which the individual is represented. One-hundred-fifty-seven public museum collections and 973 private collections have been indexed. While essentially a statistical directory, some information about other aspects of the artists' work or background is often included.

WALKER ART CENTER, INDIAN ART ASSOCIATION, and MINNEAPOLIS INSTITUTE OF ART. *American Indian Art: Form and Tradition.* New York: Dutton, 1972. 154pp. Illustrated. Bibliography.

Based on an exhibition, this volume is designed to serve as a catalog and function as a survey of current attitudes and information on many aspects of Native American art and cultures. Specialists have contributed essays, some of which deal with aesthetic attitudes and are speculative in nature, while others describe various stylistic manifestations and object-types associated with American Indian art, or stress the strong relationship of Indian art to daily life. Illustrations are grouped and discussed under: artist and artisan, visions of eyes and hands (poetic image), tradition and aesthetics, rock art, people and nature in Pueblo architecture, Iroquois masks, Woodland Indian art, Plains Indian art, Southwest Indian art, Intermontane region, carving styles of the Northwest Coast, Asiatic sources of Northwest Coast art, and Eskimo (Inuit) sculpture.

WHITEFORD, ANDREW HUNTER. *North American Indian Arts.* New York: Golden Press, 1971. 160pp. Illustrated.

This book was compiled to assist collectors and curators with the identification of articles. Hundreds of artifacts are identified by region and tribe; materials, techniques of preparation, and designs are illustrated and explained. Pottery, basketry, textiles, items of rawhide, leather and fur, quillwork, beadwork, applique, woodwork, stonework, items of bone, antler and horn, shellwork, metalwork, and featherwork are included.

NORTHEAST

GRAND RAPIDS PUBLIC MUSEUM AND THE CRANBROOK ACADEMY OF ART MUSEUM. *Beads: Their Use by Upper Great Lakes Indians.* Grand Rapids: Grand Rapids Public Museum, 1977. 81pp. Illustrated. Bibliography.

This catalog shows how beads were used by and what they reveal about the Upper Great Lakes Indians. There are essays on beads and associated personal adornment among prehistoric Great Lakes Indians, an acculturation study of beads in the Upper Great Lakes region, glass bead manufacturing techniques, and caring for American Indian materials. The illustrations show quill and moosehair decoration, shell wampum and glass imitations, European glass trade beads, tools of the beadworker, clothing and accessories of men and women, men's tools, bags, and contemporary beadwork. There is a bibliography following each of the four essays.

SPECK, FRANK GOULDSMITH. *The Iroquois.* Bloomfield Hills, Mich.: Cranbrook Institute of Science, 1945. 94pp. Illustrated.

Speck examines decorative design and symbolism of Iroquois articles, including some Huron, Delaware, Abenaki, and Mohegan objects, and traces the evolution and diffusion of design elements and innovations. Background information on Iroquois culture is followed by consideration of ceremonial objects, musical instruments, bowls, spoons, ladles, wampum, sacred plants, medicine societies, and the modern religion of the Iroquois. Captions identify and give information concerning the objects.

SOUTHEAST

FUNDABURK, LILA, and MARY DOUGLAS FUNDABURK FOREMAN. *Sun Circles and Human Hands: The Southeastern Indian Art and Industries.* Liverne, Ala.: Emma Lila Fundaburk, 1957. 232pp. Illustrated. Bibliography.

Ceremonial objects, ornaments, projectile points, and tools discovered in the southeastern United States are arranged into four general culture periods: Paleo-Indian, Archaic, Woodland, and Mississippi. Brief descriptions of each period precede the pictures. Chief characteristics, developments and changes in craftsmanship, trade, and burial customs are discussed. Chapters cover objects of stone and copper, pottery, wood and animal products, prehistoric designs, cult motifs, stone pipes, effigies, bowls, projectile points, baskets, and shell ornaments.

GREAT PLAINS

INDIAN ARTS AND CRAFTS BOARD, U.S. Department of the Interior. *Contemporary Sioux Painting.* Rapid City, S.D.: Tipi Shop, 1970. 80pp. Illustrated. Bibliography.

An introductory essay discusses the expansion and cultural diversification of the Sioux during the eighteenth and nineteenth centuries, explains the forms and development of Sioux painting during the nineteenth century, and tells of the Sioux artists of the twentieth century. Illustrations of the artists' works have been arranged to suggest the course of development of Sioux painting during the twentieth century and to reflect the increasing experimentation of the past several decades. Twenty artists are represented by their works . There are two maps and examples of nineteenth-century Sioux painting.

SOUTHWEST

ADAIR, JOHN. *The Navajo and Pueblo Silversmiths.* Norman: University of Oklahoma Press, 1962. 220pp. Illustrated. Bibliography.

Adair describes the historical development of silversmithing in the Southwest, discusses the process of making silver jewelry, explores the social aspects of the art, how the craft is learned, the aesthetic standards of each group, and includes an account of the economics of silversmithing. The book is based on information gathered in 1938.

AMSDEN, CHARLES AVERY. *Navaho Weaving: Its Technique and History.* Glorieta, N.Mex.: Rio Grande Press, 1964. 261pp. Illustrated. Bibliography.

The author presents a resume of the archaeological knowledge of the loom and its prototypes in the prehistoric Southwest and describes and illustrates in detail the various weaves used by the Navajos. The processes employed in making natural dyes are also recorded. Navajo weaving is traced from the introduction of sheep by the invading Spaniards, through its earliest historical references in old Spanish documents, to the early 1930s when it was gradually transformed from a blanket-weaving to a rug-making industry. A closing chapter analyzes and outlines the growth of design, and gives an account of the revival movement then in progress.

DUNN, DOROTHY. *American Indian Painting of the Southwest and Plains Area.* Albuquerque: University of New Mexico Press, 1968. 429pp. Illustrated. Bibliography.

Dunn traces the traditional bases of Native American motifs and styles, considering the prehistoric and recent eras tribally and geographically. The first part of the book presents historical and archaeological data and some general statements. The second section includes an analysis and description of modern American Indian art (post-1885) and provides partial biographies of some artists. Modern Indian painting is analyzed in light of cultural heritage and ideology.

HATCHER, EVELYN PAYNE. *Visual Metaphors: A Formal Analysis of Navajo Art.* New York: West Publishing, 1974. 272pp. Illustrated. Bibliography.

This study tests the proposition that visual forms in art have meanings which can be analyzed and verbalized, and that some of the meanings are cross-culturally valid. At the core of the study is a collection of hypothesized form-meanings derived from a variety of published sources. In exploring the means by which a work of art conveys something from one person to another, the author analyzes form qualities (round, oval, square, rectangular, irregular, other) from drypainting, weaving, basketry, pottery, jewelry, and watercolors, examining their arrangement in space, their repetition, balance, symmetry, lines, linearity, color, and perspective. She finds some support for the proposition tested, concluding that different people will perceive the relative importance of the various form-qualities of a work differently based on what seems to them to be the organizing idea.

JERNIGAN, E. WESLEY. *Jewelry of the Prehistoric Southwest .* Santa Fe: School of American Research, 1978. 260pp. Illustrated.

This book presents a variety of pre-Columbian jewelry found among ruins of the Southwest. Mining methods, materials utilized, trade in such materials, and similarities and differences in individual cultures are discussed. Processes of manufacture— carving, grinding, filing, painting, inlaying—are also described.

ROBINSON, ALAMBERT E. *The Basket Weavers of Arizona.* Albuquerque: University of New Mexico Press, 1954. 164pp. Illustrated.

Robinson describes techniques, materials used, and decorative patterns in the basketry of the Pimas, Papagos, Apaches, Yavapais, Walapais, Havasupais, Chemehuevis, and Hopis. He also provides information on the history, economy, and social organization of each group. Photos show baskets and basket makers. This is not a "how to" book.

SMITH, WATSON. *Kiva Mural Decorations at Awatovi and Kawaika-a, with a Survey of Other Wall Paintings in the Pueblo Southwest.* Papers of the Peabody Museum of American Archaeology and Ethnology, vol. 37, no. 5. Cambridge, Mass.: Peabody Museum, 1952. 362pp. Illustrated.

This monograph describes mural findings at two prehistoric sites in the Southwest. After a discussion of painted decorations in the Southwest and a description of excavation, preservation, and reproduction of the paintings, the author presents an over-all description of general stylistic features and gives a detailed analysis of the component elements and their relation to art symbols extant among historic pueblos.

TANNER, CLARA LEE. *Southwest Indian Craft Arts.* Tucson: University of Arizona Press, 1968. 205pp. Illustrated. Bibliography.

An introductory chapter provides prehistoric and historic cultural backgrounds of the various Native American groups in the Southwest, discussing differences, similarities, and centuries-old traditions and new ideas that have influenced the development of arts. Subsequent chapters cover basketry, textiles, pottery, silver and jewelry, kachina dolls, carving, and "minor" crafts—drums, flutes, glass beadwork, and other items—on a village by village basis. Materials, techniques, forms, styles, designs, and design elements are discussed.

NORTHWEST COAST

GUNTHER, ERNA. *Art in the Life of the Northwest Coast Indians.* Oregon: Portland Art Museum, 1966. 274pp. Illustrated. Bibliography.

This book presents 458 items from the Rasmussen Collection of Northwest Indian art in the Portland Art Museum. The author gives ethnological data on the objects, discusses the motivation for their production, and explains them in terms of those facets of the Northwest Coast cultures which were the basis for their use and meaning. Material is organized according to general features: art in daily occupations, art in daily dress and accessories, art in social and ceremonial life, art for secret societies and winter dances, and art made for strangers.

HOLM, BILL. *Northwest Coast Indian Art: An Analysis of Form.* Seattle: University of Washington Press, 1965. 115pp. Illustrated. Bibliography.

This monograph examines the system of rules and principles that governed certain aspects of Northwest Coast Indian art. The author coded and analyzed elements characteristic of surface decoration on 400 examples of Northwest Coast art. Historical background, symbolism and realism, uses of two-dimensional art, elements of the art style, and principles of form and organization are discussed. The author concludes that a highly developed system for the organization of form and space in two-dimensional design governed Northwest Coast art.

ALASKA

RAY, DOROTHY JEAN. *Eskimo Art: Tradition and Innovation in North Alaska.* Seattle: University of Washington Press, 1977. 298pp. Illustrated. Bibliography.

This encyclopedic work covers the historic and recent arts and crafts from northwestern Alaska, including St. Lawrence Island, from 1778 to 1977 and offers a comprehensive description, analysis, and interpretation of objects made in all media. The author presents the historical and cultural contexts of Eskimo (Inuit) arts and looks at traditional art and market art. Material and genre are treated in approximate chronological order in each section, and then each genre is discussed briefly with regard to history, materials, and outside influences. Academic and subsidized programs, beginning in 1965, are discussed. "Hand-made" and "Eskimo-looking" arts created for the market demand and the problems of authenticity are explored.

BIBLIOGRAPHIES

DAWDY, DORIS O. *An Annotated Bibliography of American Indian Painting.* Museum of the American Indian, Contributions vol. 21, part 2. New York: Museum of the American Indian, 1968. 27pp.

This bibliography lists articles giving critical comments on artists and their exhibitions. There are over 250 items listed.

HARDING, ANNE D., and PATRICIA BOLLING, eds. *Bibliography of Articles and Papers on North American Indian Art.* Mamaroneck, N.Y.: Kraus Reprint Co., 1969. 365pp.

The titles are mainly from periodical publications of museums and universities. Sections include: articles and papers arranged alphabetically by author; articles dealing with all of North America; articles dealing with only one tribe or region; and a list of articles arranged by craft or art form. The material is drawn from over 100 publications.

INDIAN ARTS AND CRAFTS BOARD, U.S. Department of the Interior. *Bibliography of Contemporary American Indian and Eskimo Arts and Crafts.* Washington, D.C.: Indian Arts and Crafts Board, 1964. 4pp.

This pamphlet lists general works and provides titles for regional areas including the Arctic, the Northwest Coast, the West Coast, the Plains, the Southwest, and the eastern Woodlands. Some items have one sentence annotations. The Indian Arts and Crafts Board also has other brief fact sheets on American Indian art.

OPPELT, NORMAN T. *Southwestern Pottery: An Annotated Bibliography and List of Types and Wares.* Occasional Publications in Anthropology, Archaeology Series, no. 7. Museum of Anthropology. Greeley, Colo.: University of Northern Colorado, 1976. 179pp.

Part 1 consists of an annotated bibliography of over 600 references to Southwestern ceramics. Articles cover prehistoric, historic, and contemporary pottery of the greater Southwest. Material that describes and illustrates pottery types is emphasized. Part 2 lists over 900 names of types of wares and provides references to relevant titles in an annotated section. Synonyms are given and an index to the volume is appended.

See also: Dorothy Dunn, *American Indian Painting of the Southwest and Plains Area* (p. 266). The bibliography lists over 600 references.

25   SCIENCE

The early inhabitants of the American continent were interested in scientific knowledge as well as their economic, political, and social needs. Kidwell asserts however that "It must be born in mind that most of the practices of Indian tribes in relation to nature cannot by any means be considered scientific in terms of modern science and scientific method."[1] By this the author means that Indians did not practice a science with the modern connotations of replicability, predictability, and experimentation.[2]

Astronomy was particularly important to pre-Columbian native societies. Many of the materials written about Native American scientific thought concern the astronomical knowledge of aboriginal Indians. Williamson (p. 270) treats the Native American structures which were used to track the movements of the sun and stars to set agricultural and religious calendars. Aveni edits two collections of essays on astronomy, one of which (p. 269) contains essays on archaeoastronomy (astronomical records in Chaco Canyon, New Mexico, rock art records, early Navajo pictographs, Great Basin petroglyphs, etc.) and the other (p. 269), essays on a wide range of astronomical topics. Chamberlain (p. 269) considers astronomy themes in Native American art and oral tradition. Hudson and Underhay (p. 270) investigate the astronomical knowledge of the Chumash. Coller and Aveni (p. 271) list 1,480 titles, written in several languages, in a bibliography of materials about the astronomies of aboriginal peoples of North and South America.

Indians possessed a great knowledge of the edible and nonedible plants in their environment. Kidwell argues that in the field of botany "There is the strongest basis for attributing to Indians the use of scientific method in connection with nature. The observation of plants and knowledge of their uses indicates a pragmatic concern with natural phenomena...."[3] Weiner (p. 270) explains how Indians were expert at gathering and utilizing plants, how they knew when plants were most potent and best suited for collecting. His chapter on subsistence patterns contains titles of books and articles that describe in great detail the ways Indians all over North America used different parts of plants for food or nonfood products. Schultes

1. Clara Sue Kidwell, "Science and Ethnoscience," *The Indian Historian* 6, no. 4 (Fall 1973):45.
2. Ibid., p. 52.
3. Ibid.

(p. 270) has written about the scientific knowledge of Native Americans in their use of plants as hallucinogens and Kempton (below) writes of their domestication of maize, considered to be the most important and widespread cultivated food plant in North America. It is perhaps in their medicinal use of plants that the Indians achieved their most systematic attempts to deal with nature. They possessed a great knowledge of the healing properties of plants. Weiner considers the plant remedies, drugs, and natural foods of North American Indians. "Approximately 170 drugs which are now, or were once, official in the U.S. Pharmacopoeia or the National Formulary were utilized by Indians of North America. Further, hundreds of other plant medicines which have not become accepted in our official books on plant medicines are also used by the American Indian."[4]

AVENI, ANTHONY F., ed. *Archaeoastronomy in Pre-Columbian America*. Austin: University of Texas Press, 1975. 436pp. Illustrated. Bibliography.

This is a collection of eighteen essays by scholars in the multidisciplinary field of archaeoastronomy. The focus is on Meso-American cultures but five of the essays deal with cultures north of the Rio Grande. Subjects include general Native American astronomy in Meso-America, astronomical records in Chaco Canyon, New Mexico, possible rock art records of the Crab Nebula Supernova in the western United States, the Pueblo sun-moon star calendar, early Navajo astronomical pictographs in Canyon de Chelly, star-patterns in Great Basin petroglyphs, probable astronomical projections in Meso-American architecture, and numerous specific Meso-American topics. There are numerous maps, diagrams, and illustrations.

————, ed. *Native American Astronomy*. Austin: University of Texas Press, 1977. 286pp. Illustrated. Bibliography.

A sequel to *Archaeoastronomy in Pre-Columbian America,* this is a collection of fifteen essays written by specialists in archaeology, astronomy, architecture, art history, mathematics, solar physics, and anthropology. Topics include concepts of positional astronomy in Meso-American calendrics, astronomical signs in the codices, Palenque, Mayan astronomical tables and inscriptions, current Mayan astronomy, Plains Caddoan astronomy, medicine wheels and Plains Indian astronomy, the Inca calendar, and Anasazi solar observations. There are numerous maps and diagrams.

BROWN, JANET. "Native American Contributions to Science, Engineering, and Medicine." *Science* 129 (July 4, 1975):38–40, 70. Bibliography.

Briefly, the author cites examples of Native American contributions to science, engineering, and medicine, and enunciates the need for interdisciplinary research in appropriate areas of ethnoscience. She discusses the role of specialists in native societies comparing them to specialists in

Euro-American society and notes the lack of separation of religious belief from science and empirical knowledge in many Native American societies. In addition she points out that one-third of the world's most important economic crops are of native origin including maize, brown beans, peanuts, potatoes, sweet potatoes, and cassava. Tzeltal plant classification, Shoshone birth control "pill" development, Pueblo homes and microclimate engineering, Meso-American architecture and hydraulic engineering, and North and South American medicine and astronomy are briefly described.

CHAMBERLAIN, VON DEL. "American Indian Interest in the Sky as Indicated in Legend, Rock Art, Ceremonial and Moon Art." *The Planetarian* (Fall/Winter 1974):89–123. Illustrated.

This general work considers astronomy themes in Native American art and oral tradition. The comments are divided into the following categories: the sky and its relationship to the earth, atmospheric phenomena, the sun, the moon, planets and comets, the stars, the Milky Way, and meteors and meteorite falls. Tribes referenced include Zuñi, Hopi, Navajo, Wyandot (Huron), Otoe, Sioux, Chumash, Menominee, Ojibway, Flathead, Chilcoot, Cree, Blackfeet, and Comanche. There are eight figures showing pictographs dealing with the themes discussed in the book, extensive documentation, and a number of legends that are reproduced in translation.

KEMPTON, J. H. "Maize: Our Heritage from the Indian." *Smithsonian Institution Annual Report 1937*, pp. 385–408. Washington, D.C.: Government Printing Office, 1938. Illustrated.

This article deals with corn (Arawak: maize), one of the most widely distributed cultigens of Native America. The author describes the New World at contact as having a highly developed agriculture extending over most of the two Americas and the outlying islands. Corn is the only domesticated plant which can grow from Canada south to Chile, and it produces more food value per unit of area

4. Michael A. Weiner, *Earth Medicine—Earth Food: Plant Remedies, Drugs, and Natural Foods of the North American Indians* (New York: Collier Books, 1980), p. 7.

than any of the grains. The depiction of corn in Native American art is reviewed along with archaeological evidence of species development, use as a human food, and recorded history. Sections deal with the birthplace of maize and theories of its origin. There are numerous photographs of corn and related species, and one map of Guatemala and Mexico showing where corn's relative teosinte has been found growing wild.

KIDWELL, CLARA SUE. "Science and Ethnoscience." *The Indian Historian* 6, no. 4 (Fall 1973):43–54. Bibliography.
Kidwell reviews Western philosophies of science and compares them with a generalized description of the metaphysical basis of Native American cultures, that people are a product of nature, nature being conceived of as made up of forces acting upon the life of people. Ethnoscience is defined as an explication of the world view of a culture and an examination of the metaphysical basis for that world view. References are made to Makah, Hopi, and Menominee peoples, but most of the discussion relates to Ojibway culture. Considerable emphasis is given to botany, where "there is the strongest basis for attributing to Indians the use of [Western] scientific method in connection with nature."

MORRILL, SIBLEY S. "Pre-Columbian Indians Used the Wheel." *The Indian Historian* 1, no. 4 (September 1968):18–21.
Morrill discusses the body of evidence that shows the wheel had practical use in some American Indian civilizations, despite the feeling to the contrary among Anglo-Saxon scientists and scholars. He examines the evidence for discovery and use of the wheel by American Indians prior to the arrival of whites and concludes by discussing why archaeologists and anthropologists are reluctant to admit Indians had wheels and the roads to use them on.

SCHULTES, RICHARD EVANS. "Hallucinogens of Plant Origin." *Science* 163 (1969):245–54. Illustrated. Bibliography.
The author notes the rarity of hallucinogenic plants, probably no more than sixty species of cryptogams and phanerogams out of an estimated 400,000 to 800,000 total plant species. Of the sixty species, he postulates that only twenty may be considered important. Plants used by cultures all over the world are considered, but Native American societies seem to dominate the discussion. Plants are divided by phylum. Tribes or groups cited along with plant substance include Chukchi (fly agavic, *Amanita muscaria*), Mayan-speaking groups of Mexico and Guatemala (*teonanacatl*, twenty species of mushroom), Waiká and other tribes of Brazil, Venezuela, and Colombia (*yakee, paricá, epená, Nyakwana, Virola* species), tribes of the Orinoco area of Columbia and Venezuela (*yopo, cohoba, Anadananthera peregrina*), Kaviví and Pankaravú *(Yurema)*, Arapaho and Iowa (mescal beans, *Sophora secundiflora*), Oaxacan (Mexican) peoples (piule), Yaquí *(Cytisus canariensis)*, numerous North American tribes *(peyote)*, Aztec *(ololiuqui)*, Mazatec

(Datura), and numerous others. There are illustrations of the tribes using hallucinogens.

WEINER, MICHAEL A. *Earth Medicine—Earth Food: Plant Remedies, Drugs, and Natural Foods of the North American Indians*. Rev. ed. New York: Collier Books, 1980. 230pp. Illustrated. Bibliography.
This is a guide to wild plants used for healing and survival by the American Indians. The remedies described in this book are a translation of the records of the writings of travelers, missionaries, soldiers, anthropologists, and botanists. Usually more than one plant remedy is described for problems such as backache, colds, dandruff, insect bites, and poison ivy and diseases such as bronchitis, diabetes, and influenza. There are over 150 black-and-white illustrations of the plants and 16 in color. There is a small section on food plants of Indians divided by plant families, an index to plants, and a bibliography of botanical and medical sources.

WILLIAMSON, RAY. "Native Americans Were the Continent's First Astronomers." *Smithsonian*, October 1978, pp. 78–88. Illustrated.
Williamson deals in general with Native American structures which were used to track the movement of the sun and stars in order to set agricultural and religious calendars. References and discussion are made of the Mayan calendar and its use to predict eclipses, the Hovenweep castle in the American Southwest (constructed by the Anasazi culture, probably about A.D. 1200), contemporary Hopi astronomy, the Chaco Canyon Anasazi and pictographs representing the Supernova of 1054, Casa Rinconada, Pueblo Bonito, the Bighorn Medicine Wheel, and sites at the great mound city of Cahokia, near present-day St. Louis. Numerous color photographs depict archaeological sites.

GREAT PLAINS

EDDY, JOHN A. "Astronomical Alignment of the Big Horn Medicine Wheel." *Science* 184 (1974):1035–43. Bibliography.
The Bighorn Medicine Wheel is a well known stone archaeological structure in the Bighorn Mountains of northern Wyoming. It is a twenty-five meter diameter, imperfect circle with an inner circle of four meters, and twenty-eight unevenly spaced spokes connecting the two rings. Its construction is attributed to an early Plains culture (Crow, Sioux, Arapaho, Shoshone, or Cheyenne possibly), and the date of construction is unknown. Some theorize that the geometry relates to the geometry of the Medicine Lodge (San Don Lodge). The author suggests the structure may also have been aligned to the summer solstice. Figures include photographs, maps, and diagrams.

CALIFORNIA

HUDSON, TRAVIS, and ERNEST UNDERHAY. *Crystals in the Sky: An Intellectual Odyssey Involving Chumash Astronomy, Cosmology and Rock Art.*

Ballena Press Anthropological Papers No. 10. Socorro, N. Mex.: Ballena Press, 1978. 163pp. Illustrated. Bibliography.

The authors have pieced together data drawn from a wide variety of sources—including the unpublished ethnographic notes of John P. Harrington, archaeological excavations and sites, rock art motifs, comparative ethnographies, and modern astronomy—in order to reconstruct the elaborate cosmological beliefs and astronomical knowledge of the Chumash, a group of hunting and gathering peoples in southern California. They describe a recently discovered winter solstice "observatory," identify important astronomical motifs found in Chumash pictographs and petroglyphs, and unravel many of the allusions to celestial phenomena that constitute a significant part of both myth and ritual throughout southern California. Illustrations of Chumash rock art are included.

BIBLIOGRAPHIES

CHAMBERLAIN, VON DEL. *American Indian Sky Lore: A Bibliography.* Planetarium Directors Handbook No. 33 (Sept./Oct. 1975):17–20. Chadds Ford, Pa.: Spitz Space Systems, Inc. 1975.

The work describes about sixty relevant works, most of them collections of oral traditions. The author provides standard bibliographic information, a general description of the work, and, where appropriate, specific sections and page numbers, but little attention is paid to the quality of the translations.

COLLER, BETH A. and ANTHONY F. AVENI. *A Selected Bibliography on Native American Astronomy.* Hamilton, N.Y.: Colgate University, 1978. 148pp.

This work includes materials from the fields of astronomy, archaeology, ethnology, geography, and architecture on the astronomies of the aboriginal peoples of North and South America. Books and articles published between 1850 and 1977, doctoral dissertations available in the University of Michigan microfilm series, and a few early postcontact historical documents appear also. The authors summarize primary reference sources in the introduction. There are 1,480 titles written in general languages listed without annotation. The work includes a cross-reference index.

26 LAW

The studies in this chapter concern the traditional law of tribes. The authors of the works describe the techniques of solving disputes and conflict resolution used by different Native American peoples. They explain how traditional tribal law is inextricably intertwined with native social, economic, and political organization as well as with personal values, religion, and magic.

Aboriginal laws and legal procedures provide an important picture of aboriginal society. Reid (p. 273) indicates clearly that the aboriginal Cherokee law, which he calls a law of blood, provides important insights into the character of the early Cherokee Nation. Richardson (p. 273) notes that social status among the Kiowa determines behavior and legal settlements. Thus, legal procedures reflect or perhaps help to form a vital element of Kiowa society. Finally, Hippler and Conn's two works on the Alaska Eskimo (p. 274) point out that they placed a high value on personal responsibility and avoiding conflict. Consequently their formal aboriginal legal system was almost nonexistent. Whether law forms a community or the community forms the law is not clear. But in any case the legal systems of these tribes gives us an intimate look at their society.

However, with the appearance of whites, Eskimo and other Indian legal ways changed. In Alaska the whites introduced state law, a magisterial system, state troopers, and city police. For the Eskimos, Hippler and Conn suggest, these additions are actually a step backward and certainly create problems. The Cherokee, on the other hand, seem to have responded differently to Anglo-American legal influences. Strickland's work (p. 273) describes the gradual development of the Cherokee legal system from an aboriginal system to a court system. The development was apparently a gradual fusing of aboriginal and Anglo-American legal ideas and practices. Thus the Cherokee court system bore the imprint of both legal traditions.

NORTHEAST

FENTON, WILLIAM N., ed. "Book Three." In *Parker on the Iroquois*. Syracuse: Syracuse University Press, 1968.

The third section of this book contains the Constitution of the Five Nations, or the "Great Binding Law," originally transmitted orally from one generation to another and put into written form by the Iroquois based on two principal manuscripts found in Canada in 1910. Included in this section are documents about the Dekanawida legend, the Code of Dekanawida, the origin of the Confederacy of the Five Nations, the Condolence Ceremony, and the

Hiawatha tradition. There are five appendixes. The section is illustrated with a photograph of wampum which served to recall each law or regulation.

and papers of the Cherokee Nation, supplemented by primary and secondary accounts and federal records.

SOUTHEAST

REID, JOHN PHILLIP. *A Law of Blood: The Primitive Law of the Cherokee Nation*. New York: New York University Press, 1970. 340pp.

Reid examines the law of the Cherokee in the eighteenth century which helped hold together the Cherokee Nation, gave a degree of unity to a people regionally divided but who held a trichotomy of languages, and who were decentralized due to a system of government based on towns and not on nation. Discussing the constitutional principle that every Cherokee was equal and had an equal right of participation, he also notes how Cherokees, although free of rules by official law, were hemmed in by norms of private law. He describes the substantive rules of their law including the law of homicide, or a right to vengeance, which he stresses was the foundation of most "primitive" legal systems, the mechanics of vengeance; the mitigation of liability; the laws of property, inheritance and status; the law of the Nation in matters of war; the law of visitors and retaliation; and the law of captives and adoption. He also examines the Cherokee war machine and the making and keeping of peace as well as reconstructing the Cherokee legal system and jurisprudence and the Cherokee legal mind before this people adopted a penal system based on courts, fines, and imprisonment. There are extensive notes based largely on unpublished sources.

STRICKLAND, RENNARD. *Fire and the Spirits: Cherokee Law from Clan to Court*. Norman: University of Oklahoma Press, 1975. 260pp. Illustrated. Bibliography.

This book focuses on how the Cherokee court system emerged, not from a single act, but by a gradual acculturation process fusing tribal law ways and Anglo-American legal institutions. After enacting the early laws in Georgia, the Cherokees were removed to Indian Territory in 1838–39. Their traditional law ways, with overtones of religion and magic, played a vital role in the development of their legal system, which was abolished by the federal government at the end of the nineteenth century. However, traditional Cherokee law ways survived even in the Oklahoma court system which replaced the Cherokee courts. There are four tables that list the spirit, community, clan, and individual deviations from Cherokee law; the authority determining the deviation; the agent enforcing the punishment; and the punishment itself. There are five maps, photographs, and facsimiles of documents. There are four appendixes: one which summarizes Cherokee legal history in a chronology, 1540–1907; one which summarizes 201 laws of the Cherokees, 1808–29; one which contains the Cherokee Constitution; and the last which contains a letter from Thomas Jefferson to the Cherokee Deputies in 1809. The book is largely based on official records

GREAT PLAINS

HOEBEL, E. ADAMSON. *The Political Organization and Law-Ways of the Comanche Indians*. Memoirs of the American Anthropological Association no. 54. Menasha, Wis.: American Anthropological Assn., 1940. 149pp.

This study of traditional Comanche legal institutions is based on case histories. First the author discusses the basis of Comanche society, the Peace Chief, war and war leadership, and associations and their governmental role. He then focuses on case histories which show Comanche legal mechanisms at work in the areas of adultery, wife stealing, homicide, and criminal offenses. Also considered are ritual and evidence, abnormal conduct that does not require explicit sanctions, and property, inheritance, and contract. There is a table that illustrates the development of Comanche political and legal institutions compared with three other Shoshone groups and four appendixes, one of which includes notes on the political-juridicial behavior of Northern Shoshones.

LLEWELLYN, K. N., and E. ADAMSON HOEBEL. *The Cheyenne Way: Conflict and Case Law in Primitive Jurisprudence*. Norman: University of Oklahoma Press, 1941. 360pp.

Llewellyn and Hoebel begin with a theoretical discussion of "primitive" and modern law and the background of general thinking against which they set the law ways of the Cheyennes. Their study of Cheyenne law ways includes the Council of Forty-Four, the military societies, homicide and the supernatural, marriage and sex, property and inheritance, and informal pressures and the integration of the individual, all illustrated by case studies. They also set forth the skeleton of a general theory of the nature and function of law-stuff and of the law-jobs with which any group is faced in the process of becoming and remaining a group. In the last chapter they critique the Cheyenne legal system. There is a case-finder to the fifty-three histories presented in the book.

RICHARDSON, JANE. *Law and Status among the Kiowa Indians*. American Ethnological Society Monograph no. 1. New York: J. J. Augustin, 1940. 136pp. Bibliography.

Richardson's premise is that the Kiowas had well defined legal procedures which they were obligated to observe on pain of losing the respect of their fellows. First she presents a background of Kiowa society, follows with a discussion of criminal actions and procedures, then considers dispute and grievance situations with a special consideration of the role of status as a determinant of behavior in Kiowa legal settlements. Ninety-two cases are enumerated.

SOUTHWEST

COLTON, HAROLD S. "A Brief Survey of Hopi Common Law." *Museum Notes of the Museum of Northern Arizona* 7, no. 6 (December 1934):21–24.

This study focuses on the political organization, settlement of disputes, real property, personal property, personal relations, criminal law, and communal tasks of Hopi Indians in northern Arizona.

SMITH, WATSON, and JOHN M. ROBERTS. *Zuñi Law: A Field of Values.* Papers of the Peabody Museum of Archaeology and Ethnology, vol. 43, no. 1. Cambridge, Mass.: Peabody Museum, 1954; reprint ed.: Millwood, N.Y.: Kraus Reprint Co., 1974. 175pp. Bibliography.

This is an investigation of the law ways and values which are inextricably interwoven in the culture of the Zuñi Indians of New Mexico. The introduction discusses the problem, research methods, and background information while the main body of the text contains a straightforward treatment of aspects of Zuñi law. There is a brief section on values, a discussion of the conclusions, and implications of the study for further research. The legal scope of the monograph is limited to a presentation of ninety-seven cases ranging in date from 1870 or earlier to 1952 bearing primarily on the modern legal concepts and legal procedures of Zuñi Indians as exemplified in the activities of the Bow priesthood and the Tribal Council, the latter functioning as a true judicial court. There is an appendix containing a Zuñi orthography.

VAN VALKENBURGH, RICHARD. "Navajo Common Law I: Notes on Political Organization, Property, and Inheritance." *Museum Notes of the Museum of Northern Arizona* 9, no. 4 (October 1936):17–22.

The author discusses the early political organization of the Navajos and the archaic tribal assembly, the Nah-sit, and late political organization in which Navajos had to restructure themselves because their entire governmental structure was destroyed during their exile at Bosque Redondo. He discusses the organization of the Navajo Tribal Council in 1922 and considers personal property and inheritance among Navajos.

———. "Navajo Common Law II: Navajo Law and Justice." *Museum Notes of the Museum of Northern Arizona* 9, no. 10 (April 1937):51–54.

The author discusses the basic points of Navajo conceptions of law and justice according to traditional rules of conduct. He explains witchcraft, "the most heinous of all Navajo crimes," homicide, and incest. He also notes how closely related Navajo law and justice are to taboos and to normal social customs of the Navajos.

———. "Navajo Common Law III: Etiquette-Hospitality-Justice." *Museum Notes of the Museum of Northern Arizona* 10, no. 12 (June 1938):37–42.

The author discusses Navajo etiquette and hospitality and tribal concepts and methods of handling

extramarital behavior, sexual irregularities, theft-robbery, and intoxication. The three articles are based on informants.

ALASKA

HIPPLER, ARTHUR E., and STEPHEN CONN. *Northern Eskimo Law Ways and Their Relationships to Contemporary Problems of 'Bush Justice': Some Preliminary Observations on Structure and Function.* ISEGR Occasional Paper, no. 10, July 1973. Fairbanks: Universty of Alaska Institute of Social, Economic, and Government Research, 1973. 68pp. Bibliography.

In this paper, the authors assert that the absence of a system of social control or Eskimo law in aboriginal times in northern Alaska was largely a function of the personality system and value structure of Eskimo culture that led people to avoid conflicts. They describe how the basis of aboriginal Eskimo law was in behavioral norms and sanctions used to resolve conflicts and explain that the northern Eskimo's reluctance to create intervening judicial authorities for dispute resolution and social control relates to Eskimos vesting critical importance in the individual. They describe the Eskimos' precontact system of dispute solving which stressed individual responsibility for obtaining redress and which did not support formal coercive authority. In addition they analyze the influence of Anglo-American agents of change (missionaries, white laws in the person of the U.S. Commissioner, state troopers, and local magistrates). They describe the Eskimo legal system at the turn of the century, the village council based on traditional Eskimo ways and procedures that developed to resolve disputes, consider the formal intervention of state law in the 1960s through the magisterial system which supplanted the village council system as a forum for dispute resolution, and analyze the success of the village councils and the shortcomings of the magisterial courts. They conclude by explaining reasons why the magistrate's court which attempts to solve disputes by applying Alaskan state law is a step backward in bush justice. There is a bibliography of psychology and anthropology literature. See: E. Adamson Hoebel. "Law Ways of Primitive Eskimos." *Journal of the American Institute of Criminal Law and Criminology,* vol. 31 (1941):663–83.

———. *Traditional Athabascan Law Ways and Their Relationship to Contemporary Problems of 'Bush Justice': Some Preliminary Observations on Structure and Function.* ISEGR Occasional Paper, no. 7, August 1972. Fairbanks: University of Alaska Institute of Social, Economic, and Government Research, 1972. 19pp. Bibliography.

Hippler and Conn analyze Alaskan Athapaskan aboriginal law ways to discuss discontinuities between them and contemporary Anglo-American law. They first explain how traditional law ways were derived from the personality, economic organization, and social structure of the Athapaskans. Then they consider three primary assumptions upon which the resolution of conflicts and disputes are based in aboriginal society, major offenses and their resolution, and summarize some aspects of structure and function of traditional law ways. They conclude by citing some disfunctions between past and present (white state troopers and city police) law ways. There is a bibliography of law and anthropology sources.

BIBLIOGRAPHIES

NADER, LAURA; K. F. KOCK; and BRUCE COX. "South America" and "North America." In "Ethnography of Law: A Bibliographic Survey." *Current Anthropology* 7 (1966):284–88.

This is a selected and annotated bibliography of literature on law in North and South America. The focus is on English and German works but sources in French, Dutch, Portuguese, and Spanish are also included. The authors' purpose is to "encourage and facilitate contemporary social science research in law." Some sources deal with Euro-Americans but the majority relate to Native American law topics. The emphasis is on traditional legal matters and systems rather than on European imposed legal structures. Over one hundred sources are cited and include the work of anthropologists, missionaries, imperialist administrators, lawyers, judges, travelers, and lay observers. Works dealing solely with written laws or codes are not included.

27   LITERATURE

It is not at all clear exactly how one ought to analyze or criticize Native American literature. It is even unclear exactly what American Indian literature is. Traditional native literature contains much oral story telling and mythology. Neither of these forms of expression is as prevalent in Western literature. Yet scholars generally use Western-influenced methods to approach this body of work. Furthermore, one can even raise the question of whether there is such a thing as American Indian literature. Since American Indians come from so many distinct tribes and cultures it is perhaps difficult to justify lumping all of their poetry and stories together into one group.

Several scholars included here attack the usual approach to Native American literature. Bevis, in his book on verse translation (p. 278), suggests that translation is nearly impossible because anything but the most literal translation completely distorts the poem. Ramsey (p. 280) discusses the dilemma of those who study Native American literature in virtual ignorance of the culture, raising the question of how accessible native literature can possibly be to one who does not have an extensive training in Indian culture. Cook (p. 279) decries the "all-out violence" done to American Indian literature by scholars who, she claims, completely misunderstand oral literature, treating it as a stage in the progression toward literacy. She argues that oral literature can be properly studied only in its original context and oral form. Chapman, in his book (p. 278), compares side-by-side Indian and non-Indian approaches to native literature. This work closely examines the difference between the work of someone approaching literature from within the culture and someone studying it from outside.

However, scholarship that is primarily Western is not the only kind currently being used with Native American literature. Buller (p. 278) discusses the work of contemporary American Indian writers. In the process he develops and urges a non-Western method of criticism. Momaday (p. 280), himself a prominent contemporary Native American author, discusses native literature and one of his own novels. In the course of this discussion the relationship between ecology, story telling, and imagination plays a central role in the exposition of his work.

Although some scholars may think that the field of Native American literature does not exist because it is so diverse in styles, cultures, and genres, perhaps contemporary Native American literature can more easily be studied. Because of the inescapable confrontation between white and native culture, much of contemporary Indian literature is in some way a response to that confrontation. In her essay "A Stranger in My Own Life . . . 1" (below), Allen argues that alienation is a major theme in contemporary Native American prose and poetry.

Because Native American literature encompasses such a voluminous amount of published materials, it is impractical to list every single work on tribal mythologies, traditional poetry and songs, folktales, legends, etc. These works can be located in any one of the five bibliographies listed (Dorris, Jacobson, Haywood, Smith, and Ullom, p. 284–85), in the annual reports and bulletins of the U.S. Bureau of American Ethnology, a department of the Smithsonian Institution (Rexroth, p. 280), or in learned publications such as the *American Anthropologist,* the American Museum of Natural History Bulletins, Columbia University Contributions to Anthropology, Field Museum of Natural History Anthropological Series, IJAL Native American Text Series, Journal of American Folklore, the American Folklore Society Memoirs, University of California Publications in American Archaeology and Ethnology, University of Pennsylvania University Museum Anthropological Publications, and the University of Washington Publications in Anthropology.

ALLEN, PAULA GUNN. "The Mythopoeic Vision in Native American Literature: The Problem of Myth." *American Indian Culture and Research Journal* 1, no. 1 (1974):3–13. Bibliography.
Allen dismisses the contemporary usage of myth as a synonym for lie and contends that it is both a means of transmitting information of a particular sort and a particular kind of narrative related to religious systems in Native American cultures. She begins by defining Native American myth as a profoundly sacred story that recounts a special experience which transcends ordinary consciousness-experiencing, relies preeminently on symbolism as a vehicle of articulation, and requires a supernatural or nonordinary figure as its central character. She also explains how myth and ceremony (ritual) are based on visionary experience. Black Elk's vision is described and analyzed in detail because it was written down white-style, because it is one of the most complete accounts of a vision ever available, and because through examining it one can discover the workings of a metaphysical statement and how myth relates to sacred songs, ceremonies, objects, and ornaments. The author concludes by defining myth as a presentation of a vision told in terms of the vision's symbols, characters, chronology, and import; a vehicle of transmission, of sharing, and of renewal which plays an integral part in the ongoing psychic life of a people.

————. "A Stranger in My Own Life: Alienation in Native American Prose and Poetry. (1)" *Newsletter of the Association for Study of American Indian Literatures* 3, no. 1 (Winter 1979):1–10.

Allen focuses on one of the major themes in modern or individually written Native American literature, that of alienation or "otherness." She tells of traditional literatures, "one of the more attractive qualities of which is the almost total absence of a sense of 'otherness.'" Maintaining that alienation as a theme, an articulation of a primary experience characteristic of biculturated Indians, preoccupies the contemporary imaginative writings of Indians, she views the experience that creates the sense of alienation and illustrates how the theme is portrayed in poetry by Maurice Kenny, Nila Northsun, Jeff Saunders, Simon J. Ortiz, Wendy Rose, Betty Oliver, and Marnie Walsh.

————. "A Stranger in My Own Life: Alienation in Native American Prose and Poetry. (2)" *Newsletter of the Association for Study of American Indian Literatures* 3, no. 2 (Spring 1979):16–23.
This article describes the way alienated Native Americans see the world in terms of antagonistic principles, good against bad, Indian against white, tradition against modernism and tells how the confusion of dualities is played out in poetry and prose. The author discusses Silko's *Ceremony* in some detail, explaining Tayo's feelings of strangeness and separateness.
See other issues of *Studies in American Indian Literature (SAIL),* formerly the *Newsletter of the Association for Study of American Indian Literatures,* edited by Karl Kroeber. This quarterly contains studies of American Indian prose and poetry, bibliographical reports, discussions of Indians in film, recent historical writings, and reviews of

books dealing with all aspects of Indian affairs. *SAIL* is published by the Department of English, Columbia University, New York, NY 10027.

BERNER, ROBERT L. "N. Scott Momaday: Beyond Rainy Mountain." *American Indian Culture and Research Journal* 3, no. 1 (1979):57–67.
The author discusses the structure of the three main divisions in *The Way to Rainy Mountain,* "The Setting Out," "The Going On," and "The Closing In," as well as the structure of each of the twenty-four sections which comprise these three divisions. He maintains that the book, which is built of small pieces of myth, legend, and history, is "the journey of the Kiowas from the hollow log of their origin myth to their destiny on the Southern plains" and that it also is "the author's own journey from his first discovery of what it means to be a Kiowa descendant to the recognition of common mortality with the Kiowa dead . . ." Berner feels that it is the story of Momaday's real journey, "the process by which his separation from his Kiowa identity was healed by his own journey to Rainy Mountain," and he concludes by suggesting that "we must recognize that all people . . . are on the way to Rainy Mountain." See also Thekla Zachrau, "N. Scott Momaday" (p. 281).

BEVIS, WILLIAM. "American Indian Verse Translation." *College English* 35, no. 6 (March 1974): 693–703. Bibliography.
Bevis measures translations of Plains and Southwest poetry against the highest documentary standards to determine how well they allow us to enter the imaginative world of the Indian's art. After discussing how some translations drastically change the length, images, and forms of the originals, he analyzes in some detail a Pawnee poem found in a Brandon anthology to show how it has been distorted from the original oral form in images, form, and dramatic situation. He looks at misleading representatives of Indian language arts in printed anthologies and argues that the translations are untrustworthy and the anthology form misleading. The anthologies of Curtis, Rothenberg, Brandon, Cronym, Day, Astrov, and Bierhorst are evaluated and Bevis suggests that "extensive changes of the original in order to 'totally translate' the 'feeling' or 'hidden meanings' should be practiced as little as possible." He indicates that he prefers extensive notes on a literal text to a rewriting of the content because it gives one a sense of the Indian art forms. His bibliography of anthologies categorizes them into Recommended, Uneven, and Not Recommended.

BOAS, FRANZ. *Race, Language, and Culture.* New York: Macmillan, 1940. 647pp.
This volume contains eight essays on Native American literature. These include "The Development of Folk-Tales and Myths" (1916), "Introduction to James Teit, 'The Traditions of the Thompson Indians of British Columbia' " (1898), "The Growth of Indian Mythologies" (1895), "Dissemination of Tales among the Natives of North America" (1891), "Mythology and Folk-Tales of the North American

Indians" (1914), "Stylistic Aspects of Primitive Literature" (1925), "The Folk-Lore of the Eskimo" (1904), and "Romance Folk-Lore among American Indians" (1925).

BROTHERSTON, GORDON, and EDWARD DORN. *Images of the New World: The American Continent Portrayed in Native Texts.* London: Thames & Hudson, 1979. 324pp. Illustrated. Bibliography.
This book concentrates on Native American texts in native script. It shows what native signs and symbols look like, how they are put together and may be read, what purposes they were and are used for, and how they are related to each other. Included are translations of pictographs, ideograms, and other written documents, such as the Mide scrolls of the medicine men of the Ojibway Nation. The authors have arranged their book in chapters ranging from the conquest to the roles of shaman and priest in different societies, addressing the American Indian sense of both time and space. There are 118 documentary texts from the literatures of the natives of the Western Hemisphere divided into chapters entitled: "Invasion from the Old World," "Defense of Traditional Values and Forms," "Ritual," "Calendars," "Cosmogony and the Birth of Man," "Hunting and Planting," "Conquest," "Healer," and "Singer and Scribe." There are four maps, six tables, and examples of Indian signs and symbols.

BULLER, GALEN. "New Interpretations of Native American Literature: A Survival Technique." *American Indian Culture and Research Journal* 4, nos. 1 and 2 (1980):165–77.
The author discusses the literature produced by contemporary American Indian writers and suggests that it has unique characteristics compared to non-Indian literature. Defining these characteristics as the relationship between the land and the Indian, the ceremony, and the medicine linked to the past, he suggests that contemporary literature has a structure and thematic content related to traditional ritual, and that novels affirm the existence of and the need for a sense of community as an integral part of an Indian determination to survive. He explains how American Indian literature differs as a body of literature from American literature in five areas: a reverence for words, a sense of place and a dependence on that sense, a feeling for a sense of ritual (ceremony), an affirmation of the need for community, and a significantly different world view. Each area is illustrated with excerpts from literature written by contemporary American Indians. Buller advocates the development of methods of criticism of American Indian literature that are distinct from Western influence. There are notes from the literature of American Indians.

CHAPMAN, ABRAHAM, ed. *Literature of the American Indian: Views and Interpretations. A Gathering of Indian Memories, Symbolic Contexts, and Literary Criticism.* Introduction by Abraham Chapman. New York: New American Library, 1975. 357pp.
In this collection of twenty-six pieces, the editor

brings together "two currents of thinking and expression: first, traditional and contemporary Indian views and interpretations of the Indian cultures, literature, and symbolism from older and recent writings ... Secondly is included a historical sequence of older and contemporary non-Indian interpretations of Indian literature and the cultures out of which it grew by American writers and anthropologists outside the Indian cultures ..." The book begins with selections by Indians including a Seneca legend, and pieces by George Copway, Charles Eastman, John Stands in Timber, John Fire/Lame Deer, N. Scott Momaday, Paula Gunn Allen, Vine Deloria, Jr., Hyemeyohsts Storm, and Rupert Costo. Some of the essays by non-Indians are entitled "Literature and Art among the American Aborigines," "Aboriginal American Authors and Their Productions," "The Significance of American Indian Myths, Legends, and Tales," "The Relation of Indian Story and Song," "Stylistic Aspects of Primitive Literature," "The Indian Background of American Theatricals," "The Oral Poetry of the Indians," "American Indian Songs," "Total Translation," "American Indian Verse Translations," "The Indian Treaty as Literature," "Remarks on Reading *Indian Tales of North America*," and "N. Scott Momaday: Racial Memory and Individual Imagination."

COOK, LIZ. "American Indian Literature in Servitude." *The Indian Historian* 10, no. 1 (Winter 1977):3–6.

Cook discusses the "all-out violence" done to American Indian literature by academics who treat native oral literature as a stage in the progression toward literacy. She asserts that Indian literatures can be properly experienced only in the context of their utterances and that any interpretation of Indian literature jeopardizes its integrity. She also discusses some of the problems in interpreting oral literature, maintaining that the process renders the literature useless and/or corrupt.

FELDMANN, SUSAN, ed. *The Story Telling Stone: Myths and Tales of the American Indians.* Introduction by Susan Feldman. New York: Dell, 1965. 271pp. Bibliography.

In a lengthy introduction Feldmann considers the elements of myths and tales that describe the origins of the earth and mankind, the theft of fire, the flood, the establishment of human institutions, and the adventures of heroes in the world familiar to Indians. The stories are grouped to emphasize the ways various tribes handle a particular theme, to illustrate how the same story may be used by several tribes to explain different facts, and to invite comparison with myths of different cultures.

HASLAM, GERALD. "Literature of the People: Native American Voices." *CLA Journal* 15, no. 2 (December 1971):153–70.

This is a survey of the oral poetry and prose of American Indians in the past and the present. Haslam begins by describing characteristics of traditional Indian oral poetry which include general areas of symbolism and stylistic devices, such as repetition. He then considers the oral prose of Indi-

ans, maintaining it was a method for passing on "survival information" of the tribe "be it secular, mythic, or legendary." Finally, he examines the contemporary prose and poetry being created by contemporary Indians as well as some of the compelling novels being written by non-Indians about Indians.

IJAL Native American Text Series. Eric P. Hamp, gen. ed. Chicago: Univesity of Chicago Press, 1976.

The IJAL Native American Texts Series is a monograph series established to disseminate and preserve accurate, valuable specimens of American Indian language and literature. The Series publishes all languages indigenous to North and South America. Selections are limited neither by form nor content and include myths, legends, and fiction as well as personal narratives, descriptions from daily life, correspondence, and other casual texts. Texts are printed either in close phonetics, in systematic phonological representations, or in philologically faithful reflections of source material. Whenever possible, texts are accompanied by word-by-word translations, free translations in English, grammatical commentary, or other explanatory material. The contents of each monograph are united thematically or by a particular language or language group. Issues appear irregularly, three or four per volume, but regardless of the number of issues, each volume comprises at least 320 pages. The Series is under the general editorship of Eric P. Hamp. The first volume contains three articles which present transcriptions and translations from three distinct language groups. The first comprises twenty-four texts in eight Mayan languages. The second deals with Otomi parables, folktales, and jokes. The last offers at least one text in each of the ten Yuman languages still spoken. Subsequent volumes present texts in Caddoan, Jaqi-Aymara, Kitsa, northern Californian, and Northwest Coast.

LARSON, CHARLES R. *American Indian Fiction.* Albuquerque: University of New Mexico Press, 1978. 208pp. Bibliography.

Larson has written the first critical and historical account of novels by American Indians. Tracing the development of Native American fiction through four phases from the nineteenth century to the present, he discusses three early novelists (Pokagon, Oskison, Mathews) who wrote assimilationist novels which reflect estrangement from the land, two novelists (McNickle, Momaday) who reject the white world, three novelists (Chief Eagle, Storm, Bedford) who tell history from the Indian point of view, and four recent novelists (Pierre, Welch, Silko, Nasnaga) who are harder to categorize because they emphasize character and technique more than politics. He also surveys the white Pocahontas myth and the emergence of Native American fiction. The appendix includes information on an early novel by an American Indian woman who wrote her book with a collaborator and a novel written by an American Indian man whose identity cannot be authenticated.

LINCOLN, KENNETH R. "Tribal Poetics of Native America." *American Indian Culture and Research Journal* 1, no. 4 (1976):14–21.

The author explores shared natural poetics among Native American tribes. Rather than isolating one region, tribe, or poet, he considers Native American tribal literatures as a collective voice and focuses on common characteristics of the poetics. He contends that the literatures, given their diversity, intersect in a common and organic aesthetic. His method is impressionistic, responding to the tones and states of mind implicit in the native literatures.

LOWIE, ROBERT H. "The Test Theme in North American Mythology." *Journal of American Folklore* 21, no. 81–82 (April–September 1908):97–148. Bibliography.

Lowie discusses the test theme in North American mythology, the imposition of a difficult or dangerous task and a mutual or competitive trial of strength evidently derived from human experience, and shows that the celestial hero's traits are not uniform but of indefinite variability. There is a summary of test tales from various parts of America and a summary of North American hero tales from various tribes. The author investigates the extent to which the test theme is found in connection with visits to the sky or underworld, examines traits in the celestial trial tales that differentiate them from those of earthly plots, and considers whether tested heroes can be safely identified with the heavenly bodies.

MAYS, JOHN BENTLEY. "The Flying Serpent: Contemporary Imaginations of the American Indian." *Canadian Review of American Studies* 4, no. 1 (Spring 1973):32–47.

In this article, the author discusses translations of American Indian literature since Schoolcraft (1851) and Brinton (1882–90), criticizes several anthologies of Indian poetry, and appraises the signinicance of Rothenberg's anthologies for the whole of contemporary poetry and poetics. He also praises Rothenberg's collections for their "commentaries" section, discusses the way to an encounter with structures of "primitive imagination," and tells how we can discover in the thousands of pages of investigations of scholars the "otherwise-extinct forms of consciousness which may inform our responses to the future which is being created by global imperialism." (See also William Bevis, "American Indian Verse Translation," page 278.)

MOMADAY, N. SCOTT. "The Man Made of Words." In *Indian Voices: The First Convocation of American Indian Scholars,* pp. 49–84. San Francisco: Indian Historian Press, 1970.

Momaday, a Kiowa Indian, delivers a paper in which he discusses the relationship of ecology, storytelling, and the imagination. He tells how an "ancient, one-eyed woman Ko-sahn stepped out of the language and stood before" him on the paper, talked with him, and finally "receded into the language" that he had written. He feels that people should activate an ethical regard for the land because that is the only alternative to not living at all. He considers the meanings of oral tradition, language, and literature. Examining the principles of narration and the device of the journey in *The Way to Rainy Mountain,* he illustrates the way in which the narrative works by quoting from the text. Following the paper is the transcript of a discussion held between Momaday and different members of the Convocation about oral tradition and its relevancy to our time and place.

RAMSEY, JAROLD. "The Teacher of Modern American Indian Writing as Ethnographer and Critic." *College English* 41, no. 2 (October 1979):163–69.

Ramsey considers the dilemma of a teacher: whether to be a scholar or a critic of Native American literature. He tells how young Indian writers are becoming impatient with the role being defined for them by ethnographically slanted criticism and teaching. Also he warns against critical commentary and teaching that is indifferent to, or ignorant of, ethnological facts, asserting that a general sense of the "knowledge of the history and culture in which works by Native Americans are and have been made can help us to understand their character." He suggests that teachers elucidate "the geography of modern Indian fiction and poetry" and proposes that the most valuable ethnological resources teachers and students can turn to on behalf of modern Indian writing are the traditional oral literatures of the tribes or groups in question.

REXROTH, KENNETH. "American Indian Songs: The United States Bureau of Ethnology Collection." In *Literature of the Amerian Indian: Views and Interpretations,* edited by Abraham Chapman, pp. 278–91. New York: New American Library, 1975.

The author discusses the publications of the Bureau of American Ethnology, a department of the Smithsonian Institution. The author explains that this is "the largest body of anthropological literature ever published by one institution, private or public." There are a large number of texts and translations of Indian oral literature: myths, legends, lengthy ceremonies, and songs. He considers the collections of Indian music recorded by Frances Densmore, which he characterizes as "the largest body of primitive lyric poetry in the original language and in translation in existence." He describes the texts of these songs as "pure poems" and cites their resemblance to Japanese poetry. The essay concludes with examples of American Indian songs, translated by Densmore. See also entry under Smithsonian Institution, page 281.

ROESLER, MAX. "Discussion: Enough Is Enough." *The Indian Historian* 11, no. 3 (Summer 1978): 25–28. Bibliography.

This is Roesler's response to essays of several recent contributors to *The Indian Historian* (Sobosan, Cook, and Ortiz) who have variously endorsed the proposition that Indian people "do not always mean what they say nor say what they mean." He suggests it is better to interpret Indian literatures with as much fidelity as possible to their literal meanings and that the term "pictorial," embracing all the senses and not just vision, be used to understand Indian literatures. He discusses how some writers make the distinction between Indian and European literatures, that the former pictures and the latter explains. He cites Sobosan's reluctance to credit Black Elk's literal meaning, discusses Ortiz's contention that space is a central issue in the consideration of many non-Indian world views, and maintains that there is a difference in the way one makes sense of the state of affairs expressed metaphorically.

ROSEN, KENNETH. "American Indian Literature: Current Condition and Suggested Research." *American Indian Culture and Research Journal* 3, no. 2 (1979):57–66.
Rosen considers some of the poems, short stories, and novels witten by American Indians in the last decade as well as some of the journals and chapbooks in which the material appears. He makes suggestions throughout concerning the needs and opportunities for scholarly and critical research in the field of American Indian literature. The bulk of the essay analyzes novels by Momaday, Bedford, Pierre, Storm, Nasnaga, Silko, and McNickle.

SMITHSONIAN INSTITUTION. Bureau of American Ethnology Bulletins and Annual Reports. Washington, D.C.: Government Printing Office, 1887–1971.
Most of the traditional American Indian verse was gathered between 1880 and 1940 by scholars in the field and published in reports of the Bureau of American Ethnology, a department of the Smithsonian Institution. "There are forty-seven annual reports, from 1881 to 1932, averaging around 800 pages each. After the forty-seventh report, the ethnological and anthropological material has been published separately. There are about 150 bulletins . . . these run from thirty-two to 1,000 pages, and include the annual anthropological papers— about ten articles to each volume—published each year since the forty-seventh annual report. Besides this there have been a couple of hundred other miscellaneous publications." The field material includes original texts, interlinear translations, and freer translations. These materials in the Bureau of American Ethnology Bulletins and Annual Reports are the source for almost all subsequent "editions" of Indian verse. See Bulletin 200, 1971, for a list of publications of the Bureau of American Ethnology with an index to authors and titles. See Annual Report vol. 48 (1930–31), which contains a general index to 48 Annual Reports of the Bureau of American Ethnology (1879–1931). See also under Rexroth, page 280.

VELIE, ALAN R. *Four American Indian Literary Masters: N. Scott Momaday, James Welch, Leslie Marmon Silko, and Gerald Vizenor.* Norman: University of Oklahoma Press, 1981. 176pp. Bibliography.
This critical work shows how Momaday, Welch, Silko, and Vizenor have drawn on tribal antecedents and how they have been affected by modern American and European literary movements. An introductory chapter traces the major periods of Native American literature and identifies common themes and misconceptions. Three following chapters portray N. Scott Momaday's Kiowa heritage, his boyhood experiences among the Tanoan tribe in New Mexico, and the influence of Yvor Winters and the post-symbolists on his poetry. In two chapters on Blackfeet poet and novelist James Welch, the author looks at Blackfeet mythology and the work of modern South American surrealists and relates Welch's work to the poetry of James Wright, Robert Bly, and other contemporary poets. In an essay on Leslie Marmon Silko he describes Silko's Laguna Indian heritage and her use of Laguna myths, which closely resemble the medieval legends of the Holy Grail. In a final chapter Velie traces the life of Chippewa fiction writer Gerald Vizenor and analyzes his post-modern fiction in terms of Chippewa Trickster myths.

WATERMAN, T. T. "The Explanatory Element in the Folk-Tales of the North American Indians." *Journal of American Folklore* 27, no. 103 (January–March 1914):1–54. Bibliography.
This article focuses on the part played by explanations in the folktales or stories of twenty-three tribes from seven culture areas in America north of Mexico. The author discusses the data in tables that show what phenomena are the subject of explanations in the various mythologies and explains data in tables that show "terrestrial" explanations outnumber "celestial" ones. Contending that cosmic forces are not the chief subject of folklore, either as actors or as subjects for explanation, he also discusses his findings that less than half of the tales have explanatory value and concludes that explanations in folktales are not of primary significance.

ZACHRAU, THEKLA. "N. Scott Momaday: Towards an Indian Identity." *American Indian Culture and Research Journal* 3, no. 1 (1979):39–56.
The author discusses how, on a literary level, N. Scott Momaday's works "reflect a sociological development which seems to indicate a reversal of roles: today it is the Indian way of life which is praised as an example to be followed by the white man." He examines three works by Momaday, tracing the theme of the search for identity in each. He begins with *House Made of Dawn,* Momaday's first novel awarded the Pulitzer Prize in 1969; considers the variation on the identity theme in *The Way to Rainy Mountain,* his second novel; and concludes with *The Names,* designated as "A Memoir," again the story of a quest for identity. See also Robert L. Berner, "N. Scott Momaday" (p. 278).

NORTHEAST

RADIN, PAUL. *The Evolution of an American Indian Prose Epic: A Study in Comparative Literature.* 2 Parts. Special Publications of the Bollingen Foundation, nos. 3, 5. Baltimore: Waverly Press, 1954–56.
Radin analyzes a specific prose epic of the Winnebago Indians of Wisconsin and Nebraska entitled *The Two Boys* from the viewpoint of its literary qualities and its possible history. The first part of

the study contains the text in English, together with a number of supplementary narratives closely connected with it; the second part contains analysis and commentary. The introduction contains a brief discussion of Winnebago history, religion, myth, hero cycles, general characteristics of *The Two Boys* cycle, and the history of the text of *The Two Boys*.

————. *The Trickster: A Study in American Indian Mythology.* London: Routledge & Kegan Paul, 1956. 211pp.

This book includes an authentic, translated version of a Trickster myth found among Siouan-speaking Winnebagos of Wisconsin and Nebraska in 1912, the Winnebago Hare myth, and summaries of the Assiniboine and Tlingit Trickster myths. The author analyzes the Winnebago Trickster myth and compares it with Trickster cycles of other parts of the North American continent, asserting that the creation of the Trickster figures is an attempt by people to solve their problems inwardly and outwardly. In other essays Kerenyi relates the Trickster to Greek mythology and Jung discusses the psychology of the Trickster figure.

GREAT PLAINS

VELIE, ALAN R. "James Welch's Poetry." *American Indian Culture and Research Journal* 3, no. 1 (1979):19–38.

Velie focuses on two elements in the poetry of James Welch which trace back to his Montana Blackfeet Indian heritage. First he discusses how Welch was influenced by surrealism, the use of the unconscious and the radical change in the use of language to convey images, and the surrealist fascination with the world of dreams. He considers important direct influences, the surreal poetry of his friend, James Wright, and the works of Peruvian poet, Cesar Vallejo. He analyzes the poems entitled "Magic Fox," "Dreaming Winter," "Picnic Weather," and "Getting Things Straight." He also discusses the relationship between Blackfeet visions and surrealist dreams, as well as Welch's comic vision, the second element of his poetry, as it is used in "Arizona Highways," "Plea to Those Who Matter," "Grandma's Man," and "In My Lifetime."

SOUTHWEST

SPENCER, KATHERINE. *Mythology and Values: An Analysis of Navaho Chantway Myths.* Philadelphia: American Folklore Society, 1957. 240pp. Bibliography.

The author examines the content of a substantial portion of Navajo myths to see what light they throw on Navajo values and interests. She finds that the value themes center on four areas: the maintenance of health, the acquisition of supernatural power, the maintenance of harmony in family relationships, and the process of the young person's attainment of adult status. She also examines the myths to see what can be learned about the valua-

tion of specific actions, character traits, and life situations, then considers explanatory elements that contain statements which set forth a rule of conduct together with the expected penalty for its violation and mythological elements that show the operation of sanctions and standards of conduct. One section includes abstracts of chantway myths and the author considers their position in the formal Navajo ceremonial system as well as the time and energy devoted to their performance. There is a bibliography of anthropological sources.

TEDLOCK, DENNIS. "On the Translation of Style in Oral Narrative." *Journal of American Folklore* 84, no. 331 (January–March 1971):114–33.

In this study Tedlock examines narratives of Zuñi Indians to show that something has gone wrong in the translation from the oral performance to the printed page. He discusses how past translations of Zuñi narratives suffered from neglect of "linguistic" features of style and from neglect of "oral" or "paralinguistic" features such as voice quality, loudness, and pausing. Finally, he recommends that oral narrative be treated as dramatic poetry.

TYLER, HAMILTON A. *Pueblo Animals and Myths.* Norman: University of Oklahoma Press, 1975. 274pp. Illustrated. Bibliography.

The importance of certain major animals to the Pueblo Indians and the form they take in their myths are the focus of this book. Tyler explains how Pueblo animal gods intermix with lesser animals, spirits, pets, and other deities, how they may be the forms taken by gods in epiphanies, and how they often work as spirit messengers between gods and men. The animals discussed are badgers, pronghorn antelopes, deer, bison, American elk, mountain sheep, rabbits, coyotes and their kin, bears, and mountain lions. The author briefly describes each animal and its ecology, Pueblo hunting techniques, the Pueblo myths, songs, and dances in which the animal figures, and how the animal fits into Pueblo daily life as a source of food or clothing. He concludes with a discussion of the place of animals in Pueblo religion. There is a map of Pueblo territory. There is a bibliography of works on mammals and hunting, archaeology and history, anthropology and mythology. See also: Hamilton Tyler, *Pueblo Birds and Myths* (Norman: University of Oklahoma Press, 256pp.), a cultural study of the role of birds as messengers to the gods.

WALTON, EDA LOW, and T. T. WATERMAN. "American Indian Poetry." *American Anthropologist* 27, no. 1 (January–March 1925):25–52. Bibliography.

Initially these authors point out that Indians are poets and that they are not "untrammeled" children of nature. They cite the many forms of poetry which members of every tribe practice according to the style and viewpoint of the tribes to which they belong, discuss tribal patterns in versification, and focus on Navajo poetry explaining its meter, use of simple predication as its main feature of verse form, and parallels. Pueblo songs with their brief established list of ideas and Pima poetry with its mixture of magical phrases and pictures of nature are examined. Poetry is viewed from the standpoint of culture areas and differences are noted in the poetry of tribes residing in the same area, illustrated by Navajos, Pueblos, and Pimas all of whom live in the Southwest. The authors also discuss the problems in recording poetry from Indians, especially the alteration of the original form.

GREAT BASIN–PLATEAU

JACOBS, MELVILLE. *The Content and Style of an Oral Literature: Clackamas Chinook Myths and Tales.* Chicago: University of Chicago Press, 1959. 285pp.

Jacobs presents eight stories as illustrative samples of the procedures he adopted in interpreting sixty-four stories in the field notebooks of Mrs. Victoria Howard, a Clackamas Chinook. He attempts to reconstruct for each story as much as he can of what he deduced was happening before, during, and after the narrator's recital. He tries to see the literature as it appeared to the Chinooks, to show the reciprocal processes between the stories and the culture, between the particular event and the people themselves. The introduction includes background sketches of the sources and the nature of the information about the sociocultural heritage of the Clackamas Chinook. In part 1, the author discusses each of the eight stories isolated from analyses of other Clackamas stories. He first gives a useable version in translation, makes deductions about interpersonal relationships and personalities which were present in the literature and society, and suggests the intent of the raconteur and the responses of the people. In part 2, he examines the collection of sixty-four stories as a unitary literature. He studies the titles, stylized introductions, closing sentences, humor, values, types of plays, formalized actions or plot expediters, and other traits of content style. In addition, he assembles and discusses important recurrent features that characterize the literature. See: Jacobs. *The People Are Coming Soon: Analyses of Clackamas Chinook Myths and Tales.* Seattle: University of Washington Press, 1960. 359pp. Also see Jacobs. "Titles in an Oral Literature." *Journal of American Folklore* 70, no. 276 (April–June 1957):157–72. The author analyzes and categorizes titles of fifty-nine Clackamas myths into five types.

STERN, THEODORE. "Some Sources of Variability in Klamath Mythology." *Journal of American Folklore* 69, no. 271 (January–March 1956):1–9; no. 272 (April–June 1956):135–46; no. 274 (October–December 1956):377–86.

In these articles Stern examines the principal sources of variation in the mythology of the Klamath Indians. First he remarks on Klamath life in the aboriginal and early historical periods, then he discusses the manner in which cultural context and social function affect mythic form, illustrated by transformations wrought in the Klamath way of life. He explains how plot organization and arrangement of component episodes are fields for variation and analyzes the role of variability played by the cultural setting in which the myth appears as well as by the character and past experience of the narrator. Finally, the manner in which the formal components (plot, episode, element, and dramatic personae) enter a myth are considered, as are the stylistic dimensions in which Klamath myths may be said to vary.

STROSS, BRIAN. "Serial Order in Nez Percé Myths." *Journal of American Folklore* 84, no. 331 (January–March 1971):104–13.

The author analyzes some of the order relationships that may be found within forty Nez Percé myths collected by Archie Phinney, a Nez Percé. He shows that the order of some things, such as the structuring of events and actor appearances, can reflect the organization of other elements of the myths and the patterns of status relationships likely occurring in the society producing the myths. He examines the specification of ordered rules for the determination of actor sequences in myth titles, the relationship of the myth-initial and myth-final sequence to titles, and the unexpected common sequence of three rather than five. There is a list of myth titles in Phinney's collection as well as notes on other folklore studies.

CALIFORNIA

BLACKBURN, THOMAS C., ed. *December's Child: A Book of Chumash Oral Narratives.* Berkeley: University of California Press, 1975, 1980. 359pp. Illustrated. Bibliography.

The editor of this volume has published and analyzed the main body of oral literature that John Peabody Harrington collected from the Chumash Indians of Santa Barbara and Ventura counties in California between 1912 and 1928. The 111 texts range from aboriginal narratives centering on Old Man Coyote to nineteenth-century tales borrowed from Mexico. In the first part of the book, Blackburn analyzes the structure and meaning of the oral narratives, explaining what the Chumash thought and why. Maintaining that folklore is much more than storytelling, he shows the relationship of Chumash oral narratives to all aspects of their culture. In a chapter entitled "Background of the Study," he discusses sources of information on Chumash culture, describes the Harrington papers, and gives data on the informants. The second part of the book contains the narratives, some as short as a paragraph. There is an appendix of sources and comparative notes, a glossary of Chumash and Spanish words and phrases, and a map of some historic Chumash villages. The bibliography contains largely anthropological works.

RAMSEY, JAROLD. "The Bible in Western Indian Mythology." *Journal of American Folklore* 90, no. 358 (October–December 1977):442–54.

Exploring the impact of Catholic and Protestant evangelism and preaching on the mythologies of the Indians of the West, Ramsey explains how the Indians accepted the stories from the Christian

Bible into their oral repertoires with or without accepting the doctrines that the stories embodied for the Christians. He describes how tribes of California, the Northwest, and the Plateau were introduced to the stories of the Bible and cites three kinds of assimilation of Bible stories into native texts: incorporation, adaptation, and mythopoesis.

NORTHWEST

HYMES, DELL. "Some North Pacific Coast Poems: A Problem in Anthropological Philology." *American Anthropologist* 67, no. 2 (April 1965):316–41. Bibliography.

Hymes shows that poems may have a structural organization and "nonsense" vocables which serve a structural function. Analyzing six north Pacific Coast poems, he relates them to the perspectives of folklorists, anthropologists, linguists, literary scholars, and poets. He discusses the validity of translations and the structure of the originals in anthologies by Astrov and Day, cites faults in a poem collected and translated by Schoolcraft and says similar faults can be found in more recent translations, and maintains that the true structure of the original poem is essential to the knowledge of it in ethnographic and aesthetic terms. Each of the six poems is presented in the format of text, literal translation, literary translation and comment, and literary translation in light of specific comments and structural analysis. The author suggests that for the true value of the original structures and the contents of poems to be realized, the perspectives and tools of linguistics are indispensable.

BIBLIOGRAPHIES

CLEMENTS, WILLIAM M., and FRANCIS M. MALPEZZI. *Native American Folklore: An Annotated Bibliography.* Chicago: Swallow Press, Forthcoming. 1982/1983.

This work covers materials in English dealing with the folklore of Native Americans north of Mexico. Folklore is defined in the anthropological sense as verbal art, so the work includes books, articles, and government documents dealing with myths, legends, other oral narratives, songs, chants, prayers, speeches, formulas, and similar art forms. The material is arranged by culture area and tribal group, and a system of cross-referencing entries is used. An index provides guides to the entries by author and subject. Unpublished works are not included in the bibliography.

DORRIS, MICHAEL. "Native American Literature in an Ethnohistorical Context." *College English* 41, no. 2 (October 1979):147–62.

The author describes the linguistic and cultural diversity of Indian North America, contrasting this with the history of relative cultural homogeneity in Europe. He reviews the derivation of the misnomer Indian, and discusses the reasons why the term "Native American literature" is ambiguous and misleading. The importance of understanding the cultural context in which a literature is created and functions is illustrated with a Tanaina tale. The author reviews ethnocentric works about native peoples by Europeans and contemporary works in English by Native American writers. A bibliography of Native American literature contains sections on bibliographies, history and culture, language, non-Indian views of Native Americans, literary history and criticism, general anthologies, oral literature and traditional materials, contemporary literature, and periodicals.

See: Jarold Ramsey, "A Supplement to Michael Dorris' 'Native American Literature'" *College English* (April 1980):933–35.

HAYWOOD, CHARLES. *A Bibliography of North America Folklore and Folksong.* Vol. 2, 2nd ed. New York: Dover, 1961. 1,301pp. Illustrated.

This volume is devoted to Amerian Indian and Eskimo folklore and music, excluding Mexican native peoples. The first chapter is concerned with general bibliographies; the remaining divisions are geographical (Northeastern Woodland, Southeastern, Plains, Southwestern, California, Great Basin-Plateau, Northwest Coast, Mackenzie-Yukon, and Arctic Coast). Within each geographic region, listings are by tribe and by subject category ("folklore" and "music" with numerous subcategories). Recordings are also indexed. Some of the entries are annotated. The work contains an index and two general maps, one of contemporary North America and one of culture areas of the North American Indians.

JACOBSON, ANGELINE, comp. *Contemporary Native American Literature: A Selected and Partially Annotated Bibliography.* Metuchen, N.J.: Scarecrow, 1977. 262pp.

This bibliography brings together the literary works (poetry, fiction, autobiography, personal reminiscences, biography, short stories, essays, and humor) of Native American authors which have been written and published from 1960 to mid-1976 in periodicals, collections of works by several authors, or as a title of an individual author's collected works, or as a single work. In some cases, the works of authors such as Momaday, written earlier than 1961, have been included, and some writers of the earlier years of the twentieth century have been selected whose writings reflect their assimilation. The 2,024 sources, many of which are annotated, are organized under the following headings: "Poets and Their Poetry," single poem titles of an author and collections of poems by a single author, arranged in one alphabet by author; "Native American Spiritual Heritage," including a Selection of Traditional Narratives; "Autobiography, Biography, and Letters and Personal Narratives"; "Fiction"; "Present Day Realities Which Recall Memories of an Earlier and Better Time"; "Interviews, Letters, Stories and Other Prose Selections"; and "Humor and Satire." In the concluding chapters, the compiler analyzes some collections of native writings and lists bibliographies, indexes, and periodicals that include native prose and poetry. There is a title and first line index to single poems and an author index.

SMITH, WILLIAM F., JR., comp. "American Indian Literature." *English Journal* (January 1974):68–72.

This bibliography lists works created by Indians, no matter who collected or edited them into a written English form. The compiler selected the best works he could find in four different categories: "Anthologies," "Autobiographies," "Poetry," and "Traditional Narratives: Myths, Tales, and Legends." In each category the works are first listed, then discussed.

ULLOM, JUDITH C. *Folklore of the North American Indians: An Annotated Bibliography.* Washington, D.C.: Library of Congress, 1969. 126pp.

This collection of 152 titles with annotations does not aim to be comprehensive. The author states that selection criteria include: (1) a statement of sources and faithfulness to them, (2) a true reflection of Indian cosmology, and (3) a written style that retains the spirit and poetry of "the Indian's" narrative style. Sections include general bibliographies and works by culture areas. Each section includes a special listing of children's editions.

AUTHOR-TITLE INDEX

Physical Anthropologist's View of the Peopling of the New World," 231

Stineback, David C., *Puritans, Indians, and Manifest Destiny*, 136

Stoltman, James B., *The Southeastern United States*, 29

Stone, Peter, *The Far North: 2000 Years of American Eskimo and Indian Art*, 263

Storms Brewed in Other Men's Worlds: The Confrontation of Indians, Spanish, and French in the Southwest, 1540–1795, E. A. H. John, 158–59

The Story Telling Stone: Myths and Tales of the American Indians, S. Feldmann, 279

"A Stranger in My Own Life: Alienation in Native American Prose and Poetry," P. G. Allen, 277–78

Strangers Devour the Land, B. Richardson, 60

The Stratigraphy and Archaeology of Ventana Cave, Arizona, E. W. Haury, 31

Strickland, Rennard, *Fire and the Spirits: Cherokee Law from Clan to Court*, 273

Strong, B. Stephen, *Circumpolar Peoples: An Anthropological Perspective*, 18

Strong, William Duncan, *Aboriginal Society in Southern California*, 226

Stross, Brian, "Serial Order in Nez Percé Myths," 283

"The Structure and Causation of Mohave Warfare," G. H. Fathauer, 219

"The Structure of Social Organization among the Eskimo," E. M. Weyer, 70

Struever, Stuart, *Koster: Americans in Search of Their Prehistoric Past*, 29; "Koster Site, the New Archaeology in Action," 29

Studies in American Indian Literature, 277–78

Studies in Californian Linguistics, W. Bright, 235

Studies in Southwestern Ethnolinguistics, D. H. Hymes and W. E. Bittle, 235

A Study of Pueblo Architecture in Tusayan and Cibola, C. Mindeleff, 213

"The Study of Race," S. L. Washburn, 231

Stull, Donald D., "Native American Adaptation to an Urban Environment: The Papago of Tucson Arizona," 229

Sturgis, Henry F., *A Review of Texas Archaeology*, 30

Sturtevant, William C., "Preliminary Bibliography on Eastern North American Agriculture," 196; "Spanish-Indian Relations in Southeastern North America," 145

"A Suggested Typology of Defensive Systems of the Southwest," M. F. Farmer, 219

"Suicide and the American Indian," P. A. May and L. H. Dizmang, 180

Suicide, Homicide, and Alcoholism among American Indians: Guidelines for Help, National Institute of Mental Health, 180

Sullivan, Robert J., *The Ten'a Food Quest*, 195

Sun Chief: The Autobiography of a Hopi Indian, D. C. Talayesva, 50

Sun Circles and Human Hands: The Southeastern Indian Art and Industries, L. Fundaburk and M. D. F. Foreman, 265

"The Sun Dance of the Plains Indians: Its Development and Diffusion," L. Spier, 241–42

The Sun Dance Religion: Power for the Powerless, J. G. Jorgensen, 239

"The Sun's Influence in the Form of Hopi Pueblos," J. W. Fewkes, 212

"A Supplement to Michael Dorris' 'Native American Literature,' " J. Ramsey, 284

Suttles, Wayne, *The Current Status of Anthropological Research in the Great Basin, 1964*, 16–17

Sutton, Imre, *Indian Land Tenure: Bibliographical Essays and a Guide to the Literature*, 61

Swadesh, Morris, "Motivations in Nootka Warfare," 220–21

Swanton, John R., "Housing," 209; *The Indian Tribes of North America*, 14; *The Indians of the Southeastern United States*, 15, 189; "Social Organization," 224

Sweet Medicine: The Continuing Role of the Sacred Arrows, the Sun Dance, and the Sacred Buffalo Hat in Northern Cheyenne History, P. J. Powell, 155, 241

Sweezy, Carl, *The Arapaho Way: A Memoir of an Indian Boyhood*, 49

Sylvestre, Guy, *Indian-Inuit Authors: An Annotated Bibliography*, 52

Systems of North America: Witchcraft and Sorcery, D. E. Walker, 240

Szasz, Margaret Connell, *Education and the American Indians: The Road to Self-Determination*, 255–56

Szathmary, Emöke, "Are the Biological Differences between North American Indians and Eskimos Truly Profound?" 231

Talayesna, Don C., *Sun Chief: The Autobiography of a Hopi Indian*, 50

Tanis, Norman Earl, "Education in John Eliot's Indian Utopias, 1646–1675," 256

Tanner, Clara Lee, *Southwest Indian Craft Arts*, 266

Tanner, Helen Hornbeck, *Atlas of Great Lakes Indian History*, 20; *The Ojibwas: A Critical Bibliography*, 6

"Taos Blue Lake Controversy," J. J. Bodine, 242

Tax, Sol, "The Impact of Urbanization on American Indians," 229

Taxing Those They Found Here: An Examination of the Tax Exempt Status of the American Indian, J. V. White, 58

Taylor, Graham D., *The New Deal and American Indian Tribalism*, 94

Taylor, R. E., *Chronologies in New World Archaeology*, 26

Taylor, Theodore W., *The States and Their Indian Citizens*, 96

"The Teacher of Modern American Indian Writing as Ethnographer and Critic," J. Ramsey, 280

The Technique of Porcupine Decoration among the Indians of North America, W. C. Orchard, 264

Tedlock, Dennis, "On the Translation of Style in Oral Narrative," 282

The Ten'a Food Quest, R. J. Sullivan, 195

Tennessee's Indian Peoples, R. N. Satz, 144–45

A Tentative Bibliography for the Colonial Fur Trade in the American Colonies: 1608–1800, J. P. Donnelly, 170

SUBJECT INDEX

This index lists the tribes, individuals, place names, and a limited number of topics mentioned in the annotations in this bibliography. It is designed to be used in conjunction with the Contents and the essays at the beginning of each section. Asterisks identify Native Americans.